VICTORIAN CROCHET

by Weldon and Company

with a new introduction by Florence Weinstein

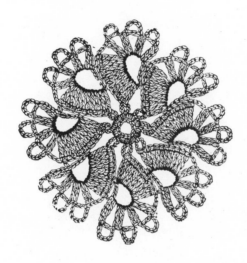

Dover Publications, Inc.

New York

Published in Canada by General Publishing Company, Ltd., 30 Lesmill Road, Don Mills, Toronto,
Ontario.
Published in the United Kingdom by Constable
and Company, Ltd., 10 Orange Street, London WC 2.

This Dover edition, first published in 1974, is an
unabridged republication of *Weldon's Practical
Crochet,* First through Nineteenth Series, originally
published by Weldon & Co., London, England,
circa 1895. A new introduction has been especially
prepared for this edition by Florence Weinstein.

International Standard Book Number: 0-486-22890-8
Library of Congress Catalog Card Number: 72-81611

Manufactured in the United States of America
Dover Publications, Inc.
180 Varick Street
New York, N. Y. 10014

Introduction
to the Dover Edition

The art of crocheting was first practiced in ancient times by shepherds who retrieved the sheep's wool which had been snagged on bushes in the fields. After spinning the wool, they were able to make warm garments for themselves using a stick with the end carved into a hook.

These crude sticks evolved into the bone or ivory hooks which the nuns in sixteenth-century Ireland used to make their exquisite crocheted lace. We still use many antique Irish stitches in our Irish Point or Irish Crochet, but now we have a choice of steel, plastic, wood or aluminum needles.

In England various schools were founded and sponsored by princesses and other members of the royal household. These schools taught needlework, crocheting and lacework, and then, where necessary, made arrangements for the finished pieces to be sold. In the nineteenth century, needlework became more fashionable, as the newly created middle class sought to emulate the upper classes and royalty. As crocheting became more popular, it became easier to procure yarns. This development, in turn, stimulated the publication of numerous excellent books with carefully worked-out designs for all manner of clothing and household items.

One of the best of these publications is the present work which dates from the late nineteenth century. Originally issued as a series of newsletters distributed on a subscription basis, it is admirably thorough in its coverage and includes numerous examples of the Victorian genius for design.

To the modern crocheter, who will recognize at a glance that this book is a treasure trove of ideas, Victorian terminology may seem strange, and so I have briefly explained some of the more obscure terms.

Andalusian wool.	Came from Southern Spain; it is roughly comparable to our sports yarn.
Antimacassar.	Cover to protect the back or arms of furniture from Macassar oil or other hair preparations.
Berlin wool.	Worsted which got its name from the fact that it was originally distributed from a Berlin depository. This wool was meant for use with Berlin needlepoint, similar to modern needlepoint on canvas, but worked from a colored chart.
Boa.	Long fluffy scarf.
Capote.	Long, hooded cloak or overcoat, or small bonnet with tie strings and a long mantle.
Comforter.	Warm wrap for the neck; long narrow scarf.
Couvrepied.	Literally a cover for the feet, similar to a small afghan.
Fascinator.	Light head scarf of crochet or lace.
Pelerine.	Short shaped shoulder cape; usually with long ends hanging down in front.
Pelisse.	Full-length lightweight cloak or coat, often fur-trimmed and fur-lined.
Tippet.	Cape worn over a cloak.

Page one of the text illustrates the basic repetoire of stitches used in the book. These stitches are the same stitches we use today, but we generally call them by different names. The following table supplies the current American name for these stitches.

Weldon's name	*Current American name*
Chain stitch	Same
Single crochet	Slip stitch
Short or Double crochet	Single crochet
Long double crochet	Half double crochet
Ordinary treble	Double crochet
Double treble	Treble
Treble treble	Double treble
Tricot crochet	Afghan stitch

The threads specified in the text are no longer available—at least not under the names indicated in the text. In the following table I have supplied the names of available threads that I find make acceptable substitutes for basic materials indicated in the text. I have also indicated the appropriate size and type of needle that I recommend for the various yarns.

Victorian wool	Modern substitute	Recommended aluminum needle
Fleecy wool Double Berlin 3 Thread Lady Betty	worsted or mohair	H - J
Andalusian Pompadour	sports yarn	F
Single Berlin Berlin fingering Shetland*	fingering	E
Saxony Single Berlin	baby zephyr or baby pompadour	E

Victorian cotton	Modern substitute	Recommended steel needle
Macramé thread	Speed-cro-sheen	1
Maltese thread	Knit cro-sheen	5
Adams Ivory crochet	Bedspread cotton	6
Coats crochet cotton	Crochet cotton #20	8
Evans crochet cotton	Crochet cotton #30	10

FLORENCE WEINSTEIN

Brooklyn, New York
March, 1974

---

*The Victorian Shetland, usually a 2-ply, was a much finer yarn than the bulkier wool we now associate with the name.

VICTORIAN CROCHET

WELDON'S
PRACTICAL CROCHET.

(FIRST SERIES.)

How to Crochet 36 Useful Articles for Ladies, Gentlemen, and Children.

FORTY-FIVE ILLUSTRATIONS.

Telegraphic Address—
"Consuelo," London.

The Yearly Subscription to this Magazine, post free to any Part of the World, is 2s. 6d. Subscriptions are payable in advance, and may commence from any date and for any period.

[Telephone—1745.

The Back Numbers are always in print. Nos. 1 to 87 now ready, Price 2d. each, or post free for 15s. 6d. Over 5,000 Engravings. The sizes of Crochet Hooks mentioned in descriptions are regulated by Walker's Bell Gauge.

DETAILS OF CROCHET.

CROCHET, or, as it was called by the Scotch, "shepherd's knitting," has really only been practised during the last half century. and, in fact, barely that, for it was about 1838 that it became publicly known in Great Britain; for, although it dates back from the 16th century, it was then called "nun's work," simply because it was only known to the nuns, who made most lovely laces and different articles. But of late years nothing has met with such success as this simple yet most durable work, which is now found so useful for such articles as ornamental laces, edging, mats, antimacassars, as well as articles of apparel—in fact, crochet may be applied to an almost endless variety of useful purposes, as these pages will show.

SHORT OR DOUBLE CROCHET STITCH.

Illustration 3 shows clearly how this useful stitch is executed, by putting the hook through a stitch, drawing the cotton through, thus forming two loops on the needle, when the cotton has to be thrown over the hook and drawn through both loops, which you repeat till the row is done.

LONG DOUBLE CROCHET.

This is very useful for many purposes, being close and strong, and Illustration 4 being so clearly given will enable any one to copy it.

The cotton has to be passed over the crochet hook, then pass the hook through a stitch, draw the cotton which brings 3 loops on the needle. You now

No. 2.

No. 1.

No. 3.

No. 4.

No. 5.

The simple stitches of crochet are now so well known as to scarcely need explanation, still this little work would not be complete without a few remarks, and therefore we commence with

CHAIN STITCH,

which is the foundation of all crochet work, and for which you make a loop, and with the hook draw the cotton through it, as clearly shown by Illustration 1.

SINGLE CROCHET STITCH.

Illustration 2 shows exactly the mode of working, and you put the crochet hook through the foundation chain stitch, or, in the course of the work, through a stitch of the preceding row, throw the cotton over the crochet hook, and draw through both the stitch and loop on the hook.

pass the cotton over the hook again, and draw it through the 3 loops, and repeat till end of row.

ORDINARY TREBLE STITCH.

This is a much-used stitch, and is simple to work, as Illustration 5 will show. Pass the crochet cotton over the hook, then draw the cotton through a stitch to get 3 loops on the hook, after which you again pass cotton on the hook and draw it through the two loops, which makes another 2 loops remaining on the hook. Pass cotton again over the hook and draw it through the 2 loops, when the stitch is completed.

DOUBLE TREBLE CROCHET AND TREBLE CROCHET STITCHES.

These are worked in exactly the same manner as the ordinary treble stitch,

[1]

except that in double treble crochet you pass cotton twice round the hook previous to putting it in a stitch, which makes 4 loops on the hook, while with treble crochet stitch the cotton is passed over or round the hook 3 times, in each case drawing the cotton through two stitches only at a time.

To Make a Stitch.

At the beginning and ending of a row you make a stitch of chain before the first stitch and after the last which in the following row are to be crocheted.

To Increase a Stitch.

To accomplish this you make two stitches in the same loop.

To Decrease.

In this you can either crochet two stitches together, or miss a stitch; and, of course, decreasing is done in the same ratio as increasing.

To Fasten Off.

Draw the cotton or wool that you may be crocheting with through the last stitch.

Tricot Stitch.

Illustration 6 shows this pretty stitch, which is worked as follows: Having made a chain, pass hook through first foundation loop, draw wool through, making a stitch on the hook for each one picked up. For the return row throw wool over the hook and draw through two loops. Repeat over and over again till they are all worked off.

Hair-pin or Krotchee Crochet.

Many very durable and pretty trimmings can be made of hair-pin work, which can be executed in fine or coarse cotton, wool, or silk, according to the purpose to which it is to be applied.

It derives its name from the fork or hair-pin like article upon which it is worked, and which may be had in metal or bone, or even a coarse hair-pin can be employed.

In white crochet cotton with a row of chain along one side it makes a durable trimming for undergarments, or with chain on either side it serves well for an insertion. In coloured crochet cottons it can be used as a dress trimming, while in silk it is particularly lacey and useful. To commence hair-pin crochet, hold the hair-pin like article or krotchee, as it is sometimes called, in the left hand, the round part upwards. Now make a loop on the crochet hook and twist the cotton round the left prong, drawing it through the loop on the hook from the centre of the hair-pin, take the hook out and turn the hair-pin or krotchee, as Illustration 7 shows, which brings * the cotton to the front, put it over the right-hand prong to the back, put the crochet hook into the loop from which you have just taken it, and draw the cotton through, which makes a fresh loop on your needle, then do a double crochet, which secures the loop and forms a firm centre to the work, as shown by Illustration 8. Take out the hook and turn the hair-pin, then repeat from *.

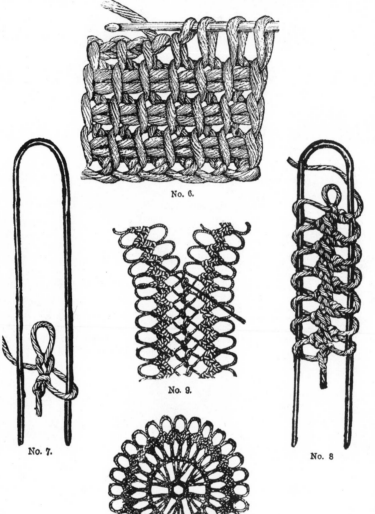

No. 6.

No. 7.

No. 9.

No. 8.

No. 10.

When the fork is filled slip off the work to within two or three loops. The beauty of hair-pin work consists in its firm centre and even loops.

Illustration 9 shows two strips of work joined together by crochet to make a broad edging for trimming undergarments. On the one side you must crochet a row of chain to give firmness and something to sew it on by, while the other edge can have any fancy pattern crocheted on it that fancy may suggest. By joining strips of this hair-pin work together a very pretty border to a shawl is formed, or, indeed, the entire shawl can be made of it by using wool; in fact, scarfs and many pretty and useful articles can be made with hair-pin crochet.

Illustration 10 gives a rosette or wheel made of hair-pin work, and which is arranged thus:—To form rosettes fasten off after 26 or 28 loops on each side are made, tying one side of them together to form a centre, and when several are thus prepared, make a crochet foundation with 2 rows of double square crochet, and catch 4 or 6 of the loops in each rosette to it. When the first set of rosettes are thus secured, another set beyond them is added by sewing the loops together where they touch, or form vandykes by sewing rosettes above and between every second one of the first set. Scalloped and vandyked braid is often used for foundations to these ornamental trimmings instead of square crochet.

CROCHET SKIRT.

MATERIALS—11 ozs. of grey and 5 ozs. of red knitting worsted. Medium crochet hook. Make a chain of 240 stitches with grey wool. **1st row**—* 11 long crochets in fourth foundation stitch, miss 3 stitches, 1 short crochet stitch in next stitch. Repeat from * to end of chain. **2nd row**—Like the first, but worked on other side of foundation chain, the eleven long crochet stitches coming in same stitch as the other, and join this row of wheels together. **3rd row**—5 single crochet stitches in first five stitches *, 1 short crochet stitch in next stitch, 3 chain, 11 long crochet stitches in next eleven stitches, retaining the last stitch of each on hook, you now have twelve stitches on hook, draw wool through all the stitches, 4 chain. Repeat from * all the length. **4th row**—* 11 long crochets in the stitch that joined the eleven long crochets in last row, 1 short crochet in the short crochet of last row. Repeat from * all the row. **5th row**—Like the third row. **6th row**—Like fourth row. **7th row**—With red wool, like third row. **8th row**—With red, like fourth row. **9th and 10th rows**—With grey wool, like third and fourth rows **11th row**—With red, like third row. **12th row**—With red wool, 9 long crochet stitches in stitch where you joined the eleven long crochets in last row, 1 short crochet stitch in short crochet. **13th row**—Like third row, work in only nine stitches instead of eleven. **14th row**—Like twelfth row. **15th row**—Like thirteenth row, with red wool. **16th row**—Like fourteenth row. **17th row**—With grey wool, like thirteenth row. **18th row**—Like fourteenth row. **19th row**—With red wool, like thirteenth row. **20th row**—Like fourteenth row. **21st row**—With grey, like thirteenth row. **22nd row**—Like fourteenth row. **23rd row**—With red, like thirteenth row. **24th row**—7 long crochets in the stitch that joins the nine long crochets in last row, 1 short crochet in short crochet stitch of last row. From here the skirt is made with grey wool. **25th row**—Like thirteenth row, but work only seven instead of nine. The next twelve rows are made with 7 long crochets, the rest with 5, finish with a cord and tassel.

COMFORTABLE HOOD.

MATERIALS—4 ozs. of any coloured wool, bone hook No. 2. On a chain of 128 stitches work thirty-two squares of crazy stitch. **2nd row**—Turn work, make 3 chain, pass hook through first stitch and draw wool through loosely, same with second and third stitches. You will now have 4 stitches on hook, throw wool over, and draw through all four at once, wool over and draw through single stitch. Make 1 single crochet stitch into the last of the 4 long crochet stitches in preceding row. This is to fill up the little triangular space, which would otherwise leave the edges uneven and with which every row is commenced. You then work on with regular crazy stitch. Work back and forward nineteen times, and fill in the uneven squares which will be left after last row, by chaining one, then throwing wool over hook and taking up first stitch, wool over and take up second, and so on till the 6 stitches between the two points are on hook, then wool over and draw through all the stitches at once quite tightly, chain one loosely and fasten with short crochet in second point. Continue this filling-in all across the row. For Border—Turn work, chain 3 and work 2 long crochet stitches in second stitch of foundation, chain 1 and work two more long crochets in same stitch, making a shell. Work next shell in end of second square, and continue these shells all around hood. **2nd row** of border—Work shells in centre of preceding shells. Across ends of hood work a third row of shells, after which the last row of border is made. Work 8 long crochet stitches in centre of shell, and fasten down by short crochet between shells on second row of border, then chain 3, and fasten between shells on first row of border, chain 3 more and fasten on edge of hood, turn and chain 3 and fasten at top of first row of shells, chain 3 and fasten on top of second row of shells, when you then make 8 long crochet stitches in centre of next shell, and so continue all around hood, making the two lines of little chains between each row of shells. When this is done, turn this border back on to hood, along the front and back, and fasten wool with needle and wool. Next, double hood evenly and sew the back up, commencing about the fifth square from the bottom. Fasten wool on front edge of hood and work a row of shells all across to finish front. Trim with ribbon bows and strings.

GIRL'S CROCHET COAT.

REQUIRED 12 ozs. of white single Berlin wool for the body of the coat, and 6 ozs. double Berlin for the border. Bone crochet needles, No. 12 and No. 8. These directions are for a coat to fit a child of six, it is worked all in one piece in plain treble stitch. A smaller size can be produced by using a finer wool such as Penelope, and a larger and stronger jacket may be made by combining 3 thread and 4 thread Fleecy, using the latter for the border. Commence on the shoulder with 7 chain, work 2 treble in the fourth chain from the needle, 2 treble in the next, 2 in the next, and 3 in the last. Break off at the end of every row and recommence on the right-hand side. Work into the two top threads of the stitches of previous row and the work lies flat without any ridge. **2nd row**—3 treble on the first treble stitch of last row, 3 consecutive treble, 3 on the next, 3 on the next, 3 consecutive, 3 on the last. **3rd row**—3 treble on the first, 7 consecutive, 2 on the next, 2 on the next, 7 consecutive, 3 on the last. And now before proceeding any further, work a second shoulder piece the same as the above. **4th row**—3 treble on the first, 10 consecutive, 3 on the next, 3 on the next, 10 consecutive, 3 on the last, 9 chain for the back of the neck, and take the second shoulder piece and work upon it 3 treble on the first stitch, 10 consecutive, 3 on the next, 3 on the next, 10 consecutive, 3 on the last. **5th row**—3 treble on the first, 14 consecutive, 2 on the next, 2 on the next, 14 consecutive, 2 on the next, 1 on each of the first four chain stitches, 2 in the next chain, 1 on each of the next four chain, 2 on the first treble of the other shoulder, 14 consecutive, 2 on the next, 2 on the next, 14 consecutive, 3 on the last. **6th row**—9 chain, 3 treble on the first treble stitch, 17 treble, 3 on the next, 3 on the next, 42 treble straight across the back, 3 on the next, 3 on the next, 17 treble, 3 on the last, 9 chain. **7th row**—2 treble in the first of the chain, 8 consecutive, 2 treble on the first treble of last row, 21 treble, 2 on the next, 2 on the next, work straight across the back and the opposite shoulder the same as the one just done, ending with 2 treble in the last stitch of the nine chain. **8th row**—34 treble, 3 on the next, 3 on the next, work straight across the back, and work the opposite shoulder the same. **9th row**—2 treble on the first, 35 treble, 2 on the next, 2 on the next, straight across the back, and the opposite shoulder the same. **10th row**—38 treble, 3 treble on the next, 3 treble on the next, straight across the back, and the opposite shoulder the same. **11th row**—2 treble on the first, 39 treble, 2 on the next, 2 on the next, straight across the back and the opposite shoulder the same. **12th row**—42 treble, 3 on the next, 3 on the next, straight across the back, and the opposite shoulder the same. **13th row**—2 treble on the first, 43 treble, 2 on the next, 2 on the next, straight across the back and the opposite shoulder the same. **14th row**—44 treble, and break off for the armhole. **15th row**—Re-commencing at the front—42 treble. **16th row**—41 treble. **17th row**—40 treble. Work 6 more rows the same as the last. **24th row**—39 treble, 2 treble on the last. **25th row**—40 treble, 2 treble on the last. **26th row**—41 treble, 2 treble on the last. This finishes the armhole. Next work the other front, beginning three stitches from the increase on the opposite shoulder, and work 44 treble straight along. Proceed with the next 12 rows, working to correspond with the front already done. Then work 13 rows of plain trebles for the back, sloping round the armholes the same as for the fronts. **27th row**—Beginning again on the right-hand side of the work, 42 treble, 3 treble on the last stitch of the front piece, 3 chain, 3 treble on the first stitch of the back, treble across the back, and 3 treble on the last stitch, 3 chain, 3 treble on the first stitch of the other front, 42 treble to the end of the row. Now work 3 rows of plain treble, then 1 row, increasing 2 treble under each arm, and repeat till 19 rows are done. **Next row**—in which the Beehive pattern worked with double Berlin and the coarse needle commences in the middle of the back—work as before plain treble, increasing 2 stitches under the arm, and plain to within fifteen stitches of the middle of the back, here break off, and take the double Berlin, and work 1 double crochet on the next stitch, * miss two, 6 treble on the next (but instead of working these six treble in the usual way, draw through all three loops of each stitch at once loosely), miss two, 1 double crochet on the next, and repeat from * four times, making five groups of six trebles, the centre group of which comes on the centre stitch of the back of the coat, take single Berlin again and work plain treble, increasing 2 stitches under the arm and plain to the end of the row. **2nd row**—Plain treble to within three treble of the Beehive pattern of last row, then with double Berlin 1 double crochet, * wool over the needle and insert the hook in the space between the two next stitches of last row and draw the wool through loosely, wool over the needle and draw through two stitches on the needle, raise 5 more stitches in the same manner, making 7 stitches on the needle, and this brings you half way up the six treble stitches of last row,

draw the wool through all the stitches on the needle, 1 double crochet between the third and fourth trebles of last row, and repeat from * five times, take single Berlin and work plain trebles to the end of the row. **3rd row**—Plain treble on both fronts, and at the back work 7 groups of six trebles the same as the first row, making the 6 treble in the stitch that draws together the raised stitches of last row. You will have to work an additional row or two of plain trebles on the fronts to keep the rows level, as the Beehive pattern takes more room than the plain treble work does. **4th row** and **5th row**—The same as the second and third rows, working the Beehive pattern a little further out each time. Then again work an additional row or two of plain trebles on the fronts to keep the rows level. **6th row**—Commence the Beehive pattern upon the front, and work it all along from end to end, bringing it in nicely to meet that already worked at the back. **7th row**—Same as the second row. Work another repeat of the pattern. Then commence at the neck, and work Beehive pattern down the front, ease round the corner, and continue along the bottom of the coat and up the other front. Work 2 more rows, which completes the border. Strengthen the neck with a row of double crochet, and work 3 or 5 rows of the Beehive pattern for a collar. For the **Sleeve**—Commence with 18 chain, and break off. **1st row**—4 chain, 18 treble in the foundation chain, 4 chain, and break off. **2nd row**—4 chain, 26 treble, 4 chain, and break off. Proceed in this way, increasing 4 stitches at the beginning and end of every row till you have a length sufficient for the armhole, then join round, and continue working in rounds for ten rounds, afterwards decrease 2 stitches in each round till the sleeve is nearly the length required, and finish with 3 rows of the Beehive pattern to match the bottom of the coat. Work the other sleeve the same. Sew the sleeves in. Put buttons on the left front, and a nice ribbon bow on the back.

GIRL'S CROCHET COAT AND HOOD.

GIRL'S CROCHET HOOD.

FOUR ozs. of white single Berlin wool. Bone crochet needle, No. 12. Commence with 4 chain, join round, and work 6 double crochet in the circle. **2nd round**—2 double crochet on each double crochet of last round. **3rd round**—2 double crochet on the first stitch, 1 double crochet on the next, and repeat. Continue thus round and round, increasing in each round sufficiently to keep the work in slightly concave shape till the crown measures 7 inches across. Then turn the work and double crochet a row, inserting the hook in the back of the stitches of last row so as to form a rib, leave about 24 stitches of the crown unworked, and turn and work 7 more rows of ribbed crochet, increasing 2 stitches in each rib as you go round the top of the bonnet, break off the wool. Now work 4 rows of treble stitches, increasing 1 stitch

BOY'S CROCHET TURBAN HAT.

at the beginning and end of each alternate row, and keep a right side, breaking off at the end of each row, then work 10 rows of ribbed double crochet, increasing 1 at the end of each row, and now 6 rows of ribbed crochet without any increase, and fasten off. For the **Frilled Edging** round the face—Commence with 1 double crochet on the outside row of ribbed crochet at the end of the bonnet, and work 1 double crochet on each of the first five ribs straight along with 4 chain between each double crochet, turn and work the same back to the front edge again, and so on all round the face. For the **Curtain**—Hold the right side of the work towards you, and commence working double crochet upon the eight rows of ribbed crochet, along the bottom of the crown, and upon the eight rows of ribbed crochet on the other side, * turn and double crochet back and work 5 stitches further along the hood, repeat from * till you get the curtain the entire length of the hood, then work 4 rows of ribbed crochet the whole length, and break off. Work 3 rows of trebles, keeping a right side to the work, and then work 5 or 7 rows of the Beehive pattern as described above for the border of the coat. Make two nice ribbon bows, one to place on the head of the bonnet, the other at the back on the curtain.

BOY'S CROCHET TURBAN HAT.

THIS pretty hat requires 2½ ozs. of white double Berlin wool. Bone crochet needle, No. 9. Commence with 3 chain, join round, and work 6 double crochet in the circle. Run a cotton in to mark the beginning of each round. **2nd round**—2 double crochet in every stitch of last round, working into two threads of the wool. **3rd round**—2 double crochet in the first stitch, 1 double crochet in the next stitch, and repeat. **4th round**—The same. **5th round**—1 double crochet in each of the first two stitches, and 2 double crochet in the third stitch, and repeat. **6th round**—2 double crochet in the first stitch, and afterwards 2 double crochet in every seventh stitch. After the first six rounds the crown is not intended to lie quite flat, as the hat is gradually to assume a convex shape. **7th round**—2 double crochet in every tenth stitch. **8th round**—2 double crochet in every thirteenth stitch. **9th round**—2 double crochet in every sixteenth stitch. Now work for the **Border** in looped crochet, which is done as follows : Twist the wool round a mesh 1½ inches wide, and work a double crochet stitch, the wool round the mesh again, and work another double crochet, and so on all round, letting the loops off the mesh when it gets full. Work 12 rounds of this looped crochet. Very little increase will be necessary, not more than 2 stitches at intervals in the fourth, sixth, and ninth rounds. The hat should measure about 20 inches round the head, but if too large can be drawn in with a ribbon at the back part, and will stretch the size required if too small. Put in a cap, and strings to tie under the chin.

BABY'S LONG CROCHET BOOT.

CARDINAL and white single Berlin wool, 1 oz. of each. Fine bone crochet needle. Commence with white wool, at the heel, with 22 chain, miss the first of the chain stitches and work 21 double crochet; 1 chain to turn and work 21 double crochet again, taking up the small loop at the back of the stitches, as the work is to set in ribs. Work 16 rows of double crochet. At the end of the sixteenth row work 10 chain for the instep, join across to the opposite side of the work, and now proceed with the toe in rounds. **1st round**—Double crochet in every stitch, making 21 double crochet on the work already done, and 10 double crochet on the chain stitches; 31 double crochet in all. **2nd round**—18 consecutive double crochet, work 1 double crochet on next *two* double crochet of preceding round, 9 double crochet, 1 double crochet on next *two* double crochet of preceding round. **3rd round**—Plain. **4th round**—18 consecutive double crochet, 1 double crochet on next two of last round, 7 double crochet, 1 double crochet on next two of preceding round. **5th round**—Plain. **6th round**—18 consecutive double crochet, 1 double crochet on next two of last round, 5 double crochet, 1 double crochet on next two of last round. Now continue double crochet working every fifth stitch 1 double crochet on *two* of the last round, until the toe is reduced to 10 stitches, break off the wool, and with a wool needle draw the wool through the ten stitches, and sew them up close and round. **For the Instep**—with Cardinal wool—Work 10 double crochet on the instep chain, and continue working 10 double crochet backwards and forwards for 10 rows, at the end of each row catching up the side stitch of the foot part. Break off when 10 rows are done, and recommence with the cardinal wool at the heel, working double crochet on each rib of the foot part, 10 double crochet along that side, 10 double crochet on the instep stitches, and 10 double crochet on the opposite side of the foot. Crochet 10 rows of ribbing backwards and forwards, without either increase or decrease. **11th row**—Increase 1 at the beginning and 1 at the end of the row; then 3 plain rows. **15th row**—Increase 1 at the beginning and 1 at the end of the row; then 4 plain rows. **20th row**—Increase 1 at the beginning and 1 at the end of the row; and now work 8 plain rows, and the boot will be sufficiently long. Sew it up the leg, making the raised ribs meet one another. **For the Trimming.**—**1st row**—With cardinal wool — 1 double crochet in the centre of the instep in the fourth depressed rib, 5 treble on the fifth raised rib of the instep (to make these treble, instead of working in the usual way, draw the wool through all three loops of each stitch at once), 1 double crochet in the next depressed rib, 5 treble in next depressed rib, and so on, working 8 groups of five trebles up the leg, then work the same, making 9 groups of trebles, 1 double crochet between each group, round the top of the leg. **2nd row**—with white wool—1 single crochet on the double crochet of last row, 1 more single crochet, 1 double crochet on the second stitch of trebles of last row, * wool over the needle, insert the hook in the next stitch of last row and draw the wool through, repeat from * four times, draw the wool through all the stitches on the needle together, 1 double crochet on the second stitch of next group of trebles of last row, and repeat. The groups of raised stitches are always to come between the trebles of previous row. **3rd row**—with white wool—Same as the first row, working the 5 treble stitches in the stitch which draws together the five raised stitches of last row. The trimming down the front is now complete, but work the last two rows again round the top of the leg, once with cardinal wool, and once with white. And the boot is finished. Of course any two shades of wool can be employed, or one colour even if preferred, while the trimming down the front and along top of boot can be varied according to the maker's fancy; or a ribbon run in and tied in a bow at the side adds a pretty finish.

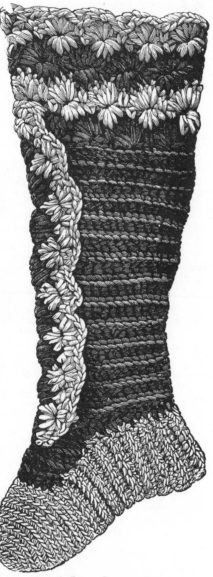

BABY'S LONG CROCHET BOOT.

LADY'S HOOD.

THIS becoming hood will take 3 ozs. of single Berlin wool, white or any colour preferred. It is worked in the Scotch fashion with no ridge, inserting the hook so as to take up both the top threads of the previous row. Bone crochet needle, No. 10. Commence with the **crown** by working 4 chain, join round, and work 7 double crochet in the circle. **2nd round**—2 double crochet on each double crochet of last round. **3rd round**—2 double crochet on the first stitch, 1 double crochet on the next, and repeat. **4th round**—The same. **5th round**—1 double crochet on each of the two first stitches, 2 double crochet on the next, and repeat. Continue increasing where necessary, and the work after the sixth round should be just a little drawn in, that is, not so perfectly as the crown of a Tam o' Shanter. When the crown measures eight inches across, break off the wool and recommence about 27 stitches farther on, the missed stitches will form the bottom of the crown. Work round with a slight increase at the top, and again break off at the same place as before. Continue thus working in rows for the front part of the hood till it is as large as is required. For the **frill**—1 treble on the outside row of the double crochet, 1 chain, 1 treble on the next row, 1 chain, 1 treble on the next row, 1 chain, 1 treble on the next row, 1 chain, 1 treble or the next row, all straight along, 1 chain, turn and work the same back, and so on up and down 5 trebles in a line with 1 chain between each treble round the entire front of the hood. Work the same, but only 4 stitches wide round the centre of the hood. Having done this, work 1 double crochet under loop of one chain, 4 chain, 1 double crochet under next one chain, and so on all over the frill, which when finished tack down in its place.

LADY'S HOOD.

For the **curtain**—Hold the hood the right side towards you, and work a row of double crochet loosely and just a little full, break off at the end of the row. Work 3 more rows of double crochet the same way as the hood is worked. Then a row of double long treble (the wool turned three times round the needle), increase 1 double long treble in every eighth stitch. Then 4 rows of double crochet, and another row of double long treble, and finish with a row of edging, 1 double crochet on one long treble, * 4 chain, 2 treble in the first of the chain, miss three long treble, 1 double crochet on the next, and repeat from *. Make a chain and tassels to tie round the front, and the same on the back of the curtain, make a nice ribbon bow on the top of the hood.

BABY'S CROCHET HAT.

THIS most becoming little hat will take 2½ ozs. of pale blue double Berlin wool. Bone crochet needle, No. 8. Commence with 3 chain, join round, and work 8 treble in the circle; do not join again, but continue working round and round like a serpent for 6 rounds, closely and evenly; in the first of the rounds increase upon the foundation by working 2 treble on each of the eight treble stitches, inserting the hook in the top loop, and afterwards increase here and there wherever necessary to make the work lie flat. This will complete the crown. Then to shape the head, work 3 rounds straight on without any increase. **10th round**—To commence the brim—1 double crochet,* 3 chain, miss two treble, 1 double crochet on the third, and repeat from *, and join at the end of the row. **11th round**—Work 6 treble under every loop of three chain of previous row; join and break off. **12th round**—Turn the work so as to get the wrong side of the treble stitches to the right side of the crochet already done, work 1 treble on each consecutive stitch, and join at the end of the round. **13th round**—1 treble on each consecutive treble of last round. **14th round**—2 long treble on two consecutive stitches of previous round,* 4 chain, 1 double crochet in the fourth chain from the needle, 1 chain, miss two treble of last row, and work 2 long treble on the next two consecutive stitches; repeat from *; join round and fasten off neatly. Procure 2½ yards of pale blue ribbon and 1½ inch wide, trim with a plain band of ribbon round the head joined together in front with a small bow, also a small bow on the crown towards the front. Fold 30 inches of the ribbon in half lengthways and run it in through the holes round the brim of the hat, join neatly. Use the remainder of the ribbon for strings, sew in a little white cap and the hat will be finished.

CROCHETED IMITATIONS OF FUR.

WITH a fine bone hook and single Berlin wool make a chain. **1st row**—Double crochet at the end, 1 chain. **2nd row**—1 double crochet in the first double crochet, taking up the back of the loop, which is done throughout the work; take up the back of the second loop, draw the wool through, pass the wool round the needle, take up the same loop again, making 3 loops on the needle in this one stitch, draw the wool through these three, then through the two on the needle; take up the whole of this row in this manner. **3rd row**—Plain double crochet worked from the back of the loop as before. Repeat the second and third rows.

CHILD'S FROCK.

THIS pretty frock is worked with pale blue Beehive wool, and bone crochet needle, No. 12, and will fit a child of two. It will take about 14ozs. of wool, and is worked throughout in ribbed Russian crochet, inserting the hook into the back of the stitches of the preceding row. If worked with a thicker wool it will be large enough for an older child. Commence for the right side of the back, at the neck, with 38 chains, turn, work 8 double crochet, 3 double crochet in the next, 5 consecutive double crochet, miss two, 5 consecutive double crochet, 3 double crochet in the next, 5 consecutive double crochet, miss one, 8 double crochet to the end: this is the shoulder side. **2nd row**—1 chain to turn, miss the first stitch of last row, 7 double crochet, 1 double crochet on two of last row, 4 double crochet, 3 double crochet on the centre stitch of the three double crochet of last row, 4 double crochet, 1 double crochet on two, 1 double crochet on two, 4 double crochet, 3 double crochet on the centre stitch of the three double crochet

CHILD'S FROCK.

of last row, 8 double crochet, working the last stitch of the eight upon two of last row. **3rd row**—1 chain to turn, miss the first stitch of last row, 8 consecutive double crochet, 3 double crochet on the centre stitch of the three double crochet of last row, 4 double crochet, 1 double crochet on two, 1 double crochet on two, 4 double crochet, 3 double crochet on the centre stitch of the three double crochet of last row, 4 double crochet, 1 double crochet on two, 8 double crochet. Repeat the second and third rows till you can count 16 ridges, then being on the shoulder side, work 1 chain to turn, miss the first stitch of last row, 1 double crochet on each of the two next stitches, 3 double crochet on the next, 5 consecutive double crochet, 1 double crochet on two, 4 double crochet, 3 double crochet on the centre stitch of the three double crochet of last row, 4 double crochet, 1 double crochet on two, 1 double crochet on two, 4 double crochet, 3 double crochet on the centre stitch of the three double crochet of last row, 8 double crochet, working the last stitch of the eight upon two of last row. **Next row**—1 chain to turn, miss the first stitch last row, 8 consecutive double crochet, 3 double crochet on the centre stitch of the three double crochet of last row, 4 double crochet, 1 double crochet on two, 1 double crochet on two, 4 double crochet, 3 double crochet on the centre stitch of the three double crochet of last row, 4 double crochet, 1 double crochet on two, 1 double crochet on two, 4 double crochet, 3 double crochet on the centre stitch of the three double crochet of row, 4 double crochet. Continue as these last two rows, and you will find two more double crochet coming like a gore upon the shoulder side at the end of each alternate row, and when you get 12 double crochet at the end, turn, and begin another scalloped pattern the same as the last, and work on till that scallop comes to 6 double crochet at the end of the row after the 3 double crochet at the point, and this completes the right back of the dress. Commence again with 38 chain, and work the left back exactly the same, only reversing the work by beginning at the *end* of each row. When the second half of the back is finished begin for the front, which is worked all in one piece, commencing with 16 chain. **1st row**—8 double crochet, miss one, 5 consecutive double crochet, 3 double crochet in the next, 5 consecutive double crochet, miss two, 5 consecutive double crochet, 3 double crochet in the next, 8 consecutive double crochet, miss two, 8 consecutive double crochet, 3 double crochet in the next, 5 consecutive double crochet, miss two, 5 consecutive double crochet, 3 double crochet in the next, 5 consecutive double crochet, miss one, 8 double crochet. **2nd row**—1 chain to turn, miss the first stitch of last row, 7 consecutive double crochet, 1 double crochet on two of last row, 4 double crochet, 3 double crochet on the centre stitch of the three double crochet of last row, 4 double crochet, 1 double crochet on two, 1 double crochet on two, 4 double crochet, 3 double crochet on the centre stitch of the three double crochet of last row, 7 consecutive double crochet, 1 double crochet on two, 1 double crochet on two, 7 consecutive double crochet, 3 double crochet in the centre stitch of the three double crochet of last

row, 4 double crochet, 1 double crochet on two, 1 double crochet on two, 4 double crochet, 3 double crochet on the centre stitch of the three double crochet of last row, 4 double crochet, 1 double crochet on two, 8 double crochet. Repeat the second row forwards and backwards till you can count 16 ridges. Then increase out for the gores exactly the same as the back pieces are increased, of course making a gore on each side. Now sew the back pieces together about four inches up from the bottom, then sew up the sides, leaving spaces for the sleeves. Proceed to shape the neck by beginning on the left-hand back, work 2 single crochet on the point, 2 double crochet and 1 treble down the side of the hollow, 1 long treble in the stitch that was missed in the commencing chain, 1 treble and 2 double crochet on the other side the hollow, and 2 single crochet on the point, and so on, work 14 chain for the shoulder piece, then work along the front and the other shoulder and back the same. Now work two ridges of plain double crochet round the neck, decreasing in the centre of each shoulder piece, and also decreasing a stitch at intervals of every nine or ten stitches to get the neck a nice shape, finish with an edge of 1 double crochet, miss one, 3 treble in the next, miss one, and repeat. This done, proceed with the tufted trimming which is worked round the neck and sleeves, round the bottom of the dress, and straight up the back and front to the width of 1½ inches, work 1 double crochet, 4 chain, and repeat in a line five times, and work close together and forwards and backwards. For the **Flounce**—Commence with a chain about half as wide again as the bottom of the skirt, as the scallops contract it so much, and work in ribbed crochet the same as the dress. **1st row**—5 consecutive double crochet, 3 double crochet in the next, 5 consecutive double crochet, miss two, and repeat. **2nd row**—1 chain to turn, miss the two first stitches of last row, * 4 consecutive double crochet, 3 double crochet on the centre stitch of the three double crochet of last row, 4 consecutive double crochet, 1 double crochet on two, and repeat from *. Work the same as the second row till you have 12 ridges worked, and the flounce is deep enough. Join it round. Tack the commencing chain on the skirt under the tufted crochet, placing the scallops flat and even and so as to fall loosely, making the flounce resemble a box pleating, keep the pleats in place by means of two tacking threads lower down. For the **Sleeve**—Commence with 8 chain, turn, and work 7 double crochet, and work in ridges like the dress. **2nd row** and 5 succeeding rows—1 chain to turn, and work 7 double crochet. **8th row** and 5 succeeding rows—1 chain to turn, and work 8 double crochet. **14th row** and 5 succeeding rows—1 chain to turn, and work 9 double crochet. **20th row** and 10 succeeding rows—1 chain to turn, and work 10 double crochet. Now decrease on the same side as you have increased, and work back from the 19th row to the 1st row. Work the other sleeve the same, and edge both on the straight side with a row the same as that that edges the neck. Sew the sleeves up, the seam comes on the top of the arm, work the tufted trimming the same as round the neck, and sew the sleeves in. Trim the dress with a pretty Valenciennes lace round the neck and sleeves.

CROCHET SHAWL.

To be worked with single Berlin wool or a fine make of fingering yarn, as preferred. Bone crochet needle, No. 9. Commence with a chain sufficient for the width of the shawl; turn, work 1 treble in the third chain from the needle, * 1 chain, miss one stitch of the foundation, 1 treble in the next, and repeat from * to the end of the row. **2nd row**—2 chain to turn, 1 treble under the first one chain, 1 chain, 1 treble under the next one chain, and repeat, the last treble stitch at the end of the row is to be worked upon the chain that turned. Work the entire centre of the shawl the same as the second row, keeping the same number of treble stitches in every row. For the **Border**. **1st row**—Work 6 treble at the corner, 1 chain and 1 treble alternately, the same as the centre of the shawl along the side, and repeat. **2nd row**—6 treble between the third and fourth treble stitches of last row at the corner, 1 chain and 1 treble alternately along the side, and repeat. **3rd row**—6 treble between the second and third treble stitches at the corner, 1 chain, 6 treble between the fourth and fifth trebles, * 1 chain, miss the next one chain hole, 1 treble in the next, 1 chain, 1 treble in the next, 1 chain, miss the next one chain hole, 6 treble in the next, and repeat from * to the corner, where again increase. **4th row**—6 treble between the third and fourth treble stitches in the first group at the corner, 1 chain, 6 treble under the one chain, 1 chain, 6 treble between the third and fourth trebles of the second group at the corner, * 1 chain, 1 treble on the

CROCHET SHAWL.

treble of last row, 1 chain, 1 treble on the next treble of last row, 1 chain, 6 treble between the third and fourth treble stitches of the group, and repeat from * to the corner, where again increase. Work 6 more rows of bordering in the same way as the last row, only increasing to turn the corner as shown in the illustration. **11th row**—1 double crochet under the chain stitch between the two treble stitches, 7 chain, * wool over the needle, insert the hook in the fourth chain from the needle, and draw the wool loosely through, repeat from * seven times, wool over the needle, and draw through all the stitches on the needle, 1 single crochet in the next stitch of the chain to secure the ball, 2 chain, 1 double crochet between the third and fourth treble stitches of the group, 7 chain, make another ball, 2 chain, and repeat

NICELY FITTING HOOD FOR LADY OR CHILD.

THE crown of this hood is worked in Point Neige, and can be made to fit any head. About 4ozs. of white Peacock Fingering or single Berlin will be required, and a No. 7 bone crochet-needle, also 2 yards of 1½-inch wide satin ribbon for strings and bows. Commence with chain sufficient to reach at the back of the neck from ear to ear; our model is begun with 65 chain, in which 31 points of neige are worked. Point Neige is worked in this manner:—**1st row**—Raise 5 loops in 5 successive stitches of the chain, wool over the needle, and draw through all the loops and the stitch on the needle together, 1 chain, * raise a loop in the thread that lies under the chain, another in the thread at the back of the last stitch of the group, another in the same chain the last group was worked into, one in the next chain, and another in the next chain, there will be 6 stitches on the needle, wool over the needle and draw through all, 1 chain, repeat from *, and fasten off at the end of the row. **2nd row**— Beginning on the right-hand side, 1 single in the first stitch of previous row, 2 chain, raise a loop in the first chain, another in the single stitch, another in the top thread of the first group of stitches of previous row, another in the hole formed by the one chain, and another in the top thread of the next group of stitches, there will now be 6 stitches on the needle, wool over the needle, and draw through all, 1 chain, * raise a loop in the thread that lies under the chain, another in the thread at the back of the last stitch of the group, another in the same stitch the last group was worked into, another in the hole formed by the one chain, and another in the top thread of the next group of stitches, wool over the needle and draw through all, 1 chain, repeat from *, and fasten off at the end of the row. Work another row the same as the second row, and be careful to have the same number of points in the row. The 4th row is worked in the same manner, but commence upon the third point and fasten off, leaving two points unworked at the end of the row, so you will have 4 points less in this row than in the preceding ones. Work another row with the same number of points as in the fourth row. In the 6th row increase 1 point in the middle of the row, and increase again at the same place in the next row, and two successive rows; there will now again be 31 points of neige in the row. Work 4 or 5 rows straight along, having the number of points in a row, and this should bring you far enough to begin the rounding for the head. In the next row decrease 2 points in the middle of the row, and do likewise in every row till only 12 points of neige remain, fill up this small triangular space with points to fit in straightly with the edges of the work, and the crown of the hood is complete. Now holding the work the right side towards you, and commencing at the beginning of the fourth row of the point neige, work 8 treble, catch the last of the treble into the first, so making a tuft of treble stitches, then 1 treble by itself in the fifth row of the point neige, and repeat the tuft and the single treble stitch alternately all round the front and to the opposite side of the crown and fasten off. Now join on at the beginning of the third row of the point neige and work a row of double long treble stitches (wool three times over the needle), one double long treble on the tuft and one on the treble stitch alternately with 1 chain between each, go all round the front of the hood and join on to the other end of the third row of the point neige, and then go round the back of the hood on the third row of point neige in loops of 3 chain 1 double crochet and fasten off at the same place as you began. Recommence and work another row of tufted treble in front, the same as before, and fasten off. Again begin on the right-hand side, and upon the first treble stitch (which here will be the first one of the group of eight) work 2 treble, 2 long treble, 4 double long treble, 2 long treble, 2 treble (all together), then 1 double crochet on the single treble stitch of last row, and repeat the bunch of stitches and the 1 double crochet stitch alternately on the successive treble stitches of last row, not working into the tufts at all, continue the same in the loops of 3 chain round the back of the hood. Next round—1 double crochet on the double crochet of last row, and 4 chain 1 double crochet repeated on each successive stitch of last row. Now the head part is finished, and you proceed to work the curtain. First of all, under the frilled rows you have done at the back of the head, and into the *same* place as the row of 3 chain 1 double crochet is worked, work a row of double long treble stitches like that in the front, commencing at the *end* of the front double long treble row, and working to meet the *other* end of the same row, and between every stitch of this double long treble, instead of 1 chain, work 3 double crochet stitches into the foundation row of the point neige. For the **Curtain**—Upon the last row of double crochet and double long treble stitches work 4 rows of point neige as described for the crown, but increasing 1 point seven stitches from the beginning and end of each row, 1 point at each quarter, and 2 points in the centre of the back, so making it nice and full.

NICELY FITTING HOOD FOR LADY OR CHILD.

5th row—Work 1 double crochet, 2 chain, 3 long treble, into the stitch at the beginning of last row, and the same into every alternate shell, and break off at the end of the row. **6th row**—Begin on the 2 chain of last row with a double crochet stitch, and into the next 2 chain work * 4 double long treble, 3 chain, 1 double crochet, and repeat from * into every loop of chain of last row. **7th row**—Beginning under the 3 chain of last row work 1 double crochet, 3 chain, 4 double long treble, and repeat the same under every 3 chain of last row, omitting the *last*. **8th row**—Working on the curtain from the first row of the crown on one side to the first row of the crown on the other side, 1 double crochet to begin, then * 4 chain 1 double crochet, and repeat from *, the double crochet at the bottom of the curtain goes into the first stitch of each group of double long treble stitches, and at the sides it goes in each alternate row of the work. **9th row**—Work a group of 7 treble stitches under every loop of 4 chain of last row, drawing up the first thread of each stitch very long and loose. **10th row**—A group of 10 treble stitches worked in the same way upon the centre stitch of the 7 trebles of last row, 1 double crochet in between each of the groups of last row. Run 1 yard of ribbon in through the long stitches at the front of the hood to tie for strings, and make a bow of part of the remaining ribbon and sew on at the top. Run the rest of the ribbon in through the long stitches at the back in two pieces so that they tie under the crown. Tack the row of frilling down over these pieces of ribbon, just leaving a little up at the back to show the bow.

CHILD'S CROCHET PETTICOAT.

THIS Petticoat measures 14 inches in length, and will take 3 ozs. of white and 1 oz. of pale blue single Berlin wool. Fine bone crochet needle. Commence for the waist with 171 chain, turn, miss the first of the chain stitches, *3 consecutive double crochet, 3 double crochet in the next stitch of the chain, 3 consecutive double crochet, miss the next two chain stitches and repeat from*. Turn the work at the end of the row, and for the remainder of the petticoat take up the small loop at the back of the stitches as the work is to set in ribs. **2nd row**—Miss the first double crochet stitch, work* 3 consecutive double crochet on the next three double crochet, 3 double crochet in the centre stitch of the three double crochet of last row, 3 consecutive double crochet, miss the two next double crochet stitches, and repeat from*. Work 5 more rows the same as the last. **8th row**—Miss the first double crochet stitch, work *1 double crochet in each of the two next stitches, 2 double crochet in the next, 3 double crochet in the centre stitch of the three double crochet of last row, 2 double crochet in the next, 1 double crochet in each of the two next stitches, miss the two next double crochet stitches, and repeat from*. **9th row**—Miss the first double crochet stitch, work *4 consecutive double crochet, 3 double crochet in the centre stitch of the three double crochet of last row, 4 consecutive double crochet, miss the two next double crochet stitches, and repeat from*. Work 9 more rows the same as the last. **19th row**—Miss the first double crochet stitch, work * 1 double crochet in each of the three next stitches, 2 double crochet in the next, 3 double crochet in the centre stitch of the three double crochet of last row, 2 double crochet in the next, 1 double crochet in each of the three next stitches, miss the two next double crochet stitches, and repeat from*. **20th row**—Miss the first double crochet stitch, work *5 consecutive double crochet, 3 double crochet in the centre stitch of the three double crochet of last row, 5 consecutive double crochet, miss the two next double crochet stitches, and repeat from*. Work 4 more rows the same as the last, then join on the blue wool and work 6 rows the same with blue; then 4 rows with white, and 7 rows with blue. **Last row**—with blue wool—Miss the first double crochet stitch, work *5 consecutive double crochet, 5 double crochet in the centre stitch of the three double crochet of last row, 5 consecutive double crochet, miss the two last double crochet stitches, and repeat from*. For the **Band**—Work into the commencing chain—with white wool—1 double crochet on the first stitch, 1

DETAILS OF CHILD'S CROCHET PETTICOAT.

treble on the next stitch, 1 long treble in the same stitch as the three double crochet of the first row is worked into, 1 treble on the next stitch, 1 double crochet on the next stitch, 1 double crochet under the two missed chain stitches, and repeat. Work 2 rows of plain double crochet. **4th row**—1 double crochet, *1 chain, miss one double crochet of last row, 1 double crochet in the next, and repeat from*. **5th row**—Plain double crochet. Sew the petticoat up the back, joining the raised ribs together neatly, and leaving sufficient space for the placket hole. Make a crochet chain and draw it through the holes in the waistband, to tie with a tassel at each end.

TUFTED PATTERN.

THIS pattern is very useful and pretty for shawls and scarfs, being alike on both sides. Use fingering wool and a bone crochet needle, No. 7, and commence with chain sufficient for the width of the shawl. **1st row**—1 double crochet in the first chain from the needle, 1 double crochet in the next, * wool over the needle, and insert the hook in the next chain, and draw the wool through, wool over the needle again and draw through two stitches on the needle, this makes half a treble stitch, make two more half treble stitches in the same place, wool over the needle and draw through the three half trebles and through the other stitch that is on the needle, 2 double crochet in two consecutive chain, and repeat from * to the end of the row, turn. **2nd row**—2 double crochet above the two double crochet of previous row, * 3 half treble above the three half trebles, and 2 double crochet above the two next double crochet, repeat from *. Every succeeding row is worked the same as

TUFTED PATTERN.

the second row. The shawl may be fringed, or finished off with the crochet edging.

BOY'S CROCHET HAT.

MATERIALS—3 ozs. of Berlin wool, any colour preferred, and a suitable crochet hook. Make a chain of 4 stitches and join in a circle. **1st round**—In each foundation stitch 2 short crochets. **2nd round**—Again 2 short crochets in each stitch, take up the back part of each stitch. **3rd round**—* 1 short crochet in first stitch, 2 short crochets in next stitch, repeat from * seven times. **4th round**—* 2 short crochets in first two stitches, 2 short crochets in next stitch, repeat from * all the round. **5th round**—* 3 short crochets in first three stitches, 2 short crochets in next stitch, repeat from * seven times. In like manner widen in each row until the twentieth row has 18 stitches between the widenings. **21st and 22nd rounds**—Without widening. **23rd round** —* 8 long crochets, miss 1 stitch, repeat from * to end of round. **24th round** —In each stitch 1 long crochet. **25th round**—14 long crochets, miss 1 stitch, repeat from * to end of round. **26th round**—1 double crochet stitch in every stitch. **27th round**—* 12 double crochets in next 12 stitches, miss 1 stitch, repeat from * all the round. **28th round**—In every stitch of last row 1 double crochet. **29th round**—Like twenty-seventh. **30th round**—Like twenty-sixth. This finishes the cap. For the **Trimming**, which is a looped border, make a chain of 10 stitches, and work 1 short crochet in each foundation stitch. **1st round**—Put hook through first stitch, taking up both upper parts of stitch, wind the wool around the hook and forefinger of right hand six times, bring them all through the stitch, and draw wool through all the stitches. Repeat this in every stitch. Turn work. **2nd round**—1 chain, 1 short crochet in every stitch of last row. When this stripe is long enough sew it neatly around the cap. Make four rosettes, two for the ear-laps and two for the front and side of cap; for these make a chain of 4 stitches, join in a circle and work 1 loop stitch in every one in the next row, 2 stitches in every loop, stitch, &c., until the rosette is the desired size.

CROCHET EDGING.

1st round—* 22 chain, close the last eight into a circle, 12 double in circle, 1 slip stitch in first of 12 double, 7 chain, 5 long treble with 3 chain between each in the next double stitches, 7 chain, 1 double in next stitch, twice alternately 5 chain, 1 double in every second stitch, then 5 chain, 1 slip stitch in last slip stitch, 2 double, 1 treble, 2 long treble in next 7 chain, 3 chain, 2 long treble, 1 treble, 1 double in same chain, 4 times alternately 1 double, 1 treble, 2 long treble with 2 chain between, 1 treble in one double in 3 chain, then 1 double, 1 treble, 1 long treble in 7 chain, 3 chain, 2 long treble, 1 treble, 2 double in same 7 chain, repeat from *, joining as you proceed. **2nd round** —* 1 treble in centre of five chain scallops, 9 chain, 1 treble in centre of 13 chain, 9 chain, repeat from *. **3rd round**—* 1 long treble, 1 chain, miss 1, 1 long treble, joining the centre stitch to centre of last long treble, 3 chain, miss 3, repeat from *.

CROCHET EDGING.

CROCHET as follows—**1st row**—* 14 chain, 1 leaf as follows—going back along the chain, 1 slip stitch, 1 single, 1 double, 2 treble, 1 double, 1 single, 1 slip stitch, repeat from *. **2nd row**—* 1 double in fourth of the six free chain stitches, 3 chain, 7 treble in centre 7 stitches of the leaf, working the centre of the 7 treble in the point of the leaf, 3 chain, repeat from *. **3rd row**—* 1 double in 3 chain, 5 chain, 1 double in centre of 7 double, 5 chain, 1 double in next 3 chain, 1 purl of 5 chain and 1 double, repeat from *. **4th row** —* 1 double in 5 chain, 5 chain, 1 double in 5 chain, 5 chain, 1 double in next purl, 5 chain, repeat from *.

STYLISH WALKING COAT.

THIS coat can be made of a size to fit any child by cutting a paper pattern to shape the work by. The plain part of the coat is executed throughout in a stitch of one double crochet 1 chain, turning at the end of every row, and working the double crochet always under the chain stitch of preceding row. The work must not be too loose; it is elastic, and will therefore stretch. If done with peacock fingering, single Berlin wool or other wool about the same thickness. Use a No. 12 crochet needle. A No. 5 crochet needle will be required for the border. A coat 24 inches in length from the neck to the bottom of the trimming will take about 1 lb. of wool. Commence at the bottom of the plain part of the skirt, making as many chain as you require for the entire width of the coat. **1st row**—1 double crochet in the third chain from the needle, * 1 chain, miss one of the foundation, 1 double crochet in the next, and repeat from * to the end of the row. **2nd row**—2 chain to turn, 1 double crochet under the first chain stitch of last row, and work 1 chain, 1 double crochet all along. Work 4 more rows the same as the second row. Then fold the work and put in a mark at the quarters where the side seams should come, and where by-and-by the sleeve holes will be formed, and here decrease in each alternate row by working 1 double crochet in each of 2 holes, but drawing the 2 double crochet stitches together at the top so as to form only 1 stitch instead of 2. When you have decreased sufficiently, according to your paper pattern, work several rows straight on for the waist, and increase a little as you get towards the armholes, the increase will be made by working an extra 1 chain 1 double crochet into a hole. There is no decrease or increase whatever at the fronts or on the back. Having done a sufficient length to reach the armholes, work to the paper pattern in 3 sections, first the piece for the right front, then the piece for the back, and afterwards the piece for the left front. Then work 2 rows the entire length, and having done that, begin the slope for the shoulders and also a little slope in the middle of the back, decreasing in the same way that the side seams were decreased and keeping to the shape of paper pattern. Finish round the neck with a row of 1 chain 1 long treble, by which holes are made to run in a ribbon. Now into the foundation chain at the bottom of the skirt work, first of all, a row of double crochet with the wool passed once round a 1 inch mesh between every stitch, so making a kind of fringed edge. Then, again, into the foundation chain work a row of 2 chain, miss 2, 1 treble, and repeat these stitches, working loosely, and increasing where necessary to shape for a little fulness, for about 9 rows. This is intended merely as a ground for the shell-stitch trimming, and will not show when the coat is worn. Now for the **Shells**—With a No. 5 crochet needle commence again upon the foundation chain, and keeping the fringe under your thumb out of the way, work 1 double crochet, * 12 chain, wool over the needle, insert the hook in the chain nearest the needle and draw the wool through in a long loose stitch, do the same in each succeeding stitch of the chain, also in the first stitch but one of the foundation. There will be 25 stitches on the needle, wool over the needle and draw through all, then do 1 chain to keep the shell in place, and 1 double crochet in the next stitch but one of the foundation, and repeat from * to the end of the row, and fasten off; this will produce a series of long loose scallops resembling shells. Recommence on the right-hand side and proceed with another row in the same way, working into the first row of the treble groundwork. Then a row the same stitch worked into the next row of the groundwork. In the four following rows work 14 chain for each shell and draw up 29 stitches on the needle. In the next two rows work 16 chain and draw up 33 stitches on the needle, working if possible longer and looser stitches so as to make larger shells. Commence the last row of shells at the same place as the first row is begun, and work along the side of the front to the bottom, and finish up the other front to the place where the first row is ended. For edge to the last row of shells, commence again in the same place and work 1 double crochet in every stitch of the stitch of the shells, and finish with a little scalloped edge up the right-hand front, doing 1 treble, 3 long treble, 1 treble, 1 double crochet consecutively, in consecutive stitches of the front. Now for the **Cape**—Make a fringed edge and a groundwork of treble and chain like you did for the flounce, but with more increasings, so as to bring it to a pretty circular shape, five or six rows will make it sufficiently large, and cover the same with the same number of rows of shells, edging the last row the same as the flounce is edged. For the **Sleeves**—Commence with sufficient chain for the wrist, and work in the same stitch as used for the coat, increase at the beginning and end of the rows, in about every sixth row as you get beyond the elbow, and when the sleeve is sufficiently long on the inner side slope off to fit in the shoulder, working two double crochet less at the end of every row, till only six double crochet remain, fasten off, sew up the sleeve and sew it in the armhole. The other sleeve is worked in the same way. The trimming for the sleeve consists of 6 rows of smaller shells worked upon a treble and chain foundation, 3 rows with 8 chain for a shell and 3

STYLISH WALKING COSTUME.

rows with 9 chain, and the last row edged the same as the flounce is edged You will see that the shells hang about rather loosely, particularly the large ones on the flounce and cape. With a rug needle and wool tack every shell down in its place upon the foundation, one row turning to the right, the next row turning to the left. Sew five white satin buttons on the left front, and run in a yard of inch-wide satin ribbon to tie round the neck in a bow.

SMALL WHEEL PATTERN.

For Pincushion Covers, Toilet Mats, &c.

Required, a skein of Ardern's crochet cotton, No. 14. Steel crochet needle, No. 20. Begin with 12 chain, join round, work 5 chain, cotton twice round the needle, insert the hook in the circle and draw the cotton through, cotton over the needle and draw through two stitches on the needle, cotton over the needle and draw through two stitches on the needle, 3 chain, * cotton twice round the needle, insert the hook in the circle and draw the cotton through, cotton over the needle and draw through two stitches on the needle, cotton over the needle and draw through two stitches on the needle, cotton twice round the needle, insert the hook again in the circle and draw the cotton through, and now cotton over the needle and draw through two stitches on the needle four times, thus making 2 double long treble stitches joined into one, 3 chain, and repeat from *, work 16

SMALL WHEEL PATTERN.

groups of stitches in the circle, and fasten off. Make other round wheels in the same manner, joining them together in process of working, as shown in the illustration. The crossed stitches between the wheels are sewn in afterwards in point-lace stitch with a needle and cotton.

WOOLLEN CROSSOVER.

¼ LB. of black, 1 oz. of violet Scotch fingering. Bone crochet needle, No. 9. Commence at the bottom of the back, with black wool, with 16 chain, turn, and work 1 treble in the fourth chain from the needle, 1 treble, 1 chain, miss 1 of the foundation, 3 consecutive treble, 1 chain, miss 1, 3 consecutive treble, 1 chain, miss 1, 1 treble in the next, and 2 treble in the last stitch, 2nd row—2 chain to turn, 2 treble in between the first and second trebles of last row, * 1 chain, 3 treble under the one chain of last row, and repeat from * to the end of the row, where work the three last trebles under the chain stitches that turned at the end of the preceding row. Proceed the same as the second row, increasing the work gradually on each side till 17 rows are done, then work 4 chain to turn, and the 3 treble under the first one chain of last row, so making no increase, continue the pattern, and end the row with 1 chain, 1 treble. Next row—2 chain to turn, and 3 treble under the one chain of last row, and so work straight on forwards and backwards for 16 rows. There should now be 33 rows from the commencement, and be 20 groups of 3 trebles along the last row. For the Shoulder Turn the same way as before, and repeat the pattern till you have done 8 groups of 3 trebles, then 1 chain, 1 treble under the next 1 chain of previous row, turn the work, 2 chain, 2 treble under the 1 chain of last row, and work 1 chain, 3 treble, all along. Increase at the commencement of the next row, and increase at the end of the next succeeding row, and increase again in the next two rows in the same way on the outside of the crossover, keeping the front edge, where you divided for the neck, perfectly straight. After these four increasings, work straight on for 20 rows. Now, still keeping the front edge of the work quite straight, decrease the outside at the ending of every alternate row, which is done by working after the last three trebles, 1 more treble into the chain that turned, then turn with 3 chain and work the first group of 3 trebles under the one chain of last row. Continue decreasing on that one side of the work until you have only 3 groups of 3 trebles remaining, and fasten off. Re-commence where you divided for the neck, missing one loop of chain and beginning by working 1 treble in the next loop of chain. Continue the pattern, making 8 groups of 3 trebles along the row, and 1 chain 1 treble at the end. Work this shoulder of the crossover to correspond with that already done, increasing where that is increased, then doing 20 straight rows, and afterwards decreasing to 3 groups of 3 trebles. For the Edging—With violet wool—Work first of all 1 treble 1 chain alternately and easily, all round the crossover. 2nd row—1 single crochet on the treble stitch of last row, * 5 chain, 1 double crochet in the third from the needle, insert the hook in the next chain stitch and draw the wool through, insert the hook in the other chain stitch and draw the wool through, miss two stitches of previous row, insert the hook in the next stitch and draw the wool through, insert the hook in the next stitch of last row and draw the wool through, there will be 5 stitches on the needle, draw the wool through all, and repeat from *. This completes the crossover. Work two pieces of chain about 20 inches long, make a tassel at one end, and affix the other end to the front end of the crossover to tie round the waist.

HALF-SQUARE SHAWL IN RUSSIAN CROCHET.

This shawl is easily worked, and is very warm and useful either for personal wear or to give to the poor. Grey and blue single Berlin wool in quantity according to the size of the shawl, the chief part of which is worked with grey, the blue being used for the border. Bone crochet needle, No. 9. Commence with grey wool with 4 chain, turn, and work 3 double crochet in the third chain from the needle, 1 double crochet in the last of the chain. The double crochet throughout the shawl is to be worked by inserting the hook into the small horizontal loop at the back of the stitches of the preceding row so as to form ridges. 2nd row—1 chain to turn, 1 double crochet in the first double crochet of last row, 1 double crochet in the next, 3 double crochet in the centre stitch of the three double crochet of last row, 1 double crochet in the next, and 2 double crochet in the chain that turned. 3rd row—1 chain to turn, 1 double crochet in the first double crochet of last row, 3 double crochet in three consecutive stitches, 3 double crochet in the centre stitch, 3 double crochet in three consecutive stitches, and 2 double crochet in the chain that turned. 4th row—1 chain to turn, 1 double crochet in the first double crochet of last row, 5 double crochet in five consecutive stitches, 3 double crochet in the centre stitch, 5 double crochet in five consecutive stitches, and 2 double crochet in the chain that turned. Proceed in this manner, increasing two consecutive stitches on each side of every row till the centre part of the shawl is as large as you wish it to be. Then join on the blue wool and work 4 rows in the same manner, join on the grey wool and work 6 rows, join on the blue again and work 4 rows, now return to the grey wool and work 4 more rows. For Edging round two sides of the shawl—With grey wool, 1 treble in the first double crochet stitch of last row, 2 chain, another treble in the same place, miss three double crochet of last row, and repeat. Increase a little round the point by missing only one stitch instead of three, and work the 2 treble stitches into the centre stitch of the three double crochet. 2nd row—1 treble under the two chain of last row, 5 chain, 1 double crochet in the first of the chain stitches, 4 chain, 1 double crochet in the lower part of the last double crochet, 1 treble under the same two chain the last treble is worked into, and repeat.

SHELL STITCH IN LINE.

This is a pretty and effective stitch for an antimacassar or sofa blanket, and may be applied to scarfs, jackets, and many other useful articles. If working with wool about the thickness of single Berlin, use a No. 10 bone crochet needle. Commence with chain for the length required. 1st row—Insert the hook in the third chain from the needle and draw the wool through, and do the same in the three next consecutive chain-stitches, you now have 5 stitches on the needle, wool over the needle and draw through the four raised stitches, wool over the needle and draw through the two stitches on the needle, 1 chain, * insert the hook in the lower back loop of the shell just made and draw the wool through, insert the hook in the same chain-stitch the last shell is raised from and draw the wool through, insert the hook in the next chain-stitch and draw the wool through, and again in the next chain-stitch and draw the wool through, you now again have 5 stitches on the needle (as shown in the illustration), wool over the needle and draw through the 4 raised stitches, wool over the needle and draw through the 2 stitches on the needle, 1 chain, and repeat from *. Fasten off at the end of this and every row, and re-commence on the right-hand side. 2nd row—Double crochet in every stitch of last row, working under both top threads. 3rd row—Double crochet on every stitch of last row, taking up one top thread of the work. 4th row—Commence with a single crochet on the first stitch of last row, 2 chain, insert the hook in the first stitch of the chain and draw the wool through, insert the hook in the first stitch of last row and draw the wool through, raise a loop also in each of the two next stitches of last row, and there will be 5 stitches on the needle, wool over the needle and

SHELL STITCH IN LINE.

draw through the 4 raised stitches, wool over the needle and draw through the 4 stitches on the needle, 1 chain, and proceed with a row of shell stitches as directed in the first row. Repeat from the second row. When you have worked sufficient of the pattern, border the piece all round with 2 rounds of double crochet, and add a fringe or bordering as preferred.

BABY'S JACKET WORKED IN POINT NEIGE.

POINT neige, or shell pattern, as it is sometimes called, makes a lovely stitch for a jacket, being close and firm in texture, and therefore very warm. These directions are for a jacket large enough for a child of twenty months, and will also do for an older child by working a few additional rows before dividing for the armholes. 5 ozs. of white, 1 oz. of salmon pink single Berlin wool, or a soft make of German fingering. Bone crochet needle, No. 5. Commence at the bottom of the jacket with 129 chain. 1st row—Raise 5 loops loosely in five successive stitches of the chain, draw the wool through all the loops and the

BABY'S JACKET WORKED IN POINT NEIGE.

stitches of the needle together, 1 chain, * raise a loop in the little round hole formed by the chain, another in the lower thread at the back of the last stitch of the group, another in the same chain the last group was worked into, one in the next chain, and another in the next chain, there will be six stitches on the needle, draw the wool through all, 1 chain, repeat from * and fasten off at the end of the row, there should be 62 shells in the row. Tie three threads of coloured wool at the half and the quarters of the jacket, decreasings are to take place exactly straight above these ties. 2nd row—Beginning again on the right-hand side of the work, join into the first stitch of previous row, 2 chain, raise a loop in the first chain, another in the joined on stitch, another in the top thread of the group of stitches of previous row, another in the hole formed by the one chain, and another in the top thread of the next group of stitches, there will now be 6 stitches on the needle, draw the wool through all, 1 chain, * raise a loop in the little round hole formed by the chain, another in the lower thread at the back of the last stitch of the group, another in the same stitch the last group was worked into, another in the hole formed by the one chain, and another in the top thread of the next group of stitches, draw the wool through all, 1 chain, and repeat from *, decrease when you come to the ties by imperceptibly working 2 shells over 3, thus there will be 59 shells in this row; fasten off at the end. 3rd row—In which the salmon pink wool is introduced as a bordering mixed with the white, beginning on the right-hand side, 1 shell white, 1 shell pink, * 3 white, 1 pink, 3 white, 1 pink, and repeat from * to the end. 4th row—3 shells pink, 1 white, 3 pink, 1 white, and repeat, notice the middle stitch of the three pink always comes over the pink stitch of last row. 5th row—1 shell pink, 1 white, * 3 pink, 1 white, 3 pink, 1 white, and repeat from *. 6th row—3 shells white, 1 pink on the centre stitch of the three pink of last row, 3 white, 1 pink, and repeat. 7th row—With all white wool, work shells straight along, decreasing 1 over each of the ties, and there will be 56 shells in the row. 8th and 9th rows—Plain shells. 10th row—Decrease over the ties, making 53 shells in the row. 11th and 12th rows—Plain. 13th row—Decrease over the ties, and work 50 shells in the row. 14th and 15th rows—Plain. 16th row—Decrease over the ties, and work 47 shells in the row. 17th row—Plain. Now for the Right-hand Front of the jacket—Commence again at the right-hand side and work 11 shells and fasten off. Work 5 more rows upon these eleven shells. 7th row—Commence on the fifth shell from the beginning and work 7 shells. 8th row—Commence on the second shell and work 6 shells. 9th row—Commence on the first shell and work 5 shells. 10th row—Work 5 shells, which completes the shoulder. For the Back—Re-commence where you divided for the armhole, and leaving two shells unworked, begin on the third, and work 21 shells. Work 5 more rows upon these 21 shells. 7th row—Work 7 shells. 8th row—Work 7 shells. 9th row and 10th row—5 shells. Now sew this shoulder to the shoulder on the right-hand front. Miss seven shells on the back-piece and work another shoulder to correspond with the above. For the Left-hand Front—Re-commence where you divided for the armhole, and leaving two shells unworked, begin on the third, and work 11 shells. Work 5 more rows upon these eleven shells. 7th row—Work 7 shells. 8th row—Work 6 shells. 9th row—Commence on the second shell and work 5 shells. 10th row—Work 5 shells. Now sew this shoulder to the shoulder on the back-piece. For the Sleeve—Work in the armhole 3 rounds of 22 shells, then decrease 1 shell in each alternate round until you have done 12 rounds of the sleeve. 13th round—Work 1 stitch white and 1 stitch pink alternately. 14th round—All pink. 15th round—1 stitch white and 1 stitch pink alternately. 16th round—All white, and decrease 2 shells in the

round. Work the other sleeve in the same way. Now, holding the right side of the jacket towards you, work a row of double crochet round the neck, 1 double crochet in each shell and 1 chain between each double crochet. 2nd row—Beginning on the right-hand side, 1 treble under each chain stitch of last row, turn the corner, and continue down the front and entirely round the jacket with a row of shell pattern. 3rd row—Work a picot edging round the jacket and along the neck, 1 double crochet in a shell, 1 double crochet in the first of the chain, and repeat. Make a crochet chain and run it in the row of trebles to tie round the neck with a nice tassel at each end.

FROCK FOR CHILD OF TWO.

THE body of this frock is worked in plain treble stitch lengthways. Our model by which these instructions are given measures 18 inches from the neck to the bottom of the flounce and 18 inches round the waist. If a larger size be required it can easily be managed by working a few additional treble stitches of each row of the body and a few extra rows on the flounce. Required, 3 ozs. in white, 1½ ozs. of pink single Berlin wool. Bone crochet needle, No. 10. Commence with white wool for the right-hand back with 42 chain, turn, miss the first two chain, and work 40 treble stitches. 2nd row—2 chain to turn, then 40 treble, taking up the thread at the back of the stitches of last row so that the work sets in ridges. Work the same as the second row till you have 13 rows done from the commencement, then to heighten for the shoulder, do 7 chain, turn, 1 treble in the third chain from the needle and treble along to the end of the row, 46 treble in all, 2 chain to turn, and work to the neck end again, then 22 chain for the armhole, turn, 1 treble on the twenty-third treble of last row, and work 1 treble on each stitch to the end, 25 treble in all, 2 chain to turn, work treble on the treble stitches of last row and 22 more treble on the twenty two chain stitches, 46 treble in all, 2 chain to turn, and treble to the end, and now work a straight piece of 17 rows, 40 treble in a row, forwards and backwards, for the front of the frock. Form the other shoulder in the same way, heightening with 7 chain, and working 2 rows with 46 treble in a row, then 22 chain for the armhole, and a short row of 25 treble, then 2 rows with 46 treble in a row, and then a piece of 13 rows with 40 treble in a row, for the left-hand back. This completes the body. To shape the Neck—First of all sew the small shoulder-pieces together. Then for the 1st row—With white wool work plain double crochet, doing 5 double crochet to three ribs of the treble so as to tighten in a little. 2nd row—With pink wool, treble in every stitch of last row, but taking up two stitches in one twice on each shoulder. 3rd row—Treble, working into both top threads of last row, and again reducing twice on each shoulder. 4th row—The same. 5th row—1 double crochet between the first and second treble stitches, * 4 chain, 1 single in the double crochet just done, miss two treble, 1 double crochet in the next space, and repeat from *. For the Sleeves—With white wool—Commence at the lower part of the arm hole, work 3 treble under the treble stitch at the top of the short row of trebles, 22 treble on one side the armhole and 22 treble the other side, and join round. 2nd round—With pink wool—Treble in every stitch of last round, but taking up two stitches in one twice under the arm. 3rd round—The same. 4th round—1 double crochet between the first and second treble stitches, * 4 chain, 1 single in the double crochet just done, miss 2 treble, 1 double crochet in the next space and repeat from *. Work the other sleeve the same. For the Flounce—1st row—With white wool—Work 2 double crochet on each rib of the trebles of the body part, and join round, taking two rows of the right-hand side of the body over like a placket. 2nd round—With pink wool—Treble in every stitch of last round, working into one top thread. 3rd round and 4th round—The same. 5th round—With white wool—2 double crochet in every stitch of last round, working into both top threads. 6th round—3 double crochet in the first double crochet of last round, 1 double crochet in each of the four next consecutive double crochet, working into one top thread, and repeat. 7th round—3 double crochet on the centre one of the three double crochet of last round, 1 double crochet on each of the two next stitches, miss 2 double crochet, 1 double crochet on each of the two next stitches, and repeat. Work 7 more rounds the same. 15th round—Increase by working 3 double crochet instead of 2 on each side the three centre stitches. 16th round—3 double crochet in centre stitch of the three double crochet of last round, 1 double crochet on each of the three next stitches, miss 2 double crochet, 1 double crochet on each of the three next stitches, and repeat. Work 5 more rounds the same. 22nd round—With pink wool—3 double crochet in the centre stitch of the three double crochet of last round, 1 treble on each of the three next stitches, miss 2 double crochet, 1 treble on each of the three next stitches, and repeat. Sew five or six buttons on the left-hand back, they will fasten in between the treble stitches on the other side. Crochet a chain with a small tassel at either end, and run in through the last row of treble stitches at the neck to draw in and tie. Tack a frilling of white lace round the neck and sleeves.

FROCK FOR CHILD OF TWO.

"WELDON'S ILLUSTRATED DRESSMAKER." 1d. monthly, post free 1½d. A Coloured Fashion Plate given away every month, 28 pages of letterpress, 50 illustrations, Practical Art of Dressmaking at Home, &c.

BABY'S CROCHET PETTICOAT WITH KNITTED BODY.

PROCURE 3ozs. of cardinal and 1oz. of white single Berlin wool, or Saxony wool. Knitting needles, No. 14. Bone crochet needle, No. 12. Commence knitting at the back of the body, which is knitted all in one piece lengthways. With cardinal wool cast on 40 stitches. **1st row**—Plain. **2nd row**—Purl. **3rd row**—Knit 11, knit 2 together, make 2, knit 2 together, knit 10, knit 2 together, make 2, knit 2 together, knit 11. **4th row**—Purl 13, knit 1, purl 13, knit 1, purl 12, the two holes thus made are for button-holes, and there are now 40 stitches on the needle again. Knit 59 rows plain. **64th row**—Cast off 18, knit 21. Knit 14 rows upon the 22 stitches. **79th row**—Knit 22, cast on 36. Knit 16 rows upon the 58 stitches, this is for the shoulder-strap. **96th row**—Cast off 19, knit 39. Knit for the front of the body 100 plain rows upon the 40 stitches. Next row—knit 40, cast on 18. Knit 16 rows upon the 58 stitches for the other shoulder-strap. Next row—Cast off 37, knit 21. Knit 14 rows upon the 22 stitches. Next row—Knit 22, cast on 18, and knit 58 rows. Next a purl row, a plain row, a purl row, then 3 plain rows, and cast off. Sew the shoulder-straps over on to the back pieces. For the **Sleeve**—Pick up 20 stitches on the shoulder-strap, and knit 2 plain rows. **3rd row**—Knit 20, pick up 3 more stitches. **4th row**—Knit 23, pick up 3 more stitches, and so on till you have picked up all the stitches round the armhole, you will require four needles for this, as the sleeve is knitted round. Arrange the stitches so that the 7 stitches picked up under the arm come to be knitted first. **1st round**—Knit 7, knit 2 together, knit all round, and knit the last 2 together. **2nd round**—Plain. **3rd round**—Knit 7, knit 2 together, knit all round, and knit the last 2 together. **4th round**—Plain. **5th round**—Knit 7, knit 2 together, knit all round, and knit the last 2 together. **6th round**—Plain. **7th round**—With white wool, plain. **8th round**—Purl. **9th round**—make 1, knit 2 together, and repeat. **10th round**—Purl. **11th round**—Plain. **12th round**—Cast off. Knit the other sleeve the same. Now with white wool and holding the right side of the knitting towards you, pick up the stitches round the neck, knitting each stitch as you pick it up. **1st row**—Plain. **2nd row**—Purl. **3rd row**—Slip, knit 1, * make 1, knit 2 together, repeat from *. **4th row**—Purl. **5th row**—Plain. **6th row**—Cast off. Fin-

BABY'S CROCHET PETTICOAT WITH KNITTED BODICE.

ish the neck and sleeves with a crochet edge with white wool, working 1 double crochet in the first stitch of the knitting, 3 chain, 1 treble in the first of the chain, miss 2 of the knitting, 1 double crochet in the next, and repeat from *. Now holding the right side of the work towards you, with white wool pick up the stitches round the waist, knitting each stitch as you pick it up. **1st row**—Plain. **2nd row**—Purl. **3rd row**—Plain. **4th row**—Purl. **5th row**—Slip 1, knit 1, * make 1, knit 2 together, and repeat. **6th row**—Purl. **7th row**—Plain. **8th row**—Purl. **9th row**—Plain. **10th row**—Cast off. For the **Skirt**—With cardinal wool—Crochet a row of treble stitches into the white waistband, getting in a number divisible by 9, as the scollops commence upon 9 stitches, and 18 scollops will be found wide enough, break off at the end of the row. **2nd row**—Commence again on the right-hand side, miss the first treble of last row, * 1 treble on each of next three consecutive treble, 3 treble on the next, 1 treble on each of next three consecutive treble, miss 2 treble of last row, repeat from *, there will be one treble to leave at the end of the row. Work 9 more rows the same, then join round, and henceforth work in rounds. **12th round**—Miss 1 treble, * 1 treble on each of next two stitches, 2 treble on the next stitch, 3 treble on the centre stitch of the three trebles of last row, 2 treble on the next, and 1 treble on each of the two next trebles, miss 2 treble of last row, repeat from *. **13th round**—Miss 1 treble, * 1 treble on each of four next stitches, 3 treble on the centre stitch of the three trebles of last row, 1 treble on each of four next stitches, miss 2 treble of last row, repeat from *. Work 5 more rows the same as the last. **19th round**—Miss 1 treble, * 1 treble on each of three next stitches, 2 treble on the next, 3 treble on the centre stitch of the three trebles of last row, 2 treble on the next, 1 treble on each of three next stitches, miss two treble of last row, repeat from *. **20th round**—With white wool—Miss one treble, * 1 treble on each of next five trebles, 3 treble on the centre stitch of the three trebles of last row, 1 treble on each of next five trebles, miss two treble of last row, repeat from *. **21st round**—The same. **22nd round**—With cardinal—The same. Work 3 more rounds the same. **26th round**—With white wool—1 double crochet on the first treble of the scallop, * miss one, 2 treble on the next, 3 chain, 2 more treble in the same place, miss one, 1 double crochet on the next, repeat from * twice more, and work the same round each scallop. **27th round**—With cardinal—1 double crochet on the double crochet of last round, 3 treble under the three chain, 3 chain, 3 more treble in the same place, and repeat. Finish off with a white crochet chain run in through the holes round the waist, neck, and sleeves, to tie, with nice tassels at the ends, and sew on two buttons to meet the button holes. Work double crochet round the placket hole to strengthen it.

TAM O' SHANTER.

WORKED IN TUFTED TRICOT.

THIS novel Tam o' Shanter is exceedingly pretty for children of the ages of six or eight. It consists of ten sections of tufted tricot with ten lines of open worked tricot between, through which a narrow ribbon is run. Our model is worked in pale blue, but a pretty cardinal can be used if preferred, and will look equally well. Procure 3 ozs. of single Berlin wool. A tricot needle, No. 8. 2 yards of ¼-inch wide corded ribbon to match the wool, and a silk pompon for the centre of the crown. Commence with 30 chain, pick up 24 stitches (25 in all

TAM O' SHANTER.
Worked in Tufted Tricot.

on the needle), leave 5 chain, and work back, wool over the needle and draw through one stitch, * 4 chain, wool over the needle and draw through the last of the chain and one stitch, wool over the needle and draw through the stitch so formed and the next stitch of tricot, and repeat from * to the end of the row. There should be 12 tufts of tricot with 3 plain stitches between each tuft. **2nd row**—Pick up 22 stitches, and work back, wool over the needle and draw through one stitch, * 4 chain, wool over the needle and draw through the last of the chain and one stitch, wool over the needle and draw through the stitch so formed and the next stitch of tricot, and repeat from * to the end of the row, and there should be 11 tufts of tricot. Continue working in this way, picking up two stitches less in each row till you have worked off all the stitches, when you should be able to count 12 tufts every way. **13th row**—Pick up the stitches all along right to the end of the commencing chain, and having 30 stitches in all on the needle, work straight back as in ordinary tricot. **14th row**—Pick up 27 stitches, and pick up the last two together as 1, and having 29 stitches on the needle, work back in ordinary tricot. **15th row**—Pick up 25 stitches, inserting the hook in the small loop at the *back* of the stitches of last row, pick up the last three together as 1, and having 27 stitches on the needle, work back as usual, by picking up at the back of the stitches, this will be an open work row. **16th row**—Pick up 23 stitches in the usual manner, pick up the last three together as one, and having 25 stitches on the needle, draw back as ordinary tricot. **17th row**—Pick up 21 stitches, then two together as 1, and having 23 stitches on the needle, work back in the usual way. This completes one section of the cap. Work nine more sections, ten sections in all forming the crown of the cap, join it round. For the **Underpart**—Work 1 round of double crochet round the extreme edge of the tricot rather tightly. Then work 8 rounds of double crochet, inserting the hook into both upper loops of the double crochet of last round, and decreasing all the time just sufficiently to make the work lie flat, which will be about one stitch in eight. The two outside rounds of tufted tricot should turn over and show upon this underpart. For the **Band**—Into the last round of double crochet work in this manner: wool over the needle as if about to make a treble stitch, insert the hook, taking up both upper loops of double crochet stitch of previous round and draw the wool through, wool over the needle and draw through the three stitches on the needle, and repeat, join at the end of the round. And now work a round of single crochet thus: insert the hook, taking up both upper loops of stitch of previous round and draw the wool through and through the next stitch on the needle, insert the hook in the same manner in the next stitch of previous round and complete the stitch in the same way, and repeat. This makes a row which looks like a row of chain stitches on the front of the work. Repeat these two rounds three more times. Run the narrow ribbon in the open sections of the crown, and place the pompon in the centre, and the cap is finished.

TAM O' SHANTER.

REQUIRED, 4 ozs. of good navy blue fingering wool, and a bone crochet needle No. 10. Commence with 3 chain, join round, and work 2 double crochet in each stitch of the chain. **2nd round**—2 double crochet in every stitch, working into the top and back threads of the stitches of the previous round. **3rd round**—2 double crochet in the first stitch, 1 double crochet in the next stitch, and repeat. **4th round**—The same. **5th round**—1 double crochet in each of the first two stitches, and 2 double crochet in the third stitch, and repeat. **6th round**—2 double crochet in the first stitch, and 1 double crochet in each of the three next stitches, and repeat. **7th round**—2 double crochet in every fifth stitch. **8th round**—2 double crochet in every seventh stitch. And now continue the double crochet, always working into the top and back threads of the stitches of the last round, and increasing at intervals as often as necessary to make the work lie flat, until you have a circle measuring ten inches in diameter. Then work 4 rounds of double crochet without increasing. In the next round, to bring the cap into shape for the head, decrease

TAM O' SHANTER.

by missing every ninth stitch, and afterwards for about 10 rounds, or until the cap is the size required for the head, decrease about six times in each round. For the **Band**—Work 8 rounds of plain double crochet. A tuft of wool is to be added in the centre of the crown, to make which wind a good quantity of wool over a piece of card about three inches wide, tie it strongly together, sew it on the cap, and cut and pull it into shape. The cap should be lined with silk to match the wool with which it is worked.

SCALLOP EDGING.

VERY pretty edging in coloured silks for fancy articles, or can be done in fine crochet cotton. Commence with *, 24 chain, 16 of these join into a loop, in this work 16 treble, join this to the chain remaining of the 24, turn, into the 16 treble put the same with 1 chain between, turn, 5 chain, 1 double, join to the chain as before, last round 6 chain, 1 double, repeat from *. When working the next round join the last row to the first pattern. Foundation, 1 treble, 1 chain.

CROCHET EDGING.

THIS is extremely pretty when worked with crochet cotton of a fine make. Commence with 13 chain, turn, 1 double in the 6th, 2 chain, 2 treble, 3 chain, 2 treble in the 4th, 2 chain, miss 2, 1 treble, turn, 5 chain, 2 treble, 3 chain, 2 treble in the 3 chain of former row; 10 chain, 1 double in the chain made when turning in the 1st row, turn, 18 double, then 2 treble, 3 chain, 2 treble in the 3 chain; 2 chain, 1 treble, turn, 2 chain, 2 treble, 3 chain, 2 treble in the 3 chain, 2 chain, 1 treble, 1 chain 9 times into the double, turn, 3 chain, 1 double into the spaces of former row 8 times, 2 chain. This completes the 1st scallop. The illustration shows on which 3 chain the next is joined.

POINT LACE BRAID AND CROCHET EDGING.

MEDALLION braid is employed for the lace itself, while a row of plain braid forms a heading to give firmness to the work. 1st row—1 double treble joining two medallions about half-way down, 3 chain, 1 double crochet at end of medallion, 3 chain, 1 double in next, 3 chain, and repeat. On the other side of braid work 1 double treble between two medallions, 4 chain, 1 double at point of medallion, 7 chain which form into a loop by working 1 treble in top of last double, 4 chain, and repeat. 2nd row—12 double treble in each loop, with 1 chain between each, treble on treble and finish with an edging of double all along

---

CROCHET EDGING WITH LOOP BORDER.

MAKE a chain of 22, * turn with 7 more, miss these 7 and work 4 treble, 2 chain, miss 2, 1 treble, 2 chain, miss 2, 1 treble, 2 chain, miss 2, 4 treble, 2 chain, miss 2, 1 treble. 2nd row—Turn with 7 chain, 1 treble over second treble of last row, 2 chain, miss 2, 6 treble, 3 chain, miss 3, 4 treble, 2 chain, miss 2, 4 treble, 1 on last of previous row and 3 more in the last hole, 2 chain, 1 treble in same, repeat from *. Round the edge work double crochet with 3 chain between each stitch, which forms a small picot.

CROCHET AND BEAD PURSE.

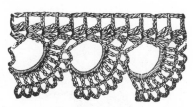

CROCHET EDGING.

CROCHET EDGING WITH LOOP BORDER.

CROCHET FRINGE.

SCALLOP EDGING.

CHILD'S CROCHET BALL.

POINT LACE BRAID AND CROCHET INSERTION.

POINT LACE BRAID AND CROCHET EDGING.

KROTCHEE AND CROCHET EDGING.

CROCHET STAR.

IF worked with very fine cotton looks like lace, and is very effective. Commence with 14 chain, form into a loop, in this work *, 4 chain, 1 long treble, 6 chain, 1 treble into the edge of the long treble, repeat the 6 chain and 2 long treble 3 times more, now 3 chain, 10 long treble into the 12 chain, turn, 4 chain, then double all along the 10 treble, turn, 4 chain, 1 double into the 4th double, turn, 8 chain, 1 single into the 1st of the 4 chain, in this 8 chain, work from *, when 8 of these points are done, join the last to the first, then fasten off. To draw them into a circle, fasten the cotton on to the 4 chain of each point, work enough chain from point to point to make them lay flat, then into this double crochet.

POINT LACE BRAID AND CROCHET INSERTION.

THIS requires rather fine cotton, and then makes a pretty trimming suitable for fancy aprons and pinafores as well as under-clothing. 1st row—*, 1 double treble between two medallions, 1 treble half-way up next 5 chain, 1 double near top, 6 chain, 1 double on next, 5 chain, 1 treble half-way, and repeat from *. For centre—Work **, 4 treble down one side of a medallion, 4 treble on next, 3 chain, 1 double at end of medallion, 5 chain, 1 double on next, 3 chain, and repeat from **. When a sufficient length is worked fasten off, and repeat this last row on another length of braid, only joining at commencement of 4 treble, as shown in illustration. As a finish to make the work stronger, a row of 5 chain, 1 double, is worked on each side.

KROTCHEE AND CROCHET EDGING.

HAVING worked a few yards of " krotchee " or hair-pin work, cut off 16 points more or less, according to size of cotton and purpose for which required; join into a round with needle and fine cotton, drawing up the centre loops by passing the needle and cotton through them and fasten securely. Having done the length of stars required, crochet the foundation, putting a treble between two stars, 5 chain, join to loop of star, missing one, 3 chain join to next loop. Next row, work 1 treble, 2 chain, miss 2.

CROCHET AND BEAD PURSE.

THIS pretty little sovereign purse is worked with crimson silk twist and small gold beads. Thread the beads on the twist, take some very fine black cotton cord and work double crochet over it, slipping up a bead at every stitch; the beads will come on the side of work farthest from you. Commence with 1 double crochet, working round and round to the size desired, then fringe with beads and fasten on clasp.

CHILD'S CROCHET BALL.

TAKE a large ball of yarn or a very thin rubber one, commence the cover of worsted by making a chain of 4 stitches joined in a circle, and work in double stitches, increasing at regular intervals till the work is large enough to cover one half the ball; then work a few rows without increase, draw the cover over the ball, letting the wrong side of the work be outside, and work the other half to correspond with the first half, decreasing at regular intervals, and putting the needle in from the inside. A pattern of bright flowers worked with worsted round the centre adds greatly to the ball's attraction for a child.

KALEIDOSCOPE STAR FOR WOOLLEN ANTIMACASSARS.

CENTRE star black, 6 chain join; in this work 12 double, next round increase to 24, round this work 8 blocks of 1 double, 1 treble, 1 long treble, 1 treble, 1 double. Round this centre are six blocks of red, green, orange, brown, pink, and blue; the blocks are double crochet worked thus: 10 chain, on this 2 rows of ribbed double crochet, in the middle of third row insert the needle one row below, and work 5 long treble, 5 more double, turn and work back, putting chain at back of long treble; in the next row make 5 long treble the right-hand and 5 long treble the left-hand side of the first little clump, work back, and in the next row make another little clump just over the first one, finish the row with double, turn and do 2 more rows of double; tie on another colour and work another block, fastening it on to the centre star before turning to do the first row of double. Edge the star with black wool chain and double, putting 3 loops of 5, 7, and 5 chain into the corners.

CROCHET FRINGE.

THIS can be made in white or coloured crochet cottons, as well as wool or silk, with good effect for edging curtains, bed hangings, antimacassars, shawls or dresses. It is worked the short way. On 5 chain work 5 double, turn, * 5 chain, on this 1 double, 2 treble, 3 treble, taking up both stitches, 4 chain, 1 single in last double, turn, 2 double, 2 chain, 6 double (the 2 chain are for looping in the fringe), 3 double over the first 3 treble, repeat from *. Cut the fringe the desired length and knot firmly into the 2 chain, then a little lower down knot again.

CROCHET STAR FOR ANTIMACASSAR.

A PRETTY star for cotton or woollen antimacassars in three shades of green or amber. With light amber work 12 chain, in this round 7 chain, 1 double, 4 chain, 1 long treble, 4 chain, 1 double 5 times, making in all 6 small points, 6 large points, fasten off. With next shade of amber work enough chain from one large point to the other to lay flat but in a point, on this chain work 3 rows of ribbed or Russian crochet —that is, insert the hook through both of the chain stitches of the double, 2 double in the middle of the chain to form a vandyke. This done, fasten off, then join on the next shade of amber and work 5 long treble divided by 5 chain into top of each point, 7 chain and 1 double into the lower part of vandyke. The number of chain in this pattern must depend on the size of wool used and the method of working, either tightly or loosely.

CHILD'S NECK FRILL AND WRISTLETS.

1 OZ. of white, 1 oz. of pink single Berlin wool. Fine bone crochet needle. Commence with pink wool, with 15 chain, turn, and work 14 double crochet, and continue working backwards and forwards in ribbed double crochet, 14 stitches in each row, for the length required to meet round the neck. Now with white wool, and beginning on the first of the fourteen stitches, work 1 treble *, 1 chain, miss 1 double crochet stitch, 1 treble on the next, and repeat from * seven times; turn along the next ridge of the double crochet stitches and work the same along there, and so on till the strip of crochet is covered with white frilling. 2nd row—With pink wool—1 double crochet under the chain stitch of last row, 1 chain, and repeat all along the frilling. Sew a piece of white ribbon 1 inch wide at each end of the neck frill to tie in a nice bow. For the wristlets, work two pieces the same as above, but only 10 stitches wide; make them just long enough to slip easily over the hand, and join round.

KALEIDOSCOPE STAR FOR WOOLLEN ANTIMACASSARS.

CROCHET STAR.

BABY'S CROCHET BIB.

KNITTING cotton No. 12 is best for this bib, as it washes so well, and you wil require a steel crochet hook. Make a chain of 162 stitches, miss the first chain, and begin, always taking up the back edge of the stitch only. 1st row—On the first 10 chain of foundation work 10 short crochets, miss 2 chain, 10 short crochets, 3 short crochets in the next stitch. Repeat these directions across the row, not widening at the end. Turn your work. 2nd row—9 short crochets in the first nine short crochets of the last row, * miss 2, 10 short crochets in the next ten stitches, 3 short crochets in the next stitch, 10 short crochets in the next ten stitches. Repeat across the row from *. The next ten rows are worked like the second, except that each row decreases at the beginning and end by one stitch At the end of the tenth and eleventh rows new foundation-chains of eleven stitches are added, and missing the first chain, the directions are repeated from the first row until eight vandyke points, containing eight rows, are completed, when we are ready for the shoulders. The pattern is repeated for the shoulders, each being pointed and having two vandykes on the outside. The directions for one Shoulder are as follows:—1st row—Having made 11 foundation chain at the end of the eightieth row, begin with 10 short crochets on the ten chain, miss 2, 10 short crochets, 3 short crochets in next stitch, 10 short crochets, miss 2, 10 short crochets. 2nd row—Turn and work like the last. The shoulder is carried up the length of two vandykes, with which the outer edge is finished like the rest of the bib. There would be four vandykes across the breast of the bib, but those next the shoulders instead of stopping in a sharp point, have the side next the shoulder slanted up to the side of the strap, making the lower part of the shoulder wider. The inner side has no vandyke to correspond to the top one on the outer side of the shoulder. The bib is finished with a row of open-work crocheted edging. The Collar is formed by turning down the two vandykes that finish the breast, together with about a quarter of an inch of the slanted sides of the shoulder, and, of course, all the edging up to the shoulder-points. The Edging on our design is thus worked:—1st row—Fasten the thread and go all round the bib, making seven chain, fastened with short crochet in every fourth stitch of the work. 2nd row—7 chain, fastened by a short crochet in every loop of last row. 3rd row—5 chain, miss 1 and fasten with short crochet in the third stitch of the chain, a long crochet in the second stitch of the chain, short crochet in next loop. Repeat this picot in every loop.

DOUBLE CRAZY-STITCH EDGING.

MAKE a chain the desired length. 1st row—Miss 3 chain, 4 long crochets in next stitch, * miss 3 chain, 1 short crochet in next stitch, 3 chain, 4 long crochets in same stitch, repeat from * to end of row, turn work. 2nd row—6 chain, * 1 double crochet in loop formed by three chain in last row, 4 chain, repeat from * to end of row, turn work. 3rd row—3 chain, 4 long crochets in first stitch *, 1 short crochet in next double crochet, 3 chain, 4 long crochets in same stitch, repeat from * to end of row, turn work. 4th row—3 chain, 4 long crochets in first stitch *, 1 short crochet n next loop formed by three chain in last row, 3 chain, 4 long crochets in same chain, repeat from * to end of row, turn work. 5th row—3 chain, * one short crochet in first loop formed by three chain, 2 chain, 1 long crochet in same loop, 1 picot formed by four chain, fastened back in first chain, 1 long crochet in same loop, 1 picot, 1 long crochet, 1 picot, 1 long crochet in same loop, 1 picot, 1 long crochet in same loop, 1 picot, 1 long crochet in next loop formed by three chain in last row, repeat from * to end of row, break wool. Any kind of wool can be used for this pretty stitch, and naturally the crochet hook will vary with the wool; such as with Andalusian wool a No. 9 hook would be correct. It is a useful pattern for shawls, stripes, for antimacassars worked in various colours, hoods for ladies or children, infants' head squares in white, pink, pale blue, or cream Andalusian wool, finished round with a scalloped border, or a crochet fringe, while tassels only can be placed at the corners. Before attempting to fashion any article, it is better to try the stitch with any odd piece of wool.

CROCHET STAR FOR ANTIMACASSAR.

WELDON'S
PRACTICAL CROCHET.

(SECOND SERIES.)

How to Crochet 47 Useful Articles for Ladies, Gentlemen, and Children.

THIRTY-FIVE ILLUSTRATIONS.

The sizes of Crochet Hooks mentioned in descriptions are regulated by Walker's Bell Gauge.

Telegraphic Address—] "Consuelo," London.]

The Yearly Subscription to this Magazine, post free to any Part of the World, is 2s. 6d. Subscriptions are payable in advance, and may commence from any date and for any period.

[Telephone— 2745.

The Back Numbers are always in print. Nos. 1 to 84 now ready, Price 2d. each, or post free for 15s. Over 5,000 Engravings.

CROCHET SLIPPERS.

A VERY pretty pair of crochet slippers can be made as follows, and for which you will require four skeins of double Berlin wool, any colour preferred, six skeins of single Berlin wool to match, one skein of filoselle, and such a hook as one uses for tricot crochet; not too large, however, as this stitch for slippers must be worked close and firm. The stitch is a kind of double tricot, and is worked in the same way, but the wool is always put around the hook before taking-up two loops, and again to draw it through these two loops; and in going back the wool is always drawn through three loops. To make the **Toe** of the slipper—**1st row**—Make 10 chain, miss 1, wool round the hook; draw through the next, wool around the hook; take-up in this way nine stitches from the chain, there will be ten with the first loop on the hook. Go back, wool around the hook, draw through three loops every time. **2nd row**—* Wool around the hook, take up two stitches, the straight one and the slanting one beyond it, draw the wool through these two, repeat from *. The last stitch must be taken up double, through to the back of it, to make the edge firm. Go back, draw through three loops. **3rd row**—Increase wool around the hook, take up the little slanting stitch close to the top on the hook. At the end of the row, with the wool around the hook, take up a second time the slanting stitch of the one worked the last but one before the end. Go back, draw through three loops, **4th row**—Plain. Increase at both ends every other row till eleven rows are worked, then do two plain rows between each increasing. There will be twenty-four stitches across the foot. In the eighteenth row, work to six from the end, and go back to eight from the beginning; then work eight and go back to the beginning. Now work the side of the shoe upon eight stitches. There will be eight left for the front and eight for the other side. Work from forty-five to fifty rows, according to the length of the sole, taking care always to work the last stitch through to the back. Join this piece to the shoe with a large wool needle, taking the edge-stitch singly, then two stitches, one from each edge. With the silk, work looped stars, according to fancy; one on the toe, one on each side of this, a little above, one in the middle below the rosette, and three continued at each side. Sew the shoe to a double sole to the inside leather, hold the fluffy part nearest to you, and take up the inside edge stitch, together with the loop above it. Work one tight row of double crochet on the side piece (not across the front), taking-up the inside loop at the edge. The rosette is made of the single Berlin wool. Upon the end of the wool held in the left hand, work sixty long crochet; turn and between each of these do three chain of the last row. Draw this up tightly, to form an irregular rosette, and sew it to the shoe.

HOOD FOR A LADY.

MATERIALS.—Four ounces of Andalusian wool, bone hook, No. 9. On a chain of 128 stitches work thirty-two squares of crazy stitch. **2nd row**—Turn work, make three chain, pass hook through first stitch and draw wool through loosely; same with second and third stitches. You will now have 4 stitches on hook; throw wool over, and draw through all four at once, wool over and draw through single stitch. Make one single crochet stitch into the last of the 4 long crochet stitches in preceding row. This is to fill up the little triangular space which would otherwise leave the edges uneven and with which every row is commenced. You then work on with regular crazy stitch. Work backward and forwards nineteen times, and fill in the uneven squares which will be left after last row, by chaining one, then throwing wool over hook and taking up first stitch; wool over and take up second, and so on till the 6 stitches between the two points are on hook; then wool over hook and draw through all the stitches at once quite tightly; chain one loosely and fasten with short crochet in second point. Continue this filling-in all across the row. For **Border**—Turn work, chain 3, and work 2 long crochet stitches in second stitch of foundation; chain one and work two more long crochets in same stitch, making a shell. Work next shell in end of second square, and continue the shells all around hood. **2nd row of Border**—Work shells in centre of preceding shells. Across ends of hood work a third row of shells, after which the last row of border is made. Work 8 long crochet stitches in centre of shell, and fasten down by short crochet between shells on second row of border; then chain three, and fasten between shells on first row of border; chain three more, and fasten on edge of hood; turn and chain three, and fasten at top of first row of shells; chain three, and fasten on top of second row of shells, when you then make 8 long crochet stitches in centre of next shell, and so continue all around hood, making the two lines of little chains between each row of shells. When this is done, turn this border back on to hood, along the front and back, and fasten worsted with needle and wool. Next, double hood evenly and sew the back up, commencing about the fifth square from the bottom. Fasten wool on front edge of hood and work a row of shells all across to finish front. Trim with ribbon bows and strings.

TULIP PATTERN.

THIS design is suitable for the border of a counterpane, the counterpane itself, or any article for which solid work is required. Materials—Strutt's crochet cotton, No. 6, and a fine steel crochet hook. Make a chain of length equal to the width of the article to be made. **1st row**—1 double crochet in each stitch of foundation. Break off the cotton and begin again on the right side for every row. **2nd row**—5 double crochets in first five of preceding row, * 3 loops of nine chain each, fastened by a single crochet in the same stitch with the last double crochet, 9 double crochets, repeat from *. Note that only the lower or wrong sides of the stitches are taken up, leaving the upper edge of every row of stitches as a line across the right side of the work. **3rd** and **4th rows**—Double crochet. **5th row**—2 double crochets, * 1 double crochet in first loop of nine chain of second row, 4 double crochets, miss the second loop of nine chain, 1 double crochet in third loop, 2 double crochets, repeat from * to end of row. **6th, 7th,** and **8th rows**—Double crochet. **9th row**—5 double crochets, * 5 long crochets in the middle loop of nine chain, which was missed in the 5th row, 7 double crochets, repeat from *. **10th row**—Double crochet, taking care to make the stitches, not in the top of the tulip, but making it, upon the four stitches of the eighth round, which were missed in making the flower cup. Repeat from the first row, taking care to make the tulips in the second row come over the spaces between the flowers in the row below.

CROCHETED HERRING-BONE STITCH.

THIS pattern will be found serviceable for making scarfs, comforters, clouds, &c. It should be worked with a coarse needle and fine wool, it then represents a lattice or herring-bone stitch. Make a chain the length required. **1st row** —* The wool before the needle, take up the next chain, draw the wool through the loop, keeping it before the needle, the wool on the needle, draw through the two loops on the needle, repeat from * in every stitch. **2nd row**—Work like the preceding row, always taking up the back of the chain.

CHILD'S VEST IN TREBLE CROCHET.

THIS will be found a strong serviceable vest, and is quickly made. If required about 12 inches long, procure 2½ ozs. of white Merino wool, a smaller size can be made by using 3 balls of Cocoon wool. Bone crochet needle, No. 12. Commence with 62 chain, turn, 1 treble in the third stitch from the needle, and treble all along, making 60 treble in all. **2nd row**—2 chain to turn, and work 60 treble again. **3rd row**—2 chain to turn, work 60 treble again, and this completes the half of one shoulder. **4th row**—2 chain to turn, and work 50 treble stitches. Repeat this row till 15 of these short rows are done, and at the end of the fifteenth row make 12 chain, turn, and again work 60 treble up and down for 3 rows. This completes the front of the vest. Recommence, and work a similar piece for the back. Then sew up the shoulder straps, and sew the sides together, leaving sufficient space for an armhole. For the little edge round the neck and armholes, work 1 double crochet in one ridge of the treble work, 7 treble in the next ridge, and repeat. Run a ribbon in to confine the neck and to tie with a bow in front.

CHILD'S VEST IN TREBLE CROCHET.

CROCHET SQUARE FOR QUILT.

WITH FOUR DIAMONDS OF RAISED TREBLE STITCHES.

THIS handsome square is worked with Strutt's knitting cotton, No. 6, and a steel crochet needle, No. 15. Commence with 4 chain, join round, and for the **1st round** work 2 double crochet in each chain stitch; 8 double crochet in all, and join at the end of this and every round. **2nd round**—Working into the one top thread of the stitches of last round, 3 double crochet on the first double crochet of last round, 1 double crochet on the next, * 3 double crochet on the next, 1 double crochet on the next, and repeat from * twice. **3rd round**—3 double crochet on the centre stitch of the three double crochet of last round (which will be a corner stitch), 3 consecutive double crochet along the side of the square, * 3 double crochet on the next corner stitch, 3 double crochet along the next side of the square, and repeat from * twice ; 24 double crochet in all. **4th round**—3 double crochet on the corner stitch, 2 consecutive double crochet, 1 treble on the front of the work in the centre stitch along the side of the *second* round, 2 consecutive double crochet, and repeat three times. **5th round**—3 double crochet on the corner stitch, 2 consecutive double crochet, 1 treble into the third round, 1 double crochet, 1 treble into the third round, 2 consecutive double crochet, and repeat. **6th round**—3 double crochet on the corner stitch, 2 consecutive double crochet, 1 treble into the fourth round, 1 double crochet, 1 treble over the treble in the fourth round, 1 double crochet, 1 treble into the fourth round, 2 consecutive double crochet, and repeat. **7th round**—3 double crochet on the corner stitch, 2 consecutive double crochet, 1 treble into the fifth round, 1 double crochet, 1 treble over the treble in the fifth round, 1 double crochet, 1 treble over the treble in the fifth round, 1 double crochet, 1 treble into the fifth round, 2 consecutive double crochet, and repeat. Continue working in this manner, increasing the diamond of raised treble stitches until you have done six rounds of the raised trebles. **10th round**—3 double crochet on the corner stitch, 4 consecutive double crochet, 1 treble into the eighth round, then 1 double crochet and 1 treble alternately four times, 4 consecutive double crochet, and repeat. Contract the raised diamond in this manner, until in the fourteenth round it is reduced to a point of 1 treble stitch. **15th round**—3 double crochet in the corner stitch, 27 double crochet along the side of the square, and repeat. **16th round**—1 single crochet to shape the corner, which tighten in to render the junction invisible, 4 chain, 1 treble in the corner stitch,* 1 chain, miss one double crochet, 1 treble on the next stitch, and repeat from * until you have 14 treble stitches along the side, then 1 chain, and work 3 treble in the corner stitch with a chain between each treble, and repeat from the first asterisk*. **17th row**—1 treble on every stitch along the sides of the square, and for the corners work 3 treble on the corner stitch and 2 treble on the stitch on each side the corner stitch. **18th round**—The same as the sixteenth round, only there will be 18 treble to come in along each side.

CROCHET SQUARE FOR QUILT.

WITH FOUR DIAMONDS OF RAISED TREBLE STITCHES.

POINT NEIGE SUPERBE. CROCHET.

AS will be inferred from the name, this stitch is a variation of the ordinary point neige or shell stitch, it is beautifully close and thick, and is a most charming pattern for sofa blankets and bassinette covers. Required, double Berlin wool, five shades of art green, or any colour that may be preferred. Bone crochet needle, No. 6. Commence with the darkest shade of green with a chain as long as required, and work the **1st row** in ordinary point neige as follows:—Insert the hook successively in the first five stitches of the chain, raising a loop loosely in each, wool over the needle and draw through all the loops and the stitch on the needle together, 1 chain, * insert the hook in the small hole formed by the one chain just made, and draw the wool through, insert the hook in the lower thread at the back of the last stitch of the group and draw the wool through, insert the hook in the same stitch of the commencing chain as the last group of point neige is worked into and draw the wool through, insert the hook successively in the two next stitches of the chain, drawing the wool through each, there will now be 6 stitches on the needle, wool over the needle and draw through all, 1 chain, repeat from *, fasten off at the end of the row. **2nd row**—With the next lightest shade of green, join on at the right-hand side of previous row, work 2 chain, insert the hook in the first of the chain and draw the wool through, insert the hook in the stitch at the commencement and draw the wool through, insert the hook in the top of the first point neige stitch of previous row and draw the wool through, insert the hook in the small hole formed by the one chain of previous row and draw the wool through, insert the hook *below* the chain stitch and *through* the work where the bunch of six threads appears to be tied up and draw the wool through, insert the hook still *lower* down in the work and draw the wool through, there will be 7 stitches on the needle, wool over the needle and draw through all, 1 chain, * insert the hook in the small hole formed by the one chain just done and draw the wool through, insert the hook in the same place as the last group of point neige is worked into and draw the wool through, insert the hook in the top of the point neige stitch of previous row and draw the wool through, insert the hook in the small hole formed by the one chain of previous row and draw the wool through, insert the hook *below* the chain stitch and *through* the work where the bunch of six threads appears to be tied up and draw the wool through, insert the hook still lower down in the work and draw the wool through, there will be 7 stitches on the needle, wool over the needle and draw through all, 1 chain, repeat from *, fasten off at the end of the row. **3rd, 4th, and 5th rows**—Worked with the next lightest shades of green in succession, and in the same manner as described for the working of the second row, only that you will draw up the sixth loop from the second previous row of the work. **6th, 7th, 8th, 9th, and 10 rows**—Worked in the same manner, and shaded successively from light to dark. Continue the repetition of the shades till you have done a piece of work sufficiently wide for the purpose required.

POINT NEIGE SUPERBE.

CHILD'S CROCHETED SLIPPERS.

MATERIALS. — One ounce grey single Berlin, one medium steel hook, one pair No. 8 cork soles, one yard of narrow ribbon. Size for a child about five years. They are very durable and useful for nursery wear. The pattern is worked throughout in short crochet stitch. The increase is made in each row on the centre or odd stitch, and the effect produced is a pointed or reversed Λ-shaped vamp. The top of slipper is edged with blue scallops, through which the ribbon is run and fastened on the vamp in a pretty bow. Make a chain of 3 stitches. Turn the work (always work into loop of previous chain furthest from you). Crochet into first chain stitch once ; into the second chain three times; into third chain once, thus giving 5 stitches in this row. The next row when finished, should be 7 stitches ; next, 9 stitches ; always an uneven number, that is increase by twos, or work in every centre stitch of each row 3 stitches. Continue working back and forward until you have made eight ribs, which form vamp part of slipper. Now crochet the first 9 stitches back and forward until you have a strip long enough to pass around sole and join to other side of vamp. Make joining by crocheting the two edges together on wrong side. Then crochet an edge of close short crochet once around the portion of slipper that comes next to sole.

TRICOT VANDYKE.

This is a pretty and very durable pattern for chair-backs, sofa-cushions, and other purposes. Procure single Berlin wool in two good contrasting colours, say red and white, the same quantity of each, and a bone tricot needle, No. 10. For the **First Wide Stripe**—Make 14 chain with red wool and 6 chain with white wool all in a piece. **1st row**—Pick up 6 white tricot stitches, then 14 red stitches, and draw back in the usual way, through each stitch with its own colour, but pass the white wool across the red wool where the colours are to change. **2nd row to the 9th row**—Pick up 1 white tricot stitch more in each row and 1 red stitch less, and in the 9th row there should be 14 white and 6 red stitches. **10th row**—13 white stitches and 7 red. **11th row to the 17th row**—Pick up 1 white stitch less in each row and 1 red stitch more, and in the 17th row there should be 6 white stitches and 14

TRICOT VANDYKE.

red stitches. Repeat from the second row till you have a stripe as long as required. For the **Second Wide Stripe**—Make 6 chain with white wool and 14 chain with red wool all in a piece. **1st row**—Pick up 14 red tricot stitches, then 6 white stitches, and work back, drawing through each stitch with its own colour. **2nd row to the 9th row**—Pick up 1 red stitch less in each row and 1 white stitch more, and in the 9th row there should be 6 red and 14 white stitches. **10th row**—7 red stitches and 13 white. **11th row to the 17th row**—Pick up one red stitch more and 1 white stitch less in each row, and in the 17th row there should be 14 red stitches and 6 white stitches. Repeat from the second row till you have a stripe the same length as the first stripe. For the **Narrow Stripe**—Commence with red wool with 6 chain, and work 3 rows of plain tricot. **4th row**—Pick up 6 stitches, and in working back draw through 3 stitches (one at a time), then do 3 chain, and draw through the remaining 3 stitches. **5th row**—Pick up 6 stitches, keeping the three chain stitches to the front, and in working back draw through 2 stitches, 3 chain, draw through 2 stitches, 3 chain, draw through the remaining 2 stitches. **6th row**—The same as the fourth row. **7th row to the 11th row**—Plain tricot. Repeat from the fourth row for the same number of rows as worked for the wide stripes. With a wool needle work a small star between each raised spot of chain stitches in the narrow stripes. Sew the stripes together stitch by stitch, a narrow stripe (alternately one red and one white) goes between each wide one.

ROUND MAT FOR LAMP.

The centre of this mat is composed of plain double crochet worked over a wire, and afterwards ornamented with fancy stitches, as shown in the engraving; the border is worked in a pretty stitch of coiled crochet. The mat complete should measure about 9 inches in diameter. Required—double Berlin wool, five shades of maize or olive browns, the lightest shade being quite a golden-yellow, about ½ oz. of each, also ½ oz. of black, and a little gold-coloured filoselle. A No. 4 bone crochet needle for the border, No. 7 for the centre of the mat. A piece of rather thick bonnet wire. Commence with the border, and with the darkest shade of wool work 80 chain, loosely, for the extreme size of the outside edge of the mat. Join round. And for the **1st round**—Work * 1 double crochet in the first stitch of the chain, insert the hook in the next stitch of the chain, draw the wool through, work 5 chain loosely, wool over the needle and draw through the two stitches on the needle, repeat from *, and fasten off at the end of the round. **2nd round**—With next lightest shade of wool * 1 double crochet on the double crochet of last round, working into both top loops, insert the hook in the loop formed by the five chain of last round, draw the wool through, and work 5 chain loosely, wool over the needle and draw through the two stitches on the needle, repeat from *, and fasten off at the end of the round. **3rd round**—With next lightest shade of wool, work the same as the second round. **4th round**—With next lightest shade, the same, but doing only 4 chain instead of 5 chain. **5th round**—With the lightest shade, work the same as the fourth round. **6th round**—With the same shade of wool, plain double crochet working 2 consecutive stitches, then missing 1 stitch of previous round, and so on. This finishes the border. The centre of the mat is worked entirely in double crochet over the wire, which keeps it firm and flat. Commence with the second darkest

shade of maize, and work 2 rounds of double crochet, inserting the hook into the *top* loop only. Then 2 rounds with the next lightest shade. Then 1 round with the yellow. Then take black, and continue working for 5 rounds. Again take the yellow and work 1 round. Then 2 rounds with the third lightest shade, and 2 rounds with the same shade with which you began. Now the centre of the mat ought to be just the right size to fit into the border. Sew the border on neatly on the wrong side, and in such a way that the double crochet stitches of the border show uninterruptedly on the right side of the mat. Work fancy stitches on the black double crochet with gold filoselle and yellow wool, as shown in the illustration, or according to fancy.

CROCHET SHAWL. OMEGA PATTERN.

Procure Shetland or Andalusian wool of the colour preferred, and in sufficient quantity for the size of the shawl. Work with a bone crochet needle, No. 10 or No. 9. Begin by working a chain for the length required. **1st row**—1 double crochet in the first of the foundation chain,* 5 chain, miss five of the foundation, 1 double crochet in the next, and repeat from *. Turn at the end of this and every row. **2nd row**—2 chain, 3 treble in the centre stitch of the five chain of last row, 2 chain, 1 double crochet on the double crochet of last row, and repeat. **3rd row**—2 chain to turn, 1 double crochet on the middle one of the three trebles of last row, * 5 chain, 1 double crochet on the middle one of the next three trebles of last row, repeat from *, and at the end of the row work 2 chain and a double crochet on the chain stitch at the end of last row. **4th row**—2 chain to turn, 1 treble on the double crochet stitch, * 2 chain, 1 double crochet on the next double crochet stitch, 2 chain, 3 treble in the centre stitch of the five chain of last row, repeat from *, and end the row with 2 chain, 1 treble on the double crochet at the end of last row. **5th row**—1 double crochet on the treble stitch, * 5 chain, 1 double crochet on the middle one of the three trebles of last row, repeat from * ; the double crochet at the end of the row is to be worked upon the treble stitch. Repeat from the second row. For the Border—**1st row**—Work treble all round the shawl increasing at the corners. **2nd round**—1 treble on the first treble of last round, * 1 chain, 1 treble on the next treble, 1 chain, 1 long treble in the same place, 2 chain, another long treble in the same place, 1 chain, 1 treble in the same place, 1 chain, 1 treble on the next treble, miss three trebles of last row, and in the next work 2 half trebles, thus—wool over the needle, insert the hook in the stitch and draw the wool through, wool over the needle and draw through two stitches on the needle, wool over the needle, insert the hook again in the same place and draw the wool through, wool over the needle and draw through two stitches on the needle, wool over the needle and draw through the three stitches on the needle, miss three trebles of last row, 1 treble on the next treble; and repeat from *. **3rd round**—1 treble under the one chain between the treble and first long treble of last round, 1 chain, 1 treble under the two chain, 1 chain, 1 long treble in the same place, 2 chain, another long treble in the same place, 1 chain, 1 treble in the same place, 1 chain, 1 treble under the next one chain of last round, 1 chain, 2 half treble stitches between the half trebles of last round, 1 chain, and repeat. **4th round**—1 treble under the first one chain of last round, 1 chain, 1 treble under the chain between the treble and first long treble of last round, 1 chain, 1 treble under the two chain, 1 chain, 1 long treble in

the same place, 2 chain, another long treble in the same place, 1 chain, 1 treble in the same place, 1 chain, 1 treble under the next one chain of last round, 1 chain, 1 treble under the next one chain, 1 chain, 2 half trebles between the half trebles of last round, 1 chain, and repeat. **5th round**—The same as the fourth round, working an additional 1 chain, 1 treble on each side the scallop. **6th round**—1 treble under the first one chain of last round, * 5 chain, 1 single crochet picot into the first of the chain, 1 treble under the next one chain of last round, repeat from *, working four treble stitches with a picot between each under the two chain at the head of the scallop, and working the half trebles as before.

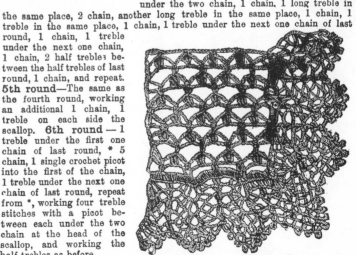

CROCHET SHAWL IN OMEGA PATTERN.

This pretty and quickly worked shawl looks effective, and wears well in fawn or grey, Shetland or Andalusian wool, while for evening wear, pale blue, pink, or cream would be preferable. In black it makes a useful shawl for indoors, more especially if made with Pompadour wool, which lends a rich appearance, or if this is not procurable combine with the wool a ball of soft silk, crocheting both together.

ROUND MAT FOR LAMP.

CROCHET SHAWL. OPEN CHAIN NET-WORK PATTERN.

THIS shawl is worked with Shetland wool, and bone crochet needle, No. 10. Commence with chain for the length required. **1st row**—1 double crochet in the twelfth chain stitch from the needle, *7 chain, miss six of the foundation chain, 1 double crochet in the seventh, and repeat from *. Turn at the end of this and every row. **2nd row**—7 chain, 1 double crochet on the double

CROCHET SHAWL IN OPEN CHAIN NET-WORK PATTERN.

crochet stitch of last row, and repeat. **3rd row**—7 chain, 1 double crochet in the centre chain stitch of the seven chain in the first row, working over the loop of seven chain in the second row; repeat. **4th row**—7 chain to turn, 1 double crochet on the first double crochet of previous row, *7 chain, 1 double crochet on the next double crochet of previous row, repeat from *; and at the end of the row work 3 chain, 1 double crochet in the chain stitch that turned. **5th row**—7 chain, 1 double crochet in the centre chain stitch of the seven chain in the third row, working over the loop of seven chain in last row; repeat; at the end of the row the double crochet stitch comes in the fourth chain stitch that turns. **6th row**—7 chain, 1 double crochet on the double crochet stitch of last row, and repeat. Repeat from the third row for the length required. **For the Border**—**1st round**—Work 1 double crochet, 7 chain, alternately, all round the shawl. **2nd round**—3 long treble in the centre stitch of the seven chain of last round, 3 chain, 3 more long treble in the same place, and repeat. **3rd round**—3 treble under the three chain of last row, 3 chain, 3 more treble in the same place, 1 double crochet in the space between the scallops, and repeat. **4th round**—3 long treble under the three chain of last row, 3 chain, 3 more long treble in the same place, and repeat. **5th round**—3 treble under the three chain of last row, 3 chain, 3 more treble in the same place, 1 double crochet in the space between the scollops, and repeat. **6th round**—Same as the fourth round. **7th round**—Same as the fifth round.

BOY'S CRICKETING CAP.

THIS strong, useful cap for boys is worked in star-pointed sections of plain tricot. Required, 2 ozs. of blue, 1½ ozs. of white, single Berlin wool. Bone tricot needle No. 8. Begin with the blue wool, with 36 chain; raise a tricot stitch in each stitch of the chain, and having 36 stitches on the needle, work back, wool over the needle and draw through 1 stitch, * wool over the needle and draw through the stitch so formed and through the next stitch on the needle, and repeat from * till all the stitches are worked off. **2nd row**—Insert the hook in the perpendicular stitches of last row and raise 35 stitches, leaving the last stitch unraised, and work back as directed in the first row. **3rd row**—Raise 34 stitches, and work back. And proceed in this manner, working one stitch less in every row, till in the 15th row you raise only 22 stitches, and work back. This forms one section of the cap. Join on the white wool, pick up the 22 stitches of last row, and the 14 unraised stitches forming the gore, 36 stitches in all, and work another piece of 15 rows. And proceed in this way till you have done four sections of blue and four sections of white tricot. **For the band**—with blue wool—Pick up all the stitches along the straight side of the cap, 15 stitches on each section, and work 16 rows of all plain tricot. Then sew up the cap, drawing the top together so as to leave no hole, and place a blue silk button on the centre. Fold the band double and hem it down on the wrong side.

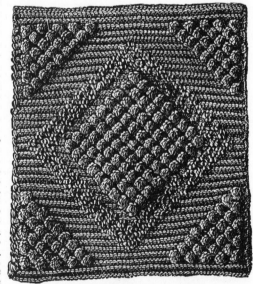

BOY'S CRICKETING CAP.

CROCHET SQUARE FOR A QUILT.

WITH A DIAMOND IN THE CENTRE AND FOUR TUFTED CORNER PIECES.

THE working of this rather large square will result in a very handsome quilt. Use Strutt's best knitting cotton, No. 6, and a steel crochet needle, No. 15. Commence with 62 chain, and work the first five rows forwards and backwards in plain double crochet, 62 stitches in each row, and inserting the hook in the back thread of the stitches of previous row, so as to make the work set in ridges. **6th row**—3 double crochet, 4 treble into the second row of the work,

missing a double crochet of previous row and catching the last of the treble stitches into the first to bind them together in a tuft, 3 double crochet, another tuft into the second row, 3 double crochet, tuft, 3 double crochet, tuft, 3 double crochet, tuft, 22 double crochet, tuft, 3 double crochet, tuft, 3 double crochet, tuft, 3 double crochet, tuft, 3 double crochet, tuft, 3 double crochet. **7th row**—Double crochet, and working 1 treble on each double crochet stitch that was missed in last row, 62 stitches in all. **8th row**—5 double crochet, tuft into the fourth row of the work, 3 double crochet, tuft, 3 double crochet, tuft, 3 double crochet, tuft, 26 double crochet, tuft, 3 double crochet, tuft, 3 double crochet, tuft, 3 double crochet, tuft, 5 double crochet. **9th row**—Same as the seventh row. **10th row**—3 double crochet, tuft, 3 double crochet, tuft, 3 double crochet, tuft, 3 double crochet, tuft, 14 double crochet, 2 treble on the last row but one, 14 double crochet, tuft, 3 double crochet, tuft, 3 double crochet, tuft, 3 double crochet. **11th row**—Same as the seventh row. **12th row**—5 double crochet, tuft, 3 double crochet, tuft, 3 double crochet, tuft, 14 double crochet, 2 treble on the last row but one, 2 double crochet, 2 treble on the last row but one, 14 double crochet, tuft, 3 double crochet, tuft, 3 double crochet, tuft, 5 double crochet. **13th row**—Same as the seventh row. **14th row**—3 double crochet, tuft, 3 double crochet, tuft, 3 double crochet, tuft, 14 double crochet, 2 treble, 2 double crochet, 2 treble, 2 double crochet, 2 treble, 14 double crochet, tuft, 3 double crochet, tuft, 3 double crochet. **15th row**—Same as the seventh row. **16th row**—5 double crochet, tuft, 3 double crochet, tuft, 14 double crochet, 2 treble, 2 double crochet, 2 treble, 2 double crochet, 2 treble, 2 double crochet, 2 treble, 14 double crochet, tuft, 3 double crochet, tuft, 5 double crochet. **17th row**—Same as the seventh row. **18th row**—3 double crochet, tuft, 3 double crochet, tuft, 14 double crochet, 2 treble, 2 double crochet, 2 treble, 6 double crochet, 2 treble, 2 double crochet, 2 treble, 14 double crochet, tuft, 3 double crochet, tuft, 3 double crochet. **19th row**—Same as the seventh row. **20th row**—5 double crochet, tuft, 14 double crochet, 2 treble, 2 double crochet, 2 treble, 5 double crochet, tuft, 4 double crochet, 2 treble, 2 double crochet, 2 treble, 14 double crochet, tuft, 5 double crochet. **21st row**—Same as the seventh row. **22nd row**—3 double crochet, tuft, 14 double crochet, 2 treble, 2 double crochet, 2 treble, 5 double crochet, tuft, 3 treble, tuft, 4 double crochet, 2 treble, 2 double crochet, 2 treble, 14 double crochet, tuft, 3 double crochet. **23rd row**—Same as the seventh row. **24th row**—16 double crochet, 2 treble, 2 double crochet, 2 treble, 5 double crochet, tuft, 3 double crochet, tuft, 3 double crochet, tuft, 4 double crochet, 2 treble, 2 double crochet, 2 treble, 16 double crochet. **25th row**—Same as the seventh row. **26th row**—14 double crochet, 2 treble, 2 double crochet, 2 treble, 5 double crochet, tuft, 3 double crochet, tuft, 3 double crochet, tuft, 4 double crochet, 2 treble, 2 double crochet, 2 treble, 14 double crochet. **27th row**—Same as the seventh row. **28th row**—12 double crochet, 2 treble, 2 double crochet, 2 treble, 5 double crochet, tuft, 3 double crochet, tuft, 3 double crochet, tuft, 3 double crochet, tuft, 4 double crochet, 2 treble, 2 double crochet, 2 treble, 12 double crochet. **29th row**—Same as the seventh row. **30th row**—10 double crochet, 2 treble, 2 double crochet, 2 treble, 5 double crochet, tuft, 3 double crochet, tuft, 3 double crochet, tuft, 3 double crochet, tuft, 3 double crochet, tuft, 3 double crochet, tuft, 4 double crochet, 2 treble, 2 double crochet, 2 treble, 10 double crochet. **31st row**—Same as the seventh row. **32nd row**—8 double crochet, 2 treble, 2 double crochet, 2 treble, 5 double crochet, tuft, 3 double crochet, tuft, 3 double crochet, tuft, 3 double

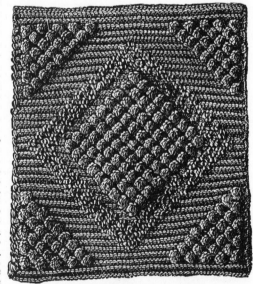

CROCHET SQUARE FOR A QUILT.
With a Diamond in the Centre and Four Tufted Corner Pieces.

treble, 2 double crochet, 2 treble, 5 double crochet, tuft, 3 double crochet, tuft, 3 double crochet, tuft, 3 double crochet, tuft, 4 double crochet, 2 treble, 2 double crochet, 2 treble, 8 double crochet. **33rd row**—Same as the seventh row. **34th row**—6 double crochet, 2 treble, 2 double crochet, 2 treble, 5 double crochet, tuft, 3 double crochet, tuft, 3 double crochet, tuft, 3 double crochet, tuft, 3 double crochet, tuft, 3 double crochet, tuft, 3 double crochet, tuft, 3 double crochet, tuft, 4 double crochet, 2 treble, 2 double crochet, 2 treble, 6 double crochet. **35th row**—Same as the seventh row. **36th row**—4 double crochet, 2 treble, 2 double crochet, 2 treble, 5 double crochet, tuft, 3 double crochet, tuft, 3 double crochet, tuft, 3 double crochet, tuft, 3 double crochet, tuft, 3 double crochet, tuft, 3 double crochet, tuft, 3 double crochet, tuft, 3 double crochet, tuft, 4 double crochet, 2 treble, 2 double crochet, 2 treble, 4 double crochet. **37th row**—Same as the seventh row. Now work the same as the 34th row, and work thence backwards, ending with the five rows of plain double crochet, which will complete the square.

CROCHET SHAWL. PICOTEED PATTERN.

THIS light, lacy-looking shawl may be worked with Shetland or Pompadour wool—the latter gives it a very rich appearance. Bore crochet needle, No. 10. The shawl is worked lengthways, therefore commence with chain sufficient for the length required. **1st row**—1 double crochet in the ninth chain from the needle, 4 chain, another double crochet in the same place,* 3 chain, miss three of the commencing chain, 1 double crochet in the fourth, 4 chain, another double crochet in the same place; repeat from *. Turn at the end of this and every row, **2nd row**—5 chain, 1 double crochet under the three chain of last row, and repeat. **3rd row**—5 chain, 1 double crochet in the centre

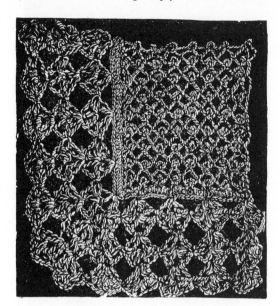

CROCHET SHAWL IN PICOTEED PATTERN.

stitch of the five chain of last row, 4 chain, another double crochet in the same place, * 3 chain, 1 double crochet in the centre stitch of the next loop of five chain of last row, 4 chain, another double crochet in the same place; repeat from *. **4th row**—5 chain, 1 double crochet under the three chain of last row, and repeat. Repeat the third and fourth rows alternately till the desired size is obtained for the centre of the shawl. **For the Border**—First of all, to get the two sides and the finishing off row perfectly straight, work 3 chain, 1 double crochet, along these three sides. **1st round of the Border**—1 treble in every stitch all round the shawl, increasing at the corners. **2nd round**—1 long treble, 2 chain, 1 long treble, 2 chain, 1 long treble, 2 chain, 1 long treble, all four of these long treble stitches to be worked into one treble stitch of previous round, then miss nine treble of previous round, and repeat. **3rd round**—1 treble, 2 chain, 1 treble, 2 chain, 1 treble, 2 chain, 1 treble, all four of these treble stitches to be worked into the centre loop of two chain of last round, 1 double crochet in the space between the scallops, and repeat. **4th round**—The same as the third round, working the four long treble stitches into the centre loop of two chain of last round. **5th round**—The same as the third round. **6th round**—The same as the fourth round. **7th round**—The same as the third round.

PLUM LATTICE PATTERN. CROCHET.

THIS is a good pattern for antimacassars and couvrepieds. Required, double Berlin wool, four shades of crimson or any colour that may be preferred. Bone crochet needle, No. 6. With the darkest shade of wool make a chain as long as required, and work 4 rows of plain double crochet forwards and backwards. **5th row**—With the next lightest shade of wool, and commencing the same end of the work as you left off, work 3 consecutive double crochet, * wool three times over the needle, insert the hook in the work so as to take up the first double crochet of the first row, draw the wool through, wool over the needle and draw through two loops, wool over the needle and draw through two loops, wool over the needle and draw through two loops again, wool twice over the needle and insert the hook in the work so as to take up the fourth double crochet of the first row, draw the wool through, wool over the needle and draw through two loops, wool over the needle and insert the hook in the same place, draw the wool through, wool over the needle and draw through two loops, wool over the needle and insert the hook in the same place, draw the wool through, wool over the needle and insert the hook in the same place, draw the wool through, wool over the needle and draw through four loops, you now have 3 stitches on the needle, wool three times over the needle, insert the hook in the work so as to take up the third double crochet from the last stitch so picked up in the first row, draw the wool through, wool over the needle and draw through two loops, wool over the needle and draw through two loops, wool over the needle and draw through the 4 stitches on the needle, work 5 consecutive double crochet, missing 1 at back as the fancy stitch on needle occupies the space of one, repeat from *, now inserting the hook into the same stitch of the first row of double crochet as the last long lattice stitch is worked into. There must be 3 double crochet to work at the end of the row. **6th, 7th and 8th**

PLUM LATTICE PATTERN CROCHET.

rows—Plain double crochet with the same shade of wool. **9th row**—With the next lightest shade of wool, and commencing the same side of the work as you left off, insert the hook in the first stitch of previous row and draw the wool through (but not finish working a double crochet stitch), wool three times over the needle, insert the hook right under the loop of raised stitches made in the fifth row, draw the wool through, wool over the needle and draw through two loops, wool over the needle and draw through two loops, wool over the needle and draw through two loops, wool over the needle and draw through the 3 stitches on the needle, 5 double crochet, wool three times over the needle, and work as directed from * to * in the fifth row, this time inserting the hook through the work in the lower part of the long lattice stitch just raised where it encircles the bunch of raised loops made in the fifth row. **10th, 11th, and 12th rows**—Plain double crochet with the same shade of wool. Then work from the 5th row to the 8th row with the next lighter shade of wool, and from the 9th row to the 12th row with the lightest shade. This done you can recommence with the darkest shade of wool, and repeat the work gradually to the lightest shade, or take the second lightest shade and graduate therefrom to the darkest.

CROCHET SQUARE FOR QUILT.

REQUIRED, Strutt's knitting cotton, No. 6, and a steel crochet needle, No. 15. Commence on the outside of the square with 252 chain, which gives 63 chain for each side of the square, join round, and for the **1st round**—Work 1 treble, * 2 chain, miss 2 of the foundation, 1 treble in the next, repeat from * eighteen times, making 20 treble stitches to form one side of the square, miss 5 of the commencing chain, 1 treble in the sixth, and repeat from the first asterisk *. Join neatly at the end of the round. **2nd round**—Miss the first treble and 2 chain stitches of last round, 1 treble on the next treble stitch, and work treble (52) to the corner, where miss the last 2 chain and the treble stitch, and repeat. **3rd round**—Miss the first 3 treble stitches, 1 treble on the fourth, and work 46 treble along each side of the square. **4th round**—The same working 40 treble along each side of the square. **5th round**—Miss the first 3 treble stitches, 1 treble on the fourth, 5 more consecutive treble, a tuft of 5 treble in the next stitch, catching the last of the 5 treble into the first, 3 treble, a tuft, 3 treble, tuft, 3 treble, tuft, 3 treble, tuft, miss 1 stitch of last round, 6 consecutive treble, leave 3 stitches at the end of last round, and repeat. **6th round**—Miss the first 3 treble stitches, 1 treble on the fourth, 4 consecutive treble, a tuft, 3 treble, tuft, 3 treble, tuft, 3 treble, tuft, 3 treble, tuft, 5 consecutive treble, leave 3 stitches at the end of last round, and repeat. **7th round**—Miss the first 3 treble stitches, 1 treble on the fourth, 3 consecutive treble, tuft, 3 treble, turf, 3 treble, tuft, 3 treble, tuft, 4 consecutive treble, leave 3 stitches at the end of last round, and repeat. **8th round**—Miss the first 3 treble stitches, 1 treble on the fourth, 2 more consecutive treble, tuft, 3 treble, tuft, 3 treble, tuft, 3 treble, leave 3 stitches at the end of last round, and repeat. **9th round**—Miss the first 3 treble stitches, work 2 treble, tuft, 3 treble, tuft, 2 treble, leave 3 stitches at the end of last round, and repeat. **10th round**—Miss the first 3 treble stitches, work 1 treble, tuft, 1 treble, leave 3 stitches at the end of last round, and repeat. Join neatly, and fasten off. Work the outside edge of the square with a round of double crochet, making 3 double crochet in each corner stitch.

CROCHET SQUARE FOR QUILT.

WELDON'S LADIES' JOURNAL. Contains every month a Cut-Out Paper Pattern, 60 Illustrations of Latest Fashions in Costumes, Mantles, Jackets, Dolmans, Underclothing, &c., for Ladies and Children; about 40 pages of Letterpress; plain instructions for cutting out and making up each Garment; how to Knit, Crochet, &c.; a vast amount of useful information on the Household, &c. Price 3d. monthly; postage 1½d. Yearly subscription, 4s. 6d. post free.

HOOD AND SHAWL COMBINED.
WORKED IN CRAZY PATTERN.

THIS is a comfortable close-fitting hood, and the shawl comes down nicely over the neck and shoulders. It is equally suitable for a lady's opera hood, or for a baby to wear out in the garden, and can be made either size by the following directions. From 2 oz. to 4 oz. of best white Shetland wool will be required, a bone crochet needle, No. 9, and 2½ yards of 1½ inch wide ribbon. Commence with 4 chain. Join round. **1st round**—1 double crochet, 2 chain, and 3 treble in the circle; repeat three times, working rather loosely, and then join by drawing the wool through the first double crochet stitch. This is not worked round and round in the usual way, but the work is to be *turned* at the completion of every round, and both sides are alike. **2nd round**—Make 3 chain and turn, and under the first two chain of last round work * 1 double crochet, 2 chain, 3 treble, twice in the same place, and repeat from * twice under *each* two chain of previous round, and join by drawing the wool through the first double crochet stitch. **3rd round**—3 chain and turn,* and work 1 double crochet, 2 chain, 3 treble, under the first two chain of last round, and 1 double crochet, 2 chain, 3 treble, twice under the next two chain of last round, and repeat from *, and join round as before. **4th round**—3 chain and turn, and work 1 double crochet, 2 chain, 3 treble, under the first two chain of last round, and the same under the next two chain, then for the corner work the same twice under the next two chain of last round, and repeat, and join when the round is completed. Continue every round the same, working straight along the four sides and increasing at the four corners, until you have a square piece, of 12 rounds if for a baby, or 16 rounds for a lady's hood. Then work along *two sides* only, increasing at both ends where you turn, and in the centre, for 16 rows. Then work all the way round for 8 rounds, increasing still at the two corners where you just now turned, and also in the centre, but *not* at the fourth corner, which is to be rounded for the top of the hood. Cut the ribbon into two equal lengths, and divide one piece in half again. The longest piece is to be run exactly across the centre of the square through the increasings at the corners, and is to tie round the neck; the two shorter pieces are to be run four rounds from the front of the hood to confine it in shape, commencing where the ribbon is already run in for the neck, and being sewn down thereto, and the other ends tied in a bow on the top of the head.

HOOD AND SHAWL COMBINED.
(Worked in Crazy Pattern.)

CRAZY PATTERN.

WORKED in straight rows, as shown in the illustration, this is a useful stitch for long scarves, shawls, and various other purposes. The crochet needle will of course be selected of proper size for the wool with which it is to be used, say Andalusian wool and No. 9 needle. Commence with a chain rather longer than needed for the piece of work, as part of it contracts. **1st row**—2 treble in the fifth chain from the needle, 2 treble in the next, miss two chain, 1 double crochet in the next, * 2 chain, 2 treble in the next chain of the foundation, 2 treble in the next, miss two chain, 1 double crochet in the next, and repeat from *. **2nd row**—3 chain to turn, 1 double crochet on the last one of the four treble stitches, 2 chain, 4 treble under the two chain of last row, * 1 double crochet on the last one of the next group of four trebles, 2 chain, 4 treble under the next two chains of last row, and repeat from *. Every succeeding row is worked the same as the second row.

BABY'S BOOTS.
IN RIBBED CROCHET AND POINT MUSCOVITE STITCH.

PROCURE 1 oz. each of blue and white single Berlin wool; a bone crochet needle, No. 10; and 1 yard of narrow blue ribbon. With the blue wool commence for the toe by working 10 chain. **1st row**—Insert the hook in the second chain from the needle and work 4 consecutive double crochet stitches along the chain, 3 double crochet in the next stitch of the chain, and 4 consecutive double crochet to the end of the row. It is intended that all this double crochet be worked very closely and tightly. **2nd row**—1 chain to turn, miss the first double crochet of last row, and inserting the hook always at the back of the stitches of previous row, so that the work may set in ridges, work 11 double crochet, the last of the double crochet being worked into the chain stitches that turned the previous row. **3rd row**—1 chain to turn, miss the

first double crochet of last row, and work 5 consecutive double crochet, 3 double crochet in the next, and 5 consecutive double crochet to the end of the row. **4th row**—Same as the second row, working 13 double crochet. Continue thus till you have 25 stitches in the plain row. Then proceed for the side of the boot, work 12 double crochet, turn, and continue on these twelve stitches till 24 little rows are done. Work the same for the opposite side of the boot, and join both pieces together at the heel. **For the Sock** —Take the white wool, and holding the right side of the foot part towards you, work 1 double crochet on the first rib by the heel, * insert the hook in the furrow and draw the wool through, do 4 chain, wool over the needle and draw the wool through the chain stitch and through the stitch on the needle, 1 double crochet on the next rib, and repeat from * all round the foot part. In the next round work the "points" upon the double crochet stitches and the new double crochet stitches upon the points of last round. And continue for 8 rounds. Then join on the blue wool and work 3 rounds the same, and also work a round for a heading thus—1 double crochet, * 4 chain, 1 treble in the double crochet stitch just done, miss one stitch of last row, 1 double crochet on the next, and repeat from*. **For the Sole**—With blue wool commence at the toe with 8 chain, turn, and work in double crochet, inserting the hook in both top threads of last row, 2 rows of 7 stitches, 2 rows of 8 stitches, 4 rows of 9 stitches, 8 rows of 7 stitches, 6 rows of 9 stitches, 2 rows of 7 stitches, 2 rows of 5 stitches; break off the wool, and sew the sole to the shoe. Run a ribbon in to tie round the instep.

HANDSOME CROCHET HOOD.

THIS pretty hood is made with Berlin wool any colour desired, some large glass beads, and a bone crochet hook. You must commence with a chain of 35 stitches (taking care to crochet loosely), turn, make 2 double crochet stitches in the third stitch of chain, chain 1, make 2 more double crochet stitches in same place, which forms a shell *, skip 2 stitches and make another shell in third stitch as before, * repeat from * to * all across. You will have 11 shells, which will make the front the right width. Turn the work and chain very loosely four stitches; then put the hook through a bead, drawing the wool through; then chain 4 stitches and fasten between the shells. Work across in this way, making 8 chain with a bead in the middle between each shell. Turn, and chain 1 and make shells exactly as in the first row, and fasten in the middle of the shells of the first row, and continue in this way across. The next row is loops with beads. The shells will all be on wrong side, loops and beads on right side. Work in this way till the piece is long enough for one side of the head, allowing for the cape. Make the other side exactly like this, and join at the top. Make the crown the same number of stitches as the front, and sew in, commencing at the bottom, leaving the top of the crown square across; that is, not narrowing any. Run in satin ribbon far enough from the bottom to leave a cape. Lay the top in a box pleat above the forehead. This will make the crown come higher than the front. Place a satin bow back of the pleat and another at the back of the neck.

BABY'S CROCHETED SOCKS.

ONE oz. each of white and blue zephyr wool will be required, also a fine steel hook. Make 36 chains of the blue wool and join same, then crochet around 3 times, taking up only one half the stitch. Now fasten on the white wool, and crochet 24 rows, taking up both loops of the stitch, crochet back to the 24th stitch, then turn and go back twelve stitches, and work those 12 stitches backwards and forwards till you have 14 rows. For the instep, take up only the upper half of the stitch, join on the blue wool, and work all round the sock, taking up only the outside half of the stitch. Work round 16 rows, then crochet together at the bottom, drawing the wool through 10 stitches at the heel, and the same at the toe to form the shape of the foot; finish the top with two rows of chain loops, and a scallop of 3 stitches of blue wool. Crochet a cord and add tassel to draw up the sock, or run in narrow blue ribbon.

BABY'S BOOTS.
(In Ribbed Crochet and Point Muscovite Stitch.)

BORDER FOR QUILT, SHOWING A CORNER.

THIS border may either be worked upon the quilt itself, or separately on a length of commencing chain. Use Strutt's knitting cotton, No. 6, and a No. 15 steel crochet needle. 1st row—1 treble, 2 chain, miss two, and repeat; at the corner work 3 chain and another treble in the same stitch the last treble is worked into. 2nd row—Double crochet on every stitch of previous row, and 3 double crochet on the centre stitch of the three chain at the corner. 3rd row—The same. 4th row—3 double crochet, 5 treble on the next stitch, and catch the last of the treble stitches into the first to bind them together in a tuft, repeat, and at the corner work 1 double crochet, 3 double crochet in the corner stitch, 1 double crochet, and continue working a tuft and a double crochet alternately. 5th row—Double crochet, and 1 treble stitch worked at the back of each tuft; 3 double crochet in the corner stitch. Fasten off the cotton at the end of the row, and re-commence on the right-hand side. 6th row—Same as the first row. 7th row—Same as the second row. 8th row—Same as the second row. 9th row—Same as the fourth row, but working 2 double crochet instead of one on each side the corner stitch. 10th row—Same as the fifth row. Repeat the last five rows. 16th row—1 treble into the first stitch of last row, 3 chain, another treble in the same place, * miss three stitches of last row, 1 treble in the next, 3 chain, another treble in the same place, and repeat from *. 17th row—1 treble in the first loop of three chain of last row, 5 chain, 1 double crochet in the first of the chain just done, 5 chain, 1 double crochet in the first of the chain just done, another treble in the first loop of three chain of last row, and work the same under every loop of three chain to the end of the length.

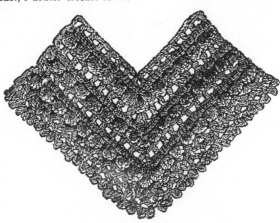

BORDER FOR QUILT, SHOWING A CORNER.

SQUARE FOR QUILT.
OPEN DIAMOND PATTERN.

THIS is more especially intended for a summer quilt, as being open work, it requires lining with pink or blue twill, which gives it a light and elegant appearance. Work with Strutt's knitting cotton, No. 6, and steel crochet needle, No. 15. Begin with a chain of 4 stitches, and join round. At the beginning of every round 3 chain are to be worked in place of the first treble stitch, therefore in the number of stitches stated at the beginning of a round 3 chain is done and counts as the first of the treble. 1st round—3 treble, 3 chain, and repeat this three times more; join round, slip into the middle of the three chain stitches, and work 3 more chain to simulate a treble for the commencement of the next round. Every succeeding round is to be joined in the same way. 2nd round—7 treble, 3 chain, and repeat. 3rd round—5 treble, 1 chain, miss 1, 5 treble, 3 chain, and repeat. 4th round—5 treble, 1 chain, miss 2, 3 treble in the one chain of last round, 1 chain, miss 2, 5 treble, 3 chain, and repeat. 5th round—5 treble, 1 chain, miss 2, 3 treble in the next one chain, 1 chain, 3 treble in the next one chain, 1 chain, miss 2, 5 treble, 3 chain, and repeat. 6th round—5 treble,

SQUARE FOR QUILT.
(Open Diamond Pattern).

1 chain, miss 2, 3 treble in the next one chain, 1 chain, 3 treble in the next one chain, 1 chain, 3 treble in the next one chain, 1 chain, miss 2, 5 treble, 3 chain, and repeat. 7th round—5 treble, 1 chain, miss 2, 3 treble in the next one chain, 1 chain, 3 treble in the next one chain, 1 chain, 3 treble in the next one chain, 1 chain, miss 2, 5 treble, 3 chain, and repeat. 8th round—5 treble, 1 chain, miss 2, 3 treble in the next one chain, 1 chain, 3 treble in the next one chain, 1 chain, 3 treble in the next one chain, 1 chain, 3 treble in the next one chain, 1 chain, miss 2, 5 treble, 3 chain. 9th round—9 treble, 1 chain, 3 treble in the next one chain, 1 chain, 3 treble in the next one chain, 1 chain, 3 treble in the next one chain, 1 chain, 9

treble, 3 chain, and repeat. 10th round—13 treble, 1 chain, 3 treble in the next one chain, 1 chain, 3 treble in the next one chain, 1 chain, 3 treble in the next one chain, 1 chain, 13 treble, 3 chain, and repeat. 11th round—17 treble, 1 chain, 3 treble in the next one chain, 1 chain, 3 treble in the next one chain, 1 chain, 17 treble, 3 chain, and repeat. 12th round—21 treble, 1 chain, 3 treble in the one chain, 1 chain, 21 treble, 3 chain, and repeat. 13th round—25 treble, 1 chain, miss 1, 25 treble, 3 chain, and repeat. Fasten off now, and this completes the square.

CROCHET SQUARE FOR QUILT.
WITH A BORDER OF TUFTS, AND A TUFTED DIAMOND IN THE CENTRE.

THIS pretty square should be worked with Strutt's best knitting cotton, No. 6, and a No. 15 steel crochet needle. Commence with 51 chain, and work the first 3 rows forwards and backwards in plain double crochet, 51 stitches in each row, and inserting the hook in the back thread of the stitches of previous row, so as to make the work set in ridges. 4th row—5 double crochet,* 5 treble into the next stitch and catch the last of the treble stitches into the first to bind them together in a tuft, 3 double crochet, and repeat from *, ending the row with 5 double crochet as it began. 5th row—Double crochet, and 1 treble stitch worked at the back of each tuft. 6th row—3 double crochet, tuft, 7 double crochet, tuft, 3 double crochet, tuft, 7 double crochet, tuft, 3 double crochet, tuft, 7 double crochet, tuft, 3 double crochet, tuft, 7 double crochet, tuft, 3 double crochet. 7th row—Same as the fifth row. 8th row—13 double crochet, tuft, 11 double crochet, tuft, 11 double crochet, tuft, 13 double crochet. 9th row—Same as the fifth row. 10th row—3 double crochet, tuft, 43 double crochet, tuft, 3 double crochet. 11th row—Same as the fifth row. 12th row—5 double crochet, tuft, 39 double crochet, tuft, 5 double crochet. 13th row—Same as the fifth row. 14th row—3 double crochet, tuft, 3 double crochet, tuft, 13 double crochet, tuft, 3 double crochet, tuft, 3 double crochet, tuft, 13 double crochet, tuft, 3 double crochet, tuft, 3 double crochet. 15th row—Same as fifth row. 16th row—5 double crochet, tuft, 13 double crochet, tuft, 3 double crochet, tuft, 3 double crochet, tuft, 3 double crochet, tuft, 13 double crochet, tuft, 5 double crochet. 17th row—Same as the fifth row. 18th row—3 double crochet, tuft, 13 double crochet, tuft, 3 double crochet, tuft, 7 double crochet, tuft 3 double crochet, tuft, 13 double crochet, tuft, 3 double crochet. 19th row—Same as the fifth row. 20th row—15 double crochet, tuft, 3 double crochet tuft, 11 double crochet, tuft, 3 double crochet, tuft, 15 double crochet. 21st row—Same as the fifth row. 22nd row—3 double crochet, tuft, 9 double crochet, tuft, 3 double crochet, tuft, 15 double crochet, tuft, 3 double crochet, tuft, 9 double crochet, tuft, 3 double crochet. 23rd row—Same as the fifth row. 24th row—5 double crochet, tuft, 9 double crochet, tuft, 9 double crochet, tuft, 9 double crochet, tuft, 9 double crochet, tuft, 5 double crochet. 25th row—Same as the fifth row.

CROCHET SQUARE FOR QUILT.
(With a Border of Tufts, and a Tufted Diamond in the Centre).

26th row—3 double crochet, tuft, 3 double crochet, tuft, 5 double crochet, tuft, 9 double crochet, tuft, 3 double crochet, tuft, 9 double crochet, tuft, 5 double crochet, tuft, 3 double crochet, tuft, 3 double crochet. 27th row—Same as the fifth row. Now work the same as directed for the 24th row, and continue thence backwards, ending with 3 rows of plain double crochet, which completes the square. Without breaking off the cotton proceed to work round all four sides of the square, do a treble stitch at the corner, 5 chain, another treble in the same place, 2 chain, miss two stitches of the square, 1 treble in the next, and repeat the 2 chain, 1 treble, with increase in turning the corners. 2nd round—Double crochet in every stitch of last round, working 3 double crochet in the stitch at the corners. When a sufficient number of squares are worked they should be sewn together, and a border added such as is shown on page 11, otherwise a knotted fringe gives a finish.

COSY ANTIMACASSAR.

This Antimacassar will be found most useful, as it fits closely to the back of an easy chair, and cannot by any possibility fall off or get disarranged. Required, double Berlin wool, 5 shades of crimson, 5 shades of art green, some sky blue, and amber; the quantity will depend upon the size the antimacassar is to be, the model, which is a large one, takes a little over 1 lb. in all. Bone crochet needle, No. 8. The antimacassar is worked throughout in Point Muscovite stitch. **1st row**—With amber wool, commence with 29 chain, 1 double crochet on the first of the chain, insert the hook in the next chain and draw the wool through, work 4 chain stitches, wool over the needle, and draw through the two stitches on the needle, 1 double crochet in the next foundation chain, a point in the next, 1 double crochet in the next, and so on, a point and a double crochet alternately all along. Break off the wool at the end of this and every row, and re-commence on the right hand side which is the bottom of the antimacassar, and is to be kept quite straight; the left hand side of the work (where the wool is broken off) is to be shaped to the back of the

chair. **2nd row**—With blue wool, a point stitch upon the first stitch of last row, and a double crochet over the point stitch, and repeat a point and a double crochet alternately, always working the point stitch over the double crochet of last row, and working into two threads of last row; increase 1 stitch at the end of the row. **3rd row**—With amber, a double crochet upon the point stitch of last row, and a point upon the double crochet, and repeat, and again increase a stitch at the end of the row. Next you work 9 rows with crimson wool, beginning with the darkest, and shading gradually to the darkest again. Then a row of amber, of blue, and of amber again. Then 9 rows with green wool, beginning with the darkest, and shading gradually to the darkest again. In all these rows it will require the stitch increased at the end of the row to shape to the back of the chair. Do the next fifteen rows, a row of amber, blue, and amber again, then 9 rows with crimson, and again amber, blue, and amber, straight on without any increase. Next you will work 9 rows with green wool, decreasing a stitch at the end of every row. Then a row of amber, blue and amber again. Then 9 rows with crimson, and then amber, blue and amber; and the work should now be reduced to 29 stitches as it began, and one half of the antimacassar is completed. The other half is to be worked exactly the same. Sew both pieces together round the semicircle, leaving the straight side of the work open. With amber wool crochet over the join, working 1 double crochet, * 4 chain, 1 single crochet in the first of the chain, 1 double crochet in the next stitch of the anti-macassar, and repeat from *. Cut some pieces of wool into lengths of seven inches, and fringe all along the straight side of the work, knotting four strands of wool (respective shades) into each row of the antimacassar.

BOY'S CAP, WITH FLUTED CROWN AND TUFTED BAND.

Required, 4 ozs. of dark crimson single Berlin or fingering wool and a bone crochet needle, No. 11. Commence with a loop, in which work 4 double crochet. **2nd round**—Work 2 double crochet in every stitch, taking up both front threads of the stitches of previous round. **3rd round**—2 double crochet in every stitch of previous round, making 16 stitches, worked into the front threads as before. **4th round**—2 double crochet in the first stitch, 1 double crochet in the next, and repeat. **5th round**—2 double crochet in the first stitch, and 1 double crochet in each of the two next stitches, and repeat, making 32 double crochet in all. **6th round**—Here the fluted crown commences, and now work into the one top thread of previous round, * 3 double crochet, 1 double crochet in the next stitch, and repeat from * fifteen times more. **7th round** and 10 following rounds—Work 3 double crochet in the centre stitch of the three double crochet of last round, and 1 double crochet in each other stitch. Now having seventeen rounds worked from the commencement, fasten off the wool. Take the fluted circle, and having the right side towards you, fold two points together with the wrong side out, and work into the second last row, taking up the centre stitch of the plain double crochet between the points, 1 double crochet, 6 chain, fold the next points, and again into the second last row work 1 double crochet in the centre stitch of the plain double crochet between the points, 6 chain, and repeat the same round the fluted circle, making 16 loops of 6 chain in the round. **19th round**—Work in double crochet over

the chain stitches of last round, making 8 double crochet under each loop **20th round**—Plain double crochet all round, working into both top threads of the stitches of last round. **21st round. 22nd round**—Again plain double crochet, and here the fluted circle is to be arranged into folds, and each point is to be caught down when working the centre double crochet stitch between the flutes, that is, in working every eighth double crochet stitch you must catch down a point—thus, commence the round exactly over the stitch where the round of loops of chain began, * work 3 double crochet, insert the hook in the centre stitch of the point and also in the next double crochet stitch of last round, and work another double crochet stitch, then 4 more double crochet, and repeat from *. Work 20 rounds of plain double crochet, 1 double crochet in every stitch of previous round, and inserting the hook always into the two top threads. Then turn the work so as to bring the wrong side towards you, and work 8 more rounds of double crochet in the same way for the turn-over band. Finish the band with 5 rounds of tufted stitch. Tufted stitch is worked as follows : * wool over the needle as if about to make a treble stitch, insert the hook in a stitch of the last round of double crochet and draw the wool through, wool over the needle, insert the hook in the same place, and again draw the wool through, wool over the needle, insert the hook a third time in the same place and draw the wool through, there are now seven stitches on the needle, draw the wool through all, and work a chain stitch, miss one double crochet of the cap, and repeat from *. In the second and succeeding rounds of tufts you insert the hook under the chain stitch between the tufts of last round. Having worked 5 rounds of the tufted crochet, fasten off. Procure a good-sized button, and cover it with crochet worked in the same manner as directed for the first 4 rounds of the cap, then 2 rounds without increasing, and slip in the button, having first covered it with silk the same colour as the wool, and crochet it up. Sew it on the centre of the crown of the cap. Next cut a round piece of silk to line the crown, and cut a piece about 20 inches in length and 2 inches in width to line the band, sew them together and work to the inside of the cap. If greater strength be desired you can have a leather band sewn in. A good bicycle cap can be made from these directions by working three additional rounds in the fluted centre of the crown, then doing 9 chain instead of eight chain in the first round of the plain part, and 9 or 10 double crochet under each loop of chain, and also working a few more rounds of double crochet before beginning the rounds of plain double crochet for the band.

CROCHETED CLOVER-LEAF LACE.

1st row—Make a chain of 9 stitches, turn back and work 2 single stitches in sixth stitch, 3 chain, 2 single in third stitch, 3 chain, and 2 single in last stitch. **2nd row**—Work 2 single stitches in first bar, 3 chain and 2 single stitches in the next bar, 3 chain and 2 single in the last bar. **3rd row**—2 stitches in first bar; 3 chain, 2 in next bar, 3 chain, 2 single, 3 chain, in last bar work a chain of eight and fasten to the first row, work 16 stitches of single crochet over the chain. **4th row**—2 stitches in first bar, 3 chain, 2 in next bar, 3 chain, 2 in last bar, 3 chain, and 2 single stitches. **5th row**—2 stitches in first bar, 3 chain, 2 in next bar, 3 chain and 2 single stitches, 3 chain and 2 stitches in last bar. Make a chain of 8, and fasten to the end of the other loop, turn back and work 8 single stitches over the chain, then make 8 chain and fasten to centre of first leaf, work sixteen on that and 8 more on the one already begun, and the trefoil is complete. **6th row**—2 stitches in first bar, 3 chain, and 2 stitches in next, 3 chain, and 2 in last bar. To repeat the trefoil begin at first row.

JOSEPHINE STITCH.

This is a pretty variety of tricot stitch, and being light and lacey comes in very handy for shawls, scarfs, antimacassars, &c. It is necessary with this pattern to first make a chain the full length of the article required, as the rows are worked backwards and forwards after the tricot style; and any make of wool can be employed. **1st row**—Insert the hook in the fourth chain stitch, draw a loop through it, draw another loop through the loop already on hook, retaining this last loop on the hook. Repeat this again in the same stitch, insert the hook again in the stitch and draw a loop through This leaves 3 loops on the hook, also the loop which was there at

BOY'S CAP, WITH FLUTED CROWN AND TUFTED BAND

the beginning. Draw a loop through the three loops, and let that loop remain on the hook, repeat in every chain stitch you have made for the foundation. **2nd row**—Work off exactly as you would for ordinary tricot. **3rd row**—Make 2 chain stitches, and work just as for the 1st row, with the exception, however, of working under instead of into the stitches. Work off just as for the 2nd row, after which you continue to repeat the 3rd and 2nd rows until the article is finished. Only work the two chain stitches at the commencement of the rows to keep them even.

COSY ANTIMACASSAR.

ENLARGED DESIGN FOR MAKING THE COSY ANTIMACASSAR.

BORDER FOR QUILT.

THIS border had better be worked separately upon a length of commencing chain, and sewn to the quilt when finished. Use Strutt's knitting cotton, No. 6, and a steel crochet needle, No. 15. The chain should contain some multiple of 63, as 63 stitches are required for each pattern. You turn at the end of every row as in the quilt squares, and work in ridges. Work the first 3 rows in plain double crochet.

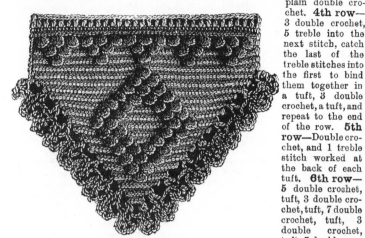

BORDER FOR QUILT.

4th row—3 double crochet, 5 treble into the next stitch, catch the last of the treble stitches into the first to bind them together in a tuft, 3 double crochet, a tuft, and repeat to the end of the row. **5th row**—Double crochet, and 1 treble stitch worked at the back of each tuft. **6th row**—5 double crochet, tuft, 3 double crochet, tuft, 7 double crochet, tuft, 3 double crochet, tuft, 7 double crochet, tuft, 3 double crochet, tuft, 7 double crochet, tuft, 3 double crochet, tuft, 7 double crochet, tuft, 3 double crochet, tuft, 5 double crochet, and repeat. **7th row**—Same as the fifth row. **8th row**—7 double crochet, tuft, 11 double crochet, tuft, 11 double crochet, tuft, 11 double crochet, tuft, 11 double crochet, tuft, 7 double crochet, and repeat. **9th row**—Same as the fifth row. **10th and 11th rows**—Plain double crochet. **12th row**—31 double crochet, tuft, 31 double crochet, and repeat. **13th row** — Begin on the third double crochet stitch and work same as the fifth row, working 61 stitches in the row, then turn, and work backwards and forwards to complete this scallop before going on to the next. **14th row**—27 double crochet, tuft, 3 double crochet, tuft, 27 double crochet, and leave two stitches unworked at the end of this and every row till the scallop is completed. **15th row**—Same as the fifth row, working 57 stitches. **16th row**—23 double crochet, tuft, 3 double crochet, tuft, 3 double crochet, tuft, 23 double crochet. **17th row**—Same as the fifth row, working 53 stitches. **18th row**—19 double crochet, tuft, 3 double crochet, tuft, 3 double crochet, tuft, 3 double crochet, tuft, 19 double crochet. **19th row**—Same as the fifth row, working 49 stitches. **20th row**—15 double crochet, tuft, 3 double crochet, tuft, 7 double crochet, tuft, 3 double crochet, tuft, 15 double crochet. **21st row**—Same as the fifth row, working 45 stitches. **22nd row**—11 double, crochet, tuft, 3 double crochet, tuft, 11 double crochet, tuft, 3 double crochet, tuft, 11 double crochet. **23rd row**—Same as the fifth row, working 41 stitches. **24th row**—7 double crochet, tuft, 3 double crochet, tuft, 15 double crochet, tuft, 3 double crochet, tuft, 7 double crochet. **25th row**—Same as the fifth row, working 37 stitches. **26th row**—7 double crochet, tuft, 3 double crochet, tuft, 11 double crochet, tuft, 3 double crochet, tuft, 7 double crochet. **27th row**—Same as the fifth row, working 33 stitches. **28th row**—7 double crochet, tuft, 3 double crochet, tuft, 7 double crochet, tuft, 3 double crochet, tuft, 7 double crochet. **29th row**—Same as the fifth row, working 29 stitches. **30th row**—7 double crochet, tuft, 3 double crochet, tuft, 3 double crochet, tuft, 7 double crochet. **31st row**—Same as the fifth row, working 25 stitches. **32nd row**—7 double crochet, tuft, 3 double crochet, tuft, 3 double crochet, tuft, 7 double crochet. **33rd row**—Same as the fifth row, working 21 stitches. **34th row**—7 double crochet, tuft, 3 double crochet, tuft, 7 double crochet. **35th row**—Same as the fifth row, working 17 stitches. **36th row**—7 double crochet, tuft, 7 double crochet. **37th row**—Same as the fifth row, working 13 stitches. **38th row**—11 double crochet. Continue in double crochet, working 2 stitches less in each row till all are worked off. Now work all the other scallops in rotation the same as this scallop. When the whole length is complete, proceed to edge the scallops, beginning with 1 treble into the twelfth row of the border, 5 chain, another treble into the same stitch, * 3 chain, 1 treble into the next point but one, 5 chain, another treble in the same place, repeat from *, an extra repeat will have to be made on the point, and continue to the end of the length. **2nd row**—1 treble in the middle of the five chain, 3 chain, another treble in the same place, twice over, 3 chain, 1 double crochet in the middle of the three chain, 3 chain, and repeat. Along the top of the border work a row thus : 1 treble into the first stitch, * 1 chain, miss one stitch, 1 treble in the next, and repeat from * to the end of the length.

FISHERMAN'S CAP.

REQUIRED, 4 ozs. of navy-blue single Berlin or peacock fingering wool. Bone crochet needle, No. 9. Begin by making a chain of 4 stitches, join round, and work 12 double crochet in the circle. **2nd round**—2 double crochet into every

stitch of last round, taking up both top threads of the work. **3rd round**—2 double crochet on the first stitch, 1 double crochet on next stitch, and repeat. **4th round**—2 double crochet on every third stitch. **5th round**—2 double crochet on every fifth stitch. **6th round**—Increase only 6 stitches in the round. Henceforward increase only 4 stitches in the round for 4 rounds. Then increase only 3 stitches in the round till you have 95 double crochet stitches in the round, or till the size required for the head; the rest of the cap is not increased, but worked in plain double crochet round and round, always working into the two top threads till the work measures about 11 inches from the commencement. This done, *turn* the cap, and work with the wrong side of the head piece towards you, now taking up the *one* top thread of the previous round, for 32 rounds. This is for the band which is double. Turn in half the band and iron down flat. The top of the cap is finished off with a thick tassel of wool.

FISHERMAN'S CAP.

CROCHET SQUARE FOR A QUILT.

WITH BORDER OF RAISED TUFTS, AND SPOT OF FIVE TUFTS IN THE CENTRE.

THIS is a pretty small square, and may be worked with Strutt's knitting cotton, No. 6, and steel crochet needle, No. 15, for a quilt, or with much finer cotton for a bassinette cover. Commence with 30 chain, turn, insert the hook in the third chain from the needle, and work 28 double crochet all along. **2nd row**—1 chain to turn, miss the first double crochet stitch, and again work 28 double crochet, inserting the hook so as to take up both top threads of the stitches of previous row. **3rd row**—1 chain to turn, miss the first stitch of last row, 1 double crochet in the next, * 4 treble in the next, and catch the last of the treble stitches into the first to bind them together in a tuft, 3 consecutive double crochet, and repeat from *, there will be 2 double crochet to work at the end of the row. **4th row**—Same as the second row. **5th row**—1 chain to turn, miss the first stitch, * work 3 consecutive double crochet, then a tuft of 4 treble, and repeat from *, there will be 4 double crochet to work at the end of the row. **6th row**—Same as the second row. **7th row**—1 chain to turn, miss the first stitch, 1 double crochet in the next, 4 treble in the next, 3 consecutive double crochet, 4 treble in the next, 15 double crochet, 4 treble in the next, 3 double crochet, 4 treble in the next, 2 double crochet. **8th row**—Same as the second row. **9th row**—1 chain to turn, miss the first stitch, 3 consecutive double crochet, 4 treble in the next, 19 double crochet, 4 treble in the next, 4 double crochet. **10th row**—Same as the second row. **11th row**—1 chain to turn, miss the first stitch, 1 double crochet in the next, 4 treble in the next, 3 double crochet, 4 treble in the next, 5 double crochet, 4 treble in the next, 3 double crochet, 4 treble in the next, 5 double crochet, 4 treble in the next, 3 double crochet, 4 treble in the next, 2 double crochet. **12th row**—Same as the second row. **13th row**—1 chain to turn, miss the first stitch, 3 consecutive double crochet, 4 treble in the next, 9 double crochet, 4 treble in the next, 9 double crochet, 4 treble in the next, 4 double crochet. **14th row**—Same as the second row. **15th row**—The same as the eleventh row, and thence work backwards, ending with the first row, which will complete the square. Then for an edge, without breaking off the cotton, work 4 chain (three of these chain will stand for a treble), 1 treble in the corner stitch, and 1 chain 1 treble alternately all round the square, having 3 treble with 1 chain between each at each corner, and 13 treble with 1 chain between each treble along each side.

PANSY MATS.

FOR two mats, it will be necessary to purchase four different shades of single zephyr—white, black, bright yellow, and purple; a quarter of an ounce of each except the yellow, of this half an ounce will be necessary. Crochet 6 stitches with the white. Join the ends ; into this ring crochet 12 long stitches, alternating with 1 chain stitch between ; fasten the last stitch very securely, and make 3 chain stitches for the next row. **3rd row**—Work this by crocheting 2 long stitches into every loop of the second row. **4th row**—Make 2 long stitches with 1 chain between, and alternate with 1 long into every loop (not stitch). **5th row**—By turns work 2 long and 2 separate stitches, with 1 chain between. **6th row**—Crochet 2 long stitches with 3 separate chain stitches between. **7th row** — Now use the black zephyr, working 2 long crochets into every loop of the white. **8th row**—Crochet with the yellow 2 long stitches into every loop of the black. **9th row**—Crochet with the purple zephyr the same as the last 2 rows. Now thread a needle with black silk and lightly catch down the fulness, the process gives the effect of pansies.

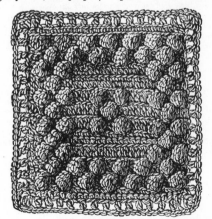

CROCHET SQUARE FOR A QUILT.
(With Border of Raised Tufts, and Spot of Five Tufts in the Centre.)

DOLL'S COSTUME IN CROCHET.

THIS pretty dress is intended for a doll about 14 inches high. It will require 2 ozs. of pale blue and 1 oz. of white Berlin wool. Tricot needle, No. 10, Commence at the bottom above the border, with blue wool, with 72 chain, raise 71 stitches in the chain, keeping them all on the needle, and to work back draw the wool through one stitch, and then through two stitches together, till all the stitches are worked off. Work 5 rows of plain tricot. 6th row—Raise 7 stitches, raise 2 together, raise 7, raise 2 together, raise 7, raise 2 together, raise 16, raise 2 together, raise 7, raise 2 together, raise 7, raise 2 together, raise 8, work back the same as before. Now 4 rows of plain tricot. 11th row—Raise 6 stitches, raise 2 together, raise 7, raise 2 together, raise 6, raise 2 together, raise 7, raise 2 together, raise 7, raise 2 together, raise 6, raise 2 together, raise 6, raise 2 together, raise 7, and work back the same. Work 4 more rows of plain tricot. Then decrease again. Work 4 more rows and decrease again. Then 4 more rows, and the skirt will be sufficiently long. For the **Body**—Commence with chain sufficient to meet round the waist. Work 4 rows of plain tricot, next row increase one stitch under each arm, a plain row, and next row increase again under the arms. Now work the right front, shaping round the arm and shoulder to the neck. Then do the back, then the other front. Make 9 chain for the sleeve, work 2 plain rows of tricot, then increase at the end of each row till the sleeve is long enough. Sew the body up, and stitch the sleeves in their place. Work with white wool a row of 1 double crochet, 1 chain, round the wrists. For the trimming round the bottom of the skirt, with white wool, work 9 chain, and do a straight piece of tricot 9 stitches wide and long enough to go round the skirt. On this strip, with blue wool, work a chain stitch up and down, inserting the hook under the loops of plain tricot, and drawing the wool through so that the wrong side of the chain stitches lies at the top, work down through one row of the perpendicular loops of the tricot, miss the next row, chain stitch again on the next, then miss two rows, and so on, turning each time at top and bottom. When this is done, crochet along the top edge with white wool, 4 treble, 1 double crochet, in between each turn of the blue chain stitches. Along the bottom edge work 1 double crochet in the first turn of the blue chain stitches, 4 treble in the intermediate space between the turns, and repeat. Sew this trimming on to the bottom of the skirt. Now arrange the dress on the doll, and sew it down where necessary, as it is not to be taken off and on. For the trimming down the front, with white wool, and No. 12 knitting pins, cast on 3 stitches, and knit in looped knitting as follows: 1st row—Plain. 2nd row—Twist the wool 3 times round a blacklead pencil and knit the twists of wool in together with the first stitch of the knitting, twist the wool round the pencil three times again, and knit in with the next stitch, and so again with the third stitch. Repeat these two rows till you have sufficient to reach from the top of the trimming to the neck. Sew it down, and arrange a blue ribbon sash round the waist, passing under the looped knitting in front, and made up in a nice bow at the back. **Doll's Bonnet**—With blue wool, commence with 4 chain, join round, and work 12 treble in the circle. 2nd round—Work 22 treble. 3rd round—20 treble round the front two-thirds of the bonnet, 8 double crochet round the back third. 4th round—Treble, just slightly increased. Now on the front two-thirds of the bonnet work 3 rows of trebles, the work being right side inwards, carry it on with double crochet round the back. Cover a piece of fine bonnet wire with blue wool and sew it on the outer rim of the bonnet, bending it to shape. Put a little blue ribbon bow on the left side of the bonnet, and on the right side a white feather made of looped knitting the same as the trimming down the front of the dress. Put little blue ribbon strings to tie under the chin. **Doll's Boots**—With blue wool, commence with 9 chain, and work 3 rows of ribbed double crochet, on the fourth stitch work 7 chain, and join across to the fourth stitch on the opposite side, this is for the instep, double crochet backwards and forwards, decreasing each time, and joining each turn to the sole, till you get to the toe, which sew up as nice and round as possible. For the **Leg**—With white wool work 6 chain, join to the centre of the instep, and work ribbed crochet up and down, at each turn connecting the leg to the foot part, work round the heel to the instep again. Sew the leg up in front and round the top work a row of 1 double crochet, 3 chain. Run in a thread of blue wool to tie round the ankle.

DOLL'S COSTUME IN CROCHET.

the next 3, 1 treble in each of the next 3, 1 long in each of the remaining stitches, repeat from (c) to (c) once, 1 short crochet in each stitch on the one side of square formed by preceding row (d), repeat from (c) to (d) three times more. 5th row—5 chain, and passing back of the three leaves fasten on the edge at the other side of third leaf, (e) skip 2 stitches, 1 long crochet, 1 chain, skip 1, 1 long crochet, make 5 more long crochets in like manner, 1 chain, and fasten the first and second leaves together by a short crochet in the fifth stitch, 3 chain, and fasten the second and third leaves in like manner, three chain, and fasten on edge of third leaf, (e) repeat from (e) to (e) three times. 6th row—(f) 6 long crochet with 1 chain between made above the 7 long crochets in the same manner, and fastened to edge of first leaf, third stitch from top, 3 chain, and fasten to opposite side of same leaf, 3 chain, and fasten to edge of second leaf, 3 chain, and fasten to opposite side of leaf, 3 chain, and join to third leaf, 3 chain, and fasten to opposite side of leaf, repeat from (f) three times more. 7th row—(g) Make 5 long crochets with 1 chain between above the six long ones in preceding row, 2 chain, and fasten at top of first leaf, 8 chain, and fasten to top of second leaf, 8 chain, and fasten at top of third leaf, (g) repeat from (g) to (g) three times more. 8th row—Chain 8, (h) 1 long crochet at the top of second long crochet of seventh row, 2 chain, skip 2, 1 long crochet, chain 2, skip 2, 1 long crochet, chain 4, 1 long crochet at top of leaf, 5 chain, and fasten in centre of chain between first and second leaves in preceding row, 5 chain, and fasten in top of middle leaf with long crochet, 5 chain, 1 long crochet in same stitch, 5 chain, and fasten in centre of chain between second and third leaves, 5 chain, 1 long crochet in top of leaf, 5 chain, (h) repeat from (h) to (h) entire row. 9th row—From the centre stitch of the three long crochet stitches of preceding row make 8 chain, (i) one long crochet in the third stitch of the five chain, 5 chain, 1 long crochet in centre of next five chain, 1 long crochet in centre of third five chain, 1 long in the centre stitch of chain between the two long crochet, 5 chain, and 1 long crochet in same stitch, 5 chain, 1 long crochet in the centre of 5 chain, 1 long crochet in centre of next chain, 5 chain in centre of next 5 chain, 5 chain, (i) the centre of the three long crochets over, repeat from (i) to (i) the entire round. 10th row—3 chain, 1 long crochet in each of the next six stitches (j), 5 chain, 1 long crochet over the one long crochet of preceding row, 5 chain, one long crochet in each of the next ten stitches, in the eleventh stitch make 4 long crochets to turn corner, 1 long crochet in the next ten stitches, 5 chain, 1 long crochet over the next long crochet, 5 chain, 1 long crochet in the next thirteen stitches (j), repeat from (j) to (j) the entire round. 11th, 12th, and 13th row—Same as tenth. Remember to put the four long crochets in same place at the four corners to turn. 14th row—(k) 1 long crochet, 5 chain, skip 5 (k), repeat from (k) to (k) all round at the corners, put two long crochets in the same stitch with 5 chain between. 15th row—Same as fourteenth row, only putting the long crochet between the long crochets in preceding row.

BABY'S CROCHET MITTEN.

To make these pretty mittens you will require half an ounce of white or cream Berlin wool, and a fine bone crochet hook. Commence with a chain of 36 stitches, which join, and for the first three rounds do single crochet. 4th round—Treble. 5th round—16 treble, and take up the 17th and 18th stitches together. 6th round—Treble without increasing. 7th round—Like the 5th round. 8th round—Like the 6th round. 9th round—Like the 5th round. 10th round—One treble, one chain, miss one: repeat. There should now be 32 stitches. 11th round—Single crochet, but increase two in the 16th stitch (i.e., work three in it). 12th round—Treble and increase two in the middle stitch. 13th and 14th rounds—Increase three in each round at the centre. The twelve stitches in the part where you have been increasing are to be joined for the thumb, which is to be done separately, thus: Four rounds single crochet, three rounds decreasing, two rounds decreasing twice, and sew up the point of the thumb. There should now be left 30 stitches for the hand. Work two rounds treble, then two rounds treble, decreasing above the thumb, and at the thirteenth stitch (on the opposite side of the hand) work two more rounds, decreasing four stitches in each round. Sew up on the wrong side, and run narrow white ribbon round the wrist, forming it into a small bow on the top.

SQUARE FOR PINCUSHION IN CLOVER-LEAF PATTERN.

THIS pretty design may also be employed for a counterpane, &c., according to the cotton used. For a pincushion cover you require a fine cotton and hook to make it lacey looking. Make a chain of 8 and join in a circle. 1st row—In the circle work 8 long crochets with 3 chain between each stitch. 2nd row—Chain 5, (a) skip 1, 1 long crochet, chain 2, (a) repeat from (a) entire row. 3rd row—Chain 6, (b) skip 1, 1 long crochet, chain 3, skip 2, 1 long crochet, chain 4, skip 2, 1 treble crochet, chain 4, (b) repeat from (b) to (b) three times more, break off cotton. 4th row—Fasten cotton in the corner and (c) chain 10, in second stitch of chain make 1 short and 1 long crochet in each succeeding stitch, join in same stitch, (c) chain 13, 1 short in first stitch, 1 long in each of

BICYCLE CAP.

MATERIALS required are Berlin wool and a fine bone crochet hook. Make a chain of 5 stitches, join in a circle. 1st round—2 treble crochets in every foundation stitch. 2nd round—Like first. 3rd round—2 treble crochets in every alternate stitch. 4th round—2 treble crochets between every increase. 5th round—3 treble crochets between every increase. 6th round—4 treble crochets between every increase. 7th round—5 treble crochets between every increase. 8th round—6 treble crochets between every increase. 9th round—7 treble crochets between every increase. 10th round—8 treble crochets between every increase. This finishes the crown of the cap. For the **Band** around the head—1st round—10 treble crochet, miss 1 all around. 11 rounds of treble crochet, without increase or decrease. Line it with silk, and work in the centre of band the initials of the club.

RICE STITCH.

This is a pretty open stitch suitable for shawls and clouds, and is also introduced in some of the coarse Maltese crochet edgings that are now so much used for dress trimmings. Commence with a chain the length required, turn the cotton five times round the needle, insert the hook in the fourth chain stitch from the needle, draw the cotton through, and also through all the stitches on the needle in the manner shown in the illustration, this forms a group of small twisted stitches, make 1 chain, miss one of the foundation, and work another rice stitch in the next, and so on to the end of the row, turn with 4 chain, and in each succeeding row the rice stitches are worked under the chain stitch of preceding row.

TAM-O'-SHANTER.
WORKED IN POINT MUSCOVITE STITCH.

This exceedingly pretty Tam O'Shanter is crocheted in Point Muscovite stitch with white Pompadour wool, or if this is not procurable use white single Berlin combined with a ball of soft white silk, crocheting the two together; about 3 ozs. of wool will be required, a bone crochet needle, No. 9, 1½ yards of quarter inch wide corded satin ribbon to run in the band, and a white silk pompon. Commence with 6 chain, join round, and in the circle work 12 double crochet; then, always taking up both top threads of previous round, 1 double crochet in the first stitch of last round, insert the hook in the next stitch of last round, draw the wool through and do 3 chain, wool over the needle and draw through the last stitch of the chain and through the stitch on the needle, 1 double crochet in the next double crochet of last round, and to increase work a point Muscovite stitch in the same place in which this double crochet is worked, and repeat, working a double crochet and a point stitch alternately, making 9 double crochet stitches and 9 point stitches in the round. The same stitch is continued throughout the cap, and produces a surface of little raised knobs. In the 3rd round there should be 12 double crochet stitches and 12 point stitches; in the 4th round 15 double crochet stitches and 15 point stitches, and afterwards you only "increase" (by working double crochet and point Muscovite stitch in one) where necessary to keep the work flat. For a boy work a crown measuring 10 inches across, for a gentleman 12 inches. Then continue the point Muscovite for the underneath brim, decreasing occasionally to bring the work in to the size required for the band, about 9 rounds will accomplish this. For the Band—1st round—Plain double crochet. 2nd round—1 double crochet and 1 point stitch alternately. 3rd round—Treble. 4th round—1 double crochet and 1 point stitch alternately. 5th round—Treble. 6th round—1 double crochet and 1 point stitch alternately. 7th round—Double crochet. This completes the band. Cut the ribbon into two pieces and run a piece through each round of the treble stitches, taking up two trebles and leaving two on the inner side, tie in small pretty bows. Sew the pompon in the centre of the crown.

BEEHIVE PATTERN.

This pattern, as shown in the illustration, is worked in straight rows forwards and backwards, and is useful for jackets, petticoats, cuffs, sofa blankets, antimacassars, &c., and also as a bordering for articles made in some other pattern. It looks equally well in fine and thick wool, and requires to be rather loosely worked. Commence with chain the length required. 1st row—Wool over the needle and insert the hook in the third chain from the needle and work a treble stitch, do 6 more treble in the same place, miss one of the foundation, 1 double crochet in the next, * miss one of the foundation, 7 treble in the next, miss one of the foundation, 1 double crochet in the next, and repeat from * to the end of the row; turn. 2nd row—In this row insert the hook always in the top and back threads of the stitches of last row; insert the hook in the top and back threads of the first treble stitch of last row and draw the wool through loosely, do the same in the two next stitches, wool over the needle and draw through the four stitches on the needle, 1 chain, 1 double crochet on the centre one of the seven trebles of last row, now raise 7 loose loops in the seven next consecutive stitches, wool over the needle and draw through all the stitches (8) on the needle, 1 chain, and repeat from *. Raise 3 loops at the end of the row to match the beginning, draw through the four stitches on the needle, and finish with one chain to secure the group; turn. 3rd

RICE STITCH.

TAM O' SHANTER.
(Worked in Point Muscovite Stitch.)

BEEHIVE PATTERN.

row—3 treble in the loop of one chain at the beginning of last row, * 1 double crochet in the same place as the double crochet of last row is worked into, 7 treble in the next loop of one chain of last row, and repeat from *, doing 3 treble at the end of the row to correspond with the beginning. 4th row—Working as in the second row into the top and back threads of the stitches of last row, raise 7 loops in seven consecutive stitches, wool over the needle and draw through all, 1 chain, * 1 double crochet on the centre stitch of the seven trebles of last row, raise 7 loops in seven consecutive stitches, wool over the needle and draw through all, 1 chain, repeat from * to the end of the row, and there catch by a single crochet to the end of last row; turn. 5th row—7 treble under the chain stitch at the beginning of last row, * 1 double crochet in the same place as the double crochet of last row is worked into, 7 treble under the next chain stitch of last row, and repeat from *, and at the end of the row catch by a single crochet to the end of last row to keep the edge even. Repeat from the second row for the length required.

INFANT'S BOOT IN TRICOT.

This pretty boot has a long leg, and therefore is very warm and protective for infants. Any coloured wool desired can be employed, and for example we give 1½ ozs. of white Andalusian wool; three skeins of pale pink Berlin wool, a bone tricot hook, No. 16, 24 small pearl or silk buttons, and 1 yard of pale pink ribbon. You commence at the top of the leg part, making a chain of 39 stitches. 1st row—Work up and off in ordinary tricot. 2nd and 3rd rows—Work up the back perpendicular loop of each stitch, work off in the usual way. 4th to 8th rows—Plain tricot. 9th row—Work up the back perpendicular loop of each of seventeen stitches, work up the front loop of the five next stitches, then work up the back loop of the seventeen next stitches, work off in the usual way. 10th to 14th rows—Like the eighth row. 15th to 20th rows—Like the eighth row, but decrease by passing over the first and last stitches of each row. 21st to 24th rows—Like eighth row without decrease. 25th to 33rd rows—Increase by working up two loops through the stitch before the plain tricot front and the stitch after it. 34th to 39th rows—Work throughout through the back perpendicular loops. To decrease for the toe, work up all but the 3 last stitches of each row. 40th to 43rd rows—Work quite across the sides and toe of boot, working up a loop through each of the stitches not worked on in the previous rows, work off in the usual way. With pink Berlin wool work in chain stitch a Grecian pattern in the plain stripe up the front of leg and round the top, sew on the buttons, sew up the leg and sole of the foot. The ribbon has to be made into two bows, one being placed nearly at the top of the leg in front and one on the toe. For the crochet edge work one double into a stitch at top of boots, 3 chain, pass over one stitch, and repeat all round.

BABY'S CROCHET BOOT.

Zephyr or Berlin wool can be used for this pretty boot, using a No. 8 or 9 hook. Commence with a chain of seven stitches, which work back in tricot, which is used for the entire foot, except the leg. Increase one stitch at each end, making 9. Crochet another row like this; then work on the 11 stitches for 5 rows. Narrow at each end, then crochet 4 rows on the nine stitches left. Next row you increase again to 11 stitches, and work 6 rows thus; then decrease at each end for the 2 next rows, which finishes the sole, and which has afterwards to be sewn to the upper part. For the upper part of the boot, make a chain of 16 stitches; work back, making 16 tricot. 2nd row—Increase at the end of this row, and the two next, then work twenty-two rows. 26th row—Narrow at the end of this and the two next rows. 27th row—Raise the first 16 stitches as usual, then instead of turning back, pick up the sixteen stitches at the beginning, which are your original 16 chain. Work back in the entire 32 stitches. Narrow for 2 rows by taking the two centre stitches together. Afterwards narrow every row by taking the 3 centre stitches together. When only 7 are left, finish off and fasten the sole in the wrong side. For the Leg—1st row—Take up 28 stitches in double crochet. 2nd row—1 treble, 1 chain, miss 1, repeat 10 more rows of double crochet. 12th row—Turn the work round so as to make the wrong side of the crochet outside instead of inside, 1 treble, 1 chain, miss 1, repeat. 13th row—* work 4 chain, work a double on the third chain, a treble on the second and first, a double into the third stitch of the leg, one double into the next stitch, * repeat from * to *, then fasten off. Turn down this upper part into the holes and scallops, and fasten here and there to keep it in place. Add a ribbon round the ankle and a bow of ribbon in front.

CHILD'S CROCHET FROCK.

THIS pretty frock is suitable for a child of two or three years; it measures 21 inches in length, but can be made longer if desired by working additional rows on the flounce. Materials required—5 ozs. of cardinal, 2 ozs. of black and white mottled Scotch yarn. Crochet needle, No. 9. Commence for the body at the back, lengthways, with cardinal wool, with 53 chain, turn, miss the first three chain stitches, 1 treble in the next, and work 50 treble stitches. **2nd row**—3 chain to turn, and work treble on every stitch of preceding row, inserting the hook at the back of the stitches, so as to make the work sit in ribs. Do 9 rows of trebles, and at the end of the 9th row make 12 chain to lengthen for the shoulder, turn, 1 treble in the fourth from the needle, and work 3 rows of treble the whole length of 59 stitches, next row 30 treble only, and at the end make 32 chain for the armhole and other side of shoulder, turn into the fourth from the needle, and work 3 rows of trebles the whole length of 59 stitches again. **17th row**—Work 50 treble stitches, and work upon these 50 treble backwards and forwards for 16 rows. At the end of the 33rd row make 12 chain to lengthen for the shoulder, and work three rows of trebles the whole length of 59 stitches, then a row of 30 treble only, at the end of which make 32 chain for the armhole and other side of shoulder, and work 3 more rows of treble the whole length, then 9 rows of 50 treble in each row. This completes the body. Sew up the shoulders, and sew up about 3 inches from the bottom, leaving the rest open. Now for the **neck band**, with black and white mottled wool—Work 5 rows of treble, breaking off at the end of every row, and working into the top loops of previous row. **1st row**—Work 3 treble stitches upon each rib of the ribbed crochet, and 1 treble on each treble along the top of the shoulder. **2nd row** and 3 following rows—Work 1 treble on each treble stitch of previous row successively, but on each shoulder make three decreasings, one exactly above the join and others a few stitches away on each side; this will be effected by inserting the hook in two treble stitches of previous row, and working both into one. **6th row**, with cardinal wool—1 double crochet on the first treble stitch * miss two trebles, 5 treble on the next, miss two trebles, 1 double crochet on the next; repeat from *. For the **sash band**, with black and white mottled wool—Do a round of double crochet, working 3 stitches on every rib of the body part, then work 5 rounds of plain treble stitches, working into the top loops of previous round. For the **Flounce**, with cardinal wool—**1st round**—double crochet all round, working 2 double crochet stitches into every stitch of the treble. **2nd round**—3 consecutive double crochet, 3 double crochet together in the next, 3 consecutive double crochet, miss 2 double crochet of previous round, and repeat. Work the same as this for 11 rounds. Then do 1 round with the mottled wool, 1 round with cardinal, and finish with 2 rounds with mottled. For the **Sleeve**, with crimson wool, worked lengthways—30 chain, turn. **1st row**—1 treble in the third from the needle, 11 consecutive treble, 15 double crochet. **2nd row**—Treble all along and 2 treble in the stitch at the end of the row. **3rd, 4th, and 5th rows**—Treble, each time increasing one stitch at the same end, therewith to produce a slope for the shoulder. **6th row** and 3 following rows—Decrease 1 treble in each row at the same end as the increasings were made. **10th row**—15 double crochet and 12 treble. Sew up the sleeve, and for the cuff work 3 rounds of treble stitches with the mottled wool, and 1 round of edging, same as that round the neck, with cardinal wool. Sew the sleeves in. Sew three or four buttons down the back of the frock. Run in a ribbon to tie round the neck, and make a nice wide ribbon bow to place at the back on the sash-band.

CHILD'S CROCHET FROCK.

INFANT'S BOOTS IN CROCHET TRICOTÉE.

USE Berlin wool and a No. 10 hook, and you commence at the toe, working the foot part in crochet tricotée and the leg in honeycomb tricotée. **1st row**—Begin with 5 chain, and raise 5 loops. Work back, first through one loop, and then through two, to the end. **2nd row**—Raise 2 loops, increase by raising a loop between the second and third loop, raise the third loop, increase as before, raise the fourth and fifth loops. You have now 7 loops on your hook. Go on increasing thus till you have 13 loops on your hook. Repeat this row without increasing. Now go on as before, increasing two in each row until you have 17 loops on your hook. Repeat this row without increasing. Go on as before, until you have 21 loops on your hook, and then begin the sides by picking up only 8 loops. Do nine rows of 8 loops, and cast off. Tie your wool now on the sixth loop on the instep, raising 8 loops, and leaving 5 unworked on the instep. Do nine rows on your 8 loops, and cast off. The shoe part is now finished, and these sides will by-and-by be joined up the back. Now tie on the wool afresh at the back, and pick up 25 loops thus: 10 on each side, and 5 across the instep, and work back in looped stitch, which is done thus: Draw the wool through 1 loop *, 3 chain, draw the wool through the next 2 loops, 3 chain *, and repeat from * to * to the end. Now pick up 25 loops again, and when you come to the three chains, bend them forward as they form little rosettes. This being the row for the ribbon to run through, you pick up your twenty-five thus: Raise a stitch, do 2 chain, and repeat to the end. Work back as usual. Now do five rows of loops, taking care that the rosettes of one row come between the rosettes of the preceding one. Cast off. Edge with a row of double crochet in coloured

wool if your boot is white, and sew up your sock before putting in the sole. For the **Sole**—Chain of 5. Raise 5 loops. Work back. Increase, and raise 7, repeat. Next row raise 9. Then 2 sevens again, by taking in twice. You then go on thus: 4 fives, 3 sevens, 1 nine, 2 sevens, 2 fives, and cast off. This makes a shapeable little sole, and must be carefully fitted and sewed in.

BRASS RING CROCHET.

RINGS used for this kind of crochet work are the small-sized curtain rings, three quarters of an inch in circumference. They are covered either with silk or single Berlin wool, and are used for mats or small hand-bags. The manner of covering the rings with crochet for both articles are similar, the only difference being in the making up and the number of rings required. For a **Mat**—Thirty-seven curtain rings and four shades of one colour, either of wool or silk, are necessary. Commence by covering one ring for the centre of mat with the lightest shade of wool; work fifty double crochets over the rings; cover six rings in the same way with the next shade, then twelve with the third shade, and eighteen with the last. Place the lightest shade in the centre, arrange the six rings of the next shade round it, and sew them to the centre ring where they touch it, and to each of the others at their junctions. Arrange the twelve rings round the six and sew as before, and eighteen round the twelve. The side of the mat where the rings are sewn together will be the wrong side, keep it still upon that side, and finish the rings with working an eight-pointed star in filoselle in the centre of each. Make a fringe round the mat by cutting filoselle in length of four inches, and looping these lengths into the outer edges of the outside circle of rings. The rings can be ornamented with a cross of white beads in their centres, and a fringe of white beads an inch long round the outside. **To Form a Bag**—One hundred and one rings are required, covered with double crochet in colours, according to taste. Sew the rings together in the shape of a cup. **1st or centre**—1 ring. **2nd row**—6 rings. **3rd row**—12 rings. **4th row**—16 rings. **5th row**—20 rings. **6th row**—22 rings. **7th row**—24 rings. Above the last ring work a row of crochet, 3 trebles into the top of a ring, 5 chains and 3 trebles into the next ring. Repeat 5 chains and 3 trebles to the end of row. **2nd row**—1 treble and 2 chains into every third stitch on foundation. Repeat second row 11 times. **14th row**—2 trebles and 3 chains, missing 3 foundation stitches for the 3 chains. Line the bag with soft silk, run a ribbon in and out of the last crochet row to draw it up, and finish the lower part with a silk tassel.

CHILD'S CROCHET BIB.

MATERIALS.—Crochet cotton, No. 16 steel hook. Make a chain of 36 stitches. **1st row**—Miss 1 stitch, 35 short crochets in next thirty-five stitches of foundation chain. **2nd row**—1 chain, 2 short crochets in first stitch, 34 short crochets in next thirty-four stitches, taking up the back part of the stitches. **3rd row**—1 chain, 2 short crochets in first stitch, 4 short crochet in next four stitches, *, 1 long crochet in next short crochet of *first* row, miss the short crochet in preceding row, 5 short crochet in next five stitches. Repeat from * four times. **4th row**—2 short crochets in first stitch, and 1 short crochet in each remaining stitch of last row. **5th row**—2 short crochets in first stitch, 2 short crochets in next two stitches *, 1 long crochet stitch in next short crochet stitch in *third* row, miss next short crochet in preceding row, 5 short crochets in next 5 stitches. Repeat from * to end of row. Continue the pattern, increasing at beginning of every row one stitch until you have twenty-six rows, now in the next sixteen rows decrease one stitch; now work the pattern on the first ten stitches and the last ten stitches of each row twelve times. Surround the bib with two rows of short crochet stitches, one row of loops, two rows short crochet stitches, one row loops, two rows short crochets, and a narrow lace or scallops in crochet. Run in ribbons through the loops all round bib, adding a bow at each corner in front.

SQUARE SHAWL WORKED IN CRAZY STITCH.

SHETLAND wool any colour preferred, and a crochet needle No. 10 will be required for this pretty shawl. Make four chain, join, and into circle work four times one double crochet, two chain, and three treble, and join by drawing wool through the first double crochet stitch. This shawl is not worked round in the usual way, but the work is to be "turned" at the completion of each round. **2nd round**—Make 3 chain, and turn, and under the first two chain of last round work, *, 1 double crochet, 2 chain, and 3 treble, twice in same place, and repeat from * under each 2 chain in previous round, and join by drawing wool through the first double crochet stitch. **3rd round**—3 chain, turn, and under first 2 chain of last round, work *, 1 double crochet, 2 chain, 3 treble under the first 2 chain of last round, and 1 double crochet, two chain, and 3 treble twice under next 2 chain, and repeat from *; join as before. **4th round**—3 chain, turn, work 1 double crochet, 2 chain, and 3 treble under first 2 chain, and same under next; then for the corner work the same twice under next 2 chain, and repeat. Continue each round the same, always increasing at the 4 corners, and work straight along the 4 sides. For border, work 3 or 4 rounds in different coloured wool from that used for ground of shawl.

WELDON'S
PRACTICAL CROCHET.

(THIRD SERIES.)

How to Crochet 47 Useful Articles for Ladies, Gentlemen, and Children.

THIRTY-EIGHT ILLUSTRATIONS.

The sizes of Crochet Hooks mentioned in descriptions are regulated by Walker's Bell Gauge.

Telegraphic Address—] "Consuelo," London.]

The Yearly Subscription to this Magazine, post free to any Part of the World, is 2s. 6d. Subscriptions are payable in advance, and may commence from any date and for any period.

[Telephone— 2745.

The Back Numbers are always in print. Nos. 1 to 84 now ready, Price 2d. each, or post free for 15s. Over 5,000 Engravings.

BABY'S OVER-ALL BOOTS IN RUSSIAN CROCHET.

REQUIRED, 2½ ozs. of white, 1 oz. of blue single Berlin, and a bone crochet needle No. 12. Begin for the leg with white wool, with 42 chain, in which work 41 double crochet. Turn, and work 41 double crochet again, inserting the hook in the back thread of the stitches of last row, so that the work may sit in ridges. Do 5 more rows the same. In the **7th row** work 1 stitch upon 2 at each end to decrease. Do 3 rows with 39 double crochet in the row. In the **11th row** decrease again. Do 3 rows with 37 double crochet in the row. In the **15th row** decrease again. Do 3 rows with 35 double crochet in the row. In the **19th row** decrease again. Do 7 rows with 33 double crochet in the row. **27th row**—14 double crochet, 2 on the next, 2 on the next, 1 double crochet, 2 on the next, 2 on the next, 14 double crochet. **28th row**—18 double crochet, 3 on the next, 18 double crochet. **29th row**—16 double crochet, 2 on the next, 2 on the next, 3 double crochet, 2 on the next, 2 on the next, 16 double crochet. **30th row**—21 double crochet, 3 on the next, 21 double crochet. **31st row**—20 double crochet, 3 on the next, 3 double crochet, 3 on the next, 20 double crochet. **32nd row**—24 double crochet, 3 on the next, 24 double crochet. **33rd row**—23 double crochet, 3 on the next, 3 double crochet, 3 on the next, 23 double crochet. **34th row**—27 double crochet, 3 on the next, 27 double crochet. **35th row**—26 double crochet, 3 on the next, 3 double crochet, 3 on the next, 26 double crochet. **36th row**—30 double crochet, 3 on the next, 30 double crochet. **37th row**—29 double crochet, 3 on the next, 3 double crochet, 3 on the next, 29 double crochet. **38th row**—33 double crochet, 3 on the next, 33 double crochet. **39th row**—32 double crochet, 3 on the next, 3 double crochet, 3 on the next, 32 double crochet. **40th row**—36 double crochet, 3 on the next, 36 double crochet. **41st row**—35 double crochet, 3 on the next, 3 double crochet, 3 on the next, 35 double crochet. **42nd row**—Plain double crochet. **43rd row—For the Sole**—Work now on the top thread of stitches of previous row, 1 chain, 1 double crochet on the third stitch from the end, take in (by working 1 double crochet upon 2 stitches of last row), take in again, plain double crochet along the side, take in 10 times round the toe, plain along the other side, take in when close to the end, and leave the last stitch unworked. **44th row**—Plain double crochet. **45th row**—1 chain, 1 double crochet on the third stitch from the needle, take in, plain along the side, take in 8 times round the toe, plain along the other side, take in when close to the end, and leave the last stitch unworked. **46th row**—Miss the first stitch of last row, plain double crochet along the side, take in 4 times round the toe, plain along the other side, and leave the last stitch unworked. Fasten off. Sew the boot in the middle of the sole and up the leg, making the ridges round the leg meet one another. Then with blue wool work a frilling round the leg, perpendicularly up and down upon the four top ridges, thus : 1 double crochet on stitch at the top, 3 chain, 1 double crochet on stitch of the first ridge, 3 chain, 1 double crochet on stitch of next ridge, 3 chain, 1 double crochet on stitch of the next ridge, 3 chain, 1 double crochet on next stitch of the same ridge, then crochet back to the top in the same way, and continue same all round. Place a rosette of blue ribbon upon the instep, and the boot is finished. Boots for wearing in the house may be made in the same way, but using Eider or some other fine make of wool.

BABY'S CROCHET SHOE.

PINK AND WHITE SINGLE BERLIN WOOL.

THE sole is to be cut out in white kid, with an inner lining of fine white flannel, and bound round the edge with a piece of narrow white ribbon. **For the Toe**—Make 15 chain with the pink wool, turn, miss 1, and work 14 double crochet. **2nd row**—1 chain to turn, and miss the first double crochet of last row, work 1 double crochet in the loop at the *back* of each stitch, and increase by working 3 double crochet in the centre stitch. **3rd row**—1 chain to turn, and miss the first double crochet of last row, then plain double crochet all along (no increase), taking up the back loops. Repeat these two rows 8 times. **For the Side**—1 chain to turn, and miss the first double crochet of last row, 10 double crochet. Repeat this row until you have 20 ribs done, then join the last row to the opposite side of the instep. **With white wool**—Work a row of double long treble round the top of the shoe, 1 stitch of double long treble in each rib, and immediately over the instep miss one of the double crochet between each of the double long treble. Next, with the *inside* of the shoe towards you, work 12 rows of single crochet round and round, fasten off. With black silk, work a stitch here and there on the right side of the single crochet, which is to be turned and rolled over the shoe. Sew the shoe neatly on to the kid sole. Twist a cord of the pink wool, and run it through between the double long treble · finish with a small tufted tassel at each end.

RINGS. CROCHET FOR ANTIMACASSAR.

DOUBLE or single Berlin wool, three shades of crimson, three shades of green, and the same of any other colours that may be desired, also some black wool. **1st ring**—Commence with lightest shade of crimson, with 30 chain, join round, do 4 chain to stand for the beginning of the first round, and work 1 treble in every stitch of the chain with one chain between each treble. **2nd round**—With next lightest shade of crimson, work 1 treble, 1 chain alternately, the treble stitches being worked one under each chain stitch of preceding row. **3rd round**—With darkest shade of crimson, to be worked the same as the second round. **2nd ring**—Commence with lightest shade of green with 30 chain, pass the tag end of the chain through the centre of the crimson ring so that the two rings encircle each other, join round, and then work on with green the same as directed above for crimson. **3rd ring**—Violet, or any other colour, and to be worked each encircling the previous one the same as the green ring. When you have worked rings sufficient to make a strip as long as required, take the black wool, and commencing on the right-hand side of the lowest ring, work 1 treble, 1 chain as heretofore up the entire length of the side, round the top ring, and down the opposite side, and then round the lower ring. Keep each ring down in its respective position as you work.

CAPOTE.

THIS is an exceedingly pretty capote for wearing to the theatre, or on any occasion when a comfortable warm wrap is required for the head and shoulders. It must be worked very loosely, and will take nearly 1 lb. of single Berlin or best soft fingering wool, cherry colour, or whatever colour preferred. 2 yards of 2-inch wide ribbon to match. Bone crochet needle No. 6. Commence for the neck with 56 chain. Work 8 long treble stitches (wool twice round the needle) in the fourth chain from the needle, * miss three chain, 1 double crochet in the next, miss three chain, 9 long treble in the next, and repeat from * ; making in all seven shells of nine long trebles in the row ; these long trebles should stand up

Capote.

loosely and quite an inch high. Turn the work at the end of this and every following row. 2nd row—Slip along to the centre one of the nine trebles, there work a double crochet stitch, and work * 9 long treble on the double crochet stitch of last row, and 1 double crochet on the centre stitch of the group of nine trebles, and repeat from * ; making six shells of nine long trebles in the row. 3rd row—3 chain to turn, and again work 7 shells in the row. 4th row—Same as the second row. 5th row—Same as the third row. 6th row—Same as the second row. The work is now to narrow gradually towards a point. 7th row—5 shells in the row. 8th row—6 shells in the row. 9th row—5 shells. 10th row—4 shells. 11th row—3 shells. 12th row—3 shells. 13th row—3 shells. 14th row—2 shells. 15th row—1 shell, and fasten off. This completes the hood. Now for the Cape—Holding the right side of the work towards you, recommence upon the foundation chain, and work 7 groups of 9 long trebles opposite the groups in the first row, and double crochet opposite the double crochet in the first row. 2nd row—3 chain to turn, work 9 long treble on the first long treble stitch of last row, * 1 double crochet on the centre stitch of the group of nine long trebles, 9 long treble on the double crochet stitch, and repeat from *, making 8 shells of nine long trebles in the row. 3rd row—3 chain to turn, and work as instructed for the second row, making 9 shells of nine long trebles in the row. Proceed thus, increasing one shell in every row, till you have done 18 rows, and have 24 shells of nine long trebles in the row. Continue the pattern along the side of the capote, round the hood, and along the other side. The Fringed Edging is done thus : 1 double crochet in a stitch of last row, * 20 chain, 1 double crochet in next stitch of last row, and repeat from *, all round the capote. Take 16 inches of ribbon and run in the first row of the hood to secure the neck. Cut the remaining ribbon into two pieces, run it in the front of the hood, and tie in a bow at the top : sew the ends of the neck ribbon underneath where the ribbons cross, and leave the ends of the front ribbons to tie under the chin.

PETTICOAT FOR CHILD OF TWO.

THIS petticoat is worked in single and double crochet, and is quickly and easily made, at the same time being very pretty, the single crochet forms the upper part, and is intended to be set into a linen bodice, the double crochet forms scallops round the bottom, so no edging is required. The work *must* be executed with *thick* wool, either double Berlin or 4 thread Fleecy, or the pattern does not show up. Crochet needle No. 6. Commence with 48 chain for the length of the petticoat. 1st row—Miss three chain stitches, work 28 double crochet, and finish the row with 17 single crochet stitches, turn the work. 2nd row—Inserting the hook in the top thread of the stitches of last row, do 17 single crochet over the single crochet of last row, then 28 double crochet, 3 chain, turn the work. 3rd row—Again working into the top thread of the stitches of previous row, work 28 double crochet and 17 single crochet stitches. Repeat these last two rows till the petticoat is as wide as required, then sew the last row to the commencing chain as far as the double crochet extends, and leave the

single crochet open for a placket hole. Any scraps of thick wool may be utilised for this work, doing two rows or four rows of a colour, and the little petticoats will be acceptable gifts for Christmas.

NECK HANDKERCHIEF OR SHAWL.

PROCURE a sufficient quantity of Shetland wool, and a bone crochet needle No. 12, and commence by making a chain as long as desired for one side of the shawl. 1st row—1 treble in the seventh chain from the needle, * 1 chain, miss one, 1 treble in the next, and repeat from * to the end of the row. 2nd row—4 chain to turn, 1 treble on the treble of last row, * 1 chain, 1 treble on the next treble of last row, and repeat from * to the end, working the last treble stitch on the second chain of the turn. Continue the same as the second row until you have worked a perfect square. For the Border—1st round—Work 1 treble 1 chain alternately all round the centre piece, doing 3 chain and 1 extra treble stitch at the corners. 2nd round—1 treble on the last treble but one on the side of the shawl, 1 chain, 1 treble on the last treble on the side, 3 treble under the three chain at the corner, 3 chain, 3 more treble in the same place, 1 treble on the treble stitch, 1 chain, 1 treble on the next treble stitch, * 1 chain, 3 treble in the second space, 2 chain, 3 more treble in the same place, 1 chain 1 treble three times on consecutive trebles of last round, and repeat from *, work all corners like the corner already done. 3rd round—1 treble on the first treble of previous round, 1 chain, 1 treble on chain stitch, 1 chain, 1 treble on treble stitch, 3 treble under the three chain at the corner, 3 chain, 3 more treble in the same place, 1 chain, 1 treble on the last of the group, 1 chain, 1 treble on chain stitch, 1 chain, 1 treble on the next treble stitch, 1 chain, 1 treble on the next treble * 3 treble in the loop of two chain, 2 chain, 3 more treble in the same place, 1 treble on the first single treble stitch, 1 chain 1 treble twice on consecutive trebles of last round, and repeat from *. 4th round—1 treble on the first treble of previous round, 3 treble under the chain stitch, 2 chain, 3 more treble in the same place, 1 treble on the treble stitch, 1 chain, 1 treble on the single treble stitch, 1 chain, 3 treble under the three chain at the corner, 3 chain, 3 more treble in the same place, 1 chain, 1 treble on the single treble stitch, 1 chain, 1 treble on the next, 3 treble under the chain stitch, 2 chain. 3 more treble in the same place, 1 treble on the treble stitch, 1 chain, 1 treble on the next treble stitch, and continue the same as from * to * in the third round, doing each corner the same as the corner just done. 5th round—1 treble on the first treble of the previous round, 3 treble under the two chain, 2 chain, 3 more treble in the same place, 1 treble on the last of the group, 1 chain, 1 treble on the single treble stitch, 1 chain, 1 treble on the first of the three treble stitches, 3 treble under the three chain at the corner, 3 chain, 3 more treble in the same place, 1 treble on the last of the group, 1 chain, 1 treble on the single treble stitch, 1 chain, 1 treble on the first of the three treble stitches, 3 treble under the two chain, 2 chain, 3 more treble in the same place, 1 treble on the last of the group, 1 chain, 1 treble on the single treble stitch, and proceed same as from * to * in last round. 6th round—1 treble on the first treble of previous round, 3 treble under the two chain 2 chain, 3 more treble in the same place, 1 treble on the single treble stitch

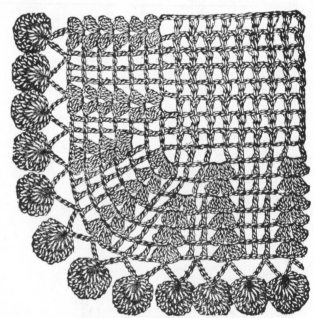

Neck Handkerchief or Shawl.

1 chain, 1 treble twice, 1 chain, 3 treble under the three chain at the corner 3 chain, 3 more treble in the same place, 1 chain, 1 treble on the single treble stitch, 1 chain 1 treble twice, and continue same as last round. 7th round—Same as last round, and break off the wool. 8th round—1 double crochet under the two chain of previous round, 6 chain, * wool over the needle, insert the hook in the first chain from the needle and draw the wool through, repeat from * seven times as loosely as possible, wool over the needle and draw through all the stitches on the needle, wool over the needle, and draw tightly through the one stitch on the needle to keep the bunch firm, 1 double crochet in the next chain stitch, 4 chain, 1 double crochet on the square, 6 chain, and proceed with making another bunch of stitches, and so on, all round the shawl.

GENTLEMAN'S SMOKING CAP.

THE model of this pretty cap is worked with navy blue and amber single Berlin wool, 1 oz. of each being required, and a No. 12 bone crochet needle. Commence with navy blue wool with 7 chain, and join round in a circle. **1st round**—Do 3 chain at the beginning of this and the following seven rounds to stand for a treble stitch, work 16 treble closely and evenly in the circle, and join round. **2nd round**—Inserting the hook into the two upper threads of the stitches of previous round, work 2 treble on every stitch, 32 treble in the round. **3rd round**—1 treble on the first stitch of previous round, 2 treble on the next, and so on alternately; be particular as to the number of stitches, there should be 49 treble. **4th round**—1 treble on each of the first two stitches of last round,

Gentleman's Smoking Cap.

2 treble on the next, and repeat, making 66 treble in the round. **5th round**—1 treble on each of the three first stitches of last round, 2 treble on the next, and continue, making 83 treble in the round. **6th round**—Work 1 treble on each of the first two stitches of last round, but stop before the last time of drawing the wool through the second treble and take the amber wool and finish the stitch with amber, work the first part of a treble with amber on the next stitch of previous round, and finish it with blue, * then 2 blue treble on the next stitch of last round, and 1 treble on the next, but finish this last stitch with amber, and work the first part of a treble with amber on the next stitch of last round, and finish it with blue, and repeat from * to the end of the round; this method of pro- cedure makes the stitches of each colour clear and distinct, work *over* the wool that is not in use, and so pass it on from stitch to stitch invisibly, there are to be 28 amber treble stitches in the round, and 3 blue stitches between. **7th round**—No increase, work 1 blue treble over the centre stitch of the three blue treble of last round, then 3 amber treble, and repeat. **8th round**—All amber, 6 consecutive treble, 2 treble on the next, and repeat, and there will be 127 treble in the round. **9th round**—With blue wool, 1 double crochet on each stitch of last round, which, working a double crochet on the chain that stands for a treble, makes 128 double crochet in the round, and this number is to be adhered to till the cap is finished; you now work for the band. **10th round**—Also with blue wool, double crochet, inserting the hook into the *lower* thread at the *back* of the stitches of last round. Work 4 rounds of blue double crochet, taking up both threads of the stitches of last rounds. **15th round**—Work 3 double crochet with blue, 1 double crochet with amber, changing the wools in the manner described in the sixth round. **16th round**—1 blue double crochet over the centre stitch of the three blue double crochet of last round, 3 amber double crochet, and repeat. Work 5 rounds of plain double crochet with amber wool. **22nd round**—1 blue double crochet to come exactly above the one blue double crochet in the sixteenth round, 3 amber double crochet, and repeat. **23rd round**—1 amber double crochet over the centre stitch of the three amber double crochet of last round, 3 blue double crochet, and repeat. Now work 6 rounds of plain double crochet with blue wool, and strengthen the edge with a round worked into the lower thread at the back of the stitches of the last round, and the cap is finished. It may be lined or not as preferred.

CHILD'S PETTICOAT WITH BODICE.

THIS petticoat is easy of execution, and at the same time is very neat and pretty, it is alike on both sides. Procure 2½ ozs. of blue, 2½ ozs. of white single Berlin wool, or other wool of about the same consistency, or odd scraps may be used, as the petticoat is worked throughout two rows in a colour. Crochet needle No. 10. Commence with white wool with 90 chain, turn, miss the first 2 chain, and work 88 treble. **2nd row**—2 chain to turn, 55 treble for the skirt, 32 double crochet for the body; break off the white wool. **3rd row**—With blue wool work 88 treble. **4th row**—2 chain to turn, 55 treble for the skirt, 32 double crochet for the body; break off the blue wool. Continue the 3rd and 4th rows alternately with each coloured wool till you have done five stripes of white and five of blue, and this makes the right back. Now with white wool, instead of working into the first 21 double crochet, make 21 chain for an armhole, and then do 67 treble; next row, 2 chain to turn, 55 treble, and 32 double crochet. Work for the front the same as the back piece until you have done eight stripes of white and seven of blue. Now with blue wool, instead of working into the first 21 double crochet, make 21 chain for the other armhole, and then do 67 treble; next row, 2 chain to turn, 55 treble, and 32 double crochet. Work for the left back five stripes of

white and six of blue. Then sew up the skirt as far as the treble stitches extend, also sew together about two stripes on each shoulder to shape the neck. Round the neck and armholes, with white wool, work an edging of 1 double crochet. * 3 chain, 1 double crochet into the double crochet just done, and missing 1 stitch of the petticoat 1 double crochet into the next. Work the same edge with blue wool round the bottom of the skirt. Make a crochet cord to run in round the neck and waist to tie with tassels at the ends.

EDGING.

BEGIN with 10 chain, join round; work 4 chain, 5 long treble in the circle, 5 chain, 6 long treble, 5 chain, 6 long treble, 5 chain, 6 long treble, 5 chain, and join round; now work double crochet on every stitch of last round and 3 double crochet in the centre stitch of the five chain, and fasten off. Work another small square in the same manner, and in doing the last round join it from above the centre of the six long treble stitches by 5 chain to the corresponding place on the first square, 9 chain, and continue the double crochet joining by a single crochet to the first square cornerways. For the **Heading**—**1st row**—3 single crochet on the three centre stitches of the square, * 7 chain, 1 double crochet under the loop of chain stitches, 7 chain, 3 single crochet on the three centre stitches of the next square, and repeat from *. **2nd row**—1 treble, 1 chain, miss 1, alternately to the end of the row. For the **Scallop**—1 treble on the seventh stitch before the centre of the point, 3 chain, another treble in the same place, miss two stitches, 1 treble on the next, 3 chain, another treble in the same place, miss one stitch, 1 treble on the next, 3 chain, another treble in the same place, miss one stitch, 1 treble on the centre stitch of the point, 3 chain, another treble in the same place, continue thus three more times, then cross over to the next square and work the same, and continue.

LADY'S OVER-BOOT.

WORKED IN RUSSIAN CROCHET.

Lady's Over-Boot.
Worked in Russian Crochet.

REQUIRED, 1½ ozs. of claret, 1½ ozs. of white double Berlin wool, or 4 thread Fleecy, a No. 8 bone crochet needle, ten buttons, and a pair of cork soles. Wind the claret wool in two balls. Begin for the toe with claret with 8 chain. **1st row**—3 consecutive double crochet, 3 double crochet in the centre stitch, 3 con- secutive double crochet, turn the work. **2nd row**—4 double crochet, 3 double crochet in the centre stitch, 4 double crochet, all worked into the back threads of the stitches of last row, so as to form ridges. **3rd row**—5 double crochet, 3 double crochet in the centre stitch, 5 double crochet. **4th row**—3 double crochet with claret, but draw through the *last* of these with white, do 3 consecutive double crochet, 3 double crochet in the centre stitch, and 3 more consecutive double crochet with white, but take the other ball of claret wool, and draw through the *last* of these stitches with claret, and finish with 3 claret double crochet. The stitch is the same throughout, and the centre of every row is white, the ends claret, do 1 more claret stitch each end till you have 7, then do 1 less each end till you have only 3, and when changing colours, keep the wool always on the same side, whichever side you choose for the inside of the boot. At the **12th row** go only to the centre, where you still increase, and work backwards and forwards till 24 rows are done, end the **24th row** with 20 chain and now there is no more increasing, but you work straight on for 34 rows. At

Edging.

the end of the next row leave 20 white stitches unworked, and now decrease in every row at the white end to match the other side of the boot, till you meet the instep, and sew together. For the **Frilling** round the front and top of the boot—Begin with claret wool, insert the hook at one corner, and draw the wool through, * insert the hook a little farther along, and draw the wool through, do 4 chain, draw the wool through the last of the chain, and through the stitch on the needle, insert the hook again in the work, and draw the wool through, and repeat from * all round for 5 rows. Then place five buttons on one side this frilling, and add 5 loops of crochet chain the other side to button into.

COMFORTER.

THIS splendid warm wrap for the neck is worked in Dutch crochet with white Peacock wool, of which 4 ozs. will be required and a No. 8 bone crochet needle. Begin with 45 chain. 1st row—1 double crochet in the fourth chain from the needle, * 1 chain, miss one stitch of the foundation, 1 double crochet in the next, and repeat from * to the end of the row. 2nd row—2 chain to turn, * wool over the needle, insert the hook under the chain stitch of last row and draw the wool through, wool over the needle and raise another loop in the same place, wool over the needle and raise a third loop (all the loops to be as long and as loose as possible), wool over the needle and draw through all these loops, wool over the needle and draw through 2 stitches on the needle, 1 chain; repeat

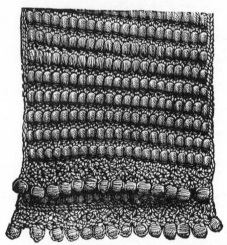

Comforter.

from *; there should be twenty-one clumps in the row. 3rd row—3 chain to turn, 1 double crochet above the first clump of loops taking up both top threads of wool, * 1 chain, 1 double crochet above the next clump, and repeat from *. 4th row—2 chain to turn, and work twenty-one clumps the same as the second row. Repeat the last two rows till 34 rows of clumps are done for the half of the comforter, or it may be longer if so desired. Proceed with the edging without breaking off the wool. 1st row—The same as the third row of the comforter. 2nd row—2 chain to turn, 1 double crochet under first space of last row, 2 chain, 1 treble in the same place, * miss the next space, 1 double crochet in the next, 2 chain, 1 treble in the same place, and repeat from *. 3rd row—2 chain to turn, 1 double crochet under first space of last row, * 4 chain, wool over the needle, insert the hook in the second chain from the needle, and draw the wool through; do this six times; wool over the needle and draw through all the stitches on the needle, 1 chain to keep the ball firm, 1 single crochet in the next chain stitch ,1 treble in the same place the double crochet stitch is worked into, 1 double crochet in the next space, and repeat from *; and fasten off. Now re-commence on the foundation chain and work the other half of the comforter to correspond.

BOY'S COLLEGE CAP.

REQUIRED, 3 ozs. of navy blue single Berlin wool and a bone crochet needle No. 10. Commence with 4 chain, join round, and work 8 double crochet in the circle. 2nd round—Inserting the hook so as to take up the two top threads of the stitches of previous round, work 3 double crochet on the first stitch, 1 double crochet on the next, and repeat. 3rd round—3 double crochet on the centre stitch of the three double crochet of last round (which centre stitch is always a corner stitch), 1 double crochet on each of the three next stitches, and repeat. 4th round—3 double crochet on the corner stitch, 1 double crochet on each of the five next stitches, and repeat. 5th round—3 double crochet on the corner stitch, 7 consecutive double crochet, and repeat. 6th round—3 double crochet on the corner stitch, 9 consecutive double crochet, and repeat. 7th round—3 double crochet on the corner stitch, 4 consecutive double crochet, insert the hook in the next stitch, draw the wool through and work 4 chain, draw the wool through the last of the chain and through the stitch on the needle, 4 consecutive double crochet, and repeat. 8th round—3 double crochet on the corner stitch, 4 consecutive double crochet, a "point" same as that in last round, 1 double crochet, another "point," 4 consecutive double crochet, and repeat. 9th round—3 double crochet on the corner stitch, 4 consecutive double crochet, a point, 1 double crochet, a point, 1 double crochet, a point, 4 consecutive double crochet, and repeat. Continue thus enlarging the diamond for 7 more rounds, when there will be ten point stitches across it, then decrease to only one point as it began Work 4 rounds of plain double crochet, only increasing as usual in the corner stitches. Then work 5 rounds without any increase. Then 14 rounds of double crochet, taking 3 stitches together at each corner, and so reducing the cap to the size required for the head, 20 inches or thereabouts. For the Band—Work 8 rounds of Point Muscovite, 1 double crochet and 1 point alternately, the point being always worked over the double crochet stitch of previous round and the double crochet over a point. Strengthen the inside of the band with a strip of lining Cut a number of strands of wool twelve inches in length, loop a number of shorter strands across the centre and tie in a tassel, fold the long strands double, twist them, and secure to the centre of the crown.

BABY'S OVER-BOOTS.

REQUIRED, 2 ozs. of white, and rather more than 1 oz. of scarlet single Berlin wool, a bone crochet needle No. 11, and 1½ yards of narrow scarlet corded ribbon for bows. The boots are crocheted in point Muscovite stitch, for which commence with white wool with 35 chain, and work rather loosely in rows, breaking off at the end of the row, and re-commencing on the right-hand side. 1st row—1 double crochet in the first stitch of the chain, insert the hook in the next chain, draw the wool through, work 3 chain, wool over the needle, and draw through the two stitches on the needle, repeat, making 17 tufts with a double crochet between each, and end the row with a double crochet stitch, as it began. 2nd row—Work a tuft upon the double crochet stitch, and a double crochet upon the tuft stitch of previous row, inserting the hook to take up the two front threads of last row. And continue thus—17 tufts in one row, 18 tufts in the next row, till 10 rows are worked. 11th row—For the instep, begin on the ninth stitch from the end, and work still in Muscovite stitch, leaving nine stitches unworked at the other end; this produces 9 tuft stitches. 12th row—10 tuft stitches. 13th row—Leave two stitches unworked at each end and work 7 tuft stitches. 14th row—8 tuft stitches. 15th row—Leave two stitches unworked at each end, and work 5 tuft stitches. 16th row—6 tuft stitches. 17th row—Again leave two stitches at each end, and work 3 tuft stitches. 18th row—4 tuft stitches and 3 double crochet between them completed the instep. Sew up the leg. Now work round and round in the same stitch for the foot, doing 2 rounds; then a round decreasing twice at the points of the toe, then a round decreasing at both toe and heel. Sew up the foot. The top of the leg is now worked with scarlet wool in looped crochet, using the wool double. Insert the hook into a stitch, and before drawing it through, put the wool three times round the forefinger and hook, and next time round the hook only, and draw the wool through all the threads on the hook, and make a chain stitch to keep all together tightly; work 15 of these looped stitches round the top of the leg. Do 5 rows. 6th round—Still with scarlet wool, work 3 treble 1 chain 3 treble all into the same stitch of previous round, 1 double crochet in the next stitch, and repeat. Work the other boot in the same way. Make up the ribbon into bows and place in front.

HONEYCOMB CROCHET FOR A SHAWL.

To be worked with Andalusian or Shetland wool; crochet needle No. 10. Commence with chain for the length required, and work in rows forwards and backwards, turning at the end of every row. 1st row—1 treble in the 6th chain from the needle, * 1 chain, miss 3, 1 treble in the next, 3 chain, 1 treble in the same place last treble is worked into; repeat from * to the end of the row. 2nd row—1 double crochet, 5 treble, 1 double crochet, all under every loop of 3 chain. 3rd row—4 chain, * 1 treble between the 2 double crochet stitches of last row, 3 chain, another treble in the same place, 1 chain, and repeat from *, and it should come 1 chain 1 treble at the end of the row. 4th row—1 double crochet, 5 treble, 1 double crochet under every loop of 3 chain; at the end of the row make 1 extra double crochet in the corner loop. 5th row—6 chain, 1 treble between the 2 double crochet at the corner of last row, * 1 chain, 1 treble between the next 2 double crochet stitches, 3 chain, another treble in the same place; repeat from *. Repeat from the 2nd row f r the length required, and when the shawl is large enough carry on the 4th row down the side along the commencing chain and up the other side, and fasten off. No other bordering is required, as the pattern sits in little scallops all round; if fringe is liked, knot one thread of wool in every stitch of the crochet.

RAISED DIAMOND LATTICE CROCHET.

DOUBLE Berlin wool, four shades of any colour preferred; crochet needle No. 7. With the darkest wool make a chain the length required. 1st row—Plain double crochet. 2nd row—1 chain to turn, and double crochet to

Boy's College Cap.

Baby's Over-Boots.

the end of the row, working into *both* loops of the previous row. 3rd row—1 chain to turn, 3 double crochet, wool twice over the needle, and insert the hook so as to take up the second stitch of the commencing chain, draw the wool through 2 loops, then through 2 again, wool twice over the needle, miss 5 stitches of the commencing chain, take up the next, draw the wool through 2 loops, then through 2 loops twice more; insert the hook in the next stitch of the double crochet of previous row, draw the wool through, and then through the 3 stitches on the needle; 5 double crochet, and then 2 more long treble, the first of them in the next chain to the long treble already done, and the other at an interval of 5 stitches beyond, repeat, and fasten off at the end of the row. 4th row—Next lightest shade of wool, and commencing on the right-hand side, plain double crochet. 5th row—Plain double crochet. 6th row—2 double crochet, make a long treble the same as in the 3rd row, inserting the hook under the *second* long treble of that row, 5 double crochet, then 2 long treble, for the first put the needle underneath the one just made, and round the *first* of the two long trebles in the 3rd row, for the 2nd long treble take up the 4th long treble of 3rd row, and continue, with 5 double crochet between the long trebles. Fasten off at the end of the row. Care must be taken to finish off the long trebles like a double crochet stitch, and fasten off after every fancy row (that is every 3rd row), commencing again with the next shade at the right-hand side.

LADY'S PETTICOAT—TRICOT.

REQUIRED, 1 lb. of best cardinal Scotch fingering and a long bone tricot needle No. 6. Commence at the bottom of the plain part of the petticoat, with chain sufficient for the whole width; 336 chain will make a width of nearly two yards. Work 9 rows of plain tricot having 336 stitches in a row. **10th row**—Pick up the stitches as usual, and in working back make 8 decreasings in the row, thus—draw through 15 stitches, through 2 stitches together, through 40, through 2 together, through 40, through 2 together, through 40, through 2 together, through 50, through 2 together, through 40, through 2 together, through 40, through 2 together, through 40, through 2 together, through 15. Work 5 plain rows

Lady's Petticoat in Tricot.

16th row—Pick up the stitches as usual, and again in working back make 8 decreasings in the row, thus—draw through 15 stitches, through 2 stitches together, through 39, through 2 together, through 39, through 2 together, through 39, through 2 together, through 48, through 2 together, through 39, through 2 together, through 39, through 2 together, through 39, through 2 together, through 15. Work 3 plain rows. Next row, and every fourth row, decrease again 8 times in the row, always making the decreasings in a straight line with those already done, working 15 stitches always at the beginning and end of the row, 1 stitch less upon each side gore, and 2 stitches less upon the front gore, each time, till the petticoat (not including the flounce) is as long as desired. **For the Waistband**—**1st row**—Plain double crochet, taking up 2 tricot stitches together occasionally as frequently as necessary to decrease to size of the waist. Work 3 more rows of plain double crochet. **5th row**—3 double crochet on three consecutive stitches of last row, * wool over the needle, insert the hook in the double crochet stitch of the second row, and work a treble stitch, work 2 more trebles in the next stitches of the second row, 3 double crochet on the last row, and repeat from *. A string is afterwards run in through the treble stitches of this row. Work 5 more rows of plain double crochet, sew up the skirt, and continue the last row of double crochet round the placket hole. **For the Flounce**—Commence with 25 chain, and work 6 rows of plain tricot. **7th row**—Insert the hook so as to pick up from the *back* of the stitches of previous row, and work back as usual. **8th row**—3 double crochet on three first stitches of the tricot, * insert the hook in the next stitch, draw the wool through, and work four chain, wool over the needle and draw through the two stitches on the needle, 1 double crochet, and repeat from *, at end of the row work 3 double crochet. **9th row**—4 double crochet, and proceed as from * to * in the eighth row, 4 double crochet at the end. **10th row**—The same as the eighth row. **11th row**—The same as the seventh row. Then work 5 rows of plain tricot. Repeat from the seventh row till you have a piece sufficient to go round the skirt. Now work a crochet edging upon each side of the flounce. **1st row**—1 double crochet on the first row of tricot, 1 chain, 5 treble on the fourth row of tricot, working a chain stitch between each treble, 1 chain, 1 double crochet on the seventh row of tricot, 1 chain, 5 treble on the centre row of raised knobs, working a chain stitch between each treble, 1 chain, 1 double crochet on the eleventh row of tricot, 1 chain, 5 treble on the fourteenth row of tricot, working a chain stitch between each treble, 1 chain, 1 double crochet on the seventeenth row of tricot, and continue in this manner. **2nd row**—1 double crochet under loop of one chain, 4 chain, 1 double crochet in the first of the chain, and repeat. Turn the edging to the front at the top of the flounce, and sew the edge of the tricot to the skirt.

OPEN-WORK SQUARE.

THESE squares are useful either for a quilt or a cushion, and look well made up over a lining of coloured sateen. Of course a quilt would be worked with white cotton for the sake of washing, but for a cushion brown cotton might be used, with a lining of peacock-blue. Select a steel crochet needle of size to suit the cotton, and commence with 16 chain, join round, and in the circle work 24 double crochet, join round; then * 6 chain, miss two of the double crochet, 1 double crochet in the next, 14 chain, 1 long treble in the eighth from the needle, 7 chain, 1 double crochet in the same place, 8 chain, 1 double long treble in the same place, 8 chain, 1 double crochet in the same place, 7 chain, 1 long treble in the same place, 7 chain, 1 double crochet in the same place, 1 double crochet in the next chain stitch, 4 chain, miss two double crochet of the circle, 1 double crochet in the next; repeat from * three times, and fasten

off; this forms the centre, and you now work it into a square. **1st round**—Beginning at the corner—1 double crochet on the double long treble stitch, 1 double crochet on the following chain stitch, * 7 chain, 3 double crochet on the top of the next leaf, 11 chain, 3 double crochet on the top of the next leaf, 7 chain, 3 double crochet on the top of the corner leaf, and repeat from *. **2nd round**—3 double crochet on the centre stitch of the three double crochet at the corner, 33 double crochet along the side of the square, and repeat. **3rd round**—3 treble on the centre stitch of the three double crochet at the corner, 1 chain, 1 treble on the next stitch, 1 chain, miss one, 1 treble seventeen times, 1 chain, and repeat. **4th round**—3 treble on the centre stitch of the three treble at the corner, 2 treble on the next, 1 treble on the next, 1 chain, 1 treble on the next, 1 chain, 1 treble on the next, 1 chain, miss one, 1 treble on the next sixteen times, 1 chain, 1 treble on the next, 1 chain, 1 treble on the next, 1 treble on the next, 2 treble on the next, and repeat; break off cotton at the end of the round. **5th round**—1 treble on each of the two stitches next after the corner stitch, * 3 chain, miss three, 2 treble, repeat from * eight times, 5 chain to round the corner, and repeat. **6th round**—Same as last round, with the addition of two extra groups of 2 treble at each corner with 5 chain between the groups. **7th round**—Double crochet all round, working 3 double crochet in the corner stitch. **8th round**—1 double long treble in the centre stitch at the corner, 5 chain, 3 long treble in the next stitch, 6 chain, miss eight stitches of last round, 5 long treble in the next,* 4 chain, miss six, 3 treble in the next, repeat from * five times, 6 chain, miss eight, 3 long treble in the next, 5 chain, and repeat. **9th round**—1 treble on the corner stitch, * 6 chain, 1 single crochet in the fifth chain from the needle, 1 chain, miss two stitches of last row, 1 treble on the next, and repeat from *, and do three of the little pique stitches to turn the corner. This round completes the square.

BABY'S JACKET.

REQUIRED, 3 ozs of white Shetland wool; bone crochet needle, No. 12. Commence with 89 chain for the neck, turn, work 1 treble in the fifth chain from the needle, 2 chain, 1 treble, alternately, all along. This jacket is worked in "sets," and "a set" is 1 treble, 1 chain, 1 treble, all worked into the same hole, an "increase" is 1 treble, 1 chain, 1 treble, 1 chain, 1 treble, all worked into the same hole; make 3 chain to turn at the end of every row. **2nd row**—Work 6 sets, increase, 6 sets, increase, 1 set, increase, 6 sets, increase, 6 sets. **3rd row**—Work sets all along, increasing only one at the beginning and end of the row. **4th row**—6 sets, increase, 2 sets, increase, 18 sets, increase, 2 sets, increase, 6 sets. Every alternate row is the same as the third row. **6th row**—7 sets, increase, 4 sets, increase, 7 sets, increase, 1 set, increase, 7 sets, increase, 4 sets, increase, 7 sets. **8th row**—8 sets, increase, 6 sets, increase, 19 sets, increase, 6 sets, increase, 8 sets. **10th row**—9 sets, increase, 8 sets, increase, 8 sets, increase, 1 set, increase, 8 sets, increase, 8 sets, increase, 9 sets. **12th row**—10 sets, increase, 10 sets, increase, 21 sets, increase, 10 sets, increase, 10 sets. **14th row**—11 sets, increase, 12 sets, increase, 9 sets, increase, 1 set, increase, 9 sets, increase, 12 sets,

Open-Work Square.

increase, 11 sets. After doing the **15th row** work the Sleeves: Do 12 chain across from the increases on the shoulder to make the under part of the sleeve; work 3 rounds in sets, 20 sets in a round; in the next 5 rounds decrease under the arm, and bring it in the 25th round to 14 sets; then work the remainder of the sleeve in sets round and round for the length required, the *last* round is to be 1 double crochet in one set, and 5 treble in the next set, alternately. When sleeves are both finished proceed with the skirt part of the jacket. **16th row**—Sets all along. **17th row**—Sets, increasing one set at the beginning and one at the end of the row. **18th row**—29 sets, increase, 1 set, increase, 29 sets. **19th row**—Same as the seventeenth row. Then work six or seven more rows the same, and finish by working 3 rows of sets all round the jacket, rounding by a little increase at the corners, and for the last round work same as the last round of the sleeves.

LADY'S FANCY WORK BASKET.

To make this novel basket you will require two reels of Evans' brown crochet cotton No. 2, a steel crochet needle No. 16, a yard of inch-wide blue corded ribbon, and a small piece of blue satin. Commence with 28 chain, work 1 double crochet in every stitch of the chain, 3 double crochet in the last stitch to turn,

Lady's Fancy Work Basket.

and 1 double crochet in every stitch along the opposite side of the foundation chain, 3 double crochet at the end, and join round, having 58 double crochet in the round; and continue working double crochet, inserting the hook in the one top thread of previous row, making an oblong square for the bottom of the basket, plain double crochet along the four sides and 3 double crochet in the centre stitch at each corner, till 10 rounds are done. Then work straight round with no increase for 8 rounds. **1st round of the Open Pattern**—2 treble, 1 chain, 2 treble, *all* in one stitch of the double crochet, miss three double crochet, and repeat. **2nd round**—2 treble, 1 chain, 2 treble, all under the one chain stitch of last round, and repeat. **3rd round**—in which to run a ribbon—1 double long treble (cotton three times round the needle), 2 chain, 1 double long treble, all under one chain stitch of last round, and repeat. **4th round**—2 treble, 1 chain, 2 treble, all under the loop of chain of last round. **5th round**—Same as the second. **6th round**—Same as the third, but do 3 chain between the double long trebles. **7th round**—Same as the fourth round. **8th round**—5 treble under one chain of last round, 1 double crochet between the group of treble stitches, and repeat. Break off the cotton and fasten off neatly. **For the Handles**—Begin with 60 chain, work 6 rows of plain double crochet, fold lengthways, and sew together, and sew on the basket. The basket must now be stiffened. Make some thick starch into which put a little glue, and let the basket lie in it till thoroughly saturated and nearly cold, then draw the crochet into shape, blocking it as it were with the hand, and drawing up each point of the crochet in place. Dissolve 1 oz. of shellac in spirits of wine (it takes at least a day to dissolve), do not have it too thin, with this mix some Brunswick black or brown Japan varnish, according to the colour you desire the basket to be, and brush it over the crochet outside and inside carefully, not to allow a bit of white starch to be seen. After it dries, varnish it with clear spirit varnish. Cut the ribbon in two pieces and run in through the double long treble stitches, finishing off the top ribbon in the centre with a bow. Make a small padded cushion to fit the bottom of the basket and cover it with the piece of blue satin.

SCARF.

This pretty and useful scarf is worked throughout in crossed treble stitch. Procure 3½ ozs. of white and 1 oz. of pale blue Peacock wool, and a bone crochet needle, No. 8. For the commencement with white wool work 39 chain. **1st row**—1 treble in the fourth chain from the needle, * miss the next stitch, 1 treble in the next, pass the hook in front of the treble just done, insert it in the missed chain stitch and work a treble loosely across the other; repeat from * to the end of row, making in all eighteen groups of treble stitches; break off the wool at the end of this and every row. **2nd row**—Beginning on the right hand side, 1 treble in the first space of previous row, pass the hook in front, insert it at the top of the first treble of last row and work a treble loosely across the first treble, * then a treble in the next space of previous row and another treble across that into the space to the right where a treble is already worked into; repeat from * to the end of the row, and there for want of another space work a treble on the last treble of last row and cross it as the others are crossed. Every succeeding row is the same as the second row, working alternately 1 treble forwards and 1 treble backwards, and always making eighteen "crossed" stitches in the row, as loosely and evenly as possible. Continue with the white wool till 36 rows are done, then work 3 rows with blue, 3 rows with white, 3 rows with blue, and again 3 rows with white for the end. Re-commence

upon the foundation chain and work the other side of the scarf in the same manner. Fasten all the ends of wool in securely. For edging round the scarf, work with white wool, 1 double crochet into a space of the scarf, * 4 chain, 1 double crochet in the double crochet just done, 1 double crochet into the next space, and repeat from *. Fringe the ends by knotting four strands of wool into the loops of four chain.

BED SOCKS IN RUSSIAN CROCHET.

For these 3 ozs. of good quality Scotch Fingering will be required, and a No. 10 bone crochet needle. Commence for the toe with a chain of 28 stitches, and in this work 27 double crochet. **2nd row**—Double crochet, inserting the hook into the thread at the back of the stitches of last row, and increase by working 3 stitches into the centre stitch of last row. **3rd row**—Plain double crochet worked into the back thread of the stitches of preceding row. Repeat these two rows till 33 rows are done, when you have to work 59 stitches in the plain row. **34th row**—Work 30 double crochet and make 20 chain for the leg. Now work backwards and forwards upon 50 stitches for 48 rows to reach round the leg. Break off the wool, and sew the first 20 stitches to the 20 commencing chain of the leg, sew the remainder stitch by stitch to the 29 stitches you left unworked at the end of the thirty-third row. Sew up the toe, rounding it as nicely as possible, and sew up underneath the sole, keeping the ribs to meet one another. For edge round top of the leg work 1 double crochet in a depressed ridge of the foundation, * 5 chain, 1 double crochet in the first of the chain, 1 double crochet in the next depressed ridge, and repeat from *. Work the other sock in the same way.

BAG FOR KNITTING.

This handy little bag will be acceptable to knitters, as needles of any length can be accommodated in it. Procure 1 oz. of cherry colour and ½ oz. each of two shades of green single Berlin wool, 2 yards of inch-wide ribbon to match the cherry-coloured wool, 2 brass rings about an inch in diameter, and a No. 10 bone tricot needle. Begin with the cherry-coloured wool, with 50 chain, and work 4 rows of plain tricot, then 1 row of tricot with the lightest shade of green, 2 rows with the darker green, and 1 row again with light green, and repeat till 4 green stripes and 5 cherry-coloured stripes are worked, cast off the tricot stitches with a row of single crochet. This piece forms the front, back, and bottom of the bag. Take the cherry-coloured wool and crochet a row of long loose treble stitches along one *side* of the tricot, fold the tricot double, and join the last treble stitch to the first; do 4 chain to stand for a treble and work a round of long loose treble stitches inserting the hook between the stitches of last row; join round, and break off with a long thread, and with a rug needle work a button-hole stitch from each treble stitch over one of the brass rings, so that the ring is entirely covered with stitches, and the ends of the bag are secured in a circle. Do the other end in the same way. Now the top of the bag is to be crochet. **1st round**—With dark green wool, 1 treble on the first stitch of tricot, * 1 chain, miss one, 1 treble on the next, and repeat from * to the end of the row of tricot, down the two treble stitches at the end of the bag, along the opposite side of the tricot, and down the two treble stitches at the other end of the bag, join round. **2nd round**—Begin with 4 chain to stand for a treble, 1 treble in first space of last round, * 1 chain, 1 treble in the next space, and repeat from *, and join

Bag for Knitting.

at the end of the round. **3rd round and 4th round**—Same as the second round. **5th round**—With light green wool, work 1 treble, 1 chain, 1 treble, under each chain stitch of previous round. Cut the ribbon into two pieces, and run a piece in the second row and a piece in the fourth row of treble stitches and tie the ends in a knotted bow at opposite sides of the bag.

Scarf.

SQUARE PINCUSHION COVER.

REQUIRED, a ball of Evans' ecru Maltese thread No. 10, and a steel crochet needle No. 16. Commence with 4 chain, join round, and work 3 double crochet in each stitch of the chain, 12 double crochet in all, and join round. 2nd round—3 double crochet in the centre stitch of the three double crochet of last round, 1 double crochet in each of the two next stitches, and repeat, working 20 double crochet in the round, and join neatly at the end of this and every

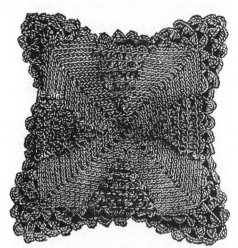

Square Pincushion Cover.

round. 3rd round—3 double crochet in the centre stitch of the three double crochet of last round, 1 double crochet in each of the two next stitches, 6 chain, 1 double crochet in each of the two next stitches, and repeat three times. 4th round—3 double crochet in the centre stitch of the three double crochet of last round (this being always a *corner* stitch), 6 consecutive double crochet, and repeat. 5th round—3 double crochet in the corner stitch, 3 consecutive double crochet, 6 chain, 2 consecutive double crochet, 6 chain, 3 consecutive double crochet, and repeat. 6th round—3 double crochet in the corner stitch, 10 double crochet along the side of the square, and repeat. 7th round—3 double crochet in the corner stitch, 4 double crochet, 6 chain, 2 double crochet, 6 chain, 2 double crochet, 6 chain, 4 double crochet, and repeat. 8th round—3 double crochet in the corner stitch, 14 double crochet along the side of the square, and repeat. 9th round—3 double crochet in the corner stitch, 5 double crochet, then 6 chain and 2 double crochet four times, 3 more double crochet, and repeat. 10th round—3 double crochet in the corner stitch, 18 double crochet along the side of the square, and repeat. 11th round—3 double crochet in the corner stitch, 6 double crochet, then 6 chain and 2 double crochet five times, 4 more double crochet, and repeat. 12th round—3 double crochet in the corner stitch, 22 double crochet along the side of the square, and repeat. 13th round—3 double crochet in the corner stitch, 7 double crochet, then 6 chain and 2 double crochet six times, 5 more double crochet, and repeat. 14th round—3 double crochet in the corner stitch, 26 double crochet along the side of the square, and repeat. 15th round—3 double crochet in the corner stitch, 8 double crochet, then 6 chain and 2 double crochet seven times, 6 more double crochet, and repeat. 16th round—3 double crochet in the corner stitch, 30 double crochet along the side of the square, and repeat. This completes the square. For the Border—Commencing at the first corner stitch of last round with a single crochet,* work 4 chain, cotton over the needle, insert the hook in the third chain stitch from the needle, and draw the cotton through loosely, cotton over the needle, insert the hook in the next chain stitch and draw the cotton through loosely, cotton over the needle, and draw through the five stitches on the needle, 1 chain, miss two double crochet of last round, 1 single crochet in the next, and repeat from * ; and work *two* of these "points" upon each *corner* stitch, to turn it nicely. Work two more rows in "points" the *same* as this row, working the single crochet stitches at the top of the points of last row. The pincushion is made of two pieces of lining 4½ inches square, sewn together, and stuffed with bran, and covered with red twill or satin ; the crochet square is stitched lightly in place on the top.

DRAWING-ROOM TABLE MATS.

THE centre of these mats may be worked with double Berlin wool in double crochet over blind-cord. The border is of tufted fringe, or, as some call it, Daisy fringe, to make which, procure skeins of single Berlin wool of five shades of any colour, either crimson or green being the prettiest, and the best to harmonise with the usual surroundings of furniture. Lay the wool evenly in strands of ten ; thread a rug needle with some of the wool, tie the end round the end of the strands,

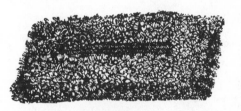

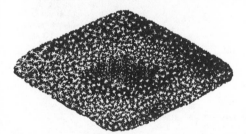

Drawing-room Table Mats.

beginning on the left-hand side, and with the wool in the needle, again tie the stranded wool tightly twice round, about an inch distant from the first tie, sewing it in a firm knot. Proceed in this way till you have tied it at regular intervals all along. Then break off the wool with which you have been sewing, and cut the strands in the centre of every space between the ties. This leaves a series of little tufts on the wool you have been sewing with, and the fringe is complete. Make as much fringe as will be sufficient for the bordering of your mat, and sew it on, arranging it in loops of any length preferred, and mixing the shades to produce a good effect.

ROUND PINCUSHION COVER.

REQUIRED, a ball of Evans' ecru Maltese thread, No. 10, and a steel crochet needle, No. 16. Commence with 4 chain, join round, and work 2 double crochet in each stitch of the chain, 8 double crochet in all, and join the last stitch neatly to the first stitch at the end of this and every round. 2nd round—2 double crochet in the first stitch of last round, 1 double crochet in the next, and repeat, inserting the hook to take both top threads of the stitches of last round, and working 12 double crochet in the round. 3rd round—2 double crochet in the first stitch, 1 double crochet in each of the two next stitches, and repeat. Continue working thus round and round in double crochet, increasing where necessary to make the work lie flat, until there are 51 double crochet stitches in the circle, then join neatly, and break off the cotton. For the Border—Recommence by working * 2 treble in one stitch of the double crochet circle, 3 chain, 2 more treble in the same place, miss two stitches, and repeat from *, working 17 patterns in the circle, and join round. 2nd round—12 treble in every loop of three chain of last round. 3rd round—1 double crochet on every treble stitch of last round, inserting the hook so as to take both top threads of the stitches. 4th round—Same as the first round, but working the 4 treble stitches between the eighth and ninth trebles of the twelve treble of the second round, and taking the stitches *over* the round of double crochet. 5th round—12 treble in every loop of three chain of last round, making 17 scallops. 6th round—Same as the third round. Break off the cotton. 7th round—1 double crochet at the *back* of the trebles between the scallops of the fifth round, * 7 chain, 1 double crochet at the back between the two next scallops, and repeat from *, making 17 loops of seven chain. 8th round—1 treble on double crochet stitch of last round, 11 long treble in loop of seven chain, with 1 chain stitch between each long treble, and repeat. 9th round—1 double crochet in first loop of one chain of last round, * 3 chain, 1 double crochet in next loop of one chain, and repeat from * nine times, and work the same in each scallop of last round. Join at the end of the round, fasten off neatly, and the cover is finished. The pincushion is made of two circular pieces of lining measuring 4½ inches across, and joined together by a band about ¾ of an inch wide, the turnings-in being extra, it is stuffed with bran, and covered with red sateen or satin.

EIS WOOL SHAWL.

THE shawl is commenced in the centre. Make a chain of 5 stitches, join round. 1st round—3 chain, 1 double crochet in the circle, repeat three times more. 2nd round—3 chain, 1 double crochet in the centre of the three chain of last round, 3 chain, 1 double crochet in the same place, repeat three times

Round Pincushion Cover.

more. 3rd round—3 chain, 1 double crochet under the three chain of last round, 3 chain, 1 double crochet under the next three chain, 3 chain, 1 double crochet in the same place, repeat three times more. Continue working in the same manner, straight along the four sides and increasing at each corner until the shawl is large enough. Add a border or fringe.

CHILD'S PETTICOAT.

REQUIRED 11 ozs. of Scotch fingering wool and a No. 9 bone crochet needle. This petticoat is large enough for a child of six or seven years, the skirt is worked in scallop shells, and the body is a close stitch. Commence with chain sufficient to go round the waist, and on this first of all work 6 rows of plain double crochet forwards and backwards for the waistband, taking up both top threads of the stitches of previous row. **7th row**—1 double crochet on the first double crochet stitch of last row, * miss one, 4 treble on the next, miss one, 1 double crochet on the next, and repeat from * to the end of the row. Break off at the end of this row and every succeeding row till you have done the length required for the placket-hole, then join round, and work in rounds for the remainder of the skirt. **8th row**—3 treble on the double crochet stitch, * 1 double crochet in between the second and third trebles of last row, 4 treble on

Child's Petticoat.

the double crochet stitch, and repeat from *, and do 3 treble on the double crochet stitch at the end of the row. **9th row**—1 double crochet on the first stitch of treble, * 5 treble on the double crochet stitch, 1 double crochet in between the second and third trebles of last row, and repeat from *, and end the row with a double crochet on the treble stitch as it began. **10th row**—3 treble on the double crochet stitch, * 1 double crochet on the centre stitch of the five trebles of last row, 5 treble on the double crochet stitch, and repeat from *, ending the row with 3 treble. **11th row**—1 double crochet on the first stitch of treble, * 5 treble on the double crochet stitch, 1 double crochet on the centre stitch of the five trebles of last row, and repeat from *, doing the last double crochet on the last stitch of treble. Repeat the tenth and eleventh rows alternately three times more. This probably will be a sufficient length for the placket-hole, join round, and work 8 rounds with 6 treble in a shell, then 12 rounds with 7 treble in a shell, and if required longer work 4 or 6 more rounds with 8 treble in a shell. Now again on the foundation row of chain work 4 rows of double crochet. **The Body** is worked separately and sewn on. Begin with 110 chain, and work alternately a row of treble and a row of double crochet, doing 108 stitches in a row, forwards and backwards for 22 rows. Then for the left side of the back work in the same manner upon 30 stitches for 9 rows (ending with a treble row); work 48 stitches forwards and backwards for 9 rows for the front; and the remaining 30 stitches in the same way for the other half of the back. When the ninth row of this last piece is finished, turn, and work a row of double crochet along all three pieces, then a row of treble stitches, and another row of double crochet, and finish round the neck with an edging, thus, 1 treble on the first stitch of last row, * miss two, 1 treble on the next, 3 chain, another treble in the same place, and repeat from *. Work the same edging round the armholes. Sew the body to the waistband. Do a row of double crochet to strengthen the ends of the waistband and round the placket hole, and run a piece of narrow ribbon round the neck and waist to tie.

STAYS FOR CHILD OF THREE.

THESE stays are worked as closely and firmly as possible in Russian crochet, and being strong and comfortable wear for a young child will prove an acceptable gift for distribution to the poor. Procure 4 ozs. of 4 thread Fleecy wool and a No. 8 bone crochet needle, also ten buttons. Commence for the back with 39 chain, turn, and work double crochet, doing 38 stitches in the row. Work 7 more rows of double crochet, taking the stitches into the back thread of the stitches of previous row so as to form ridges, and working 38 stitches in each row. **9th row**—Work 14 double crochet, turn, and work back. Work 8 more rows of 38 stitches in a row. **19th row**—Work 30 double crochet, turn, and work back, and do 4 more rows on these 30 stitches. At the end of the 25th row

make 9 chain, and work 4 rows of 38 double crochet in a row. **30th row**—Work 14 double crochet, turn, and work back. **32nd row**—Work 38 double crochet. **33rd row**—Work 14 double crochet, turn, and work back. Work 6 rows of 38 double crochet in a row. **41st row**—14 double crochet, turn, and work back. **43rd row**—Work 38 double crochet. **44th row**—14 double crochet, turn, and work back. Work 5 rows of 38 double crochet in a row. **51st row**—Work 30 double crochet, turn, and work back, and do 4 more rows on these 30 stitches. **57th row**—Work 30 double crochet, 9 chain, turn, and work 38 double crochet back. Work 6 more rows of 38 double crochet in a row. **65th row**—Work 14 double crochet, turn, and work back. **67th row**—Work 38 double crochet, and work 7 more rows of 38 double crochet, and fasten off. For **Edge**, along the top and bottom of the stays, work 1 double crochet in the first ridge, * 2 chain, 2 treble in the same place, 1 double crochet on the next ridge, and repeat from *. For shoulder straps, make 20 chain, and work 6 rows of Russian crochet: sew the shoulder straps neatly at the back of the edging. Sew four buttons down the left back, and with a rug needle work button-hole loops on the opposite back to button into. Place six buttons on the waist for the purpose of attaching a petticoat, and the stays are complete.

WARM PETTICOAT IN PLAIN TRICOT.

REQUIRED, 1½ lbs. of grey 3 thread Fleecy wool, long tricot needle No. 7. The petticoat is worked lengthways, from bottom to top, and is gored to measure four times as much round the bottom as it measures round the waist. Begin with 100 chain. **1st row**—Pick up a stitch in each stitch of the chain, and draw back as in ordinary tricot. **2nd row**—Raise 85 stitches, and draw back. **3rd row**—Raise 70 stitches, and draw back. **4th row**—Raise 55 stitches, and draw back. **5th row**—Raise 100 stitches, and draw back. **6th row**—Same as second row. **7th row**—Same as third row. **8th row**—Same as fourth row. And continue these four rows till the top of the petticoat measures (without stretching) sufficient to go round the waist. Sew up the petticoat, leaving space for a placket hole, and sew the petticoat on a band. For edge round bottom of the petticoat, draw the wool through the first tricot stitch by the seam of the petticoat, do 3 chain, insert the hook in the chain next the needle and draw the wool through, insert the hook in the next chain and draw the wool through, raise stitches likewise in the same stitch you first drew the wool through, and in the two next tricot stitches; there now are 6 stitches on the needle, wool over the needle and draw through all, 5 chain, 1 single in the fourth chain from the needle; * raise a stitch in the little hole where the stitches of last group are drawn together, raise a stitch in the lower part of the group, one in the same tricot stitch the group is worked into, and one in each of the two next tricot stitches, 6 stitches on the needle, wool over the needle and draw through all, 5 chain, 1 single in the fourth chain from the needle, and repeat from * all round the petticoat.

CLOUD.

FOR this light and elegant wrap procure 8 ozs. of white 3 thread Lady Betty wool and a bone crochet needle No. 9. Commence with 96 chain in which work 95 double crochet; turn, and inserting the hook into the back thread of the stitches of preceding row, again work a row of 95 double crochet. **3rd row**—3 chain, insert the hook in the chain next the needle and draw the wool through, insert the hook in the chain stitch and draw the wool through, do the same in the back threads of the first, second, and third stitches of last row, you now have 6 stitches on the needle, wool over the needle and draw through all, 1 chain, * insert the hook in the little hole formed by the one chain

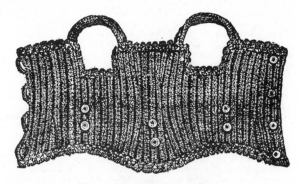

Stays for a Child of Three.

stitch and draw the wool through, do the same in the lower part of the group just worked, in the same stitch of last row as the group was worked into, and in the back thread of the two next stitches of last row, now there are 6 stitches on the needle, wool over the needle and draw through all, 1 chain, and repeat from * to the end of the row. **4th, 5th, and 6th rows**—Ridged double crochet, 95 stitches in each row. Continue these four rows till you have about three quarters of a yard done for half the cloud. For edge work 1 double crochet on first double crochet of last row, * 10 chain, wool over the needle, insert the hook in the fourth chain from the needle and draw the wool through loosely, raise 6 more loops in the same way, wool over the needle and draw through all the stitches on the needle, 1 chain to keep the ball firm, 1 single crochet in first chain stitch from the ball, 2 chain, miss two chain, 1 double crochet in the next, 2 chain, 1 treble on the third double crochet of last row, 2 chain, another treble in the same place, and repeat from * to the end of the row. Fasten off. Then recommence with 2 rows of double crochet on the foundation chain, and work the other half of the cloud to correspond.

CROSSOVER.

REQUIRED, 3½ ozs. of dove colour and ½ oz. each of three shades of blue Andalusian wool, a long bone tricot needle, No. 9, and a crochet needle the same size. Commence with grey wool, with 240 chain, pick up 239 stitches on the needle, and work 1 row of plain tricot; this is the entire size round the bottom of the shawl above the border. Continue working in plain tricot, but pick up 2 stitches together at the beginning of every row, 3 stitches together in the exact centre of the row, and 2 stitches together at the end of the row, till the shawl is reduced to about 9 stitches in the centre, so forming a triangular-

Crossover.

shaped piece of work. Now along the top of the crossover with grey wool work 2 rows of double crochet loosely. **For Border** along two sides of the crossover. **1st row**—With darkest blue wool, plain double crochet, 1 stitch in every stitch of the foundation chain. The second row and six following rows are worked in Point Neige, which has already been described in these pages. **2nd row**—With palest blue. **3rd row**—With medium blue, and working 2 point neige stitches on the first stitch of previous row, 2 or 3 additional stitches to round the point of the shawl, and two stitches on the last stitch of previous row. **4th row**—With grey, increasing in the same manner. **5th row**—Darkest blue. **6th row**—Grey. **7th row**—Medium blue. **8th row**—Palest blue. **9th row**—With darkest blue, plain double crochet, working 2 stitches on every stitch of point neige. **10th row**—With grey, wool over the needle and insert the hook in the first stitch of last row and draw the wool through, wool over the needle, insert the hook in the next stitch and draw the wool through, wool over the needle, insert the hook in the next stitch and draw the wool through, 6 loops are on the needle, draw the wool through all, do * 1 chain, wool over the needle, insert hook in the same stitch the last loop was worked into and draw the wool through, wool over the needle, insert the hook in the next stitch and draw the wool through, wool over the needle, insert the hook in the next stitch and draw the wool through, draw the wool through the 6 loops on the needle, then draw the wool through 2 stitches on the needle, and repeat from *. **11th row**—With grey, plain double crochet all along, turn at the end of the row, and work another row of double crochet, inserting the hook in the small thread at the back of the stitches. **13th row**—Same as the tenth row. **14th row**—Same as the eleventh row. Now on the ends of this border and along the entire top of the shawl work with grey wool a row of plain double crochet, then a row thus—1 double crochet on the first stitch, * 3 chain, 1 treble in the same place the double crochet is worked into, miss 1 stitch, 1 double crochet on the next, and repeat from *. Cut the remainder of the grey wool into strands five inches long, and fringe by knotting 2 threads into every alternate stitch of the border, and the crossover is finished.

TUFTED BORDER.

THIS is a handsome border, and may be used as an edging for any of the quilts worked in tufted squares, directions of which appeared in our last Crochet number. Begin with 20 chain; turn, work 1 treble in the sixth chain from the needle, * 1 chain, miss one, 1 treble, and repeat from * six times; turn. **2nd row**—1 double crochet on every stitch of last row, doing 17 double crochet in all, and inserting the hook into the back threads of previous row as the work is to set in ridges, 3 chain at the end of the row. **3rd row**—1 double crochet on each of the two last chain, and 1 on the first stitch of double crochet, 5 treble in the next stitch (this makes a "tuft"), 15 consecutive double crochet. **4th row**—15 double crochet on the fifteen of last row, 1 treble behind the tuft into a stitch of the second row, 3 consecutive double crochet, 3 chain at the end. **5th row**—1 double crochet on each of the two last chain, and 1 on the first stitch of double crochet, a tuft of 5 treble in the next stitch, 3 consecutive double crochet, another tuft, 13 consecutive double crochet. **6th row**—13 double

crochet, 1 treble, 3 double crochet, 1 treble, 3 double crochet, 3 chain. **7th row**—1 double crochet in each of the two last chain and 1 on the first stitch of double crochet, a tuft, 3 double crochet, a tuft, 3 double crochet, a tuft, 11 double crochet. **8th row**—11 double crochet, 1 treble, 3 double crochet, 1 treble, 3 double crochet, 1 treble, 1 double crochet, leave 2 stitches unworked. **9th row**—3 double crochet, tuft, 3 double crochet, tuft, 13 double crochet. **10th row**—13 double crochet, 1 treble, 3 double crochet, 1 treble, 1 double crochet, leave 2 stitches unworked. **11th row**—3 double crochet, tuft, 15 double crochet. **12th row**—15 double crochet, 1 treble, 1 double crochet, leave 2 stitches unworked. **13th row**—4 chain, 1 treble in the third stitch of double crochet, * 1 chain, miss 1, 1 treble, repeat from * six times. Repeat from the second row for the length required. **For the Edging round the Scallops**—Work 1 double crochet on the last stitch of the last row of the border, 5 chain, 2 treble in the double crochet just worked, 1 double crochet on the last stitch of the next little point, 5 chain, 2 treble in the double crochet just worked, and so on making 7 of these little piqués round each scallop, and 3 chain to pass over the open row. **For the Heading at the top—1st row**—1 treble, 1 chain, alternately all along, working a treble stitch in each depressed rib of the bordering, turn. **2nd row**—Work 2 double crochet under each chain stitch of last row. **3rd row**—Plain double crochet, 1 double crochet on each stitch of last row, working into the back threads. **4th row**—1 treble, miss one, 1 chain, and repeat. **5th row**—1 double crochet on each stitch of last row.

CROCHET SHAWL—THE FASCINATOR.

THIS pattern is one that is generally used for making those pretty light coverings for the head known by the name of "Fascinators." It is also suitable for small three-cornered shawls and neck handkerchiefs. Work with Shetland wool or fine Eider yarn and good-sized bone crochet needle. Commence in the middle of the back with 5 chain, join round, make 4 chain, and work 13 long treble in the circle. Long treble are formed by putting the wool twice round the needle. Now make 5 chain to turn, 13 long treble in the last stitch of the 13 treble just done, 1 double crochet in the middle stitch of the 13 treble, and 13 more long treble on the chain stitch at the end of the row. **3rd row**—5 chain to turn, 13 long treble in the last treble stitch of previous row, 1 double crochet in the middle stitch of the 13 treble of previous row, 13 long treble in the double crochet stitch, 1 double crochet in the middle of the last group of 13 treble of previous row, and 13 long treble on the chain-stitch at the end of the row. Every succeeding row is worked in the same manner as the third row, always remembering to increase at the beginning and end of every row, and work 13 long treble in every double crochet stitch and a double crochet in the middle stitch of every 13 long treble. When the Fascinator is the size required, finish it off by working a pattern row along the straight side where the rows are turned.

BASKET PATTERN. TRICOT.

THIS is a useful pattern for antimacassars, sofa blankets, and cushions. It is best worked in stripes of medium width, the stripes to be afterwards joined together with a row of double crochet. Procure double Berlin wool of the colour preferred, and a No. 8 bone tricot-needle. Begin with a chain of 15 or 16 stitches.

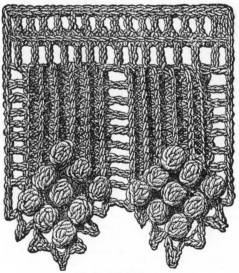

Tufted Border.

1st row— * miss one chain, raise a stitch in the next chain, put the wool over the needle and raise another stitch in the same place; repeat from *, keeping all the stitches on the needle; to work back, wool over the needle and draw through 3 stitches, 1 chain, wool over the needle and draw through the chain and the next 3 stitches, and so on, till all the stitches are worked off. **2nd row**—1 chain to turn, * raise a stitch under the chain stitch of last row, wool over the needle, and raise another stitch in the same place, repeat from *, and at the end of the row raise one extra stitch to keep the work even; to work back, do 1 chain, wool over the needle and draw through the chain and the 3 first stitches and repeat, till at the end of the row you draw through the chain and 1 stitch only. Every succeeding row is worked in the same manner. Be careful to keep the same number of stitches in each row.

TIPPET WORKED IN POINT MUSCOVITE.

REQUIRED, 3 ozs. of white double Berlin wool and a bone crochet needle No. 10. Commence for the neck with 50 chain. **1st row**—1 double crochet in

Tippet and Muff Worked in Point Muscovite.

the first stitch from the needle, * insert the hook in the next stitch, draw the wool through and do 4 chain, draw the wool through the last of the chain and through the stitch on the needle, 1 double crochet in the next stitch of foundation, and repeat from *; break off the wool at the end of this and every row and re-commence at the right-hand side. Put in a thread of cotton to mark the half and quarters of the work where increasings are to be made. **2nd row**—Begin with a point stitch over the double crochet stitch, and work a double crochet over the point stitch of last row, and continue. **3rd row**—Work in the same manner, but increase five times in the row by working twice into the first stitch, and last stitch, and at the quarters and half. Increase in the same manner in every alternate row till 15 rows are done. Next work a row of plain double crochet in the foundation chain to strengthen the neck, break off at the end. On this do a row of 1 treble, 1 chain, miss one, and repeat. Then begin at the lower right-hand corner and work up the side along the neck and down the other side, thus—1 double crochet in the first stitch, * 3 chain, 1 treble on the double crochet just done, miss one stitch of the tippet, 1 double crochet on the next, and repeat from *. Now work the edging of tufts round the bottom of the tippet, holding the work the wrong side towards you do 1 double crochet on the first stitch, * 5 chain, wool over the needle, insert the hook in the third chain from the needle and draw the wool through loosely, do this five times, wool over the needle and draw through all, 1 chain, 1 single crochet in the next stitch of the chain, 1 treble worked in the lower back thread of the double crochet stitch, miss two stitches of the tippet, 1 double crochet on the next, and repeat from *. Make a double foundation chain thus—make a stitch on the needle, 1 chain, draw up a loop through the first stitch, draw through both stitches on the needle, * draw up a loop through the left loop, draw through both stitches on the needle, repeat from *: draw this chain through the row of treble stitches round the neck and finish it off with tassels to tie. Sew a button and a loop on the lower corners of the tippet and there place a small ribbon bow

MUFF.

THIS is worked in Point Muscovite to match the tippet. 2 ozs. of white double Berlin wool will be required, also 2 yards of inch-wide white satin ribbon, and a piece of white silk for the lining. Commence with 29 chain, and work the first and second rows as directed for the tippet. Then continue working a point stitch over a double crochet and a double crochet over a point till 36 rows are done. Join the last row to the commencing chain. Line the muff, and place a bow on each side and ribbon to tie round the neck.

PRETTY HAT FOR BABY BOY.

REQUIRED, 3 ozs. of ivory-coloured Peacock fingering or Berlin wool. Bone crochet needle No. 11. A skein of ivory-coloured thick embroidery silk, 1½ yards

of corded ribbon for strings and bow, 2 yards of very narrow ribbon to match, and a cap front. The hat is worked throughout in a small close stitch of point neige or shell stitch. Commence with 4 chain, join round; work 1 chain, insert the hook in the chain stitch and draw the wool through, insert the hook in the back of the chain stitch and draw the wool through, insert the hook in the circle and draw the wool through, wool over the needle and draw through the four stitches on the needle, 1 chain, * insert the hook in the small hole formed by the one chain and draw the wool through, insert the hook in the back of the shell just made and draw the wool through, insert the hook in the circle of foundation chain and draw the wool through, wool over the needle and draw through the four stitches on the needle, 1 chain, and repeat from * till you have seven shells done in the foundation circle. Then continue working round and round in the same stitch of three raised loops. The increasings are made by working two shells over one shell of last round wherever necessary to make the work lie flat; for instance, in this second round work 2 shells on the first shell of last round, 1 shell in the chain stitch, 1 shell on the next shell, 1 shell in the next chain stitch, and 2 shells again on the next shell of last round, and so on to the end of the round. In successive rounds work shell over shell and you will not have to increase so frequently. Work till you have a flat circular piece measuring 7½ inches across. Then work 5 rounds without any increase. These done, work 2 rounds with 2 shells on every alternate shell to make a full border. Now take the embroidery silk, and crochet a round of plain double crochet all round the hat; then a round of * 4 double crochet in four consecutive stitches, 3 chain, 1 single into the last double crochet, and repeat from *. Embroider in feather stitch round and round upon the first six rounds of the crown, and between these rounds of feather stitching work at intervals a French knot stitch. Cut the narrow ribbon into two pieces and run a piece in the fifth and sixth rounds from the edge of the hat to tie at the back and draw in to the size of the child's head. Put on the strings, make a pretty bow for the front, line the hat with a piece of white sarscenet, and sew in the cap front.

CHILD'S BIB.

THIS useful bib is worked with Strutt's knitting cotton No. 16, and rather fine steel crochet needle. Commence with 25 chain, turn, work 12 consecutive double crochet, 3 double crochet in the centre stitch, and 12 more consecutive double crochet. **2nd row**—Insert the

Child's Bib.

hook to take up the threads at the back of the stitches of last row, so that the work sits in ridges, 13 consecutive double crochet, 3 double crochet on the centre stitch of the three double crochet of last row, 13 more consecutive double crochet. Continue in this manner, doing one more double crochet stitch each side in every successive row, and always three double crochet in the centre stitch, till 26 ridges are done. In the next row, instead of three double crochet in the centre stitch, do 5 chain as a button-hole to fasten down the flap. Then work on as before till 29 ridges are done; and for the shoulders work 31 double crochet on each side forwards and backwards for 12 ridges. The border is worked all round the bib. **1st row**—1 double crochet on every ridge, and 3 chain between the double crochet. **2nd row**—1 double crochet on double crochet of last row, 4 chain, and repeat

Pretty Hat for Baby Boy.

Sew a white ribbon string on each shoulder-piece, and also one on each side of the bib to tie round the waist; sew a pearl button in position to fasten down the flap.

BABY'S BIB.

REQUIRED, 2 reels of Evans' crochet cotton, No. 10, and a steel crochet needle, No. 16. Commence with 56 chain. **1st row**—Miss two chain, work 26 consecutive treble, 4 treble in the next stitch, and 27 consecutive treble to finish the row. **2nd row**—2 chain to turn, and inserting the hook into the one back

Baby's Bib.

thread of the stitches of previous row so as to form ridges, work 27 consecutive treble, 4 treble in the next stitch, and 28 consecutive treble to finish the row **3rd row**—2 chain to turn, 28 consecutive treble, 4 treble in the next stitch, 29 consecutive treble to finish the row. **4th row**—2 chain to turn, 29 consecutive treble, 4 treble in the next, 30 consecutive treble to finish the row. Continue in this manner, increasing one stitch each side in every row, and always working 4 treble in the centre of the rows, till twenty-two rows are done, when there should be 99 treble stitches in the row. Turn, and **For the Armholes** work 10 treble, turn, and work 10 treble forwards and backwards for 10 rows, and fasten off. Recommence again upon the twenty-second row, missing twelve stitches from the half shoulder-piece just done, and work 10 treble, turn, and work these 10 treble forwards and backwards for 10 rows; do not break off the cotton, but slip along the side of this little strip, and work 17 treble on the next seventeen stitches of the twenty-second row, 4 treble in the next, and 28 treble on the next twenty-eight stitches, turn, and work 10 treble forwards and backwards till 10 rows are done; fasten off. Now work 10 treble forwards and backwards upon the last 10 stitches of the twenty-second row till 10 rows are done; fasten off. This completes the centre of the bib. **For the Border**—Commence at the bottom right-hand corner, 1 double crochet, * 3 chain, miss two stitches of the foundation, 1 double crochet in the next, and repeat from * all round the bib to the corner again, going up and down the shoulder-pieces. **2nd row**—1 double crochet in the first loop of three chain of last row, 2 treble, 3 chain, 2 treble, all in the next loop of three chain, and repeat all round the bib. Sew a button on each of the two back shoulder-straps, catch them into the crochet edge on the opposite shoulder-strap, and tie over the button with a pretty ribbon bow.

SEE-SAW CAP.

MATERIALS required, 3½ ozs. of white or coloured single Berlin wool, and a bone crochet needle, No. 11. Begin with 4 chain for the bag-like end that hangs over the brim, join round, and work 6 double crochet in the circle, work a round of 6 double crochet, inserting the hook so as to take up both top threads of previous round, in the 3rd round increase three stitches, work 2 plain rounds, in the next round again increase 3 stitches, work one plain round, and continue thus till you have 78 stitches in the round. Then keep working plain double crochet round and round till you have done seven inches from the commencement. In working the last round make 20 chain at the end, and break off the wool. Again make 20 chain, work a double crochet on the next double crochet consecutive to that last worked on, continue double crochet all round the bag-end and also along the 20 chain stitches, and break off the wool. Now work in rows from end to end, 118 stitches in the first row ; the part that juts out upon the chain stitches is for the head-band underneath the brim. The centre of the work is the top of the cap, mark it with a bit of coloured cotton and here double-crochet 2 stitches together in every 3rd row till you have reduced to 108 stitches, then decrease every row (always in the centre of the work) to 66 stitches. Sew the 14 end stitches together, and work round and round on the centre of the cap decreasing 3 stitches in every 3rd round, till brought to a point of 6 stitches, and fasten off. Sew the chain stitches together. Now for the turn-over brim, hold the wrong side of the cap towards you, and commencing at the back, where 14 double crochet stitches are seamed together, work 2 rounds of plain double crochet, always now taking up the one top thread of the stitches of last round. Mark the front and the quarters, * leave the wool with which you are working at the back for the

See-Saw Cap.

present, and with another ball of wool work double crochet across the front from quarter to quarter and break off. Continue now from the back and work 2 rounds. Repeat from * three times, each time beginning and ending the odd row 4 stitches nearer to the front, this will cause the front of the brim to stand higher than the back in the manner shown in the illustration. Finish by working double crochet round and round, till you have 32 rounds in front and 28 at the back. Turn 8 or 9 rounds in at the top. Arrange the ends to fall as illustrated, and finish off with tassels.

CROCHET SPILL CASE.

THESE are pretty novelties to work for bazaars or presents. Required a ree of Evans' brown Maltese crochet thread No. 2, a steel crochet needle No. 16, and ½ yard of inch-wide ribbon. Commence with 4 chain ; work 2 consecutive double crochet, 3 double crochet in the last of the chain, 2 double crochet on the opposite side, and 3 double crochet at the end, 10 double crochet in all, making a small square, and continue double crochet round and round, doing 3 double crochet in the centre stitch at each corner, till 12 rounds are completed. Then work double crochet straight on without any increase for 8 rounds. **1st round of the open pattern**—2 treble, 1 chain, 2 treble, all in one stitch of the double crochet, miss three double crochet, and repeat. **2nd round**—2 treble, 1 chain, 2 treble, all under the one chain stitch of last round, and repeat. Work two more rounds the same as the second round. **5th round, in which to run a ribbon**—1 double long treble (cotton three times round the needle), 2 chain, 1 double long treble, all under one chain stitch of last round, and repeat. **6th round**—2 treble, 1 chain, 2 treble, all under the loop of chain of last round. **7th round**—Same as the second round, and work two more rounds the same. **10th round**—5 treble under one chain of last round, 1 double crochet between the group of treble stitches, and repeat. Break off the cotton, and fasten the end neatly. **For the Handles**—Begin with 30 chain, work 6 rows of plain double crochet, fold lengthways, and sew together, and sew on the case. The Spill Case must now be stiffened. Make some thick starch, into which put a little glue, and let the work lie in it till thoroughly saturated and nearly cold, then draw the crochet into shape, blocking it with the hand or stretching it over a small box, and pulling each point of the crochet in place. Dissolve 1 oz. of shellac in spirits of wine (it takes at least a day to dissolve), do not have it too thin ; with this mix Brunswick black or brown Japan varnish, according to the colour you desire the Spill Case to be, and brush it over the crochet outside and inside carefully, not allowing a bit of white starch to be visible. After this dries, varnish it with clear spirit varnish. Run ribbon in through the double long treble stitches, covering the join with a pretty bow, and the Spill Case is finished.

SQUARE FOR BABY'S QUILT.

REQUIRED, three shades of pale pink or blue, and some white Berlin wool. With the white, make a circle of 5 chain. Into this work 4 treble 1 chain 4 times, making 16 treble in all, the chain to form the corners of square. Take the lightest shade of wool, and with it work in each corner 3 treble, 1 chain, 3 treble, then with the next work in one corner 3 treble, 2 chain, 3 treble, then 3 treble between the pale shade of previous row, and again 3 treble, 2 chain, 3 treble at the next corner ; repeat this all round. Now take the darkest wool, and with it make 6 treble in each corner, and 2 clumps of 3 treble on each side, repeating it

Crochet Spill Case.

all round, which completes the square. Be careful when joining the different colours to work the ends of the wool in neatly. This same pattern is also pretty for couvrepieds or sofa blankets, the colours being chosen with reference to the furniture, or a mixture of colours, white, blue, red, olive, and gold, looks very well if the squares are arranged diagonally. For a baby's quilt however, nothing is prettier than pale blue or pink.

GIPSY BONNET FOR A BABY.

THIS stylish little bonnet is crocheted with white single Berlin wool, of which 2 ozs. will be required, also 1½ ozs. of pale blue single Berlin for pompons, a No. 12 bone crochet needle, and 3 yards of inch-wide pale blue ribbon for trimming. Commence with 6 chain for the centre of the crown, join in a circle. **1st round**—Work rather loosely, 3 treble in the first of the chain, 2 treble in each of the two next stitches, in the next, and 2 treble in each of the two next, and join round. **2nd round**—5 treble on the centre stitch of each of the three trebles of last round, 2 treble on each of the other stitches, making 34

Gipsy Bonnet for a Baby.

Baby's Bootikins.

treble in the round, worked into the two top threads of the stitches of last round, and drawn up long and loosely; join. **3rd round**—5 treble on the centre stitches at bottom and top, and 1 treble on each of the other stitches; join round, and break off the wool. Now work in rows forwards and backwards. Still in trebles, beginning on the first stitch where you broke off the wool, work 1 treble loosely on every stitch to the top, work 5 treble in the centre stitch, and 1 treble on every stitch down the other side. **2nd row**—Long treble stitches, the wool being turned twice round the needle, work 1 long treble on every stitch of last row, and 3 on the centre stitch. **3rd row**—Double long treble with the wool three times round the needle. **4th, 5th, and 6th rows**—Ordinary treble, no increase. Now work a row of scallops all round the head-piece, doing 1 double crochet, 4 chain, 5 long treble in every alternate stitch. For the frill which goes all round the head-piece, and which forms the front and the curtain, begin with 12 chain, and work plain tricot for a length of nearly 1½ yards, this allows plenty for pleats over the face, at the corners, and at the centre of the back. Work a row of chain stitch with blue wool, as an edging on the side where the tricot stitches appear like a row of chain, or you can do this with a rug needle, like the chain stitch in appliqué work: on every third stitch of the tricot, one stitch from the blue edge, work a cross-stitch with blue wool. Run a piece of blue ribbon on this tricot strip, join the ends together, and sew the strip to the head-piece, the join coming at the back. Run a piece of ribbon in the row of double long treble stitches, 1 stitch above the ribbon, and 3 stitches underneath. Make a ribbon bow for the front, and also one for the back of the bonnet, and further ornament the front with 6 small blue pompons, made by winding blue wool over circles of cardboard, tying tightly together in the centre, and clipping into shape. Put in strings, and a bit of white sarscenet for head-lining.

BABY'S BOOTIKINS.

FOR these pretty bootikins which come nicely up the leg and are very warm and comfortable, 2 ozs. of white and 1 oz. of scarlet single Berlin wool, a No. 11 crochet needle, four knitting pins No. 16, and 16 white pearl buttons are required. Commence with white wool, making 32 chain for the top of the leg, and join round. Work a round of 32 treble stitches. Then 10 rounds of double crochet, 32 stitches in a round, inserting the hook so as to take up the top thread and the thread at the back of that which makes a strong stitch. In the next round of double crochet decrease at the centre of the back by working one stitch over two, then a plain round, and next round decrease again in same manner. Work 5 double crochet rounds, 30 stitches in the round. Now work 3 rows of double crochet upon the 18 front stitches for the instep; you must break off at the end of each of the instep rows, and re-commence at the right-hand side to keep the right side of the work uppermost, leave the 12 back stitches till the instep is finished. * Decrease a stitch at the beginning and at the end of the 4th row of the instep, then 2 rows plain, and repeat from * till you have only 10 stitches left. From the last instep row work round and round for the foot, 14 being picked up on each side the instep rows, making 50 double crochet in the round, work 4 rounds plain, then 3 rounds decreasing at the toe on each side the eight centre stitches, and crochet the sole together on the wrong side. The top of the leg is knitting, with scarlet wool, pick up 56 stitches with three pins on the commencing chain, knitting each stitch as you pick it up, and knit a round, purl 2 rounds, knit a round, purl a round, knit a round. **7th round**—Make 1, knit 2 together, and repeat all round. **8th round**—Plain. **9th round**—Knit 1, * make 1, knit 2 together, and repeat from *, ending the round with knit 1. **10th round**—Plain. Repeat the last 4 rounds and cast off. Now with scarlet wool work a crochet scallop at the top, 1 double crochet, 2 treble, 1 double crochet, all into the same stitch of the knitting, miss three stitches of the knitting, and repeat. With a piece of scarlet wool threaded in a rug needle work a straight line of chain stitch (like embroidery chain stitch) down the front of the boot from the knitting to the toe. At distance of two stitches of the crochet away from this line work a row of double crochet stitches on the boot with scarlet wool. Sew four pearl buttons down each side between the chain and the double crochet.

GLOVES FOR BOY OF TEN.

PROCURE 1 oz. of cardinal and ½ oz. of fawn-coloured Scotch fingering and a bone crochet needle No. 11. Begin for the wrist of the left-hand glove. With fawn colour make 40 chain, join round, and work 2 rounds of single crochet,

taking the top thread only; then 2 rounds with cardinal; and repeat the two colours, doing 2 rounds with each till 9 stripes are done. The fawn colour is now finished with, and the remainder of the glove is worked with cardinal. Work 1 round the same as before, the next and following rounds are done in shepherd's stitch—that is, single crochet inserting the hook in the front thread of the stitches of previous round. With a thread of white cotton mark the first stitch in the round and work 4 rounds of shepherd's stitch, after the fourth stitch in the 5th round increase 1 by making a chain, and repeat this every other round till you have 45 stitches. Now for the **Thumb**, work 10 single crochet, 4 chain, and join round, and work 13 rounds, after which take 2 stitches together till you have only 4 left, pull these together and fasten off. Continue the hand part, working all round and four stitches over the thumb, for 8 rounds. For the **First Finger**, crochet 8 stitches over the thumb, make 2 chain, and crochet 4 stitches from the inside of the hand, work 14 rounds, and decrease and finish off the top the same as the thumb is finished. For the **Second Finger**, crochet 6 stitches on the back of the hand, make 2 chain, crochet 4 stitches on the inside of the hand and 2 stitches on the two chain belonging to the first finger, work 16 rounds, and finish the top. For the **Third Finger**, crochet 5 stitches on the back of the hand, make 2 chain, crochet 4 stitches on the inside and 2 stitches on the chain belonging to the second finger, work 13 rounds, and finish the top. For the **Little Finger**, crochet the remaining stitches and 2 stitches on the chain belonging to the third finger, work 11 rounds, and finish the top. You now strengthen the edge of the wrist by working a round of single crochet upon the foundation chain stitches. The right-hand glove is worked in the same manner as far as the increasing for the thumb, instead of making the chain stitch at the beginning of the 5th round make it four stitches from the end of the round, and when beginning the fingers be careful to take the stitches right from the inside and outside. Ornament the back of the hand with three rows of chain stitches.

CROCHET EDGING.

COMMENCE with 9 chain, join round by working 1 double crochet in the first stitch of the chain. **2nd row**—4 chain to turn, 12 long treble (cotton twice round the needle) in the loop formed by the commencing chain. **3rd row**—4 chain to turn, 1 treble and 1 chain alternately twelve times, the treble stitches being worked *between* the long trebles of last row. **4th row**—4 chain and 1 double crochet alternately twelve times, the double crochet being worked under the chain stitches of last row. **5th row**—6 chain and 1 double crochet into the second loop of four chain of last row. **6th row**—4 chain to turn, 12 long treble under the six chain of last row. **7th row**—Same as the third row, and at the end connect to the first scollop by a single crochet worked in the fifth loop of four chain. **8th row**—Same as the fourth row. Repeat from the fifth row for the length required. For the heading along the top of the scallops work a row of 1 treble, 2 chain.

BECTIVE CAP.

THIS cap is a variety of the now universally popular Tam O'Shanter, from which it varies only by having the increasings worked in straight line one above another, thus giving the crown the appearance of being worked in seven divisions. Procure 4½ ozs. of navy blue fingering wool, and a bone crochet needle, No. 12, and work rather closely, inserting hook in the one top thread of the stitches of previous round. Commence with 4 chain, and join round. **1st round**—Work 7 double crochet in the circle. **2nd round**—2 double crochet in every stitch of last round. **3rd round**—2 double crochet on the first stitch, 1 double crochet on the next stitch, and repeat. **4th round**—2 double crochet on the first stitch, 1 double crochet on each of the two next stitches, and repeat. **5th round**—2 double crochet on the first stitch, 1 double crochet on each of

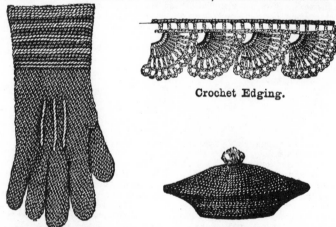

Crochet Edging.

Gloves for a Boy of Ten.   **Bective Cap.**

the three next stitches, and repeat. **6th round**—2 double crochet on the first stitch, 1 double crochet on each of the four next stitches. **7th round**—2 double crochet on the first stitch, 1 double crochet on each of the five next stitches. **8th round**—2 double crochet on the first stitch, 1 double crochet on each of the five next stitches. And continue thus, working one more plain stitch between the increasings in every round, till the crown measures 10 inches in diameter. Then work 4 rounds of double crochet without increasing. And for the next 11 rounds decrease 7 times in each round by missing a stitch, always keeping in straight line with the stitches where you before increased. This should now be the right size for the head. For the **Band**—Work 12 rounds of plain double crochet, inserting the hook so as to take up both top threads of the stitches of previous round; this band will curl over, and does not require lining. For the **Tuft**—Wind a good quantity of wool over a card about 3 inches wide, tie it firmly together, trimming it in a nice rosette shape, and sew on to the centre of the crown.

WELDONS
PRACTICAL CROCHET.

(FOURTH SERIES.)

How to Crochet 28 Useful Articles for Ladies, Gentlemen and Children.

THIRTY-EIGHT ILLUSTRATIONS.

₊ *The Sizes of Crochet Hooks mentioned in descriptions are regulated by Walker's Bell Gauge.*

Telegraphic Address—] "Consuelo," London.]

The Yearly Subscription to this Magazine, post free to any Part of the World, is 2s. 6d. Subscriptions are payable in advance, and may commence from any date and for any period.

[Telephone— 2745.

The Back Numbers are always in print. Nos. 1 to 84 now ready, Price 2d. each, or post free for 15s. Over 5,000 Engravings.

OUTDOOR PELISSE FOR A YOUNG CHILD.

FOR a walking pelisse for a child aged two or three years, nothing can surpass this in elegance and durability; it measures about 24 inches in length, and is a perfect fit, shaped to figure. Every stitch of the working is here given, so that not the slightest difficulty can be experienced. The pelisse is worked in plain tricot, the trimming is looped knitting in imitation of astrachan. 1¼ lbs. of best white single Berlin or best white peacock wool will be required, a long wooden tricot needle No. 8, and a pair of steel knitting needles No. 12. Commence with 213 chain for the bottom of the pelisse above the trimming, and work 4 rows of plain tricot. **5th row**—Raise 53 stitches, then raise 2 together, 22 stitches and then 2 together, 53 stitches and then 2 together, 22 stitches and then 2 together, and thence raise 54 stitches to the end, and draw back in the usual manner. Work 3 plain rows. **9th row**—Raise 52 stitches, then raise 2 together, 22 stitches and then 2 together, 51 stitches and then 2 together, 22 stitches and then 2 together, and thence raise 53 stitches to the end. Work 3 plain rows. **13th row**—Raise 51 stitches, then raise 2 together, 22 stitches and then 2 together, 49 stitches and then 2 together, 22 stitches and then 2 together, and thence raise 52 stitches to the end. Work 2 plain rows. **16th row**—Raise 50 stitches, then raise 2 together, 22 stitches and then 2 together, 47 stitches and then 2 together, 22 stitches and then 2 together, and thence raise 51 stitches to the end. Work 2 plain rows. **19th row**—Raise 49 stitches, then raise 2 together, 22 stitches and then 2 together, 45 stitches and then 2 together, 22 stitches and then 2 together, and thence raise 50 stitches to the end. Work 2 plain rows. **22nd row**—Raise 48 stitches, then raise 2 together, 22 stitches and then 2 together, 43 stitches and then 2 together, 22 stitches and then 2 together, and thence raise 49 stitches to the end. Work 2 plain rows. **25th row**—Raise 47 stitches, then raise 2 together, 22 stitches and then 2 together, 41 stitches and then 2 together, 22 stitches and then 2 together, and thence raise 48 stitches to the end. Work 2 plain rows. **28th row**—Raise 46 stitches, then raise 2 together, 22 stitches and then 2 together, 39 stitches and then 2 together, 22 stitches and then 2 together, and thence raise 47 stitches to the end. Work 1 plain row. **30th row**—Raise 45 stitches, then raise 2 together, 22 stitches and then 2 together, 37 stitches and then 2 together, 22 stitches and then 2 together, and thence raise 46 stitches to the end. Work 1 plain row. **32nd row**—Raise 44 stitches, then raise 2 together, 22 stitches and then 2 together, 35 stitches and then 2 together, 22 stitches and then 2 together, and thence raise 45 stitches to the end. Work 1 plain row. Continue working in this manner, working one stitch less on each front and two stitches less across the back, keeping 22 stitches for each sidepiece, and doing one plain row between each row of decreasings, until you have completed 54 rows from the commencement, when there should be 34 stitches on each front, 13 stitches across the back, and 22 stitches on each sidepiece, which with the 4 seam stitches will make 129 stitches altogether. Work 5 plain rows. **60th row**—Raise 57 stitches, increase 1 by raising a stitch in the chain before the next perpendicular thread, raise 13 stitches, increase 1 again, and thence raise 58 stitches to the end. Work 2 plain rows. **Now for the First Front— 1st row**—Raise 33 stitches (which with the stitch on the needle makes 34 in all), and work back. **2nd row**—Raise 32 stitches, take up the last 2 together, and work back. **3rd row**—Raise 31 stitches, take up the last 2 together, and work back. Work 13 plain rows. Work 4 plain rows, increasing 1 stitch at the end of each row by raising a stitch in the chain before the last perpendicular thread. **21st row**—Raise 34 stitches, and work back. **22nd row**—Raise 31 stitches, then raise 3 together at the end, and work back. **23rd row**—Raise 30 stitches, then 2 together at the end, and work back. **24th**

row—Raise 28 stitches, then 3 together at the end, and work back. **25th row**—Raise 27 stitches, then 2 together at the end, and work back. **26th row**—Raise 26 stitches, then 2 together at the end, and work back. **27th row**—Cast off 8, then raise 2 together, raise 15, raise 2 together at the end, and work back. **28th row**—Cast off 1, raise 2 together, raise 12, then 3 together at the end, and work back. **29th row**—Cast off 1, raise 2 together, raise 8, then 2 together at the end, and work back. **30th row**—Cast off 1, raise 2 together, raise 5, then 2 together at the end, and work back. **31st row**—Cast off 1, raise 2 together, raise 2, then 2 together at the end, and work back. **32nd row**—Cast off 1, raise 1 stitch, raise 2 together, and work back. **33rd row**—Raise 2 stitches together, and finish off. **For the other Front—1st row**—Raise 34 stitches (counting them from the *end* of the row), and work back, drawing through the last 2 together. **2nd row**—Raise 32 stitches, and work back, drawing through the last 2 together. Work 14 plain rows. Work 4 plain rows, increasing 1 stitch at the beginning of each row by raising a stitch in the chain in front of the first perpendicular thread, and work back. **21st row**—Cast off 2 stitches, raise 33, and work back drawing through the last 2 together. **22nd row**—Raise 32 stitches, and work back drawing through the last 2 together. **23rd row**—Raise 31 stitches, and work back drawing through the last 2 together. **24th row**—Cast off 1, raise 29, and work back drawing through the last 2 together. **25th row**—Raise 28 stitches, and work back drawing through the last 2 together. **26th row**—Cast off 1, raise 26, and work back drawing through the last 2 together. **27th row**—Raise 17 stitches (leaving 8 unraised), and work back drawing through 2 together at the beginning, and 2 together at the end. **28th row**—Cast off 1, raise 13, raise 2 together, and work back drawing through 2 together at the beginning, and 2 together at the end. **29th row**—Raise 11 stitches, raise 2 together, and work back drawing through 2 together at the beginning, and 2 together at the end. **30th row**—Cast off 1, raise 3 together, and work back drawing through 2 together at the beginning, and 2 together at the end. **31st row**—Raise 5 stitches, raise 2 together, and work back drawing through 2 together at the beginning, and 2 together at the end. **32nd row**—Cast off 1, raise 2, raise 2 together, draw back through 2 together, and through 2 together, and finish with a row of slip stitches to shape round the neck. **For the Back—1st row**—Leave one perpendicular loop under the armhole, raise 23 stitches, increase 1, raise 15 stitches, increase 1, raise 23 stitches, and work back drawing through the last 2 together. **2nd row**—Raise 59 stitches, raise the last 2 together, and work back drawing through the last 2 together. **3rd row**—Raise 57 stitches, raise the last 2 together, and work back drawing through the last 2 together. **4th row**—Raise 19 stitches, increase 1, raise 17, increase 1, raise 19, raise the last 2 together, and work back drawing through the last 2 together. **5th row**—Raise 55 stitches, raise the last 2 together, and work back drawing through the last 2 together. **6th row**—Raise 17 stitches, increase 1, raise 19, increase 1, raise 17, raise the last 2 together, and work back drawing through the last 2 together. **7th row**—Raise 53 stitches, raise the last 2 together, and work back drawing through the last 2 together. **8th row**—Raise 15 stitches, increase 1, raise 21, increase 1, raise 15, raise the last 2 together, and work back; and *not* draw through 2 together at the end. Work 1 plain row. **10th row**—Raise 15 stitches, increase 1, raise 23, increase 1, raise 15, and work back. Work 1 plain row. **12th row**—Raise 15 stitches, increase 1, raise 25, increase 1, raise 16, and work back. Work 1 plain row. **14th row**—Raise 15 stitches, increase 1, raise 27, increase 1, raise 16, and work back. Work 2 plain rows. Work 3 rows, increasing 1 stitch at the beginning, and 1 stitch at the end of each row. **20th row**—Cast off 2, raise 61, raise 3 together at the end, and work back drawing through the last 2 together. **21st row**—Raise 59 stitches, raise the last 2 together, and work back drawing through the last 3 together. **22nd row**—Raise 55 stitches, raise the last 2 together, and work back drawing through the last 2 together. **23rd row**—Raise 54 s itches, raise the last 2 together, and work back drawing through the last 2 together. **24th row**, raise the last 3 together, and work back drawing through the last 2 together. **25th row**—Raise 49 stitches, raise the last 2 together, and work back drawing through the last 3 together. **26th row**—Raise 45 stitches, raise the last 3 together, and work back drawing through the last 2 together. **27th row**—Raise 43 stitches, raise the last 2 together, and work back drawing through the last 2 together. **23th row**—Raise 41 stitches, raise the last 2 together, and work back drawing through the last 2 together. **29th row**—Raise 12 stitches, raise 2 together, and work back drawing through the last 2 together, this little piece is to heighten the shoulder. **30th row**—Raise 9 stitches, raise 3 together, and work back drawing through the last 3 together. **31st row**—Raise 5 stitches, raise 3 together, and work back drawing through the last 2 together. **32nd row**—Raise 2 stitches, raise 3 together, and work back drawing through 2 together and through 2 together; work a few slip stitches down the slope of the neck till you come within 15 stitches of the opposite shoulder, then raise 12 stitches, raise the last 3 together, and work back drawing through the last 2 together. **2nd little row**—Raise 9 stitches, raise 2 together, and work back drawing through the last 3 together. **3rd row**—Raise 5 stitches, raise 3 together, and work back drawing through the last 3 together. **4th row**—Raise 2 stitches, raise 2 together, and work back drawing through 2 together and 2 together, and fasten off. Sew up the sides and shoulders of the pelisse. **For the Sleeves**—Begin with 54 chain, and break off. **1st row**—Miss 20 chain, commence on the twenty-first and raise 14 stitches, work back ; slip the wool stitch by stitch backwards a'ong 4 of the commencing chain. **2nd row**—Raise 3 stitches in the 4 you have just slipped (which with the 1 on the needle makes 4 in all), raise 14 stitches above the fourteen of last row and 4 stitches in the chain on the opposite side, and work back ; slip the wool along 4 more of the foundation chain. **3rd row**—Raise 3 stitches in the chain, raise 22 stitches above the 22 of last row, raise 4 in the chain on the opposite side, and work back ; slip the wool along 4 more of the foundation chain. **4th row**—Raise 3 stitches in the chain, raise 30 stitches above the 30 of last row, raise 4 in the chain on the opposite side, and work back ; slip the wool along 4 more of the foundation chain. **5th row**—Raise 3 stitches in the chain, raise 38 stitches, raise 4 in the chain on the opposite side, and work back ; slip the wool along 4 more of the foundation chain. **6th row**—Raise 3 stitches in the chain, raise 46 stitches, raise 4 in the chain on the opposite side, 54 stitches in all, and work back. *Work 4 plain rows. In drawing back in the fourth row stop 6 stitches from the end, raise again to within 6 stitches of the other end, and draw back through all. Repeat from * 3 times more. Work 1 plain row. **24th row**—Raise 23 stitches, raise 2 together, raise 2 stitches, raise 2 together, raise 24 stitches, and work back. **25th row**—Plain, and in drawing back stop 6 stitches from the end, raise again to within 6 stitches of the other end, and draw back through all. **26th row**—Raise 22 stitches, raise 2 together, raise 2 stitches, raise 2 together, raise 23, and work back. Work 1 plain row. **28th row**—Raise 21 stitches, raise 2 together, raise 2, raise 2 together, raise 22, and in drawing back stop 6 stitches from the end, raise again to within 6 stitches of the other end, and draw back through all. Work 1 plain row. **30th row**—Raise 20 stitches, raise 2 together, raise 2, raise 2 together, raise 21, and work back. **31st row**—Plain, and in drawing back stop 6 stitches from the other end, raise again to within 6 stitches of the other end, and draw back through all. **32nd row**—Raise 19 stitches, raise 2 together, raise 2, raise 2 together, raise 20, and work back. Work 1 plain row. **34th row**—Raise 18 stitches, raise 2 together, raise 2, raise 2 together, raise 19, and in drawing back stop 6 stitches from the end, raise again to within 6 stitches of the other end, and draw back through all. Work 1 plain row. **36th row**—Raise 17 stitches, raise 2 together, raise 2, raise 2 together, raise 18, and work back. **37th row**—Plain, and in drawing back stop 6 stitches from the end, raise again to within 6 stitches of the other end, and draw back through all. **38th row**—Raise 16 stitches, raise 2 together, raise 2, raise 2 together, raise 17, and work back. Work 1 plain row. Then work a row of crochet for edging, 1 double crochet in the first stitch of tricot, miss 1 stitch of tricot, 2 treble 1 long treble 2 treble all in the next, miss 1, and repeat, and fasten off. Make another sleeve similar to this one, sew them up, and sew them into the pelisse. **Now for the Border round the Bottom of the Pelisse**—With a No. 9 crochet needle work a chain of 215 stitches,

Outdoor Pelisse for a Young Child.

and do 4 rows of trebles, 213 trebles in a row, breaking off at the end of every row and keeping the work perfectly flat (you cannot see these four rows in the engraving ; they are underneath the astrachan trimming, and are worked thus for the sake of lightness). **5th row**—Tricot, beginning on the second stitch, raise 11 stitches on consecutive stitches of the treble, and work back, drawing through the first 2 together and the last 2 together. **6th row**—Raise 8 stitches, taking up the small horizontal thread that lies at the *back* of previous row, and work back, drawing through the first 2 together and the last 2 together. **7th row**—Raise 6 stitches in the same way, and draw back as before. **8th row**—Raise 4 stitches in the same way, and work back, drawing through the first 3 together and the last 2 together. Do 1 double crochet in the middle of the stitches just drawn together, then slip along in four loose stitches down the side of the scallop so that the last of the four goes into the treble stitch, work 1 single crochet on the next treble, 1 single crochet on the next; raise 10 stitches (there will be 11 with the one on the needle), and work a second scallop like the first. There should be 17 scallops in all round the bottom of the pelisse. **9th row**—Begin again on the right-hand side, work 1 double crochet on the first stitch of the trebles, * 4 double crochet up the side of the scallop, 3 double crochet on the point of the scallop, 4 double crochet down the opposite side of the scallop, and 1 double crochet between the two single stitches of last row, and repeat from *. **10th row**—Re-commence on the right-hand side, and insert the hook always into the top and back thread of the stitches of last row, 1 double crochet on the first stitch, * miss 1, 1 double crochet on the next, 3 chain, another double crochet in the same place, miss 1, 1 double crochet on the next, 3 chain, another double crochet in the same place, miss 1, 1 double crochet on the centre stitch of the three double crochet of last row, 3 chain, another double crochet in the same place, miss 1, 1 double crochet on the next, 3 chain, another double crochet in the same place, miss 1, 1 double crochet on the next, 3 chain, another double crochet in the same place, miss 1, 1 double crochet on the double crochet between the scallops, and repeat from *, and fasten off at the end of the row. **For the Trimming** — Take the knitting needles, and cast on 12 stitches for the astrachan trimming round the bottom of the pelisse. **1st row**—Plain. **2nd row**—Slip the first stitch, insert the needle in the next stitch, put the wool over the point of the needle and round the first finger of the left hand twice, then wool over the needle, and knit the stitch in the usual manner drawing all 3 threads of wool through, knit 9 more stitches in the same way, knit the last stitch plain. Repeat these two rows for the length required, and cast off. Sew the border of treble stitches upon the pelisse and place this astrachan trimming over the 4 rows of treble and just above the scallops. Knit the trimming for the fronts of the pelisse and for the sleeves in the same way, but cast on only 6 stitches. Sew hooks and eyes to fasten down the front of the pelisse.

CUFFS FOR A LADY.

REQUIRED, 1 oz. of violet and ½ oz. of black single Berlin wool. A bone crochet needle, No. 9, will be a good size for the cuff itself, as the stitch looks better, and is more elastic if not worked too closely, and No. 12 needle for the border. Commence with the largest needle and violet wool, with 37 chain, turn, and work all along in single crochet, that is, insert the hook in a stitch and draw the wool through and also through the stitch on the needle. Turn the work, and now insert the hook so as to take up the one top thread of the single crochet stitches of the previous row drawing the wool through as before ; turn the work, and again work single crochet, taking up the one back thread of the stitches of last row. Proceed in this manner, working one row on the top threads and the following row on the back threads till 19 rows are done. Fasten off, and sew up. The right side of the work is the side on which the ridges appear furthest apart, turn this side outside. Now for the **Frill round the Wrist**—With the fine crochet needle work first with violet wool round the margin of the commencing chain, 1 double crochet in the first stitch, * 5 chain, 1 double crochet in the third chain from the needle, 1 chain, miss two of the foundation, 1 double crochet in the next, and repeat from * to the end of the round, join to the first double crochet stitch and fasten off. Take the black wool and work a similar edge upon the ridge of single crochet just about half an inch from the margin. Then an edge with violet wool upon the ridge next above, and another edge with black wool upon the next ridge above. The colours used can of course be varied according to taste, as brown and gold, or red and fawn, and the result will be a pretty and useful pair of cuffs either for personal wear or for a present.

HOOD.

Required, 2 ozs. of white, and 1 oz. of pale blue single Berlin wool, and a bone crochet needle No. 8. With white wool make a chain of 68 stitches rather loosely for the front of the hood. **1st row**—1 treble in the third stitch from the needle and treble to the end, making 65 treble in all. **2nd row**—2 chain to turn, and work a treble on each stitch of previous row, inserting the hook in the small thread that lies below the top thread of every stitch, this is done that the two front threads of previous row may appear like a row of chain stitches on the right side of hood. **3rd row**—2 chain to turn, and work 65 treble, inserting the hood in the two top threads of last row. **4th row**—3 chain to turn, and work 65 long treble stitches (wool twice round the needle), taking up as described in the second row. **5th row**—Same as the third row. **6th**

Hood.

row—Same as the second row. **7th row**—Decrease on each side of the four centre stitches. And work 9 more rows in the same manner, decreasing in every row on each side the four centre stitches. Break off the wool, fold the work, and sew up the last row for the centre of the crown. The frill-like appearance is given by rows of double crochet worked with blue wool in zigzag across 2 rows of the treble. For the **Curtain**—Hold the hood the right side towards you, and beginning at the left corner of the front, work 64 treble along the neck of the hood. **2nd row**—2 chain to turn, 2 treble, increase (by working 2 treble in the same stitch), 29 treble, increase, 29 treble, increase, 2 treble. Work 6 more rows increasing in the same way. Then with blue wool work a scallop border all round the hood and curtain, 1 double crochet, miss 2, 6 treble on the next, miss 2, and repeat. Run a ribbon in the row of long treble stitches and tie in a bow at the top. Crochet a chain with blue wool to tie at the back of the crown and also under the chin, finish all 4 ends of this with tassels, and place a tassel at each corner of the curtain.

TRICOT STRIPE FOR ANTI-MACASSAR.

In Pattern of Raised Diamonds.

The quantity of wool required will of course depend upon the size the antimacassar is to be, 12 ozs. of white and 2 ozs. of blue single Berlin will make one sufficiently large for a sofa or small easy-chair; procure also a bone tricot needle No. 9, and two shades of blue filoselle for filling in the diamonds. With white wool make 26 chain, and work 2 rows of plain tricot. **3rd row**—Pick up the stitches as usual, and coming back draw through 13, make 4 chain, draw through 13. **4th row**—Pick up the stitches, and coming back draw through 12, 4 chain, through 2, 4 chain, through 12. **5th row**—Pick up the stitches, and draw back through 11, 4 chain, through 2, 4 chain, through 2, 4 chain, through 11. **6th row**—Pick up the stitches, and draw back through 10, 4 chain, through 2, 4 chain, through 2, 4 chain, through 2, 4 chain, through 10. **7th row**—Pick up the stitches, and draw back through 9, 4 chain, through 2, 4 chain, through 2, 4 chain, through 2, 4 chain, through 9. **8th row**—Pick up the stitches, and draw back through 8, 4 chain, through 2, 4 chain, through 6, 4 chain, through 2, 4 chain, through 8. Continue thus increasing the width of the raised diamonds till you have to draw through only 3 stitches at the beginning and 3 stitches at the end, when you will count 11 rows of raised tufts; now decrease the diamond till you bring it again to a single tuft. Repeat from the third row for the length required. With two shades of filoselle work a cross-stitch star to fill the centre of the diamonds. For the Edge—With blue wool—Holding the tricot the right side towards you work a row of double crochet along the side of the strip, turn, and work double crochet back. **3rd**

row—1 double crochet on the first stitch of previous row, 1 treble inserting the hook down in the tricot in the place where a double crochet stitch is worked into, another treble in the same place, a double crochet on stitch of last row, 2 treble in the tricot, and repeat. Work a similar edge along the other side of the strip. Make as many more stripes as required, and join them together. Finish off the top and bottom of the antimacassar thus, with blue wool, 1 double crochet, * 5 chain, 1 treble on the top part of the double crochet just done, miss three tricot stitches, 1 double crochet in the next, and repeat from *. Fringe with white wool, 2 strands knotted in every loop of five chain, and again knotted together in itself.

THISTLE PATTERN.

This pattern is especially suitable for cotton crochet, for pincushion covers, insertion round quilts, or any purpose for which a close ground is required. Commence with a chain the necessary length. **1st row**—12 consecutive double crochet, * 10 chain, 1 double crochet in the same place last double crochet is worked into, 10 chain and a double crochet twice more in the same place, 12 double crochet, and repeat from * to the end of the foundation. **2nd row**—Plain double crochet working into the one top thread of the stitches of preceding row, and do one stitch only at the back of the thistle, holding down the loops of chain in the front of the work. **3rd row**—Plain double crochet. **4th row**—8 double crochet,* 1 double crochet on the next catching in the first loop of ten chain, 5 double crochet, 1 double crochet on the next catching in the third loop of ten chain, 5 double crochet, and repeat from *. **5th row**—Double crochet. **6th row**—11 double crochet, 6 treble on the next, catching down the middle loop of ten chain, and repeat. **7th row**—6 double crochet, * 10 chain, 1 double crochet in the same place last double crochet is worked into, 10 chain and a double crochet twice more in the same place, 12 double crochet, and repeat from *. **8th row**—Plain double crochet, same as the second row. **9th row**—Double crochet. **10th row**—2 double crochet, * 1 double crochet on the next catching in the first loop of ten chain, 5 double crochet, 1 double crochet on the next catching in the third loop of ten chain, 5 double crochet, and repeat from *. **11th row**—Double crochet. **12th row**—5 double crochet, * 6 treble on the next catching down the middle loop of ten chain, 11 double crochet, and repeat from *. Repeat from the first row for the length required.

SLEEVE HOLDER.

Ever since fashion demanded tight sleeves for wraps as well as for dresses, the feminine mind has been in a perturbed state regarding the donning of garments. An under-sleeve lodged half way to the elbow is a source of great annoyance, and anything to prevent this inconvenience is exceedingly welcome, especially if it be so simple a contrivance as a crocheted cord to each end of which a ring is attached. One ring is slipped on the first finger and the cord brought down and wound tightly around the sleeve near the wrist, leaving enough of the cord to allow the other ring to slip over the thumb, and the sleeve is drawn on without any difficulty and the holder removed. To make the cord, use worsted or zephyr of any colour you desire, olive, blue, pink, or brown are suitable, work 5 chain stitches, join them and make one single crochet in the back of each loop of the foundation; work on with single crochet in continuous rounds until your strip is 27 inches long. Fasten to each end a ring worked around with single crochet.

Tricot Stripe for Antimacassar. In Pattern of Raised Diamonds.

BEAN STITCH.

Make a loose chain for the foundation; in the third loop draw the thread through with an Afghan needle, as if to make a single crochet, put the thread over the needle, draw the thread through the

Thistle Pattern.

loop again; you have now 4 stitches, 1 remaining from foundation and the 3 made in this first loop. Leave them all on your needle and repeat the 3 stitches in each loop of the foundation chain until you reach the end and work a single crochet in the last foundation stitch. **2nd row**—Work back as in Afghan stitch, only draw the thread each time through the 3 stitches made in each foundation stitch. **3rd row**—Make 1 single crochet and between first and second group of stitches in the first row, work similar groups of three and continue to end of this row. The following rows are worked as described for second and third rows

BABY'S JACKET IN RUSSIAN CROCHET.

This very pretty and comfortable little jacket is worked with white Andalusian wool, of which 4 ozs. will be required, and a bone crochet needle No. 12. Commence with 61 chain. **1st row**—Work 60 double crochet. **2nd, 3rd, and 4th rows**—The same, inserting the hook in the back thread of the stitches of preceding row, as the work is to form ridges. **5th row**—7 double crochet, a tuft, which is made by working 5 treble into the corresponding double crochet stitch of the next row below, and catch the last of the treble stitches into the first, double crochet to the end of the row, and work 2 double crochet in the last stitch to heighten for the neck. **6th row**—53 double crochet, 1 treble (worked into the second preceding row at the back of the tuft), 7 double crochet. **7th row**—5 double crochet, a tuft, 3 double crochet, a tuft, double crochet to the end of the row, and again work 2 double crochet in the last stitch. **8th row**—52 treble crochet, 1 treble, 3 double crochet, 1 treble, 5 double crochet. **9th**

Baby's Jacket in Russian Crochet.

row—3 double crochet, tuft, 3 double crochet, tuft, 3 double crochet, tuft, double crochet to the end of the row, and work 2 double crochet in the last stitch. **10th row**—51 double crochet, 1 treble, 3 double crochet, 1 treble, 3 double crochet, 1 treble, 3 double crochet. **11th row**—5 double crochet, tuft, 3 double crochet, tuft, double crochet to the end of the row, and work 2 double crochet in the last stitch. **12th row**—54 double crochet, 1 treble, 3 double crochet, 1 treble, 5 double crochet. **13th row**—7 double crochet, tuft, double crochet to the end of the row, and work 3 double crochet in the last stitch. **14th row**—58 double crochet, 1 treble, 7 double crochet. **15th row**—Plain double crochet, working 2 double crochet in the last stitch, 67 double crochet in all. **16th row**—67 double crochet. **17th row**—Plain double crochet, working 3 double crochet in the last stitch. **18th row**—69 double crochet. **19th row**—7 double crochet, tuft, double crochet to the end of the row, doing 2 double crochet in the last stitch. **20th row**—62 double crochet, 1 treble, 7 double crochet. **21st row**—5 double crochet, tuft, 3 double crochet, tuft, double crochet to the end of the row, doing 3 double crochet at the end. **22nd row**—62 double crochet, 1 treble, 3 double crochet, 1 treble, 5 double crochet. **23rd row**—3 double crochet, tuft, 3 double crochet, tuft, 3 double crochet, tuft, double crochet to the end of the row, doing 2 double crochet in the last stitch. **24th row**—61 double crochet, 1 treble, 3 double crochet, 1 treble, 3 double crochet, 1 treble, 3 double crochet. Now proceed with tufts at bottom of jacket, and decrease at the shoulder every other row till reduced to 66 double crochet. Next row work 40 stitches, leave the remaining 26 stitches for the armhole, and turn, and work back. Work 15 stitches and back. Work 15 stitches and back. Work 40 stitches, then do 26 chain to compensate for the 26 unworked stitches, and work back. Now increase every other row at the shoulder till 73 double crochet. Decrease every other row to 70 double crochet. Then do 10 rows on the 70 stitches, and this forms one-half the jacket: work the other half to correspond. **For the Sleeves**—Commence with 50 chain. Work ridged double crochet forwards and backwards, increasing 1 stitch at the end of every other row for 20 rows, then work 18 rows without increase or decrease, and afterwards decrease at the end of every other row till reduced to 50 stitches again. Sew up the sleeve, and round the edge work a scallop, 1 double crochet on a ridge of the sleeve, 5 treble on the next ridge, and repeat : turn this up about an inch to form a cuff. Work the other sleeve the same. Sew up the shoulders and sew in the sleeves. The little tufts are tiny bits of wool sewn on with a needle and cotton. Place strings of narrow ribbon to tie the jacket.

Mr. HAYWARD, of 10 and 12, Arcade, Briggate, Leeds, has introduced an excellent quality vest yarn in such lovely shades as shell-pink, pale blue, delicate fawn, and white, which is much to be recommended for either knitted or crochet vests, as well as other garments which require repeated washing. It is beautifully soft, makes up evenly, wears well, and is in every way an excellent and inexpensive wool for general use. It costs 4s. 11d. the lb. in any of the above shades.

BABY'S BIB.

REQUIRED, Evans's crochet cotton No. 14, steel crochet hook No. 16. Begin for the **Neck** with 166 chain, and on both sides of this chain work 165 double crochet stitches; break off the cotton. **For the Front**—Hold the work the wrong side of the double crochet towards you, and work into the back thread of the stitches, so as to form ridges; leave the first 58 stitches, and, beginning or the 59th stitch, work 4 consecutive double crochet, 6 treble in the next, and catch the last of the treble stitches into the first to form a "tuft," 3 double crochet, another tuft, 15 consecutive double crochet, 3 double crochet in the next, which is the centre stitch, 15 consecutive double crochet, a tuft, 3 double crochet, a tuft, 4 double crochet, and leaving 58 stitches unworked, turn. **2nd row**—Miss the first double crochet of last row, and work 49 double crochet straight along, taking up the back thread of previous row. **3rd row**—Miss the first double crochet, work 24 consecutive double crochet, 3 double crochet in the centre stitch, 24 consecutive double crochet. **4th row**—Same as the second row, 49 double crochet. Repeat these four rows four times, keeping 49 stitches in a row. **21st row**—Not miss the first stitch, work 4 double crochet, a tuft, 3 double crochet, a tuft, 16 double crochet, 3 double crochet in the centre stitch, 16 double crochet, a tuft, 3 double crochet, a tuft, 4 double crochet. **22nd row**—Miss the first stitch, and work 51 double crochet. **23rd row**—Not miss the first stitch, work 25 double crochet, 3 double crochet in the centre stitch, 25 double crochet. **24th row**—Miss the first stitch, and work 53 double crochet. Now continue the four pattern rows, but not missing any more stitches at the beginning or end of the rows, so you will increase 2 stitches in every row, and in the 40th row you will work 85 double crochet. **41st row**—4 double crochet, a tuft, * 3 double crochet, a tuft, repeat from * eight times, 1 double crochet in the centre stitch, 1 double crochet, a tuft, * 3 double crochet, a tuft, repeat from * eight times, 4 double crochet. **42nd row**—Plain double crochet (87). **43rd row**—43 double crochet, 3 double crochet in the centre stitch, 43 double crochet. **44th row**—Plain double crochet (89). **45th row**—4 double crochet, a tuft, * 3 double crochet, a tuft, repeat from * eight times, 3 double crochet, 3 double crochet in the centre stitch, 3 double crochet, a tuft, * 3 double crochet, a tuft, repeat from * 8 times, 4 double crochet. **46th row**—Plain double crochet (91). **47th row**—45 double crochet, 3 double crochet in the centre stitch, 45 double crochet. **48th row**—Plain double crochet (93). **For the Border**—**1st row**—1 treble on a double crochet stitch of last row, * 1 chain, miss 1 stitch of the work, 1 treble in the next, and repeat from * all round the bib, and round both sides of the commencing rows of the neck; fasten off the cotton. **2nd row**—Begin with 1 double crochet at the extreme right hand of the neck band, 13 chain, miss 2 spaces of last row, 1 double crochet in the third, and continue round the bib and along the opposite side of the neck band, but not on the top of the neck. **3rd row**—1 double crochet over double crochet of last row, 13 chain, and repeat. **4th row**—The same. **5th row**—1 double crochet taking up the centre of all chains of last 3 rows, 7 chain, 1 double crochet taking up the centre of all next chains, and repeat. **6th row**—1 double crochet over double crochet of last row, 7 chain, and repeat. **7th row**—The same. **8th row**—1 double crochet over 2 last rows by inserting the hook in the double crochet of the fifth row, 13 chain, and repeat. **9th row**—1 double crochet over double crochet of last row, 13 chain, and repeat. **10th row**—The same. **11th row**—1 double crochet taking up the

Baby's Bib.

centre of all chains of last 3 rows, 7 chain, 1 double crochet taking up the centre of all next chains, and repeat. **12th row**—1 treble at the right-hand corner of the neck band, 1 chain, 1 treble 6 times along the beginning of the last 9 rows, 1 chain, miss 1, 1 treble all along the side of the neck band, round the bib, and along the opposite side of the neck band, 1 chain 1 treble 6 times along the ending of the 9 chain rows, and fasten off at the left-hand corner of the neck band. **13th row**—1 double crochet under first space of last row, * 1 double crochet, 4 treble, 1 double crochet, all under next space of last row, and repeat from * entirely round the bib and neck.

LADY'S BODICE IN RUSSIAN CROCHET.

THIS is intended to wear as a winter bodice under the dress. 8 ozs. of white Scotch fingering will be required, a No. 11 bone crochet needle, and nine white bone buttons. Commence with a chain of 96 stitches, and on this work double crochet forwards and backwards for 6 rows, inserting the hook so as to take up the back thread of each preceding row, as the work is to set in ridges. In the next row work only 18 double crochet, and turn, and double crochet back. This short row is to supply the necessary fulness round the hips, and though for the sake of brevity it is not again alluded to in the directions, it is to be worked after *every sixth* row. Work 10 full length rows. Then decrease 1 stitch at the shoulder end every other row till 38 rows in all are done. Now leave 30 stitches unworked at the shoulder end, and work on the other stitches for 6 rows. At the end of the next row make 30 chain to compensate for the thirty unworked

Lady's Bodice in Russian Crochet.

stitches, and afterwards increase at this end 1 stitch every other row till you work 95 double crochet. Then decrease 1 stitch every row at the same end till brought to 80 stitches. In the next row make buttonholes thus, 8 double crochet, * 3 chain, 6 double crochet, and repeat from * seven times; then a row of double crochet all along as before, and fasten off. Work the other half of the bodice the same, and sew up the shoulders and back. **For the Neck-band** —Work 6 rows of double crochet along the top of the bodice, doing 60 double crochet in a row; in the third row of this, on the button-hole side, make another buttonhole. **For the Sleeves**—Begin with 16 chain, and work in ridged double crochet, increasing 1 stitch at the end of every other row to 25 stitches, on these work 25 rows without either increase or decrease, and then decrease on the same side one stitch at the end of every other row to 15 stitches; fasten off, and join the last row to the commencing chain. Work the other sleeve in the same way. Sew the sleeves in the armholes. **For the Border** round the Bodice and Sleeves—Work first a row of double crochet, and then this scallop, * 2 treble, 1 chain, 2 treble, all into one stitch of previous row, miss 1, 1 double crochet in the next, miss 1, and repeat from *. Sew the buttons down the other side of the front opposite the buttonholes.

CHILD'S JACKET WORKED IN CRAZY STITCH.

REQUIRED, 2 ozs. of white, 1 oz. of pink Shetland wool, and a bone crochet needle, No. 11. With white wool, commence with 50 chain, work 2 treble in the third chain from the needle, * miss one chain, 2 treble in the next, 1 treble in the next, and repeat from *, making 48 treble stitches in the row. The jacket is worked throughout in picots of crazy stitch, that is, each picot is composed of 1 double crochet, 3 chain, and 2 treble, *all* worked into the same stitch of previous row; turn at the end of every row, beginning the next row with 3 chain and ending with a double crochet into the three chain. To increase, work two picots into the same place. **2nd row**—Work a picot upon every alternate treble stitch, 24 picots in all. **3rd row**—Again work 24 picots. **4th row**— 1 picot, increase, 22 picots, increase, 1 picot. **5th row**—26 picots. **6th row**—13 picots, increase, 13 picots. **7th row**—and every alternate row—to be worked in crazy picots all along, no increase. **8th row**—7 picots, increase, 13 picots, increase, 7 picots. **10th row**—7 picots, increase, 15 picots, increase, 7 picots. **12th row**—7 picots, increase, 7 picots, increase, 7 picots, increase, 7 picots. **14th row**—7 picots, increase, 10 picots, increase, 10 picots, increase, 7 picots. **16th row**—7 picots, increase, 12 picots, increase, 11 picots, increase, 7 picots. **18th row**—7 picots, increase, 6 picots, increase, 7 picots, increase, 7 picots, increase, 6 picots, increase, 7 picots. **20th row**—7 picots, increase, 8 picots, increase, 8 picots, increase, 7 picots, increase, 8 picots, increase, 7

picots. **22nd row**—7 picots, increase, 10 picots, increase, 8 picots, increase, 8 picots, increase, 10 picots, increase, 7 picots. **24th row**—7 picots, increase, 12 picots, increase, 9 picots, increase, 8 picots, increase, 12 picots, increase, 7 picots. **26th row**—7 picots, increase, 14 picots, increase, 9 picots, increase, 9 picots, increase, 14 picots, increase, 7 picots. **28th row**—9 picots, miss 14 picots for the armhole, 10 picots, increase, 9 picots, miss 14, 9 picots. Now work 13 more rows of the crazy stitch, increasing only in the centre of the back in every alternate row: continue the last of these rows all round the jacket. Then for a border, work with pink wool 4 rows of crazy stitch all round, and finish with one round of white, increasing a picot or two at the corners to keep the work flat. **For the Sleeves**—First work 3 rows of 2 or 3 picots under the arm in shape of a gusset, then work 10 rounds with 12 picots in a round; take the pink wool and work 4 rounds, and finish with 1 round of white. Crochet a chain with one strand of white and one strand of pink wool together, and having turned down the border round the neck to simulate a collar, run this chain in through the treble stitches and through the collar, make tassels at the ends, and the jacket will be finished.

LADY'S VEST.
POINT DE CHANTILLY.

THIS is a warm, comfortable vest worked in tricot, the stitch being a pretty variation of the ordinary tricot stitch. Procure 12 ozs. of white Peacock fingering, and a No. 8 bone tricot needle. Begin for the bottom of the vest with a chain of 99 stitches. **1st row**—Insert the hook in the second chain from the needle, raise a loop, and work a chain stitch in it, then raise a loop in the next stitch and work a chain in that, and so on to the end of the row, keeping all the chain stitches on the needle; to work back, draw the wool through the last stitch, and then through 2 stitches together, until all are worked off. **2nd row** —1 chain to begin, insert the hook in the first perpendicular loop and also in the thread at the back of it, raise a loop, and work a chain stitch in it, * insert the hook in the next perpendicular loop and also in the thread at the back of it, raise a loop, and work a chain stitch in it, repeat from *, keeping all the chain stitches on the needle, and work them off the same as before. Every succeeding row is worked the same as the second row. Decrease a stitch at the beginning and at the end of the seventh row. This is done by picking up 2 stitches together of the previous row. Repeat these 7 rows, decreasing again in the seventh row. Work 6 rows, and decrease again at the beginning and at the end

Lady's Vest. Point de Chantilly.

of the last of these. Repeat these 6 rows, again decreasing in the sixth row Then work 5 rows four times, decreasing in every fifth row. Then 4 rows three times, decreasing in every fourth row. Then work 4 rows. There are now 62 rows done, and it is time to begin the sleeves, which are worked all in the piece. **63rd row**—Increase a stitch at the beginning and a stitch at the end of the row. In the next and following rows increase 2 stitches on each side until there are 114 stitches in the row. Then work 9 rows on these 114 stitches. Now for the shoulder work 49 stitches only, and draw back. Do 9 rows decreasing in each row at the neck end. Then do 5 rows without further decrease, and fasten off. Leave 16 stitches in the middle for the neck. On the other side work 49 stitches to correspond for the other shoulder. This completes the front. Commence again with 99 chain, and work a similar piece for the back of the vest. Sew up the two sides and join the shoulder pieces together. Finish round the neck and sleeves with an edging; thus, 1 double crochet in one stitch of the tricot, 5 treble in the next.

PETTICOAT WITH BODICE FOR CHILD OF TWO.

PROCURE 4 ozs. of white and 2 ozs. of ruby Scotch fingering wool, and a long tricot needle No. 7. With white wool commence with 200 chain for the bottom of the petticoat. Pick up each stitch of the chain as in ordinary tricot, and draw back in the usual manner. Work another row with white wool. Then 2 rows with ruby and 2 rows with white. 7th row—With ruby. 8th row—Also with ruby, pick up 20 stitches (with the first stitch already on the needle, this makes 21 stitches on now), pick up 2 together, 21 stitches, 2 together, 12 stitches, 2 together, 21 stitches, 2 together, 34 stitches, 2 together, 21 stitches, 2 together, 12 stitches, 2 together, 21 stitches, 2 together, 21 stitches, and draw back as usual. Work 2 rows with white, 192 stitches in each row. Then 2 rows with ruby. 13th row—With white. 14th row—Also with white, pick up 19 stitches, 2 together, 20 stitches, 2 together, 12 stitches, 2 together, 20 stitches, 2 together, 32 stitches, 2 together, 20 stitches, 2 together, 12 stitches, 2 together, 20 stitches, 2 together, 20 stitches, and draw back. Work 2 rows with ruby. 17th row—With white. 18th row—Also with white, pick up 18 stitches, 2 together, 19 stitches, 2 together, 12 stitches, 2 together, 19 stitches, 2 together, 30 stitches, 2 together, 19 stitches, 2 together, 12 stitches, 2 together, 19 stitches, 2 together, 19 stitches, and draw back. Work 2 rows with ruby. 21st row—With white. 22nd row—Also with white, pick up 17 stitches, 2 together, 18 stitches, 2 together, 12 stitches, 2 together, 18 stitches, 2 together, 28 stitches, 2 together, 18 stitches, 2 together, 12 stitches, 2 together, 18 stitches, 2 together, 18 stitches, and draw back. Work 2 rows with ruby. The remainder of the petticoat is worked entirely with white. In the 26th row decrease 8 times in the row in a straight line above the previous decreasings, and at the end of the drawing back work 8 chain to make a "lap"

row—5 chain to turn, 2 treble under each chain stitch of last row, 1 treble on the last of the long treble stitches, 1 treble on each of the two next treble stitches, 2 treble under the 3 chain, 3 chain, 2 more treble in the same place. 4th row—5 chain to turn, 2 treble under the three chain of last row, 3 chain, 2 more treble in the same place, 1 double crochet on each stitch to the end of the row, making 21 double crochet in all. 5th row—1 chain to turn, double crochet on every double crochet of last row and on two treble stitches, inserting the hook so as to take up the back threads of last row, 2 treble under the three chain, 3 chain, 2 more treble in the same place. 6th row—5 chain to turn, 2 treble under the three chain of last row, 3 chain, 2 more treble in the same place, 3 chain, miss one stitch, 1 double crochet on the next, 5 chain and 1 double crochet on each alternate stitch to the end of the row. 7th row—6 chain to turn, 1 double crochet under first loop of five chain of last row, 5 chain, 1 double crochet under next loop of five chain, and continue 5 chain 1 double crochet under every loop round the scallop, then 3 chain, 2 treble under the three chain, 3 chain, 3 more treble in the same place. 8th row—5 chain to turn, 2 treble under the three chain of last row, 3 chain, 3 more treble in the same place. 9th row—5 chain to turn, 2 treble under the three chain of last row, 3 chain, 2 more treble in the same place. Repeat from the second row for the length required, and to make the scallops sit nicely catch at the end of the 2nd, 4th, and 6th rows by a single crochet stitch into a chain loop of preceding scallop. Twenty scallops will be a sufficient length to go round the neck of a chemise, and eight scallops for each sleeve. The top is done when you have crocheted the length required, it is as follows: 1st row—2 treble under loop of five chain that turned, * 5 chain, 2 treble under the next loop, and repeat from *. 2nd row—1 treble on the second treble of last row, 4 treble under the 5 chain, and repeat to the end. 3rd row—1 treble on first treble stitch of last row, * 2 chain, miss 2 stitches, 1 treble on the next, and repeat from *. Run a narrow ribbon in and

Petticoat with Bodice for Child of Two.

Chemise Trimming.

Gentleman's Waistcoat.

underneath the placket hole. Beginning next row on the "lap," work 3 rows of plain tricot. Next row decrease again. Continue thus decreasing every fourth row till in the 46th row you pick up 12 stitches between each decrease, excepting in the front where there will be 16 stitches. Decrease again in the 48th row. Now the petticoat is reduced to 120 stitches for the waist. Work 30 rows on the 120 stitches; this brings you to the armhole. For the first half of the back, pick up 32 stitches, work 16 rows, and fasten off; pick up the last 12 stitches and work 8 rows thereon for a shoulder-strap, and fasten off. Miss six stitches from where you divided for the armhole, pick up 50 stitches for the front, and work 16 rows; then for the shoulder-strap pick up 11 stitches (one already on the needle makes 12), on which work 8 rows, and fasten off; pick up the last 12 stitches for another shoulder-strap, work 8 rows, and fasten off. Miss six stitches from the division for the armhole, pick up thence to the end, 25 stitches, and work 16 rows; then for the shoulder-strap pick up 11 stitches, on which work 8 rows, and fasten off. Sew up the shoulder pieces, and join the back of the skirt as far as the additional eight stitches for the "lap," sew these under the right-hand side. Work a row of single crochet round the neck and shoulders, and down the right-hand side of the placket hole, also round the armholes. And round the neck and armholes and bottom of the skirt work an edge thus: 1 double crochet into a stitch of the single crochet, * 2 chain, 2 treble on the double crochet, miss a stitch of the single, 1 double crochet on the next, and repeat from *. Sew five or six buttons down the back of the bodice, and on the opposite side work buttonholes with a rug needle.

CHEMISE TRIMMING.

THIS is worked with Evans' crochet cotton, No. 16, and a fine steel crochet needle. Commence with 7 chain, work 2 treble in the first of these chain stitches, 3 chain, 2 more treble in the same place. 2nd row—5 chain, turn the work, 2 treble under the three chain of last row, 3 chain, 2 more treble in the same place, then 9 long treble into the next hole with 1 chain between each. 3rd

out through the first row of this heading, tying it in a pretty bow in the front and on the top of the sleeves.

GENTLEMAN'S WAISTCOAT.

To make this warm, comfortably fitting waistcoat, procure 10 ozs. of double Berlin wool, brown, or any colour preferred, and a No. 7 bone crochet needle, or No. 8 for a small size. The work is plain double crochet forwards and backwards, turning at the end of every row, and inserting the hook so as to take up the two top threads of the stitches of the preceding row. Begin for the front with 46 chain, and work 3 rows of double crochet, 45 stitches in each row. 4th row—Which commences at the neck end—Increase a stitch at the beginning by working 2 double crochet in the first stitch. 5th row—Increase a stitch at the end. Repeat these two rows till 11 rows are done. 12th row—Decrease a stitch at the end. 13th row—Increase at the end. Repeat the last two rows till 22 rows are done. Then decrease at the end of every row till 31 rows are done. 32nd row—Work only 8 double crochet, turn, and decrease a stitch at the end of each little row till all are worked off. Break off the wool. And leaving 12 stitches for the armhole, double crochet thence on the remaining stitches for three rows; then work 14 stitches from the bottom, turn, and work back; next row work all up to the armhole. This completes one front. Commence with 46 chain for the other front, and in the second row of this make buttonholes thus: 4 double crochet, * 1 chain, miss 1, 5 double crochet, and repeat from *. Next row double crochet all along, and proceed, shaping the same as the front already done. For the Back—Work 60 chain, and do 5 rows of double crochet from end to end; then decrease at the end of the next row and every alternate row till 16 rows are done. Then decrease at the end of every row till 25 rows are done. Finish off the shoulder, and work the rows under the arm the same as directed for the front of the coat. Then re-commence on the 60 chain, and work the other half of the back to correspond. Sew up the shoulders, and sew under the arms, leaving about three inches open at the bottom. Bind the whole with mohair braid, and place two rows of buttons down the front.

HAND-BAG.

For this useful bag procure 6 ozs. of Macramé twine, a bone crochet needle, No. 8, and a yard of 2-inch wide dark green ribbon. Commence for the bottom of the bag with 4 chain, turn, and work 3 double crochet, and turn, and working into both top threads of the stitches of last row, do double crochet, increasing a stitch at the end of every row till 11 stitches are attained, then work 14 rows forwards and backwards on the 11 stitches, and afterwards decrease a stitch at the end of every row till brought to 3 double crochet again. This forms the base or foundation; fasten off. Now catch the thread into the tenth row of the foundation, and work for the sides in point neige stitch; beginning with 3 chain, raise a loop in the second of the chain stitches, raise a loop in the first chain stitch, another in the place you caught the thread into, and raise 2 more loops in the foundation. There will be 6 stitches on the needle, draw through all, 1 chain, * raise a loop in the thread that lies under the chain, another in the lower thread at the back of the group, another in the same stitch as the group is worked into, and 2 more along the foundation, draw the thread through all, 1 chain, and repeat from *. Continue this stitch round and round till 10 rounds are done. Then work 1 chain, 1 treble all round to make a series of holes in which to run the ribbon. Then finish off with a round of plain double crochet, and having joined the last double crochet stitch neatly to the first, make a length of 45 chain for a handle, catch the thread into a double crochet stitch on the same side of the bag, and an equal distance from the end, and crochet back on it 45 single crochet, and fasten off. Make a similar handle on the opposite side of the bag. Cut the ribbon in two pieces, and run it through the holes in such a manner that you can tie a nice bow on each side of the bag.

with a row of single crochet, inserting the hook below the margin of the treble stitches; also with a rug needle work a scarlet long stitch upon each of the treble stitches. Next sew up the back of the leg and the under part of the sole. With the rug needle and with scarlet wool work a row of cross stitches below the row of holes, and also do 3 rows of cross stitches down the front of the leg, stopping at the instep, where place a ribbon rosette with a steel ornament in the centre. Run ribbon through the holes round the leg, and tie in a pretty bow in front.

SOFA BLANKET.

This warm, useful sofa blanket is composed of squares of fancy tricot, worked with 2 good contrasting colours, the squares being joined together in process of working the open crochet that surrounds each square. Procure an equal quantity of fawn and of blue double Berlin wool, and a bone tricot needle No. 7. Begin with blue wool with 17 chain. 1st row—Pick up each stitch of the chain as for ordinary tricot, and draw back in the usual manner. 2nd row— Bring the wool to the right of the needle, pass it round the outer edge of the tricot, and along the front of the stitch on the needle, and under the hook towards the back and draw the wool through the stitch on the needle, * bring the wool to the front of the work, insert the hook in the next perpendicular tricot stitch of last row, pass the wool to the front and under the hook and draw the wool through the stitch, repeat from * to the end of the row, and draw back as usual. Work every row the same as the second row till the tricot forms a perfect square. Then do a row of single crochet all round the square, the same number of stitches

Hand-Bag.

Baby's Long Boots.

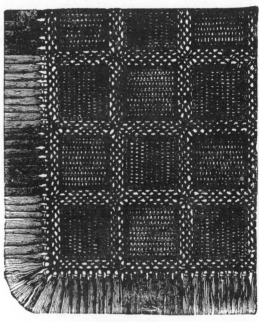

Sofa Blanket.

BABY'S LONG BOOTS.

Required, 2 ozs. of best white and ½ oz. of scarlet Scotch fingering, a bone tricot needle, No. 9, and 1½ yards of ⅜-inch wide scarlet ribbon for trimming. Commence with white wool with 36 chain. 1st row—Pick up all the stitches as in ordinary tricot and draw back. 2nd row—Bring the wool in front under the needle, insert the hook in the perpendicular loop of tricot, put the wool back under the hook and draw wool through the stitch as usual, proceed to the end of the row in this manner, 36 stitches on the needle, and draw back. Work 6 rows thus. Then 3 rows, decreasing 1 stitch at the beginning and 1 stitch at the end of each row. Then 5 rows with 30 stitches in each row, always keeping to the fancy stitch as detailed in the second row. Next row work 12 stitches, increase 2 by pulling up two stitches before the next loop of tricot, work 6 stitches, increase 2, work 12 stitches, and draw back. Increase in this manner in every row, keeping always 6 stitches in the centre between the increasings, till you have 66 stitches on the needle, and draw back. Next row decrease a stitch at the beginning and a stitch at the end; and then to shape the sole of the foot do 3 rows decreasing at the beginning and end and also at each side of the 6 centre stitches each side for 2 more rows. Next row work all 36 stitches, and break off the wool. For the top of the Boot—1st row—To make the row of holes in which to run a ribbon, insert the hook in the first stitch of the commencing chain, draw the wool through and * work 8 chain, miss 1 of the foundation, 1 single crochet in each of the 2 next stitches, and repeat from *; break off wool at end of the row. 2nd row—Work same as the second row of the boot, picking up the 4 centre stitches of every loop of 8 chain, making in all 36 stitches on the needle, and draw back. Work 2 more rows. Then miss 3 stitches each side for 2 more rows. Next work all 36 stitches again. Then for the last row work a scallop, 6 treble in the second stitch of tricot, miss 1, 1 double crochet in the next, and repeat. With scarlet wool edge this last row

on each side. 1st row of the open border—Work 1 double crochet on the corner stitch of the square, 4 chain, another double crochet in the same place, * 4 chain, miss three, 1 double crochet on the next, and repeat from * to the corner, where work 2 double crochet with 4 chain between as at the first corner and proceed the same along each side of the square. 2nd row—1 double crochet under the corner loop of four chain, 4 chain, another double crochet in the same place, 4 chain, 1 double crochet under the next loop of four chain, and continue the same all round, doing an extra loop of chain at each corner. Break off, and fasten off the wool. Work the next square in the same manner, but using fawn wool. When doing the last open round, place this square in proper position beside the square already done—by reference to the engraving it will be seen the tricot lies lengthways in one square and widthways in the next—where the squares touch catch from each 4 chain loop of this (when on the second chain of the four) to a corresponding loop of the other square.

WAISTCOAT IN TRICOTEE.

Required, 10 ozs. of black 3-thread fleecy wool or double Berlin, and a long bone tricot needle, No. 8. Commence with a chain of 66 stitches, or as many as are required to make the width of one of the front pieces, measuring from a cloth waistcoat. Pick up each stitch in succession and work back in the ordinary manner, and continue in plain tricotee row by row till you have a length of 24 inches. Work the other front similarly. Send to a tailor to be made up. A pretty variation is to use wool of two colours, say black and violet, or brown and navy, and work alternately a row with each, not breaking off the wool at the completion of the rows, but carrying it on from one alternate row to the next.

ANTIMACASSAR STRIPE OF PLAIN AND TUFTED TRICOT.

With Cornflower Crewel Worked in the Centre.

Required, ½ lb. of blue and ½ lb. of white single Berlin wool, a bone tricot needle No. 9, and a skein of white filoselle and two shades of b'ue. Use white wool for the centre stripe, beginning with 21 chain, and work all plain tricot, 21 stitches in every row, for the length desired; on this embroider the cornflower spray as shown in the illustration. The narrow stripes are worked with blue wool, commencing with 10 chain, do 2 rows of plain tricot 10 stitches in a row. **3rd row**—Pick up the stitches as usual, and coming back draw through 3, work 4 chain, draw through 2, 4 chain, draw through 5. **4th row**—Pick up as usual, and coming back draw through 7, work 4 chain, draw through 6. **5th row**—Same as the third row. **6th row**—Plain tricot. **7th row**—Pick up the stitches, and coming back draw through 6, work 4 chain, draw through 2, work 4 chain, draw through 2. **8th row**—Pick up as usual, and coming back draw through 7, work 4 chain, draw through 3. **9th row**—Same as the seventh row. **10th row**—Plain tricot. Repeat from the third row for the length required. In each space between the tufts work a leviathan cross stitch with white filoselle. Make another stripe of blue tricot and sew them stitch by stitch on each side of the white stripe. Then continue a white stripe and a blue one for the width of the antimacassar. Strengthen each outside edge with a row of chain stitches worked as single crochet on the margin of the tricot. Fringe each stripe with its own colour, two strands of wool together, and placing 3 fringes in each blue and 6 fringes in each white stripe, and make a heading of two rows of knots.

CURTAIN BAND.

The rosettes of this curtain band are graduated in size; the largest, which is in the centre, has twelve points, the next ten and the other two have eight points each. Procure ecru or navy blue crochet cotton, Evans' No. 2, or corresponding size in any other make, and a steel crochet needle No. 18. Commence for the largest rosette with 12 chain, join round, and work 24 double crochet in the circle, join; 13 chain, 1 treble in the fourth from the needle and 4 more treble in next consecutive stitches, 4 double crochet, 1 single crochet; turn, 1 chain. 5 double crochet on five first stitches of last row, 2 treble in each of the next four stitches, 3 long treble in the last stitch; turn, 1 chain, 1 double crochet on the first stitch, * 3 chain, 1 double crochet in the same stitch as last double crochet is worked into, 1 double crochet on each of the three next stitches, repeat from * four times, 1 single crochet on the last stitch, join to the next stitch but one on the circle, and work 11 more points like this point; break off the cotton. To keep the points lying in place one over the other, work at the back of the rosette 1 double crochet under the chain stitch at the turn of the first row, 5 chain, 1 double crochet under the same chain stitch of the next point, and repeat; break off the cotton. Now outside the rosette work 1 double crochet under the loop of three chain at the corner of a point, 11 chain, 1 double crochet under the three chain at the corner of the next point, and so on, and join round; next round, 1 double crochet in each stitch of previous round, and 3 double crochet in the centre stitch of the eleven chain. Work two rosettes commencing with 10 chain for the circle, in which work 20 double crochet, and finish off the same as the rosette already done, but making only ten points. Work four rosettes commencing with 8 chain, doing 16 double crochet in the circle, and making eight points; two of these rosettes are edged the same as the large one, and two have 1 double crochet 9 chain worked from point to point on *five* points, leaving three points loose. Sew the rosettes together in a row, the largest in the centre, and the loose points at either end. **For the Border**—Begin on the middle one of the three loose points, work 3 treble, 4 chain, 3 treble, all under the three chain at the corner, 4 chain, 3 treble, 4 chain, 3 treble, all under the three chain at the corner of the next point, 9 chain, 1 double crochet at the top of the rosette in the same double crochet where you began the chain that edges the rosette, 8 chain, 1 treble, 1 long treble, 1 double long treble, all on the stitch

at the top of the next point, 1 double long treble, 1 long treble, 1 treble, all on the seventeenth double crochet *before* the centre of the top of the next rosette, 4 chain, miss three, 3 treble on three next consecutive stitches, 8 chain, 1 double crochet on centre stitch of the rosette, 8 chain, miss twelve, 1 treble, 1 long treble, 1 double long treble on the next three consecutive stitches, and 1 double long treble, 1 long treble and 1 treble on three consecutive stitches of the third rosette, 8 chain, 1 double crochet on centre stitch of the three double crochet, 9 chain, 1 double crochet on centre stitch of next three double crochet, 8 chain, miss eight, 1 long treble on the next, 4 chain, miss four, 1 double long treble on the next three double crochet of the next three double crochet, 5 chain, miss four, 1 double long treble on the next, 4 chain, 1 treble on centre stitch of next three double crochet, 9 chain, 1 double crochet on centre stitch of the next three double crochet; this is the exact centre of the band, work to the end corresponding to this beginning, turn round the last rosette, and work the other side in the same way. **2nd row**—1 treble on every stitch of last row. **3rd row**—Begin with 20 chain for the button-hole loop at the end, 1 single crochet in the eighth from the needle, and work 2 double crochet in each stitch of the little circle and 12 treble along the remaining chain stitches; then on to the previous row work 6 consecutive double crochet, 5 chain, and repeat all round; when at the other end work another button-hole loop like that at the beginning.

BASSINETTE COVER.
Shell Pattern.

To be worked with white and pink single Berlin wool and rather fine bone crochet needle. Commence for the first shell with white wool, with 2 chain, turn, and do 3 double crochet in the first of the chain; turn the work, and inserting the hook so as to take up the back thread of the stitches of preceding row that the shell may sit in ridges, work 1 double crochet in the first stitch, 3 double crochet in the centre stitch, and 1 double crochet in the last stitch; turn the work; do 1 double crochet in each of the first two stitches, 3 double crochet in the centre stitch, 1 double crochet in each of the last two stitches; turn the work, and now do 3 consecutive double crochet, 3 double crochet in the centre stitch, and 3 more consecutive double crochet; and so on, always increasing in the centre stitch till you can count five ridges on each side of the shell. Then work a pink shell in the same manner. And proceed till you have done a sufficiency of each colour. Join the shells in such a way that the commencement of a shell comes always on the increased point of the shell beneath, pink above white, and white above pink. Half shells will be required to fit in round the outside. When the margin is straight border the cover with a pretty edging or knotted fringe.

CROCHET FRINGE.

This is intended to be produced with cotton to border quilts, toil et-covers, tray-cloths, &c., and it may either be worked round and round upon the article itself, or commenced on a foundation chain of the length required; if the latter break off at the end of every row and re-commence on the right-hand side. **1st row**—1 treble, * 2 chain, miss 2 stitches of the foundation, 1 treble in the next, and repeat from *. **2nd row**—3 treble under the first loop of two chain, * miss the next loop, 3 treble in the next, and repeat from *. **3rd row**—1 double crochet on the centre stitch of the first group of 3 treble of last row, * 3 chain, 1 treble on the first stitch of the next group of treble, 2 chain, another treble in the same place, 2 chain, 1 treble on the centre treble stitch, 2 chain, 1 treble on the third treble stitch, 2 chain, another treble in the same place, 3 chain, 1 double crochet on the centre stitch of the next group of three treble, repeat from *. **4th row**—1 double crochet on the double crochet of last row, 3 chain, 1 treble under the first loop of two chain, 3 chain, 1 treble under the next loop, 3 chain, 1 treble on the centre treble stitch of last row, 3 chain, 1 treble under the next loop of two chain, 3 chain, 1 treble under the next loop, 3 chain, and repeat. **5th row**—1 double crochet under the second loop of three chain, * 5 chain, 1 double crochet under the next loop of three chain, do from * twice more, 3 chain, miss the next two loops of last row (those on each side of the double crochet stitch), 1 double crochet under the next, and repeat from *. Now cut a skein of cotton into lengths of 7 inches, and knot 7 threads together in each loop of five chain.

Antimacassar Stripe of Plain and Tufted Tricot.

Curtain Band.

INSERTION.

COMMENCE with chain sufficient for the length required. **1st row**—1 treble, * 2 chain, miss two of the foundation, 1 treble in the next, and repeat from * to the end of the row. **2nd row**—1 treble on the first chain stitch of last row, * 2 chain, 1 treble on the first of the next two chain stitches of last row, and repeat from *. **3rd row**—1 treble on the first chain stitch of last row, * 2 chain, 1 double crochet and 1 treble both on the treble just done, 1 treble on the first of the next two chain stitches, and repeat from *. Repeat the same three rows on the other side of the commencing chain

VENETIAN CAP.

REQUIRED, 1½ ozs. of rose colour and ½ oz. of white single Berlin wool. A bone crochet needle No. 8. Commence with rose colour with 84 chain; join round. **1st round**—3 chain to stand for a treble, * 1 chain, miss 1 stitch of the foundation, 1 treble in the next, and repeat from *; join at the end of this and every round, and *turn* the work so that the right side of the succeeding round comes to the wrong side of the round last done. **2nd round**—1 treble, 1 chain alternately, the trebles being over the treble stitches of last round. **3rd round**—The same. **4th round**—All treble, making 84 treble in the round. **5th round**—All treble, and decrease 6 times in the round, inserting the hook so as to take up every 13th and 14th stitch together, so working 1 treble over 2. **6th round**—Treble, and again decrease 6 times in the round between the decreasings of last round. **7th round**—The same, 66 treble. **8th round**—The same, 60 treble. **9th round**—The same, 54 treble. **10th round**—Decrease 8 times in the round. **11th round**—The same, 38 treble. **12th round**—The same, 30 treble. **13th round**—1 long treble on

of 7 loops, and repeat; join at end of the round and break off the wool. **6th round**—Take the white wool and work as described for the second round. **7th round**—With white wool, same as the third round, and this finishes the cap. Fold the Beehive pattern upon the cap like a band, and tack it in place; make a daisy tuft with strands of white wool and affix to the point of the cap, bending this over the side of the cap to meet the band, just a stitch will keep it in place.

DRAPE FOR BRACKET, OR MANTEL BORDER.

REQUIRED, a ball of brown Macramé thread, a piece of inch wide peacock-blue ribbon twice the length the piece of work is intended to be, and a No. 12 crochet needle. Commence with 20 chain. **1st row**—2 treble in the eighth chain from the needle, 3 chain, 2 more treble in the same place, 4 chain, miss four, 2 treble in the next, 3 chain, 2 more treble in the same place, 4 chain, miss four, 2 treble in the next, 3 chain, 2 more treble in the same place, 4 chain, turn the work. **2nd row**—2 treble under the three chain of last row, 3 chain, 2 more treble in the same place, 4 chain, 2 treble under the next three chain of last row, 3 chain, 2 more treble in the same place, 4 chain, 2 treble under the next three chain of last row, 3 chain, 2 more treble in the same place, 4 chain, turn the work. **3rd row**—Same as the second row. **4th row**—Same as the second row. **5th row**—2 treble under the three chain of last row, 3 chain, 2 more treble in the same place, 4 chain, 1 double crochet over the bars of four chain of the last two rows, 4 chain, 2 treble under the next three chain of last row, 3 chain, 2 more treble in the same place, 4 chain, 1 double crochet over the bars of two previous rows, 4 chain, 2 treble under the next three chain of last row, 3 chain, 2 more treble in the same place, 4 chain, turn the work. Repeat from the second row till 10 rows are done. Then for the scallop, after doing 4 chain, work 1 double crochet under the loop of four chain along the *side* of the

Insertion.

Venetian Cap.

Full-size Working Design of
Rosette for Curtain Band.

Drape for Bracket, or Mantel Border.

every 2 treble of last round, making 15 long treble; break off the wool, and with a rug needle secure the top of the stitches together in a circle. Next, still with rose colour, work a round of treble stitches, 84, along the opposite side of the foundation chain. And for the **Border**, which is in Beehive stitch, work for the **1st round**—Holding the round of treble stitches the right side towards you, 1 double crochet on the first treble, miss 1, 7 treble on the next, miss 1, and repeat, and join at the end of the round. **2nd round**—In this round each time of inserting the needle, put the hook in from back to front at the right-hand side of the treble stitch of last round, and bring it out from front to back at the left hand of the same treble stitch, so having the treble stitch itself upon the needle, draw the wool through in rather a loose loop or stitch; do 4 chain to stand for the first loop, then take up a loop as described in each of the 3 first treble stitches of last round, wool over the needle and draw through 4 stitches on the needle, 1 double crochet to tighten the group, 1 double crochet on the centre 1 of the 7 trebles of last round, raise 7 loops in the manner described above in the 7 next consecutive stitches, wool over the needle and draw through the 8 stitches on the needle, 1 chain, and repeat from *, and raise 3 loops at the end of the round to match the beginning, and join round. **3rd round**—Do 3 chain to stand for a treble, work 3 treble in chain stitch at junction of the round, 1 double crochet on double crochet of last round, * 7 treble on the chain stitch that unites the bunch of seven loops of last round, 1 double crochet on the next double crochet of last round, and repeat from *, do 3 treble at the end to correspond with the beginning, and join round. **4th round**—Work 1 double crochet on the chain stitch into which you have just joined, * raise 7 loops in the next 7 consecutive stitches, wool over the needle and draw through the 8 stitches on the needle, 1 chain, 1 double crochet on the centre 1 of the group of 7 trebles, and repeat from *, and join at the end of the round. **5th round**—1 double crochet on double crochet of last round 7 treble on the chain stitch that unites the bunch

work, 9 chain, 1 double crochet under the next loop of 4 chain, 9 chain, 1 double crochet under next loop of four chain, 9 chain, 1 double crochet under next loop of four chain, turn the work, 14 double crochet under the first loop of 9 chain, 7 double crochet under the next loop of nine chain, 9 chain, turn the hook in front of the work, and do a single crochet between the seventh and eighth double crochet stitches and 14 double crochet under this loop of nine chain, 7 double crochet in the same loop where seven double crochet are already worked, 7 double crochet under the next loop of nine chain, 9 chain, turn the hook in front of the work and do a single crochet between the seventh and eighth double crochet, then 7 double crochet under the nine chain just done, 9 chain, turn the hook in front of the work and do a single crochet between the seventh and eighth double crochet of last loop, then 14 double crochet under this loop of nine chain, 7 double crochet to fill up the next loop, and 7 more double crochet in the next loop; now 5 chain, turn the work, 1 treble on the third double crochet stitch, * 1 chain, miss one, 1 treble on the next, and repeat from * till 21 treble stitches are worked, 3 chain, 1 single crochet under the loop of four chain, turn the work, 5 chain, 1 single in the fourth chain from the needle, 1 chain, 1 treble on the first treble stitch of last row, * 5 chain, 1 single in the fourth chain from the needle, 1 chain, 1 treble on the next treble of last row, and repeat from *, making 22 treble stitches in all; 3 chain, 1 double crochet on the first treble stitch of the heading; 2 chain, 2 treble under the three chain of the tenth row, 3 chain two more treble in the same place, and continue the heading the same as before till another 10 rows are done, when you proceed with the working of the second scallop. Three scallops will be sufficient for a bracket; to make the commencement look the same as the last row work 1 row of the heading pattern reversely into the foundation chain. Cut the ribbon into two pieces and run it in and out through the heading in the manner shown in the illustration, sewing it firmly at the ends.

CHILD'S MUFF IN TUFTED TREBLE STITCH.

REQUIRED, 1½ ozs. of creamy-white Andalusian wool, a bone crochet needle No. 9, a piece of satin or fine flannel for lining, a layer of wadding, and 1 yard of cream satin ribbon for a bow. Commence with 32 chain, worked not too tightly, for the length of the muff; then 1 treble in the third chain from the needle, and 5 long treble (wool turned twice round the needle), and another treble in the same place; now take out the hook, insert it in the first treble, then take up again the stitch you have just let go, and draw it through the first treble stitch rather tightly, keeping the long treble stitches in a tuft to the front, 1 chain, miss one stitch of the foundation, in the next foundation chain work another tuft of 7 stitches in the same way, 1 chain, and continue to the end, making 15 tufts of trebles in all, with a chain stitch between each. Fasten off at the end of the row, and recommence on the right-hand side. The work is the same throughout, the tufts henceforward being under the chain stitch of preceding row. There should be 14 tufts in the second row, 15 tufts in the third row, and so on. Proceed till 19 rows are done. Then sew up the last row to the first. Put in the wadding and line the muff, and make a pretty wide bow to place over the join

LEWIS POINT PATTERN.

THIS stitch may be worked either in stripes or lengthways; if for an antimacassar the former is preferable, and the stripes should be of two good contrasting colours. Procure double Berlin wool, and a bone crochet needle No. 6, and com-

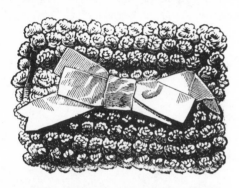

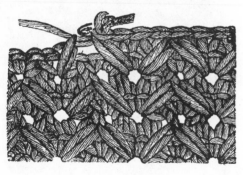

Child's Muff in Tufted Treble Stitch.

Lewis Point Pattern.

Bell-Pull.

treble in the sixth chain from the needle, 2 chain, 3 more treble in the same place, 3 chain, miss four, 3 treble in the next, 2 chain, 3 more treble in the same place, catch with a single crochet into the last stitch of foundation chain; * 5 chain, turn the work, 3 treble under the two chain of last row, 2 chain, 3 more treble in the same place, 3 chain, 3 treble under the next two chain of last row, 2 chain, 3 more treble in the same place; 5 chain, turn the work, 3 treble under the two chain of last row, 2 chain, 3 more treble in the same place, 3 chain, 3 treble under the next two chain of last row, 2 chain, 3 more treble in the same place; 5 chain, turn the work, 3 treble under the two chain of last row, 2 chain, 3 more treble in the same place, 3 chain, place hook under the three chain of the second row and work a double crochet, 3 chain, 3 treble under the next two chain of last row, 2 chain, 3 more treble in the same place; 5 chain, turn the work, 3 treble under the two chain of last row, 2 chain, 3 more treble in the same place, 3 chain, 2 treble under the next two chain of last row, 2 chain, 3 more treble in the same place; and repeat from * for the length required. Run an inch-wide ribbon in and out through the centre of the crochet, securing it at top and bottom. Cut eighteen threads ten inches long and knot three fringes in three holes of the foundation chain. The other end of the pull is to be fastened to the bell wire.

FASCINATOR.

THIS pretty fascinator is intended to be worn folded corner-ways, the corners to come on the top of the head to the front, the ends tie under the chin or pass round the neck. Procure 2½ ozs. of white Shetland wool, and a No. 10 bone

Fascinator.

mence with 13, 16, or 19 chain, in which work 1 row of plain double crochet: do not break off the wool, but *turn* at the end of this and every row. **2nd row**—2 double crochet, insert the hook in the first stitch of the commencing chain, and draw the wool up in a long loop loosely, insert the hook in the fourth stitch of the commencing chain, and draw up another long loop, wool over the needle, and draw through the 3 stitches on the needle, then 3 double crochet above three double crochet of last row, * insert the hook in the same place where the last looped stitch is worked and draw up the wool loosely, insert the hook in the fourth stitch of the commencing chain to the left hand and draw the wool up loosely, wool over the needle, and draw through the 3 stitches on the needle, 3 double crochet, and repeat from *, there will be 2 double crochet at the end of the row the same as at the beginning. **3rd row**—Plain double crochet. **4th row** is worked exactly the same as the second row, and to draw up the long loops which form the "points" you insert the hook in the double crochet stitches of the second row. **5th row**—Plain double crochet. Repeat thus for the length required, being careful to keep the "points" exactly in straight line one above the other.

BELL-PULL.

THIS is worked with medium-sized macramé thread, of which about two balls will be required if the pull is to be a long one. Use a No. 12 crochet needle, steel if procurable, if not a bone one will do. Begin with 16 chain. Work 3

crochet needle. Make a chain of 100 stitches, and work 3 treble into every third stitch. **Next row**—3 chain to turn, 3 treble in every space. Every succeeding row is the same as this last row. Continue till 52 rows are done or till your work forms a perfect square, then turn with three chain and work 3 groups of 3 treble stitches forwards and backwards for 36 rows, and **break off** wool. At the opposite corner in the chain stitches at the turning of the rows work 3 groups of 3 treble stitches, and complete another end of 36 rows to correspond. For Border all round the square and end, work **1st row**—4 treble into one space, 1 treble into the next space, and repeat, putting 6 treble at the corners. **2nd round**—4 treble in between the second and third trebles of last round, 1 treble on the previous one treble, and repeat, putting 8 treble at the corners. **3rd round**—8 treble in between the second and third trebles of last round, 1 chain, 1 treble on the previous one treble, 1 chain, and repeat, putting 10 treble at the corners. Now make little daisy tufts by winding wool about thirty times round a blacklead pencil, and sewing tightly with a needle and cotton, cut and trim to shape, and sew one tuft on the point of every scallop round the square, not round the ends.

LADY'S SHOULDER CAPE.
POINT BATTENBERG.

THIS is a lovely raised pattern, and the cape is suitable either for wearing to the opera or for general use, according to the material employed. Our model is worked with white double Berlin wool, of which 1 lb. will be required, and a bone crochet needle, No. 8. Commence with 49 chain for the front of the cape. **1st row**—1 double crochet in the second chain from the needle; insert the hook in the next stitch, draw the wool through, work 6 chain, wool over the needle, and draw through the two stitches on the needle, 1 double crochet on the next stitch of the foundation, a point on the next, and so on, and there will be 24 double crochet stitches, and 24 points in the row. Fasten off at the end of this and every row, and recommence on the right-hand side, which is the top of the cape. **2nd row**—1 double crochet on the first double crochet of last row, inserting the hook so as to take up the two top threads; insert the hook under the loop of six chain and work a double crochet, and repeat. **3rd row**—1 double crochet on the first double crochet of last row, * 1 double crochet on the next, insert the

crochet under the first one chain of last row, * 1 chain, 1 double crochet under the next one chain of last row, and repeat from *, again making 40 double crochet in the row. Work 10 more rows like the second row. Then increase, by working an additional 1 chain, 1 double crochet at the beginning of every row, till in the 32nd row you do 60 double crochet. Then do 2 rows without increase, and 2 rows with increase till you have done 64 rows and have 76 double crochet in the row. Then increase 1 at the beginning of every row till you have done 90 rows. Do 2 rows without increase, 2 rows with increase; 2 rows without increase, 2 rows with increase; and 2 rows without increase, making 100 rows done, and 106 double crochet in the row. Now decrease 1 at the beginning of the next 2 rows, then 2 rows without decrease, and continue thus till the leg is nearly the length required—130 rows or thereabouts; to slope the back, in the 131st row work 66 double crochet, turn, and work back; work 48 double crochet, turn, and work back; work 32 double crochet, turn, and work back; work 16 double crochet, turn, and work back; work forwards and back again the whole width of the leg; break off the wool. This is the left leg. Work for the right leg in the same manner, only

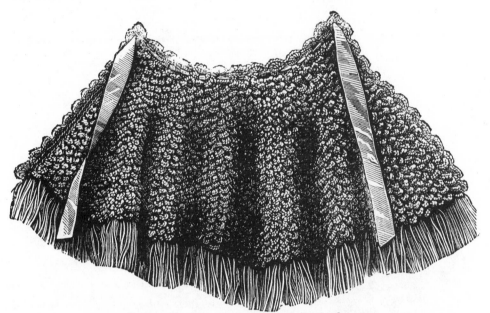

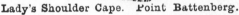

Lady's Shoulder Cape. Point Battenberg.

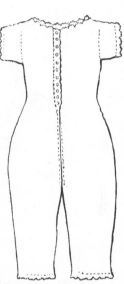

Diagram showing the Shape of Lady's Combination Garment.

hook in the next, draw the wool through, work 6 chain, wool over the needle and draw through the two stitches on the needle, and repeat from *. **4th row**—1 double crochet on each double crochet stitch of last row, and 1 double crochet under each loop of 6 chain. **5th row**—Begin on the double crochet that is worked in the fifth loop of 6 chain, and proceed as in the first row, and there will be 19 double crochet and 19 points in the row. **6th row**—Same as the fourth row. **7th row**—Begin on the double crochet that is worked in the fifth loop of 6 chain, and again work as in the first row, and there will be 15 double crochet and 14 points in the row. **8th row**—Same as the fourth row. **9th row**—Begin above the fifth point of the seventh row, and again work as in the first row, and there will be 10 double crochet and 10 points in the row. **10th row**—Same as the fourth row. **11th row**—Begin above the fifth point next ensuing, and again work as in the first row, and there will be 6 double crochet and 5 points in the row. **12th row**—Same as the fourth row. This finishes the gore. Repeat these twelve rows, and when the half of the cape is attained (which will be three gores for a small size, and four gores for full size), work four rows from the neck to the bottom, and for the t'other half proceed reversely—that is, doing the shortest go e rows first. If the cape is for a thin person, the eleventh and twelfth rows may be omitted throughout, and only ten rows worked in a gore. **To finish the Cape**, work a row of plain double crochet up each front and round the neck; then work a row of scallops thus—1 double crochet on the first stitch of last row, miss one, 5 treble in the next, miss one, and repeat. Cut the remainder of the wool into 6-inch lengths, and knot a fringe in every stitch along the bottom of the cape. Place ribbon strings at the neck, or a button, as preferred.

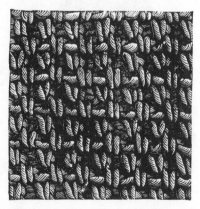

Full-size Working Design of Stitch used for Lady's Combination Garment.

LADY'S COMBINATION GARMENT.

REQUIRED, 1½ lbs. of best white Scotch fingering, and a bone crochet needle No. 13. Commence for the bottom of the leg with 81 chain. **1st row**—1 double crochet in the second stitch from the needle, * 1 chain, miss 1, 1 double crochet in the next, and repeat from *, making 40 double crochet stitches in the row; turn, with 1 chain at the end of this and every row. **2nd row**—1 double

remember the slope of the back has to come reversely to that already done. Now **for the Body**—Beginning at the right-hand front of the right leg. The legs have to be joined together at the back by overlapping 10 stitches of the right leg over 10 stitches of the left leg and crocheting both together. The decreasings are continued up each front, decreasing 1 at the beginning of the first 2 rows, then 2 rows without decrease, till you have done 168 rows in all, and you also decrease twice on the hips in every fourth row, but only *till* the work is the right dimensions for the waist. Begin and end the 168th row with 9 plain double crochet, that is, no chain stitch between these 9 edge stitches, but working a double crochet on the double crochet of last row. In the **169th row**, which should begin on the right-hand front, make a buttonhole thus—3 double crochet, 3 chain, miss 3, 3 double crochet, and proceed in stitch as before. Similar buttonholes are to be formed in every eighth successive row. In the **193rd row** increase twice on each side over the hip, also in the **197th** and **201st rows**. In the **203rd row** divide for the armholes, and work 2 front pieces and one back piece, each for 50 rows; shape the shoulders in this way, working from the *shoulder* end, do 1 chain, 1 double crochet, thirteen times, turn, and work back; 1 chain, 1 double crochet, ten times, turn, and work back; 1 chain, 1 double crochet, five times, turn, and work back; break off the wool. Sew up the shoulders. **The Sleeves** are worked in the armhole in the same pattern, 1 chain, 1 double crochet, and joined up afterwards. You begin under the armhole, decrease a stitch at the beginning of each of the first 12 rows, then do 10 rows without decrease. Sew up the round part of the legs, and work a row of double crochet to strengthen the edge along the open part. Work 3 rows of plain double crochet round the neck. **4th row**—For a scalloped edge, work 1 double crochet on double crochet of last row, miss 1, * 1 treble on the next, 1 chain and 1 treble three more times in the same place, miss one, 1 double crochet on the next, miss one, and repeat from *. **5th row**—1 double crochet on the double crochet of last row, 1 chain, 1 double crochet under one chain of last row, 3 chain, 1 double crochet under the next chain stitch, 3 chain, 1 double crochet under the next chain stitch, 1 chain, and repeat. Work these two scalloped rows round the sleeves and round the bottom of the drawers. Sew buttons down the left-hand front of the garment, one button will also be required at the back to keep the "over-lap" in its place.

POKE BONNET FOR A YOUNG CHILD.

This charming bonnet is not nearly so difficult of accomplishment as may appear at first sight, and if undertaken by a fairly good worker is sure to be very greatly admired. Materials required, a bonnet shape, 3 yards of pale blue satin ribbon for strings and trimming, a little fine muslin for head lining, 2 ozs. of white single Berlin wool, a crochet needle No. 8, and one No. 10. The brim is crocheted in a variety of Point Muscovite stitch, and the crown is Point Neige. Take the No. 10 crochet needle and begin with 57 chain, or so many as are sufficient to go from ear to ear round the outer rim at the back of the bonnet. **1st row**—1 single crochet in the first stitch from the needle, * insert the hook in the next stitch and do 3 chain, draw the wool through the last of the chain and through the stitch on the needle, 1 single crochet in the next stitch of the

Poke Bonnet for a Young Child.

foundation chain, and repeat from *; break off the wool at the end of the row. **2nd row**—Re-commence on the right-hand side, work a point stitch over the single crochet and a single crochet over the point stitch of last row, and continue. Proceed in like manner till 5 rows are done, and fasten off. Begin again with 107 chain, or so many as will go round the front of the brim and meet the piece already done, the two pieces being afterwards joined together under the strings, do 9 rows, but at each end of the second and successive rows work one stitch less to decrease to shape. For the Crown or Head-piece, use the No 8 crochet needle, and begin with 42 chain for the back of the head. Point neige has already been described in these pages, so a repetition of the manner of procedure is unnecessary. Work as far as the top of the crown, 16 or 17 rows, increasing one stitch at the beginning and at the end of each row; this done, work to *fit* your bonnet shape, 3 stitches in each row must be decreased on the top of the head, and other stitches decreased where necessary, till you have sufficient done to cover the head of the bonnet. Sew this piece on, stretching it to shape (if cleverly managed, it will fit without a wrinkle); sew the Muscovite strips on the brim, making the joins come by the ears. Neatly gather the satin for the lining of the brim, put head lining in in the usual way. Trim the bonnet with a nice looped bow in front; the strings are brought to meet in a point on the head over the bow.

BABY'S GLOVES.

Procure 1 oz. of fawn and ½ oz. of red fingering wool and a bone crochet needle, No. 10. With red wool make a chain of 30 stitches, join round, and work 8 rounds of single crochet, taking up the back threads only. After this do 8 rounds with fawn colour. Then with the red wool again work 3 rounds, reducing 2 stitches in each round, and so bringing to 24 single crochet for the wrist. Now with fawn colour, and taking up the front threads of each preceding round, work 10 rounds, in the last three rounds of these increasing by 2 stitches in a round to 30 stitches. Next round work 9 single crochet and 3 chain for the thumb, join round, and single crochet 8 rounds, 12 stitches in each round; then do 2 rounds with red, and afterwards take 2 together till only three stitches are left, sew these up with a rug needle. Proceed with the hand

on 24 stitches for 8 rounds, then do 6 rounds with red, and after this take 2 together all round, and sew up the top. For the little edge round the wrist crochet with red wool, 1 double crochet, 3 chain, alternately, and work the same edge 2 rounds above. At the back of the hand, on the red band round the wrist, sew a few loops of red wool in the form of a rosette.

COUVREPIED.

This couvrepied may be worked with double Berlin wool or AA Peacock fleecy, and a bone crochet needle No. 6. The stripes are of good contrasting colours, say fawn and blue for the narrow, and black and amber for the wide stripes. Begin with fawn wool for the narrow stripe with 16 chain. **1st row**—Plain double crochet; turn the work at the end of this and every row. **2nd row**—Double crochet, 15 stitches in the row, inserting the hook into both top threads of the stitches of preceding row. **3rd row**—2 double crochet, take the blue wool over the needle, insert the hook on the right side to take up the second double crochet stitch of the second previous row, bringing it out to the left of the same stitch and draw the wool through, blue wool over the needle, insert the hook from the front to take up the next stitch of the second previous row and draw the wool through, blue wool over the needle, insert the hook to take up the next stitch of the second previous row and draw the wool through, blue wool over the needle and draw through 5 blue stitches on the needle, fawn wool over the needle and draw through the 2 stitches on the needle, 3 double crochet with fawn, then again raise blue loops in the second previous row, the first loop at distance of one stitch from the former group and the others in next two consecutive stitches, draw through as already described, work 3 fawn double crochet, another series of blue loops, and 4 double crochet at the end of the row; break off the blue wool after doing the last tuft, and secure the tag ends with a rug needle. **4th row**—Same as the second row. **5th row**—4 double crochet, * blue wool over the needle in the manner described above, and raise loops in the three stitches between the group of loops raised in the third row, 3 double crochet with fawn, and repeat from *, and there will be 2 double crochet to work at the end of the row. **6th row**—Same as the second row. Repeat from the third row till the stripe is the length you wish it. The wide stripes are worked in the same manner, using black wool for the ground and amber for the raised loops, beginning with 24 chain to allow for five tufts in every pattern row. Work as many stripes as are required for the width of the couvrepied, and join them together with a row of double crochet. Finish off the top and bottom with a deep fringe.

WATCH GUARDS.

These guards are used by both ladies and gentlemen, and are especially appropriate for mourning. Procure 2 skeins of black purse silk and some small black beads. First of all thread the beads upon the silk. Then with a steel crochet needle commence with 6 or 8 chain, join round; insert the hook in the first stitch of the chain, push a bead close to the work, draw the silk through, then silk round the needle and draw through the 2 stitches of the needle, so making a double crochet stitch; continue in this way in each chain stitch of the foundation and go on round and round

Baby's Glove.

Couvrepied.

putting a bead at every stitch until the guard is the required length. Attach a swivel at one end and a pendant at the other if the guard is an Albert. If a long chain affix a snap to secure the ends together.

WELDON'S
PRACTICAL CROCHET. EDGINGS.
(FIFTH SERIES.)

How to Crochet 46 Useful Edgings and Insertions for all Purposes

Telegraphic Address—] "Consuelo," London.] The Yearly Subscription to this Magazine, post free to any Part of the World, is 2s. 6d. Subscriptions are payable in advance, and may commence from any date and for any period. [Telephone 2745.

The Back Numbers are always in print. Nos. 1 to 92 now ready, Price 2d. each, or post free for 16s. 4d. Over 5,000 Engravings.

No. 1.—MUSSEL-SHELL BORDER.

BEGIN with a foundation of chain the length required. **1st row**—1 treble in the fourth chain from the needle, 1 treble in the next, * 13 chain, miss thirteen of the foundation, work 16 consecutive treble, and repeat from *. **2nd row**—13 double crochet on the thirteen chain of last row, 5 chain, miss four, 8 treble on the centre eight of the sixteen treble of last row, 5 chain, miss four, and repeat. **3rd row**—11 double crochet beginning on the second double crochet of last row, 5 chain, 1 treble on the third treble stitch, 3 chain, another treble in the same place, 1 chain, miss 2, 1 treble on the next, 3 chain, another treble in the same place, 5 chain, and repeat. **4th row**— 9 double crochet beginning on the second double crochet of last row, 5 chain, 1 treble under the loop of three chain, 3 chain, another treble in the same place, 2 chain, 1 treble under the next loop of three chain, 3 chain, another treble in the same place, 5 chain, and repeat. **5th row**—9 double crochet on the nine double crochet of last row, 5 chain, 1 treble under the loop of three chain, 3 chain, another treble in the same place, 3 chain, 1 treble under the next loop of three chain, 3 chain, another treble in the same place, 5 chain, and repeat. **6th row**—7 double crochet beginning on the second double crochet of last row, 5 chain, 1 treble under the loop of three chain, 3 chain, another treble in the same place, 2 chain, 1 treble under the next loop of three chain, 3 chain, another treble in the same place, 2 chain, 1 treble under the next loop of three chain, 3 chain, another treble in the same place, 5 chain, and repeat. **7th row**—Same as last row, working 7 double crochet over the seven already worked. **8th row**—5 double crochet, beginning on the second double crochet of last row, 5 chain, 1 treble under the loop of three chain, 3 chain, another treble in the same place, 3 chain, 1 treble under the next loop of three chain, 3 chain, another treble in the same place, 3 chain, 1 treble under the next loop of three chain, 3 chain, another treble in the same place, 5 chain, and repeat. **9th row**—5 double crochet on the five double crochet of last row, 5 chain, * 1 treble under the first loop of three chain, 3 chain, another treble in the same place, 1 chain, repeat from * four times, do 4 more chain, and continue. **10th row**—3 double crochet beginning on the second double crochet of last row, 5 chain, * 1 treble under the first loop of three chain, 3 chain, another treble in the same place, 2 chain, repeat from * four times, do 3 more chain, and continue. **11th row**—1 double crochet on the centre stitch of the three double crochet, 5 chain, * 1 treble under the first loop of three chain, 3 chain, another treble in the same place, 2 chain, repeat from * four times, and continue. **12th row**—1 double crochet under the loop of five chain, 1 chain, 6 treble under the first loop of three chain, * 1 chain, 1 double crochet under the two chain, 1 chain, 6 treble under the next loop of three chain, repeat from * three times, 1 chain, 1 double crochet under the loop of five chain, and continue. This completes the border. Finish by working a row of treble stitches along the opposite side of the foundation chain.

No. 2—THE ELZY INSERTION.

COMMENCE with 22 chain. **1st row**—1 treble in the fifth chain from the needle, 1 chain, miss one, 1 treble in the next, 8 chain, miss ten, 1 treble in the next, 1 chain, miss one, 1 treble in the next, 1 chain, miss one, 1 treble at the end. **2nd row**—4 chain to turn, 1 treble under the first one chain of last row, 1 chain, 1 treble under the next one chain, 8 chain, 1 treble in the last stitch of the eight chain of last row, 1 chain, 1 treble under the next loop of one chain, 1 chain, 1 treble in the loop at the end. **3rd row**—4 chain to turn, 1 treble under the first one chain, 1 chain, 1 treble under the next, 6 chain, 1 double crochet over the three last rows of chain stitches, 6 chain, 1 treble in the last stitch of the eight chain of last row, 1 chain, 1 treble under the next loop of one chain, 1 chain, 1 treble in the loop at the end. **4th row**—4 chain to turn, 1 treble under one chain of last row, 1 chain, 1 treble under next one chain, 8 chain, 1 treble in the last stitch of the second loop of six chain, 1 chain, 1 treble under the next loop of one chain, 1 chain, one treble in the loop at the end, 7 chain, 1 double crochet at the edge of the work in the third row from the needle, 3 chain, 1 double crochet at the edge of the next row. **5th row**—Turn, and work 1 treble under the loop of seven chain, 5 chain and 3 treble under the same loop five times, 3 chain, 1 treble under the first one chain, 1 chain, 1 treble under the next, 8 chain, 1 treble in the last stitch of the eight chain of last row, 1 chain, 1 treble under the next loop of one chain, 1 chain,

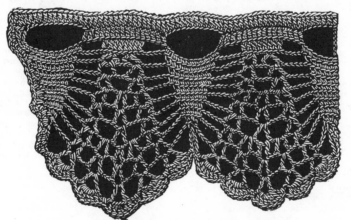

No. 1.—Mussel-Shell Border.

1 treble under the loop at the end, 7 chain, 1 double crochet at the edge of the work in the third row from the needle, 3 chain, 1 double crochet at the edge of the next row. **6th row**—Turn, work 1 treble under the loop of seven chain, 5 chain and 3 treble under the same loop five times, 3 chain, 1 treble under the first one chain, 1 chain, 1 treble under the next, 8 chain, 1 treble in the last stitch of the eight chain of last row, 1 chain, 1 treble under the next loop of 1 chain, 1 chain, 1 treble under the loop at the end. **7th row**—Same as the third row. **8th row**—Same as the fourth row. And continue the insertion, catching the centre loops together with a double crochet stitch in every fourth row, and working the scalloped edge on both sides at the end of every sixth row.

No. 3.—VICTORIA PATTERN.

IF fine white crochet cotton be used, this is a pretty pattern for edging drawers; done with ingrain thread, it is suitable for bracket draping and other purposes. Begin with 10 chain. **1st row**—2 treble in the sixth stitch from the needle, 1 chain, 2 more treble in the same place, 3 chain, 2 treble in the last stitch, 1 chain, 2 more treble in the same place. **2nd row**—5 chain to turn, 2 treble under the first loop of one chain, 1 chain, 2 more treble in the same place, 3 chain, 2 treble under the next loop of one chain, 1 chain, 2 more treble in the same place. Repeat this last row till you have 9 little rows done Then to commence the scallop, work 4 chain, 1 double crochet under the first loop of five chain, 8 chain, 1 double crochet under the next loop of five chain, 8 chain, 1 double crochet under the next, 8 chain, 1 double crochet under the next. Turn the work, and make 12 double crochet in the two first of the loops of eight chain, and 6 double crochet in the third loop. Turn, 8 chain, 1 single crochet in between the sixth and seventh double crochet stitches of the first group, 8 chain, 1 single crochet in between the sixth and seventh double crochet stitches of the other group. Turn, and do 12 double crochet in the first loop of eight chain, and 6 double crochet in the second loop. Turn, 8 chain, 1 single crochet in between the sixth and seventh double crochet stitches of the first group. Turn again, and do 12 double crochet in the loop of eight chain, and 6 double crochet in each of the two half-finished loops of chain. Then 5 chain, turn the work, and go round the scallop doing 1 treble in every other double crochet stitch with 1 chain between each treble, shaping at the top with a treble in six successive stitches. Turn, 1 double crochet in the first space, 1 chain and 1 treble three times in the second space, 1 chain, and repeat nine times, ending with 1 double crochet ; then 1 chain, 2 treble under the first loop of one chain of the ninth row, 1 chain, 2 more treble in the same place, 3 chain, 2 treble under the next loop of one chain, 1 chain, 2 more treble in the same place. Repeat from the second row. In working the successive scallops connect them by catching the first stitch of the last row into the last row of the preceding scallop. When a sufficient length is crocheted, work a row of heading along the top in this manner : 4 chain, 2 treble under loop of five chain, and repeat.

No. 4.—TRINITY EDGING.

Procure a piece of mignardese braid, a reel of Evans's crochet cotton No. 22, and a very fine steel crochet needle. Commence with two long treble stitches in the first piqué of the braid, * 8 chain, 1 single crochet in the fourth piqué of the braid, 1 chain to turn, and work 6 rows of double crochet forwards and backwards on the eight chain stitches, then 2 long treble in the fourth piqué from the one in which the single crochet is worked, and repeat from * for the length required ; this will produce the series of little square diamonds as seen in the engraving. 2nd row—Begin on the right-hand side of the row of square diamonds, and along one side of the first diamond * work 4 treble with 1 chain between each ; this brings you to the angle, where make 3 chain and another treble in the same place as the last treble stitch is worked into, then 1 chain 1 treble three times along the second side of the diamond, and repeat from * to the end of the row. 3rd row—1 treble under the first one chain of last row, * 1 chain, 1 double crochet under the next one chain, 5 chain, 1 double-crochet under the next, 5 chain, 1 double crochet under the three chain, 5 chain, another double crochet in the same place, 5 chain, 1 double crochet under the

next one chain, 5 chain, 1 double crochet under the next, 1 chain, 1 treble under the next, 1 treble under the first chain of the next square diamond, and repeat from * 4th row—1 treble under the one chain of last row, 1 chain, 1 double crochet under the first loop of five chain, 5 chain, 1 double crochet under the next loop of five chain, 5 chain, 1 double crochet under the 5 chain at the point, 5 chain, another double crochet in the same place, 5 chain, 1 double crochet under the next, 5 chain, 1 double crochet under the next 1 chain, 1 treble under the one chain, and repeat. This completes the edging. On the other side of the braid work in each piqué a double crochet stitch with 1 chain between.

No. 5.—TORTOISE EDGING.

Procure a piece of fancy braid of the kind shown in the engraving. Evans's crochet cotton No. 18, and a fine steel crochet needle. On one side of the braid for the top of the edging, work 1 treble in the first picot, 3 chain, miss one picot, 1 double crochet in the next, 1 chain, 1 double crochet in the next, 3 chain, miss one picot, 1 treble in the next, and do the same in each tab of the braid for the length desired. Work on the opposite side of the braid for the Scallops—1st row—1 treble in the first picot, 1 chain and 2 treble in each of the next four picots, 1 chain, 1 treble in the last, and continue the same in each tab to the end of the braid. 2nd row—1 double crochet under the first one chain of last row, * 8 chain, 1 treble in the seventh chain from the needle, 1 chain, 1 double crochet under the next one chain of last row, and repeat from * three times ; then 1 double crochet under the first one chain of the next scallop, and continue.

No. 6.—SPIDER-WEB EDGING.

This is a strong, pretty edging for underlinen. Use Evans's crochet cotton No. 24, and a very fine steel crochet needle. Commence with 22 chain. 1st row— 1 treble in the fourth chain from the needle, 2 chain, miss two, 1 treble five times, 3 treble on the last three chain stitches. 2nd row—12 chain to turn, 1 treble in the tenth chain from the needle, 1 treble in each of the two next chain stitches, and 1 treble on the first of the four treble of last row, 1 chain, 1 treble on the last of the four treble, 1 treble on each of the two chain, and 1 treble on

No. 2.—The Elzy Insertion.

the treble stitch of last row, 2 chain and 1 treble three times, 2 chain, 2 treble at the end. 3rd row—3 chain to turn, 1 treble on the first treble stitch, 2 chain and 1 treble three times, 3 more successive treble, 4 chain, 1 long treble under the loop of one chain, 4 chain, 1 treble on the last treble stitch, and 3 treble on three chain at the end. 4th row—12 chain to turn, 1 treble in the tenth chain from the needle, 1 treble in each of the two next chain stitches, and 1 treble on the first of the four treble of last row, 4 chain, 3 double crochet, the centre one being over the long treble stitch, 4 chain, 1 treble on the last of the four treble stitches, 3 successive treble, 2 chain, 1 treble, 2 chain, 2 treble at the end. 5th row—3 chain to turn, 1 treble on the first treble stitch, 2 chain, 4 treble, the last being over the first of the four treble of last row, 8 chain, 5 double crochet, 8 chain, 1 treble on the last treble stitch, and 3 treble on three chain at the end. 6th row—6 chain to turn, 1 treble on the last stitch of the four treble of last row, 3 successive treble, 7 chain, 3 double crochet on the centre of the five of last row, 7 chain, 3 treble on the last three stitches of the loop of chain, 1 treble on the first treble stitch, 2 chain, 1 treble, 2 chain, 1 treble 2 chain, 2 treble at the end. 7th row—3 chain to turn, 1 treble on the first treble stitch, 2 chain, 1 treble, 2 chain, 1 treble, 2 chain, 4 treble, 3 chain, 1 long treble on the centre double crochet stitch, 3 chain, 3 treble on the last three stitches of the loop of chain, 1 treble on the first treble stitch. 8th row— 6 chain to turn, 1 treble on the last stitch of the four treble, 3 successive treble, 1 chain, 3 treble on three chain stitches and 1 treble on the first treble stitch, 2 chain, 1 treble, 2 chain, 1 treble, 2 chain, 1 treble, 2 chain, 2 treble at the end. 9th row—3 chain to turn, 1 treble on the first treble stitch, 2 chain and 1 treble four times, 2 chain, 1 treble on the last of the four treble of last row, 2 treble in the one chain stitch, and 1 treble on the first of the four treble stitches. This completes one scallop. Repeat from the second row for the length desired. Now bind round the scallops with a row of double crochet, doing 1 double crochet in the treble stitch at the end of the ninth row, and 9 double crochet under each loop of chain, with 1 double crochet between.

No. 7.—THISTLE BORDER.

Procure a piece of fancy braid of the kind shown in the illustration. Evans's crochet cotton No. 18, and a fine steel crochet needle. 1st row—3 treble in

No. 3.—Victoria Pattern.

the first picot of the braid, 2 chain, miss the next picot, 2 treble in the next, working off both top loops together, 2 chain, miss the next picot, 2 treble in the next, working off both top loops together, 2 chain, miss the next picot, 3 treble in the next, and repeat the same in each tab of the braid for the length required ; break off at the end of this and every row. 2nd row—1 treble, 2 chain, miss two, and repeat. 3rd row—1 double crochet on the first chain stitch of last row, * 6 chain, miss five stitches of last row, 3 long treble in the next, working off all three top loops together, 5 chain, 1 double crochet in the same stitch as the three long treble are worked into, and repeat from *. 4th row—1 chain, * 1 double crochet on the bunch of stitches of last row, 5 chain, and repeat from *. 5th row—1 treble, 2 chain, miss two, and repeat. Now work on the other side of the braid. 1st row—Same as the first row above. 2nd row—2 treble under the first loop of two chain, 5 chain, 1 double crochet on the top of the treble stitch just done, 1 chain, * 2 treble under the second loop of two chain, 5 chain, 1 double crochet on the top of the treble stitch just done, 1 chain, repeat from * twice more in the same place, 2 treble under the third loop of two chain, and repeat.

No 8.—MIGNARDESE BORDER.

Procure a piece of mignardese braid and crochet cotton No. 18 or No. 20. Commence with 1 treble in the first picot of the braid, 2 chain and 1 treble in six successive picots, * 8 chain, 1 long treble in the next picot, 5 chain, another long treble in the same place, 2 chain, 5 long treble in five successive picots, keeping the last loop of each stitch on the needle, and then drawing through all together and doing 1 chain stitch to tighten the group. 2 chain, 1 long treble in the next picot, 5 chain, another long treble in the same place, 5 chain, again another long treble in the same place. 2 chain, 5 long treble in five successive picots as a group, 3 long treble separate, 3 long treble as a group, 3 more long treble as a group, 3 long treble separate, 5 long treble as a group, 2 chain, 1 long treble in the next picot, 2 chain, catch by a single crochet to the five chain on the opposite side of the scallop, 2 chain, 1 long treble in the same picot last long treble is worked into, 2 chain, catch by a single crochet to the other five chain on the opposite side of the scallop, 2 chain, 1 long treble in the same picot last long treble is worked into, 2 chain, 5 long treble in successive loops as a group, 2 chain, 1 long treble in the next picot, 2 chain, catch by a single crochet to the corresponding loop of five chain, 2 chain, 1 long treble in the same picot last long treble is worked into, 3 chain, catch by a single crochet to the loop of eight chain, 5 chain, 1 treble in the next picot, 2 chain and 1 treble in 9 successive picots, and repeat from * till you have a sufficient length worked; end with 7 successive treble stitches as you began. **Now for the Heading—1st row—** 1 double crochet under first two chain of last row, 3 chain and 1 double crochet under next four spaces, * 3 chain, 1 long treble under the first loop of eight chain, 4 chain, 1 long treble under the next loop, 3 chain, miss the first space of two chain, 1 double crochet in the next, 3 chain and 1 double crochet six times in successive spaces, and repeat from *. **2nd row—**1 double crochet under the first space, 2 chain and 1 double crochet twice in successive spaces, * 2 chain, 4 long treble on the three chain of last row, 1 chain, 4 long treble on the four chain, 1 chain, 4 long treble on three chain, 2 chain, 1 double crochet under the second space of two chain, 2 chain and 1 double crochet under the next three spaces, and repeat from *. **For the Scallops—**Beginning on the opposite side of the braid in the picot just to the right of the seven treble stitches ; * 3 long treble stitches in successive picots and drawn together as a group, 3 more long treble as a group, 3 long treble separate, 5 long treble as a group, 2 chain, 1 long treble in the next picot, 5 chain, another long treble in the same place, 5 chain, another long treble in the same place, 2 chain, 5 long treble as a group, 3 chain, 2 long treble in the next picot as a group, 7 chain, 1 long treble in the top thread of the long treble group just done, miss one picot, 2 long treble in the next as a group, 7 chain, 1 long treble in the top thread of the long treble group just done, repeat this till you have six groups of two long trebles, 3 chain, 5 long treble as a group, 2 chain, 1 long treble in the next picot, 5 chain another long treble in the same place, 5 chain, another long treble in the same place, 2 chain, 5 long treble as a group, 2 chain, 4 long treble separate, and repeat from * : in course of working the following scallops catch with a single crochet into the loops of preceding scallop, as shown in the illustration

No. 9.—JUBILEE BORDER.

THE centre of this handsome border is worked the short way, and the edging and heading are added afterwards. Commence with 24 chain. **1st row—** 1 treble in the sixth chain from the needle, 2 chain, another treble in the same place, 2 chain, miss two, 2 treble in the next, 2 chain, 2 more treble in the same

loop, and repeat from * twice, and fasten off. Work as many of these sectional pieces as will suffice for the length required, joining them in process of working by catching the third stitch of the last loop of five chain into the first loop of five chain of the preceding section. The side where a loop of seven chain of the second round is left vacant is the top of the border. Along this side work for the **1st row of the Heading—**3 double long treble in the first stitch of the group of double long treble stitches on the right-hand side, 4 chain, 3 treble under the loop of four chain, 4 chain, 5 long treble under the loop of five chain of the second round, 4 chain, 3 treble under the loop of four chain, 3 double long treble on the last double long treble stitch of the section, and continue the same to the end of the row. **2nd row—**Plain double crochet. **3rd row—**2 treble, 2 chain, miss two, and repeat. **4th row—**Double crochet. Work **for the Scallops** along the opposite side of the sections—**1st row—**1 double crochet on the first stitch, 5 chain, 1 double crochet on the centre stitch of the group of seven double long treble, 5 chain, 1 double crochet on the last stitch of the same group, 5 chain, 1 double crochet on the first stitch of the next group, 5 chain, 1 double crochet on the centre stitch of the group, 5 chain, 4 treble under the loop of five chain, 5 chain, 4 more treble in the same place, 5 chain and 1 double crochet five times along the opposite side of the section, and continue the same to the end of the row. **2nd row—**1 double crochet under the first loop of five chain of last row, * 5 chain, 1 double crochet in the next loop, 5 chain, another double crochet in the same place, repeat from * twice, then 5 chain, 6 treble under the loop of five chain in the centre of the scallop, 5 chain, 6 more treble in the same place, and crochet along the opposite side of the scallop to correspond. **3rd row—**1 double crochet under the first loop of five chain of last row, 6 chain, miss the next loop of five chain (the picot), 1 double crochet in the next, repeat twice, then 6 chain, 11 treble under the loop of five chain in the centre of the scallop, 6 chain and 1 double crochet three times along the side of the scallop. **4th row—**Same as the second row along both sides of the scallop, and 1 plain double crochet in each of the eleven treble at the point.

No. 11.—WILLOW PATTERN FOR SHAWL BORDER.

COMMENCE with chain sufficient for the length required, or, if preferred, the border may be crocheted upon the shawl itself. If worked in the length, break off at the end of every row, and begin again on the right-hand side. **1st row—**

No. 4.—Trinity Border.

No. 5.—Tortoise Edging.

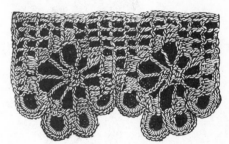

No. 6.—Spider-Web Edging.

place, 4 chain, miss five, 1 treble in the next, 2 chain and 1 treble three times in the same place, 4 chain, miss five, 2 treble in the next, 2 chain, 2 more treble in the same place, 2 chain, miss two, 1 treble in the next, 2 chain, another treble in the same place. **2nd row—**5 chain to turn, 1 treble under the first two chain of last row, 2 chain, another treble in the same place, 2 chain, 2 treble in the space between the two trebles of last row, 2 chain, 2 more treble in the same place, 2 chain, 1 double crochet in the third stitch of the loop of four chain, 5 treble in the first of the three centre loops, 3 treble 2 chain 3 treble in the next, 5 treble in the last of the three centre loops, 1 double crochet in the second stitch of the loop of four chain, 2 chain, 2 treble in the space between the two trebles, 2 chain, 2 more treble in the same place, 2 chain, 1 treble under the last loop of two chain, 2 chain, 1 more treble in the same place. **3rd row—**5 chain to turn, 1 treble under the first two chain of last row, 2 chain, another treble in the same place, 2 chain, 2 treble in the space between the two trebles of last row, 2 chain, 2 more treble in the same place, 4 chain, 1 treble under the centre loop of two chain, 2 chain and 1 treble three times in the same place, 4 chain, 2 treble in the space between the two trebles, 2 chain, 2 more treble in the same place, 2 chain, 1 treble under the last loop of two chain, 2 chain, 1 more treble in the same place. **4th row—**Same as the second row. Repeat these two rows for the length required. Now work along one side of the crochet **for the Scalloped Edging—1st row—**2 long treble, 3 chain, 2 long treble under every loop of five chain, and break off at the end of the row. **2nd row—**1 double crochet under the first three chain of last row, 1 chain and 1 treble six times under the next three chain, 1 chain, and repeat to the end. **3rd row—**1 double crochet under the first chain stitch of last row, * 5 chain, 1 double crochet under the next chain stitch, and repeat from * to the end ; and this finishes the scallops. Work for the heading of the border, 3 treble under each loop of five chain, with 3 chain to divide the groups.

No. 10.—WATERFALL BORDER.

COMMENCE with 10 chain ; join round, and work 24 treble in the circle, and join. **2nd round—**7 chain, miss two treble of last round, 1 double crochet in the next, and repeat, getting eight of these loops in the round, join. **3rd round—**3 single crochet under the first loop of seven chain, * 4 chain, 7 double long treble (cotton three times round the needle) in the next loop, 5 chain, 7 more double long treble in the same place. 4 chain, 1 double crochet in the next

Double crochet in every stitch of the foundation. **2nd row—**8 treble in the second stitch of double crochet, * wool over the needle, miss three double crochet, insert the hook in the next stitch of double crochet, draw the wool through and pull up a long stitch, wool over the needle, insert the hook in the same place and pull up another long stitch, wool over the needle, insert the hook in the same place and pull up a third long stitch, wool over the needle, insert the hook in the same place and pull up a fourth long stitch, wool over the needle and draw through all the long stitches and through the stitch on the needle, 1 chain, another bunch of long stitches in the same place, 1 chain, miss three double crochet, 8 treble in the next, and repeat from * to the end of the row. **3rd row—**1 treble on each of the six centre treble stitches of last row, * 1 chain, 1 bunch of long stitches (worked as already described) in the space between the bunches of last row, 1 chain, another bunch in the same place, 1 chain, 1 treble on each of the six centre trebles of last row, and repeat from *. **4th row—**1 treble on each of the four centre treble stitches of last row, 1 chain, 4 bunches of stitches with a chain stitch between each bunch in the space between the bunches of last row, 1 chain, and repeat. **5th row—**1 treble on each of the two centre treble stitches of last row, 1 chain, 2 bunches in the first space, 1 bunch in the next, 2 bunches in the next, 1 chain stitch being between each bunch, 1 chain, and repeat. **6th row—**1 double crochet on each treble stitch of last row, 1 chain, 2 bunches in each space between the bunches of last row, making 8 bunches in all, 1 chain between each bunch, 1 chain, and repeat. **7th row—**1 double crochet under the first one chain of last row, 2 chain, 1 double crochet in the first space between the bunches, 4 chain, 1 double crochet on the double crochet just worked, * 1 treble in the next space between the bunches, 4 chain, 1 double crochet on the treble just worked, repeat from * six times, 1 double crochet in the next space, 4 chain, 1 double crochet on the double crochet just worked, 2 chain, and work the same round the next succeeding scallops.

No. 12.—MARGUERITE BORDER.

PROCURE Evans's crochet cotton No. 24, and a very fine steel crochet needle. Commence with 30 chain. **1st row—**1 treble in the sixth chain from the needle, 2 chain, another treble in the same place, 1 chain, miss one, 1 double crochet in the next, 1 chain, miss one, 8 consecutive treble, 5 chain, miss one, 8 more consecutive treble, 1 chain, miss one, 1 double crochet in the next, 1 chain, miss one, 1 treble at the end, 2 chain another treble in the same place **2nd row—**

5 chain to turn, 1 treble under the two chain, 2 chain, another treble in the same place, 2 chain, 4 treble on the first four treble of last row, 5 chain, 1 double crochet under the five chain of last row, 5 chain, 4 treble on the last four treble stitches, 2 chain, 1 treble under the two chain, 2 chain, another treble in the same place. **3rd row**—5 chain to turn, 1 treble under the two chain, 2 chain, another treble in the same place, 1 chain, 1 double crochet under the two chain, 1 chain, 2 treble on first two treble stitches, 4 chain, 1 double crochet under the five chain, 5 chain, 1 double crochet under the next five chain, 4 chain, 2 treble on last two treble stitches, 1 chain, 1 double crochet under the two chain, 1 chain, 1 treble under the two chain 2 chain, another treble in the same place. **4th row**—5 chain to turn, 1 treble under the two chain, 2 chain, another treble in the same place, 2 chain, 4 consecutive treble beginning over the two treble of last row, 5 chain, 1 double crochet under the five chain, 5 chain, 4 consecutive treble ending over the two treble of last row, 2 chain, 1 treble under the 2 chain, 2 chain, another treble in the same place. **5th row**—5 chain to turn, and work same as the first row. And continue for the length required. **For the Scalloped Edge**—**1st row**—Work 2 long treble, 3 chain, 2 long treble, under each turn of five chain stitches ; break off at the end of the row. **2nd row**—Beginning on the right-hand side, 1 double crochet under the first loop of three chain, 1 chain, 1 treble under the next loop of three chain, 1 chain and 1 treble six times in the same place, 1 chain, and repeat to the end of the row. **3rd row**—1 double crochet under the first one chain of last row, 5 chain, 1 double crochet under the next one chain, 5 chain and 1 double crochet six more times under successive one-chain stitches, and continue. To head the top, work a row of 3 treble under each turn of five chain stitches, doing 3 chain between each group of treble.

No. 13.—WIDE HANDSOME BORDER FOR FURNITURE.

To be worked with Strutt's knitting cotton No. 10, and a fine steel crochet needle, or with other material according to the purpose for which it is required. Begin with 30 chain, turn back, and work 29 double crochet. * Turn, work 27 double crochet, inserting the hook to take up the back thread of the stitches of last row, turn back, and again work 27 double crochet in the same manner. Turn, work 22 double crochet ; turn back, and again work 22 double crochet. Turn,

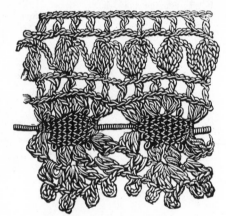

No. 7.—Thistle Border.

work 17 double crochet ; turn back, and again work 17 double crochet. Turn, work 10 double crochet ; turn back, and again work 10 double crochet. Now do 16 chain ; turn back, and work 10 double crochet, leaving five chain stitches unworked for the open part between the scallops. Turn, work 10 double crochet, 8 chain ; turn back, and work 17 double crochet. Turn, work 17 double crochet, 6 chain ; turn back, and work 22 double crochet. Turn, work 22 double crochet, 6 chain ; turn back, and work 27 double crochet. Turn, work 27 double crochet, 3 chain ; turn back, and work 29 double crochet. Repeat from * for the length required. Now to edge round these scallops, begin with 1 treble on the chain stitch at the tip of the first point, * 5 chain, another treble in the same place, 2 chain, 1 treble on the second double crochet stitch, 2 chain, 1 treble at the corner of the first ridge, 2 chain, miss two, 1 treble on the next, 2 chain, 1 treble at the corner of the next ridge, 2 chain, miss two, 1 treble on the next, 2 chain, 1 treble at the corner of the next ridge, 2 chain, miss two, 1 treble on the next, 2 chain, miss two, 1 treble on the next, 2 chain, 1 treble at the corner of the next ridge, 4 chain, miss two, 1 treble on the next, 4 chain, miss two, 1 treble on the next, 3 chain, 1 single crochet in the centre stitch of the five chain that connect the scallops, 3 chain, 1 treble in the third stitch of the next scallop, 2 chain, catch into the loop of four chain opposite, 2 chain, miss two, 1 treble in the next, 2 chain, catch into the four chain opposite, 2 chain, miss two, 1 treble at the corner, 2 chain and 1 treble nine times down the side to the point, and repeat from * and fasten off. Next the stars are to be made ; commence with 12 chain, join round in a circle ; work 4 chain to stand for a long treble stitch, 3 long treble in the same place, leaving the last loop of each on the needle, and drawing through all together when the tuft is completed, * 9 chain, miss one stitch of the circle, 4 long treble in the next, leaving the last loop of each on the needle, and drawing through all together, repeat from * twice ; then 4 chain and catch on to the second space of two chain from the point of the second scallop, 4 chain, a tuft of long treble as before, 11 chain, catch on to the seventh space of two chain of the same scallop, 5 chain, catch on to the corresponding space of the first scallop, 6 chain, 1 single crochet in the fifth chain from the star, 4 chain, a tuft of long treble, 4 chain, catch on to the second space of two chain from the point of the first scallop, 4 chain, join to the first tuft of the star, and fasten off. Fill up all the spaces between the scallops with similar stars. Work for the lower edging 1st row—1 treble in the centre stitch of five chain at the

point of the scallop, * 4 chain, 1 treble in the centre stitch of the nine chain of the star, 13 chain, 1 treble in the centre stitch of the next loop of nine chain, 13 chain, 1 treble in the centre stitch of the next nine chain, 4 chain, 1 treble in the centre stitch of five chain at the point of the next scallop, and repeat from *. **2nd row**—1 treble in the fourth chain stitch of last row, * 2 chain, miss one, 1 treble, fifteen times, miss seven over the point, 1 treble in the next, and repeat from *. **3rd row**—1 double crochet on the second treble stitch of last row, and work double crochet in every stitch, making 40 in all, which will bring you to the second treble from the point of the scallop, miss six, and repeat. **4th row**—Miss the first six double crochet stitches of last row, 1 treble on the next, * 5 chain, 1 single crochet in the fourth chain from the needle, 1 chain, 1 double crochet under the loop of last row, 1 treble on the next, repeat from * eight times, miss twelve double crochet at the point, 1 treble on the next, and repeat. This finishes the scallops. Now proceed for the heading. **1st row**—1 treble on the last row of the ridged double crochet, 2 chain and 1 treble three times, the last treble stitch being on the short row of the ridged crochet, * 2 chain 1 treble in the centre stitch of the 5 chain, 2 chain, 1 treble on the short row of the next lot of ridged crochet, 2 chain and 1 treble six times, the last of these treble stitches being on the other short row of the same lot of ridged crochet, and repeat from *. **2nd row**—1 double crochet on the first treble stitch of last row, 3 chain, 1 treble in the same place, * 1 chain, miss the next treble stitch of last row, 1 treble on the next, 3 chain, 1 double crochet in the same place, 3 chain, 1 treble in the same place, and repeat from *. **3rd row**—Same as the second row, working into each stitch of one chain. **4th row**—1 double crochet in each chain stitch of last row, with 5 chain between. **5th row**—1 treble, 2 chain, miss two, and repeat.

No. 14.—STAR EDGING.

Commence with 18 chain. **1st row**—3 treble in the fifth chain from the needle, 1 chain, 3 treble in the next, 8 chain, miss seven, 3 treble in the next, 3 chain, 3 treble in the next, 1 treble in the last. **2nd row**—3 chain to turn, 3 treble under the loop of three chain, 3 chain, 3 more treble in the same place, 4 chain, 1 double crochet over the last row and into the foundation chain, 4 chain, 1 treble under the one chain, 3 chain, another treble in the same place. **3rd**

No. 8.—Mignardese Border.

row—4 chain to turn, 3 treble under the loop of three chain, 1 chain, 3 more treble in the same place, 3 chain, 1 treble on the one treble, 2 treble under the four chain, 2 treble under the next four chain, 1 treble on the first of the three treble stitches, 3 chain, 3 treble under the loop of three chain, 3 chain, 3 more treble in the same place, 1 treble on the chain that turned. **4th row**—3 chain to turn, 3 treble under the loop of three chain, 3 chain, 3 more treble in the same place, 2 long treble in between the six treble stitches of last row, 8 chain, 2 more long treble in the same place, 1 treble under the one chain, 3 chain, 3 more treble in the same place, 3 chain, 7 treble under the loop of four chain, 1 double crochet on the treble stitch at the end of the first row. **5th row**—4 chain and 1 double crochet under each one chain stitch of last row, 4 chain, 1 double crochet under the three chain, 3 chain, 3 treble under the loop of three chain, 1 chain, 3 more treble in the same place, 8 chain, 3 treble under the next loop of three chain, 3 chain, 3 more treble in the same place, 1 treble on the chain that turned. **6th row**—3 chain to turn, 3 treble under the loop of three chain, 3 chain, 3 more treble in the same place, 8 chain, 1 treble under the one chain, 3 chain, 1 more treble in the same place. **7th row**—4 chain to turn, 3 treble under the loop of three chain, 1 chain, three more treble in the same place, 4 chain, 1 double crochet over the last three rows of eight chain, 4 chain, 3 treble under the loop of three chain, 3 chain, 3 more treble in the same place, 1 treble on the chain that turned. **8th row**—3 chain to turn, 3 treble under the loop of three chain, 3 chain, 3 more treble in the same place, 3 chain, 1 treble on the last of the three treble stitches, 2 treble under the loop of four chain, 2 treble under the next loop of four chain, 1 treble on the first of the three treble stitches, 3 chain, 1 treble under the one chain, 3 chain, 1 treble in the same place, 3 chain, 7 treble under the loop of four chain, 1 double crochet on the treble stitch at the end of the fifth row. **9th row**—4 chain and 1 double crochet under each one chain stitch of last row, 4 chain, 1 double crochet under the three chain, 3 chain, 3 treble under the loop of three chain, 1 chain, 3 more treble in the same place, 2 long treble in between the six treble stitches of last row, 8 chain, 2 more long treble in the same place, 3 treble under the loop of three chain, 3 chain, 3 more treble in the same place, 1 treble on the chain that turned. Work on in this manner, varying by one row in each pattern the position of the stars, and always catching together three rows of eight chain with a double crochet.

No. 15.—SHAMROCK PATTERN FOR SHAWL BORDER.

THIS may be commenced with chain for the length required or crocheted immediately upon the shawl; if the former, break off at the end of every row and begin anew on the right-hand side. **1st row**—Double crochet in every stitch of the foundation. **2nd row**—1 treble, 1 chain, miss one, and repeat. **3rd row**—Wool over the needle, insert the hook under the first one chain of last row, draw the wool through and pull up a long stitch, wool over the needle, insert the hook in the same place and pull up another long stitch, wool over the needle and make a third long stitch, wool over the needle and make a fourth long stitch, wool over the needle and draw through all the stitches on the needle, 1 chain, work another bunch of long stitches under the next one chain of last row, 1 chain, and repeat. **4th row**—1 treble under the one chain of last row, * 1 chain, 1 treble under the next one chain, and repeat from *. **5th row**—1 double crochet under the first one chain of last row, * 3 chain, miss the next space of one chain, 1 bunch of stitches in the next, 2 chain, another bunch in the same place, 3 chain, miss the next space of one chain, 1 double crochet in the next, and repeat from *. **6th row**—1 double crochet on the double crochet of last row, 3 chain, 1 bunch in the space between the bunches of last row, 2 chain, another bunch in the same place, 2 chain, another bunch in the same place, 3 chain, and repeat. **7th row**—1 double crochet on the double crochet of last row, 3 chain, 1 bunch in the first space between the bunches of last row, 2 chain, another bunch in the same place, 2 chain, 1 bunch in the second space between the bunches of last row, 2 chain, another bunch in the same place, 3 chain, and repeat. **8th row**—1 double crochet under the three chain of last row, 1 double crochet, 5 treble 1 double crochet all worked into each of the three spaces between the bunches of last row, 1 double crochet under the three chain, and repeat the same round every scallop of the border.

No. 16.—STAR-CROSS BORDER.

THIS handsome pattern may be worked with cotton for a quilt border or furniture trimming, and if done with wool it makes an elegant finish to a shawl.

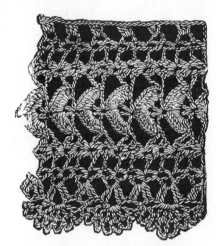

No. 9.—Jubilee Border.

Commence with 11 chain. **1st row**—1 treble in the fourth chain from the needle, 1 treble in the next, 3 chain, miss three, 1 treble in each of the three last foundation stitches. **2nd row**—6 chain to turn, 3 treble under the three chain, 3 chain, 1 treble on the chain that turned. **3rd row**—2 chain to turn, 2 treble under the three chain, 3 chain, 3 treble under the six chain, 6 chain, 3 more treble in the same place. **4th row**—6 chain, 1 single in the sixth from the needle, 6 chain, 1 single in the sixth from the needle, 6 chain, 1 single in the sixth from the needle, 3 treble under the six chain of last row, 6 chain, 3 more treble in the same place, 3 chain, 3 treble, 3 chain, 1 treble on the chain that turned. **5th row**—2 chain, 2 treble under the three chain, 3 chain, 3 treble, 3 chain, 3 treble, 6 chain, 3 more treble in the same place. **6th row**—6 chain, 1 single in the sixth from the needle, 6 chain, 1 single in the sixth from the needle, 6 chain, 1 single in the sixth from the needle, 3 treble under the six chain of last row, 6 chain, 3 more treble in the same place, 3 chain, 3 treble, 3 chain, 3 treble, 3 chain, 1 treble in the chain that turned. **7th row**—2 chain, 2 treble under the three chain 3 chain, 3 treble, 3 chain, 3 treble, 3 chain, 3 treble, 6 chain, 3 more treble in the same place. **8th row**—6 chain, 1 single in the sixth from the needle, 6 chain, 1 single in the sixth from the needle, 6 chain, 1 single in the sixth from the needle, 3 treble under the six chain of last row, 6 chain, 1 single in the sixth from the needle, 6 chain, 1 single in the sixth from the needle, 6 chain, 1 single in the sixth from the needle, 3 treble under the same three chain as last three treble are worked under, 3 chain, 3 treble, 3 chain, 3 treble, 3 chain, 3 treble, 3 chain, 1 treble on the chain that turned. **9th row**—2 chain, 2 treble under the three chain, 3 chain, 3 treble, 3 chain, 3 treble, 3 chain, 3 treble. **10th row**—6 chain, 1 single in the sixth from the needle, 6 chain, 1 single in the sixth from the needle, 6 chain, 1 single in the sixth from the needle, 3 treble under the three chain of last row, 3 chain, 3 treble, 3 chain, 3 treble, 3 chain, 1 treble in the chain that turned. **11th row**—2 chain, 2 treble under the three chain, 3 chain, 3 treble, 3 chain, 3 treble. **12th row**—6 chain, 1 single in the sixth from the needle, 6 chain, 1 single in the sixth from the needle, 6 chain, 1 single in the sixth from the needle, 3 treble under the three chain of last row, 3 chain, 3 treble, 3 chain, 1 treble on the chain that turned. **13th row**—2 chain 2 treble under the three chain, 3 chain, 3 treble under the next three chain. Repeat from the second row for the length

required. When a sufficient length is done work this heading along the straight side. **1st row**—1 double crochet and 1 chain alternately, and not too full; break off at the end of the row, and recommence on the right-hand side. **2nd row**—1 double crochet under the one chain of last row, 5 chain, 2 long treble in the same place, working off the top loops of both long trebles together with the chain stitch on the needle, miss two loops of one chain, 2 long treble in the third working off the top loops of both long trebles together, 4 chain, 1 double crochet in the same place, 11 chain, miss two loops of one chain, and repeat. **3rd row**—2 long treble stitches between the group of long trebles in previous row, working off the top loops of both long trebles together, 4 chain, 1 double crochet in the same place, 5 chain, 2 more long trebles in the same place, working off the top loops of both long trebles together with the chain stitch on the needle, 5 chain, 1 double crochet under the loop of eleven chain, 5 chain, and repeat; turn the work at the end of this row. **4th row**—1 double crochet on the first group of long treble stitches, 6 chain, 1 double crochet on the next group of long treble stitches, 6 chain, and repeat; turn the work at the end of the row. **5th row**—1 treble, 1 chain, miss one, alternately.

No. 17.—CORAL EDGING.

THIS is a pretty edging for underlinen if worked with Evans's crochet cotton No. 24 and a fine steel crochet needle. Begin with 11 chain; turn, and work 1 treble in the seventh chain from the needle, 2 chain, 1 treble in the next stitch of the foundation, 3 chain, another treble in the same place, 4 chain, 1 treble in the last of the foundation, 3 chain, another treble in the same place. **2nd row**—Turn with 3 chain, 5 treble under the loop of three chain of last row, 4 chain, 6 treble under the next loop of three chain, 2 chain, 1 treble under the loop that turned at the end, 2 chain, another treble in the same place **3rd row**—5 chain to turn, 1 treble under the first two chain of last row, 2 chain, 1 treble under the next loop, 3 chain, another treble in the same place, 4 chain, 1 treble under the loop of four chain of last row, 3 chain, another treble in the same place **4th row**—Same as the second row. Repeat the third and fourth rows for the length required.

No. 10.—Waterfall Border.

No. 18.—SCALLOPED EDGING WORKED ON PLAIN BRAID.

PROCURE a piece of plain braid, and with red ingrain cotton work thereon in cross-stitch the scroll pattern as shown in the engraving. With crochet cotton No. 20, work along one side of the braid for the Heading, 1 treble in two picots of the braid taken up together, * 3 chain, 1 treble in next two picots of the braid, and repeat from * to the end. Work for the Scallops on the opposite side— **1st row**—1 double crochet in two picots of the braid taken up together, 4 chain 1 double crochet in the two next picots, 7 chain, 1 double crochet in the two next picots, and repeat. **2nd row**—1 double crochet on the first double crochet of last row, * 1 long treble under the seven chain, 1 chain and 1 long treble six times in the same place, 1 double crochet on the double crochet stitch between the spaces of four chain, and repeat from *. **3rd row**—1 double crochet on the double crochet of last row, * 1 double crochet under the first one chain, 4 chain and 1 double crochet under the next one chain five times, 1 double crochet on the double crochet of last row, and repeat from *.

No. 19.—WIDE OPEN BORDER FOR FURNITURE TRIMMING.

THIS is worked with coarse ecru cotton or flax thread. Begin by working a hair-pin trimming four times the length required for the border. Hair-pin trimming is worked in this manner: having a stitch on the crochet needle, take the hair-pin (which should be a large one) in the left hand, the prongs upwards, hold the point of the crochet needle between the prongs of the hair-pin, the cotton falling from above to the right of the hair-pin, draw the cotton through the stitch on the needle, and * bring the needle out on the top of the hair-pin, turn the hair-pin over from right to left, at the same time slipping the needle again into position between the prongs with the cotton again to the right, draw the cotton through the stitch on the needle, and work a double crochet stitch in the loop that lies round the left-hand prong; repeat from *: when the hair-pin is full you can drop off all the stitches, replace the last three or four, and continue. A sufficiency of the hair-pin trimming being worked, commence for

No. 11.—Willow Pattern for Shawl Border.

No. 12.—Marguerite Border.

No. 17.—Coral Edging.

No. 13.—Wide Handso

No. 16.—Star Cross Border.

No. 20.—Snowdrop Edging.

Hair-

No. 24 —Honit

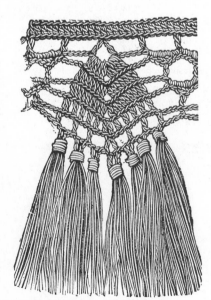

No. 22.—Fringe for Furniture Trimming.

No. 23.—Wide Scalloped Border.

No. 25.—Railw

[54]

der for Furniture.

aming.

Edging.

ing.

No. 14.—Star Edging.

No. 15.—Shamrock Pattern for Shawl Border.

No. 18.—Scalloped Edging worked on Plain Braid.

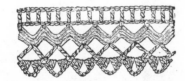

No. 21.—Narrow Wave Braid Edging.

No. 26.—Target Border.

No. 19.—Wide Open Border for Furniture.

No. 27.—Fringe for Quilts, Toilet Covers, &c.

the border with 1 double crochet in each of the four first loops, * 9 chain, 1 double crochet in the next loop, 9 chain, miss one loop, 15 consecutive treble in next successive loops of the hair-pin trimming, 4 chain, 1 single crochet in the fifth stitch of the nine loop, 4 chain, miss one loop of hair-pin trimming, 1 double crochet in the next, 3 chain, 1 single crochet in the fourth stitch of the next nine chain, 5 chain, 1 double crochet in each of four successive loops; repeat from * to the end of the hair-pin trimming. For the Heading of the Border, work on this a row of 1 treble, 1 chain, miss one, and repeat. For the Scallops, work round the other side of the hair-pin trimming, thus: leave the first loop, work 1 double crochet in the next two loops taken together, 1 double crochet in each of six successive loops, * 6 chain, 1 double crochet in the fifth chain from the needle, 1 chain, 1 double crochet in the next loop, repeat from * nine times, 1 double crochet in five next successive loops, 1 double crochet in the next two loops taken together, 1 double crochet in each of six successive loops, catch with a single crochet into the corresponding stitch of the previous scallop, then repeat the picots, and continue.

No. 20.—SNOWDROP EDGING.

COMMENCE with 8 chain; work 1 double crochet in the second chain from the needle, 1 double crochet in the next, 4 consecutive treble stitches, and 1 long treble in the last of the foundation chain; * then do 6 chain, 1 double crochet in the fifth chain from the needle, 8 chain, 1 double crochet in the second chain from the needle, 1 double crochet in the next, 4 consecutive treble, 1 long treble in the next; repeat from * till you have the length desired. Then, without breaking off, work for the Scallops, 1 double crochet on the long treble stitch just done, 6 chain, 1 single crochet in the sixth from the needle, 6 chain, 1 single crochet in the sixth from the needle, 6 chain, 1 single crochet in the sixth from the needle, 1 double crochet in the same chain-stitch that the long treble is worked into, 6 chain, 1 double crochet in the fifth from the needle, 1 chain, 1 double crochet at the top of the next long treble stitch, and continue to the end of

last row, 5 chain, and repeat from *. 5th row—2 treble in the first chain stitch of last row, 1 double crochet on each of the other chain stitches, * 5 chain, 9 consecutive treble stitches beginning over the seven treble of last row, 4 chain, 9 more consecutive treble, 5 chain, 2 double crochet 3 treble and 2 double crochet all under the centre loop of five chain of last row, and repeat from * 6th row—1 treble on the first treble of last row, * 5 chain, 1 treble on the first of the nine treble, 1 chain, miss one, 1 treble on the next, and continue 1 chain 1 treble so as to get 12 treble stitches in all round the top of the scallop, then 5 chain, 1 treble on the centre stitch of the three trebles of last row, and repeat from *. 7th row—1 double crochet on the treble stitch of last row, * 4 chain, 1 treble in the last stitch of the five chain of last row. 9 chain, 1 double crochet in the first of these chain stitches miss three stitches of last row, 1 treble on the next, work round the top of the scallop 6 more picots of 9 chain ending with a treble on the first stitch of the five chain of last row, 4 chain, 1 double crochet on the treble stitch of last row, and repeat from *. This completes the heading. For the Fringe, cut the remainder of your thread or wool into lengths of 5 inches, and knot seven strands into each loop of the picoteed edge.

No. 23.—WIDE SCALLOPED BORDER.

THIS is commenced with 21 chain. 1st row—1 treble in the fourth chain from the needle, 5 chain, miss four, 1 treble in the next, 3 chain, another treble in the same place, 5 chain, miss five, 1 double crochet in the next, 5 chain and 1 double crochet three times in the same place, 5 chain, miss four, 1 treble in the next, 1 treble in the next. 2nd row—4 chain to turn, 1 treble on the second treble stitch of last row, 5 chain, 1 treble in the centre loop of five chain of last row, 3 chain, another treble in the same place, 5 chain, 1 double crochet under the loop of three chain, 5 chain and 1 double crochet three times in the same place, 5 chain, 1 treble on the treble stitch of last row, 1 treble on the chain that turned. Repeat this last row till you have 12 rows done. Now begin for the scallop by making 8 chain and working 1 double crochet into the

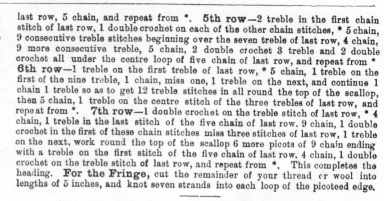

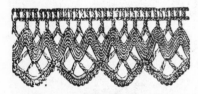

No. 28.—Picoteed Edging of Wave Braid.

No. 29.—Scalloped Edging of Wave Braid.

No. 30.—Neat Edging for Underlinen.

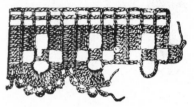

No. 31.—Polo Edging.

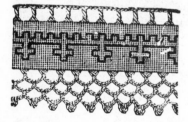

No. 32.—Simple Edging worked on Plain Braid.

No. 33.—Wave Braid Edging.

No. 34.—Narrow Mignardese Edging.

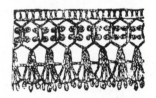

No. 35.—Juniper Edging.

the row. For the Heading—Work 1 single crochet on the one chain-stitch at the top of the point, 4 chain, 1 treble in the second treble along the side, 1 treble at base of the second treble of the next point, 4 chain, and repeat. 2nd row—Turn the work, and do * 1 double crochet in the same place the single crochet stitch is worked into, 6 chain, and repeat from *. 3rd row—Turn the work with 4 chain, 1 treble in the second chain of last row, 1 chain, miss one, 1 treble, and continue to the end of the row.

No. 21.—NARROW WAVE BRAID EDGING.

UPON a length of wave braid, and with Coats's crochet cotton No. 18 or No. 20, work for the Heading, 1 double crochet on the top of each wave of the braid and 4 chain between, for the required length, and on this do a row of 1 treble, 1 chain, miss one. On the opposite side of the braid work, 1st row—1 treble on the first wave of the braid, 5 chain, another treble in the same place, and repeat all along. 2nd row—1 double crochet, 3 treble, 3 chain, 3 treble, 1 double crochet, all under each loop of five chain of last row.

No. 22.—FRINGE FOR FURNITURE TRIMMING.

COMMENCE with chain sufficient for the length required. 1st row—Treble; break off at the end of this and every row, and recommence on the right-hand side. 2nd row—1 treble on the first treble of last row, * 5 chain, miss five treble stitches, 1 treble on the next, 5 chain, miss five, 1 treble on the next, 5 chain, another treble in the same place, 5 chain, miss five, 1 treble on the next, 5 chain, miss five, 1 treble on the next, and repeat from * to the end of the row. 3rd row—2 double crochet 3 treble and 2 double crochet all under the first five chain of last row, miss the next loop of five chain, under the next work 5 treble, 4 chain, 5 treble, miss the next loop, and work 2 double crochet, 3 treble, 2 double crochet, under the next, and repeat. 4th row—3 chain to begin,* 1 treble on the centre stitch of the three treble of last row, 5 chain, 7 consecutive treble stitches beginning over the five treble of last row, 4 chain, 7 more consecutive treble, 5 chain, 1 treble on the centre stitch of the three treble of

side of the tenth row. 2nd row of the Scallop—Turn, and do 1 double crochet under the eight loop, 9 chain and 1 double crochet six times in the same place, 4 chain, 1 treble on each of the two treble stitches of the heading, which work as before. 3rd row—Work along the heading as before, then 5 chain and one double crochet into each of the loops of nine chain round the scallop, 5 chain, and catch into the eighth row of the heading. 4th row—Turn, 5 chain and 1 double crochet under each loop of last row, and then the heading as before. 5th row—Work the heading, and then 5 chain and 1 double crochet into each loop of last row, and catch into the sixth row of the heading. 6th row—2 chain, and catch into the fifth row of the heading, work 7 treble under each loop of five chain, and the heading as before. 7th row—Work the heading, then 1 chain, 1 treble, alternately, in every other stitch of the scallop, 1 chain, and catch into the fourth row of the heading. 8th row—2 chain, and catch into the third row of the heading, 1 chain and 1 treble under each one chain of last row, and heading as before. 9th row—Work the heading, then 3 chain and 2 treble under each alternate one chain of last row, and catch into the second row of the heading. 10th row—2 chain, and catch into the first row of the heading, 2 chain, * 1 double crochet between the first two treble stitches, 2 chain, 1 treble under the three chain, do 4 chain and 1 double crochet three times for a picot on the top of the treble just done, 2 chain, and repeat from * all round the scallop, and work the heading as before. Then do 12 rows of heading only and continue.

No. 24.—HONITON LACE EDGING.

BEGIN by working a piece of hair-pin trimming about twice the length the edging is required to be. This done, commence with 18 chain, pass the cotton twice round the needle, insert the hook in the sixth chain from the needle and draw the cotton through, cotton over the needle and draw through two loops on the needle (leaving 3 on the needle), * cotton twice round the needle, miss one stitch of the foundation, insert the hook in the next stitch and draw the cotton through, cotton over the needle and draw through two loops on the needle (leaving 5 on the needle), repeat from * till you have 7 stitches worked (15 on the needle), then take the hair-pin trimming and work in the same manner 4 times in two loops of the trimming taken together, cotton once round the needle, insert the hook in the next two loops of the trimming and draw the cotton through, cotton over the needle and draw through two loops on the needle; now you work back like tricotee, cotton over the needle and draw through the first stitch, cotton over the needle and draw through the next stitch, and so on, till all are worked off. **2nd row**—2 chain to turn, miss the first treble of last row, and work the same as above on the 6 following trebles, inserting the hook so as to take up one thread only, then work same way but with cotton only once round the needle, and do 1 stitch on the space and 1 stitch on the treble for 8 stitches, do another stitch in two loops of the hair-pin trimming taken together; and work off as in previous row. **3rd row**—2 chain, miss the first treble of last row, and work 5 stitches over five treble with cotton twice round the needle, and 8 stitches over the eight with cotton once round the needle and another stitch in two loops of the hair-pin trimming taken together, and work back as in previous row. **4th row**—2 chain, miss the first treble of last row, and work 4 stitches over four treble with cotton twice round the needle, then 8 stitches over the eight of last row with cotton once round the needle, and another stitch in two loops of the hair-pin trimming taken together; and work back as in previous row. **5th row**—2 chain, miss the first treble of last row, and work 7 stitches the same as in the first row (make the last of the seven come upon the last stitch of the diamond), then take the same two loops of the hair-pin trimming as were worked into in last row, 3 more stitches taking up two loops of the hair-pin trimming each time, and 1 stitch in the next two loops with the cotton once round the needle; draw back as in the first row, and continue for the length required.

No 25.—RAILWAY EDGING.

THIS is worked upon a piece of fancy braid of the kind shown in the illustration. **For the Crochet Edging**, begin with 15 chain, work a single crochet in the eleventh chain from the needle, cross over the commencing chain, and along the under side of the circle work 6 single crochet, then do 10 double crochet in the circle, 1 double crochet in the fourth stitch from the end of the commencing chain, 4 chain, miss one, 1 double crochet in each of the two next stitches. **2nd row**—3 chain, 1 single into a picot of the braid, 2 chain, 1 single in the next picot, 2 chain, 1 treble on the first of the ten double crochet stitches, 1 chain and 1 treble nine times. **3rd row**—4 chain to turn, 1 double crochet under the first one chain, 1 double crochet under the next, 4 chain, 2 double crochet under two next chain, 4 chain, 2 double crochet under two next chain, 7 chain, turn the work, 1 single on the second double crochet at left-hand side, turn the work, do 10 double crochet under the loop of seven chain, 1 single in the same place double crochet stitch is worked into, 4 chain, 2 double crochet under next two chain: this leaves one space of one chain *not* worked into. **4th row**—3 chain, 1 single into the second picot from the one last worked into, 2 chain, 1 single in the next picot, 2 chain, 1 treble on the first of the ten double crochet stitches, 1 chain and 1 treble nine times, 6 chain, 1 single under the loop of four chain at the point. **5th row**—4 chain to turn, 1 double crochet under the loop of six chain, 4 chain and 1 double crochet five times in the same place, 4 chain, 1 double crochet under one chain, 1 double crochet under next one chain, 4 chain, 1 double crochet under one chain, 1 double crochet under next one chain, 4 chain, 1 double crochet under one chain, 1 double crochet under next one chain, 7 chain, turn the work, 1 single on the second double crochet stitch at left-hand side, turn the work, do 10 double crochet under the loop of seven chain, 1 single in the same place double crochet stitch is worked into, 4 chain, 1 double crochet under next one chain, 1 double crochet under next one chain, leave one space of one chain *not* worked into. **6th row**—3 chain, 1 single into the second picot from the one last worked

into, 2 chain, 1 single in the next picot, 2 chain, 1 treble on the first of the ten double crochet stitches, 1 chain and 1 treble nine times, 6 chain, 1 single in the third loop of four chain. **7th row**—4 chain to turn, 1 double crochet under the loop of six chain, 4 chain, 1 double crochet in the same place, 8 chain, 1 single in the fifth loop to the right, 4 chain, 1 double crochet under the loop of eight chain, 4 chain and 1 double crochet five times in the same place, 4 chain and 1 double crochet three times under the remaining part of the loop of six chain, 4 chain, 1 double crochet under 1 chain, 1 double crochet under next one chain, 4 chain, 1 double crochet under one chain, 1 double crochet under next one chain, 4 chain, 1 double crochet under 1 chain, 1 double crochet under next one chain, 7 chain, turn the work, 1 single on the second double crochet at left-hand side, turn the work, do 10 double crochet under loop of seven chain, 1 single in the same place double crochet stitch is worked into, 4 chain, 1 double crochet under next one chain, 1 double crochet under next one chain, leave one space of one chain *not* worked into. Repeat from the fourth row. **For the Heading**—On the opposite side of the braid, work **1st row**—1 single in the first picot of the braid, * 4 chain, 1 treble in the same picot, 3 chain, miss one picot, 1 single in the next, and repeat from *. **2nd row**—1 double crochet on the treble of last row, 6 chain, and repeat. **3rd row**—1 treble, 1 chain, miss one, and repeat.

No. 26.—TARGET BORDER.

BEGIN with 9 chain; join round, and work 3 long treble (cotton twice round the needle), 2 chain, eight times in the circle, join. **2nd round**—1 double crochet on the centre stitch of the three long treble, 2 chain, 1 treble in the second chain stitch, 2 chain, another treble in the same place, 2 chain, and repeat; join at the end of the round. **3rd round**—1 double crochet on the double crochet of last round, 3 chain, 1 treble, 2 long treble, and 1 treble, all under the loop of two chain between the treble stitches of last round, 3 chain, and repeat; join, and break off at the end of the round. Work a number of

No. 36.—Guipure Border.

No. 37.—Elegant Looped Border.

these circles or targets, connecting them together as you work by catching the last two long treble stitches into the first two long trebles of the preceding circle. **For the 1st row of the Heading**—Work 3 long treble in between two long treble stitches of the first circle, 7 chain, 1 double crochet in between the two next long treble stitches, which is the central point of the circle, 7 chain, 3 long treble in between the next two long treble stitches, and repeat. **2nd row**—1 treble, 1 chain, miss one, and repeat. **3rd row**—1 treble under one chain of last row, 1 chain, and repeat. Work on the opposite side of the crochet circles, **1st row** and **2nd row**—Same as the first and second row above. **3rd row**—1 double crochet on the first treble stitch, * 6 chain, miss five, 1 double crochet on the next, 3 chain, 2 long treble in the same place, miss five, 2 long treble on the next, 3 chain, 1 double crochet in the same place, and repeat from *. **4th row**—1 double crochet under the loop of six chain, 4 chain, 2 long treble on top of the two long treble of last row, 3 chain, 1 double crochet in the same place, 3 chain, 2 long treble on top of the next two long treble, 4 chain, and repeat. **5th row**—1 double crochet under the loop of three chain, 3 chain, 1 double crochet under next loop of three chain, 4 chain and repeat. **6th row**—1 treble, 1 chain, miss one, and repeat. **7th row**—1 double crochet under the first one chain of last row, 2 chain, 1 treble under the next one chain, 3 chain, another treble in the same place, 2 chain, and repeat.

No. 27.—FRINGE FOR QUILTS, TOILET COVERS, &c.

MAKE a chain the length required. **1st row**—1 treble, 1 chain, miss one, and repeat; break off at the end of this and every row. **2nd row**—1 double crochet, 7 chain, miss four stitches of last row, 1 double crochet, 9 chain, miss five, and repeat. **3rd row**—1 double crochet in the centre stitch of the seven chain, 2 chain, 5 treble in the third stitch of the nine chain, 3 chain, miss three, 5 treble in the next which is the seventh stitch of the nine chain, 2 chain, and repeat. **4th row**—1 treble on the double crochet of last row, 3 chain, 5 consecutive treble over five treble of last row, 3 chain 5 more consecutive treble, 3 chain, and repeat. **5th row**—1 treble on the treble stitch of last row, 3 chain, another treble in the same place, 3 chain, miss three chain and one treble, and work 4 consecutive treble on four treble of last row, 1 chain, 4 more consecutive treble on the four following, 3 chain, and repeat. **6th row**—1 treble on the first treble stitch of last row, 3 chain, another treble in the same place, 1 chain, 1 treble on the next treble of last row, 3 chain, another treble in the same place, 3 chain, 7 treble, the centre one of these to come over the one chain-stitch of last row, 3 chain, and repeat. **7th row**—1 treble on the first treble stitch of last row, 3 chain, another treble in the same place, 1 chain, 5 treble in the single chain stitch of last row, 1 chain, 1 treble on the fourth treble stitch of last row, 3 chain, another treble in the same place, 3 chain, 5 consecutive treble over the centre five treble of last row, 3 chain, and repeat. **8th row**—1 treble on the first treble stitch of last row, 3 chain, another treble in the same place 1 chain, 5 treble in single chain stitch, 1 chain, 5 treble in the other single chain stitch, 1 chain, 1 treble on treble stitch of last row, 3 chain, another treble in the same place, 3 chain, 3 consecutive treble over the centre three treble of last row, 3 chain, and repeat. **9th row**—1 double crochet on the first treble stitch of last row, 5 chain, * 1 treble in the single chain stitch of last row, 3 chain, another treble in the same place, 1 chain, 5 treble in the one chain between the groups of treble stitches, 1 chain, 1 treble in the single chain, 3 chain, another treble in the same place, 5 chain, 1 double crochet in the loop before the three treble of last row, 5 chain, 1 double crochet in the loop after the three treble, 5 chain, and repeat from *. **10th row**—1 double crochet on double crochet of last row, 5 chain, 1 double crochet in the last stitch of the 5 chain of last row, 5 chain, 1 treble in the single chain stitch of last row, 3 chain, another treble in the same place, 1 chain, 1 treble in the next single chain of last row, 3 chain, another treble in the same place, 3 chain, 1 double crochet in the first of the five chain of last row, 5 chain, 1 double crochet on double crochet of last row, 7 chain and repeat. **11th row**—1 double crochet under the first loop of five chain, 5 chain, 1 double crochet under the next loop of five chain, 5 chain, 1 treble in the single chain stitch, 3 chain, another treble in the same place, 5 chain, 1 double crochet under the loop of five chain, 5 chain, 1 double crochet under the next loop of five chain, 7 chain, and repeat. **12th row**—1 double crochet under the first loop of five chain, 5 chain, 1 double crochet under the next loop, 5 chain, 1 double crochet under the loop of three chain, 5 chain, 1 double crochet under the loop of five chain, 5 chain, 1 double crochet under the next loop, 7 chain, and repeat. Now to form the fringe, cut the remainder of your thread or wool into 6-inch lengths, and knot six strands into every loop of the crochet heading.

No. 30.—NEAT EDGING FOR UNDERLINEN.

COMMENCE with 17 chain. **1st row**—1 treble in the seventh chain from the needle, 1 chain, miss one, 1 treble in the next, 2 chain, miss three, 1 treble in the next, 3 chain, another treble in the same place, 2 chain, miss three, 1 treble in the next, 3 chain, another treble in the same place. **2nd row**—2 chain to turn, 9 treble under the loop of three chain, 7 treble under the next loop of three chain, 1 treble on the first of the two treble stitches, 1 chain, 1 treble on the next treble, 1 chain, 1 treble on the second stitch of the chain that turned. **3rd row**—4 chain to turn, 1 treble on the first treble stitch, 1 chain, 1 treble on the next treble stitch, 2 chain, 1 treble on the centre stitch of the seven treble, 3 chain, another treble in the same place, 2 chain, 1 treble on the fourth stitch of the nine treble, 3 chain, another treble in the same place. Repeat the second and third rows for the length required.

No 31.—POLO EDGING.

BEGIN with 16 chain. **1st row**—1 treble in the fourth chain from the needle, 8 treble worked consecutive, 1 chain, miss one, 1 treble in the next, 1 chain, miss one, 1 treble in the next. **2nd row**—4 chain to turn, 1 treble on the first treble stitch of last row, 1 chain, miss one, six consecutive treble, 3 chain, miss three, 1 treble at the end. **3rd row**—9 chain to turn, 3 treble on the three chain, 4 chain, miss four, 2 treble, 1 chain, 1 treble, 1 chain, 1 treble on the second stitch of the chain that turned. **4th row**—4 chain to turn, 1 treble on the first treble stitch of last row, 1 chain, miss one, 6 consecutive treble, 3 chain, miss three, one treble at the end. **5th row**—3 chain to turn, 9 treble in consecutive stitches, 1 chain, 1 treble, one chain, 1 treble on the second stitch of the chain that turned. Repeat from the second row. Break off when you have a sufficient length, and work for the Scallops—**1st row**—1 double crochet at the corner of the commencing chain, 2 chain, 1 double crochet at the corner of the first row, * 13 treble under the loop of nine chain, 1 double crochet at the corner of the fourth row, 2 chain, 1 double crochet at the corner of the fifth row, and repeat from *. **2nd row**—1 double crochet under the loop of two chain, 1 double crochet on the second stitch of the thirteen trebles, 3 chain, miss one, one double crochet on the next five times, 3 chain, and continue.

No. 32.—SIMPLE EDGING, WORKED ON PLAIN BRAID.

HAVING a piece of plain braid, work on it with red ingrain cotton in Holbein stitch the little pattern shown in the illustration. With crochet cotton No. 18 or

No. 38.—Mignardese Edging for Baby Things.

No. 39.—Birkbeck Edging.

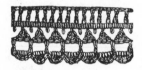

No. 40.—Pretty Narrow Edging.

No. 28.—PICOTEED EDGING OF WAVE BRAID.

PROCURE a length of wave braid and a skein of Coats's crochet cotton No. 18 or No. 20. Work for the Heading, 1 treble on the top of the first wave of the braid, * 2 chain, cotton twice round the needle, insert the hook half-way down the side of the same wave and draw the cotton through, cotton over the needle, and draw through two loops on the needle, cotton over the needle, insert the hook in the side of the next wave and draw the cotton through, cotton over the needle and draw through two loops on the needle, cotton over the needle and draw through two more loops on the needle, cotton over the needle and again draw through two loops on the needle, cotton over the needle and draw through the two last loops on the needle, 2 chain, one treble on the top of the wave, and repeat from *. On this work a row of 1 treble, 1 chain, miss one. On the opposite side of the braid work, **1st row**—1 double crochet on the top of the first wave, * 1 long treble in the side of the next wave, 3 chain, 1 treble on top of the same wave, 5 chain, another treble in the same place, 3 chain, 1 long treble in the side of the wave, 1 double crochet on the top of the next wave, and repeat from *. **2nd row**—1 double crochet in the little space between the double crochet and the long treble stitch of last row, 1 double crochet under the loop of three chain, 4 chain, 1 single in the fourth chain from the needle, 1 double crochet under the same loop of three chain, 4 chain, 1 single in the fourth chain from the needle, 1 double crochet in the same loop of three chain, and continue the piqués thus, doing 5 under the loop of five chain, and 2 under the other loop of three chain, 9 piqués in all round the scallop, 1 double crochet in the little space between the long treble and the double crochet of last row, and repeat to the end of the row.

No. 29.—SCALLOPED EDGING OF WAVE BRAID.

PROCURE a piece of wave braid and crochet cotton No. 18 or No. 20. Work for the Heading—**1st row**—1 long treble in the top of the first wave of the braid, 3 chain, another long treble in the same place, and repeat. **2nd row**—1 double crochet in every stitch of the preceding row. On the opposite side of the braid work for the Scallops—**1st row**—1 single crochet in each wave of the braid, 7 chain between. **2nd row**—1 double crochet, 9 treble, 1 double crochet, under each loop of seven chain of last row.

No. 20, work along one side of the braid for the Heading, 1 treble in two picots of the braid taken up together, * 3 chain, 1 treble in next two picots of the braid, and repeat from * to the end. On the other side of the braid work—**1st row**—1 double crochet in two picots of the braid taken up together, * 5 chain, 1 double crochet in next two picots of the braid, and repeat from *. **2nd row**—1 double crochet under loop of five chain of last row, 5 chain, and repeat. **3rd row**—1 double crochet under five chain of last row, * 7 chain, 1 double crochet in the fifth chain from the needle, 2 chain, 1 double crochet under five chain of last row, and repeat from *.

No. 33.—WAVE BRAID EDGING.

USE Coats's crochet cotton No 18 or 20, and for the Heading work 2 single crochet on the first wave of the braid, 4 chain, 2 single crochet on the next wave, and continue for the length required. On the opposite side work, **1st row**—1 double crochet on the first wave of the braid, * 2 chain, 1 long treble on the next wave, 3 chain, another long treble, 3 chain, another long treble, all in the same place, 2 chain, 1 double crochet in the next wave of the braid, and repeat from *. **2nd row**—2 double crochet under loop of two chain, * 2 double crochet under the loop of three chain, 4 chain, 1 single in the fourth chain from the needle, 2 more double crochet under the same three chain, repeat from * under each of the other loops of three chain, 2 double crochet under the two chain, and continue the same to the end of the row.

No. 34.—NARROW MIGNARDESE EDGING.

PROCURE a length of mignardese braid, and work with crochet cotton No. 18 or No. 20. **1st row**—1 double crochet in the first picot of the braid, 1 chain, 1 double crochet in the next picot, * 7 chain, miss one picot, 8 treble in next successive picots, 2 chain, catch with a single crochet in to the third chain stitch before the trebles, 4 chain, miss one picot, 1 double crochet in the next, 1 chain, 1 double crochet in the next, and repeat from *. Turn with 1 chain, work 1 double crochet under one chain of last row, 8 chain, and repeat to the end. Turn with 1 chain, and work double crochet in every stitch of last row.

No. 35.—JUNIPER EDGING.

THIS is worked lengthways; it looks best done with fine cotton, and is pretty for edging pincushion covers and other purposes. Begin with a chain the length required, and for the **1st row**—Work 1 treble, 1 chain, miss one, and repeat. **2nd row**—1 double crochet under the first space of one chain, * 9 chain, 1 single crochet in the fifth from the needle, 7 chain, 1 single in the fifth from the needle, 9 chain, 1 single in the fifth from the needle, 7 chain, 1 single in the fifth from the needle, 1 single in the fourth chain from the double crochet stitch, 3 chain, miss two spaces of one chain, 1 double crochet in the next, and repeat from * to the end of the row. **3rd row**—1 treble under the top loop of chain between the picots of last row, 6 chain, and repeat. **4th row**—2 long treble in the third chain-stitch of the preceding row, 2 long treble in the next chain-stitch, and repeat. **5th row**—1 single treble on the first stitch of the long treble of last row, 6 chain, 1 single in the fifth from the needle, 1 long treble on the next long treble, 6 chain, 1 single in the fifth from the needle, 1 long treble on the next long treble, 6 chain, 1 single in the fifth from the needle, 1 treble on the last long treble, and repeat to the end of the row.

No. 36.—GUIPURE BORDER.

THIS is a useful border for many purposes. If worked with ecru or grey linen thread it makes a handsome trimming for summer dresses. Commence by making a length of hair-pin trimming, rather more than twice as long as the length required for the border. **1st row**—1 double crochet in the first picot of the hair-pin trimming, which hold in such a way as to keep to the *right* as you work, 3 chain, miss one picot of the trimming, 1 double crochet in the next, * 19 chain (here begins the spray), 1 single in the third picot from that last worked into, and now you are on the first leaf, for which miss the first chain stitch, work 1 double crochet in the next, 2 treble, 1 long treble, 2 treble, 1 double crochet in successive stitches; then for the second leaf, 11 chain, 1 single in the fourth picot, and work the same; for the third leaf (the one at the top), 8 chain, 1 single in the fifth picot, and work the same; for the fourth leaf, 8 chain, 1 single in the fifth picot, and work the same, and do also 1 single into the second leaf and 1 single on each of the three stem stitches; for the fifth leaf, 8 chain, 1 single in the fourth picot, and work the same, and do also 1 single into the first leaf and 1 single on each of three stem stitches; for the sixth leaf, 8 chain, 1 single, 1 single in the third picot, and work the same, then 5 chain, and do the seventh leaf on the remaining chain stitches; work 1 double crochet

back, that the work may sit in ridges; do 4 rows altogether of 5 double crochet, then 6 chain, and again 4 rows of 5 double crochet; and continue till you have the length desired, when fasten off. **2nd row**—Begin with 1 double crochet on the first corner of the little square, * 9 chain, 1 double crochet in the fifth chain from the needle, 5 chain, 1 double crochet in the fifth from the needle, 8 chain, 1 double crochet in the fifth from the needle, 5 chain, 1 double crochet in the fifth from the needle, 1 double crochet in the chain stitch before the first of these piqués, 3 chain, 1 double crochet on the point of the little square; repeat from *, and after doing three chain work the double crochet stitch on the point of the next little square, and continue to the end of the row. **3rd row**—Begin with 1 double crochet in the space between the second and third piqués of last row, 9 chain, 1 double crochet in the fifth from the needle, * 5 chain, 1 double crochet in the fifth from the needle, and repeat from * till you have done 11 piqués, then do 1 double crochet in the chain stitch before the first of the piqués, 3 chain, 1 double crochet in the space in the next circle of piqué stitches and continue. This completes the loops. **Now work for the Heading**—**1st row**—1 double crochet on the point of the first little square, * 6 chain, 1 double crochet on the point of the next little square, and repeat from * **2nd row**—1 treble, 1 chain, miss one, and repeat. **3rd row**—1 treble on the treble stitch of last row, 1 chain, and repeat.

No. 38.—MIGNARDESE EDGING FOR BABY THINGS.

WORK with crochet cotton No. 20 upon a piece of mignardese braid. **1st row**—1 single crochet in the first picot of the braid, * 3 chain, miss one picot, 1 treble in the next, 6 chain, 1 double crochet in the lower part of the treble stitch, 3 chain, miss one picot, 1 single crochet in the next, and repeat from *. **2nd row**—3 double crochet under each loop of three chain, 7 double crochet under the six chain. **For the Heading**—Work on the other side of the braid, 2 double crochet in one picot, 1 double crochet in the next, and repeat.

No. 39.—BIRKBECK EDGING.

COMMENCE with 20 chain. **1st row**—1 treble in the seventh chain from the needle, 2 more treble in the same place, 2 chain, 3 treble in the next stitch of the foundation, 3 chain, miss three, 1 double crochet in the next, 3 chain, miss three, 3 treble in the next, 2 chain, 3 treble in the next, leave three stitches unworked. **2nd row**—6 chain to turn, 3 treble under two chain of last row, 2

No. 41.—Acorn Edging.

No. 42.—Serpolette Edging.

No. 43.—Scallop of Wave Braid.

under the loop of three chain, * 8 chain, 1 single in the sixth from the needle, 1 chain, 1 single in the sixth from the needle, 2 chain, turn the work, and do 1 double crochet under the loop of five chain; 8 chain, 1 single in the sixth from the needle 9 chain, 1 single in the sixth from the needle, 2 chain, 1 double crochet at the tip of the last leaf; 8 chain, 1 single in the sixth from the needle, 9 chain, 1 single in the sixth from the needle, 2 chain, 1 double crochet in the third picot from that last worked into; 8 chain, 1 single in the sixth from the needle, 1 single in the sixth from the needle, 2 chain, 1 double crochet in the third picot from that last worked into, turn the work so that you get the hair pin trimming again to the right as you work, and repeat from * for the length required. **For the Heading—1st row**—Work 2 treble in the centre of every picoted bar above the sprays of last row, 6 chain, and repeat. **2nd row**—2 treble on the first two chain stitches of last row, 2 chain, miss two, 2 treble on the last two chain stitches, 2 chain, miss two treble stitches, and repeat. **For the Edging—1st row**—Begin at the same end of the hair-pin trimming as the first spray began upon, and work 1 double crochet in the third picot of the trimming, 6 chain, 1 single in the fourth from the needle, 2 chain, miss two picots in the next, * 9 chain, 1 treble in the seventh from the needle, 1 long treble in the next, 1 chain, miss one picot, 2 treble in the next, repeat from * seven times more, then 6 chain, 1 single in the fourth from the needle, 2 chain, miss two picots, 1 double crochet in the next, 2 chain, miss two picots, 1 treble in the next, miss one picot, 1 treble in the next, 2 chain, miss two picots, 1 double crochet in the next, catch with 1 single into the double crochet stitch eight picots back, 6 chain, 1 single in the fourth from the needle, 2 chain, miss two picots, 2 treble in the next, and repeat from * to the end of the scallops. **2nd row**—2 double crochet under the first picot loop of last row, * 8 chain, 1 single in the sixth from the needle, 9 chain, 1 single in the sixth from the needle, 2 chain, 2 double crochet under the next picot loop of last row, repeat from * six times more, 2 chain, 1 double long treble (cotton three times round the needle, in the little space between the two treble stitches of last row, 2 chain, 2 double crochet under the first picot loop of the next scallop, and continue.

No. 37.—ELEGANT LOOPED BORDER.

THIS is suitable for a variety of purposes, and if worked with ecru thread or with coloured silk is pretty for dress trimming. Commence with 6 chain, turn, miss the first chain stitch, work 5 double crochet, turn with 1 chain, and again work 5 double crochet, inserting the hook to take up the thread at the

chain, 3 more treble in the same place, 3 chain, 1 double crochet on the double crochet of last row, 3 chain, 3 treble under two chain, 2 chain, 3 more treble in the same place, 1 chain, 1 treble on the second stitch of the chain that turned. **3rd row**—4 chain to turn, 3 treble under two chain, 2 chain, 3 more treble in the same place, 7 chain, 3 treble under two chain, 2 chain, 3 more treble in the same place, 1 chain and 1 treble seven times under the loop of six chain at the side of the edging, 1 single crochet in the stitch at the end of the foundation chain. **4th row**—Work 5 chain and 1 double crochet seven times under the one chains of last row, 3 chain, 3 treble under two chain, 2 chain, 3 more treble in the same place, 3 chain, 1 double crochet in the centre stitch of the seven chain, 3 chain, 3 treble under two chain, 2 chain, 3 more treble in the same place, 1 chain, 1 treble on the second stitch of the chain that turned. **5th row**—4 chain to turn, 3 treble under two chain, 2 chain, 3 more treble in the same place, 3 chain, 1 double crochet on the double crochet of last row, 3 chain, 3 treble under two chain, 2 chain, 3 more treble in the same place. **6th row**—6 chain to turn, 3 treble under two chain, 2 chain, 3 more treble in the same place, 7 chain, 3 treble under two chain, 2 chain, 3 more treble in the same place, 1 chain, 1 treble on the second stitch of the chain that turned. **7th row**—4 chain, 3 treble under two chain, 2 chain, 3 more treble in the same place, 3 chain, 1 double crochet in the centre stitch of the seven chain, 3 chain, 3 treble under two chain, 2 chain, 3 more treble in the same place, 1 chain and 1 treble seven times under the loop of six chain at the side of the edging, 1 single crochet under the three chain of the fourth row. **8th row**—Work 5 chain and 1 double crochet seven times under the one chains of last row, 3 chain, 3 treble under two chain, 2 chain, 3 more treble in the same place, 3 chain, 1 double crochet on the double crochet of last row, 3 chain, 3 treble under 2 chain, 2 chain, 3 more treble in the same place, 1 chain, 1 treble on the second stitch of the chain that turned. Continue thus: each scallop takes four rows, and you do seven chain every third row in the centre.

No. 40.—PRETTY NARROW EDGING.

WORK upon a piece of mignardese braid with crochet cotton No. 18 or No. 20. **1st row**—3 treble in every alternate picot of the braid. **2nd row**—1 treble in the little space between the groups of treble stitches, 8 chain, and repeat. **3rd row**—1 double crochet, 3 treble, 1 double crochet, under every space of three chain of last row. Then on the opposite side of the braid, for a heading, work 1 treble in every picot and 1 chain between.

No. 41.—ACORN EDGING.

COMMENCE with 9 chain. **1st row**—1 treble in the eighth chain from the needle, 2 chain, another treble in the same place, 2 chain, 1 treble in the last stitch of the foundation, 2 chain, another treble in the same place. **2nd row**—5 chain to turn, 1 treble under the centre loop of two chain of last row, 2 chain and 1 treble three more times in the same place. Repeat the second row for the length desired. When a sufficient length is done, form the scallops by working along one side of the foundation, 9 treble under every loop of five chain. And on the opposite side make a heading, 2 double crochet under loop of five chain, 4 chain, and repeat.

No 42.—SERPOLETTE EDGING.

THIS pretty edging is worked the short way. Begin with 14 chain. **1st row**—1 treble in the eighth chain from the needle, 6 treble in consecutive stitches. **2nd row**—2 chain to turn, 1 treble in the third treble stitch, 1 treble on the fifth, and 1 treble on the last of the seven treble stitches, 4 chain, 7 treble under the loop at the end. **3rd row**—4 chain to turn, 1 treble on the third treble stitch, 1 chain, 1 treble on the fifth, 1 chain, 1 treble on the last of the seven treble stitches, 5 chain, 7 treble under the four chain of last row, 1 treble in the first chain-stitch at the end of the row. **4th row**—Same as the second row. **5th row**—Same as the third row. **6th row**—2 chain to turn, 1 treble on the third treble stitch, 1 treble on the fifth, and 1 treble on the last of the seven treble stitches, 4 chain, 7 treble under the five chain of last row, 9 chain, 1 single crochet in the four chain of previous point. **7th row**—Turn, do 11 double crochet under the loop of nine chain, 1 chain, 1 treble on the third treble stitch, 1 chain, 1 treble on the fifth, 1 chain, 1 treble on the last of the seven treble stitches, 5 chain, 7 treble under the loop of four chain, 1 treble in the first chain stitch at the end of the row. **8th row**—2 chain to turn, 1 treble on the third treble stitch, 1 treble on the fifth, and 1 treble on the last of the seven treble stitches, 4 chain, 7 treble under the loop of five chain, 1 long treble on the first stitch of the eleven double crochet, * 2 chain, 1 long treble on the next, repeat from * till 12 long treble are done, the last of these will come upon the single

1 treble in the next, 2 chain and 1 treble three times in the same place. **4th row**—Same as the second row. Continue working the third and fourth rows for the length required. Then along the top of the edging work a heading of 5 chain, 1 double crochet, alternately.

No. 45.—SWISS PATTERN BORDER.

EVANS'S crochet cotton No. 24, and a very fine steel crochet needle. Begin with 26 chain. **1st row**—1 treble in the tenth stitch from the needle, cotton twice round the needle, insert the hook in the same stitch of the foundation and draw the cotton through, cotton over the needle and draw through two loops on the needle, cotton over the needle, insert the hook in the third foundation stitch from that last worked into and draw the cotton through. Now there are five loops on the needle. Cotton over the needle and draw through two loops on the needle, cotton over and draw through two loops, cotton over and draw through two loops, cotton over and draw through the two last loops, 3 chain, cotton over the needle, insert the hook to take up three threads in the centre of the twisted stitch just done and draw the cotton through, cotton over the needle and draw through two loops on the needle, cotton over the needle and draw through the two last loops, 1 treble in the same stitch of the foundation already worked into 3 chain, miss three, 1 treble in the next, cotton twice round the needle and work another cross-stitch as described above and a treble stitch adjoining, 8 chain, 1 double crochet in the last stitch of the foundation. **2nd row**—1 chain to turn, 13 treble under the loop of eight chain, 1 treble on the first treble stitch, 3 chain, 1 treble on the next treble stitch, cotton twice round the needle and work a cross-stitch and a treble adjoining, 3 chain, 1 treble on the last treble stitch, cotton twice round the needle, work a cross-stitch and a treble adjoining upon the chain that turned. **3rd row**—7 chain to turn, 1 treble on the first treble stitch of last row and work a cross and a treble stitch adjoining, 3 chain, 1 treble on the fourth treble stitch of last row, and work another cross and a treble stitch adjoining, 1 chain, 1 long treble, alternately, on each treble to the end of the scallop. **4th row**—5 chain, 1 double crochet under the first loop of one chain, 5 chain and 1 double crochet under each loop of one chain, 3 chain, one treble on the first treble stitch, 3 chain, 1 treble on the second treble stitch and work a

No. 44.—Spike Edging.   No. 45.—Swiss Pattern Border.   No. 46.—Cornflower Edging.

crochet stitch at the end, catch with a single crochet into the four chain of previous point. **9th row**—3 chain to turn, 1 double crochet on the second long treble stitch, 5 chain (here in succeeding scallops you catch into the scallop preceding) 1 single crochet in the top thread of the double crochet just done, 1 double crochet under the loop of two chain, 4 chain and 1 double crochet eight times under consecutive loops of two chain, 2 chain, 1 double crochet under the last loop of two chain, 1 double crochet on the long treble stitch, 2 chain, 1 treble on the third treble stitch, 1 chain, 1 treble on the fifth, 1 chain, 1 treble on the last of the seven treble stitches, 5 chain, 7 treble under the loop of four chain, 1 treble in the first chain-stitch at the end of the row. Repeat from the fourth row for the length desired.

No. 43.—SCALLOP OF WAVE BRAID.

HAVE a sufficient length of braid, and work with Coats's crochet cotton No. 18 or No. 20. **1st row**—1 treble on the first wave of the braid, 3 chain, another treble in the same place, 1 chain, and repeat. **2nd row**—1 treble, 1 chain, miss one, and repeat. On the opposite side of the braid work 1 double crochet on the first wave, 1 long treble on the next wave, * 4 chain, 1 single crochet in the fourth chain from the needle, 1 long treble in the same place as last long treble is worked into, repeat from * till 6 long treble are worked, then 1 double crochet in the next wave of the braid, and continue.

No 44—SPIKE EDGING.

THIS edging is worked the short way with Evans's crochet cotton No. 22 and a fine steel crochet needle; it is useful for trimming underlinen. Commence with 8 chain; turn, work 1 treble in the seventh chain from the needle, 2 chain, another treble in the same place, 2 chain, 1 treble in the last stitch of the foundation, 2 chain, another treble in the same place. **2nd row**—6 chain to turn, miss the first loop of two chain, 1 treble in the next, 2 chain and 1 treble three times in the same place, 7 chain, 1 double crochet in the loop at the end. **3rd row**—2 double crochet under the loop of seven chain, 4 chain and 2 double crochet twice in the same place, 4 chain, miss the first loop of two chain,

cross and a treble stitch adjoining, 3 chain, 1 treble on the last treble stitch and work a cross and a treble stitch adjoining on the chain that turned. **5th row**—7 chain to turn, and proceed the same as the first row, and work the double crochet at the end under the first loop of five chain stitches. Repeat from the second row for the length required.

No. 46.—CORNFLOWER EDGING.

PROCURE a piece of mignardese braid, a reel of Evans's crochet cotton No. 22, and a fine steel crochet needle. **1st row**—Work 1 double crochet in the first picot of the braid, 5 chain, another double crochet in the same place, * 4 chain, miss two picots of the braid, 1 double crochet in the next, 16 chain, 1 single crochet in the fourteenth from the needle, 2 chain, 1 double crochet in the same picot as last double crochet is worked into, 4 chain, miss two picots of the braid, 5 chain, another double crochet in the same place, and repeat from * for the length required. **2nd row**—Beginning on the right-hand side, * 1 double crochet under the first loop of five chain, 9 chain, 1 double crochet in the same place, 11 chain, 1 double crochet in the same place, 9 chain, another double crochet in the same place, then under the loop of fourteen chain work 3 long treble stitches, 4 treble, 5 double crochet, 4 treble, 3 long treble, and repeat from *. **3rd row**—1 double crochet under the loop of nine chain, 1 double crochet under the loop of eleven chain, 5 chain, another double crochet in the same place, 1 double crochet under the loop of nine chain, 4 chain, 1 double crochet on the centre stitch of the five double crochet, 5 chain, 1 single in the fifth from the needle, 5 chain, 1 single in the same place, 5 chain, 1 single in the same place, 1 double crochet in the same stitch last double crochet is worked into, 4 chain, and repeat. On the other side of the mignardese braid work a row of single crochet stitches in the picots of the braid, 1 chain between each single crochet.

WELDON'S
PRACTICAL CROCHET.

(SIXTH SERIES.)

How to Crochet Useful Articles for Personal and Home Decoration.

THIRTY ILLUSTRATIONS.

[Telegraphic Address—
"Consuelo," London.]

The Yearly Subscription to this Magazine, post free to any Part of the World, is 2s. 6d.
Subscriptions are payable in advance, and may commence from any date and for any period.

[Telephone—
2745.

The Back Numbers are always in print.   Nos. 1 to 84 now ready, Price 2d. each, or post free for 15s.   Over 5,000 Engravings.

JAR FOR PENCE.

REQUIRED, 1 skein of pale blue and a small quantity of white Berlin finger-ing, and a No. 10 bone crochet needle. Begin with blue wool, with 3 chain, join round, and work 8 double crochet in the circle, and join round. **2nd round**—2 double crochet on each double crochet stitch of last round, and join round. **3rd round**—Work 2 double crochet on the first and 1 double crochet on the next, making in all 24 double crochet in the round, and join. **4th round** —2 double crochet on the first and 1 double crochet on the next, making in all 36 double crochet in the round, and join. **5th round**—2 double crochet on the first and 1 double crochet on each of the two next, making in all 48 double crochet in the round, and join evenly. **6th round**—Do 3 chain to stand for a treble stitch, 4 treble on the first double crochet of last round, catch the crochet hook in the top stitch of the three chain to draw the treble stitches into a tuft which draw in tightly with a chain stitch, * miss one double crochet of last round, 5 treble in the next, and catch the last of these treble stitches into the first, 1 chain, and repeat from * ; make 24 tufts in the round ; join to the first tuft. **7th round**—Again 24 tufts, which work under the chain stitches of last round, and join. **8th round**— With white wool,—make 24 tufts under the chain stitches of last round, join. **9th round**—With blue wool,—the same. **10th round**—With white wool,— 1 double crochet under each chain stitch of last round, making in all 24 double crochet, and join round. **11th round**—Also 24 double crochet, worked upon the stitches of previous round. Work 2 more rounds the same. **14th round**—With blue wool,—22 double crochet, the decrease is formed by working 1 stitch over two stitches of last round at opposite sides of the jar. **15th round**—22 double crochet worked on the double crochet of last round. Work 3 more rounds the same, and fasten off. For the **Handles**—Make 15 chain with blue wool ; 1 double crochet in the first chain from the needle, 1 double crochet in the next, 1 double crochet in the next, catch into the top round of the crochet jar over the place where the decrease

Jar for Pence.

was made in the fourteenth round, work 8 consecutive double crochet, catch into the eleventh round under the place where decreased, do 3 more double crochet, and fasten off. Make the other handle to correspond.

LADY'S COLLAR.

THIS pretty collar may be worked with Strutts', Ardern's, or any of the usual makes of crochet cotton, or with Finlayson's real Scotch linen thread, which is procurable at most drapers, and is of peculiarly soft quality, un-equalled for smoothness and strength, and the cream, écru, and other shades wash splendidly.   Procure then one ball, No. 35 of this thread, and a fine steel crochet needle.   For the **Neck-band—1st row**—Begin with 16 chain, along which work 15 double crochet ; * 1 chain and turn the work, and do 15 double crochet on the previous double crochet stitches inserting the needle to take up the back thread that the crochet may sit in ridges ; 1 chain and turn the work, and again work 15 double crochet in the back threads of the last little row ; 1 chain and turn the work and once more do 15 double crochet ; now 15 chain, turn the work, take out the needle and insert it in the end

stitch of the preceding little row and draw the loop through ; 1 chain and turn the work, and do 15 double crochet along the fifteen chain ; 1 chain and turn the work, and do 15 double crochet into the back thread of the fifteen stitches last worked ; now 15 chain, turn the work, take out the needle and insert it in the end stitch of the last little row and draw the loop through ; 1 chain and turn the work, and do 15 double crochet along the fifteen chain and repeat from * till you have twenty-three of the wide and twenty-two of the narrow bars, through which by and bye to run a ribbon. **2nd row**—1 chain and 1 double crochet alternately, all along one side of the strip of insertion, putting the double crochet stitch on the turning of each little ridge, so as to get five double crochet to a pattern (two bars) of the insertion. **3rd row**—4 chain to turn, 1 treble under the one chain stitch of last row, * 1 chain, 1 treble under the next loop of one chain, and repeat from *.   **4th row** —5 chain to turn, miss four stitches of last row, 1 double crochet on the next, * 4 chain, miss three stitches, 1 double crochet on the next, and repeat from *. **5th row**—Turn, and work * 3 double crochet under the loop of four chain of last row, 5 chain, 1 single crochet in the fifth chain from the needle, and repeat from * : fasten off at the end of this row, which completes the neck-band. For the **Collar—1st row**—1 double crochet into the first stitch on the opposite side of the neck-band insertion, * 6 chain, cotton twice round the needle, insert the hook in the fifth chain from the needle and draw the cotton through, cotton over the needle and draw through two stitches on the needle, cotton over the needle and draw through two more stitches on the needle, cotton twice round the needle, insert the hook in the next chain stitch and draw the cotton through, cotton over the needle and draw through two stitches on the needle *four times*, which works off all the stitches on the needle and makes what we will call a "leaflet" ; make another leaflet in the same manner, and then work 1 double crochet into the neck-band ; repeat from *, so spacing the work that four patterns of the leaflets will come evenly with three patterns of the insertion ; there should be 32 patterns, or 64 leaflets, in the row when completed ; fasten off. **2nd row**—Beginning again on the right-hand side, 1 double crochet on the first double crochet of last row, 15 chain, make one leaflet as before, then 1 double crochet between the first two leaflets of last row, * make two leaflets, then 1 double crochet between the next two leaflets of last row, and repeat from * to the end, where finish off with one leaflet, 9 chain, 1 double crochet on the last double crochet of last row, and fasten off. **3rd row**—Turn the work and commence where last row ended, 1 double crochet in the chain stitch next the last leaflet of last row, * 8 chain, 1 double crochet between the next two leaflets, and repeat from * to the end of the row. **4th row**—3 chain to turn, work 16 consecutive treble stitches, * 2 chain, miss one stitch, 1 treble in each of the two next stitches, 2 chain, miss one stitch, work 32 consecutive treble stitches, repeat from * six times, then 2 chain, miss one stitch, 1 treble in each of the two next stitches, 2 chain, miss one stitch, do 17 treble. **5th row**—3 chain to turn, miss the first treble stitch and work 15 treble consecutively, and taking up the back thread of the stitches of the preceding row, * 2 chain, 2 treble under the two chain of last row, 2 chain, 2 more treble in the same place, 2 chain, 2 treble under the next two chain of last row, 2 chain, 2 more treble in the same place, 2 chain, 30 treble beginning upon the second stitch of the thirty-two treble of last row, repeat from * six times, then 2 chain, 2 treble under the two chain of last row, 2 chain, 2 more treble in the same place, 2 chain, 2 treble under the next two chain of last row, 2 chain, 2 more treble in the same place, 2 chain, and 16 treble beginning upon the second of the seventeen treble of last row. **6th row**—3 chain to turn, miss the first treble stitch and work consecutively and taking up the back thread of the stitches of last row, * 3 chain, 2 treble under the second loop of two chain of last row, 2 chain, 2 more treble in the same place, 3 chain, 2 treble under the fourth loop of two chain of last row, 2 chain, 2 more treble in the same place, 3 chain, 28 treble beginning upon the second stitch of the thirty treble of last row, repeat from * seven times, but at the *end* of the row you will work only 15 treble stitches. **7th row**—3 chain to turn, miss the first treble stitch and work 13 consecutive treble, * 4 chain, 2 treble under the two chain of last row, 2 chain, 2 more treble in the same place, 4 chain, 2 treble under the next two chain of last row, 2 chain, 2 more treble in the same place, 4 chain, 26 treble beginning upon the second stitch of the twenty-eight treble of last row, repeat from * seven times, but at the *end* of the row you will work only 14 treble stitches. **8th row**—3 chain to turn, miss the first treble stitch and work 12 consecutive treble, * 5 chain, 2 treble under the two chain of last row, 2 chain, 2 more treble in the same place, 5 chain, 2 treble under the next two chain of last row, 2 chain, 2 more treble in the same place, 5 chain, 24 treble beginning on the second stitch of the twenty-six treble of last row, repeat from * seven times, but at the *end* of the row work only 13 treble stitches. **9th row** —3 chain to turn, miss the first treble stitch and work 11 consecutive treble, * 6 chain, 2 treble under the two chain of last row, 2 chain, 2 more treble in the same place, 6 chain, 2 treble under the next two chain of last row, 2 chain, 2 more treble in the same place, 6 chain, 22 treble beginning on the second stitch of the twenty-four treble of last row, repeat from * seven times, but at the *end* of the row work only 12 treble stitches. **10th row**— 3 chain to turn, miss the first treble stitch and work 10 consecutive treble, * 6 chain, 2 treble under the 2 chain of last row, 2 chain, 2 more treble in the same place, 3 chain, 2 treble in the third stitch of the loop of six chain stitches, 2 chain, 2 treble in the fourth stitch of the same loop of six chain stitches, 6 chain, 2 treble under the two chain of last row, 2 chain, 2 more treble in the same place, 6 chain, 20 treble beginning on the second stitch of twenty-two treble of last row, repeat from * seven times, but at the *end* of the row work only 11 treble stitches. **11th row** —3 chain to turn, miss the first treble

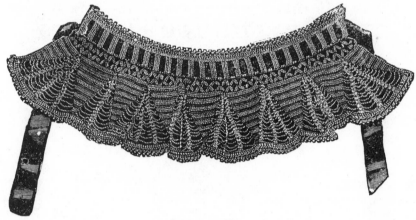

Lady's Collar.

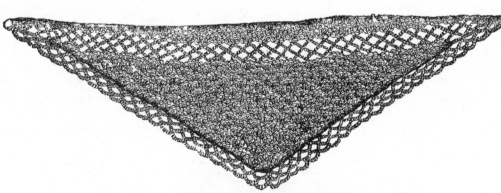

Three-Cornered Neck-Handkerchief.

stitch and work 9 consecutive treble, * 7 chain, 2 treble under the two chain of last row, 2 chain, 2 more treble in the same place, 7 chain, 2 treble under the next two chain of last row, 2 chain, 2 more treble in the same place, 7 chain, 2 treble under the next two chain of last row, 2 chain, 2 more treble in the same place, 7 chain, 18 treble beginning on the second stitch of the twenty treble of last row, repeat from * seven times, but at the *end* of the row work only 10 treble stitches. **12th row**—3 chain to turn, and beginning with 8 treble stitches, proceed in the same manner as last row, but making 8 chain where in last row there was seven, and working 16 treble instead of eighteen treble. The pattern goes on thus, increasing one stitch in every row in each of the four long loops of chain, and decreasing the solid treble stitches by one stitch at each end, until in the **19th row** you bring the latter to a point of 2 treble stitches only, and do 15 stitches in the loops of chain; the 2 treble 2 chain 2 treble worked as a group under the two chain of previous row continues the same throughout. **20th row**—4 chain to turn, miss one stitch of last row, 1 treble in the next, * 1 chain, miss one stitch, 1 treble in the next, and repeat from * to the end of the row. **21st row**—4 chain to turn, miss four stitches of last row, 1 double crochet on the next, * 4 chain, miss three stitches, 1 double crochet on the next, and repeat from *. **22nd row**—Turn, and work * 3 double crochet under the loop of four chain of last row, 5 chain, 1 single crochet in the fifth chain from the needle, and repeat from * to the end of the row. This finishes the collar. To make **Cuffs** to match the **Collar**—Work a sufficient number of patterns of the bar-like insertion to go round a sleeve, join, and then crochet the four rows of the neck-band on each side of the

insertion. Run ribbon through the insertion of both neck-band and cuffs, the widest bars of the crochet are intended to come on the right side of the collar; let the ends of each piece of ribbon be sufficiently long to tie in a pretty bow.

THREE-CORNERED NECK-HANDKERCHIEF.

REQUIRED, 2 ozs. of white Shetland wool, and a No. 10 bone crochet needle. Begin with 5 chain, which join round; work 4 chain, 6 treble in the circle; the treble stitches must be drawn up quite evenly to the height of half an inch or more. **2nd row**—4 chain, turn the work, and do 6 treble on the first treble stitch of preceding row, 1 double crochet on the fourth treble stitch, and 7 treble in the top stitch of the chain that turned; this makes two shells or groups of treble. **3rd row**—4 chain to turn, and do 6 treble on the first treble stitch of preceding row, 1 double crochet on the fourth treble stitch, 7 treble on the double crochet stitch, 1 double crochet on the fourth treble stitch of the chain that turned; and there are three shells in this row. **4th row**—4 chain to turn, do 6 treble on the first treble stitch of preceding row, 1 double crochet on the fourth treble stitch, 7 treble on the double crochet stitch, 1 double crochet on the fourth treble stitch of the next shell, 7 treble on the double crochet stitch, 1 double crochet on the fourth treble stitch of the next shell, 7 treble in the top stitch of the chain that turned; this makes four shells in the row. Continue in this manner, increasing one shell in every row, till you have done 20 rows, or more, according to the size desired for the shawl. Then for the **next row**—Work 7 chain to turn, 1 double crochet on the fourth treble stitch of the first shell of last row, * 5 chain, 1 double crochet on double crochet stitch, 5 chain, 1 double crochet on the fourth treble stitch of the next shell, and repeat from * making at the end 5 chain, and 1 double crochet in the top stitch of the chain that turned; work similar loops along both sides of the handkerchief, allotting one loop to each row, turn the bottom of the handkerchief with two loops. **Next row**—Do one double crochet under a loop of chain of last row, * 5 chain, 1 double crochet under the next loop, and repeat from * all round the handkerchief. **Next row** — The same. Now work four rows of shells along the top of the neck-handkerchief, and fasten off. This handkerchief may also be used as a fascinator, or covering for the head.

FROCK FOR CHILD OF TWO.

WORKED IN PLAIN TRICOT AND POINT MUSCOVITE.

THIS pretty little frock measures 18 inches from the neck to the bottom of the skirt. If required longer, a few more rows of plain tricot can be worked in the upper part of the skirt. Procure 6 ozs. of white and 2 ozs. of pale blue single Berlin wool, and a long tricot needle, No. 6. Commence with white wool with 168 chain. Work 6 rows of plain tricot. **7th row**—Pick up all the loops the same as before, and decrease in working back, thus—draw through 12 stitches, then through 2 stitches together, through 16 stitches, through 2 stitches together, through 16, through 2 together, through 16, through 2 together, through 32, through 2 together, through 16, through 2 together, through 16, through 2 together, through 16, through 2 together, and lastly through 12. Work 3 plain rows. **11th row**—Pick up all the loops the same as before, and again decrease in working back, draw through 12 stitches, through 2 stitches together, through 15, through 2 together, through 15, through 2 together, through 15, through 2 together, through 30, through 2 together, through 15, through 2 together, through 15, through 2 together, through 15, through 2 together, through 12. Work three plain rows. **15th row**—Pick up all the loops the same as before, and decrease in working back, draw through 12 stitches, through 2 together, 14, 2 together, 14, 2 together, 14, 2 together, 28, 2 together, 14, 2 together, 14, 2 together, 14, 2 together, 12. Work 1 plain row. **17th row**—Pick up all the loops, and working back, draw through 12, through 2 together, 13, 2 together, 13, 2 together, 26, 2 together, 13, 2 together, 13, 2 together, 13, 2 together, 12. Work 1 plain row. **19th row**—Pick up all the loops, and working back, draw through 12, 2 together, 12, 2 together, 12, 2 together, 12, 2 together, 24, 2 together, 12, 2 together, 12, 2 together, 12, 2 together, 12. Work 1 plain row. **21st row**—Pick up all the loops, and working back draw through 12, 2 together, 11, 2 together, 11, 2 together, 11, 2 together, 22, 2 together, 11, 2 together, 11, 2 together, 11, 2 together, 12. Work 1 plain row. **23rd row**—Pick up all the loops, and working back draw through 12, 2 together, 10, 2 together, 10, 2 together, 10, 2 together, 20, 2 together, 10, 2 together, 10, 2 together, 10, 2 together, 12. Work 1 plain row. **25th row**—Pick up all the loops, and working back draw through 12, 2 together, 9, 2 together, 9, 2 together, 9, 2 together, 18, 2 together, 9, 2 together, 9, 2 together, 9, 2 together, 12. **26th row**—Pick up all the loops with white wool and draw back with the blue wool, then break off, and begin again with white wool. **27th row**—Pick up all the loops by the *back* thread so that the blue stitches come quite to the front and appear like a row of raised threads, draw back stitch by stitch and fasten off. **28th row**—With blue wool. For the **Waistband**—Work a stitch of double crochet in each of the first two tricot stitches, * insert the hook in the next tricot stitch and draw the wool through, work 4 chain, and in the last stitch of chain draw the wool also through the double crochet stitch on the needle, 1 double crochet in the next stitch of tricot and repeat from * to the end of the row, and break off the wool. **29th row**—

Frock for a Child of Two Years.

Recommencing on the right-hand side, work 1 double crochet to begin, then go on with the point "Muscovite" stitch as directed above, working always a point above a double crochet stitch of last row and a double crochet over a point. **30th row**—Same as the twenty-eighth row. **31st row**—Same as the twenty-ninth row. **32nd row**—Plain tricot with white wool. **33rd row**—Pick up all the loops with white wool, and draw back with blue; then break off, and again with white. **34th row**—Pick up all the loops by the *back* thread so as again to make a row of raised blue stitches appear on the front of the work, draw back stitch by stitch. Now for the **Body**—Work 12 rows of plain tricot with the white wool, and this brings you to the opening for the armholes. **13th row**—Pick up 25 loops and work back, and work in all 9 rows on these 25 stitches for one half of the back. Recommence on the twelfth row, at a distance of five stitches from the back piece just done, pick up 43 loops and work back, and proceed upon the 43 stitches till 9 rows are done, then work only 5 stitches for 22 rows, this is for the shoulder strap, sew it over in its place to the back piece. Work 5 tricot stitches upon the other end of the 43 stitches for the other shoulder strap, doing 22 rows and break off. Again on the twelfth row recommence at a distance of five stitches from the piece worked for the front, and pick up all the remaining loops (25) and work 9 rows for the other half of the back, sew the shoulder strap last worked on to this. Now still with white wool pick up all the loops right round the neck, making 115 stitches, and work *back* with blue wool, then break off, and again with white pick up all the loops by the *back* thread, taking at each four points of the shoulders 3 stitches of last row into 1, to shape nicely for the neck draw back stitch by stitch and fasten off. With blue wool work 2 rows of point Muscovite like the waistband, still taking up 3 stitches in 1 at the points of the shoulders, then with white wool work 1 plain row of tricot again contracting 3 stitches at the shoulder corners. Next row, pick up the loops with white wool, and draw back with blue. Then work 2 rows of plain tricot with white wool, still not forgetting to contract 3 stitches together at the shoulders. Next row—With blue wool, 1 double crochet in the first tricot stitch, * 4 chain, 1 single in the first stitch of the chain, miss one tricot stitch, 1 double crochet in the next, and repeat from * all round the neck, and also down the right-hand side of the back, but

before doing this latter, work with white wool a row of double crochet up each side of the back as a strengthening. **For the Sleeves**—Commence with the white wool, with 15 chain, and work 5 rows of plain tricot. **6th row**—Pick up the loops with white wool, and draw back with blue. **7th row**—With white wool, pick up all the loops by the back thread, and draw back as in ordinary tricot. **8th, 9th, and 10th rows**—With blue wool, and worked in crochet point Muscovite, the same as already worked for the waistband. **11th row**—Plain tricot with white wool. **12th row**—Pick up all the loops with white wool, and draw back with blue. **13th row**—With white wool, pick up all the loops by the back thread, and draw back as in ordinary tricot. Now work 4 rows of plain tricot with white wool; then work from the 6th row to the 13th row inclusive, and continue in this manner till you have four stripes of white tricot and four stripes of blue crochet, when neatly sew the sleeve up. **For the Edging of the Sleeve**—With blue wool, work 1 double crochet into the stitch at the end of the little narrow line of blue tricot, 1 treble in the centre stitch of the five rows of plain white tricot, 1 chain and 1 treble four times more in the same place, 1 double crochet in the stitch at the end of the next little narrow line of blue tricot, 1 treble in the centre stitch of the three rows of blue crochet, 1 chain and 1 treble four times more in the same place, and repeat, making eight scallops round the sleeve. **2nd round of Edge**—1 double crochet under the first chain-stitch of last round, * 4 chain, 1 single in the first stitch of the chain, 1 double crochet under the next chain-stitch of last round, and repeat from *, making three picot knobs at the top of each scallop. On the other side of the sleeve, where it is to be sewn into the armhole, work 1 row of edge with blue wool like the blue edge at the top of the neck. Sew in the sleeve, tacking each little picot in place upwards towards the neck. Work the other sleeve in the same way. **For the Flounce** at the bottom of the Frock—Begin with 21 stitches (or 26, or 31 if required very deep), and work exactly the same as described for the sleeves, making in length 12 stripes of white tricot and 12 stripes of blue crochet. Join round, and work an edging at the top and at the bottom, the same as on the sleeves. Sew the flounce on to the skirt which remains open as a placket-hole as far as this flounce. Small tufts of blue wool are sewn in the centre of the five white tricot rows on the flounce and sleeves at every fifth stitch of the tricot, and extending over three rows. They are made thus : thread a wool needle and insert it into the tricot, taking up a stitch in the second row, wind the wool round a half-inch mesh, and pass the needle through the tricot stitch three times, and then sew the three round stitches so formed in such a way that they lie flat and straight upon the white tricot; make five of these tufts upon every white stripe of the flounce, and three upon every white stripe of the sleeves. Put ten or twelve small white buttons down the back of the frock, these will button into the edge which is already crocheted along the side of the back and down the placket hole.

Crochet Ball or Pincushion shaped like an Orange.

CROCHET BALL OR PINCUSHION.
SHAPED LIKE AN ORANGE.

THESE balls are greatly liked by children, and a dessert dish-full arranged as oranges makes an attractive and profitable addition to a stall at a bazaar or fancy fair. Required, ¼ oz. of orange-coloured and 1 skein of shaded-green single Berlin wool, and a No. 10 crochet needle. Begin with the orange wool with 4 chain, join round, and work 3 double crochet in each stitch of the chain. **2nd round**—Work 3 double crochet on the first stitch, 1 double crochet on the next stitch, and repeat, taking up always the two front loops of the stitches of previous round. **3rd round**—Do 3 double crochet on the centre stitch of the three double crochet of last round, and 1 double crochet on each of the three intermediate stitches. **4th round**—3 double crochet on the centre stitch of the three double crochet of last round, and 1 double crochet on each of the five intermediate stitches. **5th round**—3 double crochet on the centre stitch of the three double crochet of last round, and 1 double crochet on each of the seven intermediate stitches. **6th round**—3 double crochet on the centre stitch of the three double crochet of last round, and 1 double crochet on each of the nine intermediate stitches. **7th round**—3 double crochet on the centre stitch of the three double crochet of last round, and 1 double crochet on each of the eleven intermediate stitches. **8th round**—Work 3 double crochet on the centre stitch of the three double crochet of last round, and intermediately do 5 consecutive double crochet, take up the next 3 stitches of preceding round and work them as 1 stitch, then 5 consecutive double crochet. Work 10 more rounds the same as this last round, and fasten off. For the **leaves** at the **top** of the **Orange**—Use shaded green wool, and commence with 5 chain; miss one, and work 1 double crochet in each of the remaining chain stitches; this forms the stem of the orange, and it must be kept outside—*i.e.*, at the **top** of the leaves you are now going to work, for which * 12 chain, miss one, and work along in succession, 1 double crochet, 2 treble, 3 long treble, 2 treble, 2 double crochet, 1 single crochet, then 1 single crochet in the lower part of the stem, and repeat from * five times, which will make six leaves. Now for the **2nd row**—Miss the first stitch of the first leaf, and work 10 double crochet to reach to the tip of it, then 3 chain, miss one, and do 1 double crochet in each of the remaining chain stitches, till you reach the tip of the other side of the leaf, miss the last stitch of the leaf, and do 1 single crochet in the stem foundation, and work the same round each of the remaining five leaves, and fasten off. The **Ball** can be made of a sheet of white wadding, which cut into strips an inch wide, and wind round and round, till you get a ball large enough to fill the crochet, put it in, and bring the six points of the crochet up nicely and evenly together at the stem end, and secure the stem and leaves on by sewing them neatly over where the points are joined together.

BABY'S JACKET.

PROCURE 3 ozs. of white and 1 oz. of pale blue Scotch fingering, and a No. 12 bone crochet needle. Begin with white wool for the bottom of the right hand front piece, with 34 chain, in which work 33 double crochet, turn the work. **2nd row**—Again do 33 double crochet, working into both top threads of the stitches of previous row, turn. Work two more rows the same. **5th row**—32 double crochet, the decrease is made at the end by taking up

Baby's Jacket.

together the two last stitches of the preceding row. **6th row**—32 double crochet. Work two more rows the same. **9th row**—Decrease again at the end, doing 31 double crochet. **10th row**—31 double crochet. Work two more rows the same. **13th row**—Decrease again at the end doing 30 double crochet. **14th row**—30 double crochet. Work two more rows the same. **17th row**—Again decrease at the end, and do 29 double crochet. Work 9 more rows of 29 double crochet. **27th row**—Increase 1 at the end, the same end at which you before decreased. Work 3 rows of 30 double crochet in a row. **31st row**—Work 28 double crochet, and leave two unworked at the end to form the bottom of the armhole. Work 14 rows of 28 double crochet in a row. **46th row**—Beginning at the armhole end, for the shoulder, work 20 double crochet, leave eight unworked for the neck; turn, and work 20 double crochet back. **48th row**—18 double crochet; turn, and work 18 double crochet back. **50th row**—16 double crochet; turn, and work 16 double crochet back. **52nd row**—15 double crochet; turn, and work 15 double crochet back. Do 4 more rows on the 15 double crochet Break off the wool. Work the other front the same. **For the Back** of the **Jacket**—Commence with 62 chain, in which work 61 double crochet, and proceed shaping each side exactly as the front pieces are shaped at the sides, armholes and shoulders. **For the Sleeves**—Begin with 31 chain; work 30 double crochet forwards and backwards for 18 rows. **19th row**—Increase 1 stitch at the end. **20th row**—The same. Work 2 rows of 32 double crochet in the row. **23rd row**—Increase 1 stitch at the end. **24th row**—The same. Work 2 rows of 34 double crochet. Work 2 rows with increase at the end of each. Work 2 rows of 36 double crochet. Then shape the top of the sleeve by taking two stitches together at the end of every row till reduced to 20 double crochet, when fasten off, and sew up. Work the other sleeve the same. Sew up the sides and shoulders of the jacket, and put the sleeves in. Work a row of plain double crochet round the neck. For the **Border**—This is worked all round the jacket, using the blue wool. **1st round**—1 single crochet in a stitch of the jacket, 4 chain, 3 treble in the same place the single crochet is worked into, miss three stitches of the jacket, and

repeat. **2nd round**—1 single crochet under a loop of chain of last round, 4 chain, 3 treble in the same place, and repeat: in all the border rounds ease as much as is necessary at the corners. **3rd round**—The same as last round. **4th round**—The same with white wool. Work the same four rows of border round each wrist. Make with blue wool a crochet chain to run round the neck to tie in front, put a tassel at each end.

BABY'S HOOD AND CAPE COMBINED.

THIS is worked in point-neige, and will require 2½ ozs. of ruby and ½ oz. of white single Berlin wool, and a No. 10 bone crochet needle. Begin with ruby wool, with 10 chain, raise a stitch in each of the five chain stitches nearest the needle, wool over the needle, and draw through the six stitches on the needle, 1 chain; * raise a stitch in the little hole formed by the one chain, another in the lower part of the shell just done, another in the same stitch last shell is worked into, and another in each of the two next chain stitches, wool over the needle and draw through the six stitches on the needle, 1 chain; repeat from *, which makes three points in the row. Turn with three chain, and work another row of three point stitches. Again turn with three chain and work a similar row; and you have a little square counting three point stitches each way. Now work in the same stitch all round the little square, increasing at every corner; and continue working round till the head is large enough, about 16 points on each side. **For the Curtain**—Work along two sides only, breaking off the wool at the end of each row, and beginning each row at the right-hand side. Increase in every row at the beginning, the middle, and the end, and work as many as 18 or 20 rows. Then **for the Border**—With white wool, work 2 rows of crazy-stitch round the whole piece of work, thus, 1 single crochet, 3 chain, 2 treble in the same place the single crochet is worked into, miss one stitch, and repeat. Make three tassels, and place one at each point of the curtain. Run a ribbon round the neck tied in a bow at the back. Run a ribbon round the front, make a bow at the top, and leave sufficient as strings to tie in a bow under the chin.

SKIRT FOR A LITTLE CHILD.

PROCURE 2½ ozs. each of pink and white 3-thread fleecy wool of peacock quality, a No. 6 bone tricot needle. Commence with pink wool, with 41 chain. **1st row**—Pick up 40 tricot stitches and work back. **2nd row**—Pick up 29 tricot stitches and work back. **3rd row**—Pick up 40 tricot stitches and work back. Join on the white wool and work 3 rows the same. And continue thus

Baby's Hood and Cape Combined.

alternately, 3 rows with pink and 3 rows with white, till 14 stripes of each colour are worked. You will observe there are three rows of a colour in each stripe on the skirt and only two rows in the part which forms the band. This is for the purpose of contracting the band to the size of the waist. The wool is not to be broken off on changing colour, but passed from stripe to stripe. When the petticoat is sufficiently wide, sew up the skirt, leaving space for a placket hole at the top. Work round the bottom a crochet edge as a pretty finish and to bind in the loose threads of wool; begin with white wool, 1 double crochet on the first pink row of the skirt, 1 double crochet, 3 treble, 1 double crochet on the second pink row, then take the pink wool and do 1 double crochet on the first white row, and 1 double crochet, 3 treble, 1 double crochet on the second white row, and continue thus all round with the two colours, working over the one not in immediate use Place a button on the band

BABY'S DOUBLE CAPE AND HOOD.

THIS hood and double cape is worked in one piece, the deepest cape is 23 inches in length, the other cape falls over and makes a pretty finish, besides forming a double thickness, which is especially warm and comfortable round a baby's neck and shoulders. Procure 6 ozs. of white and 2 ozs. of blue Shetland wool, and a No. 11 bone crochet needle. Begin with white wool with 59 chain, for the neck. **1st row**—1 treble in the eighth chain from the needle, * 2 chain, miss two stitches, 1 treble in the next, and repeat from * to the end when there should be eighteen spaces in the row. **2nd row**—3 chain to turn, and work 3 treble stitches under each space of last row, making eighteen groups of three treble stitches. You turn the work, and begin every row with 3 chain, and work in groups of treble stitches; each group of 3 treble is termed a "set"; to "increase" make a group of 4 treble stitches, and then in the following row work a "set" intermediate between the second and third of these trebles. **3rd row**—1 set, increase, 6 sets, increase, 6 sets, increase, 2 sets. **4th row**—Work in plain sets, making 21 sets in the row. **5th row.**—6 sets, increase, 7 sets, increase, 6 sets. **6th row**—This, and every alternate row, is worked in plain sets. **7th row**—1 set, increase, 9 sets, increase, 10 sets, increase. **9th row**—6 sets, increase, 12 sets, increase, 6 sets. **11th row**—9 sets, increase, 8 sets, increase, 9 sets. **13th row**—5 sets, increase, 8 sets, increase, 9 sets, increase, 5 sets. **15th row**—1 set, increase, 30 sets, increase. **17th row**—14 sets, increase, 5 sets, increase, 14 sets. **19th row**—4 sets, increase, 27 sets, increase, 4 sets. **21st row**—11 sets, increase, 15 sets, increase, 11 sets. **23rd row**—1 set, increase, 38 sets, increase. **25th row**—10 sets, increase, 21 sets, increase, 10 sets. **27th row**

Skirt for Little Child.

—17 sets, increase, 9 sets, increase, 17 sets. **29th row**—23 sets, increase, 23 sets. **31st row**—4 sets, increase, 38 sets, increase, 4 sets. **33rd row**—1 set, increase, 47 sets, increase. **35th row**—19 sets, increase, 12 sets, increase, 19 sets. **37th row**—11 sets, increase, 14 sets, increase, 15 sets, increase, 11 sets. **39th row**—5 sets, increase, 45 sets, increase, 5 sets. **41st row**—20 sets, increase, 17 sets, increase, 20 sets. **43rd row**—1 set, increase, 58 sets, increase. **45th row**—18 sets, increase, 25 sets, increase, 18 sets. **47th row**—9 sets, increase, 45 sets, increase, 9 sets. **49th row**—33 sets, increase, 33 sets. **51st row**—23 sets, increase, 20 sets, increase, 23 sets. **53rd row**—1 set, increase, 67 sets, increase. **55th row**—10 sets, increase, 50 sets, increase, 10 sets. **57th row**—1 set, increase, 35 sets, increase, 35 sets, increase. **58th row**—Work in plain sets. All this has been crocheted with white wool; now fasten off. For the **Border**—Commence every row at the top of the front against the neck, and work down the front of the cape, along the bottom, and up the other front to the neck again, and fasten off; *not* work along the neck. **1st row**—With white wool,—Work one set in each space, increase three or four times in turning round the two corners, and increase twice along the bottom of the cape. **2nd row**—With blue wool,—Work in the same manner. Repeat these two rows till you have done 5 rows with blue wool and 6 rows with white wool. **12th row**—With white wool,—Work 1 double crochet in the first space, 6 treble in the next space, 1 double crochet in the next, and 6 treble in the next, and continue; do 9 treble in the three corner spaces to keep the work flat. **13th row**—With blue wool,—Work 1 double crochet in every stitch of preceding row. This completes the large cape. For the **Small Cape**—Take the white wool, and commence in "sets" the same as the second row of the large cape, working 3 treble in each space of the first row, 1 treble to come between the first and second and 2 treble to come between the second and third stitches already worked there. Continue to the end of the 36th row, and fasten off. Round this work the same border that is worked round the large cape, but when you have done eleven rows, stop, and crochet the hood before going on with the other two rows. For the **Hood**—Begin this with white wool, working into the foundation chain on which the capes are worked, of which hold the wrong side towards you. **1st row**—3 treble stitches under each space, making eighteen groups or "sets" of treble stitches in the row. **2nd row**—3 chain as before

to turn, and work 1 set, increase, 5 sets, increase, increase, increase, 5 sets, increase, 1 set. **3rd row**—4 sets, increase, 5 sets, increase, 5 sets, increase, 5 sets. **4th row**—Increase, 6 sets, increase, 8 sets, increase, 6 sets, increase. **5th row**—In plain sets, 28 sets in the row. **6th row**—Miss the first, and work 27 sets in the row. **7th row**—Miss the first, and work 26 sets in the row. And continue thus till the hood is reduced at the top to 3 sets only; when fasten off. For the **Border** round the **Hood**—Begin with white wool on the right-hand side of the hood, where, in the loop of the second row, work 3 treble, and do 3 treble in each loop all round the hood and fasten off. Then work round the hood a row with blue wool and a row with white wool like the border of the capes, till 3 rows are done with blue and 3 rows with white. Now work the 12th and the 13th rows of the border round the hood and round the small cape as well. Tie the hood in shape by running a narrow white ribbon in the first row of the border, finishing it with a nice bow at the top. The hood may hang at the back of the neck if wished instead of being worn on the head. Run a ribbon through the holes round the neck.

FROCK FOR CHILD OF THREE.

THIS is a dressy, comfortable-fitting frock, suitable for a child of three or four years. Our model is crocheted with creamy white Saxony wool (Faudel and Phillips' peacock quality), and is finished off with a surah silk sash tied lightly round below the waist, and ribbon at the neck and wrists to match. The body is worked throughout in ridged crochet and the skirt in point-neige. 10 ozs. of wool will be required and bone crochet needles No. 10 and No 7, also four rather large white bone buttons. Use No. 10 crochet needle for the body, and begin with 52 chain for the length of the left side of the back. Work 8 rows of plain double crochet, inserting the hook to take up the back thread of the stitches. Increase 1 stitch at the end of the 9th, 13th, 17th, and 21st rows. Decrease 1 stitch at the end of the 25th, 29th, 33rd, and 35th rows: this is to form the neck and shoulders, the straight side of the work goes round the waist. For the **37th row**—work 27 double crochet only and make 25 chain, and turn and double crochet back. Increase 1 stitch at the

Baby's Double Cape and Hood.

end of 39th, 43rd, and 47th rows. Decrease 1 stitch at the end of the 51st, 55th, and 59th rows. Work 5 plain rows. Increase 1 stitch at the end of the 65th, 69th, and 73rd rows. Decrease 1 stitch at the end of the 77th, 81st, and 85th rows. For the 87th row, work 27 double crochet and do 25 chain, and turn and double crochet back. Increase 1 stitch at the end of the 89th, 91st, 95th, and 99th rows. Decrease 1 stitch at the end of the 103rd, 107th, 111th, and 115th rows. Work 5 plain rows. In the 121st row make buttonholes, thus, 9 double crochet, 3 chain, miss three stitches, and repeat. Work 2 plain rows, and fasten off. For the **Skirt**—Take No. 7 crochet needle, and holding the work conveniently to begin crocheting along the straight edge of the rows of ridged crochet, commencing on the button-hole side, work in point-neige, making the stitches rather closely so that the skirt may hang nice and full; there should be 145 or 150 stitches in the row. Work 18 rows, each may be done a little more loosely than the last. Then sew up the skirt leaving just sufficient room for a placket hole, and sew up the shoulder pieces. For the **Sleeves**—Use No. 10 crochet needle, and making 36 chain for the length of the sleeve, work 3 rows of ridged double crochet. **4th row**—Increase 1 stitch at the beginning and at the end of the row, also on the tenth and thirteenth stitches. Work 3 plain rows. Repeat from the fourth row till you have done five rows of increasings. Then work 5 plain rows. **26th row**—Decrease 1 stitch at the beginning and at the end of the row, also twice at the elbow where you before increased. Work 3 plain rows. Repeat from the twenty-sixth row four times. Fasten off, and sew the sleeve up. Work the other sleeve in the same manner. Sew the sleeves into the body of the frock. For the **Edge** round the **Sleeves** and **Neck—1st row** —Point-neige. **2nd row**—The same. **3rd row**—Crazy-stitch,—1 single crochet into a stitch of the point-neige, 3 chain, 2 treble in the same place as the single crochet is worked into, and repeat: this row is carried along the buttonhole side of the bodice before working it upon the neck. Work the same crazy-stitch edge round the bottom of the skirt. Sew the buttons in their places. Fold the sash and secure it with a stitch or two in front to keep it in position. Run narrow ribbon round the neck and sleeves and tie in bows.

13 treble, 2 double crochet, and then do 1 single crochet in the top stitch of the stem; turn the work, and taking up the back thread of the stitches, work 1 double crochet on each of the two double crochet stitches of the flower, 1 treble on each of the two first treble stitches, 2 treble on each of the four next treble stitches, 3 treble on the next, 2 treble on each of the four next, 1 treble on each of the two next, 1 double crochet on each of two double crochet stitches, take the needle out and insert the hook pointing upwards in the stem and draw the loop (stitch) through, do 4 chain, miss three spaces of the preceding row, 1 double crochet in the next, 8 chain, miss three spaces, 1 double crochet in the next, and repeat from *. For a pointed chemise it must be managed that a flower comes in the exact centre at front and at back, and you miss five spaces below the flower and four spaces on each side instead of three spaces; and in all following rows a contraction must be observed to preserve the correct shaping of the two points. **3rd round**—1 double crochet on the fourth treble stitch of a flower, * 3 chain, miss one treble stitch, 1 double crochet on the next, and repeat from * till there are 8 loops of chain and 9 double crochet stitches worked round the flower, then 2 chain, 2 treble under the loop of eight chain of last row, 2 chain, 1 double crochet on the

Frock for a Child of Three.

Section of Chemise Trimming showing t**

CHEMISE TRIMMING.

PROCURE a reel of Evans' crochet cotton, No. 20, and a fine steel crochet needle, also 2 yards of very narrow pink ribbon. Commence with chain the length required to go round the top of the chemise, and join round. **1st round**—4 chain to begin, miss the first stitch of the commencing chain, 1 treble in the next, * 1 chain, miss 1 stitch, 1 treble in the next, and repeat from *; if your chemise top is cut in a point like our illustration put a stitch or two of coloured cotton in the foundation chain to mark the exact centre of the front and the exact centre of the back, and in these places miss three chain stitches instead of missing only one, but, of course, if the chemise is the ordinary round shape you will crochet all round alike; at the end of the round do 1 chain and join into the third stitch of the chain with which the round commenced; fasten off at the end of this and every round. Or supposing the chemise opens in front, the border will be worked in rows, every row beginning on the right-hand side **2nd round**—1 double crochet under the first space, * 14 chain, 1 single crochet in the eighth chain from the needle, turn the work, and for the flower work in the little circle, 2 double crochet,

fourth treble stitch of the next flower, and continue in the same way. **4th round**—1 double crochet under the first loop of three chain, 3 chain, 1 double crochet under the next loop of three chain, all round the flower, then 2 chain, and work round the next flower. **5th round**—1 double crochet under the third loop of three chain, 1 chain, 1 single crochet under the next loop, 1 chain, 1 double crochet under the next loop, 9 chain, and continue. **6th round**—1 treble in the first stitch of chain of last row, * 1 chain, miss one stitch, 1 treble in the next, and repeat from *. **7th round**—2 long treble (1 on each of the first two stitches of last round), 2 chain, miss two stitches, 2 long treble, 2 chain, miss two stitches, and repeat; this round is to admit of a ribbon being run in. **8th round**—1 treble on the first stitch of last round, * 1 chain, miss one stitch, 1 treble in the next, do this three more times, then 1 chain, miss two stitches, 1 treble on the next, and repeat from *. **9th round** —1 double crochet on a treble stitch of last round, * 2 chain, 2 treble under the third space, 3 chain, 2 more treble in the same place, 2 chain, 1 double crochet on the fifth treble stitch from that last worked upon, and repeat from *. **10th round**—1 double crochet on double crochet stitch of last round, * 3 chain, 1 treble under the loop of three chain of last round, 4 chain, 1 single crochet in the fourth chain from the needle, 1 treble in the same place last treble is worked into, do a picot and a treble twice more in the same place, then 3 chain, 1 double crochet on double crochet of last round, and repeat from *. This finishes the border for the neck of the chemise. Work two pieces for the sleeves. Then sew the trimming neatly upon the chemise, and run ribbon in and out through the long treble stitches of the seventh round.

THE LILY JACKET.

THIS pretty jacket is intended for an infant of nine or ten months old. It is worked in tricot, but always taking up the loop that lies flat along the top of the previous row instead of the usual tricot loop. Procure 4 ozs. of best white Berlin fingering, a No. 5 tricot needle, a No. 10 crochet needle, and 1½ yards of inch wide ribbon for bows. Commence for the bottom of the **Right Front** with 36 chain. **1st row**—Pick up 35 stitches along the chain, and draw back as in ordinary tricot. **2nd row**—Pick up 35 stitches, taking up the thread that lies flat between the tricot stitches of last row, and draw back. Decrease at the end of the third and following rows to 31 stitches. Work

foundation,* insert the hook in the next foundation stitch, draw the wool through, do 5 chain, wool over the needle and draw through both stitches on the needle, 1 double crochet on the next stitch of the foundation, and repeat from * all round the jacket, excepting up the left front. Do 5 rows, making the loops of chain sit as shown in the engraving. Work 5 rows in the same manner round the sleeves. Add ribbon to tie at the neck, and put a bow on each wrist

WIDE CROCHET BORDER.

FOR this handsome border commence with the stars, which are made thus:—10 chain, join round, and in the centre work 12 double crochet, 25 chain, 1 double crochet, 19 chain, 1 double crochet, 21 chain, 1 double crochet, 25 chain, 1 double crochet, 21 chain, 1 double crochet, 19 chain, 1 double crochet, 25 chain, 1 double crochet, join to the first double crochet, and fasten off. Make as many of these stars as are required for the length of the border. **1st row** of the Border—9 chain, * 1 single in the first loop of the star, 5 chain, 1 single in the next loop, 5 chain, 1 single in the next, 7 chain, 1 single in the centre loop, 7 chain, 1 single in the next, 5 chain, 1 single in the next,

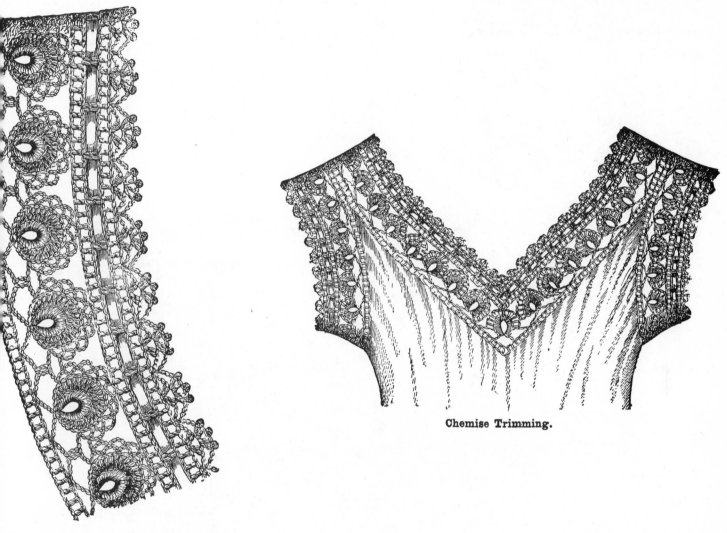

Chemise Trimming.

Arrangement of One Sleeve and Shoulder.

straight on without decreasing till the sixteenth row, when leave 3 at the end unworked for the armhole. Continue till the twenty-second row, when slip stitch along the first 7 stitches for the neck, and tricot the remainder. Afterwards slip stitch along the first 3 stitches of every row till you work 12 tricot only, which completes the front. Work the **Left Front** in the same manner, but making the decreasings come at the beginning of the rows instead of at the end. **For the Back**—Begin with 61 chain, in which work 60 tricot stitches. Then after doing another row of 60 stitches, decrease at the beginning and at the end of every row to 52 stitches. Proceed in rows to correspond with the fronts. When ready to shape the neck, work 18 tricot stitches only, and then leave 3 stitches at the end of every row till only 12 are left. Work the other neck piece to correspond. Sew up the sides of the jacket, and sew up the shoulders. **For the Sleeves**—Make 29 chain, and in this work 28 tricot stitches. Then increase at the end of every alternate row to 32 stitches. Work 6 rows plain. Decrease at the end of every alternate row back to 28 stitches. Work the other sleeve in the same way; and sew them up, and set them neatly into the armholes. The **Frilly Border** which goes round the jacket and sleeves is worked in chain crochet. **1st row**—1 double crochet on the

5 chain, 1 single in the next, 15 chain, take the second star and repeat from * till all the stars are united, end with 11 chain, and turn the work. **2nd row**—1 double crochet in the sixth chain stitch from the needle and * 1 double crochet in each consecutive stitch till 27 double crochet are done, which brings you to the single stitch at the point, 2 chain, 1 double crochet in the same single stitch and again work 27 double crochet are done, 5 chain, miss 3 stitches, 1 double crochet in the next, and continue from * to the end of the row. **3rd row**—5 chain to turn, * miss the first double crochet stitch, and taking up the back thread of the stitches of preceding row that the work may sit in ridges, do 27 consecutive double crochet, the last of these will come under the two chain at the point, do 2 chain, and beginning with 1 under the same loop of two chain, do 27 more consecutive double crochet, 3 chain, 1 double crochet under the loop of five chain, 3 chain, and repeat from *. **4th row**—4 chain to turn, work 27 double crochet up to the point and 27 down again as in last row, then 1 double crochet under the three chain of last row, 5 chain, 1 double crochet under the other three chain, and continue. Repeat the third and fourth rows nine times. Break off the cotton. Now work for the **Open Edge**, beginning on the same side as you began the last

row of double crochet :—**1st row**—1 double crochet on the first double crochet of last row, * 5 chain, miss two, 1 double crochet on the next, and repeat from * till 18 loops of 5 chain are worked round the scollop, then 3 chain, 1 double crochet under the loop of 5 chain, 3 chain, 1 double crochet on the first stitch of the next scollop, and continue ; break off at the end and re-commence on the right-hand side. **2nd row**—leave the first loop of 5 chain, 1 treble on the centre stitch of the second 5 chain, * 7 chain, 1 single in the fifth chain from the needle, 2 chain, 1 treble in the same place the last treble stitch is worked into, 7 chain, miss the next loop of 5 chain, 1 treble on the centre stitch of the next five chain, and repeat from * ; work a picot in EACH of the four top loops of the scollop with 7 chain between, so you get 5 picots on each side the scollop, then do 3 chain, 1 treble on the double crochet stitch of last row over the 5 chain of row previous. **3rd row**—1 treble on the centre stitch

The Lily Jacket.

of the first loop of 7 chain, 8 chain, 1 single in the fifth from the needle, 6 chain, 1 single in the same place, 5 chain, 1 single in the same place, 1 single in the next chain stitch (making a group of three picots), 2 chain, 1 treble on the centre stitch of the next loop of 7 chain, * 7 chain, 1 single in the fifth from the needle, 2 chain, 1 treble in the same place last treble is worked into, 8 chain, 1 single in the fifth from the needle, 6 chain, 1 single in the same place, 5 chain, 1 single in the same place, 1 single in the next chain stitch, 2 chain, 1 treble on the centre stitch of the next loop of seven chain, and repeat from * six times, then 3 chain, and go on to the next scollop. **4th row**—1 double crochet in the centre loop of the first group of picots, 11 chain, 1 double crochet in the centre loop of the next group of picots, * 10 chain, 1 single in the seventh from the needle, in the little circle thus formed work 1 double crochet, 3 treble, 2 double crochet, 3 treble, 2 double crochet, 3 treble, 1 double crochet, then 1 single in the same stitch last single is worked into, 3 chain, 1 double crochet in the centre loop of the next group of picots, 11 chain, 1 double crochet in the centre loop of the next group of picots, repeat from * twice, then 1 double crochet in the centre loop of the first group of picots on the next scollop. **5th row**—1 double crochet on the centre stitch of the 11 chain, * 7 chain, 1 single in the fourth from the needle 3 chain, 1 treble on the first treble stitch of the little circle, 5 chain, 1 single in the fourth from the needle, 5 chain, 1 single in the fourth from the needle, 5 chain, 1 single in the fourth from the needle, 1 chain, 1 treble between the two double crochet stitches, work another bar of 3 picots, 1 treble between the next two double crochet stitches, another bar of 3 picots, 1 treble on the last treble stitch of the little circle, 7 chain, 1 single in the fourth from the needle, 3 chain, 1 double crochet on the centre stitch of the 11 chain, repeat from * twice, then 1 double crochet on the centre stitch of the 11 chain on the next scollop, and continue to the end of the row. For the **Heading,**—**1st row**—work 3 double crochet under the loop of chain at the right-hand side of the end scollop, * 17 chain, 3 single crochet on the star, 17 chain, 3 double crochet under the loop of 3 chain, and repeat from *. **2nd row**—1 treble, 1 chain, miss one, and repeat. **3rd row**—2 long treble, * 3 chain, miss three, 2 long treble, and repeat from * **4th row**—1 treble, 1 chain, miss one, and repeat.

CROSS-OVER.

THIS cross-over is suitable for outdoor wear under a jacket or fur cloak, or may be worn in the house, it is double across the chest, and affords ample warmth without being heavy. Required, 2 ozs. of white and 1½ ozs. of blue peacock fingering, a No. 9 bone crochet needle, and half a dozen white pearl

buttons. With white wool make 6 chain, and join round ; work 3 chain, then do 1 treble, 1 chain, 1 treble, 1 chain, 1 treble in the circle. **2nd row**—3 chain to turn, 1 treble under the first one chain of last row, 1 chain, another treble in the same place, 1 treble 1 chain and 1 treble under the next one chain of last row, 1 treble 1 chain and 1 treble between the last treble and the chain that turned. **3rd row**—3 chain to turn, a "set" (1 treble, 1 chain, 1 treble) under each one chain of last row, and a set between the last treble and the chain that turned, there are 4 "sets" in this row. **4th row**—3 chain to turn, and work in the same manner, doing 5 sets in the row. Continue in the same way, working one more set in each successive row until 12 rows are done, when break off the wool. This three-cornered piece of crochet is the top portion of the back of the cross-over, the last row being the part by the neck. Join the blue wool to the white where you broke off, do 3 chain, and work 1 set under the treble stitch at the end of the row, and the same in every row from the corner to the circle of chain with which you began ; in this circle do a double set, viz., 1 treble 1 chain 1 treble 1 chain 1 treble, then continue in sets along the opposite side, break off the wool at the completion of the last set. Join the white wool to the blue where you broke off, work 3 chain to turn, 1 set in the first set of last row, and continue along to the point, where work one set under the chain between the first and second treble, 1 set *on* the second treble, and 1 set under the chain between the second and third treble, and proceed along the opposite side. Work 7 more rows with white wool, rounding the point each time in alternate manner as described above. After working 8 rows with white, join on the blue and work three rows, then white again and work 8 rows, and break off. For the **Front** of the **Cross-over**—Take the blue wool and begin with 1 treble worked into the same place as the first set you worked with blue wool upon the three-cornered piece with which the cross-over commenced, and work 1 set under the stitch at the end of each row from that downwards to the corner where do an extra 1 chain, 1 treble ; work 3 chain to turn, and work a set under the first one chain, and thence back along to the top, make no increase at the end of the row here ; join on the white wool, do three chain, and work the first set under the second one chain of last row, for in this row and in the 8 following rows the top, or neck, of the cross-over decreases, viz., slants downwards, and the bottom increases, *i.e.,*

Wide Crochet Border.

goes to form a point at the waist, 7 rows are worked with white wool, and then 2 rows with blue, and this is half of one side of the front ; now do 2 more rows with blue and 7 rows with white, but decreasing at the waist and increasing at the neck. Work a front upon the opposite side of the crochet the same exactly as this front. Then take the blue wool and work 2 rows all round the cross-over, the 1st round to be in pattern as before, and the 2nd round in scollops, doing 1 double crochet, 5 treble, 1 double crochet under the first one chain, and a double crochet stitch under the next one chain, and repeat. The fronts are to overlap each other. Upon the left-hand front sew the six buttons, three at each side of the front, as shown in the engraving ; the right-hand front is to button over. This completes the cross-over.

POINT D'ALENÇON.

THIS is suitable for edging quilts or for any purpose for which a wide handsome border is desired. It is worked the short way. Commence with 26 chain. **1st row**—Do 25 double crochet, turn the work. **2nd row**—Beginning on the first stitch of previous row and inserting the needle to take up the one back thread as the work must sit in ridges, work 20 double crochet, do 6 treble on the next stitch to make a tuft, then 4 more double crochet, which brings you to the end of the row, turn the work. **3rd row**—1 double crochet on each of the first 4 double crochet of last row, 1 treble worked in the second previous row at the back of the tuft of six treble, 20 double crochet straight along to the end of the row. **4th row**—18 double crochet, a tuft of 6 treble on the next stitch, 4 double crochet, and leave the last two stitches unworked. **5th row**—1 double crochet on each of the four double crochet of

Cross-Over.

last row, 1 treble in the second previous row at the back of the tuft of six treble, 18 double crochet straight along. **6th row**—16 double crochet, a tuft of 6 treble on the next stitch, 4 double crochet, and leave the last two stitches unworked. **7th row**—4 double crochet, 1 treble at the back of the tuft; 16 double crochet straight along. **8th row**—14 double crochet, a tuft, 4 double crochet, and leave the last two stitches unworked. **9th row**—4 double crochet, 1 treble at the back of the tuft, 14 double crochet straight along. **10th row**—12 double crochet, a tuft, 4 double crochet, and leave two stitches unworked. **11th row**—4 double crochet, 1 treble at the back of the tuft, 12 double crochet straight along. **12th row**—10 double crochet, a tuft, 4 double crochet, and leave two stitches unworked. **13th row**—4 double crochet, 1 treble at the back of the tuft, 10 double crochet straight along. **14th row**—8 double crochet, a tuft, 4 double crochet, and leave two stitches unworked. **15th row**—4 double crochet, 1 treble at the back of the tuft, 8 double crochet. **16th row**—6 double crochet, a tuft, 4 double crochet, and leave two stitches unworked. **17th row**—4 double crochet, 1 treble at the back of the tuft, 6 double crochet. **18th row**—4 double crochet, a tuft, 4 double crochet, and 3 chain. **19th row**—1 double crochet on each of two chain stitches and 1 double crochet on each of four double crochet stitches making 6 double crochet in all, 1 treble at the back of the tuft, 4 double crochet. **20th row**—6 double crochet, a tuft, 4 double crochet, 3 chain. **21st row**—1 double crochet on each of two chain stitches and 1 double crochet on each of four double crochet stitches, making 6 double crochet in all, 1 treble at the back of the tuft, 6 double crochet. **22nd row**—8 double crochet, a tuft, 4 double crochet, 6 chain, turn the work to get the tufted side next you, and here begin the open stars which form the scollops of the border, cotton over the needle and insert the hook in the fourth chain from the needle, draw the cotton through, cotton over the needle and draw through two stitches on the needle, cotton over the needle and insert the hook in the same chain stitch as before and draw the cotton through, cotton over the needle and draw through two stitches on the needle, cotton over the needle and draw through three stitches on the needle, catch with a single crochet into the corner of the twentieth row; 4 chain and work a similar section to that described above, 4 chain and work another section, catch with a single crochet into the corner of the seventeenth row; work 1 section and join to the corner of the thirteenth row; work 2 sections and join to the centre of the half-star in the middle of the scollop; work 2 sections and join to the corner of the first section where you commenced the open stars. **23rd row**—1 double

crochet on each of two chain stitches and 1 double crochet on each of four double crochet stitches, making 6 double crochet in all, 1 treble at the back of the tuft, 8 double crochet. **24th row**—10 double crochet, a tuft, 4 double crochet, 3 chain. **25th row**—6 double crochet, 1 treble at the back of the tuft, 10 double crochet. **26th row**—12 double crochet, a tuft, 4 double crochet, 3 chain. **27th row**—6 double crochet, 1 treble at the back of the tuft, 12 double crochet. **28th row**—14 double crochet, a tuft, 4 double crochet, 3 chain. **29th row**—6 double crochet, 1 treble at the back of the tuft, 14 double crochet. **30th row**—16 double crochet, a tuft, 4 double crochet, turn the work, and now go on with the open stars, having the tufted side of the border next you, 6 chain, cotton over the needle and insert the hook in the fourth chain from the needle draw the cotton through and complete a section as directed in the twenty-second row, catch with a single crochet into the corner of the twenty-eighth row; 4 chain, and work a similar section, 4 chain and work another section, join into the centre of the first half-star to the right; work 2 sections and catch into the centre of the next half-star to the right; work 2 sections and join to the corner of the eighth row; work 1 section and join to the corner of the fourth row; again work 2 sections and join into the centre of the first half-star to the left, 2 sections and join into the centre of the next half-star to the left, 2 sections and join into the centre of the next half-star to the left; work 3 sections and join into the centre of the first half-star to the right, 2 sections and join into the centre of the next half-star to the right, and 2 sections and join into the centre of the next half-star to the right; work 1 section, 6 chain, 1 section (4 chain to begin this beyond the six chain just done), join to the centre of the first half-star to the left, 1 section, then * 4 chain, 1 treble in the fourth chain from the needle, 3 chain, 1 single crochet in the same chain stitch the treble was worked into, 1 single crochet at the top of last section, repeat again from *, then work 1 section and join into the centre of the next half-star to the left; work 1 section, 4 chain, 1 treble in the fourth chain from the needle, 1 chain, catch with a single crochet into the top of the one treble stitch to the right, 1 single crochet in the one chain stitch, 1 single crochet on the treble stitch to the left, 3 chain, 1 single crochet in the same chain stitch the treble was worked into, 1 single crochet at the top of last section, 4 chain, 1 treble in the fourth chain from the needle, 3 chain, 1 single crochet in the same chain stitch the treble was worked into, 1 single crochet at the top of last section, 1 section and join into the centre of the next half-star to the left; 1 section, 6 chain, 1 section (beginning with 4 chain beyond the six chain just done), join to the centre of the last half-star to the left, and work 1 section and join into the tip of the section by the thirtieth row. **31st row**—1 double crochet on each of two chain stitches and 1 double

Point d'Alençon.

crochet on each of four double crochet stitches making 6 double crochet in all, 1 treble at the back of the tuft, 16 double crochet to the end of the row. **32nd row**—18 double crochet, a tuft, 4 double crochet, 3 chain. **33rd row**—6 double crochet, 1 treble at the back of the tuft, 18 double crochet. **34th row**—20 double crochet, a tuft, and 4 double crochet. **35th row**—Work 1 double crochet on each of the four double crochet stitches of last row, 1 treble at the back of the tuft, and 20 double crochet straight along to the end of the row. Repeat from the fourth row for the length required. Then work for the **Heading—1st row**—1 treble, 1 chain, alternately, the treble stitches to be placed one in each ridge of the double crochet. **2nd row**—Work from left to right,—make 2 sections of open stars, turn the hook to the right, and catch with a single crochet into the seventh stitch to the right, 2 more sections and again catch into the seventh stitch to the right, and so on to the end of the row. **3rd row**—Work from right to left,—make 3 sections and catch with a single crochet into the centre of the first half-star to the left, make 2 sections and catch into the centre of the next half-star to the left, and continue; do 1 section only at the end. **4th row**—6 chain, turn the work, 1 single crochet into the centre of the first half-star, 6 chain, 1 single crochet in the centre of the next half-star, and continue. **5th row**—5 chain, turn the work, * 1 treble, 1 chain, miss one, and repeat from *; fasten off at the end of the row. For the **Edge** round the **Scollops**—**1st row**—Commence with 1 double crochet in the centre of the point of ridged crochet, * 6 chain, catch with a single crochet into the top of the first section to the left and work 1 single crochet in each of the six chain stitches between this section and the next section, 6 chain, catch with a single crochet into the top of the next section to the left, 6 chain, 1 single crochet between the points of the next two sections, 6 chain, 1 single crochet into the top of the next section to the left, 6 chain, 1 single crochet in the top of the next section and 1 single crochet in each of the continuous six chain stitches, 6 chain, 1 double crochet in the centre of the point of ridged crochet, and repeat from * to the end of the row. **2nd row**—Re-commencing on the right-hand side,—work 1 double crochet in each stitch of preceding row. **3rd row**—Begin again on the right-hand side with 1 treble on the fourth double crochet stitch of last row, miss three double crochet, 1 treble on the next, * 5 chain, 1 treble worked into the centre two threads of the treble stitch last done, miss three double crochet, 1 treble on the next, and repeat from * ten times; then go on to the next scollop and work the same. This completes the border.

BABY'S BOOTIKIN.

THIS is a warm comfortable-fitting boot for a young infant. Procure 2 ozs. of

Baby's Bootikin.

white Berlin fingering, Beehive wool, or Victoria yarn, and a No. 11 bone crochet needle. First of all, work the ridged crochet for the top of the leg, beginning with 13 chain, work 12 double crochet forwards and backwards, inserting the hook to take up the one back thread of the stitches of the row previous; continue till 32 rows are done. Join this strip round as if for a cuff, and work on it in single crochet, doing 44 stitches in the round. Work 34 rounds for the leg. Then take 17 back stitches for the heel and work on them forwards and backwards, still in single crochet, for 14 rows; then take 2 stitches together in the middle of every row till 6 stitches remain, join these. Now work 14 single crochet along the side of the heel, do 27 stitches across the front, and 14 stitches along the other side of the heel; crochet round and round, taking 2 stitches together on each gusset for 7 rounds, then 12 rounds without decrease, and afterwards take 2 together until about an inch from the end, when take in every stitch till you have but 16 stitches left; fold these together, the top to the underpart, and join them up. Work the other bootikin in the same manner.

CROCHET TRIMMING WITH ROSARY BEADS.

FOR THE NECK AND SLEEVES OF A DRESS.

FRILLING though certainly not yet out of fashion appears to be somewhat on the wane, and a durable substitute, much more economical, will doubtless be welcome to many of our readers. Plain linen collars are suitable for tailor-made dresses, but something more dainty is required for a more dressy style. Our illustration shows a most useful little collar. Required, a skein of fine écru crochet cotton, or a ball of Finlayson's No. 35 Scotch linen crochet thread, a very fine steel crochet needle, a string of small red rosary beads, and a piece of soft écru tape about an inch wide and 14 inches long, or the

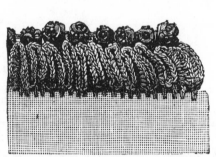

Crochet Trimming with Rosary Beads for Neck and Sleeves of a Dress.

length to fit in the band of the dress. Hem neatly the two ends of the tape. The first row of the collar is crocheted *into* the tape, and if any difficulty be experienced in getting the hook through, it may be obviated by taking a coarse sewing needle and piercing holes with it, ten holes to the inch, all along the tape. **1st row**—Hold the right side of the tape towards you, and work 1 treble in the first of the pierced holes, * 1 chain, 1 treble in the next hole, and repeat from * the length of the tape. **2nd row**—5 chain to turn, 1 double long treble under the first one chain stitch of last row (to work a double long treble pass the cotton three times round the needle, insert the hook in the space and draw the cotton through, now there are five loops on the needle, cotton over the needle and draw through two loops at a time till all are worked off), * 1 chain, 1 double long treble under the next one chain stitch of last row, and repeat from *. **3rd row**—Turn the work, and holding it sideways towards you, do 12 treble stitches along the first double long treble stitch of last row, working from the top to the bottom of the stitch, then reversing the position of the work do 12 treble stitches along the next double long treble stitch, working from the bottom to the top of the stitch, and continue thus down and up along each double long treble to the end of the row, which makes a thick flat ruching. **4th row**—Thread your beads on the crochet cotton (our model had 51 beads) and work a double crochet under the first one chain stitch of the second row, * pass down a bead, do 1 double crochet under each of the three next one chain stitches, and repeat from * to the end of the row, and fasten off. Thread a sewing needle with the crochet cotton, using it double, sew very firmly before the first bead, and then thread through each bead in succession to the last, and fasten off securely. This will keep the beads nicely in position. The trimming for the sleeves is worked exactly the same way. The rosary beads may be had in amber, brown, or black if preferred, and the trimming will look equally pretty. They should not be larger than a pea.

GLOVE.

THIS glove is crocheted in two colours. Procure 1 oz. of white and 1 oz. of brown Scotch fingering, and a No. 11 bone crochet needle. Begin with white wool, with 22 chain, and work forwards and backwards in single crochet for 46 rows, always inserting the hook to take up the one back thread of the row previous. This is for the wrist; join it round like a cuff. Now, still in single crochet and commencing at the seam, work upon the wrist, making 44 stitches in the round. Do 2 rounds with white wool and 2 rounds with brown, taking now the one top thread of the stitches of the preceding round, and being careful to join the last stitch of every round evenly to the stitch with which the round commenced, otherwise the stripes will not meet nicely. **5th round**—Begin the increase for the thumb,—work 1 single crochet, 1 chain to make increase, 1 single crochet, 1 chain to again increase, and then plain single crochet to the end of the round. Work 3 rounds without increase. **9th round**—1 single crochet, 1 chain, 3 single crochet, 1 chain, and plain single crochet to the end of the round. Work 3 rounds without increase. Proceed thus increasing every fourth round, each time with 2 more single crochet between the increasing chains. When there are 16 stripes done, Begin the **Thumb**—Work 16 stitches, 3 chain, and join round to the fourth stitch. Continue round and round on the thumb stitches till 11 stripes are worked, then finish off the thumb with white; decrease every second and third stitch; 1 round plain; decrease again till only two or three stitches are left; break off the wool, thread the end in a rug needle, draw the stitches closely together, and sew up neatly at the inside. Now continue working the **Hand**—Do 3 stitches on the chain that was made for the thumb, and work on till 23 stripes in all are accomplished. Then for the **First Finger**—Begin on the fourth stitch of the round, do 13 single crochet, 3 chain, and join round; work 12 stripes, and finish off the top the same as the thumb is finished.

Glove.

For the **Second Finger**—Work 5 stitches inside the hand, pick up 3 in the chain by the first finger, work 6 stitches outside, do 3 chain, join round; work 14 stripes, and finish the top. For the **Third Finger**—Work 5 stitches inside the hand, pick up 3 by the second finger, work 5 stitches outside, do 3 chain, join round; work 12 stripes, and finish the top. For the **Fourth Finger**—Work round all the remaining stitches and pick up 2 on the chain by the third finger, join round; work 10 stripes, and finish the top. Crochet the other glove to correspond.

BIB, WORKED IN RIDGED CROCHET.

REQUIRED, Evans' crochet cotton, No. 20, and a fine steel crochet needle. Commence with 162 chain. **1st row**—Work 10 consecutive double crochet, miss two chain stitches, 10 double crochet worked consecutively, 3 double crochet in the next chain stitch, and repeat to the end of the row, which must finish with 10 consecutive double crochet as it began. **2nd row**—Turn the work, and inserting the hook to take up the back thread of the stitches of previous row, do 1 double crochet on each of the first 9 stitches, * miss two double crochet, do 1 double crochet on each of the next 10 stitches, 3 double crochet on the next stitch which is the centre stitch of the three double crochet of last row, 1 double crochet on each of the next 10 stitches, and repeat from * to the end of the row, where finish with 9 double crochet as it began. The next following rows are worked in the same manner only decreasing one stitch at the beginning and one stitch at the end of each row. At the end of the **10th row** and at the end of the **11th row** you must make 11 chain to compensate for the stitches that have been decreased, and work as from the first row till you have done eighty rows and have eight points or scollops up each side of the bib. Make 11 chain as usual at the end of the eightieth row, and turn and do 10 double crochet along the chain, miss two stitches, 10 double crochet, 3 double crochet on the next stitch, 10 double crochet, miss two stitches, 10 double crochet, and turn, and continue backwards and forwards till two more points or scollops are complete up the side of the bib, when fasten off, and work the other shoulder piece to correspond. When this is finished you work a **Border** all round the bib, as follows,—

frequently as necessary to draw into size for the band. **For the Band**—Work 8 rounds of plain double crochet. Finish the tam o'shanter with a wool pompon in the centre of the crown.

HOOD FOR CHILD OF THREE.

THIS is a comfortable, warm hood for winter wear. Procure 3 ozs. of white and 2 ozs. of pale blue Andalusian wool, a bone crochet needle, No. 10, and a pair of steel knitting needles, No. 15. If Berlin wool be employed these directions will make a hood large enough for an older child. Commence with white wool, with 80 chain, insert the hook in the third chain from the needle and proceed with the working of a straight line of treble stitches, doing 77 treble in the row. **2nd row**—3 chain to turn, and work 77 treble in the row, inserting the hook in the one top thread of the stitches of last row. Work 5 more rows the same. Then work 3 rows of trebles, decreasing in each row by taking the 3 centre stitches together in one. Afterwards take the 5 centre stitches together in one for 4 rows. Fold the work together and crochet it up. This is the foundation, and the commencing chain is the front of the hood. Now for the frilling, of which there are three rows—one at the front, one up the middle of the hood, and one up the centre of the crown. For the first frill which goes across the five first rows of the foundation, take the blue wool, and beginning with a double crochet upon the left-hand side of the front work 10 treble stitches across the 5 rows, then 2 treble on the straight line of stitches, and 10 treble back again, and so on to the opposite side of the front. For the second frill, miss two rows of the foundation, and work 8 treble stitches forwards and backwards in the same manner. For the third frill, miss two rows of the foundation, and work 8 treble stitches forwards and backwards on the 4 rows which form the crown. Edge all these frills by working thereon a heading of double crochet with white wool. Work with blue wool a row of chain stitches over the trebles of the four missed rows. The curtain is in knitting: cast on with white wool 73 stitches, and alternately knit 2, purl 2, and purl the extra stitch at the end of the row. Every row is the same, and this is not ordinary ribbed knitting, but a pretty striped pattern. When 15 rows are done, decrease 1 stitch at each end of every row till there are 36 stitches on the pin, when cast off. With white

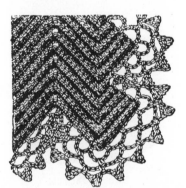

Section of Bib worked in Ridged Crochet.

Tam O'Shanter, Fluted.

Bib worked in Ridged Crochet.

1st round—1 double crochet in a stitch of the bib, * 7 chain, miss three or four stitches of the bib, 1 double crochet in the next, and repeat from *, regulating the loops of chain so as to preserve an equal degree of fulness, five loops round every scollop, and double crochet from one scollop to the next. **2nd round**—1 double crochet under the loop of seven chain of last round, 7 chain, and repeat. **3rd round**—1 double crochet under the loop of seven chain of last round, 5 chain, 1 double crochet in the third chain from the needle, 1 treble in each of the other two chain stitches, and repeat; ease round the corners, and pass from one loop to the next at intervals between the scollops. Place a loop on each side of the bib and a string of ribbon on each shoulder.

TAM O'SHANTER, FLUTED.

PROCURE 3 ozs. of single Berlin wool of any colour preferred, and a bone crochet needle No. 11 or No. 12. Begin with 4 chain, join round, and work 10 double crochet in the circle. **2nd round**—1 double crochet on the first stitch, 2 double crochet on the next, and repeat (there will be 15 double crochet in the round). **3rd round**—2 consecutive double crochet, 2 double crochet on the next, and repeat (there will be 20 double crochet in the round). **4th round**—3 consecutive double crochet, 2 double crochet on the next, and continue, increasing where necessary to make the work lie perfectly flat, till you can count 50 double crochet in the round, when seven rounds of crochet should be done. **8th round**—Work 3 double crochet in every stitch of last round. **9th round**—1 double crochet, * 3 double crochet in the next stitch, which is the centre stitch of three double crochet of last round, 5 consecutive double crochet, and repeat from *. **10th round**—3 double crochet on centre stitch of the three double crochet of last round, 3 consecutive double crochet, miss 1, 3 consecutive double crochet, and repeat. **11th round**—3 double crochet on centre stitch of the three double crochet of last round, 3 consecutive double crochet, miss 2, 3 consecutive double crochet, and repeat. Work 13 more rounds the same as the last round. **25th round**—1 double crochet on centre stitch of the three double crochet of last round, take up two stitches together four times, and repeat. **26th round**—Double crochet, taking up two stitches together as

wool crochet 4 rows of treble stitches round the *outside* of the curtain (not where the stitches are cast on), increasing where necessary to keep the work flat. **5th row**—With blue wool, work double long treble (the wool three times round the needle) on every stitch of last row, increasing one stitch in every four. **6th row**—1 double crochet on the first stitch of previous row, * miss one, 5 treble on the next, miss one, 1 double crochet on the next, and repeat from *. Work a frill forwards and backwards upon the four rows of treble stitches. Sew the curtain to the head. With double white wool crochet a chain to run in where the curtain joins the head, have it long enough to tie, and finish off the ends with blue and white tassels.

MEDALLION FOR AN ANTIMACASSAR.

PROCURE Evans' brown Maltese thread No. 10, or Finlayson's Scotch linen thread No. 25, écru colour, and a medium-sized steel crochet needle. Begin with 4 chain, which join round, and work 8 double crochet in the circle. **2nd round**—Working into the one top thread of the stitches of the previous round, do 1 double crochet on each of two double crochet stitches of last round, 2 chain, * 1 double crochet on each of the next two stitches, 2 chain, and repeat from *. **3rd round**—1 double crochet on each of two double crochet stitches, and 1 double crochet on each of two chain stitches of last round, making 4 consecutive double crochet in all, 2 chain, and repeat. **4th round**—1 double crochet on each of four double crochet stitches, and 1 double crochet on each of two chain stitches of last round, making 6 consecutive double crochet in all, 3 chain, and repeat. **5th round**—1 double crochet on each of six double crochet stitches, and 1 double crochet on each of two chain stitches, making 8 consecutive double crochet in all, 3 chain, miss one chain stitch, and repeat. **6th round**—1 double crochet on each of eight double crochet stitches, and 1 double crochet on each of two chain stitches, making 10 consecutive double crochet in all, 4 chain, miss one stitch, and repeat. **7th round**—1 double crochet on each of ten double crochet stitches, and 1 double crochet on each of two chain stitches, making 12 consecutive double crochet in all, 4 chain, miss two stitches, and repeat. **8th round**—1 double crochet on each of twelve double crochet stitches and 1 double crochet on each of two chain stitches, making 14 consecutive double crochet in all, 4 chain, miss two stitches, and repeat. **9th round—** 1 double crochet on each of fourteen double crochet stitches, and 1 double crochet on each of two chain stitches, making 16 consecutive double crochet in all, 5 chain, miss two stitches, and repeat. **10th round—**Now insert the hook to take up the two front threads of the stitches of the previous round, miss the first double crochet stitch, and work 14 consecutive double crochet, 5 chain, 1 double crochet under the loop of five chain of last round, 5 chain, and repeat. **11th round—**Miss one double crochet stitch, work 12 double crochet consecutively, 5 chain, 1 double crochet under the first loop of five chain of last round, 5 chain, 1 double crochet under the next loop of five chain, and repeat. **12th round—**Miss one double crochet stitch, work 10 double crochet consecutively, 5 chain, 1 double crochet under the first loop, 5 chain, 1 double crochet under the next loop, 5 chain, 1 double crochet under the next loop, 5 chain, and repeat. **13th round—**Miss one double crochet stitch, work 8 double crochet consecutively, 5 chain, 1 double crochet under loop of last round, this four times, 5 chain, and repeat. **14th round—** Miss one double crochet stitch, work 6 double crochet consecutively, 5 chain, 1 double crochet under loop of last round, this five times, 5 chain, and repeat. **15th round—**Miss one double crochet stitch, work 4 double crochet consecutively, 5 chain, 1 double crochet under loop of last round, this six times, 5 chain, and repeat. **16th round—**Work 1 double crochet between the second and third double crochet stitches of last round, 5 chain, 1 double crochet under loop of last round, do this seven times, 5 chain, and repeat: fasten off at the end of this round, which finishes the medallion. The medallions may be joined to each other in course of working the last round, or sewn together afterwards, as preferred.

BABY'S JACKET.

THIS elegant little jacket is worked in wicker pattern, which is a nice close

neige on the long trebles at the corner of the neck, carrying it down the front along the bottom, and up the other front, this makes three rows of point neige at the bottom, and one row up each front, break off wool. Re-commence at the corner of the neck, and finish with a row of scallops, doing 5 treble into one little hole of point neige, 1 double crochet into the next, and repeat; and work 7 treble in scallops to ease round the corners. **For the Collar—**Work first of all 1 row of double crochet on the foundation chain of the jacket, on that do 3 rows of wicker pattern, 1 row of long trebles, 2 rows of point-neige, and end with a row of scallops all round the collar. **For the Sleeves—**These are rounded at the top and fit very comfortably. Begin with 37 chain, worked loosely. **1st row—**1 treble in the second chain from the needle, * miss the next chain, 2 treble in the next, and repeat from *, making 13 sets, and turn, leaving 10 chain unworked. **2nd row—**2 treble into each of the chain stitches missed in the foundation, making 9 sets, turn. **3rd row—**1 set between the two stitches of the first row, and work 10 sets, the tenth being worked into the foundation chain, at distance of one chain from the work already done, turn. **4th row—**1 set in the chain stitch missed in the foundation, sets between the trebles of the second row, making 11 sets, the eleventh being worked into the first missed chain of the foundation, turn. **5th row—**1 set between two treble of the first row, 9 sets between the trebles of the third row, 1 set at end of the first row, and 1 set in the second foundation chain. **6th row—**1 set in the chain stitch missed in the foundation, 1 set between two treble of the second row, 9 sets between the trebles of the fourth row, 1 set at end of the second row, 1 set in the first missed chain of the foundation, 1 set in the next missed chain of the foundation. **7th row—**1 set between 2 treble of the first row, 1 set between next 2 treble of the first row, 1 set between 2 treble of the third row, 9 sets between 2 trebles of the fifth row, 1 set between 2 treble of the third row, 1 set at end of the first row, 3 sets along foundation chain. **8th row—**2 chain to turn, 1 set in missed stitch of foundation chain, 1 set in next missed stitch of foundation chain, sets along to the end of the row, 18 sets in all. **9th row—** 2 chain to turn, 1 set between 2 treble of the first row, work sets all along to the end, 18 sets. **10th row—**18 sets. **11th row—**17 sets, omitting one at the

Hood for Child of Three.

Medallion for an Antimacassar.

Baby's Jacket.

stitch, very warm and elastic; the size according to these directions will fit a child of eighteen months or two years. Required, 6 ozs. of white Peacock wool, a No. 10 bone crochet needle, and 2½ yards of inch-wide white satin ribbon. Commence for the neck with 69 chain. **1st row—**Work 68 double crochet. **2nd row—**2 chain to turn, 2 treble on the second stitch of last row, * miss 1 stitch, 2 treble on the next, and repeat from * to the end of the row. **3rd row—** 2 chain to turn, 2 treble on every double crochet that was missed in the previous row, drawing up the lower parts of the trebles rather loosely, and *over* the trebles of last row; each group of 2 treble stitches is termed a "set;" there should be 34 sets in each of these rows; turn with 2 chain at the end of this and every row. **4th row—**Insert the hook between the two treble stitches of the second row, 2 treble, * 2 treble between the next treble stitches of the second row, and repeat from *, working 34 sets. **5th row—**34 sets in the row worked into those of the third row. **6th row—**2 sets (4 treble) in the first, 7 consecutive sets, 2 sets in one, 2 sets in one, 14 consecutive sets, 2 sets in one, 2 sets in one, 7 consecutive sets, 2 sets in the last. **7th row, 8th row, and 9th row—** Each 40 sets in the row. **10th row—**10 sets, 2 sets in one, 2 sets in one, 16 sets, 2 sets in one, 2 sets in one, 10 sets. **11th row and 12th row—**Each 44 sets. **13th row—**11 sets, 2 sets in one, 19 sets, 2 sets in one, 12 sets. **14th row and 15th rows—**Each 46 sets. **16th row—**Work 13 sets, turn, and for one-half of the front, continue the pattern forwards and backwards for 18 rows, to make the length of the armhole. This done, break off the wool, and work 20 sets for the back, doing the same number of rows as you have for the front. Then work the remaining 13 sets for the other half of front. Now for the lower part of the jacket, work all across these three pieces and do 22 rows, increasing in the 3rd, 7th, 11th, 15th, and 19th of these rows under the armholes. **For the Border—**Holding the jacket the right side towards you, commence at the corner of the neck, and work one row of long treble stitches down the front along the bottom, and up the second front, easing the corners well. Now work two rows of point-neige along the bottom, break off the wool, and begin point

end of the row. 12th row—16 sets, omitting one at the end of the row. Work 4 more rows, each with 16 sets in a row. **17th row—**15 sets, omitting one at the end of the row. **18th row—**14 sets, omitting one at the end of the row. Work 4 more rows, each with 14 sets in a row. Sew up the sleeve, and round the wrist work 1 row of long trebles, 2 rows of point-neige, and end with a row of scallops. The other sleeve is worked in the same way. Sew the sleeves in the armholes. Make a crochet chain to run round the neck, to tie with a tassel at each end. Run ribbon in and out of the long treble stitches all round the jacket, the wrists, and collar.

WELDON'S
PRACTICAL CROCHET

(SEVENTH SERIES.)

HOW TO CROCHET USEFUL ARTICLES FOR PERSONAL AND HOME DECORATION

THIRTY ILLUSTRATIONS.

Telegraphic Address—]
"Consuelo," London.]

The Yearly Subscription to this Magazine, post free to any Part of the World, is 2s. 6d.
Subscriptions are payable in advance, and may commence from any date and for any period.

[Telephone—
2745.

The Back Numbers are always in print. Nos. 1 to 86 now ready, Price 2d. each, or post free for 15s. 4d. Over 5,000 Engravings.

TAM O'SHANTER.
WORKED IN POINT NEIGE AND DOUBLE CROCHET.

REQUIRED, 2½ ozs. of single Berlin wool, and a No. 8 crochet needle. Make 3 chain, join round, and work in the circle 6 stitches of point neige; the method of working point neige or shell stitch is described in No. 3 of this Needlework Series. Join every round evenly to its own commencement before beginning the next round, and always begin with 2 chain for the point neige rounds, and with 1 chain for the double crochet rounds. **2nd round**—Work 10 point neige stitches over the six stitches of previous round. **3rd round**—27 double crochet in the round, contriving always to make the increase stitches at regular intervals. **4th round**—Turn the work, do 30 double crochet **5th round**—Turn, work 25 point neige. **6th round**—33 point neige. **7th round**—66 double crochet. **8th round**—Turn the work, do 66 double crochet. **9th round**—Turn, work 58 point neige. **10th round**—64 point neige. **11th round**—120 double crochet. **12th round**—Turn the work, do 126 double crochet. **13th round**—Turn, work 86 point neige. **14th round**—94 point neige. **15th round**—154 double crochet. **16th round**—Turn the work, and again do 154 double crochet. **17th round**—Begin to draw in for the under part of the brim, work 86 point neige, making the decreasing come at regular intervals. **18th round**—80 point neige. **19th round**—110 double crochet. **20th round**—Turn the work, do 95 double crochet. **21st round**—52 point neige. **22nd round**—The same. **23rd round**—50 double crochet. Now for the **Band**, work 5 rounds of plain double crochet, taking up the one back thread of the stitches of previous round. Fasten off. Use the remainder of the wool to make a tuft to go in the centre of the crown.

Tam O'Shanter.

CHILD'S PRINCESS PELISSE, SHOULDER CAPE, AND BREWER'S CAP.
WORKED IN TRICOT AND BEAN STITCH.

THIS charming out-door costume for a girl of four or five years is worked partly in tricot and partly in a new raised crochet stitch, called "bean" stitch; the body of the pelisse is shaped to the figure and a deep full flounce is placed round the skirt, the shoulder cape hangs nearly to the waist and matches the flounce, as also does the brewer's cap, which from its becoming shape is likely to rival the ever-popular Tam o'Shanter. Required, 1 lb. of dove grey single Berlin wool, a bone tricot needle No. 6, a crochet needle No. 9, and 16 grey metal buttons the size of a farthing. Commence for the **bottom** of the **right front**, working with the tricot needle 50 chain stitches. **Work** 3 rows of plain tricot. Beginners will find directions for tricot in No. 3 of "Weldon's Practical Needlework" Series. **4th row—**

Decrease by picking up 2 stitches together at the end of the row. Repeat these four rows six times. Work 1 row of plain tricot. Now in the **30th row** you begin to form the armhole by leaving 3 stitches unworked at the end of the row. **31st row**—Plain tricot, and again leave 3 stitches unworked at the end. **32nd row**—Leave 2 stitches at the end. **33rd row**—The same Work 4 rows of plain tricot. **38th row**—and 8 following rows—Plain tricot and increase 1 stitch at the end. **47th row**—Leave 3 stitches unworked at the end. **48th row**—Begins the neck, slip stitch along the first 5 tricot stitches, plain tricot along, decrease 2 at the end. Then decrease 2 stitches at the beginning and 2 stitches at the end of every row till all are worked off Work the **left front** in the same manner, only making the decreasings on the other side the work *i.e.*, at the beginning of the rows. For the **Back**:—Begin with 55 stitches. Plain tricot, and decrease every fourth row till the twenty-fourth row, all decreasings and increasings are to be done on both sides the work. In the **26th row** and **28th row** increase 1 stitch at each side the intervening rows being plain tricot. **30th row**—Beginning of armhole, decrease 2 stitches each side. **31st and 32nd row**—The same. Work 4 rows of plain tricot Work 6 rows increasing 1 stitch each side. Work 12 rows decreasing 1 stitch each side. **Next row**—Work for the shoulder only 12 stitches, and decrease at the beginning and at the end of each little row till all are worked off Work the last 12 stitches the same for the other shoulder. Sew up the shoulders, and also sew up the sides of the body from the armholes to the bottom of the skirt For the **Sleeves**:—Do 12 chain Work plain tricot increasing 2 stitches at the beginning and 2 stitches at the end of each row till 56 stitches are attained, this shapes for the top. Work 3 rows plain, and decrease 1 stitch each side every 4th row till reduced to 44 stitches for the bottom of the arm, when with the addition of the bean-stitch crochet the sleeve will be sufficiently long, but work the flounce before doing this. For the **Flounce**:—Bean-stitch crochet: Take the crochet needle, and holding the work the wrong side towards you, do a row of double crochet stitches into the foundation chain along the bottom of the **skirt**, increasing occasionally to produce fulness, and ending with 11 chain stitches on the right side front; there should be about 213 double crochet in all in the row. **2nd row**—Turn the work, do 10 double crochet along the chain, 1 double crochet on the first double crochet of last row taking both top threads, * wool over the needle, insert the hook from right to left under two threads of the foundation chain just below next double crochet stitch, draw the wool through loosely, wool over the needle and draw through 2 stitches on the needle, wool over the needle and draw through 2 more stitches on the needle, miss a double crochet stitch of last row, 1 double crochet on the next taking both top threads, and repeat from * to the end of the row. **3rd row**—Turn and do plain double crochet, working under both top threads of the stitches of the preceding row **4th row**—Turn, work 1 double crochet in the first stitch, 1 bean stitch into the second preceding row, and repeat to the end. Repeat the last two rows, increasing 8 or 10 stitches in each double crochet row to 253 stitches; there are 29 rows in the flounce. After these 29 rows are done, work upon the upper side of the extra chain stitches, in little rows of the same pattern bean stitch, a length sufficient to go up the front of the body, and sew it to the edge of the tricot. Hold the wrong side of the neck towards you, and work a row of double crochet, drawing in slightly to shape; then a row of bean stitch and a row of double crochet, and repeat the same once. Now, for the scalloped edge round the flounce, up the front, and round the neck, work 2 treble, 1 chain, 2 treble, all on stitch over a bean stitch, 1 double crochet on stitch over the next bean stitch, and repeat. Work 11 rows of double crochet and bean stitch, and 1 row of scalloped edge, on each sleeve; sew the sleeves up, and put them into the armholes. Sew eight buttons on the right side front by the margin of the strip of crochet bean stitch, and eight buttons on the left side front to button through into small spaces you missed in working the row of edge.

CHILD'S SHOULDER CAPE.

COMMENCE for the neck with 66 chain. **1st row**—Plain double crochet. **2nd row**—Turn, 1 double crochet on the first stitch of previous row, taking both top threads, wool over the needle, insert the hook from right to left under the foundation chain just below the next double crochet, draw the wool through loosely, wool over the needle, and draw through 2 stitches on the needle, wool over the needle and draw through 2 more stitches on the needle, miss a double crochet stitch of last row, and repeat 1 double crochet and 1 bean stitch alternately to the end. **3rd row**—Work 12 double crochet stitches, increase in each of the next 6, work 29 double crochet, increase in each of the next 6, work 12 double crochet. **4th row**—Bean stitch, inserting the hook under the double crochet of the second row, between the bean stitches thereof. **5th row**—Work 18 double crochet, increase in each of the next 6, work 41 double crochet, increase in each of the next 6, work 12 double crochet. **6th row**—Bean stitch. **7th row**—Double crochet, and increase on the middle 5 stitches. **8th row**—Bean stitch. **9th row**—Double crochet, and increase on each shoulder. **10th row**—Bean stitch. Continue from the seventh row until 18 rows in all are done. Then work 5 rows without any increase whatever. For Fringe of **Picoteed Loops**—1 double crochet on double crochet stitch of last row of the cape, * 4 chain, 1 double crochet in the third chain from the needle, repeat from * seven times, 3 chain, miss 2 double crochet stitches, 1 double crochet on the next, and repeat from * to the end of the row, and fasten off. Recommence again with a double crochet upon one of the stitches missed in last row, * 4 chain, 1 double crochet in the third chain from the needle, and repeat from * four times, 3 chain, keep the fringe of last row to the back, and work a double crochet upon one of the stitches missed in last row; repeat from * to the end, and fasten off. Tighten if necessary round the neck with a row of double crochet. For scalloped edge up each front, and round the neck, work 2 treble, 1 chain, 2 treble, all in one stitch of the crochet, miss a stitch, 1 double crochet in the next, miss a stitch, and repeat. Make a cord of crochet chain to tie the cape at the neck, and put nice tassels on at each end.

CHILD'S BREWER'S CAP.

THE head of this cap is worked in plain double crochet, and the turn-over brim in bean stitch. Begin with 85 chain, or a sufficient length to go round the head of the child for whom the cap is intended, join round. Work in double crochet round and round continuously, taking up the one top thread of the stitches of previous round, until 16 rounds are done. Afterwards decrease 3 stitches in every round, at alternate intervals, till the cap is brought to a point at the top. For the **Brim**—Holding the cap the right side towards you, do a row of double crochet stitches into the commencing chain, join now at the end of every round and turn the work, and recommence the next round with one or two chains. **2nd round**—Bean stitch—1 double crochet on the first stitch of preceding row, taking both top threads, wool over the needle,

Child's Princess Pelisse.

insert the hook from right to left under two threads of the foundation chain just below the next double crochet stitch, draw the wool through loosely, wool over the needle and draw through 2 stitches on the needle, wool over the needle and draw through 2 more stitches on the needle, miss one double crochet of last round, and repeat a double crochet stitch and a bean stitch alternately to the end of the round. Work 9 rounds in all for the brim, decreasing 2 or 3 stitches in the course of the fifth, seventh, and ninth rounds. **10th round**—Scallop edge—1 double crochet on stitch above the first bean stitch, 2 treble, 1 chain, 2 treble, all on stitch above the next bean stitch, and repeat. Make a tufted wool tassel to place on the point at the top of the cap.

AMAZON STRIPE IN TRICOT FOR ANTIMACASSAR.

THIS is a remarkably bright and effective pattern for an antimacassar, and is easy to make, the ground-work being all plain tricot, which is worked upon afterwards in a cross-stitch design with bright-coloured filoselles. Materials required, ½ lb. of crimson and ½ lb. of black single Berlin wool, a tricot needle No. 9, a ball of gold-coloured knitting silk, and an assortment of filoselle, gold, white, pale blue, crimson, green, and four shades of brown. Begin for the wide stripe with crimson wool, with 24 chain; pick up each stitch on the needle, and work back as plain tricot. Do 198 or 226 rows, according to the length desired for the antimacassar. Take the black wool, and beginning with 12 chain, work a narrow stripe the same length as the first stripe. Three stripes of crimson and four stripes of black will suffice for the width of the antimacassar. You now must edge all these stripes with gold knitting silk, working double crochet along both sides and both ends, take 1 stitch in the thread by the edge of the stripe and 1 stitch one line further down alternately, which appears like a row of jagged teeth. When all the stripes are edged, proceed with the embroidery. Thread two strands of each shade of brown filoselle together into a crewel needle, and work a zigzag stitch forwards and backwards up the centre of the black stripes, and in each little triangular space on each side put three stitches in the shape of an arrow head, using crimson, blue, and green filoselle alternately; a reference to the engraving will clearly show how this is to be done. The pattern up the centre of the crimson stripe is worked in cross-stitch, the rounds with gold filoselle inside and outer margin of green, and the diamonds with gold inside and outer margin of blue; the centre of each pattern is filled in with a star worked with white filoselle and blue French knots in the middle. Join the stripes together with a row of chain stitch, using five or six strands of gold filoselle, which must be wound together on a ball for the purpose. Also with gold filoselle work a straight line of embroidery chain-stitch along the top and the bottom of the antimacassar. Then for **Fringe** at top and bottom, work crochet with gold knitting silk. **1st row**—Plain double crochet. **2nd row**—1 double crochet on first double crochet of last row, * 5 chain, miss two, 1 double crochet on the next, and repeat from *. Knot in a fringe, putting a bunch of gold silk under each stripe of double crochet joining, and alternate bunches of red and black wool in the other loops.

INFANT'S PETTICOAT.

THIS serviceable little petticoat may be worked with Berlin fingering or Beehive yarn, procuring 4½ ozs. of grey for the garment itself and of pale blue for the border, a bone crochet needle No. 9, and 2 yards of inch-wide blue ribbon. Begin with grey wool, with a chain of 167 stitches for the bottom of the skirt. Work 3 rows of plain double crochet, 166 stitches in each row, turning at the end of the rows, and working into the two top threads of the stitches of previous row. **4th row**—Work on the double crochet of last row 83 stitches of point neige, or shell stitch, instructions for which are given in No. 3 of "Weldon's Practical Needlework" series; and have also been repeated in other numbers. **5th row**—Double crochet, 166 stitches in the row. **6th row**—Point neige. Repeat these six rows three times. Then work 3 rows of plain double crochet. **28th row**—Double crochet, decreasing after every twelfth stitch. **29th row**—Plain double crochet. **30th row**—Double crochet, decreasing after every tenth stitch. **31st row**—Plain double crochet. **32nd row**—Double crochet, decreasing after every eighth stitch. **33rd row**—Plain double crochet. **34th row**—Double crochet, decreasing after every sixth stitch. **35th row**—To bring in for the waist, work 1 treble in each alternate stitch; this should bring 56 treble in the row. **36th row**—Plain double crochet. Work 3 more rows of plain double crochet. **40th row**—Do 28 stitches of point neige. **41st row**—Plain double crochet. **42nd row**—Point neige; work 2 rows of double crochet. **43rd row**—Work 14 double crochet; here begins the armhole; turn, and work 7 point neige; and continue the pattern the same as the skirt, till the **54th row**, when do only 4 point neige stitches for the shoulder; work here 2 rows of 8 double crochet stitches, and fasten off. Work the other half back to correspond. Then proceed in like manner upon the 28 stitches for the front, making a shoulder-piece on each side. Join the shoulder-pieces together. Sew up the back of the skirt. For **Edge round** the **neck—1st row**—With grey wool—Double crochet, working also down the back to join in the skirt. **2nd row**—With blue—Point neige. **3rd row**—With blue — Crazy stitch, 1 single crochet, 3 chain, 2 treble, all in the small hole of point neige stitch of last row. For **Edge round** the **Sleeves. 1st row**—With grey wool—Double crochet. **2nd round**—With blue—Point neige. **3rd round**—Also with blue—Double crochet. **4th round**—Crazy stitch. Repeat the last three rounds with blue wool round the bottom of the skirt. Run ribbon through the treble stitches at the waist, and also in the neck and sleeves. Put two or three buttons to fasten at the back.

and repeat. **15th round**—5 chain, 4 double crochet, a tuft, work 3 double crochet and a tuft five times, 4 double crochet, and repeat. **16th round**—5 chain, 5 double crochet, 1 treble, work 3 double crochet and 1 treble five times, 5 double crochet, and repeat. **17th round**—Here the diamond begins to lessen—5 chain, 8 double crochet, a tuft, work 3 double crochet and a tuft four times, 8 double crochet, and repeat. **18th round**—5 chain, 9 double crochet, 1 treble, work 3 double crochet and 1 treble four times, 9 double crochet, and repeat. **19th round**—5 chain, 12 double crochet, a tuft, work 3 double crochet and a tuft four times, 12 double crochet, and repeat. **20th round**—5 chain, 13 double crochet, 1 treble, work 3 double crochet and 1 treble three times, 13 double crochet, and repeat. **21st round**—5 chain, 16 double crochet, a tuft, work 3 double crochet and a tuft twice, 16 double crochet, and repeat. **22nd round**—5 chain, 17 double crochet, 1 treble, work 3 double crochet and 1 treble twice, 17 double crochet, and repeat. **23rd round**—5 chain, 20 double crochet, a tuft, 3 double crochet, a tuft, 20 double crochet. **24th round**—5 chain, 21 double crochet, 1 treble, 3 double crochet, 1 treble, 21 double crochet. **25th round**—5 chain, 24 double crochet, a tuft, 24 double crochet, and repeat. **26th round**—5 chain, 25 double crochet, 1 treble, 25 double crochet, and repeat. **27th round**—5 chain, 53 double crochet, and repeat. **28th round**—5 chain, 55 double crochet, and repeat. **29th round**—5 chain, 4 double crochet, a tuft, work 3 double crochet and a tuft twelve times, making 13 tufts in a line, 4 double crochet, and repeat. **30th round**—5 chain, 5 double crochet, 1 treble, work 3 double crochet and 1 treble twelve times, 5 double crochet, and repeat. **31st round**—5 chain, 4 double crochet, a tuft, work 3 double crochet and a tuft thirteen times, 4 double crochet, and repeat. **32nd round**—5 chain, 5 double crochet, 1 treble, work 3 double crochet and 1 treble thirteen times, 5

Child's Shoulder Cape.

Child s Brewer's Cap.

SQUARE FOR QUILT. DIAMOND OF RAISED TUFTS.

OUR engraving shows a particularly handsome design for a quilt square consisting of a diamond of raised tufts, with marginal border to correspond upon a smooth groundwork of plain double crochet. Procure Strutts' No. 8 knitting cotton, and a No. 17 steel crochet needle. The square is commenced in the centre with 8 chain, which join round in a circle. **1st round**—Do 3 chain, 1 double crochet in the second chain of the circle, and repeat three times. Do not join on the completion of the rounds, but go straight on round and round continuously, and take up the one top thread of the stitches of the previous round. **2nd round**—4 chain, 3 double crochet, 1 being worked on the double crochet stitch of last round, and 1 in the chain stitch on each side, repeat three times. **3rd round**—4 chain, 5 double crochet, 3 being worked on the double crochet stitch of last round, and 1 in the chain stitch on each side, repeat three times. **4th round**—4 chain, 7 double crochet, 5 being worked on the double crochet of last round, and 1 in the chain stitch on each side, repeat three times. **5th round**—4 chain, 4 double crochet, then a "tuft," which is made by working 5 treble into the *front* thread of next stitch, 4 double crochet, and repeat three times. **6th round**—4 chain, 5 double crochet, 1 treble into the back thread you missed behind the tuft of previous round, 5 more double crochet, and repeat three times. **7th round**—5 chain always in future at the corners, 4 double crochet, a tuft into the front thread of next stitch, 3 double crochet, another tuft, 4 more double crochet, and repeat three times. **8th round**—5 chain, 5 double crochet, 1 treble at the back of the first tuft, 3 double crochet, 1 treble at back of the next tuft, 5 double crochet, and repeat. **9th round**—5 chain, 4 double crochet, a tuft, 3 double crochet, a tuft, 3 double crochet, a tuft, 4 double crochet, and repeat. **10th round**—5 chain, 5 double crochet, 1 treble, 3 double crochet, 1 treble, 3 double crochet, 1 treble, 4 double crochet, and repeat. **11th round**—5 chain, 4 double crochet, a tuft, 3 double crochet, a tuft, 3 double crochet, a tuft, 3 double crochet, a tuft, 4 double crochet, and repeat. **12th round**—5 chain, 5 double crochet, 1 treble, 3 double crochet, 1 treble, 3 double crochet, 1 treble, 3 double crochet, 1 treble, 5 double crochet, and repeat. **13th round**—5 chain, 4 double crochet, a tuft, work 3 double crochet and a tuft four times, 4 double crochet, and repeat. **14th round**—5 chain, 5 double crochet, 1 treble, work three double crochet and 1 treble four times, 5 double crochet,

double crochet, and repeat. **33rd round**—5 chain, 4 double crochet, a tuft, work 3 double crochet and a tuft fourteen times, 4 double crochet, and repeat. **34th round**—5 chain, 5 double crochet, 1 treble, work 3 double crochet and 1 treble fourteen times, 5 double crochet, and repeat. **35th round**—5 chain, 69 double crochet, and repeat. **36th round**—5 chain, 71 double crochet, and repeat. **37th round**—5 chain, 73 double crochet, and repeat. **38th round**—5 chain, 1 single crochet on the fifth chain stitch of previous round, 5 chain, * 1 treble on the second double crochet of last round, 2 chain, miss two, 1 treble on the next, twenty-two times, 2 chain, miss one, 1 treble on the next, 2 chain, 1 treble in the first stitch of the five chain of last round, 2 chain, 1 treble in the corner stitch, 5 chain, another treble in the same place, 2 chain, 1 treble in the last of the five chain of last round, 2 chain, and repeat from * three times: join evenly when you get to the end of the round, and fasten off.

MARGUERITE MEDALLION PATTERN FOR ANTIMACASSAR.

THIS is a pretty design for cotton crochet and may be worked with either Evans' or Coats' crochet cotton, No. 18, and a fine steel crochet needle. Commence with 6 chain, join round; work 18 double crochet in the circle, and join round evenly. **2nd round**—6 chain, * miss one double crochet, 1 treble in the next, 3 chain, and repeat from *, and join at the end of the round into the third stitch of chain. **3rd round**—4 chain to stand for a treble,* 7 treble in the centre stitch of three chain of last round, catch the last of these into the first with a single crochet, 1 chain, 1 treble over treble stitch of last round, 1 chain, and repeat from *, making nine tufts in the round, and join into the third stitch of chain. **4th round**—Work 2 double crochet on every stitch. **5th round**—Work same as the third round, making eighteen tufts in the round. **6th round**—Do 2 double crochet in each chain stitch, 1 double crochet on each of the other stitches of last round. **7th round**—1 double crochet, 5 chain, miss three stitches, and repeat; at *four* intervals in the round miss only two stitches so that you may get twenty-eight loops of chain in the round. **8th round**—1 double crochet in the centre stitch of five chain of last round, 5 chain, and repeat; again there must be twenty-eight loops. **9th round**—1 double crochet in the centre stitch of five chain, 6 chain, and repeat. **10th round**—3 treble under the loop of six chain, 5 chain, single crochet in the fourth chain from the needle, 5 chain, single crochet in the same place, 5 chain, single crochet in the same place, 1 chain, and repeat; and fasten off at the end of the round. Work as many as twenty medallions, joining them as you work by a single crochet into a corresponding loop of medallion previously done; place four in a row for the width of the anti-macassar and five for the length. Work **Small Medallions** to fill up the spaces, beginning with five chain, join round; work 5 chain, 1 double crochet, eight times in the circle. **2nd round**—Single crochet to get to the top of first five chain, do 1 double crochet then * 3 chain, 1 double crochet under the next loop of five chain, and repeat from *. **3rd round**—Same as the tenth round of the Marguerite Medallion, joining each picot in position as you work.

CHEMISE TRIMMING.

FOR this trimming use Evans' crochet cotton, No. 18, and a very fine steel needle. Begin with the **Wheel** as shown full-size in illustration, make 8 chain, and join round in a circle. **1st round**—Do 3 chain to stand for a treble, work 23 treble in the circle, and join round. **2nd round**—8 chain, 1 double crochet in the second chain from the needle, 1 treble in each of the 4 next chain stitches, 1 treble on the second treble stitch of previous row, * 5 chain, 1 double crochet in the second chain from the needle, 1 treble in each of the 3 remaining chain st t hes, 1 treble in the top of the treble stitch that you made before doing the 5 chain, 1 treble on the second treble stitch of previous row, and repeat from * ten times, then join to the commencement of

Amazon Stripe in Tricot for Antimacassar.

the round, and fasten off. Continue working these wheels until a sufficient length is attained, and as you work unite two tips of each wheel by a stitch of single crochet to the corresponding tips of the wheel previously worked. For the **Edging—1st row**—Having all the wheels united, you will observe there are four tips along the top and four tips along the bottom of each wheel to be worked upon, begin with 1 treble on the first of these tips, 3 chain, 1 single crochet on the second tip, 4 chain, 1 single crochet on the third tip, 3 chain, 1 treble on the fourth tip, 1 chain, cotton three times round the needle, insert the hook in the *side* of the next tip and draw the cotton through, cotton over the needle and draw through 2 stitches on the needle, cotton over the needle, insert the hook in the *side* of the next tip and draw the cotton through, cotton over the needle and draw through 2 stitches on the needle, do this four times to work all stitches off the needle, then 1 chain; repeat to the end of the row. **2nd row**—1 treble, miss 1, 1 chain, and repeat. **3rd row**—Do 1 treble on each of 2 stitches of last row, 2 chain, miss 2 stitches, and repeat; every sixth or seventh time miss 3 stitches to draw in a little. **4th row**—1 treble, miss 1, 1 chain and repeat. **5th row**—1 double crochet on the first treble stitch of last row, * 2 chain, miss 4 stitches, 1 treble on the next, 3 chain, 1 double crochet in the top of the 1 treble just worked, 1 treble in the next stitch of previous row, 3 chain, 1 double crochet in the top of the treble just worked, 1 treble in the same stitch of previous row, 3 chain, 1 double crochet in the top

of the treble just worked, 1 treble in the same stitch of previous row, 3 chain, 1 double crochet in the top of the treble just worked, 1 treble in the next stitch of previous row, 2 chain, miss 4, 1 double crochet on the next, and repeat; this finishes the scalloped edge. The first and second rows of this edging are to be worked along the opposite side of the wheel insertion, but as the work is to expand for sewing upon the calico, make in the first row 2 chain stitches where directed to make 1 chain.

BOURBON ROSE PATTERN FOR ANTIMACASSAR.

PROCURE several skeins of Coats' crochet cotton No. 20, and a fine steel needle. Begin with 4 chain, join round; work 8 double crochet in the circle, and join neatly round. **2nd round**—1 double crochet on first stitch of last round, 3 chain, * 1 double crochet on next, 3 chain, and repeat from *, making eight loops of chain in the round. **3rd round**—1 double crochet, 3 treble, 1 double crochet, under each loop of three chain. **4th round**—1 double crochet at the back between the two double crochet of last round, 4 chain, and repeat. **5th round**—1 double crochet, 4 treble, 1 double crochet, under each loop of four chain. **6th round**—1 double crochet at the back between the two double crochet of last round, 5 chain, and repeat. **7th round**—1 double crochet, 5 treble, 1 double crochet under each loop of five chain. **8th round**—1 double crochet at the back, 6 chain, and repeat. **9th round**—1 double crochet, 6 treble, 1 double crochet, under each loop of six chain. **10th round**—1 double crochet at the back, 7 chain, and repeat. **11th round**—2 slip stitches along the loop of seven chain, 3 chain to stand for a treble, 1 treble under the loop, 3 chain, 2 more treble in the same place, 3 chain, * 2 treble under the next loop, 3 chain, 2 more treble in the same place, 3 chain, and repeat from *; join evenly. **12th round**—Slip stitch into the

Infant's Petticoat.

first loop of last round, 5 chain, 1 treble in the same loop, 5 chain, 1 treble, 3 chain, 1 treble, all in the same loop, 2 chain, 1 double crochet under the next loop, * 2 chain, 1 treble under the next loop, 3 chain, 1 treble, 5 chain, 1 treble, 3 chain, 1 treble, all in the same place, 2 chain, 1 double crochet under the next loop, 2 chain, and repeat from *, and at the end of the round join into the third stitch of the chain, and fasten off. **13th round**—1 double crochet under any loop of five chain, 13 chain, * 1 double crochet under next loop of five chain, 13 chain, and repeat from *. **14th round**—Double crochet on each stitch of last round. **15th round**—1 double crochet on the stitch over double crochet of the thirteenth round, 9 chain, miss six, 1 double crochet on the next, 9 chain, and repeat. **16th round**—Double crochet on each stitch of last round excepting in the centre stitch of chain, where put 2 double crochet, join evenly, and fasten off. **17th round**—2 treble in the first of the two increased stitches of last round, 3 chain, 2 treble in the next stitch, 5 chain, and repeat. **18th round**—1 treble, 3 chain, 1 treble, 5 chain, 1 treble, 3 chain, 1 treble, all under the three chain loop of last round, 1 double crochet under the five chain loop, 2 chain, and repeat. This completes rose medallion. Twenty medallions will make a fair size antimacassar; they are united, as will be seen in the engraving, by a stitch of single crochet worked (after doing 2 of the 5 chain stitches) into the corresponding five chain of another medallion. The small rose which fills the vacant space between four large roses is made by working as far as the twelfth round, in process of which join to the surrounding loops of five chain of the large roses.

WOOL DAHLIA.

A VERY pretty antimacassar may be made with twelve of these dahlias joined together. Required, three shades of crimson, and a small quantity of brown and black double Berlin wool. No. 7 bone crochet needle. Begin with brown wool, with 3 chain, join round, and work 10 treble in the circle. Join evenly at the end of every round, and throughout the dahlia work into two loops of preceding round. **2nd round**—With darkest shade of crimson—1 double crochet on a stitch of last round, insert the hook again in the same stitch and draw the wool through, do 4 chain, wool over the needle and draw through the chain and through the stitch on the needle, so making a picot, 1 double crochet and 1 picot on the next treble of last round, and repeat. There should be 10 double crochets and 10 picots in the round. **3rd round**—With medium shade of crimson—1 double crochet on the picot of last round, 1 picot on the double crochet and repeat. **4th round**—With lightest shade of crimson—work in the same manner, making 12 double crochets and 12 picots in the round. **5th round**—With the same wool—work as last round. **6th round**—With brown wool—1 double crochet, 4 chain, miss two, and repeat. There should be eight loops of four chain. **7th round**—With same wool—work 5 double crochet under each loop of chain. **8th round**—With same wool—1 double crochet on the first stitch of the five double crochet of last round, 1 treble on the next, 1 long treble on the next, 4 chain, 1 single crochet in the fourth chain from the needle, 1 long treble in the same stitch as last worked upon, 1 treble on the next, and 1 double crochet on the next, which is the last stitch of the five double crochet of last round. Repeat. There should be eight leaves in the round. **9th round**—With black wool—1 double crochet under the picot, 3 chain, 1 long treble in between the two double crochet stitches of last round, 3 chain, and repeat. **10th round**—With darkest shade of crimson—1 double crochet on the double crochet of last round, 1 treble, 1 long treble, 1 picot, 1 long treble, 1 treble, all under the next three chain, 1 double crochet on long treble stitch, do the group of stitches under the next loop of chain, and repeat, making sixteen leaves in the round. This completes the dahlia. Fill up the spaces in the antimacassar between the dahlias with small sectional buds, formed of the three first rounds of the dahlia, a fourth round of plain double crochet, and a round of 1 double crochet, 4 chain.

Square for Quilt. Diamond of Raised Tufts.

in coming back draw through 5 only; then pick up these five again, taking now the perpendicular loops, draw through 10; pick up again and draw back through 14; pick up again and draw back through 17; and now continue in the same manner, drawing through 3 more stitches each time till you draw through all. For the front of the skirt work 30 rows all plain tricot. This done repeat from the 20th row to the end of the gore described in the 43rd row. Work 19 plain rows for the back of the skirt. For the **Waistband**—**1st row**—Pick up all the loops along the top of the skirt, 103 in number, and draw back. **2nd row**—Pick up loops at the *back* of the stitches of last row, to form a ridge, and draw back. Work 4 plain rows. **7th row**—Pick up th loops at the back to form another ridge, and draw back. For the **Body**—Work 12 rows of plain tricot. **Next row**—Pick up 24 stitches, and draw back, and now work 8 rows on the 24, or rather, as 1 stitch is on, 25 stitches; break off the wool. Leave three tricot stitches where you divided for the armhole, and pick up 47, on which do 8 plain rows for the front of the body. Leave three tricot stitches at the other armhole, and pick up 25 for the opposite back, and work 8 rows. Then for the **Shoulders**—Pick up the 7 first stitches of the front, and do 17 rows; and pick up the 7 last stitches of the front, and do 17 rows. Join each of these shoulder-straps to the back of the body. For the **Neck**—Commence on the left back, and pick up all the stitches right round, about 106 in all; coming back draw through 3 together at each front corner and at each back corner of the shoulder straps, four decreases in the row. Do 5 more rows, each with the same decreasings on the shoulders. Work a row of slip-stitches, and fasten off. Sew up the skirt, leaving a small opening for the placket hole. For **Edge** round **Neck** and **Sleeves,** and down the right side of the back and placket hole—**1st round** — 4 treble worked in one stitch of the tricot, miss three, and repeat. **2nd round**—1 double crochet on the first treble stitch of last row, 2 double crochet on the next, 2 double crochet on the next, 1 double crochet on the fourth, and 1 double crochet in the centre stitch of the three missed in last row. **Border** for the **Bottom** of the **Petticoat**—**1st round** — Double crochet, 1 stitch to each stitch of the tricot, or increase a stitch here and there if the double crochet does not appear to lie flat; join at the end of this and every round to its own commencement. **2nd round**—Insert the hook to take up both front threads of the stitches of last round, * 1 double crochet on the first stitch, insert the hook in the next stitch and draw the wool through, do 4 chain, wool over the needle and draw through 2 stitches on the needle, and repeat from *. **3rd round**—Double crochet on each stitch of last round. **4th round**—4 treble in one stitch, miss three, and repeat. **5th round**—1 double crochet on the centre stitch of those missed in last row, 7 chain, and repeat. **6th round**—1 double crochet on the first treble stitch of the fourth round, 1 double crochet on the second, 1 double crochet on the third treble taking up also the loop of seven chain which must lie in front of the work, 1 double crochet on the fourth treble, and repeat. **7th row**—Same as the second round. **8th round**—Same as the third round. **9th round**—6 treble in one stitch, miss five, and repeat. **10th round**—1 double crochet on the first treble stitch, 2 double crochet on each of the 4 next stitches, 1 double crochet on the sixth treble stitch, and 1 double crochet in the centre stitch of the five missed in last row, and repeat. This completes the border. Put buttons and loops to fasten the petticoat at the back, or sew on strings to tie.

THE ETTA PETTICOAT.

THE model petticoat from which our engraving is taken is a nice size for a child of two years, or two-and-a-half years of age. It is worked with white single Berlin wool, and a No. 7 bone tricot needle, a No. 10 bone crochet needle being used for the border. Commence with 44 chain for the back of the skirt, which is worked lengthways, the body being tricoteed on afterwards. Do 19 rows of plain tricot. **20th row**—Here you begin the side gore, pick up all the loops in the usual manner, and draw back through 41, leaving 3 on the needle. **21st row**—Pick up the loops, and draw back, leaving 6 on the needle. **22nd row**—Pick up again and in drawing back leave 9 on the needle. Continue thus, till in the 29th row you pick up 17, and drawing back through 14, leave as many as 30 on the needle. **30th row**—Pick up the loops to the end, and draw back through 10, leaving 34 on the needle.—**31st row**—Pick up again to the end, and draw back through 5, leaving 39 on the needle. **32nd row**—Pick up again to the end, and now draw back through all. **33rd row**—Pick up loops at the *back* of the stitches of last row (instead of the perpendicular loops), this will form a ridge, draw back in the usual manner through all. Work 9 rows of plain tricot. **43rd row**—Pick up the loops at the back of the stitches of last row to make another ridge, and

ZULU STRIPE IN TRICOT FOR AN ANTIMACASSAR.

OUR engraving shows a particularly handsome stripe for an antimacassar, worked in diamond pattern tricot, with wool of two good contrasting colours, say crimson and black single Berlin, of which procure about 8 ozs. of each, also a little white, a No. 9 tricot needle, and two or three skeins of filoselle of each of the following colours - gold, blue, green, violet, and white. Wind two balls of black wool and one ball of crimson. Begin with black wool with 43 chain, **1st row**—With black wool, plain tricot, 43 stitches to be on the needle, and draw back through all. **2nd row**—Pick up 20 stitches with black wool, take the crimson wool and pick up 1 stitch, take the other ball of black wool, and pick up 21 stitches to the end of the row, draw back in the usual manner through each stitch with its own colour, but pass the black wool

With gold filoselle work a double set of single cross-stitches upon the crimson diamond, to represent spots, as shown in the engraving, and in the centre with white wool, embroider an aster-like flower, composed of sixteen long stitches or threads, radiating like petals in the form of a circle, the centre being left open to contain a multitude of tiny French knots worked with gold filoselle to represent the seeds of the flower; put a strand of white filoselle upon each white wool petal. The little scrolls that occupy the corners of the design are worked in pairs, the right-hand top corner to correspond with the left-hand bottom corner, and *vice versâ*, using white, gold, and violet filoselle in one position, and blue, gold, and green in the other. Join the stripes together with double crochet, when all the cross-stitch work is complete. Finish off the top and bottom of the antimacassar with an **edge**, thus—**1st row**—with crimson wool—1 double crochet in a stitch of the tricot,* 5 chain, miss three stitches, 1 double crochet in the next, and repeat from *. **2nd row**—with black—1 double crochet under the loop of five chain, 5 chain, and

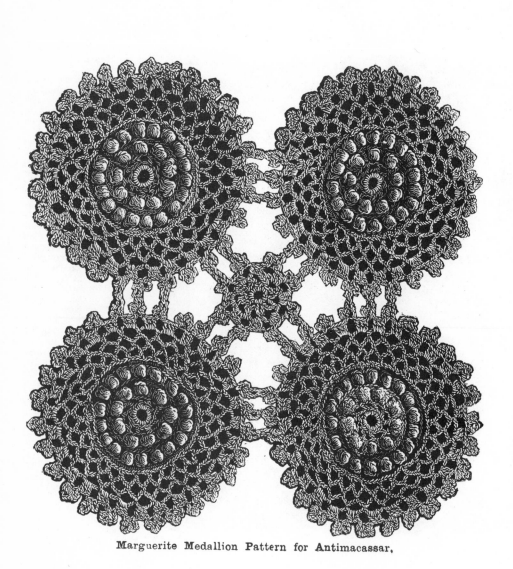

Marguerite Medallion Pattern for Antimacassar,

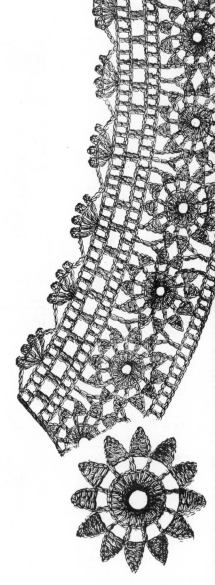

Chemise Trimming,

to the right over the crimson wool before drawing through the crimson stitch, and pass the crimson wool to the right over the other thread of black wool before drawing through the next black stitch, thus twining the wools together to keep the work firm. **3rd row**—Pick up 19 stitches with black wool, 3 stitches with crimson, and 20 stitches with black, and work back, drawing through each stitch with its own colour. **4th row**—18 stitches with black, 5 with crimson, 19 with black. **5th row**—17 stitches with black, 7 with crimson, 18 with black. And continue thus—the black stitches lessening and the crimson stitches increasing, until in the 21st row you get to the centre of the diamond, and work 1 stitch with black, 39 with crimson, 2 with black. After this decrease the crimson 1 stitch each side till the diamond is brought to a point of 1 stitch as it began. Do 1 row of tricot entirely with black wool, and then repeat from the second row until you have four or five diamonds worked for the length of the antimacassar. Work two more stripes in the same manner. Now proceed to embellish the stripes with cross-stitch.

repeat. Cut strands of crimson, black, white, and blue wool, 8 inches long, and knot as fringe in alternate bunches of colour.

BABY'S GLOVE.

PROCURE 1½ oz. of best white Berlin fingering, A A Peacock quality, a No. 12 bone crochet-needle, and one yard of very narrow pink ribbon. Begin for the wrist with 30 chain, join round, and work 3 rounds of plain double crochet, taking up both front loops; you need not join any more, but work round and round continuously, putting in a thread of cotton to denote the first stitch in each round. **4th round**—Double crochet, and increase on the first and third stitches of the round. Work 2 rounds without increase. **7th round**—Increase on the first and fifth stitches. Work two plain rounds. **10th round**—Work double crochet on the first 10 stitches, do 2 chain, join this round for the thumb, and work 8 rounds of 12 stitches in the round, then decrease by taking up 2 stitches together till only 4 stitches are left in the round, break off the wool, and sew the four stitches neatly together to close the top. Resume the hand upon the inner stitch next the thumb, do a double crochet on each of the chain-stitches, and continue round and round for 9 rounds, then take 2 together in every stitch till reduced to 4 or 5 stitches, and sew up. This is the left-hand glove. In doing the right-hand glove make the thumb increasings in corresponding stitches at the *end* of the rounds, instead of at the beginning, and when resuming the hand, let the two chain-stitches be worked upon for the two *last* stitches in the round. The **Frill** is worked in looped crochet. Begin on the foundation chain, 1 treble, 1 chain, miss one, and repeat, and join at the end of the round. **2nd round**—Plain double crochet. **3rd round**—Loop crochet, insert the hook in double crochet stitch of last round, wind the wool four times round the first finger of the left hand, and round again as far as the needle, insert the hook through

evenly. **2nd round**—3 chain to stand for a treble, 1 treble in the same stitch, 1 treble on each of the 2 next stitches, 2 treble on the next, 3 chain, * 2 treble on the first stitch, 1 treble on each of the two next stitches, 2 treble on the next, 3 chain and repeat from *, and join evenly. **3rd round**—3 chain to stand for a treble, 1 treble on each of 2 treble stitches, 6 chain, 1 double crochet on treble immediately below in the first round, 6 chain, 1 single crochet in the treble stitch last done, 1 treble on each of 3 treble stitches, 1 treble under loop of chain of last round, 3 chain, another treble in same place, * 3 treble on treble stitches, 6 chain, 1 double crochet on treble immediately below in the first round, 6 chain, 1 single crochet in the treble stitch last done, 3 treble on treble stitches, 1 treble under loop of chain, 3 chain, another treble in the same place, and repeat from *, and join evenly at the end of the round. **4th round**—You will be able to see now how the pattern stands and no more reference need be made to the joining of the rounds, work 3 treble on treble stitches of last round, a chain zigzag into the second round, 2 treble on treble

Bourbon Rose Pattern for Antimacassar.

Size of Wheel employed.

the wool round the finger, and draw the wool through the loops and through the double crochet stitch, wool over the needle and draw through 2 stitches on the needle, 1 plain double crochet in the next stitch, and repeat. **4th round**—Plain double crochet and increase one or two stitches in the round. Repeat the last two rows three times, and fasten off. Run a piece of ribbon through the open treble stitches, and tie the ends in a bow at the back of the hand.

HEXAGON FOR A QUILT.

THIS hexagon may be worked with No. 6 or No. 8 Strutts' knitting cotton, and a steel crochet needle. Commence in the centre with 8 chain, join round. **1st round**—Do three chain to stand for a treble, 2 treble in the joining place, 3 treble in each chain stitch, making 24 treble in all in the round, and join

stitches of last round, another chain zigzag into the second round, 3 treble on treble stitches of last round, and 1 treble, 3 chain, 1 treble under the loop. **5th round**—5 treble on treble of last round, a chain zigzag into the third round by the first zigzag, 5 treble on treble stitches, and 1 treble, 3 chain, 1 treble under the loop. **6th round**—12 treble over stitches of last round, and 1 treble, 3 chain, 1 treble under the loop. **7th round**—14 treble over stitches of last round, and 1 treble, 3 chain, 1 treble, under the loop. **8th round**—Work 8 treble stitches, a chain zigzag into the sixth round, 8 more treble stitches, and 1 treble, 3 chain, 1 treble, under the loop. **9th round**—8 treble stitches, a chain zigzag into the seventh round, 2 treble stitches, another chain zigzag, 8 treble stitches, and 1 treble, 3 chain, 1 treble, under the loop. **10th round**—Work 10 treble stitches, a chain zigzag into the eighth round, 10 more treble, and 1 treble, 3 chain, 1 treble, under the loop. **11th round**—22 treble over treble of last round, and 1 treble, 3 chain, 1 treble, under the loop. **12th round**—1 treble on centre stitch of three chain of last round, 3 chain, another treble in the same place, * 1 treble on first treble stitch of last round, 3 chain, another treble in the same place, miss two stitches, and repeat from * till you get to the next centre stitch of three chain, and continue the same to the end of the round. **13th round**—Work 4 consecutive treble, 3 chain, 1 single crochet in the third chain from the needle, and repeat; make increase of 3 trebles at each corner; get 9 picots along each side of the hexagon. When working the next hexagon join it at once in its place in process of crocheting by making a single crochet from picot to picot.

BORDER FOR A QUILT.

To be worked with the same sized cotton and needle as employed for the quilt upon which it is to be placed. Make a foundation of 23 chain. **1st row**—3 double crochet, 3 chain, miss three of the foundation, 16 double crochet, 3 chain. **2nd row**—Turn the work, and work this and all following rows into the back thread of the stitches of the previous row, 1 double crochet in the second chain from the needle, 1 double crochet in the next chain stitch, 16 double crochet worked consecutively, 3 chain, miss the three chain of last row, 3 double crochet. **3rd row**—3 double crochet, 3 chain, miss three chain of last row, 18 double crochet, 3 chain. **4th row**—20 double crochet, 3 chain, 3 double crochet. **5th row**—3 double crochet, 3 chain, cotton over the needle and insert the hook at the back of the work into the fifth double crochet of the third row, and draw the cotton through, cotton over the needle and draw through 2 stitches on the needle, cotton over the needle and insert the hook again in the same place and draw the cotton through, cotton

Wool Dahlia.

over the needle and draw through 2 stitches on the needle, cotton over the needle and draw through 2 more stitches on the needle, insert the hook in the next stitch of previous row and draw the cotton through, cotton over the needle, and draw through 3 stitches on the needle (this makes a tuft), do 3 double crochet, then another tuft in the fourth stitch of the third row from the last tuft, 3 double crochet, a tuft in the fourth stitch of the third row from the last tuft, 7 double crochet, 3 chain. **6th row**—22 double crochet, 3 chain, 3 double crochet. **7th row**—3 double crochet, 3 chain, 6 double crochet, a tuft at the back of the work into the seventh stitch of the fifth row, 3 double crochet, a tuft, 3 double crochet, a tuft, 7 double crochet, 3 chain. **8th row**—24 double crochet, 3 chain, 3 double crochet. **9th row**—3 double crochet, 3 chain, 8 double crochet, a tuft at the back of the work into stitch of the seventh row, 3 double crochet, a tuft, 3 double crochet, a tuft, 7 double crochet, 3 chain. **10th row**—26 double crochet, 3 chain, 3 double crochet. **11th row**—3 double crochet, 3 chain, 10 double crochet, a tuft, 3 double crochet, a tuft, 3 double crochet, a tuft, 7 double crochet, 3 chain. **12th row**—3 double crochet, 3 chain, 3 double crochet. **13th row**—3 double crochet, 3 chain, 12 double crochet, a tuft, 3 double crochet, a tuft, 3 double crochet, a tuft, 7 double crochet (no chain at the end). **14th row**—28 double crochet, 3 chain, 3 double crochet. **15th row**—3 double crochet, 3 chain, 14 double crochet, a tuft, 3 double crochet, a tuft, 3 double crochet, a tuft, 5 double crochet. **16th row**—28 double crochet, 3 chain, 3 double crochet. **17th row**—3 double crochet, 3 chain, 12 double crochet, a tuft, 3 double crochet, a tuft, 3 double crochet, a tuft, 5 double crochet. **18th row**—26 double crochet, 3 chain, 3 double crochet. **19th row**—3 double crochet, 3 chain, 10 double crochet, a tuft, 3 double crochet, a tuft, 3 double crochet, a tuft, 5 double crochet. **20th row**—24 double crochet, 3 chain, 3 double crochet. **21st row**—3 double crochet, 3 chain, 8 double crochet, a tuft, 3 double crochet, a tuft, 3 double crochet, a tuft, 5 double crochet. **22nd row**—22 double crochet, 3 chain, 3 double crochet. **23rd row**—3 double crochet, 3

chain, 6 double crochet, a tuft, 3 double crochet, a tuft, 3 double crochet, a tuft, 5 double crochet. **24th row**—20 double crochet, 3 chain, 3 double crochet. **25th row**—3 double crochet, 3 chain, 4 double crochet, a tuft, 3 double crochet, a tuft, 3 double crochet, a tuft, 5 double crochet. **26th row**—18 double crochet, 3 chain, 3 double crochet. **27th row**—3 double crochet, 3 chain, 16 double crochet. **28th row**—16 double crochet, 3 chain, 3 double crochet. Repeat from the first row for the length required. Work a **Heading** of treble stitches along the top of the border, putting 2 treble close together into each ridge. For the **Scallop**—Hold the right side of the border towards you, and for the **1st row**—Work 1 treble on the point of the first ridge, * 1 treble on the point of the next ridge, 3 chain, another treble in the same place, repeat from * nine times, which produces 11 loops of chain coming from 11 ridges of the border, do 1 treble on each of the three next ridges forming the hollow of the scallop, and repeat from * to the end of the row. **2nd row**—Recommencing on the right-hand side, 1 treble under the first loop of three chain, * 1 treble under the next loop of three chain, 4 chain, 1 double crochet in the fourth chain from the needle, 5 chain, 1 double crochet in the fourth chain from the needle, 1 treble under the same loop last treble is worked into, repeat from * eight times, 1 treble under the next loop of three chain, and 1 treble under the next, and then repeat from * to the end of the row, which finishes the border.

CROCHET D'OYLEY.

REQUIRED, Coats' crochet cotton, No. 18, and a fine steel crochet needle. Commence with 5 chain, and join round, and work continuously round and round in double crochet, taking up the two front loops of the stitches and increasing where necessary to keep the work flat, until you have done about 6 rounds, when you should have 48 stitches in the round. Make the edge even with 1 or 2 single crochet stitches, and fasten off. For the **little squares**—Begin with 10 chain, do 1 double crochet upon any stitch of the circle *, turn, and work backwards and forwards upon the 10 chain stitches, 8 rows of double crochet, inserting the hook to take up the one back thread of the

The Etta Petticoat.

stitches, that the work may sit in ridges. When the 8 little rows are done, work 10 chain, 1 double crochet in the sixth stitch of the circle from that last worked into. Repeat from * till you have worked 8 little squares, unite the corner of the last square to the corner of the first, and fasten off. Then for the **1st round**—Work 1 double crochet at the corner of a square, 10 chain, 1 long treble between the squares, 10 chain, and repeat. There should be 16 loops of 10 chain. Join evenly at the end of this and every round. **2nd round**—Double crochet in every stitch. **3rd round**—Turn the work, and do double crochet, taking up the back thread of every stitch of last round. **4th round**—Turn again, and work similarly. **5th round**—4 chain to stand for a long treble stitch, 1 long treble in the first stitch of previous round, 2 chain, 2 more long treble in the same place, 2 chain *, miss 5 stitches, 2 long treble in the next, 2 chain, 2 more long treble in the same place, 2 chain, and repeat from *. **6th round**—Slip stitch into the loop between the four long treble stitches, 5 chain, 1 treble in the same loop, 4 chain, 1 double crochet in the next loop, 4 chain, 1 treble in the loop between four long treble stitches, 2 chain, another treble in the same place, 4 chain, 1 double crochet in the next loop, 4 chain, and repeat from *. **7th round**—1 double crochet under the loop of two chain *, 5 chain and 1 double crochet three times in the same place, 4 chain, 1 double crochet under the next loop of two chain, and repeat from *. Fasten off after joining at the end of the round. **8th round**—Work 1 double crochet in the centre of the three loop of last round, 9 chain, and repeat. **9th round**—4 chain to stand for a treble, 1 treble in the second stitch of last round, 1 chain *, miss one, 1 treble in the next, 1 chain, and repeat from *. **10th round**—3 chain to stand for a treble, 2 treble in the same place, * 5 chain, miss four, 7 consecutive double crochet, 5 chain, miss four, 3 treble in the next. These 3 treble are always to come upon a treble stitch of previous round, and the centre stitch of the 7 double crochet must come upon a treble likewise. Repeat from * to the end of the round. **11th round**—3 chain to stand for a treble, 1 treble on each treble stitch and 1 treble in the first stitch of four chain, * 5 chain, 5 double crochet on double crochet of last round, missing the first and last stitches, 5 chain, 1 treble in the fourth stitch of the chain, 1 treble on each of three treble stitches, and 1 treble in the first stitch of next five chain, and repeat from * to the end of the round. **12th round**—Slip stitch on to the last but one of the treble stitches of last round, do 3 chain to stand for a treble, 1 treble on treble stitch, and 1 treble in the first stitch of five chain, * 5 chain, 3 double crochet on double crochet of

the hook into the top of the fourth double crochet stitch of the first row bring up a loop from the back of the work, keep this loop on the needle while you insert the hook in the next stitch of previous row, and work a double crochet as usual, do 3 consecutive double crochet, then bring up another claret loop from the double crochet stitch of the first row at a distance of 3 stitches from the last (the claret wool must lie smoothly at the back of the work from loop to loop), work double crochet as usual, and proceed in the same manner to the end of the row, break off the claret wool and tie the two ends together to prevent its coming out. Work 3 plain double crochet rows; then another row with claret loops, which draw up intermediately between the loops you worked in the fifth row. Continue till you have done 26 rows, making a depth of 6 coloured loops for the flounce. Now, with grey wool, commence for the **top of the skirt** with from 60 to 70 chain, calculating for the length of the petticoat, minus the flounce that is already worked, and the few rounds of crochet that have to be done for a heading. Work 2 rows of plain tricot. **3rd row**—Pick up 25 stitches only, and work back. **4th row**—Pick up 35 stitches, and work back. **5th row**—Pick up 45 stitches, and work back. **6th row**—Pick up 55 stitches, and work back. Repeat these 6 rows until you have a width round the bottom to correspond with the width of the flounce already worked. Sew up the tricot, leaving space at the top for a placket-hole. Work the flounce heading round the bottom of the tricot. **1st round**—With grey wool, 1 double crochet into a stitch of the tricot, * 3 chain, 1 double crochet in the same place, miss 1 tricot stitch, 1 double crochet in the next, and repeat from *. **2nd round**—With claret, 1 double crochet under loop of 3 chain, 3 chain, another double crochet in the same loop, 1 double crochet under the next loop, 3 chain, another double crochet in the same place, and continue **3rd round** and **4th round**—With grey wool, work the same. **5th round**—With claret, work the same. Now join up the flounce, and having a rug needle threaded with wool, sew the last round of the heading neatly over the last (the top) round of the flounce. For **Edge** round the bottom of the flounce, work 1 double crochet into one of the commencing chain stitches, miss 2, 9 treble worked loosely in the next, miss 2, and repeat. Strengthen the placket with a round of double crochet. Set the top of the petticoat into a calico waistband.

Zulu Stripe in Tricot for Antimacassar.

last round, missing the first and last stitches, 5 chain, 1 treble in the fifth stitch of the chain, 1 treble on each of two treble stitches, 5 chain, miss one, 3 consecutive treble, and repeat from *. **13th round**—Slip stitch on to first treble of last round, do 3 chain to stand for a treble, 1 treble on treble stitch, and 1 treble in the first stitch of 5 chain, * 5 chain, 1 double crochet on centre stitch of three double crochet, 5 chain, 1 treble in the fifth stitch of the chain, 1 treble on each of two treble stitches, 3 chain, 1 treble under five chain loop, 3 chain, another treble in the same place, 3 chain, miss the first treble, and work 3 treble consecutive, and repeat from *. **14th round**—Slip stitch on to first treble of last round, do 3 chain to stand for a treble, 1 treble on treble stitch and 1 treble in the first stitch of five chain, * 1 treble in the fifth stitch of next loop of chain, 1 treble on each of two treble stitches, 7 chain, 1 single crochet in the sixth chain from the needle, 1 chain, 1 treble under first loop of three chain, another picot, and 1 treble under the next loop, another picot, and another treble in the same place, another picot, and 1 treble in the next loop, another picot, and 1 treble on the second of the three treble stitches, and 2 more treble worked consecutive, and repeat from *. This completes the d'oyley.

LADY'S PETTICOAT.

THIS petticoat is composed of three different patterns; an illustration is given showing a portion of the flounce in full working size; this is done in crochet, as is also the insertion-like heading over the flounce, also illustrated full size, while the top of the skirt is worked in plain tricot. Procure 14 oz. of grey, and 4 oz. of claret petticoat fingering, a No. 6 long bone tricot needle, and a No. 9 bone crochet needle. Begin for the **Flounce**, making with grey wool a chain as long as you desire for the extreme width of the petticoat. Work forwards and backwards 4 rows of plain double crochet. **5th row**—Still with grey wool, work 3 double crochet, take the claret wool, and inserting

Baby's Glove.

FRILLING FOR THE NECK.

THIS is a strong durable frilling, and may be worked with the flax thread so much in vogue, either Harris's or Finlayson's, selecting a fine size, or if this is not procurable, a cream and a pink shade of Evans' crochet cotton, No. 22, may be employed. Use a very fine steel crochet needle, and work firmly. Commence with cream thread, with chain for the length required. **1st row**—1 treble in the sixth chain from the needle, * 1 chain, miss 1, 1 treble in the next, and repeat from *. **2nd row**—4 chain to turn, 1 treble under the first space of previous row, * 1 chain, 1 treble under the next space, and repeat from *. **3rd row**—6 chain to turn, 1 long treble under the first space, * 1 chain, 1 long treble under the next space, and repeat from *; this completes the foundation. For the **Frill**, which lies like a ruche upon the last row of the foundation; hold the foundation with the commencing chain to the right, and still using cream thread, do 9 treble under the first long treble stitch, 3 treble under the 1 chain at the top of last row of the foundation, 9 treble under the next long treble stitch, * 1 treble under the same one chain of the second row as the next long treble is worked under, do 9 treble under this long treble stitch, 3 treble under the one chain at the top of last row, 9 treble under the next long treble stitch, and repeat from *, and fasten off thread. **Next row** of the Frill—With pink thread, beginning at the same end as last row, 1 single crochet in every alternate stitch of treble, inserting the hook to take up the one top thread.

SMOKING CAP.

PROCURE 2 ozs. of brown double Berlin wool, and a No. 8 bone crochet needle. Commence with 3 chain, join round, and work 6 double crochet in the circle. **2nd round**—Work 2 double crochet on each stitch of last round, inserting the hook so as to take up both top threads of the work. **3rd round** —2 double crochet on the first stitch, 1 double crochet on the next, working into both top threads of the stitches of preceding round. Continue working round and round, increasing where necessary, to keep the work perfectly flat, till you have a circle measuring about 8 inches in diameter. Then work a round of double crochet on the front threads of the stitches of last round

Hexagon for a Quilt.

(to stand up to mark the extreme edge of the crown), and a round of double crochet on the back threads of the same stitches, and on this latter proceed for the band, working round and round in double crochet into both top threads of each preceding round, without either increase or decrease, till 12 rounds are done, which completes the cap.

BASKET PATTERN TRICOT.

THIS is a smooth, pretty pattern for antimacassars, *couvrepieds*, &c., worked with five shades of crimson double Berlin wool, and a No. 7 tricot needle. Commence with the darkest shade of wool, with any even number of stitches. **1st row**—Miss 1 chain, raise a tricot stitch in the next chain, put the wool over the needle, and raise another tricot stitch in the same chain, repeat, keeping all the stitches on the needle; to work back, wool over the needle and draw through 3 stitches together, 1 chain, wool over the needle, and draw through the chain and the 3 next stitches together, and so on till all are worked off. **2nd row**—With the same shade of wool, 1 chain to turn, * raise a tricot stitch under the one chain of last row, wool over the needle, raise another stitch in the same place, repeat from * to the end, where raise 1 stitch at the extreme corner to keep the work even; coming back wool over the needle, and draw through the first stitch, wool over the needle and draw through this stitch and the 3 next stitches together, 1 chain, wool over the needle and draw through the chain and the 3 next stitches together, and repeat, till at the end of the row you draw through the chain and 1 stitch only. Every succeeding row is worked in the same manner. Do two rows with each shade in succession to the lightest, then shade again to the dark, and continue for the length required. Finish off the work at top and bottom with a fringe of 4 strands of wool knotted under the space of one chain.

ROMAN STRIPE.

A LOVELY PATTERN FOR A CHAIR-BACK.

THIS unique chair-back is worked throughout in plain double crochet, and the beauty of the pattern consists in the arrangement of the various colours, which are artistic, and therefore will harmonise with the surroundings in almost any room, with the proviso that should blue predominate therein a pretty shade of pale China blue be substituted for the apple green here mentioned. Procure 2 oz. of each colour single Berlin wool, white, black, crimson, apple green, and amber, or rather less quantity of the last-named, and a No. 12 bone crochet needle. With black wool make a chain 28 to 30 inches in length, leaving 4 inches of wool hanging at the beginning and break off, leaving 4 inches of wool at the end; this has to be done at the beginning and at the end of *every* row and answers the purpose of a fringe, though it is advisable to knot one extra strand in each row after the chair-back is completed. Begin every row at the right-hand side, and work into the one top thread of the stitches of previous row. **1st row**—With black wool, plain double crochet. **2nd row**—1 stitch of amber double crochet, and 1 stitch of black alternately all along the row. To do this you begin with the amber wool, insert the hook in the first stitch, place the black wool at the back of the work close over the needle (leaving a 4-inch length of this also hanging as fringe) in such a position that the amber wool passes over the black and confines it close to the work when you draw the amber wool through in process of working the first half of the double crochet stitch, put the black wool round the needle and finish the stitch by drawing through the two loops on the needle with black, insert the hook in the next stitch of last row, place the amber wool at the back of the work close over the needle, draw the black wool through the stitch, put the amber wool round the needle and finish the stitch by drawing through the two loops on the needle with amber, and proceed thus all along entwining the two colours, and as you go on you will see each stitch appear in its own colour perfectly clear and distinct; leave a fringe of each colour at the end of the row. **3rd row**—Plain double crochet with amber. **4th row**—1 crimson double crochet and 1 amber double crochet alternately, worked as instructed in the second row. **5th row to the 9th row**—All crimson. **10th row**—1 stitch amber and 1 stitch crimson alternately. **11th row**—Amber. **12th row**—1 amber and 1 black alternately. **13th row** to the **15th row**—All black. **16th row**—2 green, * 5 black, 5 green, and repeat from * to the end of the row; change the colours as instructed in the second row, and work over the black wool when doing the green stitches and over the green wool when doing the black, so that the wool when not in actual use is passed along invisibly, and the stitches appear as clearly on the wrong side as on the right.

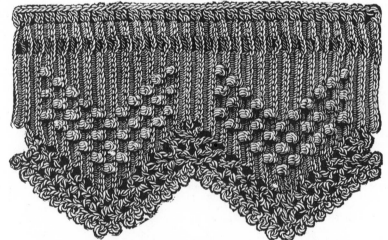

Border for a Quilt.

17th row—4 yellow, * 5 black, 5 yellow, and repeat from *. **18th row**—1 crimson, * 5 black, 5 crimson, repeat from *. **19th row**—4 white, * 5 black, 5 white, repeat from *. **20th row**—2 green, * 5 black, 5 green, repeat from *. **21st row**—4 crimson, * 5 black, 5 crimson, repeat from *. **22nd row** to the **24th row**—All black. **25th row**—1 black and 1 amber alternately. **26th row**—Amber. **27th row**—1 green and 1 amber alternately. **28th row** to the **32nd row**—All green. **33rd row**—1 green and 1 amber alternately. **34th row**—Amber. **35th row**—1 white and 1 amber alternately. **36th row to the 40th row**—All white. **41st row**—4 white, * 5 crimson,

5 white, repeat from *. **42nd row**—2 white, * 5 black, 5 white, repeat from *. **43rd row**—5 white, * 5 green, 5 white, repeat from *. **44th row**—2 white, * 5 amber, 5 white, repeat from *. **45th row**—4 white, * 5 crimson, 5 white, repeat from *. **46th row**—2 white, * 5 black, 5 white, repeat from *. **47th row** to the **51st row**—All white. **52nd row**—1 white and 1 amber alternately, the same as the thirty-fifth row. Now work the **34th row**. Then the **33rd row**. And so on backwards, and end with the first row. The four inches of wool that hang at the beginning and at the end of every row serve as a fringe, and may be thickened by the addition of as many extra strands knotted in as will suffice for the desired thickness.

LADY'S BOA.

THESE boas are very fashionable for summer wear, and are useful as well as pretty. They are generally made in black, using either Shetland wool or Ice wool,

—1 double crochet under loop of two chain, * 5 chain, 1 double crochet under next loop, and repeat from *. Work six more rows the same as last row. **9th row**—1 double crochet under the first loop of last row. 2 chain 1 treble under next loop *, 4 chain, 1 single crochet on the treble stitch last done, another treble under the same loop of five chain, repeat from * twice more, then 2 chain and 1 double crochet under the next loop of five chain, 2 chain, 1 treble under the next loop, and repeat. This finishes the boa, which hangs full and frilly.

CORISANDE STRIPE.

THIS is a new stitch of tufted tricot to work in stripes for chair-backs, sofa couvrettes, and other purposes. Procure double Berlin wool and a No. 5 bone tricot needle. Begin with 17 chain, in which pick up 16 loops and work back as in ordinary tricot. Work two more rows of plain tricot. **4th row**—Raise

Crochet D'Oyley.

but any colour may be selected and white or cream would harmonise with any dress, and with care in washing would always look fresh and becoming. Use a No. 10 crochet needle, and begin with 18 chain, work 1 treble in the eighth chain from the needle, 1 chain, miss one, 1 treble, to the end of the little row; turn with 4 chain, do 1 treble in the first space, 1 chain, 1 treble in the next space, and continue till you have six treble and six spaces in the row. Every row of the foundation is worked in this manner. Make the strip the required length of the boa. Now in this foundation work 1 treble on the chain that turned the first row of the foundation, 2 chain 1 treble on the first treble stitch, 2 chain 1 treble on the next treble stitch, and so on to the end of the little row, turn the work, and do 2 chain, 1 treble on the chain that turned the second row of the foundation, 2 chain 1 treble on the first treble stitch, 2 chain 1 treble on the next treble stitch, and continue; work in every row of the foundation in this manner, first on one side and then on the other. **2nd row**

4 loops, then insert the hook in the sixth tricot loop of the row before the last, draw the wool through, and do 6 chain, make altogether 5 loops (6 chain in each loop) all in the same stitch of the tricot, draw the wool through the 5 chain stitches on the needle, raise 5 tricot loops, and in the next (that is in the sixth from the end) insert the hook as above directed, and work 5 more loops of chain, raise 5 tricot loops; work back as in ordinary tricot. Work 2 rows of plain tricot. **7th row**—Raise 1 loop, insert the hook in the third tricot loop of the row before the last, and work a bunch of tufted chain as directed in the fourth row, raise 5 tricot loops, another bunch of tufted chain, 5 tricot loops and again another bunch, then 2 tricot loops, and work back as in ordinary tricot. Work 2 rows of plain tricot. Repeat from the fourth row for the length required.

GENTLEMAN'S VEST.

REQUIRED, 10 oz. of brown or grey double Berlin wool, and a long wooden tricot needle No. 6. Make a chain of 58 stitches, and work in plain tricot for the length of the front of the vest, about 24 inches long will be right. Work a second front in the same way. Send the two pieces of tricot to a tailor to be made up into a vest.

LADY'S MUFFLER.

THIS is an immensely becoming wrap to wind round the neck, or to pass over the head. It is 2½ yards long. Procure 10 oz. of white single Berlin for the muffler, and 1 oz. of white Shetland for making tassels, a No. 9 bone crochet needle, and a wooden hair-pin fork two inches wide. Commence for the whole length of the muffler with single Berlin, with 286 chain worked rather loosely. **1st row**—Work 5 treble in the fourth chain from the needle, then * miss 2 stitches of the foundation, 1 double crochet in the next, miss 2, 6 treble in the next, and repeat from * to the end of the row, making 48 groups of 6 treble, and fasten off. **2nd row**—Beginning on the right-hand side, 1 double crochet

the double crochet stitch, and continue. Repeat from the second row. These nine rows form the width of the centre portion of the muffler. Now take the wooden fork and do a sufficient length of hair-pin trimming to go entirely round the piece of crochet work. The method of working hair-pin trimming is detailed in No. 23 of "Weldon's Practical Work" Series. This done, take up on the crochet needle 3 loops of the hair-pin trimming and in them work a double crochet stitch, then do 2 chain, 1 double crochet on the second treble of the first group of last row, * 2 chain, 1 double crochet in the next 3 loops (taken together) of hair-pin trimming, 2 chain, 1 double crochet on the fifth treble, 2 chain, 1 double crochet in 3 loops of hair-pin trimming, 2 chain, 1 double crochet on the second treble of the next group of last row, and repeat from *: go round all four sides of the muffler and consequently join all the hair-pin trimming thereto. Now on the outer edge of the hair-pin trimming work 1 double crochet in 3 loops taken together, * 5 chain, 1 double crochet in the next 3 loops taken together, and repeat from * all round; join neatly. For the **Border**—Commence in a loop of five chain, where do 2 treble, 2 chain, 2 treble, * then 3 chain, 1 double crochet under next loop of five chain, 3 chain, 1 double crochet under next loop of five chain, 3 chain, and 2 treble

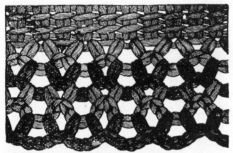

Details of Heading over the Flounce for Lady's Petticoat.

Frilling for the Neck.

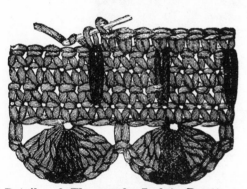

Details of Flounce for Lady's Petticoat.

Lady's Petticoat.

Basket Pattern Tricot.

Smoking Cap.

on the third treble stitch of the first group (counting the chain that turned as one), 3 chain, insert the hook in the fourth treble stitch, and draw the wool through as in tricot, but loosely; do the same in the fifth and in the sixth treble stitches, in the double crochet stitch, and in the first and second treble stitches of the next group, and you will have 7 stitches on the needle, wool round the needle, and draw through all, 1 chain to secure the group, then 3 chain, and repeat as above to the end of the row, and fasten off. **3rd row**—Commence with 3 chain, 1 double crochet on the first double crochet of previous row, * 6 treble in the loop that secures together the raised stitches of last row, 1 double crochet on the double crochet stitch, and repeat from *, and end with 3 chain as you began. **4th row**—Raise 1 stitch in each of the three chain at the beginning of last row, also in the double crochet stitch, and in the first and second treble stitches of the group, wool round the needle and draw through all, 1 chain to secure them, 3 chain, * 1 double crochet on the third treble stitch, 3 chain, raise a stitch in the fifth and sixth treble stitches, in the double crochet stitch, and in the first and second treble stitches of the next group, 7 stitches on the needle, wool round the needle, and draw through all, 1 chain to secure the group, then 3 chain, and repeat from *, and end the row as it began. **5th row**—Work 6 treble in the loop that secures together the raised stitches of last row, 1 double crochet on

2 chain, 2 treble all under next loop of five chain, and repeat from *, and fasten off at the end of the round. **2nd round**—Work 3 treble, 3 chain, 3 treble, all under loop of two chain of last round, 3 chain, 1 double crochet on double crochet stitch, 3 chain, 1 double crochet on double crochet stitch, 3 chain, and repeat. **3rd round**—Do 4 treble, 3 chain, 4 treble, all under loop of three chain of last round, 3 chain, 1 double crochet on double crochet, 3 chain, 1 double crochet on double crochet, 3 chain, and repeat. **4th round**—8 treble under the loop of three chain of last round, 4 chain, 1 double crochet on double crochet, 3 chain, 1 double crochet on double crochet, 4 chain, and repeat. **5th round**—1 treble between the first and second treble stitches of last round, 4 chain, 1 double crochet in the fourth chain from the needle, 1 treble between the second and third treble stitches, do 6 of the picots in all intermediate between 7 treble stitches worked between the eighth treble of last round, then 4 chain, 1 double crochet under chain between the two double crochet stitches of last round, and repeat. Gather in each end of the muffler and attach tassels of Shetland wool. Each tassel is made of daisy fringe of ten strands of wool, eight daisies in length, half an ounce of wool being used in each tassel, the strands are finished off with a small ball knob at each end, then folded in half, and confined together by a big ball knob where sewn to the muffler.

WELDON'S
PRACTICAL CROCHET.

(EIGHTH SERIES.)

HOW TO CROCHET USEFUL ARTICLES FOR LADIES, GENTS., & CHILDREN.

THIRTY-ONE ILLUSTRATIONS.

Telegraphic Address—]
"Consuelo," London.]

The Yearly Subscription to this Magazine, post free to any Part of the World, is 2s. 6d. Subscriptions are payable in advance, and may commence from any date and for any period.

[Telephone—
2745.

The Back Numbers are always in print. Nos. 1 to 87 now ready, Price 2d. each, or post free for 15s. 6d. Over 5,000 Engravings.

INFANT'S JACKET.

PROCURE 3 ozs. of Lady Betty wool, and a No. 9 bone crochet needle, also 2 yards of inch-wide ribbon for trimming the neck and sleeves. Begin for the front of the jacket with 41 chain. **1st row**—Work 40 double crochet along the chain. **2nd row**—1 chain to turn, and work 40 double crochet, taking up the back loop of the stitches of previous row. **3rd row**—2 chain to turn, and do 20 point neige stitches, taking up the back loop; fasten off at the end of the row, and begin the next row at the other end. **4th row**—20 point neige. **5th row**—40 double crochet, working into the front thread of the stitches of last row. **6th row**—20 point neige; always break off the wool after doing this first row of point neige and begin the second row at the other end. **7th row**—21 point neige, the increase to come at the end of the row; and increase at this same end in all other increase rows, and also decrease at the same end; the other end which is the bottom of the jacket, must be kept perfectly straight and even. **8th row**—43 double crochet. **9th row**—23 point neige.—**10th row**—24 point neige. **11th row**—49 double crochet. **12th row**—25 point neige. **13th row**—24 point neige. **14th row**—47 double crochet. **15th row**—23 point neige. **16th row**—22 point neige. **17th row**—43 double crochet. **18th row**—21 point neige. **19th row**—13 point neige, and leave the remainder for the armhole. **20th row**—Work single crochet on the first 8 stitches, then double crochet to the end. **21st row**—7 point neige. **22nd row**—13 point neige, and 17 chain for the shoulder. **23rd row**—42 double crochet. **24th row**—22 point neige. **25th row**—23 point neige. **26th row**—47 double crochet. **27th row**—21 point neige. **28th row**—25 point neige. **29th row**—50 double crochet. Now work without increasing, 11 rows for the back of the jacket, and after that shape for the other shoulder to correspond with that already done, and also the front. Sew up the shoulders. Then work round the neck, 1 row of double crochet and 1 row of treble. Work 2 rows of point neige along the lower edge of the jacket. Then all round the jacket and along the neck do a picot edge, thus, 1 single crochet in a stitch of the jacket, 3 chain, 1 single crochet in the top of last single crochet, miss one of the foundation, and repeat. For the **Sleeve**—Make 28 chain. **1st row**—Work 13 point neige stitches. **2nd row**—The same. **3rd row**—Double crochet. Repeat these three rows, in the last row increase at the beginning of the row. **7th row**—Increase at the end. **8th row**—Double crochet. Continue increasing in the same way till you are able to work 19 point neige in a row. Work 5 rows straight, and fasten off. Sew the sleeve up. Work the other sleeve to correspond. Work the same picot edge round the wrist as

Infant's Jacket.

is already worked upon the jacket. Run the ribbon in the neck and sleeves, and sew the sleeves into the armholes.

Another jacket in point neige stitch is illustrated and described in page 11 of No. 3 of "Weldon's Practical Needlework Series," and in which the stitch is fully detailed.

ANTIMACASSAR.

PATTERN OF RAISED TUFTS AND WHITE NARCISSUS FLOWERS.

THIS is a particularly handsome pattern to be worked in stripes, lengthways, and three of the wide stripes and two narrow ones will make a good-sized antimacassar. The wide stripe, as shown in the engraving, is worked entirely with ruby-red wool, and has white narcissus flowers dotted here and there upon it; the narrow stripe is worked chiefly with grey, a group of four green tufts being introduced at intervals to add a brightness of colouring; both stripes are edged all round with double crochet spike stitches worked with black wool, and the stripes are joined together with white. You will require not less than 8 ozs. of red wool, 3 ozs. of grey, 3 ozs. of black, 2 ozs. of white, ½ oz. of a rather light shade of peacock green, and a small quantity of yellow, single Berlin wool, and a No. 12 bone crochet needle. Begin for the Red Stripe with 23 chain, work 1 double crochet in the third chain from the needle, and continue along, doing 21 double crochet in all. Work two more rows of plain double crochet—viz., 1 chain to turn, miss the first stitch, and do 21 double crochet along, inserting the hook to take up both the top and the back thread of the stitches of previous row. **4th row**—1 chain to turn, miss the first stitch, 1 double crochet on the next, insert the hook through the work at the bottom of the third double crochet stitch of last row, and draw the wool through in a high loose stitch, wool over the needle, insert the hook again in the same place and draw the wool through loosely, wool over the needle and raise 4 more loops in the same manner, making 11 threads of wool on the needle besides the stitch that belongs to the double crochet, wool over the needle and draw through the 11 threads to form the raised tuft, wool over the needle and draw through 2 stitches on the needle, * 1 double crochet on each of three consecutive stitches, then insert the hook at the distance of 4 stitches (missing three) from the place where the preceding tuft was raised and make another tuft in the same way, and repeat from *, and end the row with 3 double crochet; if rightly done there will still be 21 stitches in the row—viz., 16 double crochet stitches and 5 raised tuft stitches. **5th row**—1 chain to turn, miss the first stitch, and do 21 double crochet in the row. **6th row**—

1 chain to turn, miss the first stitch, do three double crochet, then insert the hook through the work at the bottom of the fifth double crochet of last row, and drawing the wool through in a high loose stitch, work up 11 threads to form a raised tuft, wool over the needle and draw through the 11 threads, wool over the needle and draw through 2 stitches on the needle, * 3 consecutive double crochet, another tuft at the distance of 4 stitches, and repeat from *, and end the row with 5 double crochet. **7th row**—1 chain to turn, miss the first stitch, and do 21 double crochet in the row. Repeat from the fourth row to the seventh row twice. Then to leave a space in which to place the narcissus flower, omit the middle tuft in the sixteenth row, the two middle tufts in the eighteenth row, and three tufts in the twentieth row, working instead plain double crochet; in the twenty-second, twenty-fourth, and twenty-sixth rows bring these tufts gradually back again; and then repeat from the fourth row for the length required for the antimacassar, ending with six complete rows of tufts. For the **Narcissus Flowers**—Use white wool, work 7 chain, 1 double crochet in the second chain from the needle, 4 treble along, 6 treble in the top stitch, 4 treble and 1 double crochet along the other side, and a single crochet to fasten off, draw in the ends of the wool securely. Work six of these white leaves, then make a yellow dot for the centre of the flower, 4 chain, join round, work 2 double crochet in each chain stitch, and for the second round 1 double crochet upon each, and fasten off. Tack the six leaves together in the shape of a flower, the wrong side of the crochet uppermost, and place the yellow dot in the centre, then arrange the flower by means of a

Antimacassar. Pattern of Raised Tufts and White Narcissus Flowers.

few stitches in the middle of the flat space that is left among the raised tufts For the **Narrow** Stripe—Take the grey wool, and commencing with 15 chain, work 1 double crochet in the third chain from the needle, and proceed, doing 13 double crochet in all. Work two more rows of plain double crochet,—viz., 1 chain to turn, miss the first stitch, and do 13 double crochet in each row. **4th row**—1 chain to turn, miss the first stitch, 1 double crochet, a tuft, 3 double crochet, a tuft, 3 double crochet, a tuft, 3 double crochet. **5th row**—Same as the third row. **6th row**—1 chain to turn, miss the first stitch, 3 double crochet, a tuft, 3 double crochet, a tuft, 5 double crochet. **7th row.**—Same as the third row. **8th row**—1 chain to turn, miss the first stitch, 1 double crochet, a tuft, 3 double crochet, a green tuft, 3 double crochet, a tuft, 3 double crochet; the green tuft is formed by drawing the green wool up through the work and raising the looped loose stitches with it, then green wool over the needle and draw through the 11 threads of the raised tuft, grey wool over the needle and draw through the 2 stitches (one green and one grey stitch) on the needle, and leave the green wool at the back of the work. **9th row**—Same as the third row. **10th row**—Same as the sixth row, but both the tufts to be green. **11th row**—Same as the third row. **12th row**—Same as the eighth row, with one green tuft; break off the green wool, and make both ends of green wool neat by running in the work with a rug needle. **13th row**—Same as the third row. **14th row**—Same as the sixth row, and the same colour. **15th row**—Same as the third row. **16th row**—Same as the fourth row. **17th row**—Same as the third row. **18th row**—Same as the sixth row. **19th row**—Same as the third row. Repeat from the fourth row till you have worked the same number of rows as you have already done in the wide stripe, you can count easily by the tufts: then with yellow wool and rug needle work a double crossed stitch in the centre of every group of four green tufts. Work two more wide stripes with red wool, and one more narrow stripe with grey and green. Now for the **Edge** that is to surround all the stripes—Take the black wool, and * work an ordinary double crochet stitch upon the edge of the stripe, insert the hook through the work three stitches from the edge and draw the wool through, wool over the needle and draw through 2 stitches on the needle, and repeat from *; the long stitches must be drawn up loosely, and as seen in the engraving

will resemble "spike" stitches. When all the stripes are edged join them together with a row of single crochet worked with white or yellow wool. For the **Border—1st round**—With white or yellow wool as preferred,—1 double crochet in a stitch of the antimacassar, 6 chain, miss 4 stitches, and repeat the same all the way round; turn the corners by a 6 chain loop without missing any stitches. **2nd round**—With black wool—1 double crochet on the double crochet stitch of last round, 6 chain, and repeat. **3rd round**—With black wool—1 double crochet, 4 chain, 2 double crochet, 4 chain, 2 double crochet, 4 chain, 1 double crochet, *all* under every loop of six chain of last round.

TRINITY STITCH.

THIS stitch is prettier when actually worked than it appears in the illustration. If the Floss wool of the Providence Mills Company, Bradford, be used, and a No. 7 bone crochet needle, it makes a lovely scarf shawl, or Andalusian wool may be employed with the same sized needle. With No. 2 needle and double Berlin wool the stitch is suitable for a perambulator rug or a sofa blanket. Commence with a chain the length required. **1st row**—Miss the 3 first stitches, and pick up 1 stitch like tricot in each of the 3 next stitches, wool over the needle and draw through 4 stitches on the needle, 1 chain, * pick up 1 stitch like tricot in the same place as last tricot stitch was picked up and 1 stitch in each of the two next stitches, wool over the needle and draw through 4 stitches on the needle, 1 chain, and repeat from *; and at the end of the row fasten down with a double crochet into the last stitch of the commencing chain, and break off the wool. **2nd row**—Recommence on the right-hand side by drawing up the wool under the commencing chain stitch of last row, do 2 chain, pick up 1 stitch like tricot in the small space close by where you drew up the wool, and 1 in the next stitch, and 1 under the little space between the groups of last row, wool over the needle and draw through 4 stitches on the needle, 1 chain, * pick up 1 stitch in the same space as last tricot stitch was picked up, 1 stitch over the group of drawn together stitches, and 1 stitch under the next little space, wool over the needle and draw through 4 stitches on the needle, 1 chain, repeat from *; and at the end do 1 more chain and fasten down with a double crochet into the double crochet stitch of previous row. Work every succeeding row the same as the second row.

GENTLEMAN'S GLOVES.

PROCURE 2½ ozs. of brown Berlin Fingering and a No. 12 bone crochet needle, Commence with 22 chain, leaving a tag end of wool at the beginning, and work in ridged, or Russian crochet, forwards and backwards for 40 rows; this is for the wrist, join the last row to the first, sewing them together with the tag end of wool, and without breaking off the wool from the ball, proceed with the crochet for the hand. Work along the edge of the cuff, doing 41 double crochet stitches in the round. Work 5 more rounds of plain double crochet, inserting the hook to take up both the front and the top threads of the stitches

Trinity Stitch.

of previous rounds. **7th round**—Here begin to increase for the thumb, and do 2 double crochet on the first stitch and 2 double crochet on the third stitch of the round, and 1 double crochet on each of the other stitches as before. **8th round**—Plain double crochet without increase. **9th round**—Increase on the first and fifth stitches, the others plain. **10th round**—Plain, no increase. **11th round**—Increase on the first and seventh stitches, the others plain. **12th round**—Plain, no increase. Go on increasing in each alternate round till you get to 59 stitches in the round. Then for the **Thumb**—Do 17 double crochet stitches, make 5 chain, and join round to the fifth double crochet stitch, making 18 stitches in the round for the thumb; work in double crochet for 15 rounds, and decrease for the top, thus, double crochet 1 stitch, double crochet 2 stitches together, do this alternately 6 times, then 2 together 6 times, and break off the wool. Work again upon the hand part of the glove for 14 rounds, doing 51 stitches in each round. For the **First Finger**—Work the 5 stitches directly over the thumb, do 4 chain, and work 9 double crochet to the right of the first five, join round, there are 18 stitches, and work 17 rounds, and then decrease the same as the thumb is decreased. **Second Finger**—Work 6 stitches beside the first finger, do 3 chain, work 6 stitches on the other side of the hand, and 3 stitches on the chain of the first finger, making 18 stitches, work 19 rounds, and decrease as before. **Third**

Finger—Arrange the stitches the same as for the second finger, work 17 rounds, and decrease. **Fourth Finger**—Work upon all the stitches that are left, doing 2 on the chain of the third finger, work 14 rounds, and decrease. Sew up the tops of the fingers and the thumb on the side of the work as you now have it, then turn the whole thing inside out, for the inside of the work is intended to be the right side of the glove. The only difference in working the glove for the other hand is at the beginning of the first finger, where you must do the 9 stitches directly after the 5 stitches over the thumb, and then 4 chain, and join round. With a wool needle threaded with some of the wool embroider three lines of chain stitch upon the backs of the hands.

MUFF AND BOA FOR A CHILD.

REQUIRED, ¼ lb. of white and 1 oz. of grey single Berlin wool, and a No. 9 bone crochet needle. For the **Muff**—Commence with white wool with 46 chain; join round. **1st round**—Plain double crochet worked with white wool. **2nd round**—1 double crochet stitch, and 1 looped stitch alternately; a looped stitch is made by passing the wool three times round the first and second fingers of the left hand, then insert the hook in the next stitch of last

OPERA HOOD OR FASCINATOR.
FEATHERY STITCH.

OUR engraving shows a remarkably pretty covering for the head, suitable for wearing to the opera or theatre. It is made of pink Shetland wool, of which ¼ lb. is required, and, though light, it is so warm as to be a complete protection against wind and draught. Procure 1½ yards of 1½ inch wide ribbon to match the wool, and a No. 10 and No. 8 bone crochet needle. For the foundation, use No. 10 crochet needle, and begin with 48 chain, turn. **1st row**—1 treble in the sixth chain from the needle, 2 more treble in the same place, * miss two stitches of the foundation, 3 treble in the next, and repeat from * to the end. **2nd row**—Turn with 4 chain, and work 3 treble in each space between the treble groups of last row, making 15 groups of 3 treble in the row. Repeat the second row till 32 rows are done, or a length of thirteen or fourteen inches. At the beginning of the **33rd row**, miss the first space, and work along, doing 14 groups in the row. At the beginning of the **34th row** miss the first space, and work 13 groups in the row. Miss a space also at the beginning of the **35th row**, and work 12 groups in the row. Continue now without further decreasing, doing 12 groups in each row for 71 rows, making in all 106 rows from the commencement, or about 1¼ yards in length, and fasten off. Now make a piece to go cornerways on the top of the head, commencing

Gentleman's Glove.

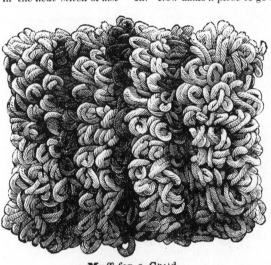

Muff for a Child

Opera Hood or Fascinator. Feathery Stitch.

Boa for a Child.

ound, and also under the wool that lies over the first finger, draw the wool through and finish as a double-crochet stitch. **3rd round**—Plain double crochet. **4th round**—Same as the second round. **5th round**—Plain double crochet. **6th round**—Join on grey wool, and work 1 double crochet stitch and 1 looped stitch alternately. Repeat from the first round twice. Then work from the first round to the fifth round, and fasten off. Make up the muff by placing inside a layer of wadding and a lining of pale blue silk, in which at each opening run an elastic to draw the lining in to shape. For the **Boa**—Begin with white wool with 4 chain; join round. Do 5 rounds with white wool the same as the first five rounds of the muff, but in the course of these rounds increase to 14 stitches, or more if a thick muffler is desired. **6th round**—Join on grey wool, and work 1 double crochet stitch and 1 looped stitch alternately. Work as directed for the muff from the first to the sixth rounds. Then work for the centre of the boa a length of 22 inches, all with white wool. **Next round**—Same as the sixth round. Work 5 rounds with white wool, 1 round with grey wool. Then 5 rounds with white wool, in the course of which decrease to 4 stitches in the round, and fasten off. Make two tassels with grey and white wool mixed, and put a tassel at each end of the boa.

---

with 48 chain, and work as first row and second row, continuing till a perfect square is attained. For the **Feathers**—Use No. 8 crochet needle, and work *loosely* over the treble foundation of the square head-piece; begin with 1 double crochet in the first space of commencing chain, 15 chain, 1 double crochet in the next space of commencing chain, and continue to the end of the row; then 15 chain, 1 double crochet in the chain that turned, 15 chain, 1 double crochet on the centre treble stitch of the first group of the first row, 15 chain, 1 double crochet on the centre treble stitch of the next group of the first row, and so on to the end of the row, and the same along each row of the foundation treble successively of the square head-piece. Then work the same feather trimming upon the scarf like piece of crochet, excepting just where the decreasings occur, as here the square is to be placed cornerways; if you arrange the square in position, diamond fashion, you will see how much space it fills up, and can judge how many treble groups to leave flat for it. When all the foundation is feathered, the square head-piece is laid in position, and retained there by a ribbon run through it, and through the top of the scarf, running from corner to corner, and tied in a bow in front.

This fascinator is also effective if the foundation is worked with Andalusian wool, and the feathers with the new ostrich wool, sold by the Providence Mills Spinning Company, Bradford, Yorks.

SEMI-CIRCULAR SHAWL.
WORKED IN SHELL STITCH.

OUR illustration shows only a section of the shawl, that the pattern may be more perceivable. A very handsome shawl may be made by using the pale blue crystal wool manufactured by the Providence Mills Spinning Co., Bradford, which is a mixture of silk and wool peculiarly twisted, light in texture, and of glossy appearance; or Shetland wool can be employed if desired. Use a No. 9 bone crochet needle. Commence with 4 chain, join round in a circle. **1st row**—Do 4 chain, miss the stitch nearest the needle, and raise a stitch as if doing tricot (loosely) in each of 3 chain stitches, raise 1 stitch in the join, and 1 stitch in the circle, now 6 stitches are on the needle, wool over the needle and draw through all, * do 3 chain, miss the stitch nearest the needle, and raise 1 stitch in each of 2 chain stitches, 1 stitch in the little hole where all six threads are drawn together, 1 stitch in the back thread of the shell just made, and 1 stitch in the circle, now 6 stitches on the needle, wool over the needle and draw through all, and repeat from * till 8 shell stitches are worked into the commencing circle, do 1 chain to hold in the last shell securely. **2nd row**—2 chain to turn the work, 1 single crochet in the top of the shell stitch point, * 2 chain, 1 single crochet in the top of the next shell stitch point, and repeat from * six times. **3rd row**—Turn the work, do 5 chain, miss the stitch nearest

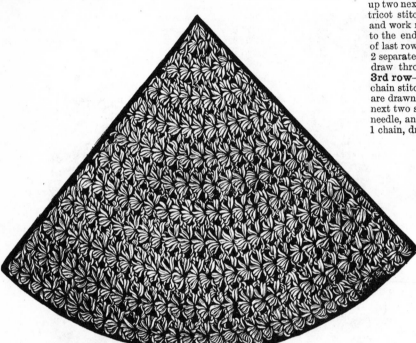

Semi-Circular Shawl, Worked in Shell Stitch.

the needle, and raise 1 stitch in each of 4 chain stitches, raise 1 on the single crochet, wool over the needle and draw through 6 stitches on the needle,* do 3 chain, miss the stitch nearest the needle, and raise 1 stitch in each of 2 chain stitches, 1 stitch in the little hole where all six threads are drawn together, 1 stitch in the back of the shell just made, and 1 stitch under the loop of two chain, wool over the needle and draw through 6 stitches on the needle, and repeat from *, doing 2 shell stitches under each loop of 2 chain, except the end loop where do only 1 shell; 16 shells in the row; and end with 1 chain to hold the shell securely. **4th row**—2 chain and turn the work, 1 single crochet in the top of the shell stitch point, * 2 chain, 1 single crochet in the top of the next shell stitch point, and repeat from * fourteen times. **5th row**—Work same as the third row, but it will be sufficient to increase in every alternate pattern, therefore in repeating from * to * work 2 shells under the first loop of two chain, 1 shell under the next, and so on, making 25 shells in the row. **6th row**—Same as the fourth row. The remainder of the shawl is worked in pattern as the last two rows, increasing always at intervals in the shell pattern row sufficiently to preserve the semi-circular shape. When the required depth is attained strengthen along the straight side of the work with a row of double crochet, and for a fringe round the shawl knot four or five strands of wool into every loop of two chain.

BABY'S BOOTS.
WORKED IN TRICOT.

PROCURE 1¼ ozs. of single Berlin wool of any colour preferred; our model is worked throughout with white wool, but the shoe may be coloured and the sock white if so desired. A No. 8 and No. 9 bone tricot needle. Using No. 9 needle, begin for the sole, at the heel end, with 5 chain; pick up 4 stitches, and draw back as in ordinary tricot. **2nd row**—Tricot 1, increase 1, tricot 1, increase 1, tricot 2, now 7 stitches on the needle, and draw back. **3rd row**—Tricot 1, increase 1, tricot 3, increase 1, tricot 2, now 9 stitches on the needle and draw back. **4th row**—Pick up 8 tricot stitches, and draw back. **5th row**—Pick up 8 tricot stitches, and in working back decrease by drawing through the 2 first stitches and the 2 last stitches together. **6th row**—Pick

up 6 tricot stitches, and again decrease in drawing back. Work 2 rows of plain tricot, 5 stitches on the needle. **9th row**—Increase like the second row. **10th row**—Same as the third row. Work 6 rows of tricot on 9 stitches in the row. **17th row**—Decrease as in the fifth row. **18th row**—Same as the 6th row. **19th row**—Tricot 4 stitches, and draw back; this brings you to the toe. **20th row**—Tricot 1, increase 1, tricot 1, increase 1, tricot 2, now 7 stitches on the needle, and draw back. **21st row**—Tricot 1, increase 1, do this 4 times, tricot 2, now 11 stitches on, and draw back. **22nd row**—Tricot 4, increase 1, tricot 1, increase 1, tricot 5, now 13 stitches on, and draw back. **23rd row**—Tricot 5, increase 1, tricot 1, increase 1, tricot 6, now 15 stitches on, and draw back. Continue thus, and increase 1 stitch each side the centre stitch in every row, till in the twenty-ninth row you have 29 stitches on the needle, and draw back. **Next row**—For the **Side of the Shoe**—Pick up 9 tricot stitches, and draw back, and work forwards and backwards till 10 little rows are worked, when fasten off. Miss the nine centre stitches of the instep, and work upon the last ten stitches for the other side of the shoe, doing 10 rows. For the **Sock**—Turn the work, do 3 chain to stand for a treble, and work 1 treble on each of 10 consecutive rows of tricot stitches, 1 double crochet taking up two instep stitches together, 1 double crochet taking up two next instep stitches together, 1 double crochet on the centre stitch, 1 double crochet taking up two instep stitches together, 1 double crochet taking up two next instep stitches together, and 1 treble on each of 11 consecutive tricot stitches to the point of the heel. **2nd row**—Take No. 8 tricot needle and work rather loosely,—turn the work with 1 chain, pick up 26 tricot stitches to the end of the row, inserting the hook to take up two threads of every stitch of last row; have 27 stitches on the needle, and work back thus,—draw through 2 separate stitches, * do 1 chain, draw through 3 stitches together, do 1 chain, draw through 2 stitches separate, and repeat from * to the end of the row. **3rd row**—Pick up 1 tricot stitch on stitch of previous row, * 1 tricot in the chain stitch, 1 tricot in the little thread at the back of the three stitches that are drawn together, 1 tricot in the next chain stitch, 1 tricot on each of the next two stitches, and repeat from * to the end of the row, 27 stitches on the needle, and to work back, draw through 2, * do 1 chain, draw through 3 together, 1 chain, draw through 2 separately, and repeat from *. **4th row**—Same as

Baby's Boot, Worked in Tricot.

the third row. **5th row**—Increase 1 tricot stitch at the beginning and at the end of the row, otherwise work the same pattern. Do 2 more rows the same as the third row, but with 1 more tricot stitch at the beginning and end. **8th row**—Increase again at the beginning and at the end, working the same pattern. Do 2 rows in pattern with extra plain stitch at the beginning and end. **11th row**—Insert the hook in the second stitch of last row, draw the wool through, and do 3 chain stitches, draw the wool through the last of the chain and through the other stitch on the needle, 1 double crochet on the next stitch, 1 picot as above on the next, 1 double crochet on the next, * a picot in the small hole over the three stitches that are drawn together, miss the next chain, 1 double crochet on the first of the two straight stitches, a picot on the second of the two straight stitches, 1 double crochet on the next stitch, and repeat from * to the end of the row, and join in a round to the beginning. **12th row**—1 double crochet, 3 chain, 1 treble, 1 double crochet, all worked on each double crochet stitch of last row, taking up two front threads. Fasten off at the end of the round. Sew up the leg and the foot of the boot. Run a narrow ribbon through the treble stitches round the ankle, and tie in a small bow in front. Work the other boot in the same manner.

CROCHET SHAWL—CANE PATTERN.

THIS is a pretty light pattern for a Shetland shawl; it also looks well worked with Pompadour wool, with spray wool, or floss wool manufactured by the Providence Mills Spinning Co., Bradford. The quantity of wool required will, of course, depend upon the size the shawl is intended to be; ½ lb. of Shetland wool or 8 or 9 balls of fancy wool will make a good-sized shawl. With a No. 10 bone crochet needle work a chain sufficient for the length of the shawl. 1st row—Wool over the needle and insert the hook in the fourth chain from the needle, and draw the wool through, insert the hook in the next chain stitch, and draw the wool through, again insert the hook in the next chain stitch, and draw the wool through, now 5 stitches on the needle, wool over the needle and draw through 4 stitches, wool over the needle and draw through 2 stitches, insert the hook through the last 3 threads of the 4 drawn together stitches and draw the wool through, wool over the needle and draw through 2 stitches on the needle, * 1 chain, wool over the needle and insert the hook in the next chain stitch and draw the wool through, insert the hook in the next chain stitch, and draw wool through, again insert the hook in the next chain stitch, and draw the wool through, now 5 stitches on the needle, wool over the needle and draw through 4 stitches, wool over the needle and draw through 2 stitches, insert the hook through the last 3 threads of the 4 drawn together stitches and draw the wool through, wool over the needle and draw through two stitches on the needle, and repeat from * to the end of the row; break off the wool at the end of this and every row, and recommence on the right-hand side. 2nd row—Work 1 treble on the first part of the cane stitch at the beginning of last row, 1 chain. * wool over the needle and insert the hook to take up 2 threads of the second part of the cane stitch and draw the wool through, insert the hook in the chain stitch and draw the wool through, insert the hook in the next stitch and draw the wool through, wool over the needle and draw through 4 stitches on the needle, wool over the

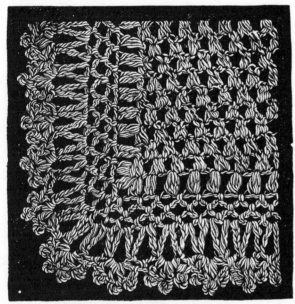

Shawl, Worked in Cane Pattern.

needle and draw through 2 stitches on the needle, insert the hook through the 3 last threads of the 4 drawn together stitches and draw the wool through, wool over the needle and draw through 2 stitches on the needle, 1 chain, and repeat from *, and do 1 treble on the last stitch at the end of the row, and fasten off. 3rd row—Knot a stitch on the needle, and putting the wool over the needle commence upon the treble stitch at the beginning of last row, and work in cane stitch to the end of the row 4th row—Same as the second row. 5th row—Same as the third row, and continue till you have a perfect square. For the Border round the shawl: 1st round—Knot a stitch upon the needle, wool over the needle, and insert the hook in the space of one of the rows along the side of the shawl and draw the wool through, wool over the needle and draw through 2 stitches on the needle, wool over the needle and insert the hook again in the same place and draw the wool through, wool over the needle and draw through 2 stitches on the needle, wool over the needle and draw through 3 stitches on the needle, 1 chain, and repeat the same bunch of stitches in the space at the end of every row along the two sides of the shawl, and in each pattern along the bottom and top. 2nd round—1 double crochet under one chain stitch of last round, * 3 chain, 1 double crochet under next chain stitch, and repeat from *; increase one loop in turning the corners. 3rd round—1 double crochet under loop of three chain, 3 chain, and repeat; no increase at the corners. 4th round—Same as last round, but increase two loops at the corners; fasten off at the end of this round, joining to the commencement. 5th round—Recommence with a stitch knotted on the needle, wool twice round the needle and insert the hook under a loop of three chain and draw the wool through *, wool over the needle and draw through 2 stitches on the needle, wool over the needle and draw again through 2 stitches on the needle, wool twice round the needle and insert the hook under the next loop of three chain and draw the wool through, wool over the needle and draw through 2 stitches on the needle, wool over the needle and draw again through 2 stitches on the needle, wool over the needle and draw through 3 stitches on the needle, 3 chain, wool twice round the needle and insert the hook under the same loop as last stitch is worked into and draw the wool through, and repeat from *; and at the end of the round join to the beginning after doing 3 chain. 6th round—1 double crochet under a loop of three chain, 1 treble under the next loop, 4 chain, 1 double crochet in the top of the treble stitch just done, another treble in the same loop as last treble, and make a picot and a treble twice more in the same place repeat, and make an extra picot and a treble in the corner loop.

CROCHET JERSEY JACKET.

THE jersey shown in our illustration is a comfortable garment for a child of two or three years. It is made with best Scotch fingering wool and a bone crochet needle No. 11. If Alloa wool be used and a No. 10 crochet needle the jersey will be large enough for an older child. Commence with 56 chain; turn, and work for the 1st row—55 plain double crochet. 2nd row—Turn with 1 chain, do 10 double crochet inserting the hook to take up both top threads of previous row, and 45 double crochet, taking up the one back thread as in Russian crochet. 3rd row—Turn with 1 chain, do 45 double crochet, taking up one back thread of the stitches of last row, and 10 double crochet taking up the two top threads. Repeat these two rows till 50 rows are done, when fasten off; this forms half the jersey, and the 10 close double stitches are the bottom edge. Work another piece the same. Join up the sides, leaving space for armholes, and join together seven ridges on the top on each side for the shoulders, leaving eleven ridges open in the centre for the neck; round this open part, work 5 rounds of plain double crochet for a neck-band, then another round, 1 double crochet on double crochet of last round, miss two, 5 treble on the next, miss two, and repeat; fasten off. For the Sleeves—Make 36 chain, and work in ribbed double crochet forwards and backwards for 40 rows. Next row—Scallop for the wrist—1 double crochet on double crochet of last row, miss two, 5 treble on the next, miss two, and repeat; fasten off. For a Gusset—Do 15 chain, and work 12 rows of ridged double crochet. Sew up the sleeve, putting the gusset in at the top. Work the other sleeve in the same manner. Sew the sleeves in the armholes. Round the bottom of the jersey work a scalloped edge the same as that already worked round the wrist. Make a length of crochet chain to run in and out through the fourth round of the neck-band to tie in to the size of the child's neck. The jersey is slipped on and off over the head.

MONEY BAG.

REQUIRED, a 1 oz. ball of fine size Imperial knitting silk, a fine steel crochet needle, a pair of gilt bars with chain and ring, and a fancy gilt tassel. Begin for the bottom of the bag with 5 chain, and join round. 1st round—Work 12 double crochet in the circle. 2nd round—Work 2 double crochet on the first double crochet stitch of last round, 1 double crochet on the next, and repeat, always inserting the hook to take up the one top thread of the stitches of last round. 3rd round—Work 2 double crochet on the first double crochet stitch of last round, 1 double crochet on each of the two next stitches,

Crochet Jersey Jacket.

and repeat. 4th round—Increase in every fourth stitch of last round. 5th round—Increase in every fifth stitch. 6th round—Increase in every sixth stitch. 7th round—Increase in every seventh stitch. 8th round—Increase in every eighth stitch. 9th round—Increase in every ninth stitch. 10th round—Increase in every tenth stitch. 11th round—Increase in every eleventh stitch. 12th round—Increase in every twelfth stitch. Work 14 rounds without any further increase. Work 6 rounds, making three decreases at equal distances in each round. On the completion of these rounds, do 2 chain to stand for a treble stitch, and work treble upon the double crochet stitches of last round until you have done exactly halfway round the purse; turn with 3 chain, and work treble over the treble stitches. Work 5 more rows of treble forwards and backwards; then take one of the gilt bars, and holding it firmly in the left hand, crochet a double crochet row, bringing the silk over the bar (not too tightly) in every stitch; fasten off Work the opposite half of the top of the purse in the same manner, and attach to it the other gilt bar. Slip the ring in proper position. Sew the tassel to the bottom of the purse.

LADY'S PETTICOAT IN ZEPHYR STITCH.

REQUIRED, ¼ lb. of blue and ¾ lb. of white single Berlin wool, or Berlin fingering, and a No. 10 bone crochet needle. Begin with blue wool for the top of the petticoat, with 141 chain. **1st row**—Miss the chain stitch nearest the needle, and do 1 double crochet in each of the 2 next stitches, * 3 double crochet in the next, 1 double crochet in each of 4 following stitches, and repeat from *, and the row will end with 2 double crochet. **2nd row**—Turn the work, and insert the hook in the back thread, and do 3 consecutive double crochet, * 3 double crochet in the next (which is the middle stitch of the three double crochet of last row), 6 consecutive double crochet, and repeat from *, and the row will end with 3 double crochet. **3rd row**—Turn, and insert the hook in the back thread of the second stitch of last row, * do 3 consecutive double crochet, 3 double crochet in the next (the middle stitch) 3 consecutive double crochet, miss two stitches, and repeat from * to the end of the row; break off the blue wool. **4th row**—Turn the work, take the white wool, and inserting the hook in the back thread of the first stitch draw up a loop with white, draw up a loop likewise in the 3 following stitches, now 4 on the needle, wool over the needle and draw through all, do 1 chain to bind the loops close, * do 3 chain, 1 single crochet in the back thread of the middle stitch of three double crochet of last row, 3 chain, raise a loop loosely in 8 consecutive stitches, wool over the needle and draw through all the stitches on the needle, 1 chain to bind the loops close, and repeat from * to the end of the row, where finish with half a pattern as you began : break off the wool. **5th row**—With white

finishing it as it began ; the looser you can draw up the loops the better the work will look, break off the wool at the end of the row. **10th row**—With white wool, beginning again on the right-hand side—Do 1 single crochet on the single crochet stitch of preceding row, and 9 treble in the stitch that binds together the bunch of loops, and repeat ; and fasten off white wool at the end of the row. **11th row**—With blue wool, commencing on the side where just fastened off, * 1 double crochet in the back thread of each of 4 treble stitches, 3 double crochet in the next, 1 double crochet in each of 4 next treble stitches, miss the single crochet, and repeat from * to the end of the row. **12th row**—Turn, insert the hook in the back thread of the second double crochet of preceding row, and do * 4 consecutive double crochet, 3 double crochet in the next (the middle stitch), 4 consecutive double crochet, miss two stitches and repeat from *. **13th row**—Turn, and work again as last row, and fasten off the blue wool. **14th row**—Take white wool, and work the same as the fourth row, but raise 5 loops at the beginning and raise 10 loops instead of only eight loops. **15th row**—Same as the 5th row. Work the next three rows in ridges with blue wool as detailed above. **19th row**—Take white wool and work the same as the ninth row. **20th row**—Same as the tenth row. Work the next 3 rows in ridges with blue wool as above. The remainder of the petticoat is a continuation of the last ten rows. **24th row**—Half zephyrs to begin and finish. **25th row**—Increase by working 6 treble at the beginning and end and 11 treble in every zephyr. Work 3 ridged rows with the necessary increase of 1 double crochet on each side of each scallop. **29th row**—Pick up 12 loops in each zephyr, and do 4 chain instead of three. **30th row**—Work 11

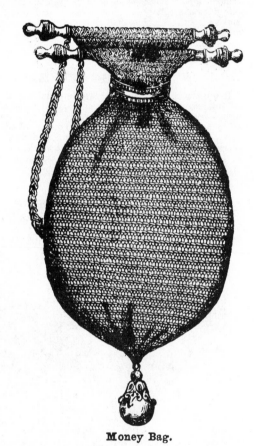

Money Bag.

Lady's Petticoat, Wor

wool, beginning again on the right-hand side, do 5 treble in the stitch that binds together the small bunch of loops, * 1 single crochet on single crochet stitch of last row, 9 treble in the stitch that binds together the bunch of loops, and repeat from * ; the row will end with 5 treble stitches as it began, break off the wool. **6th row**—With blue wool—Commencing on the side where just broken off, 1 double crochet in the back thread of each of 5 treble stitches of last row, miss the single crochet, * and do 4 consecutive double crochet, 3 double crochet in the next (the fifth stitch of the treble), 4 consecutive double crochet, miss the single stitch, and repeat from * ; the row will end with 5 double crochet. **7th row**—Turn, insert the hook in the back thread of the first stitch of last row, do 5 consecutive double crochet, miss one stitch, * 4 consecutive double crochet, 3 double crochet in the next (the middle stitch of three double crochet of last row), 4 consecutive double crochet, miss two stitches, and repeat from *, and at the end of the row miss only one stitch, and do 5 double crochet. **8th row**—Turn, and work again as last row, fasten off the blue wool. **9th row**—Turn the work, take the white wool, and beginning with a single crochet in the back thread of the first stitch of last row, do 3 chain, draw up a loop loosely in each of 9 following stitches, wool over the needle and draw through all the stitches on the needle. 1 chain to bind the loops close, 3 chain, 1 single crochet in the back thread of the middle stitch of three double crochet of last row, * 3 chain, raise a loop loosely in 10 consecutive stitches, wool over the needle and draw through all the stitches on the needle, 1 chain to bind the loops close, 3 chain, 1 single crochet in the back thread of the middle stitch, and repeat from * to the end of the row,

treble in every zephyr. Work 3 ridged rows. Repeat the last 10 rows. **44th row**—Half zephyrs to begin and finish. **45th row**—Increase by working 7 treble at the beginning and 13 treble in every zephyr. Work 3 ridged rows with increase of 1 double crochet on each side of every scallop. **49th row**—Pick up 14 loops on every zephyr. **50th row**—Work 13 treble in every zephyr. Work 3 ridged rows. **54th row**—Same as the forty-fourth row. **55th row**—Same as the forty-fifth row. Work 2 ridged rows, and then for the third ridged row thicken the stitches by passing the wool round the needle as if for a treble but draw the wool through 3 on the needle as double crochet. For the **Flounce**—Work with white wool, 3 rows of the ridged double crochet, as last row, with the wool over the needle before drawing through 3 stitches on the needle. Work 3 rows with blue wool in the same manner. Work the next row similarly, with blue wool, but here miss six stitches where you formerly missed two, this is to bring the scallops into pleats. Work another row with blue wool, this time missing two stitches as ordinarily. This completes the flounce. Sew up the skirt, leaving room at the top for a placket hole ; stitch the pleats down here and there to make them fall nice and even. For the **Waistband**—Work with blue wool 4 or 5 rows of plain double crochet along the top of the petticoat, decreasing a few stitches to bring the band in to the size of the waist. **Next row**—Form holes in which to run a ribbon to tie round the waist, 2 treble, 2 chain, and repeat. Work 4 more rows of plain double crochet, and carry on the last row to strengthen down the sides of the placket hole. This completes the petticoat.

SIMPLE V-SHAPED PELERINE.

THIS Pelerine is useful for extra warmth in the house or to wear out of doors under a jacket; it is simply made, being worked entirely in double crochet in rows forwards and backwards. Procure 5 ozs. of partridge-coloured single Berlin wool, and 1 oz. of blue wool for the border, 8 plain bone buttons, 1 larger button for the waistband, and a No. 11 bone crochet needle. Begin for the Front of the Pelerine with partridge wool, with 11 chain. **1st row—** Miss the two chain stitches nearest the needle and work 9 consecutive double crochet. **2nd row—** 1 chain to turn, miss the first stitch, and taking up both threads (the top thread and back thread) of previous row, work 9 double crochet; all the following rows are worked in the same manner, turning with 1 chain and missing the first stitch. **3rd row—** 8 consecutive double crochet, 2 double crochet to increase in the last stitch. **4th row—** Plain, 10 stitches. **5th row—** 9 consecutive double crochet, 2 double crochet to increase in the last stitch. Work 3 plain rows of 11 stitches. 9th row—10 stitches, 2 stitches in the last. **10th row—** Plain, 12 stitches. **11th row—** 11 stitches, 2 stitches in the last. Work 3 plain rows of 13 stitches. Continue increasing on the same side of the work proportionally to the last six rows, till in working the 78th, 79th, and 80th rows, you do 35 stitches in each row. **81st row—** Beginning on the straight side of the work to round for the neck—1 chain to turn, miss two stitches instead of missing one stitch, work 33 double crochet, and 2 double crochet in the last stitch. **82nd row—** Plain, 35 stitches. **83rd row—** Decrease again at the neck and

respond with the shaping of the front shoulder already done. Work the other shoulder in the same manner. Sew the shoulder pieces together. Take the blue wool, and work 3 rows of plain double crochet all round the Pelerine; in the second row of this make eight buttonholes as you go along the right-hand side of the front, by doing 3 chain and missing three stitches. For the **Waistband—** With partridge wool make 12 chain, miss the two chain stitches nearest the needle and work 10 double crochet. When 4 rows of 10 double crochet are worked, divide in the middle to form a buttonhole, do 4 rows of 5 stitches, then do the other 5 stitches for 4 rows, and finally working all across continue 10 double crochet forwards and backwards for the length required for the waistband. Edge all round the waistband with 3 rounds of double crochet worked with blue wool. Put the largest button upon the waistband, and sew the eight bone buttons upon the left-hand front of the Pelerine.

BABY'S BOOT IN FANCY TRICOT.

PROCURE 1½ ozs. of white Victoria yarn and a No. 7 bone tricot needle. Make for the top of the leg 36 chain; then with the wool in front of the needle insert the hook in the first chain stitch, pass the wool under the needle (laying the thumb on it an instant to keep it in place) then round and draw it through the stitch on the needle; pick up each succeeding chain stitch in the same way, and draw back as in ordinary tricot. You will see this method of proceeding brings a line of raised stitches upon the front of the work. The

Zephyr Stitch

Single V-shaped Pelerine.

increase at the end. **84th row—** Plain, 34 stitches, omit the last stitch. **85th row—** Decrease at the neck, do 32 double crochet, omit the last stitch. **86th row—** Plain, 31 stitches, omit the last stitch. **87th row—** Decrease at the neck, do 29 stitches, omit the last stitch. Decrease at the beginning of each row and omit working the last stitch for eight rows. **96th row—** Decrease, work to the end. **97th row—** Decrease at the neck, do 10 double crochet, omit the last stitch. **98th row—** Decrease, do 9 double crochet. **99th row—** Decrease at the neck, do 7 double crochet, omit the last stitch. **100th row—** Decrease, do 6 double crochet. **101st row—** Decrease at the neck, do 4 double crochet, omit the last stitch. **102nd row—** Decrease, do 3 double crochet. **103rd row—** No decrease, do 2 double crochet. **104th row—** 1 double crochet, and fasten off. Work the other front in the same manner; the pattern is alike on both sides, so the work may be turned to correspond. For the **Back of the Pelerine—** Make 18 chain, miss the two stitches nearest the needle, and work 16 double crochet. **2nd row—** 1 chain to turn, miss the first stitch, and taking up both threads of previous row, work 16 double crochet. **3rd row—** Increase at each end. **4th row—** Plain. **5th row—** Increase at each end. **6th row—** Plain. **7th row—** Increase at each end. Repeat last two rows twice. Work 3 plain rows. **15th row—** Increase at each end. **16th row—** Plain. **17th row—** Increase at each end. Work 3 plain rows. Work proportionably to the last six rows till in working the 83rd, 84th, and 85th rows, you do 74 stitches in each row. **86th row—** Decrease 1 stitch at each end. Work 7 more rows the same. **93rd row—** Decrease, do 20 stitches, and turn and work for the shoulder, shaping to cor-

boot is worked throughout in the same manner, picking up the tricot stitches of the preceding row. Work another row of 36 stitches, * then decrease 1 stitch at each end of the next row, then 1 row without decrease, and repeat from * till you have 30 stitches in a row. Work 12 rows. Now go upon the middle 12 stitches and work 12 rows for the instep. This done, pick up 54 stitches all round the foot, and draw back. **2nd row** of the **Foot—** Pick up 21 stitches, pick up 2 stitches together, pick up 8 stitches, pick up 2 stitches together, pick up 21 stitches, and draw back. **3rd row—** Plain. **4th row—** Decrease at the beginning, and at the end of the row, and in the middle as before. Repeat the last two rows. Sew the edges of the work together under the sole and up the leg. For the **Border** round the **Top of the Leg—** Take a rather fine bone crochet needle, and for the **1st round—** Work 3 treble, 2 chain, and 3 treble, all into one stitch of the commencing chain, miss two stitches, 1 double crochet in the next, miss two stitches, and repeat, and join evenly at the end of the round. **2nd round—** 3 treble, 2 chain, 3 treble, all under the two chain of last round, 1 double crochet on the double crochet, and repeat. **3rd round—** The same as the second round. **4th round—** This is worked oppositely to the first round, into the commencing chain, so that the little scallops fall downwards over the tricot. Work the other boot in the same way.

CROCHET MEDALLION.

USE Evans' crochet cotton No. 16, and a fine steel crochet needle. Begin with 8 chain, join round. Work 24 double crochet in the circle, and join round. **2nd round**—6 chain, 1 treble on the second double crochet stitch, * 3 chain, 1 treble on the second double crochet stitch, repeat from *, and at the end 3 chain, and join into the third chain with which the round began; fasten off. **3rd round**—Recommence with 1 double crochet in centre stitch of three chain, 3 chain, and repeat. **4th round**—1 treble on every stitch, 48 treble in the round, join. **5th round**—4 chain, 1 treble on the second treble stitch, * 2 chain, cotton over the needle and insert the hook in the same stitch as the treble is worked into and draw the cotton through, cotton over the needle and draw through 2 loops on the needle, cotton over the needle and insert the hook in the second treble stitch of last round and draw the cotton through, cotton over the needle and draw through 2 stitches on the needle, cotton over the needle and draw through 3 stitches on the needle, repeat from *, and join and fasten off at the end of the round. **6th round**—Recommence thus, do 1 treble, 1 chain, 1 treble, 1 chain, 1 treble, all in one stitch of previous round, miss three, and repeat; the third time of working same, miss four stitches instead of three, that you may bring 18 groups exactly into the round, join at end. **7th round**—3 chain to stand for a treble, work 1 treble on each stitch of last round, and increase a stitch on every third group to bring 96 treble in the round, join, and fasten off. **8th round**—Recommence, * work 3 consecutive treble, catch the last treble stitch back into the first with a single crochet, 7 chain, 3 consecutive treble caught back in the same way, 5 chain, and repeat from *, join at the end of the round and fasten off. **9th round**—1 double crochet in the centre stitch of the loop of seven chain, 2 chain, 1 treble

round. **4th round**—Again increase in every third stitch, 14 picots and 14 double crochet to make the round. **5th round**—Increase the same, and make 18 picots and 18 double crochet in the round. **6th round**—Work without any increase, doing a picot on the double crochet stitch of last round and a double crochet on the picot stitch. And continue thus till you have crocheted sufficient to draw over the rattle and reach to the base of the handle, when fasten off, and run a thread of strong cotton through the top of the stitches, and draw up, and tie securely round the handle. The handle is covered by just simply winding wool round and round it so thickly as to cover the foundation.

CHILD'S FIRST DRAWERS.

THESE drawers are most comfortable for a child's everyday wear in winter, or they may be drawn on over the ordinary calico drawers at any time when extra warmth is required. Procure 4 ozs. of soft white eider wool or merino wool of Peacock quality and a finest bone crochet needle. Commence for the bottom of the right leg with 84 chain; turn, work 1 double crochet in the fourth chain from the needle, * 1 chain, miss one, 1 double crochet in the next, and repeat from *, making 41 double crochet in the row. **2nd row**—3 chain to turn, 1 double crochet under the first chain stitch of last row, * 1 chain, 1 double crochet under the next chain stitch of last row, and repeat from * making 41 double crochet in the row. **3rd row**—Work the same as the second row, and increase at the end of the row by making an additional 1 chain 1 double crochet in the last space. **4th row**—Same as the third row. Continue in this manner increasing at the end of every row till you have done 36 rows

Baby's Boot in Fancy
Tricot.

Crochet Medallion.

Baby's Rattle.

in the second stitch of the loop of five chain, 2 chain and 1 treble three times in the next stitch, 2 chain, 1 treble in the third stitch of the same loop, 2 chain, and repeat to the end of the round, where join. **10th round**—1 double crochet on the double crochet of last round, 4 chain, 1 double crochet in the loop after the first treble stitch, 4 chain, 1 double crochet in next loop, 4 chain, 1 double crochet in next loop, 4 chain, 1 double crochet in next loop, 4 chain, and repeat; join at end, and fasten off.

BABY'S CROCHET RATTLE.

THE foundation of this rattle can be purchased at a toy shop for about twopence, it is very light, being made of wicker plaited like a basket, and of course hollow in the centre, where two small bells are placed to rattle; when covered with crochet it is so soft baby cannot hurt himself with it. Procure ¾ oz. of pink or rose-coloured wool and a No. 8 bone crochet needle. Begin with 4 chain, which join round in a circle. **1st round**—Insert the hook in the first stitch of the foundation chain and draw the wool through, do 3 chain, wool over the needle and draw through both stitches on the needle, do 1 double crochet in the same stitch, * insert the hook in the next stitch and draw the wool through, do 3 chain, wool over the needle and draw through both stitches on the needle, do 1 double crochet in the same stitch, repeat from *, twice more; you thus have 4 picots of chain stitch and 4 double crochet stitches in the round. **2nd round**—Work in the same manner, a picot and a double crochet on every stitch, and there will be 8 picots and 8 double crochet stitches in the round. **3rd round**—Do a picot on the first stitch of last round, and a double crochet on the next, then a picot and a double crochet both on the next, so you increase in every third stitch, and make 10 picots and 10 double crochet stitches in the

and get 75 double crochet in the row. Or you can work more rows still increasing to make larger size drawers. Break off the wool. Commence again with 84 chain for the left leg, and work similarly. When you have completed the thirty-sixth row, turn, and do 1 double crochet in the first space, no chain as you are now to begin to decrease for the back (the *right side* of the work is towards you as this row *begins* at the back of the drawers), 1 chain, 1 double crochet in the next space, and continue in pattern, and when you have done to the end of the row take the right leg and from the place you broke off the wool crochet in the same pattern along it. For the **2nd row** of the **Body** —Turn, 1 double crochet in the first space (no chain to turn this side either as you again decrease at the back), 1 chain, 1 double crochet in the next space, and continue all along. **3rd row**—1 double crochet in the first space, 1 chain, 1 double crochet in the next space, and continue pattern to the end of the left leg where decrease and decrease again at the beginning of the right leg, and continue pattern to the end of the row. **4th row**—Same as the second row. **5th row**—Same as the third row. **6th row**—Same as the second row. And continue these two rows till 14 rows are done, when you will want to begin the open slits at the sides of the drawers. **Next row**— 1 double crochet in the first space, 1 chain, 1 double crochet in the next space, and proceed to the centre of the left leg, where turn with 3 chain, and work back; do 14 more short rows in the same way. Then work 17 double crochet only, and turn back; 14 double crochet, and turn back; 11 double crochet, and turn back; 8 double crochet, and turn back; break off the wool. Recommence where you divided for the slit at the side, and work along the front of the drawers as far as the place for the slit on the opposite side, decreasing in the exact front (on each leg) as previously; turn with three chain, and work back; turn with 3 chain and work along again, decreasing in the centre of the front; turn and work back and proceed till 16 rows are accomplished, when break off the wool. Begin again where you divided for the second slit, and work along to the end of the row, turn, and shape this side of the back to correspond with the side already done. Sew up the legs of the drawers, sew up the back. The **Band** at the top of the drawers is worked from slit to slit, doing 8 rows of plain double crochet, and making (in the fourth row) a buttonhole at each side of the front, and put a button on each side of the back. Round the **Bottom** of the **Legs** work this Edging—**1st round**—1 double crochet in every stitch of the foundation chain, and join round. **2nd round**—3 chain to begin, wool over the needle and insert the hook in the first stitch of last round, and draw the wool through, wool over the needle, miss the next stitch of last round insert the hook in the next stitch and draw the wool through, wool over the needle and draw through four stitches on the needle, wool over the needle and draw through two stitches on the needle, 3 chain, 1 double crochet in the hole at the top of the stitches you have just drawn together, * wool over the needle, insert the hook in the same place in last row where a stitch is already worked into, and draw the wool through, wool over the needle, miss the next stitch of last row, insert the hook in the next stitch and draw the wool through, wool over the needle and draw through four stitches on the needle, wool over the

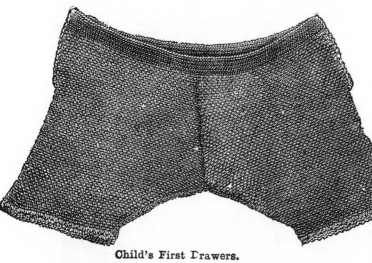

Child's First Drawers.

needle and draw through two stitches on the needle, 3 chain, 1 double crochet in the hole above the stitches you have just drawn together, and repeat from * to the end of the round, where join to the commencement and fasten off.

ECRU AND TINSEL LACE.

REQUIRED, a piece of fancy braid, a ball of ecru cotton, one of gold tinsel thread, and a fine steel crochet needle. First of all, secure the braid in circles overlapping each other in the manner shown in the illustration, bringing eight clumps of braid in the centre of every circle. Then take the tinsel thread and fill up the spaces in the circles, thus:—**1st round**—Hold the right side of the braid towards you, and work 3 half long treble stitches (cotton twice round the needle), inserting the hook in the second and third picots of the braid together and the upper loops of the long treble being pulled through all together, 7 chain, 3 long treble, inserting the hook in the fourth and fifth picots of the braid together and working in the same way, 7 chain, repeat seven times, and join round. **2nd round**—Work in the same manner 3 long treble in the centre stitch of the seven chain of last round, 1 chain, and repeat fifteen times, and join round. **3rd round**—2 double crochet under each chain stitch of last round, making 32 double crochet in all, join round. **4th round**—5 long treble in five double crochet stitches of last round, then 1 chain tightly worked, repeat four times, and there will be five groups of five long treble for the centre of the round of crochet, join, and fasten off. For the **Heading** of little **Circles**—With ecru cotton work 4 chain and join round; in the circle work 9 bunches of 3 long treble stitches pulled through all together, 5 chain between each bunch, join: work 1 chain, 1 treble in the first picot of the clump of braid to the right, 3 chain, 1 double crochet under the thick bar of braid, 3 chain, 1 double crochet under loop of five chain of the little circle, 2 chain, 1 double crochet in the first picot of the next clump of braid, 1 chain, 1 double crochet in three successive picots of braid, 2 chain, 1 double crochet under loop of five chain of the little circle, 1 double crochet into the *two* picots of braid nearest the crossing, 2 chain, 1 double crochet under loop of five chain of the little circle, 1 chain, 1 double crochet in three successive picots of braid, 2 chain, 1 double crochet in the last picot of the clump, 2 chain, 1 double crochet under loop of five chain, 3 chain, 1 double crochet under the thick bar of braid, 3 chain, 1 treble in the first picot to the left, and fasten off. Work the same to fill up the spaces between each scallop along the top of the lace. Then to bring the top to a straight heading, work a row, 1 treble under the thick bar of braid in the middle at the *top* of the big round circle of braid, 2 chain, 1 treble in the lower part of the treble just worked, 3 chain, 1 double crochet in the first picot of the braid, 2 chain, 1 double crochet in four successive picots, 2 chain, 1 long treble under the treble stitch at the beginning of the small crochet circle, 2 chain, work half a long treble in the same place and half a long treble under the

five chain of the small circle and draw both together at the top, 3 chain, 3 double crochet under the next five chain of the small circle, 4 double crochet under the next five chain of small circle, 3 double crochet under the next 3 chain, 2 half long trebles worked to correspond with those worked previously, 2 chain, 1 long treble under the treble stitch at the end of the small circle, 2 chain, 1 double crochet in four consecutive picots of the braid, and repeat along the whole length of the lace. **Top row** of the **Heading**—1 treble, 1 chain, miss one stitch of previous row, and repeat. For the **lower edge** of the **Lace**—Use ecru cotton, and holding the work the right side towards you, commence between the scallops where the braid crosses, 1 double crochet, inserting the hook in the last and first picots of each scallop, 5 chain, 1 double crochet inserting the hook in both next picots of the braid, 5 chain, 1 double crochet inserting the hook in the next two picots together, 5 chain and 1 long treble three times under the thick bar of braid, * 5 chain and 1 double crochet in the two next picots together three times, 5 chain and 1 long treble three times under the thick bar, and repeat from * ; and work up the scallop the same as it began, and go on to the next. **2nd row**—1 double crochet under the loop of five chain of last row, 5 chain, and repeat. **3rd row**—1 double crochet under the loop of five chain of last row, 5 chain, another double crochet in the same place, 4 chain, and repeat; catch in a little at the junction of the scallops. **4th row**—With tinsel thread—1 double crochet under four chain of last row, * 3 chain, 1 treble under the next loop of four chain, 5 chain, 1 double crochet at the top of the treble just done, 5 chain, 1 double crochet at the top of the double crochet just done, 5 chain, 1 double crochet on the top of the last double crochet, 1 treble under the same loop of chain as the first treble, 3 chain, 1 double crochet under the next loop of four chain of last row, and repeat from * : work 8 of these picoteed bunches along each scallop of the lace, catching in a little at the junction of the scallops.

PETTICOAT FOR CHILD OF FIVE OR SIX YEARS.

THE body and skirt of this petticoat are worked in crochet tricotee properly gored and shaped to the figure, the flounce is in treble crochet and sits in stripes. Required, 7 ozs. of grey and 2 ozs. of cardinal Fingering wool, a long bone tricot needle No. 8, a No. 10 crochet needle, and a dozen grey bone buttons. Begin for the **Flounce**, with grey wool, with 21 chain. **1st row**—1 treble in the fourth chain from the needle, and 17 treble worked consecutive.

Ecru and Tinsel Lace.

2nd row—2 chain to turn, and work 18 treble along, inserting the hook to take up the two top threads of the stitches of last row. **3rd row**—Join on cardinal and do 19 double crochet. **4th row**—2 chain to turn, and 18 treble in the row. Continue doing 2 rows with grey and 2 rows with cardinal till the petticoat is sufficiently wide; our model has twenty-four stripes of each colour. Now along the top edge of this flounce, the side that is turned with two chain, work with grey wool, 4 double crochet on each coloured stripe; the other edge of the flounce forms the bottom of the petticoat and is not proceeded with till the skirt is sewn up. For the **Tricot** of the **Skirt**, which is all done with grey wool—Pick up 192 stitches along the flounce at the *back* of the row of double crochet, and draw back through each stitch in the ordinary manner. **2nd row**—Again pick up all the stitches and draw back. **3rd row**—The same. **4th row**—Pick up 22 stitches, pick up 2 stitches together, pick up 22, pick up 2 together, pick up 22, pick up 2 together, pick up 46, pick up 2 together, pick up 22, pick up 2 together, pick up 22, pick up

2 together, pick up 23. Work 3 rows of plain tricot. **8th row**—Pick up 21 stitches, pick up 2 together, pick up 21, pick up 2 together, pick up 22, pick up 2 together, pick up 44, pick up 2 together, pick up 22, pick up 2 together, pick up 21, pick up 2 together, pick up 22. Work 3 plain rows. **12th row**—Pick up 20 stitches, pick up 2 together, pick up 21, pick up 2 together, pick up 21, pick up 2 together, pick up 42, pick up 2 together, pick up 21, pick up 2 together, pick up 21, pick up 2 together, pick up 21. Work 3 plain rows. **16th row**—Pick up 19, pick up 2 together, pick up 20, pick up 2 together, pick up 20, pick up 2 together, pick up 42, pick up 2 together, pick up 20, pick up 2 together, pick up 20, pick up 2 together, pick up 20. Work 3 plain rows. **20th row**—Pick up 18, pick up 2 together, pick up 20, pick up 2 together, pick up 19, pick up 2 together, pick up 40, pick up 2 together, pick up 19, pick up 2 together, pick up 20, pick up 2 together, pick up 19. Work 3 plain rows, and at the conclusion of the last of these rows do 8 chain stitches for an under lap. **24th row**—Pick up 6 stitches along the chain and 18 stitches upon the tricot, pick up 2 together, pick up 19, pick up 2 together, pick up 18, pick up 2 together, pick up 40, pick up 2 together, pick up 18, pick up 2 together, pick up 19, pick up 2 together, pick up 18. Work 2 plain rows.

Petticoat for a Child of Five or Six Years.

27th row—Pick up 23 stitches, pick up 2 together, pick up 18, pick up 2 together, pick up 17, pick up 2 together, pick up 40, pick up 2 together, pick up 17, pick up 2 together, pick up 18, pick up 2 together, pick up 12, do 2 chain, miss two stitches, pick up 3; in drawing back slip stitch over the two chain, which is for a buttonhole, and these buttonholes are now to be made in every fifth row to the completion of the body. Work 2 plain rows. **30th row**—Pick up 23 stitches, pick up 2 together, pick up 17, pick up 2 together, pick up 16, pick up 2 together, pick up 38, pick up 2 together, pick up 16, pick up 2 together, pick up 17, pick up 2 together, pick up 17. Work 2 plain rows. **33rd row**—Pick up 22 stitches, pick up 2 together, pick up 16, pick up 2 together, pick up 16, pick up 2 together, pick up 36, pick up 2 together, pick up 16, pick up 2 together, pick up 16, pick up 2 together, pick up 16. Work 2 plain rows. **36th row**—Pick up 22 stitches, pick up 2 together, pick up 15, pick up 2 together, pick up 14, pick up 2 together, pick up 36, pick up 2 together, pick up 14, pick up 2 together, pick up 15, pick up 2 together, pick up 15. Work 2 plain rows. **39th row**—Pick up 21 stitches, pick up 2 together, pick up 14, pick up 2 together, pick up 13, pick up 2 together, pick up 36, pick up 2 together, pick up 13, pick up 2 together, pick up 14, pick up 2 together, pick up 14. Work 2 plain rows. **42nd row**—Pick up 36 stitches, pick up 2 together, pick up 62, pick up 2 together, pick up 26, make buttonhole, pick up 3. Work 2 plain rows. **45th row**—Pick up 36 stitches, pick up 2 together, pick up 60, pick up 2 together, pick up 31. Work 10 plain rows without decreasing. **56th row—Begins the Division for the Armholes**—Pick up 35 stitches, and draw back, and proceed with 22 rows on these same stitches for the left side of the back, leave the ball of wool. With another ball of wool, and beginning on the fourth stitch from the left-hand side piece, pick up 58 stitches for the front, do 22 rows, and break off the wool. Now beginning on the fourth stitch from the front, pick up the remaining stitches and work there on 22 rows, and break off the wool. Continue working from the ball of wool on the left side of the back, pick up the stitches across all three divisions, and draw back. **Next row**—Pick up 33 stitches, pick up 2 together,

pick up 2 together, pick up 54, pick up 2 together, pick up 2 together, pick up to the end and draw back. **Next row**—Pick up 29, pick up 2 together four times, pick up 46, pick up 2 together four times, pick up to the end and draw back. Work another row with two decreasings on each shoulder, and another row with four decreasings on each shoulder; then work a row of single crochet upon the tricot stitches; and fasten off. Sew up the back of the skirt, and put buttons down the right back to fasten into the buttonholes. For the **Sleeves**—Make 45 chain. Work three rows of plain tricot. In the 4th row increase a stitch at the beginning and at the end of the row: and do the same in the 5th, 6th, 7th, and 8th rows. In the next row begin shaping the top of the sleeve, slip along 4 stitches, then pick up to within 4 stitches of the end, and draw back: and do the same till you pick up only 20 stitches in the middle of the sleeve, then single crochet all along and fasten off. Work the other sleeve the same, and sew the sleeves in the armholes. For the **Edge** round the Neck and Sleeves—**1st round**—Plain double crochet. **2nd round**—1 double crochet on the first stitch of previous row, taking up two threads of wool, * 3 chain, insert the hook in the middle part of the double crochet stitch just done, and draw the wool through, wool over the needle and draw through two stitches on the needle, miss one stitch of last row, one double crochet on the next, and repeat from *. For the **Edge** round the bottom of the Flounce—With cardinal wool. **1st round**—Plain double crochet. **2nd round**—3 chain to begin, wool over the needle and insert the hook in the first stitch of last round and draw the wool through, wool over the needle, miss the next stitch of last round, insert the hook in the next stitch and draw the wool through, wool over the needle and draw through four stitches on the needle, wool over the needle and draw through 2 stitches on the needle, 3 chain, 1 double crochet in the hole at the top of the stitches you have just drawn together, * wool over the needle, insert the hook in the same place in last row where a stitch is already worked and draw the wool through, wool over the needle, miss the next stitch of last row, insert the hook in the next stitch and draw the wool through, wool over the needle and draw through four stitches on the needle, wool over the needle and draw through two stitches on the needle, 3 chain, 1 double crochet in the hole above the stitches you have just drawn together, and repeat from *. This completes the petticoat.

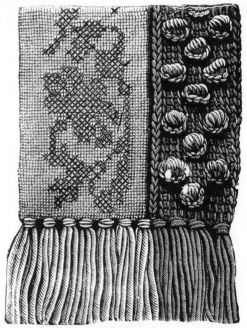

Antimacassar in Raised Ball Tricot and Cross-Stitch.

ANTIMACASSAR IN RAISED BALL TRICOT AND CROSS-STITCH.

ANTIMACASSARS worked in stripes alternately of cross-stitch and raised crochet are now very fashionable. The antimacassar shown in our illustration consists of three stripes of raised ball tricot alternated with two stripes of cross-stitch, the latter being worked in a floral scroll pattern with filoselles upon Berlin wool canvas five inches wide, this canvas is woven in various widths and colours specially for cross-stitch. White is employed for our model, and the tricot is worked with pale blue. The combination looks very light and pretty, and of course the filoselles give brightness in colouring. For the **Tricot Stripe** procure 10 ozs. or 12 ozs., of double Berlin wool, and a No. 6 bone tricot needle. Commence with 12 chain, and work 3 rows of plain tricot. **4th row**—Pick up the tricot loops in the usual manner, and work back 6 stitches only, then make 7 chain, and work back the remaining 6 stitches. **5th row**—Pick up 5 stitches, wool over the needle, and holding the 7 chain down on the front of the work insert the hook so as to take up the two small horizontal threads that lie at the top of the space, and raise a loop loosely, wool over the needle and raise another loop, wool over the needle and raise another loop, wool over the needle and raise another loop, all in the same place, wool over the needle and draw through all the loops together, insert the hook in the back thread of the second stitch of the 7 chain, and also in the next loop of the tricot, and draw the wool through both, and also through the stitch belonging to the ball that remains on the needle, pick up 5 tricot stitches, and work back as usual. **6th row**—Plain tricot. **7th row** —Pick up all the loops as before, work back 3 stitches, do 7 chain, work back 6 stitches, do 7 chain, work back the remaining 3 stitches. **8th row**— Pick up 2 stitches, then at the back of the 7 chain raise a ball of loose loops as directed in the fifth row, pick up 5 stitches, raise another ball, pick up 2 stitches, and work the row back as usual. **9th row**—Plain tricot. Repeat from the fourth row for the length required. When all the work is finished join the stripes together with single crochet. Fringe the top and bottom of the antimacassar.

SQUARE FOR A QUILT. TRIPLEX PATTERN.

THIS pretty square should be worked with rather coarse cotton, such as Strutt's best knitting cotton, No. 6, and a No. 15 steel crochet needle. Begin with a chain of 7 stitches, and join round. **1st round**—Work 16 double crochet in the circle; join this, and every round, evenly to its own commencement, and unless otherways directed, always turn the work with 1 chain to

the next side, and repeat from *; and join when you get to the end of the round. **7th round**—Plain double crochet, doing 13 stitches along each side and 3 double crochet at each corner, and repeat; join at end, and fasten off. **8th round**—Holding the right side of last round towards you, do 1 treble in the corner stitch, * 3 chain, another treble in the same place, 1 chain, miss one, 1 treble, eight times, which brings you to the next corner, repeat from * **9th round**—Plain double crochet, doing 19 stitches along each side, and 3 stitches at each corner. **10th round**—Do 21 double crochet along each side and 3 double crochet at each corner. **11th round**—Work 23 double crochet along each side and 3 double crochet at each corner. **12th round**—Work 25 double crochet along each side, and 3 double crochet at each corner, fasten off. **13th round**—Holding the wrong side of last round towards you, begin on another side of the square, so that the seam may be imperceptible, 1 double crochet on the third double crochet after the three in the corner, 1 double crochet on the next, * cotton twice round the needle, insert the hook at the back of the work into the horizontal thread of the first stitch of double crochet along the *side* of the ninth round, draw the cotton through, cotton over the needle and draw through 2 stitches on the needle, cotton over the needle and draw through 2 more stitches on the needle, repeat the same in each of 2 next stitches of the ninth row, now 4 stitches on the needle, cotton over the needle and draw through 3 stitches on the needle, insert hook in the next stitch of previous row to that last worked into, draw the cotton through, cotton over the needle and draw through 3 stitches on the needle, 1 double crochet on each of the 3 next stitches; then work another triplex into the ninth

Square for Quilt in Triplex Pattern.

re-commence a fresh round, and insert the hook to take up the one back thread of the double crochet of previous round, that the work may sit in ridges. **2nd round**—3 consecutive double crochet for a side of the square, 3 double crochet on the next stitch for a corner, and repeat three times, making 24 double crochet in the round. **3rd round**—5 consecutive double crochet, 3 double crochet on the centre stitch of the three at the corner. **4th round**—7 consecutive double crochet, 3 double crochet on the centre stitch of the three at the corner. **5th round**—9 double crochet along the side of the square, 3 double crochet on the centre stitch of the three at the corner; 40 double crochet in the round, fasten off. **6th round**—Holding the wrong side of last round towards you, begin on another side of the square so that the seam or join may be imperceptible, 1 double crochet on the third double crochet after the three in the corner, 1 double crochet on the next, * cotton twice round the needle and insert the hook at the back of the work into the horizontal thread of the first stitch of the three *straight* double crochet stitches of the second round, and draw the cotton through, cotton over the needle and draw through 2 loops on the needle, cotton over the needle and draw through 2 more loops on the needle, repeat the same in each of the 2 next stitches of the second row, now 4 stitches on the needle, cotton over the needle and draw through 3 stitches on the needle, insert hook in the next stitch of last row to that last worked into, draw the cotton through, cotton over the needle and draw through 3 stitches on the needle, do 5 double crochet consecutive, 3 double crochet in the stitch at the corner. 5 double crochet along

round of double crochet, missing 1 stitch from the stitch last worked into; then 3 double crochet along previous row, and repeat till 5 triplex are worked, the last stitch of which should come into the last double crochet along the *side* of the ninth round, be very particular to get each stitch in its proper place, then do 1 double crochet in each of the last 5 stitches of previous row, and 3 double crochet at the corner, 5 double crochet along the next side, and repeat from *; and join when you get to the end of the round. **14th round**— Plain double crochet, doing 29 stitches along each side and 3 double crochet at each corner, and join at end, and fasten off. **15th round**—Holding the right side of last round towards you, work 1 treble in the corner stitch * 3 chain, another treble in the same place, 1 chain, miss one, 1 treble, sixteen times, which brings you to the next corner, repeat from *. **16th round**— Plain double crochet, doing 35 stitches along each side and 3 stitches at each corner. **17th round**—Work 37 double crochet along each side and 3 double crochet at each corner. **18th round**—Do 39 double crochet along each side and 3 double crochet at each corner. **19th round**—Work 41 double crochet along each side and 3 double crochet at each corner. **20th round**—Work in the same manner as directed for the thirteenth round, inserting the triplex stitches into the double crochet of the sixteenth round, and getting 9 triplex along each side of the square, as shown in the engraving. **21st round**—Plain double crochet, doing 45 stitches along each side and 3 stitches at each corner; join at end, and fasten off. **22nd round**—Holding the right side of last round towards you, work 1 treble in the corner stitch, * 3 chain, another treble in

.he same place, 1 chain, miss one, 1 treble, twenty-four times, which brings you to the next corner, repeat from *. **23rd round**—Hold the same side of the work towards you, and insert the hook to take up the one top thread of the stitches of previous round, do 51 double crochet along each side and 3 double crochet at each corner. This completes the square. The squares are sewn together to make the size required for the quilt. A good **Border** for this quilt can be crocheted all round upon the quilt itself, working as directed above, from the 15th round to the 21st round; repeating the same; and then finishing with an open edge similar to that used upon the border illustrated on page 9, No. 6 of "Weldon's Practical Needlework Series."

FLUTED BORDER.

THIS may be worked either in wool or cotton and is useful for any purpose for which a full fluted border is required. Begin with chain the necessary length. **1st row**—1 treble in the third chain from the needle, and work 1 treble in each stitch of chain to the end of the row. **2nd row**—Turn the work with 5 chain, miss 4 treble stitches, 1 double crochet on the next, * 5 chain, miss 4, 1 double crochet on the next, and repeat from *: turn the work. **3rd row**—Do 1 double crochet on the first double crochet stitch of last row, * 3 chain, 5 treble in the centre stitch of five chain of last row, 3 chain, 1 double crochet on double crochet, and repeat from *. **4th row**—5 chain to turn, * insert the hook from back to front under the first loop of three chain and from front to back under the next loop of three chain, and so pressing the five treble stitches closely in a bunch work a double crochet stitch, 5 chain, and repeat from *. **5th row**—3 chain to turn, 1 treble in each stitch of preceding row. **6th row**—3 chain to turn, 1 treble between the second and third treble stitches of last row, * 2 chain, 1 treble between the second and third treble stitches, and repeat from *. **7th row**—3 chain to turn, 1 treble under the first space, * 2 chain, 1 treble under next space, and repeat from *: break off. **8th row**—Recommence at

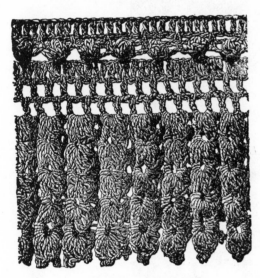

Fluted Border.

the opposite end, 2 treble under the first loop of two chain of last row, * 3 chain, 3 treble, 3 chain, 3 treble, all under the next loop, 3 chain, 2 treble under the next loop, repeat from *. **9th row**—3 chain to turn, * insert the hook from back to front under the first loop of three chain and from front to back under the third loop of three chain, and so pressing the six treble stitches closely in a bunch do a double crochet stitch, 5 chain, and repeat from * to the end of the row, where finish with 3 chain, and 1 double crochet on the last treble stitch. **10th row**—3 chain to turn, 1 treble on the second treble stitch of the eighth row, * 3 chain, 3 treble, 3 chain, 3 treble, all under the 3 chain loop between the bunches of trebles of the eighth row, 3 chain, 1 treble on each the 2 treble stitches of the eighth row and overlapping the chain stitches, and repeat from *. Repeat the last two rows three times. **18th row**—3 chain to turn, 1 treble on the second treble stitch of the sixteenth row, * 2 chain, 2 treble under the 3 chain loop between the bunches of trebles of the sixteenth row, *a* 5 chain, 1 single crochet in the fifth chain from the needle, 2 more treble stitches under the same loop, repeat from *a* twice, which makes 8 treble stitches and 3 picots in a group, do 2 chain, 1 treble on each of 2 treble stitches of the sixteenth row; repeat from *. Fasten off at the end of the row.

OPENWORK FROCK FOR A CHILD OF TWO OR THREE.

LOW NECK AND SHORT SLEEVES.

THIS frock being light and open is intended for summer wear over an underdress of pink or blue sateen. If worked with cream or ecru flax thread it will be very durable, with a gloss almost like silk, and will wash splendidly, or it may be crocheted with the Crystal wool or the Spray wool, manufactured by

the **Providence Mills** Company. Select a crochet needle to suit the material you intend working with. Commence with a chain sufficiently long to pass easily round the child a few inches below the waist. Then for the **1st row** of the **Body**—Miss the 3 chain stitches nearest the needle, and work * 3 consecutive double crochet, miss two, 3 treble in the next, 3 chain, 3 treble in the next, 3 chain, and repeat from * to the end, where complete the row with 1 treble after missing the five chain stitches. **2nd row**—3 chain to turn the work, do * 3 treble under the first loop of three chain of last row, 3 treble under the next loop, 3 chain, 3 more treble in the same place, 3 chain, and repeat from *, and at the end of the row after doing 3 chain, work 1 treble in the chain that turned. Every succeeding row is the same as the second row. As will be seen by the engraving, the body is long and straight. When you have done sufficient to reach the armhole, divide, and work in three separate pieces for the two backs and the front of the dress till enough is done to reach the neck. The **Sleeves**, which are commenced on a chain long enough to reach from the division to the top of the shoulder, are worked in the same manner as described above, and sewn in; they are six rows in depth. For the **Skirt**—Recommence upon the foundation chain, and to produce the necessary fulness, work three consecutive treble, 3 treble in the next chain stitch, 3 chain, 3 treble in the next, 3 chain, and repeat the same all along, not missing any, and at the end after doing 3 chain work 1 treble upon the last

Openwork Frock for a Child of Two or Three Years.

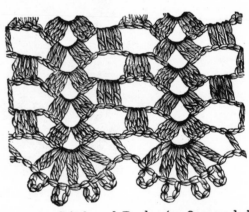

Details of the Stitch and Border for Openwork Frock.

stitch. **2nd row**—3 chain to turn, * 3 treble under the first loop of three chain, 3 treble under the next loop, 3 chain, 3 more treble in the same place, 3 chain, and repeat from *, and at the end after doing 3 chain, work 1 treble in the last stitch. Continue, every row the same, for the length required. Sew the skirt up. For the **Edge** round the **Skirt**—Work 1 treble under the first loop of three chain of last row, * 1 chain, thread twice round the needle, insert the hook under next loop of three chain (between six treble stitches) and draw the thread through, thread over the needle and draw through 2 stitches on the needle, thread over the needle and draw through 2 more stitches on the needle, thread twice round the needle insert the hook again in the same place and draw the thread through, thread over the needle and draw through 2 stitches on the needle, thread over the needle and draw through 2 more stitches on the needle, thread over the needle and draw through 3 stitches on the needle, 5 chain, 1 double crochet in the fifth chain from the needle; work 2 more double long treble and then a picot alternately, till you have 4 picots and 5 groups of double long treble in the same place, 1 chain, 1 treble under the next loop of three chain of last row, and repeat from *. Work the same edge round the neck and sleeves. Complete the little dress with a handsome broad silk sash round the waist, hooks and loops to fasten up the back, and bows of ribbon on the shoulders.

WELDON'S
PRACTICAL CROCHET.

(NINTH SERIES.)

HOW TO CROCHET HATS, BONNETS, SHAWLS, ANTIS, JACKETS, &c.

TWENTY-FIVE ILLUSTRATIONS.

Telegraphic Address—] "Consuelo," London.]   The Yearly Subscription to this Magazine, post free to any Part of the World, is 2s. 6d. Subscriptions are payable in advance, and may commence from any date and for any period.   [Telephone 2745.

The Back Numbers are always in print. Nos. 1 to 87 now ready, Price 2d. each, or post free for 15s. 6d. Over 5,000 Engravings.

BORDER FOR JACKETS, PETTICOATS, ETC.

COMMENCE with chain for the length required. Work 3 rows of plain treble stitches, inserting the hook to take up the two back threads; break off at the end of each row, and begin again on the right hand side. **4th row**—1 double crochet on the first treble stitch, * 5 chain, 1 double crochet in the top of the double crochet just worked, miss one treble stitch, 1 double crochet on the next, 7 chain, 1 double crochet in the top of the double crochet just worked, 1 double crochet on next treble stitch, 7 chain, 1 double crochet in the top of the double crochet just worked, 1 double crochet on next treble stitch, 5 chain, 1 double in the top of the double crochet just worked, miss one treble stitch, 1 double crochet on the next, and repeat from * to the end of the row. Hold the work the right side uppermost, and work the same edging of chain picots into the front threads of the treble stitches of the second row. Do the same along the treble stitches of the first row.

NIGHTCAP ANTIMACASSAR.

THIS is worked with macramé thread, and draws over the back of the chair like a cap. Procure ⅛ lb. of macramé thread of each of two good contrasting colours, as cream and pink, and a No. 9 bone crochet needle, and 4 yards of pretty pink ribbon. Begin for the **Front** of the antimacassar, lengthways, with cream-coloured thread; do 5 chain, 1 double crochet in the fourth chain from the needle, and repeat this till you have a length of 17 picots worked. **1st row**—7 chain to turn, 1 double crochet in the fourth chain from the needle, 1 treble in the chain stitch between the picots of the foundation, * 4 chain, 1 double crochet in the fourth chain from the needle. 1 treble in the chain stitch between the picots of the foundation, and repeat from * to the end of the row. **2nd row**—7 chain to turn, 1 double crochet in the fourth chain from the needle, 1 treble on treble stitch of last row, taking up both top threads, * 4 chain, 1 double crochet in the fourth chain from the needle, 1 treble on treble stitch of last row, and repeat from

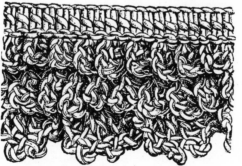

Border for Jackets, Petticoats, &c.

*, and at the end of the row work the treble stitch into the chain stitch next beyond the picot. Every successive row is worked the same as the last row. Do 6 rows with cream thread, 2 rows with pink, 4 rows with cream, 2 rows with pink, 4 rows with cream, 2 rows with pink, and 6 rows with cream, and fasten off. For the **Back** of the antimacassar, beginning with cream thread, work 50 chain. **1st row** — 1 double crochet in the second chain from the needle, * 1 chain, miss one, 1 double crochet in the next, and repeat from * to the end. **2nd row**—2 chain to turn, 1 double crochet in the back thread of double crochet stitch of last row, * 1 chain, 1 double crochet in the back thread of next double crochet stitch, that the work may sit in ridges, repeat from * to the end of the row. The remainder of the back of the antimacassar is worked in the same stitch, do 14 rows with cream thread, then 6 rows with pink, 6 rows with cream, 6 rows with pink, and 14 rows with white. This piece should be the same length and width as the piece already worked for the front of the antimacassar. For small **Side Pieces**, worked entirely with cream thread, begin with 10 chain, and work forwards and backwards in the stitch as used for the back, doing 20 rows, then decrease gradually to 4 stitches, and fasten off. Work another similar piece. Sew the two large pieces of the antimacassar together at the top, and insert a small piece on each side, the narrow part at the top. For **Curly Fringe** round the bottom of the antimacassar, working cream on the cream stripes and pink on the pink. **1st round**—1 treble, 1 chain, miss one, and repeat. **2nd round**—1 double crochet on treble stitch, * 30 chain worked very loosely, 1 double crochet on next treble stitch, and repeat from * to the end of the round. Cut the pink ribbon into four pieces, and run it into the treble row above the curly fringe, and also into the work about 2 inches from the top of the antimacassar, tying it in a nice bow on each side.

CROCHET EDGING.

To be worked with Evans' Crochet Cotton No. 20, and a fine steel crochet needle. Make a chain the length required. **1st row**—1 treble in the ninth chain from the needle, * 2 chain, miss two, 1 treble in the next and repeat from *. Break off the cotton at the end of this and every row, and recommence on the right hand side. **2nd row**—1 treble on the seventh stitch of the chain that turned, 8 chain, miss the stitch next the needle and work 1 double crochet in each of 7 chain stitches, * 1 chain, turn the work, miss the first double crochet stitch of last little row, and taking up the one back thread do one double crochet on each of 7 stitches, repeat from * three times, 1 single crochet in the second treble stitch of the first row, 1 chain, turn the work, miss the first double crochet and do 1 double crochet on each of 7 stitches, turn the work, then one treble on the second treble stitch of the first row from that last worked upon, begin another little square block with 8 chain, and proceed to the end of the row. **3rd row**—1 treble on the treble stitch of previous row, * 5 chain, 1 single crochet on the corner of the little square block, 5 chain, 1 treble on treble stitch of previous row, and repeat from *. **4th row**—1 double crochet on each of 9 consecutive stitches of last row, * 1 single crochet on the next, 10 chain, miss five stitches of last row, 1 single crochet on the next, 17 double crochet worked consecutive; repeat from star to the end. **5th row**—1 double crochet on each of 4 double crochet stitches, * 2 chain, 7 treble under the loop of ten chain, 2 chain, 7 more treble in the same place, 2 chain, miss five stitches, 7 double crochet worked consecutive; repeat from *, and end the row with 4 double crochet as it began. **6th row**—1 double crochet on each of 3 double crochet stitches, * 2 chain, 1 treble on each of 7 treble stitches of last row, 3 treble under loop of two chain, 2 chain, 3 more treble in the same place, 1 treble on each of 7 treble stitches, 2 chain, miss one double crochet stitch and do 1 double crochet on each of the 5 next stitches; repeat from *. **7th row**—1 double crochet on each of 2 double crochet stitches, * 2 chain, 1 treble on the first treble stitch of last row, 2 chain, miss two, 1 treble on the next, 2 chain, miss one, 1 treble on the next, 2 chain, 1 treble under loop at top of the scallop, 5 chain, another treble in the same place, 2 chain, 1 treble on the third treble stitch, 2 chain, miss one, 1 treble on the next, 2 chain, miss one, 1 treble on the next, 2 chain, miss two, 1 treble on the next, 2 chain, miss 1 double crochet stitch, 1 double crochet on each of the 3 next stitches; repeat from *. **8th row**—1 double crochet on the first stitch of previous row, 3 chain, 1 treble under the loop between two

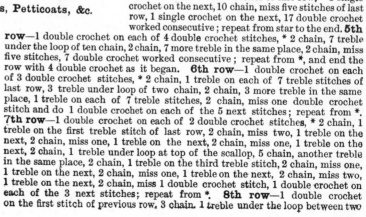

treble stitches of previous row, * 5 chain, 1 single crochet in the fourth chain from the needle, 1 chain, 1 treble under the next loop, repeat from * eight times, which gives one extra picot at the top of the scallop, then 2 chain, 1 double crochet on the centre stitch of three double crochet of last row, and continue in the same manner to the end of the row, so completing the border.

EDGING FOR UNDERLINEN.

THIS is a useful edging for putting round drawers and other underlinen and may be worked with a fine steel crochet needle and Coats' or Evans' crochet cotton No. 16 to No. 24. Commence with 20 chain. **1st row**—Do 1 treble in the seventh chain from the needle, 1 chain, miss one, 1 treble in the next, 1 chain, miss one, 1 treble in the next, 2 treble in each of the two next stitches, 1 treble in the next, 1 chain, miss one, 1 treble in the next, 1 chain, miss one, 1 treble in the next, 1 chain, miss one, 1 treble in the next. **2nd row**—7 chain to turn, 1 treble under the first one chain stitch of previous row, 1 chain, 1 treble under the next chain stitch, 1 chain, 1 treble under the next, 4 chain, 1 treble under the next chain stitch, 1 chain, 1 treble under the next chain stitch, 1 chain, 1 treble in the first stitch of the chain that turned, 1 treble in the next stitch. **3rd row**—4 chain to turn, 1 treble under the first chain stitch of preceding row, 1 chain, 1 treble under the next chain stitch, 1 chain, 6 treble under the loop of four chain, 1 chain, 1 treble under the next chain stitch, 1 chain, 1 treble under the next, 1 chain, 12 treble under the loop of seven chain at the end, and catch with a single crochet into the last stitch of the commencing chain. **4th row**—5 chain to turn, miss the first treble stitch, 1 double crochet on the next, 5 chain, miss one, 1 double crochet on the next, do this till 5 loops are made, 5 chain, 1 treble under the first one chain stitch, 1 chain, 1 treble under the next, 1 chain, 1 treble under the next, 4 chain, 1 treble under the next one chain stitch, 1 chain, 1 treble under the next, 1 chain, 1 treble in the first stitch of the chain that turned, 1 treble in the next stitch. **5th row**—4 chain to turn, 1 treble under the first chain stitch of preceding row, 1 chain, 1 treble under the next chain stitch, 1 chain, 6 treble under the loop of four chain, 1 chain, 1 treble under the next chain stitch, 1 chain, 1 treble under the next, 1 chain, 1 treble under the first loop of five chain. **6th row**—7 chain to turn, and work the same as the second row. **7th row**—Same as the third row, and after doing the 12 treble catch with a single crochet into the stitch of five chain close by the treble stitch that is already worked there. **8th row**—Same as the fourth row. Repeat the four rows for the length required.

CHILD'S JACKET WORKED IN TREBLE STITCH.

WORKED with Scotch Fingering yarn and a No. 10 crochet needle. This jacket is about the right size for a child two years old, while if petticoat wool be employed, and a No. 9 needle, it will be sufficiently large for a child of three, it is quickly and easily made, and is a serviceable little garment to give to the poor. Commence for the **Front**, lengthways, with a chain of 43 stitches. **1st row**—Insert the hook in the fourth chain from the needle and work treble to the end, doing 40 treble in the row. **2nd row**—3 chain to turn, miss the first treble stitch, and work 40 treble to the end of the row, inserting the hook to take up the back thread of the stitches of previous row. Work 4 more rows the same as the second row. **7th row**—3 chain to turn, work 20 treble, 4 double crochet, this is for a gore. **8th row**—1 chain to turn, 6 double crochet, 18 treble. **9th row**—3 chain to turn, work 40 treble, and make 11 chain at the end for the shoulder. **10th row**—Insert hook in the fourth chain from the needle, and work 48 treble stitches in the row. Work as the seventh and eighth rows for a gore. **13th row**—3 chain to turn, 48 treble. **14th row**—The same. **15th row**—3 chain to turn, 30 treble, and leave 18 treble unworked for the armhole. **16th row**—3 chain to turn, 30 treble. **17th row**—3 chain to turn, 30 treble, 21 chain. **18th row**—Insert hook in the fourth chain from the needle and work 48 treble in the row. Work a gore as the seventh and eighth rows. **21st row**—3 chain to turn, 48 treble. **22nd row**—The same. Work a gore. **25th row**—3 chain to turn, 40 treble. Work 11 more rows the same as last row for the width across the back. Work a gore. **39th row**—3 chain to turn, 40 treble, 11 chain. **40th row**—Insert hook in the fourth chain from the needle and work 48 treble in the row. Work a gore. **43rd row**—3 chain to turn, 48 treble. **44th row**—The same. **45th row**—

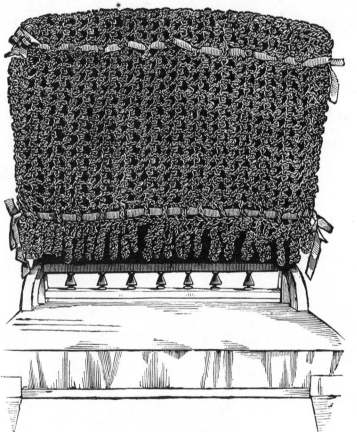

Night Cap Antimacassar.

3 chain to turn, 30 treble, and leave 18 treble unworked for the armhole. **46th row**—3 chain to turn, 30 treble. **47th row**—3 chain to turn, 30 treble, 2 chain. **48th row**—Insert hook in the fourth chain from the needle and work 48 treble in the row. Work a gore. **51st row**—3 chain to turn, 48 treble. **52nd row**—The same. Work a gore. **55th row**—3 chain to turn, 40 treble. Work 5 more rows the same. Fasten off. Sew up the shoulder pieces. Work 2 rows of treble stitches rather tightly round the neck. For **Edging** to be worked all round the jacket and neck—**1st round**—1 double crochet in a stitch of the jacket, 5 chain, and repeat. **2nd round**—1 double crochet under loop of five chain of last round, 5 chain, and repeat. **3rd round**—1 double crochet under the first loop of previous round, 7 treble under the next loop, and repeat. Make a crochet cord with tassels at the end to run in the neck. For **Sleeves**—Commence with 48 chain. **1st row**—Insert the hook in the fourth chain from the needle and work 8 treble, 2 double crochet, leave the remaining chain. **2nd row**—1 chain to turn, 4 double crochet, 6 treble. **3rd row**—3 chain to turn, 8 double crochet, 4 double crochet. **4th row**—1 chain to turn, 8 double crochet, 12 treble. **5th row**—3 chain to turn, and work 40 treble to the end of the commencing chain. Work 17 more rows the same as last row. **23rd row**—3 chain to turn, 16 treble, 4 double crochet. **24th row**—1 chain to turn, 8 double crochet, 12 treble. **25th row**—3 chain to turn, 8 treble, 2 double crochet. **26th row**—1 chain to turn, 4 double crochet, 6 treble. Fasten off. Work the other sleeve in the same manner. Work a crochet edge round the wrists the same as already worked round the jacket. Sew the sleeves into the armholes. Turn back about an inch round the wrists to simulate cuffs.

TOILET TIDY.

THIS is a small pretty tidy to hang upon the knob of a toilet glass. Our model is worked with a rather fine steel crochet needle, and pale peacock blue crochet cotton, No. 12, a small tin is placed inside to distend the work, and keep it in shape, and at the same time to form a receptacle, and a piece of narrow blue ribbon is run through the stitches at the top of the tidy, and tied in a nice bow in front. Begin for the bottom of the tidy, with 8 chain, join round. **1st round**—4 chain to stand for the beginning of the round, * 1 treble in the circle, 1 chain, repeat from * seven times, and join to the third stitch of the commencing chain. **2nd round**—1 treble, 1 chain, 1 treble under each space of last round, 1 chain, there should be 18 treble stitches in this round. **3rd round**—1 treble, 1 chain, 1 treble, 1 chain, doing the 2 treble stitches under each one chain stitch of last round. **4th round**—The same, making 72 treble stitches in the round. **5th round**—1 treble, 1 chain, 1 treble, under one chain stitch of last round, 1 chain, miss the next one chain stitch of last round, and repeat. **6th round**—1 treble, 1 chain, 1 treble, under one chain between the two treble stitches of last round, 1 chain, miss the chain stitch over the chain missed in the previous round, and repeat. Continue the same as last round until 26 rounds are worked from the commencement. **27th round**—Work in the same manner, but doing long treble stitches (the cotton twice round the needle) instead of treble. **28th round**—Same as the sixth round. **29th round**—The same. **30th round**—The same. **31st round**—Between the two treble stitches of last round work 1 treble, 2 chain, 1 long treble and 2 chain three times, 1 treble, and work 1 double crochet under the other one chain of last round, and repeat. Do a length of chain, about 120 stitches, as a string to hang the bag upon the knob of the toilet glass. Make a nice thick tassel, and secure it to the bottom of the tidy by a loop of about 20 chain stitches. Run a narrow blue ribbon through the long treble stitches of the twenty-seventh round, and tie it in the front of the tidy in a pretty bow.

DERWENT BORDER.

THIS border is very suitable for dress trimmings, collars, and revers on cuffs, for which purposes it will look best worked with fine ecru linen thread, such as Finlayson's Scotch linen thread, No. 40; this thread possesses a gloss that is not found upon cotton. Use a fine steel crochet needle, and commence with 56 chain. **1st row**—Work 1 treble in the third chain from the needle, 1 chain, miss one, 2 consecutive treble, 1 chain, miss three, 3 treble in the next, 3 chain, 3 treble in the next, * 1 chain, miss five, 3 treble in the next, 3 chain, 3 treble in the next, repeat from * five times, and leave three chain at the end of the foundation. **2nd row**—

6 chain to turn, 1 treble under the loop of three chain, 3 chain, another treble in the same place, * 5 chain, 1 treble under the next loop of three chain, 3 chain, another treble in the same place, repeat from * five times, 3 chain, 1 treble on each of two treble stitches, 1 chain, 1 treble on the treble stitch, and 1 treble on the chain that turned. **3rd row**—3 chain to turn, 1 treble on the treble stitch, 1 chain, 1 treble on each of two treble stitches, * 1 chain, 3 treble under the loop of three chain, 3 chain, 3 more treble in the same place, repeat from * six times, do 1 chain and one treble seven times in the loop of six chain that turned at the end of the row, and do 1 single crochet in the chain stitch at the end of the foundation. In future rows you will catch the single crochet stitch into the three-chain-loop of the preceding pattern. **4th row**—3 chain, 1 double crochet under loop of one chain, do this 7 times, 3 chain, 1 treble under the loop of three chain of previous row, 3 chain, another treble in the same place, * 5 chain, 1 treble under the loop of three chain,

the needle and draw through 2 stitches on the needle for three times, * 2 chain, miss three of the foundation, wool over the needle and insert the hook in the next chain stitch of the foundation and draw the wool through, wool over the needle and draw through two stitches on the needle, wool over the needle and insert the hook again in the same place and draw the wool through, wool over the needle and draw through 2 stitches on the needle for three times, 3 chain, wool over the needle and insert the hook in the next stitch of the foundation chain and proceed as before to work the 2 combined treble stitches; and repeat from * to the end of the row. **2nd row**—6 chain to turn, wool over the needle and insert the hook in the sixth chain from the needle and draw the wool through, wool over the needle and draw through 2 stitches on the needle, wool over the needle and insert the hook again in the same place and draw the wool through, wool over the needle and draw through 2 stitches on

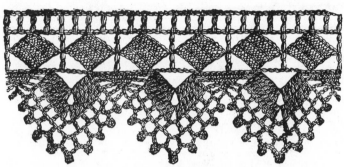

Crochet Edging.

Child's Jacket worked in Treble Stitch.

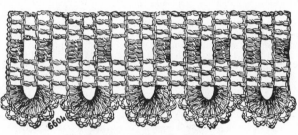

Edging for Underlinen.

3 chain, another treble in the same place, repeat from * five times, 3 chain, 1 treble on each of two treble stitches, 1 chain, 1 treble on the treble stitch, and one treble on the chain that turned. **5th row**—3 chain to turn, 1 treble on the treble stitch, 1 chain, 1 treble on each of two treble stitches, * 1 chain, 3 treble under the loop of three chain, 3 chain, 3 more treble in the same place, and repeat from * six times. Continue the pattern from the second row, and repeat for the length required.

CHILD'S MUFF.

THIS comfortable muff for a little girl is crocheted with 2½ ozs. of single Berlin wool of any colour that may be preferred, using a No. 10 bone crochet needle. Procure also a yard of ribbon to match the wool to make a bow for the front of the muff, a piece of wadding, and flannel or twill for lining. Commence working with 57 chain. **1st row**—Do 56 double crochet; turn the work at the end of this and every row. **2nd row**—Loop crochet—Twist the wool three times round the first and second fingers of the left hand, going first over and then under and ending with the wool over the first finger, insert the hook to take two top threads of the stitch of the previous row, and also under the four threads of wool that lie over the first finger, draw all threads through the stitch, let the loop off the fingers, wool over the needle and draw through all on the needle, 1 double crochet taking two top threads of the next stitch of previous row, and repeat, and there will be 28 loop stitches and 28 double crochet stitches in the row. Repeat the first and second row four times more. **11th row**—Double crochet. Work 16 or 18 rows of double crochet in ridges, that is, inserting the hook to take up the one back thread of the stitches of the preceding row, there should be 56 stitches in each row. Then work 10 rows of the looped crochet the same as at the commencement of the muff. End with a row of plain double crochet, and fasten off. Arrange the lining for the muff; join the crochet in a round, and sew it neatly to the lining; make a bow of ribbon to put in front of the muff over the join.

LIGHT OPEN PATTERN FOR A SHAWL.

THIS pretty open pattern can be worked to form a square shawl or a scarf shaped shawl as desired. Procure 7 or 8 ozs. of Shetland wool, Pompadour wool, or Crystal wool, and a No. 10 bone crochet needle. Commence with a chain the length required. **1st row**—Wool over the needle, insert the hook in the sixth chain from the needle and draw the wool through, wool over the needle and draw through two stitches on the needle, wool over the needle and insert the hook again in the same place and draw the wool through, wool over

Toilet Tidy.

the needle for three times, * 2 chain, wool over the needle, and missing the three chain loop, work the combined treble stitches under the loop of two chain, 3 chain, work 2 more combined treble stitches in the same place, and repeat from * to the end of the row. Every succeeding row is worked the same as the second row. You will observe that the edges of the shawl are not straight where the rows turn, therefore when the shawl is large enough, proceed to make these edges straight and even by working thus, 1 double crochet under the loop of five chain that turned the rows, 3 chain, 1 treble in the side of the treble stitch of the alternate row, 3 chain, and repeat. For the **Border**— **1st round**—Knot a stitch upon the crochet needle, and to work along the side of the shawl, pass the wool twice round the needle, insert the hook under a loop of three chain and draw the wool through, wool over the needle and draw through 2 stitches on the needle, wool over the needle and draw through 2 more stitches on the needle, wool twice round the needle and insert the hook in the same place and draw the wool through, wool over the needle and draw through 2 stitches on the needle, wool over the needle and draw through

2 more stitches on the needle, wool twice round the needle and insert the hook under the next loop of three chain and draw the wool through, wool over the needle and draw through two stitches on the needle, wool over the needle and draw through 2 more stitches on the needle, wool twice round the needle and insert the hook in the same place and draw the wool through, wool over the needle and draw through 2 stitches on the needle, wool over the needle and draw through two more stitches on the needle, now 5 stitches are on the needle, wool over the needle and draw through all, 3 chain, work two long treble in the same manner under the same loop of chain, and 2 long treble under the next loop, and draw through all together, and proceed similarly all round the shawl, increasing a pattern in turning the corners; when working along the top of the shawl insert the hook under the loops of two chain as you did in crocheting the rows. **2nd round**—1 double crochet under loop of three chain of previous round, 6 chain, and repeat, and make one extra loop when turning the corners. **3rd round**—The same as last round, but no increase at the corners,

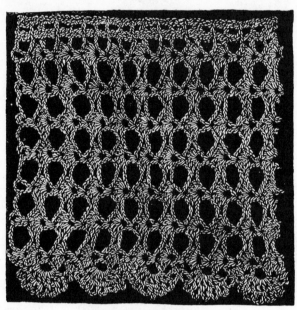

Derwent Border.

fasten off at the end of this round. **4th round**—Recommence, and work the same as the first round, but making two increasings at each corner. **5th round**—1 treble under a loop of three chain, 4 chain, 1 single crochet in the top of the treble stitch just done, 4 chain, another single crochet in the top of the treble stitch, 4 chain, another single crochet in the same place, 4 chain, 1 double crochet under the same loop of three chain, 4 chain, and repeat the same under the next loop of three chain and continue to the end of the round which completes the shawl.

FRENCH HAT FOR A BABY BOY.

To make this very pretty hat for a baby boy procure 2¼ ozs. of white single Berlin wool and a No. 10 bone crochet needle. Begin in the centre of the crown with 4 chain, and join in a circle. **1st round**—1 double crochet in the circle, insert the hook in the circle and draw the wool through, do 3 chain, wool over the needle and draw through 2 stitches on the needle, repeat four times, which will make 5 double crochet stitches and 5 bobbin stitches alternately in the round, and join evenly. **2nd round**—3 chain to stand for a treble, and work 2 treble on the first stitch and 3 treble on the next stitch alternately, that is 26 treble in the round, always taking up two threads of the stitches of the preceding round, and join evenly. **3rd round**—1 double crochet on the first stitch, insert the hook in the next stitch and draw the wool through, do 3 chain, wool over the needle and draw through 2 stitches on the needle, and repeat, and increase three times, so that you get 16 double crochet and 16 bobbin stitches in the round. **4th round**—Treble, doing 52 treble in the round, and join evenly. **5th round**—A double crochet and a bobbin stitch alternately, and you will get 26 double crochet and 26 bobbin stitches in the round. **6th round**—Treble, doing 74 treble in the round, and join evenly. **7th round**—A double crochet and a bobbin stitch alternately. **8th round**—Treble, with increase on every sixth stitch, making 86 treble in the round. **9th round**—A double crochet and a bobbin stitch alternately. **10th round**—Treble, 86 stitches. **11th round**—A double crochet and a bobbin stitch alternately. **12th round**—Same as the tenth round. **13th round**—Same as the eleventh round. **14th round**—Work 1 double crochet, 35 treble, 1 double crochet, and fasten off; this is the front of the hat. **15th round**—Begin at the commencement of last round and work a double crochet and a bobbin stitch alternately over those 37 stitches. **16th round**—Recommencing 6 stitches further to the right, do 1 double crochet, 47 treble, 1 double crochet, and fasten off. **17th round**—Begin again in the same place, and work a double crochet and a bobbin stitch alternately over those 49 stitches, and fasten off. Make a length of crochet chain, which take and hold level with the last round of the crochet, and beginning at the back of the hat, work loosely double crochet into the last round and over the chain, all round the hat,

and then draw the crochet cord up and tie it to the size of the head. Now work 1 chain 1 treble all round this, making just sufficient stitches to bring the round to fit the work as it is drawn up. Pompons made of about 50 strands of wool are sewn each pompon separately and at regular distances apart all round the margin of the hat, about 18 pompons will suffice. Then three larger pompons are made, each hanging from a crochet cord, which cord is sewn in loops upon the twelfth round of treble stitches in front of the hat. A feather is formed by winding 30 or 40 loops of wool round three fingers of the left hand and securing the loops together with one or two double crochet stitches, then 3 chain, and another bunch of loops, and so on till eight bunches of loops are made, when arrange the feather to fall prettily from behind the pompons at the front top of the hat.

DOROTHY FROCK FOR CHILD OF FOUR.

THE body of this frock is worked in a pretty twisted stitch, the skirt is "crazy" stitch, and the trimming is "looped" crochet. The frock is warm and comfortable and sufficiently large to fit a girl of four or five years. Procure 10 ozs. of white or coloured single Berlin wool, a bone crochet needle No. 9 and also one No. 7, 4 yards of inch-wide ribbon to match the wool, and a few linen buttons which should be covered with small pieces cut from the ribbon. Use No. 9 crochet needle, and begin for the back of the body with 43 chain. **1st row**—Work 42 double crochet. **2nd row**—Turn, and work 42 stitches thus—put the needle behind the wool so as to bring the wool in front under the needle, insert the hook to take up two threads of a stitch of last row, draw the wool through, wool over the needle and draw through the two stitches on the needle, every stitch is worked in the same manner, and the result is a peculiarly pretty twisted stitch something resembling "cross" stitch; break off the wool at the end of this and every succeeding row (except where otherwise directed) and recommence on the right-hand side. **3rd row**—Work in the same manner 42 stitches. Work 6 rows increasing a stitch at the end of each row to shape for the shoulder. **10th row**—To consist of 48 stitches. Work 6 rows decreasing a stitch at the end of each row. **17th row**—Work only 24 stitches for under the arm. **18th row**—Work 24 stitches and end with 18 chain for the shoulder. **19th row**—Work 42 stitches. Work 6 rows increasing a stitch at the end of each. Work 6 rows decreasing a stitch at the end of each. Turn the work at the end of the 31st row, and for the **32nd row** do 2 chain to turn, 1 treble on the second stitch of preceding row, * 1 chain, miss 1 stitch, 1 treble on the next, and repeat from * to the end, turn the work. **33rd row**—Work in the fancy stitch. Repeat the last two rows twice. **38th row**—Same as the thirty-second row, and this makes four rows of open stitches down the front of the body in which to run ribbon. Work 6 rows of fancy crochet increasing a stitch at the end of each row. Work 6 rows decreasing a stitch at the end of each row. **51st row**—Work only 24 stitches for under the arm. **52nd row**—Work 24 stitches and end with 18 chain for the shoulder. **53rd row**—To consist of 42 stitches. Work 6 rows increasing a stitch at the end of each row. Work 6 rows decreasing a stitch at the end of each row. Work 4 rows on 42 stitches.

Child's Muff.

Turn the work, do 42 plain double crochet, and fasten off. If you have not worked neatly over the tags of wool at the beginning and end of each row draw them in now with the crochet hook that no ends may be visible. For the **Skirt**—This is worked round and round, there is no placket hole, for the dress will pass readily over the child's head, still if the placket opening is desired it can be managed by *not* joining at the end of the first round; the pattern requires for the work to be turned on the completion of every round, therefore the instructions hold good for working either in rounds or rows as preferred. **1st round or row**—With No. 7 crochet needle, work double crochet along the lower edge of the body, overlap a stitch or two at the end if you join round. **2nd round**—4 chain to turn, 1 long treble on stitch of last round, * 1 chain, miss one stitch, 1 long treble on the next, repeat from *; join round. **3rd round**—1 chain to turn, and work along in double crochet, increasing by doing 2 double crochet in every fifth stitch. **4th round**—1 chain to turn, do 1 double crochet and 2 treble on a double crochet stitch of last round *, miss two stitches, 1 double crochet and 2 treble on the next, and repeat from *; this is the beginning of the "crazy" stitch in which the skirt is worked. **5th round**—On each double crochet stitch of last round do 1 double crochet and 3 treble. Every succeeding round is the same as this round, but in each of the next three or four rounds increase a group of stitches here and there for the proper widening of the skirt, which when brought to 58 or 60 groups of stitches will be wide enough. At the end of the sixth or seventh row from the body, you had better, if you have left a placket hole, join now in a round to avoid sewing a seam at the back of the skirt. There are 19 rounds of crazy stitch in all to form the length of the skirt. After this proceed for the **Border**, working in looped crochet. **1st round**—Double crochet. **2nd round**—1 double crochet on stitch of last round, twist the wool three times round the first and second fingers of the left hand, going first over then under and ending with the wool over the first finger, insert

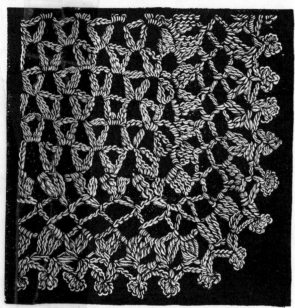

Light Open Pattern for a Shawl.

the hook in the next stitch of the previous row and also under the four threads of wool that lie over the first finger, draw all threads through the stitch, let the loop off the fingers, wool over the needle and draw through all on the needle, repeat alternately to the end. **3rd round**—Double crochet. Repeat these two rounds four times; a looped crochet stitch is always to come over a looped crochet of former round. **12th round**—Work in scallops, thus—1 double crochet on double crochet stitch of last round, miss one stitch, 1 double crochet, 3 treble, 1 double crochet, all on the next, miss one stitch, and repeat; fasten off at the end of the round. Now the shoulder pieces are to be joined together, and 9 rows of the looped crochet, and the scalloped row are to be worked round the neck, decreasing occasionally to contract to shape. For the **Sleeves**—With No. 9 crochet needle. Commence at the wrist end, with 30 chain, and join round. Work the first round in plain double crochet, and the succeeding rounds in the twisted stitch the same as the body. Do 4 rounds upon 30 stitches; then increase 1 stitch in every round (always in a different place) till brought to 40 or more stitches. Work 7 or 8 rounds without increase. **Next round**—To shape for the top of the Sleeve— Work in the same twisted stitch, and leave 5 stitches unworked at the end of the round, and fasten off. Work now in rows, omitting 2 stitches at the beginning and 2 stitches at the end, for 4 rows. Next, work round the wrist 9 rounds of the looped crochet, and end with a round worked in scallops. Shape the other sleeve to correspond. Work buttonholes up the right-hand side of the body, thus, 3 double crochet stitches, * 3 chain, miss two, 5 double crochet, and repeat from *; then put the buttons on the opposite side to meet the buttonholes. Divide the ribbon and run pieces in the four open rows down the front of the body, also run a piece round the waist, unless you prefer a broad silk sash loosely tied, and make up the remainder into small bows to place down the front of the dress.

NOISETTE ROSE PATTERN FOR ANTIMACASSAR.

THIS is a pretty design for a cotton crochet antimacassar, and may be worked with Evans' or Coats' crochet cotton, No. 12 or No. 14, and a fine steel crochet needle. Commence with 8 chain, join round; do 6 chain, 1 treble in the circle, 3 chain and 1 treble in the circle six times, 3 chain, and join to the third stitch of the chain with which the round commenced. **2nd round**—Work 1 double crochet, 4 treble, 1 double crochet, all under every loop of three chain. **3rd round**—1 single crochet at the back of the work on top of the treble stitch of the first round, 4 chain, and repeat. **4th round**—1 double crochet, 6 treble, 1 double crochet, under every loop of four chain. **5th round**—1 single crochet at the back of the work on top of the single crochet stitch of the third round, 5 chain, and repeat. **6th round**—1 double crochet, 8 treble, 1 double crochet, under every loop of five chain. **7th round**—1 single crochet at the back of the work on top of the single crochet stitch of the fifth round, 10 chain, 1 single crochet in the seventh chain from the needle, 3 chain, and repeat. **8th round**—Single crochet up to the round

loop of chain, where do 1 double crochet, 5 chain and 1 double crochet five times, then 5 chain, * 1 double crochet in the next round loop, 5 chain and 1 double crochet five times in the same place, 5 chain, and repeat from *, making 8 groups of picots round the rose, join evenly, and fasten off. Work another rose, and in process of crocheting the eight round, join the fourth picot of the seventh group to the second picot of the seventh group of the first rose and the middle picot of the eighth group to the middle picot of the sixth group of the first rose. The third rose is joined in the same way to the seventh and sixth groups of the second rose, and the fourth rose is joined in place to the first and third; and now as seen in the illustration you have a square of four roses. For the **Border** round the **Square of Roses—1st round**— 1 double crochet in the middle picot of the first group of picots on one of the roses, 8 chain, 1 double crochet in the middle picot of the next group, 9 chain, 1 double crochet in the middle picot of the corner group, 9 chain, 1 double crochet in the middle picot of the next group, 8 chain, 1 double crochet in the middle picot of the next group, 7 chain to pass from rose to rose, and repeat, and join evenly at the completion of the round. **2nd round**— 1 double crochet on every stitch of preceding round, 3 double crochet on each corner stitch, join, and break off the cotton. **3rd round**—Beginning on a corner stitch of last round, 1 long treble on the centre stitch of three double crochet, 3 chain, another long treble in the same place, 1 treble on each of the 2 next stitches, 1 double crochet on next, 1 treble on each of 2 next stitches, * 1 long treble on the next, 3 chain, another long treble in the same place, 1 treble on each of 2 next, 1 double crochet on next, 1 treble on each of 2 next, and repeat from * to the end of the round, and join to the commencement. **4th round**—1 double crochet under the loop of three chain, 5 chain and 1 double crochet three times in the same place, 5 chain, and repeat; fasten off at the end of the round. Twelve squares will make a good-sized antimacassar; they are joined to each other by the middle picots in process of working the last round of the border.

LADY'S JACKET.

THIS jacket is intended to wear as a winter bodice under the dress, or out of doors for extra warmth under a mantle. Required, 8 ozs. cardinal and 2 ozs. of brown Berlin fingering, a No. 6 long bone tricot needle, and eight brown bone buttons. Begin with cardinal wool, with 29 chain, for one of the back tabs, and do 3 rows of plain tricot. **4th row**—Decrease 1 stitch at each end, but not the outside stitch, do always 1 plain stitch at each end and decrease the following by picking up 2 stitches together. Work 3 plain rows. **8th row**—Decrease as before. Work 3 plain rows. **12th row**—Decrease again. Work 3 plain rows. In the **16th** and **17th rows** increase a stitch at each end. Work 1 plain row. **19th row**—Increase 1 stitch at each end. Break off the wool. Make another back tab the same. Then make two tabs for the fronts. Work the same as the back tabs for 14 rows. **15th row**—Increase 1 stitch at the beginning of the row which is the part to go below the arm, keep the front straight. **16th row**—Increase again under the arm. **17th row**—

French Hat for a Baby Boy.

Plain. **18th row**—Increase again on the same side. Break off the wool. Make the other tab similarly as far as the fourteenth row, and in the following rows keep the work straight at the beginning of the row which is the right side front of the jacket, and increase at the end. **19th row**, which is the 1st row of the **Body**—Plain tricot, taking up the stitches of all four of the tabs. **2nd row**—Increase 1 stitch at the beginning, increase 1 stitch under each arm, and also increase 1 stitch at the end. Work 3 plain rows. **6th row**—Increase 1 stitch at the beginning, 2 stitches under each arm (working 1 plain stitch between the 2 increased), and 1 stitch at the end. Work 3 plain rows. **10th row**—Increase 1 stitch at the beginning, 2 stitches under each arm (working 3 plain stitches between the 2 increased), and 1 stitch at the end. Work 3 plain rows. **14th row**—Increase 1 stitch at the beginning, 2 stitches under each arm (working five plain stitches between the 2 increased), and 1 stitch at the end. Work 4 plain rows. **19th row**—Here divide for the armholes, increase 1 stitch at the beginning, and pick up 34 stitches beyond, and work back. **20th row**—Omit 2 stitches at the end of the row. **21st row**—Omit 2 stitches at the end. **22nd row**—Omit 1 stitch at the end. Do 2 more rows the same as last row. Work 7 plain rows. **32nd row**—Decrease 1 stitch at the beginning. **33rd row**—Plain. **34th row**—Decrease 1 stitch at the beginning, and increase 1 stitch at the end to shape the shoulder. **35th row**—Plain. Repeat the last two rows twice.

40th row—Decrease 1 stitch at the beginning, and increase 1 stitch at the end. **41st row**—Decrease 1 stitch at the beginning. **42nd row**—Decrease 1 stitch at the beginning, and increase 1 at the end. **43rd row**—Decrease 1 stitch at the beginning. **44th row**—The same. **45th row**—Plain. **46th row**—Omit 4 stitches at the end. **47th row**—Decrease 1 stitch at the beginning, and omit 4 stitches at the end. Now leave this piece of work, and using wool from another ball, proceed with the opposite side of the front to correspond. For the **Back**—**1st row**—Leave two stitches from the right side front, and pick up all the stitches to within two of the left front, and draw back. **2nd row**—Decrease 2 stitches on each side. Work 4 rows, decreasing 1 stitch on each side. Work 2 plain rows. Next row again decrease 1 stitch on each side. Work 10 plain rows. Work 8 rows, decreasing 1 stitch on each side. Break off the wool. Resume on the right side front, work along, join at the shoulder, work along back, join the other shoulder, and work along the left side front, and draw back. Do 6 or 8 rows, according how high you wish to make the neck, in one row decrease 3 stitches on each shoulder and work the alternate row plain. Finish with a row of slip stitch. For the **Sleeves**—Make a chain the length of the armhole and work, **1st row**—Plain tricot. **2nd row**—Omit 4 stitches at the beginning and 4 stitches at the end. Work 3 more rows the same as last row. **6th row**—Plain tricot all along from beginning to the end. **7th row**—Decrease 1 stitch at the beginning and 1 stitch at the end. **8th row**—Plain. Repeat the last

GLADYS JACKET.

THIS is a very pretty jacket worked in ridged double crochet to fit a child of eighteen months or two years. Procure 5 ozs. of best white Peacock fingering, a No. 11 bone crochet needle, and three-quarters of a yard of inch-wide white ribbon for a bow. Commence at the neck with 69 chain. **1st row**—Plain double crochet, 68 stitches in the row. **2nd row**—Turn the work, and double crochet 68 stitches, inserting the hook in the back thread of the stitches of last row. Work 2 more rows the same. **5th row**—Do 8 double crochet, increase (which in this pattern means work 2 double crochet into each of four consecutive stitches of last row), 8 double crochet, increase, 20 double crochet, increase, 8 double crochet, increase, 8 double crochet. Work 2 rows of plain double crochet, 84 stitches in each row. **8th row**—36 double crochet, increase, 4 double crochet, increase, 36 double crochet. Work 2 rows of plain double crochet, 92 stitches in each row. **11th row**—Increase, 4 double crochet, increase, 12 double crochet, increase, 36 double crochet, increase, 12 double crochet, increase, 4 double crochet, increase. Work 3 rows of plain double crochet, 116 stitches in each row. **15th row**—16 double crochet, increase, 16 double crochet, increase, 36 double crochet, increase, 16 double crochet, increase, 16 double crochet. Work 3 rows of plain double crochet. **19th row**—16 double crochet, increase, 24 double crochet, increase, 36 double crochet, increase, 24 double crochet, increase, 16 double crochet.

Dorothy Frock for a Child of Four.

Noisette Rose Pat

2 rows three times. **15th row**—Slip stitch, and fasten off. Sew up the sleeve, and sew it in the armhole. Work the other sleeve the same. For the **Border**—With brown wool, and a No. 10 crochet needle. **1st row**—Work round the bottom and up both fronts of the jacket in plain double crochet, and slip stitch along the neck. **2nd row**—Work down the left-hand front as far as the buttons are to extend in plain double crochet, work to the end of the left-hand front, round the bottom, and up the right front, thus, * insert the hook in the next double crochet of previous row and draw the wool through, do 4 chain, wool over the needle and draw through 2 stitches on the needle, 1 double crochet on next stitch, and repeat from *, and work single crochet along the neck, decreasing a stitch here and there. **3rd row**—Plain double crochet round the jacket, and slip stitch along the neck. **4th row**—Double crochet on left-hand front as far as the double crochet of the second row, * 6 treble on the next stitch, miss five, and repeat from *, and work single crochet along the neck. **5th row**—Double crochet on the left-hand front as before, then 1 double crochet on the first treble stitch, 2 double crochet on each of 4 treble stitches, 1 double crochet on the sixth treble stitch, 1 double crochet into the third missed stitch of previous row, and repeat from *; work edge along the neck of * 3 treble in one stitch, miss one, 1 double crochet in next, miss one, and repeat from *. Work the same border round the sleeves. Sew eight buttons down the left front.

Work 3 rows plain. **23rd row**—20 double crochet, increase, 28 double crochet, increase, 36 double crochet, increase, 28 double crochet, increase, 20 double crochet. Work 3 rows plain. **27th row**—26 double crochet, miss 36 stitches to form an armhole, 40 double crochet, miss 36 stitches for the other armhole, 26 double crochet. Work 5 rows of plain double crochet, 92 stitches in each row. **33rd row**—8 double crochet, increase, repeat this six times, end with 8 double crochet. Work 4 rows of plain double crochet, 120 stitches in each row. **38th row**—12 double crochet, increase, 8 double crochet, increase, 12 double crochet, increase, 12 double crochet, increase twice (that is, in eight stitches), 12 double crochet, increase, 12 double crochet, increase, 8 double crochet, increase, 12 double crochet. Work 6 rows plain. **45th row**—74 double crochet, increase, 74 double crochet. Work 4 rows of plain double crochet. Work 1 row of double crochet down one side front, along the bottom of the jacket, and up the other side front. For the **Sleeves**—Double crochet 36 stitches in the space left for the armholes, and work similarly 12 rows forwards and backwards. **13th row**—Decrease by missing 1 stitch at the beginning and 1 stitch at the end of the row. Work 3 rows plain. Repeat from the thirteenth row till there are 30 stitches. **25th row**—For the **Border**—Work 1 double crochet stitch and 1 looped crochet stitch alternately; a looped stitch is formed by twisting the wool three times round the first and second fingers of the left hand and working it in with the stitch. **26th row**—Plain double crochet. Repeat the last 2 rows six times. Work the other sleeve to correspond. Crochet the same **Border** round the bottom of the jacket, up the right side front, and round the neck, increasing in the plain crochet rows as you turn the corners. Make a nice ribbon bow and put on the neck in front. Sew on either hooks and loops, or buttons, to fasten up the front of the jacket.

OPEN CROCHET FOR A STRIPE OR INSERTION.

THIS may be worked with cotton or wool according to the purpose for which it is required, for instance, if Strutt's No. 12 knitting cotton be employed the pattern is very suitable for long window curtains, being light and lacy, and worked with Shetland wool it makes a nice scarf-shaped shawl. Commence with chain for length required. **1st row**—1 single crochet in the ninth stitch from the needle, * 5 chain, miss three, 1 single crochet in the next, and repeat from *; the number of loops made in this row must be an even number divisible by four. **2nd row**—7 chain to turn, 1 single crochet in the centre stitch of the first loop of five chain of last row, 5 treble on the single crochet stitch, 1 single crochet in the centre stitch of the next

Antimacassar.

ANTIMACASSAR.

VENETIAN LATTICE STRIPE, WITH WHITE NARCISSUS FLOWER.

THIS is a particularly pretty pattern for an antimacassar, and the original is worked with single Berlin wool, a pale sky blue, white, grey, and amber being the colours employed. Bone crochet needle, No 12. Commence with blue wool for the **Wide Stripe** with 25 chain. **1st row**—Work 1 double crochet in the third chain from the needle, and double crochet all along the row, 23 stitches in all. Work 4 more rows of plain double crochet, doing 1 chain, miss the first stitch, and work 23 double crochet, taking up two threads. **6th row** —1 chain to turn, miss the first stitch, work 2 double crochet, wool twice round the needle, insert the hook in the work from right to left of the sixth stitch of the second row and draw the wool through, wool over the needle and draw through 2 stitches on the needle, wool over the needle and draw through 2 more stitches on the needle, wool twice round the needle, insert the hook again in the same place and draw the wool through, wool over the needle and draw through 2 stitches on the needle for three times, insert the hook in the next stitch of the previous row and draw the wool through, wool over the needle and draw through 3 stitches on the needle, 4 consecutive double crochet, wool twice round the needle, insert the hook in the work from right to left of the seventh stitch of the second row, and work 2 long treble stitches as before, finishing them off in the next stitch of the previous row, then 2 long

Lady's Jacket.

loop of chain, 5 treble on the single crochet stitch, 1 single crochet in the centre stitch of the next loop of chain, 5 chain, 1 single crochet in the centre stitch of the next loop, * 5 chain, 1 single crochet in the centre stitch of the next loop, 5 treble on the single crochet stitch, 1 single crochet in the centre stitch of the next loop, 5 chain, 1 single crochet in the centre stitch of the next loop, 5 chain, 1 single crochet in the centre stitch of the next loop, and repeat from * to the end of the row. **3rd row**—7 chain to turn, 1 single crochet in the centre stitch of the first loop of five chain, 5 chain, 1 single crochet on the centre stitch of the group of five trebles, 5 chain, 1 single crochet on the centre stitch of the next group of five trebles, 5 chain, 1 single crochet in the centre stitch of the loop of five chain, * 5 chain, 1 single crochet in the centre stitch of the next loop, 5 chain, 1 single crochet on the centre stitch of the group of five trebles, 5 chain, 1 single crochet on the centre stitch of the next group, 5 chain, 1 single crochet in the centre stitch of the loop of five chain, and repeat from * to the end of the row. **4th row**—Same as the second row, working the 5 trebles over the groups already made. Repeat the third and fourth rows alternately for the length required.

---

treble in the twelfth double crochet of the second row, 4 double crochet, 2 long treble in the thirteenth stitch of the second row and 2 long treble in the eighteenth stitch, 4 double crochet, 2 long treble in the nineteenth stitch of the second row, 3 double crochet. Work 3 rows of plain double crochet. **10th row**—1 chain to turn, 4 double crochet, wool twice round the needle and do 2 long treble in the manner directed in the sixth row over the first long treble of that row and 2 long treble over the next long treble (in this way the lattice diamonds are formed), 4 double crochet, 2 long treble over the third long treble of the sixth row and 2 long treble over the next long treble, 4 double crochet, 2 long treble over the fifth long treble of the sixth row and 2 long treble over the next long treble, 5 double crochet. Work 3 rows of plain double crochet. Repeat from the sixth row. When working the **26th row** do plain double crochet in the middle of the row, working only 4 long treble at the beginning and 4 long treble at the end; in the **30th row** work only 2 long treble at the beginning and 2 long treble at the end; and in the **34th row** work 4 long treble at the beginning and 4 long treble at the end; this is to give a flat space for the Narcissus Flower, as will be seen in the engraving. Afterwards, repeat from the sixth row for the length required; and when the stripe is complete, take the grey wool, and work all round it a row of double crochet, doing alternately 1 stitch upon the edge and 1 stitch deeply down, which gives a pretty "saw tooth" like effect. For the **Narrow Stripe**

Use white wool, and a No. 9 bone tricot needle, and beginning with 17 chain, work a stripe of plain tricot the same length as the lattice stripe, and go round this also with grey wool in the "saw tooth" double crochet stitch. Upon this stripe of white tricot is worked a diamond pattern with grey wool, as shown in the illustration, working each stitch to lie like a twisted chain upon the surface of the tricot; commence the diamond by inserting the hook from right to left under the ninth tricot stitch of the second row of the tricot and draw the wool through, then with this stitch on the needle insert the hook under the tenth tricot stitch of the third row of the tricot, bringing it up through the stitch on the needle and drawing the wool through it, do 3 more twisted stitches in the same way slanting to the left, then slant to the right till within 4 stitches of the edge, and continue the same the whole length of the stripe, when turn, and work twisted stitch back, so forming the diamonds; make tiny dots with grey wool, 4 chain, join in a circle, and work round, 12 double crochet; and place a dot in the centre of each diamond. For the

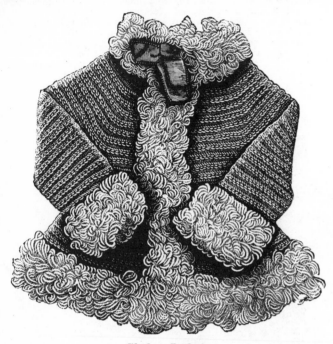

Gladys Jacket.

Narcissus Flowers to embellish the Lattice Stripe—Take white wool and with the bone crochet needle, work 7 chain, 1 double crochet in the second chain from the needle, 4 consecutive treble stitches, 6 treble in the top stitch, 4 treble and 1 double crochet down the opposite side, and a single crochet to fasten off; make 6 of these white leaves and arrange them together; then for the petals in the centre of the flower, take amber wool, work 4 chain, join in a circle, and work 2 rounds of 12 double crochet. Sew the flower down nicely on the plain crochet part of the lattice stripe. It will require three lattice stripes and two tricot stripes to make an antimacassar; crochet the stripes together with amber wool. For the Border—1st round—With grey wool—1 double crochet, 6 chain miss four stitches of the foundation, and repeat. 2nd round—1 double crochet on the double crochet of previous round, 7 chain, and repeat. 3rd round—With blue wool—Work 1 double crochet, 4 chain, 2 double crochet, 4 chain, 2 double crochet, 4 chain, 1 double crochet all under every loop of seven chain of last round. This finishes the antimacassar.

ANTIMACASSAR IN FANCY TRICOT AND CROSS STITCH.

A VERY effective antimacassar may be worked in alternate stripes of fancy tricot and Berlin wool canvas, the latter being embroidered with cross stitch with coloured filoselles in a floral scroll design. Berlin wool canvas specially intended for this work is manufactured in 4-inch, 5-inch, and 9-inch widths, in all the fashionable art colours, and is retailed at most fancy shops by the yard. A stripe of art green wool canvas about a yard in length, and a stripe of fancy raised tricot on each side worked with double Berlin wool of a bright ruby shade, will make a medium sized antimacassar that will blend admirably with the surroundings in almost any room, or other colours may be selected according to taste; two stripes of wool canvas and three stripes of tricot will suffice for a large antimacassar. Use a No. 6 tricot needle. Commence with 20 chain; raise tricot loops all along, making 20 stitches in all, and work back as in ordinary tricot. 2nd row—Pick up all the tricot stitches in the usual manner, and in working back draw through 6 stitches, work 12 chain, draw through 2 stitches, 12 chain, draw through 4 stitches, 12 chain, draw through 2 stitches, 12 chain, draw through 6 stitches. Work 2 rows of plain tricot keeping the loops of chain in front of the work. 5th row—Pick up 4 stitches, * pull the second loop of chain up and insert the hook through it and in the next tricot stitch and draw the wool through both, raise 2 stitches, pull the first loop of chain across the second, insert the hook through it and

in the next stitch of tricot and draw the wool through both, raise 2 stitches, repeat from *, and raise 5 stitches at the end of the row; now coming back, draw through 3 stitches, work 12 chain, draw through 2 stitches, 12 chain, draw through 4 stitches, 12 chain, draw through 2 stitches, 12 chain, draw through 4 stitches, 12 chain, draw through 2 stitches, 12 chain, draw through 3 stitches. 8th row—Pick up 1 stitch, * pull the second loop of chain up and insert the hook through it and in the next tricot stitch and draw the wool through both, raise 2 stitches, pull the first loop of chain across the second, insert the hook through it and in the next stitch of tricot and draw the wool through both, raise 2 stitches, repeat from *; now coming back, draw through 6 stitches, work 12 chain, draw through 2 stitches, 12 chain, draw through 4 stitches, 12 chain, draw through 2 stitches, 12 chain, draw through 6 stitches. Work 2 rows of plain tricot keeping the loops of chain in front of the work. Repeat from the fifth row till the stripe is the length required. Hem each end of the Berlin wool canvas stripe, and after having worked the cross-stitch design thereon with filoselles of various colours, do a row of "saw tooth" double crochet along each side, working 1 stitch close upon the edge, and the next stitch four or six threads lower down, this makes a pretty finish; and besides forms a line of stitches by which to join the Berlin wool stripe to the tricot stripe by a row of chain worked with wool of a good contrasting colour. Fringe the antimacassar at top and bottom with strands of wool knotted in at even distances.

WOOL ASTER.

THESE asters may be used for an antimacassar, or if a number be joined together in a long strip, and fringed and set into a heading, they make a good border for a gipsy table. Procure a sufficient quantity of three distinct shades of crimson, and a little yellow and green and black double Berlin wool, and a No. 7 bone crochet needle. Commence with the yellow wool, with 5 chain, join round, and work 12 double crochet in the circle. 2nd round—With the same wool—3 chain to stand for a treble, 1 treble on each double crochet stitch taking up both the top and back threads, join round evenly, and fasten off. 3rd round—With darkest shade of crimson—1 single crochet into the one top thread of a stitch of previous round, 1 chain, and repeat, making 12 loops of one chain in the round, join at end. 4th round—With same wool, —1 double crochet, 3 chain, 1 treble, a picot of 4 chain, 1 single crochet in the fourth chain from the needle, 1 treble, 3 chain, 1 double crochet, all to be worked under the one chain loop of last round, and repeat 11 times, which will give twelve petals in the round. 5th round—With same wool—1 double crochet in the back thread of the single crochet stitch of the third round, 3 chain, and repeat, join at end, and fasten off. 6th round—With

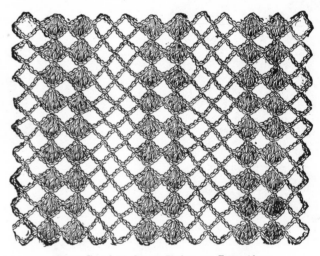

Open Crochet for a Stripe or Insertion.

medium shade of crimson—work under the three chain loop of last round in the same manner as the fourth round is worked. 7th round—With darkest shade of crimson—1 double crochet under the three chain loop of the fifth round, inserting the hook at the back and between the two treble stitches of last round, 3 chain, and repeat, join evenly at end, and fasten off. 8th round—With lightest shade of crimson—1 double crochet, 1 treble, 1 long treble, 1 picot, 1 long treble, 1 treble, 1 double crochet, all to be worked under three chain loop of last round, making twelve petals in the round. 9th round —With black wool—1 double crochet into the picot of last round, 2 chain, 1 long treble at the back into the top thread of double crochet of the seventh round, 2 chain, and repeat to the end of the round, and join evenly. 10th round—With green wool—1 double crochet under the loop to the left of the double crochet stitch of last row, 1 double crochet under the next loop, then 5 chain, 1 single crochet in the fifth chain from the needle, work three of these picots, and repeat. Twelve of these asters will make a good sized antimacassar, and to fill up the spaces between, work with darkest crimson wool the two rounds as directed for yellow wool, and a third round with green of 1 double crochet, 3 chain.

INFANT'S HOOD.

MATERIALS required, 4½ ozs. of white Shetland wool, a steel or very fine bone crochet needle, a pair of No. 10 knitting needles, a ball of white knitting silk, 2 yards of inch wide ribbon for bows and strings, 3 yards of quarter inch wide ribbon to run through the treble rows of the crochet, a lace cap front, and a piece of thin silk for head lining. Begin in the centre of the crown with 2 chain stitches, and work 4 double crochet in the second stitch from the needle. **1st round**—Do 2 double crochet on each of the four double crochet stitches, taking the one top thread only. **2nd round**—Do 2 double crochet on each of the eight stitches of the previous round, working always into the one top thread. **3rd round**—Do 2 double crochet on the first stitch, 1 double crochet on the next, and repeat, which will bring 24 stitches in the round. **4th round**—2 double crochet on the first stitch, 1 double crochet on each of the two next stitches, and repeat seven times. **5th round**—2 double crochet on the first stitch, 1 double crochet on each of the three next stitches, and repeat

Antimacassar—Venetian Lattice Stripe, with White Narcissus Flowers.

seven times. **6th round**—2 double crochet on the first stitch, 1 double crochet on each of the four next stitches and repeat seven times. Continue thus, increasing eight times in each round, and always above the last increase, till in the 13th round you do 11 double crochet between the increasings. **14th round**—Do 3 chain to commence to stand for a treble, and work treble, doing 1 treble stitch on each double crochet, rather loosely, and bringing the wool up so that the stitches stand nearly half an inch high, 104 treble in the round, and join evenly at the end, and fasten off. You now begin to work for the head— **1st row**—Knot a stitch upon the needle, wool over the needle, and insert the hook in the first stitch of one of the eight divisions of the crown and draw the wool through, wool over the needle and draw through two stitches on the needle, insert the hook in the next stitch of previous row and draw the wool through, wool over the needle and draw through 2 stitches on the needle, wool over the needle and draw through the remaining two stitches on the needle, 1 chain, and repeat this fancy stitch till you have worked over *seven* of the eight divisions of the crown, and fasten off. **2nd row**—Beginning again on the right hand side, treble worked tall and rather loosely, and increase about 6 stitches in the row. **3rd row**—Fancy stitch, the same as the first row. **4th row**—Treble. **5th row**—Fancy stitch. **6th row**—Treble. Now for the **Front** of the **Hood**—Do a strip of looped knitting on No. 10 needles. Cast on 4 stitches. **1st row**—Plain. **2nd row**—Loops, insert the needle in the stitch to be knitted, pass the wool over the point of the needle and round the three first fingers of the left hand ten or twelve times, then wool over the needle and knit the stitch in the usual manner, but drawing *all* the threads of wool through, and knit the other 3 stitches in the same way. Repeat the two rows till 10 rows of loops are done; then increase a stitch at the end of the next plain row, and knit 9 rows of loops; in the next plain row again increase a stitch at the end, and now knit as many rows of loops as will reach just beyond the middle of the last row of the crochet; then decrease a stitch at the end of the next plain row, and knit 9 rows of loops; decrease again, and knit 10 rows of loops ending with a plain row, and cast off. Sew the straight edge of this strip of knitting to the last row of the crochet, it should just reach from end to end. For the **Curtain**—Hold the work the right side towards you, and begin at the corner edge of the looped knitting; work a row of treble crochet round the bottom of the hood to the opposite corner of the looped knitting, putting in just so many treble as will let the curtain hang moderately full; break off at the end. **2nd row**—Fancy stitch like that on the hood, and break off at the end. Repeat the treble row and the fancy row twice. **7th row**—Begin this row at the corner of the looped knitting where you began before, and work treble down the side of the curtain, along the bottom thereof, and up the other side to the opposite corner of the looped knitting and fasten off. **8th row**—Work all round the curtain, 1 double crochet on each of 2 treble stitches, miss one stitch, 2 treble 2 chain 2 more

treble on the next, miss one stitch, and repeat. **9th row**—1 double crochet on each double crochet of last row, 2 treble 2 chain and 2 treble under the loop of two chain. **10th row**—With silk,—Do 1 single crochet between the two double crochet stitches, 4 chain, 1 double crochet under the loop of 2 chain, 4 chain, another double crochet in the same place, 4 chain, and repeat. Next, do the same silk edging along on the top of the second line of loop stitches at the front of the hood. Next, make three feathers of looped knitting, 3 stitches wide and 9 rows of loops in each; ornament these likewise with the silk edging, and place them in front on the top of the hood, as shown in the engraving. Line the hood and put in the lace cap. Put a bow of ribbon in front and another at the back of the crown, and put on strings to tie. Run the narrow ribbon in and out through every row of treble stitches in the hood and curtain.

SHETLAND JACKET FOR A CHILD OF TWELVE OR EIGHTEEN MONTHS.

FOR this comfortable nicely fitting little jacket, procure 2½ ozs. of best white and ½ oz. of salmon-pink Shetland wool, a No. 10 or No. 11 bone crochet needle, and 1½ yards of inch wide ribbon. Begin for the neck, with white wool, with 89 chain. **1st row**—Work 1 treble in the fourth chain from the needle, 1 treble in the next stitch, * 2 chain, miss two stitches, 1 treble in each of the 2 next, and repeat from *, making 22 groups of treble stitches. **2nd row**—3 chain to turn, do 2 treble, 1 chain, 2 treble under the first loop of two chain stitches, 2 treble, 1 chain, 2 treble, 1 chain, 2 treble, *all* under the next loop of chain, then 2 treble, 1 chain, 2 treble, to be worked under each of the next 17 loops, and 2 treble, 1 chain, 2 treble, 1 chain, 2 treble, *all* under the next loop, and 2 treble, 1 chain, 2 treble, under the last loop of the previous row; these groups of stitches are henceforth called respectively "groups" and "double groups" and are invariably to be worked under a loop of one chain; every row commences with 3 chain to turn. **3rd row**—3 chain to turn, and work in "groups," that is 2 treble, 1 chain, 2 treble, making 23 groups in the

Antimacassar in Fancy Tricot and Cross Stitch.

row. **4th row**—Do 1 group, 1 double group, 2 groups, 1 double group, 2 groups, 1 double group, 1 group and 1 double group alternately four times, 2 groups, 1 double group, 2 groups, 1 double group, 1 group. **5th row**—Work in groups, making 32 groups in the row. **6th row**—1 double group, 3 groups, 1 double group, 3 groups, 1 double group, 3 groups, 1 double group, 6 groups, 1 double group, 3 groups, 1 double group, 3 groups, 1 double group. **7th row**—Work 40 groups in the row. **8th row**—6 groups, 1 double group, 4 groups, 1 double group, 16 groups, 1 double group, 4 groups, 1 double group, 6 groups. **9th row**—Work 44 groups in the row. **10th row**—6 groups, 1 double group, 6 groups, 1 double group, 16 groups, 1 double group, 6 groups, 1 double group, 6 groups. **11th row**—Work 48 groups in the row. **12th row**—7 groups, 1 double group, 7 groups, 1 double group, 16 groups, 1 double group, 7 groups, 1 double group, 7 groups. **13th row**—Work 52 groups in the row. **14th row**—8 groups, miss nine groups for an armhole, work 18 groups, miss nine groups for the other armhole, 8 groups. Now work 7 rows without increase, doing 34 groups in each row. **22nd row**—6 groups, 1 double group, 2 groups, 1 double group, 14 groups, 1 double group, 2 groups, 1 double group, 6 groups. Work 5 rows in groups, 38 groups in each row. **28th row**—13 groups, 1 double group, 10 groups, 1 double group, 13 groups. **29th row**—Work 40 groups in the row. **30th row**—8 groups, 1 double group, 6 groups, 1 double group, 8 groups, 1 double group, 6 groups, 1 double group, 8 groups. Work 3 rows, doing 44 groups in each row. **34th row**—12 groups, 1 double group, 18 groups, 1 double group, 12 groups. Work 3 rows, doing 46 groups in each row. After the last of these rows fasten off the white wool. The **Border** is worked partly with pink and partly with white wool. For the **1st round**—Take the pink wool, and holding the right side of the jacket next you, begin by the neck to work down the left side of the front, and go all round the jacket in groups of 2 treble, 2 chain, 2 treble, increasing two groups at the corners. Then do 2 rounds with white wool in the same stitch (no increase); and also with white wool go once again round the jacket but break off at the opposite corner by the neck, as the two rows already done are sufficient there. For the **last round**—Take the pink wool, and * do a group of 3 treble, 2 chain, 3 treble, under a chain loop of previous round, 2 chain, 1 single crochet in the space between the groups of treble stitches, 2 chain, 1 single crochet in the space of the preceding row, 2 chain,

Wool Aster.

1 single crochet in the space of the next row preceding, 2 chain, 1 single in the space of the next row preceding which is the pink row so that now a line of pink stitches forms a connecting link between the first and last rows of pink wool, 3 chain, 1 single crochet in the space of the first white row (to come back to the edge), 2 chain, 1 single crochet in the space of the next row, 2 chain, 1 single crochet in the space of the last previous row, 2 chain, and repeat from *; the direction the pink wool takes is clearly visible in the illustration, and the looping of chain between the groups gives a very pleasing effect. For the **Sleeves**—Work round the armhole with white wool, doing 12 groups of stitches in a round for 4 rounds. Decrease in the **5th round** by working 2 treble as a group under the arm, and in the **6th round** decrease again, doing only 1 treble. Work 11 groups in a round for 4 rounds. Decrease as before in each of the two next rounds. Work 10 groups in a round for 4 rounds. Then work the **Border** as described above, doing the first round with pink wool, two rounds with white, and the last round with pink. Put a button on at the neck of the jacket, and finish by running a piece of ribbon in at the neck and wrists, tying the ends in a pretty bow.

SQUARE MEDALLION FOR AN ANTIMACASSAR.

A VERY pretty crochet antimacassar can be made with these medallions, using Strutt's No. 24 crochet cotton and a fine steel crochet needle. Commence with 4 chain, join round, and work 8 double crochet in the circle, and again join round. **2nd round**—Work 2 double crochet on each stitch of last round, and join evenly. **3rd round**—8 chain, miss one stitch of last round, 1 treble on the next, * 5 chain, miss one stitch, 1 treble on the next; repeat from * six times; then 5 chain, and join into the third chain with which the round commenced. **4th round**—5 chain, 1 treble in the centre stitch of the five chain of last round, 5 chain, 1 single crochet in the top of the treble stitch just done, 5 chain, 1 single crochet in the same place, 5 chain, 1 single crochet again in the same place, 5 chain, 1 double crochet on treble stitch of last round, and repeat the same, and join neatly at the end of the round, and fasten off. **5th round**—Recommence with 1 treble under a centre loop of chain picot stitches of previous round, 7 chain, another treble in the same place, 9 chain, 1 single crochet under the next centre loop of chain picot, 9 chain, * 1 treble under the next centre loop of chain picot, 7 chain, another treble in the same place, 9 chain, 1 single crochet under the next centre loop of chain picot, 9 chain, and repeat from *, and join evenly at the end of the round. **6th round**—4 chain to stand for a treble, miss one

chain stitch, 1 treble in the next, 1 chain, miss one stitch, 1 treble in the next, 5 chain, another treble in the same place *, 1 chain, miss one, 1 treble in the next, repeat from * thirteen times, which will bring you to the next corner, 15 treble being along the side of the square and 1 chain stitch between the trebles, 5 chain, do another treble in the same place as the last treble, and continue to the end of the round, and join neatly to the third stitch of the chain with which the round began. **7th round**—4 chain to stand for a treble, 1 treble on treble stitch of last round, 1 chain, 1 treble on treble stitch, 1 chain, miss one chain stitch of last round, 1 treble in the next, * 5 chain, miss one, 1 treble in the next, 1 chain, 1 treble on treble stitch, and continue 1 chain and 1 treble alternately till 17 treble are done along the side of the square, then repeat from *, and join neatly when you come to the end of the round. **8th round**—The same as the seventh round, but doing 19 treble along each side of the square. **9th round**—The same, but 21 treble along each side of the square. **10th round**—The same, but 23 treble along each side of the square. **11th round**—Slip stitch to the next treble stitch of last round, that is to the sixth treble stitch from the end of the side of the square, do 4 chain, miss three stitches, 1 treble on the fourth treble stitch from the end, 5 chain, 1 single crochet in the top of the treble stitch just done, 5 chain, 1 single crochet in the same place, 5 chain, another single crochet in the same place, 4 chain, miss four stitches, 1 single crochet in the 1 chain stitch at the end of the side of the square, 4 chain, 1 treble in the centre stitch of five chain at the corner, 5 chain, 1 single crochet in the top of the treble stitch just done, 5 chain, 1 single crochet on the single crochet, do this twice more, 1 treble in the same place that last treble is worked into, 4 chain, 1 single crochet in the one chain stitch at the beginning of the side of the square, 4 chain, 1 treble on the fourth treble stitch along the side of the square *, 5 chain, 1 single crochet in the top of the treble stitch just done, 5 chain, 1 single crochet in the same place, 5 chain, another single crochet in the same place, 4 chain, miss three stitches, 1 single crochet on the next, 4 chain, miss three stitches, 1 treble on the next (which is the eighth treble stitch along the side of the square), repeat from * till you have five sets of pique loops along the side of the square, and then shape the second corner the same as the first corner, and proceed to the end of the round. The succeeding squares are joined by the pique loops in the course of working the last round.

ANTIMACASSAR TRICOT

THIS antimacassar is worked in stripes of plain tricot with double Berlin wool of two good contrasting colours, and is embroidered in cross stitch with filoselles in the very effective design shown in our illustration. Use No 5 tricot needle, and begin for the wide stripe with fawn coloured wool with 25 chain. **1st row**—Pick up 24 stitches, retaining them all on the needle, there

Infant's Hood.

will be 25 stitches in all, counting the one at the beginning; to work back, wool over the needle and draw through one stitch, wool over the needle and draw through two stitches together to the end. **2nd row**—Insert the hook in each of the perpendicular stitches of last row and draw the wool through, making again 25 stitches on the needle, and work back as directed in the first row. Every succeeding row is worked the same as the second row. The stripe should measure about a yard in length; work single crochet along the stitches of the last row, and fasten off. Then for the narrow stripe take blue wool and commencing with 12 chain, proceed with tricot in the same manner as you worked the wide stripe, doing the same number of rows exactly, and fasten off. The cross-stitch design is clearly shown in the engraving, the pattern on the wide fawn-coloured stripe may be worked with blue filoselle, and that on the narrow blue stripe with fawn and grey filoselle. Two wide stripes and three narrow ones will be sufficient for a nice sized antimacassar. Join the stripes neatly together. Fringe the antimacassar at the top and bottom with strands of wool knotted in bunches at regular intervals.

CHILD'S TRICOT SKIRT.
(Not Illustrated.)

PROCURE petticoat wool or 3 thread Fleecy, AA Peacock quality, from 8 ozs. to 12 ozs., according to the size the skirt is required to be. Tricot needle, No. 6. Commence with chain sufficient for the width of the bottom of the skirt, any number divisible by 6 and 2 over. **1st row** and **2nd row**—Plain

Shetland Jacket for a Child of Twelve or Eighteen Months.

tricot. **3rd row**—Pick up all the stitches on the needle in the usual manner, and in coming back, draw through 4 consecutive stitches, * then 3 chain, draw through 6 consecutive stitches; repeat from * to the end of the row, where will be 4 stitches to draw through to finish. **4th row**—Pick up all stitches, bringing the picot of three chain to the front of the work; in coming back, draw through 3 stitches, * 3 chain, draw through 2 stitches, 3 chain, draw through 4 stitches, and repeat from *, and there will be 3 stitches to draw through at the end of the row. **5th row**—Pick up all stitches, and, in coming back, draw through 2 stitches, * 3 chain, draw through 2 stitches, and repeat from * to the end of the row. **6th row**—Pick up all stitches, and in coming back draw through 1 stitch, * 3 chain, draw through 2 stitches, and repeat from * to the end, where will be 1 stitch only. **7th row** and **8th row** —Plain tricot. **9th row**—Pick up all stitches, and in coming back draw through 1 stitch *, 3 chain, draw through 6 stitches, repeat from *, and there will be 1 stitch to draw through after 3 chain at the end. **10th row**—Pick up all stitches, and in coming back draw through 2 stitches, * 3 chain, draw through 4, 3 chain, draw through 2, and repeat from * to the end of the row. **11th row**—Pick up all stitches, and in coming back draw through 1 stitch, * 3 chain, draw through 2 stitches, and repeat from * to the end, where will be only 1 stitch to draw through. **12th row**—Pick up all stitches, and in coming back draw through 2 stitches, * 3 chain, draw through 2 stitches, and repeat from * to the end of the row. **13th row** and **14th row**—Plain tricot. **15th row**—Here begin decreasing to shape the top of the skirt; fold the skirt in half, and with a thread of coloured cotton, mark each half in three equidistant places to show where the decreasings are to come, six in the course of the row by picking up 2 stitches together above the cotton marks. Work 3 rows of plain tricot; then next row decrease again over the decreasings of the fifteenth row. Continue thus for the length of the skirt; the centre decreasings will gradually get closer to each other. Join up the back of the petticoat, leaving space at the top for a placket hole; strengthen round the placket hole with double crochet. Set the skirt into a calico waistband. Finish off the bottom of the skirt with a **Crochet Edge**. **1st row**—1 double crochet into a stitch of the commencing chain, * miss 2 stitches, 6 treble in the next, miss 2 stitches, 1 double crochet in the next, and repeat from *. **2nd row**—1 single crochet in every stitch of last round. For **Chain-stitch Heading** to the crochet edge—Hold the skirt the right side towards you, the crochet edge being to the left; insert the hook from the front to the back of the work in the stitch of commencing chain that the double crochet is worked into, draw the wool through the work, * insert the hook from the front to the back of the work through the next chain stitch, and draw the wool loosely through the work and through the stitch on the needle, repeat from * all round the skirt, and do the same along the top of the first row of tricot stitches.

PRETTY PATTERN FOR USING UP ODDS AND ENDS OF WOOL.
(Not Illustrated.)

IT is often very desirable to find a use for remnants of wool that have been left from time to time from large pieces of work, and very pretty antimacassars and sofa coverings may be made in this pattern if the colours be selected with taste. The work is crocheted in squares which are afterwards joined together. In our model the centre of each square is white surrounded by yellow, this gives a bright and cheerful appearance which would otherwise be missing. With No. 9 bone crochet needle and white wool commence with 4 chain, join round, do 3 chain to stand for a treble, then in the circle work 2 treble, 3 chain, 3 treble, 3 chain, 3 treble, 3 chain, 3 treble, 3 chain, and join round into the first group of stitches; break off the wool and secure the ends neatly at the completion of this and every round. **2nd round**—With yellow —3 treble, 3 chain, 3 treble, under each loop of chain of last round. **3rd round**—With crimson, green, or any other colour that may be at command— 3 treble, 3 chain, 3 treble, all under the first loop of three chain of last round, 1 chain, 3 treble under the next loop, 1 chain, and repeat. **4th round**—With black—3 treble, 3 chain, 3 treble, all under the loop of three chain of last round, 1 chain, 3 treble under loop of one chain, 1 chain, 3 treble under next loop of one chain, 1 chain, and repeat. This finishes the square. Get a number of squares made and sew them together with a needleful of black wool. When the piece of work is sufficiently large the following **Ball Edging** will make a very pretty finish. **1st round**—Work with amber wool the same as the fourth round above. **2nd round**—With green—1 double crochet on a stitch of last round, * 3 chain, insert the hook in the top of the double crochet just done and draw the wool through, wool over the needle and draw through one stitch, wool over the needle and draw through two stitches, miss two stitches of last row, 1 double crochet on the next, and repeat from * to the end of the round; ease the corners by missing only one stitch. **3rd round**—With crimson—1 double crochet in the centre one of the three chain stitches of last round, * 4 chain, wool over the needle (to make the ball) insert the hook in the second chain stitch from the needle and draw the wool through, wool over the needle and draw through one stitch, wool over the needle, insert the hook again in the same chain stitch and draw the wool through, wool over the needle, insert the hook again in the same chain stitch and draw the wool through, wool over the needle and draw through one stitch, wool over the needle, insert the hook again in the same

Square Medallion for an Antimacassar.

chain stitch and draw the wool through, there are now 9 stitches on the needle, draw through all rather loosely, now do 1 single crochet in the next stitch of chain beyond the ball, and work 1 treble into the top of the double crochet stitch, then 1 double crochet in the centre of the next three chain stitches of last round, and repeat from *.

PETTICOAT WORKED IN TREBLE STITCH.
(Not Illustrated.)

THIS is a good petticoat to work for charity purposes, as it is quickly and easily made, and wool of any colour may be employed, so that odds and ends of wool may be used, provided there is enough of any one colour to work an entire round of the petticoat. Scotch Fingering is a strong wool for wear; from 4 ozs. will be required, according to the size of the petticoat, and use a No. 11 bone crochet needle. Begin with chain sufficiently long to go round the waist. **1st row**—Plain treble: turn the work at the end of every row, doing 3 chain stitches, and work into the two top threads of the row previous. **2nd row**—Work 2 treble in every third or fourth stitch to increase the fulness. Continue working rows of treble, increasing gradually as required, until sufficient length is done for the placket. Then join round, and henceforth work in rounds, and turn the work at the end of every round, always joining the last stitch of the round to the first with a single crochet; increase as before, till the petticoat is wide enough, when work as many more rounds as are needed to make the required length. Work for the **last round** a scalloped edge, 1 double crochet in the first stitch, miss one, 5 treble in the next, miss one, and repeat. Strengthen round the placket with a row of double crochet. Set the petticoat into a calico waistband, or work a few rows of double crochet for a band.

WAISTCOAT, TENT STITCH, TRICOT.
(Not Illustrated.)

THIS pretty striped stitch is very suitable for a waistcoat, being close and firm. You may have a paper pattern and shape the tricot to the exact size, or you may work a long straight piece and have it cut to shape when made up; the latter is the easiest plan unless you are an experienced worker. Procure 10 ozs. of double Berlin wool, and a long bone tricot needle No. 7. Commence for the bottom of the waistcoat with chain sufficient to reach from the edge of the front to the seam under the arm, any even number of stitches. **1st row** —Raise a series of stitches in the chain keeping them all on the needle, and work back as in ordinary tricot. **2nd row** —Insert the hook in the second perpendicular thread of last row and raise a stitch, insert the hook in the first perpendicular thread and raise a stitch, this forms a little cross, raise a stitch in the second thread from where you now are, then raise one in the first thread, and continue in this manner crossing all the threads to the end of the row, where do the last stitch plain, and work back as in ordinary tricot. Every succeeding row is the same as the second row, and the threads that are crossed impart a striped pattern on the work. The pocket-holes are formed in the required place by missing ten or twelve stitches of the tricot, and when working back do an equal number of chain in substitution. When this front is long enough, finish it off with a row of single crochet stitch, and work the other front in the same way. Send the work to a tailor to be made up.

HOOD FOR A LADY OR CHILD.
(Not Illustrated.)

THIS is a warm pretty hood for a child, and is also comfortable for a lady to wear when driving late at night or when travelling. If worked with cheap strong wool a hood is a useful gift for a poor person. Procure 3 ozs. of white or coloured single Berlin wool, or German fingering, a No. 11 and No. 9 bone crochet needle, a pair of No. 8 knitting needles, and 3 yards of inch-wide and 2 yards of half-inch wide ribbon for bows and strings. Use No. 11 crochet needle, and commence with 6 chain for the centre of the crown, and join round. **1st round** —Do 4 chain to stand for a long treble stitch, and work 5 long treble stitches (wool twice round the needle) in each stitch of the commencing chain, 30 long treble in all, and join round. Now proceed round and round in double crochet, increasing as frequently as necessary to make the crown lie perfectly flat, and always taking up the one top thread of the stitches of the preceding round, and do altogether 7 rounds of double crochet, and end with a single crochet on the last stitch to make an even join. **9th round** —Take the No. 9 crochet needle, and work round the crown in "Shell" stitch, otherwise termed "Point Neige" stitch, thus—do 3 chain, insert the hook in the second chain from the needle and draw the wool through, insert the hook in the next chain and draw the wool through, insert the hook in the top thread of stitch of previous round and draw the wool through, insert the hook in the back thread of the same stitch and draw the wool through, now 5 stitches on the needle, wool over the needle and draw through all, do 1 chain to secure the group, * insert the hook in the small hole formed by the one chain and draw the wool through, insert the hook in the back of the shell stitch just made and draw the wool through, insert the hook in the top thread of the next stitch of previous round and draw the wool through, insert the hook in the top thread of the next stitch and draw the wool through

Antimacassar Tricot.

now 5 stitches on the needle, wool over the needle and draw through all, do 1 chain, and repeat from *; increase where necessary to keep the work flat, which increase is managed by inserting the hook in the back thread and drawing the wool through instead of inserting it in the *next* stitch of double crochet; join evenly at the end of the round. Work 2 more rounds of shell stitch with only increase of 5 or 6 stitches in the round. Next, work shell stitch upon shell stitch (no increase), till within three inches of the end of the round, where break off the wool, the three inches being left for the back of the neck, and henceforward work in rows, for the head, doing 7 rows, and in the first and third of these rows increase 3 stitches on the top of the head. For the **Curtain** —Use No. 9 crochet needle, and make a chain the same length as the bottom of the hood. **1st row** —Work 1 double crochet in the second chain from the needle, * miss two stitches, 4 long treble in the next, 3 long treble in the next, miss two, 1 double crochet in the next, and repeat from * to the end. **2nd row** —3 chain to turn, work 4 long treble on the double crochet stitch, 1 double crochet on the centre stitch of the group of seven long treble stitches, * seven long treble on the next double crochet stitch, and 1 double crochet on the centre stitch of the next group of seven long treble stitches, and repeat from *, and end the row with 4 long treble as it began. **3rd row** —Turn, and do 1 double crochet on the first long treble stitch, * 7 long treble on the next double crochet of previous row, 1 double crochet on the centre stitch of the group of seven long treble, and repeat from *, and end the row with 1 double crochet on the last long treble stitch. Repeat the last two rows, and then fasten off. Hold the right side of the curtain towards you, and along the opposite side of the commencing chain work 1 double crochet, * miss one stitch, 3 treble in the next, miss one stitch, 1 double crochet in the next, and repeat from * to the end. Sew the commencing chain to the edge of the bottom of the hood in such a way that the curtain hangs downwards, and the little scalloped edge stands up over the edge of the hood. Now holding the work the right side towards you, work all round the curtain and along the front of the hood in the same pattern as before, but doing 8 long treble in a group in the first round, and 9 long treble in a group in the second round. Now the half-inch wide ribbon is to be cut into two lengths, and each length is puckered or fluted upon the hood on the two last rows of the shell stitch. Work for head-lining with the knitting needles, casting on 20 stitches, and knit a strip of plain knitting, which sew from end to end of the hood reaching from the edge of the shell stitch crochet to the crown, which latter is not lined. Make up the inch-wide ribbon into bows for the top of the head, putting one small bow at the back over the curtain, and sew on strings to tie.

COMFORTER.
(Not Illustrated.)

PROCURE single Berlin wool, 4 ozs. of grey and 2 ozs. of ruby, and a bone crochet needle No. 8. Begin with grey wool, with chain the width you desire the comforter to be. **1st row** —Wool over the needle and raise a stitch loosely as if for tricot in 3 successive stitches of the chain, wool over the needle and draw through 5 stitches on the needle, do 1 chain, insert the hook through the 3 stitches you have just raised and draw the wool through, wool over the needle and draw through 2 stitches on the needle, do 1 chain, and repeat; break off the wool at the end of the row. **2nd row** —With ruby—Work 1 treble at the beginning of last row to keep the edge even, 1 chain, * wool over the needle and raise a stitch loosely as if for tricot in 3 successive stitches of last row (the centre of the 3 being in one chain stitch), wool over the needle and draw through 5 stitches on the needle, do one chain, insert the hook through the three stitches you have just raised and draw the wool through, wool over the needle and draw through 2 stitches on the needle, do 1 chain, and repeat from * to the end of the row, where work 1 treble to keep the edge even. Repeat the first and second rows till about 7 inches length is done for the end of the comforter, then work the centre all in grey, and do the other end to correspond with the commencement. Work an edge all round the comforter with grey wool, 1 double crochet, 3 chain, and repeat. The ends of the comforter should be fringed by cutting strands of wool and knotting three or four strands under the loops of chain stitches.

WELDON'S
PRACTICAL CROCHET.
(TENTH SERIES.)

HOW TO CROCHET MITTENS, CAPES, PETTICOATS, QUILTS, CHEMISE TRIMMINGS, ETC.

TWENTY-FOUR ILLUSTRATIONS.

Telegraphic Address—
"Consuelo," London.]
The Yearly Subscription to this Magazine, post free to any Part of the World, is 2s. 6d.
Subscriptions are payable in advance, and may commence from any date and for any period.
[**Telephone—**
2745.

The Back Numbers are always in print. Nos. 1 to 86 *now ready, Price* 2d. *each, or post free for* 15s. 4d. *Over* 5,000 *Engravings.*

DOLL'S WALKING COSTUME.

THIS costume consists of pelisse, cape, hat, muff, shoes, and handkerchief bag, worked in wool crochet, with a pair of knitted drawers, and a knitted petticoat with bodice, and fits a doll measuring 11 inches high. Procure 8 ozs. of Eider wool of a light fawn colour for the out-door apparel, 1 oz. of white Beehive wool, 1 oz. of white Andalusian, and ½ oz. of white Shetland for the underclothing, a fine bone crochet needle, a pair of steel knitting needles No. 13, four knitting needles No. 14, nine or ten small hooks and eyes, and a few small ornamental buttons.

Commence with the fawn wool and fine crochet needle for the **Pelisse,** which excepting the looped crochet rows at the bottom is worked throughout in plain double crochet, in rows forwards and backwards, closely and firmly, taking up the two top threads of the stitches of the preceding row, and always doing 1 chain to turn at the end of every row. Make 115 chain for the width round the bottom. **1st row**—Loop crochet—Twist the wool four times, over the first finger of the left hand, insert the hook in a stitch of the work and draw all four threads of wool through, wool over the needle and draw through all on the needle; every stitch is worked in the same way, and forms a loop of three strands of wool on the side of the work farthest from you. **2nd row** —Plain double crochet. **3rd row**—Looped crochet **4th row**—Double crochet. **5th row**—Looped crochet. Work 4 rows of double crochet of 114 stitches. **10th row**—Work 32 double crochet, miss one stitch, 48 double crochet, miss one stitch, 32 double crochet. Work 3 rows of double crochet of 112 stitches. **14th row**—Work 31 double crochet, miss one stitch, 48 double crochet, miss one stitch, 31 double crochet. Work 3 rows of double crochet of 110 stitches. **18th row**—30 double crochet, miss one stitch, 48 double crochet, miss one stitch, 30 double crochet. Work 3 rows of 108 stitches. **22nd row**—29 double crochet, miss one stitch, 48 double crochet, miss one stitch, 29 double crochet. Work 3 rows of double crochet, 106 stitches. **26th row**—28 double crochet, miss one stitch, 48 double crochet, miss one stitch, 28 double crochet. Work three rows of double crochet, 104 stitches. **30th row**—13 double crochet, miss one, 13 double crochet, miss one, 48 double crochet, miss one, 13 double crochet, miss one, 13 double crochet. Work 4 rows of double crochet, 100 stitches. **35th row**—12 double crochet, miss one, 12 double crochet, miss one, 48 double crochet, miss one, 12 double crochet. Work 3 rows of double crochet, 96 stitches. **39th row**—11 double crochet, miss one, 11 double crochet, miss one, 48 double crochet, miss one, 11 double crochet, miss one, 11 double crochet. Work 3 rows of double crochet, 92 stitches. **43rd row**—10 double crochet, miss one, 10 double crochet, miss one, 48 double crochet, miss one, 10 double crochet, miss one, 10 double crochet. Work 3 rows of double crochet, 88 stitches. **47th row**—9 double crochet, miss one, 9 double crochet, miss one, 48 double crochet, miss one, 9 double crochet, miss one, 9 double crochet. Work 1 row of

Doll's Walking Costume.

double crochet, 84 stitches. **49th row**—25 double crochet, * wool over the needle and insert the hook in the next stitch and draw the wool through, wool over the needle and draw through 2 stitches on the needle, repeat from * till you have done 13 stitches in this way, then wool over the needle and draw through all on the needle, 6 double crochet, 13 stitches as before, 25 double crochet; the groups of 13 stitches drawn together form two pleats at the back of the pelisse **50th row**—Plain double crochet, 60 stitches. **51st row**—8 double crochet, miss one, 8 double crochet, miss one, 8 double crochet, miss one, 6 double crochet, miss one, 8 double crochet, miss one, 8 double crochet, miss one, 8 double crochet. **52nd row**—Double crochet. **53rd row**—24 double crochet, miss one, 4 double crochet, miss one, 24 double crochet. **54th row**—Double crochet **55th row**—7 double crochet, miss one, 7 double crochet, miss one, 20 double crochet, miss one, 7 double crochet, miss one, 7 double crochet. Work 3 rows of double crochet, 48 stitches. **59th row**—6 double crochet, 2 double crochet on the next, 6 double crochet, 2 double crochet on the next, 20 double crochet, 2 double crochet on the next, 6 double crochet, 2 double crochet on the next, 6 double crochet. **60th row**—Double crochet, 52 stitches. **61st row**—6 double crochet, 2 double crochet on the next, 38 double crochet, 2 double crochet on the next, 6 double crochet. **62nd row**—Double crochet. **63rd row**—7 double crochet, 2 double crochet on the next, 8 double crochet, 2 double crochet on the next, 20 double crochet, 2 double crochet on the next, 8 double crochet, 2 double crochet on the next, 7 double crochet. **64th row**—Double crochet. **65th row**—7 double crochet, 2 double crochet on the next, 42 double crochet, 2 double crochet on the next, 7 double crochet. **66th row**—Double crochet. **67th row**—7 double crochet, 2 double crochet on the next, 7 double crochet, 1 chain to turn the work, and now proceed for the first half of the front. **68th row**—Miss the first stitch, do 15 double crochet. Work 2 more rows of 15 double crochet. Work 4 rows of 14 double crochet. **75th row**—14 double crochet, 2 chain. **76th row**—2 double crochet into second chain stitch, 8 double crochet, 1 chain, and turn. **77th row**—9 double crochet. **78th row**—Miss two stitches, 7 double crochet. **79th row**—7 double crochet. **80th row**—Miss two stitches, 5 double crochet. **81st row**—5 double crochet. **82nd row**—Miss two stitches, 3 double crochet. **83rd row**—3 double crochet. **84th row** —Miss two stitches, do 1 double crochet, and fasten off. Recommence upon the sixteenth stitch from the end of the sixty-sixth row that is, missing twenty-nine stitches from the half front already done, and work for the other half of the front, for the **67th row**—7 double crochet, 2 double crochet on the next, 8 double crochet. **68th row**—15 double crochet, omit the last stitch. **69th row**—15 double crochet. **70th row**—14 double crochet, omit the last stitch. Work 5 rows of 14 double crochet. **76th row**—14 double crochet, 2 chain. **77th row**—1 double crochet in the second chain stitch, 8 double crochet. **78th row**—9 double crochet. **79th row**—Miss two stitches, 7 double crochet. **80th row**—7 double crochet. **81st row**—Miss two stitches, 5 double crochet. **82nd row**—5 double crochet. **83rd row**—Miss two stitches, 3 double crochet. **84th row**—3 double crochet. **85th row**—Miss two stitches, 1 double crochet, and fasten off. Now work for the **Back** of the **Pelisse**: Miss two stitches on the sixty-sixth row from the first half of the front, and for the **67th row**—Work 9 double crochet, 2 double crochet on the next, 5 double crochet, 2 double crochet on the next, 9 double crochet, 1 chain to turn. **68th row**—26 double crochet. **69th row**—Miss one stitch, 24 double crochet. **70th row**—Miss one stitch, 22 double crochet. Work 4 rows of 22 double crochet. **75th row**—Miss two stitches, 20 double crochet. **76th row**—Miss 2 stitches, 18 double crochet. **77th row**—Miss two stitches, 16 double

Pelerine in Ice Wool.

crochet. **78th row**—Miss two stitches, 14 double crochet. **79th row**—Miss two stitches, 12 double crochet. **80th row**—Miss two stitches, 10 double crochet. **81st row**—Miss two stitches, 8 double crochet. **82nd row**—Miss two stitches, 6 double crochet, and fasten off. Sew up the shoulder pieces. For the **Right Sleeve**—Work 24 double crochet stitches round the armhole, beginning under the arm at the lowest part of the hole, do not join in a round, but crochet backwards and forwards to match the stitch used for the pelisse. Do 4 rows with 24 double crochet in each row. **5th row**—5 double crochet, miss one stitch, 2 double crochet, miss one, 2 double crochet, miss one, 2 double crochet, miss one, 2 double crochet, miss one, 6 double crochet. Work 3 rows of 19 double crochet. **9th row**—7 double crochet, miss one, 3 double crochet, miss one, 7 double crochet. Work 10 rows of 17 double crochet. **20th row**—Work 2 stitches of looped crochet, miss one stitch, 11 looped crochet, miss one, 2 looped crochet. **21st row**—15 looped crochet. **22nd row**—14 looped crochet. **23rd row**—14 double crochet; fasten off, and sew up the sleeve. The **Left Sleeve** is the same, except in the **5th row**, which should be thus—6 double crochet, miss one stitch, 2 double crochet and miss one stitch 4 times, end with 5 double crochet. Stitch back the corners of the breast of the pelisse to imitate a coat front. Fasten the pelisse with hooks and eyes, and sew a row of ornamental buttons down the front.

For the **Cape**—which is worked in **Looped Crochet**—Begin with a chain of 72 stitches. **1st row**—Looped crochet as already instructed in the first row of the pelisse. **2nd row**—Plain double crochet. **3rd row**—Looped crochet. **4th row**—Double crochet. **5th row**—Looped crochet. **6th row**—Double crochet. **7th row**—Work 16 stitches of looped crochet, miss one stitch, 2 looped crochet, miss one, 31 looped crochet, miss one, 2 looped crochet, miss one, 16 looped crochet. **8th row**—Double crochet. **9th row**—15 looped crochet, miss one, 2 looped crochet, miss one, 29 looped crochet, miss one, 2 looped crochet, miss one, 15 looped crochet. **10th row**—Double crochet. **11th row**—14 looped crochet, miss one, 2 looped crochet, miss one, 27 looped crochet, miss one, 2 looped crochet, miss one, 14 looped crochet. **12th row**—Double crochet. **13th row**—13 looped crochet, miss one, 2 looped crochet, miss one, 25 looped crochet, miss one, 2 looped crochet, miss one, 13 looped crochet. **14th row**—12 double crochet, miss one, 2 double crochet, miss one, 23 double crochet, miss one, 2 double crochet, miss one, 12 double crochet. **15th row**—11 looped crochet, miss one, 2 looped crochet, miss one, 21 looped crochet, miss one, 2 looped crochet, miss one, 11 looped crochet. **16th row**—10 double crochet, miss one, 2 double crochet, miss one, 19 double crochet, miss one, 2 double crochet, miss one, 10 double crochet. **17th row**

—Single crochet along 5 stitches, and beginning at the sixth stitch, do 4 looped crochet, miss one, 2 looped crochet, miss one, 6 looped crochet, miss one, 3 looped crochet, miss one, 6 looped crochet, miss one, 2 looped crochet, miss one, 4 looped crochet. **18th row**—3 double crochet, miss one, 2 double crochet, miss one, 13 double crochet, miss one, 2 double crochet, miss one, 3 double crochet. **19th row**—2 looped crochet, miss one, 2 looped crochet, miss one, 5 looped crochet, miss one, 1 looped crochet, miss one, 5 looped crochet, miss one, 2 looped crochet, miss one, 2 looped crochet. **20th row**—2 double crochet, miss one, 1 double crochet, miss one, 18 double crochet, miss one, 1 double crochet, miss one, 2 double crochet, and fasten off. **21st row**—To finish the **Neck**—Begin at the left-hand side of the front, that is holding the work the wrong side towards you, and work a row of loop stitch, missing one stitch at each corner, so as to render the shape more even; fasten off the wool.

For the **Muff**—which also is worked in **Looped Crochet**—Make a chain of 10 stitches, and work alternately a row of looped crochet and a row of double crochet till you have sufficient rows done to make the muff a proper size. Fold the crochet over on the wrong side and join it. Turn it, and run a thread of wool on each side to draw in the edge a little, and fasten off. The muff is hung round the doll's neck with a strand of fawn wool.

For the **Hat**—Make 2 chain, work 4 double crochet in the second chain from the needle, proceed in rounds. **1st round**—2 double crochet on each stitch of the double crochet with which you commenced. **2nd round**—Increase by working 2 double crochet on each alternate stitch. Work 2 more rounds in the same manner. **5th round**—Increase on every third stitch. **6th round**—The same. Work 5 rounds of plain double crochet, no increase. **12th round**—Double crochet, and miss every fifth stitch. **13th round**—Double crochet, and miss every fourth stitch. Work 2 rounds of double crochet, and fasten off.

For the **Shoes**—Begin with 3 chain. **1st row**—1 chain to turn, do 1 double crochet, 3 double crochet in the next, 1 double crochet in the end stitch. **2nd row**—1 chain to turn, 2 double crochet on consecutive stitches, 3 double crochet on the centre stitch, 2 more double crochet. **3rd row**—1 chain to turn, 3 consecutive double crochet, 3 double crochet in the centre stitch, 3 consecutive double crochet. **4th row**—1 chain to turn, 4 consecutive double crochet, 3 double crochet in the centre stitch, 4 consecutive double crochet. **5th row**—1 chain to turn, 5 consecutive double crochet, 3 double crochet in the centre stitch, 5 consecutive double crochet. This is sufficient for the front of the shoe. For the **6th row**—Do 1 chain to turn, 4 consecutive double crochet; and repeat the same till you have enough to go round the doll's heel and meet at the other side, where join it to the front. Proceed thus for the **Sole**—8 chain, work double crochet down one side of the chain, 3 double crochet in the end stitch, and double crochet down the other side increasing at the end, and continue round till the sole is the right size to fit nicely in the upper part; then sew them together. A few loops of red wool on the front of each slipper, on the muff, and on the hat, is a set-off to the doll's costume.

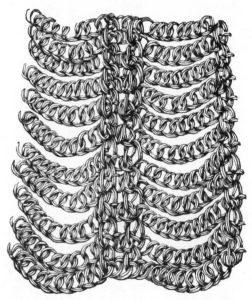

Full Size Working Design of Pelerine.

For the **Petticoat**.—This is knitted partly with white Beehive wool and partly with Andalusian, with No. 13 knitting needles; it has a fluted flounce round the bottom, and a beautifully shaped body and sleeves. Begin for the flounce with Beehive wool by casting on 24 stitches. **1st row**—Plain. **2nd row**—Plain. **3rd row**—Purl, and leave the last 2 stitches unknitted on the left-hand needle. **4th row**—Plain 22 stitches. **5th row**—Purl 22, knit 2. **6th row**—Knit 2, purl 22. **7th row**—Plain, and leave the last 2 stitches unknitted. **8th row**—Purl 22 stitches. **9th row**—Plain 24 stitches. Repeat from the second row twenty-three times more, and end by casting off instead of knitting the last plain row. Join the flounce round. For the back of the petticoat, take the Andalusian wool, and along 13 ribs of the flounce pick up 29 stitches. Knit alternately purl and plain for 9 rows. **10th row**—Knit 2, slip 1, knit 1, pass the slipped stitch over the knitted one, knit plain till you come within 4 stitches of the end, then knit 2 together, knit 2. **11th row**—Purl. **12th row**—Plain. **13th row**—Purl. **14th row**—Same as the tenth row. Knit purl and plain rows alternately until you have done about 48 rows.

Next row, cast off all but 5 stitches, and continue purl and plain rows alternately on the 5 stitches for 5 rows, and cast off. Next work the front of the petticoat, pick up 25 stitches along the 11 ribs of the flounce, and work alternately purl and plain rows until you have done about 48 rows, when cast off all but 5 stitches, and knit those for 5 rows, and cast off. Sew the shoulder pieces to the corresponding place on the opposite side. Now fashion the **Sleeves,**— thus, commence at the thirty-sixth row to pick up stitches along the side of the body, in this way, * pick up 3 stitches knitting each as you pick it up, make a stitch by passing the wool round the needle, repeat from * till you have 19 stitches. **1st row**—Purl. **2nd row**—Plain. **3rd row**—Purl. **4th row**—Plain, decreasing a stitch at the beginning and at the end of the row **5th row** —Purl. **6th row**—Same as the fourth row. **7th row**—Purl. **8th row**—

Child's Tricot Petticoat.

Cast off. Knit the other sleeve in the same manner. When both sleeves are knitted sew up the sides of the petticoat. Finish the petticoat with a crochet edge round the neck and sleeves. **1st round**—1 double crochet, * 2 chain, miss one stitch, 1 double crochet in the next, and repeat from *. **2nd round** —1 double crochet under the loop of two chain, 3 chain, and repeat ; fasten off at the end of the round. Make a cord of chain stitch, and run it through the holes round the neck, and tie in front.

For the **Drawers.**—Use white Shetland wool and four No. 14 knitting needles. Cast 9 stitches on each of two needles, and twelve stitches on a third needle, and work round and round like a stocking, doing first of all a ribbing of 2 stitches plain, 1 stitch purl, for ten rounds. **11th round**—Plain knitting. **12th round**—Knit 2, increase 1, knit plain to within 2 stitches of the end of the round, increase 1, knit 2. **13th round**—Plain. **14th round**—The same as the twelfth round. Repeat the last two rounds till you get 40 stitches on the needles. Then you commence to work in rows, alternately purl and plain, till you have completed 48 rows from the beginning. **49th row**—Purl. **50th row**—Knit 2, knit 2 together, knit plain to within 4 stitches of the end, knit 2 together, knit 2. **51st row**—Purl. **52nd row** —Plain. **53rd row**—Purl. **54th row**—Plain. **55th row**—Purl. **56th row**—Same as the fiftieth row. Repeat the last six rows. **63rd row**—Purl. **64th row**—Slip 1, * make 1, knit 2 together, repeat from * seven times, knit plain to the end. **65th row**—Purl. **66th row**—Cast off 17 stitches, make 1, knit 2 together, knit plain to the end. **67th row**—Purl. **68th row**—Cast off 2 stitches, make 1, knit 2 together, knit plain to the end. Repeat the last two rows till all the stitches are cast off ; this is the right leg. Work for the left leg the same as for the right until you have completed the sixty-third row. **64th row**—Knit 17, make 1, knit 2 together ; turn, and purl back. **66th row**—Knit 15, make 1, knit 2 together ; turn, and purl back. Continue thus knitting 2 stitches less at the beginning of every forward row, till you come to knit 1, make 1, knit 2 together, and turn, and purl back. **Next row**—Plain the whole way across. **Next row**—Cast off in purling. Now make a gusset ; cast on 5 stitches, and knit a row and purl a row alternately till you have a perfect square, when cast off. Sew the gusset into its place, and join up the seams of the drawers. Run a crochet cord through the holes at the top of the drawers.

Dolls' Handkerchief Bag.—Begin with 6 chain, and work double crochet down each side thereof, and go on crocheting round and round, without increasing, until you have finished four rounds. **5th round**—12 chain, 6 double crochet, 12 chain, 6 double crochet, and fasten off ; the loops of chain stitches form the handles. This completes the costume of this pretty doll.

PELERINE IN ICE WOOL.

THE foundation of this pretty pelerine is worked in plain tricot, in two pieces, which subsequently are joined together down the back ; the frills are fashioned separately, and afterwards sewn upon the tricot, there are six frills upon the pelerine, and a narrower frill is made to form a kind of ruching round the neck. You will require ½ lb. of double Berlin wool for the founda-

tion, and 5 or 6 balls of ice wool for the frills, and the colour may be a pretty pale blue, or light grey, or any colour in which you can get the two wools of a shade to match ; procure also a No. 5 bone tricot needle, and a No. 9 bone crochet needle. Commence with the foundation, using double Berlin wool and the tricot needle, and work 21 chain for the half of the neck of the pelerine. **1st row**—Plain tricot ; work rather loosely. For the following 14 rows increase a stitch at the beginning of each row for the front of the pelerine, increase a stitch in the middle of every row for the shoulder, and increase a stitch at the end of every alternate row for the back, therefore on the completion of the fifteenth row you will have 56 tricot stitches in the row. **16th row**—Pick up 32 stitches for the front of the pelerine (leaving 24 stitches to be worked upon presently for the back) and draw through in the usual manner. For the following 5 rows increase a stitch at the beginning of each row and decrease a stitch at the end of every alternate row. **22nd row**—Pick up 18 stitches and draw back. For the following 5 rows increase a stitch at the beginning and decrease a stitch at the end of each row. Then keep the beginning straight and still decrease a stitch at the end for 16 rows, which will reduce to 2 stitches for the corner of the left-hand side front of the pelerine. Next resume the working of the 16th row—Pick up the 24 stitches you left, and draw back ; then for 8 rows increase a stitch every fourth row at the beginning, and increase a stitch every alternate row at the end ; and then for 5 rows keep straight at the beginning and leave 3 stitches unworked every row at the end ; the last row consists of 15 tricot stitches, and completes this portion of the back of the pelerine. Next leave 5 stitches from the 18 stitches you picked up in the twenty-second row, and pick up thence to the end of the front portion, 10 stitches, and draw back. **Next row**—Slip along the first two stitches, pick up to the end, and draw back. Work three more rows the same, and fasten off. Join this portion of the front to the corresponding portion of the back of the pelerine. Recommence with 21 chain for the other half of the pelerine. **1st row**—Plain tricot. For the following 14 rows increase a stitch at the beginning of every alternate row for the back of the pelerine, increase a stitch in the middle of every row for the shoulder, and increase a stitch at the end of every row for the front, and on the completion of the fifteenth row you will have 56 stitches in the row. **16th row**—Pick up 24 stitches for the back of the pelerine (leaving 32 stitches to be worked afterwards for the front) and draw through in the usual manner ; then for 8 rows increase a stitch every alternate row at the beginning and increase a stitch every fourth row at the end ; and then for 5 rows slip along 3 stitches at the commencement of every row, and keep straight at the end ; the last row consists of 15 tricot stitches, and completes this portion of the back of the

Vest for a Child of Five.

pelerine. Next resume the working of the **16th row**—Pick up the 32 stitches you left, and draw back. For the following 5 rows decrease a stitch at the beginning of each alternate row and increase a stitch at the end of each row. **22nd row**—Pick up 10 stitches, and draw back. **Next row**—Pick up 8 stitches and draw back. And for the three following rows pick up 2 stitches less each time, and fasten off. Resume where you left off in the 22nd row—Omit 5 stitches from the ten already worked, and pick up thence to the end, 18 stitches and draw back. For the following five rows decrease a stitch at the beginning and increase a stitch at the end of each row. Then still decrease a stitch at the beginning for 16 rows but keep the end straight, which will reduce to two stitches for the corner of the right-hand side front of the pelerine. Join together the two portions of the tricot where divided below the shoulders ; and crochet the two pieces of work together down the back of the pelerine. For the **Frills.**—Work with ice wool and No. 9 crochet needle. Commence for the bottom frill with 530 chain **1st row**—Work 1 double crochet in the second chain from the needle, 1 chain, 1 double crochet in the next stitch of the foundation, * 7 chain, miss six of the foundation, 1 double crochet in the next, 1 chain, 1 double crochet in the next, and repeat from *, making 66 scallops in the row; break off at the end of this and every row, and recommence on the right hand side. **2nd row**—Work 1 double crochet on double crochet stitch of last row, 1 chain, 1 double crochet on double crochet, 7 chain, and continue the same to the end. **3rd row**—1 double crochet on double crochet stitch of last row, 1 chain, 1 double crochet on double crochet, 8 chain, and proceed thus to the end. Work 2 more rows the same as last row. Work 3 rows in the same manner, but doing nine chain instead of eight chain. Work 2 rows doing 10 chain in each long loop. **11th row**—Work in the same manner, but doing 11 chain in each loop. This finishes the first frill. Do another frill on a foundation of 387 chain stitches, making 48 scallops. Do two frills on foundations of 323 chain, making 40 scallops. Do two frills on foundations of 227 chain, making 28 scallops. Do another frill on 168 chain as a foundation, and work only 6 rows. You will observe that the first frill is the longest; thread a rug needle with a strand of the ice wool, and tack this frill all along the bottom of the pelerine and round the narrow ends of the front to where the tricot on eighteen stitches begins, the edge of the frill falls just upon the edge of the tricot and does not extend any lower whatever. The second frill is tacked a little higher upon the pelerine, and is so arranged as to entirely fill in the centres of the two front end pieces, which so far are finished. The third frill is placed a little higher still upon the pelerine. And the other three frills rise successively and cover the tricot to the neck; the last and smallest frill being tacked

with ruby and 25 stitches with grey (leaving 6 unworked), and draw back. Repeat from the second row till you have done 112 rows, that is, 14 whole points round the bottom of the skirt. Sew up the back of the skirt, leaving about twelve stitches open at the top for a placket hole; strengthen the placket with a row of single crochet. For the **Edge** round the bottom of the skirt—Work with a crochet needle, 1 double crochet in a stitch of the tricot, miss 1 stitch, 4 treble in the next, miss 1, and repeat all round. This edge should be done with ruby wool. For the **Waistband**—Use two No 14 steel knitting needles, and pick up stitches along the top of the skirt, about 100 stitches or 104 stitches, missing a stitch here and there; work in ribbing, 2 stitches plain and 2 stitches purl for 16 rows, and cast off. Put on a button, and sew a hole for a buttonhole, or if liked have ribbon to tie round the waist.

VEST FOR CHILD OF FIVE.

THIS is worked simply in treble stitch, and is a comfortable and nice fitting vest. Required, 2½ ozs of the best pink unshrinkable vest wool, and a No 11 bone crochet needle. Commence across the chest with 65 chain. **1st row**—Work 1 treble in the fourth chain from the needle, and continue in treble stitches to the end of the row, doing 62 stitches. **2nd row**—3 chain to turn. 1 treble on the second treble stitch of preceding row, inserting the hook to take up the two top threads, and work altogether 62 treble stitches to the end

Handsome Wide Border.

along the edge of the neck by one of its middle rows so that the foundation chain stands up loosely round the neck, while the last row falls level with the commencing chain of the previous frill. The neck should have previously been strengthened with a row of double crochet worked along it.

CHILD'S TRICOT PETTICOAT.

WORKED IN TWO COLOURS.

FOR this little petticoat procure 4 ozs. of grey and 1½ ozs. of ruby single Berlin wool, or the best Scotch fingering, or Petticoat fingering, and a No 7 long bone tricot needle. Or a larger petticoat can be made by using fleecy wool and a No. 5 needle. Commence with grey wool with 30 chain, take the ruby wool and joining into the grey do 13 chain. **1st row**—Pick up 12 tricot stitches with ruby wool, and pick up 31 stitches with grey wool, and draw back as in ordinary tricot, through each stitch with its own colour. **2nd row**—Pick up 10 tricot stitches with ruby, and 33 stitches with grey, and draw back as in the previous row. **3rd row**—Pick up 8 tricot stitches with ruby, and 35 stitches with grey, and draw back. **4th row**—Pick up 6 tricot stitches with ruby, and 37 stitches with grey, and draw back. **5th row**—Pick up 4 tricot stitches with ruby, and 33 stitches with grey (leaving 6 unworked), and draw back. **6th row**—Pick up 6 tricot stitches with ruby, and 37 stitches with grey, and draw back. **7th row**—Pick up 8 tricot stitches with ruby, and 35 stitches with grey, and draw back. **8th row**—Pick up 10 stitches with ruby and 33 stitches with grey, and draw back. **9th row**—Pick up 12 stitches

of the row, the last stitch being upon the chain that turned. Do 4 more rows the same as the last row, and break off the wool. Begin again with 65 chain, and work another piece of 6 rows in the same manner. **7th row**—3 chain to turn, 1 treble on the second treble stitch of previous row, and work 62 treble stitches in the row, take the first piece of crochet and do 1 treble on the first treble stitch by the tag of wool, and continue in treble to the end, in all 63 stitches, the last stitch being upon the chain that turned, work 1 single crochet in the top stitch of chain on the second piece of crochet to join the work round. **1st round**—3 chain to stand for a treble stitch, turn the work, and do 125 treble stitches in the round, and when you get to the end join with a single crochet stitch to the top stitch of chain with which the round commenced. Work each successive round in the same manner In the **6th round** increase a stitch on each side (that is, under each armhole), and increase in the same place every third round five times. Then proceed without increasing till you can count 29 lines of treble stitches from the commencement Work for the **last round**—1 double crochet on a treble stitch, * 5 chain, 1 double crochet in the fourth chain from the needle, 1 double crochet on the next treble stitch, 1 double crochet on the next, and repeat from * to the end of the round and fasten off. Now work for the **Shoulders**—Hold the work with the wrong side of the first row towards you, and do a row of treble stitches along the commencing chain. **1st Shoulder row**—3 chain to turn, miss the first stitch, do 10 consecutive treble. **2nd row**—3 chain to turn, miss the 2 first stitches, do 9 treble. **3rd row**—3 chain to turn, miss the first stitch, 8 treble. **4th row**—3 chain to turn, miss the two first stitches, 7 treble. **5th row**—3 chain to turn, miss the first stitch, 6 treble. **6th row**—3 chain to turn, miss the first stitch, 6 treble, and fasten off. Miss 41 stitches from the shoulder you have just worked, and for the **1st row** of the other shoulder do 11 treble stitches. **2nd row**—3 chain to turn, miss the first stitch, do 9 treble, omit the last. **3rd row**—3 chain to turn, miss the two first stitches, 8 treble. **4th row**—3 chain to turn, miss the first stitch, 7 treble. **5th row** —3 chain to turn, miss the two first stitches, 6 treble. **6th row**—3 chain to turn, miss the first stitch, 6 treble, and fasten off. Work shoulders upon the other half of the vest in the same way. Sew the shoulder pieces together. For the **Neck**—Work 1 round of treble stitches. **Next round**—1 single crochet on a stitch of last round, 3 chain, 1 double crochet in the same place as the single crochet is worked into, miss 1 stitch, and repeat; fasten off at the end of the round. For the **Sleeves**—Work 3 rounds of treble stitches; then 1 round of edging the same as you have just worked round the neck Make a crochet chain to run through the treble stitches at the neck to tie in a bow in front; put a little tassel on each end of the chain.

Baby's Pilch.

HANDSOME WIDE BORDER.

THIS border is useful to go round quilts, or may be employed for a mantle drape, or for any purpose for which a handsome wide border is required. Select a crochet needle of suitable size, and cotton, silk, or wool, as is considered most desirable for the article it is intended to make. The border is worked in separate scallops which are joined together previous to working the last row, and before the heading is put on. Commence with **7 chain**; work 1 treble in the seventh chain from the needle, 3 chain, another treble in the same place, 3 chain, another treble in the same place. **2nd row**—Turn the work, and do 1 double crochet, 5 treble, and 1 double crochet under the first loop of three chain, and the same under each of the other two loops. **3rd row**— Turn the work, 5 chain, 1 double crochet on the treble stitch of the first row, 5 chain, 1 double crochet on the next treble stitch, 5 chain, 1 double crochet on the treble stitch at the end. **4th row**—Turn, do 1 double crochet, 7 treble, 1 double crochet under the first loop of five chain, and the same under each of the other two loops. **5th row**—Turn, do 4 chain, 1 double crochet on the first double crochet of the third row, 6 chain, 1 double crochet on the next double crochet of the third row, 6 chain, 1 double crochet on the double crochet at the end. **6th row**—Turn, do 8 chain, 1 single crochet in the sixth chain from the needle, do 9 treble and 1 long treble under the first loop of six chain, do 1 long treble, 8 treble, and 1 long treble under the second loop of six chain, and do 1 long treble and 9 treble under the third loop. **7th row**—Turn, do 6 chain, 1 single crochet on the first treble stitch of last row, 3 chain, 1 treble on each of 9 consecutive stitches taking up the one top thread only, 2 treble on the next stitch, 4 consecutive treble, 2 treble on the next, 4 consecutive treble, 2 treble on the next, 9 consecutive treble to the end. **8th row**—Turn, do 6 chain, 1 single crochet on the first treble stitch of last row, 1 treble on each of 6 consecutive stitches taking up the back thread only; turn the work, 6 chain, 1 single crochet on the first treble stitch of last row, 3 chain, 6 treble worked consecutively and taking up the one top thread; turn the work, make a picot as before (*i.e.*, 6 chain, 1 single crochet on the first treble stitch of last row), 3 chain, 7 treble worked consecutively and taking up the back thread; turn, make a picot, 3 chain, 8 consecutive treble taking up the one top thread; turn, a picot, 8 chain, 1 single crochet in the sixth chain from the needle, and taking up the top thread work 1 treble on each of the first 2 treble stitches, a picot, 5 consecutive treble, a picot, 2 treble, a picot, another picot, and fasten off evenly; this forms one of the four divisions. You will notice the little rows are crocheted on the back thread and on the top thread alternately of previous rows, and the "ridge" so formed always shows on the right side of the scallop. Turn the work, and first making a picot by doing 6 chain, 1 single crochet in the sixth chain from the needle, resume working upon the stitches of the seventh row, miss two stitches from the first division and do 1 treble on the

third treble stitch, and 6 more treble consecutively, taking up the back thread; turn the work, make a picot, 3 chain, 8 consecutive treble taking up the one top thread; turn, 8 chain, 1 single crochet in the sixth chain from the needle, 9 consecutive treble taking up the back thread; turn, make a picot, 8 chain, 1 single crochet in the sixth chain from the needle, and taking up the top thread work 1 treble on each of the second and third treble stitches, make a picot, 5 consecutive treble, a picot, 2 treble, a picot, and fasten off evenly. The third division is worked the same as the second division. For the fourth division, after turning the work, first make a picot by doing 6 chain, 1 single crochet in the sixth chain from the needle, miss two stitches from the third division and do 7 consecutive treble to the end of the row taking up the back thread; turn, make a picot, 3 chain, 7 consecutive treble taking up the one top thread, turn, 8 chain, 1 single crochet in the sixth chain from the needle, 8 consecutive treble taking up the back thread; turn, make a picot, 8 chain, 1 single crochet in the sixth chain from the needle, 6 chain, 1 single crochet in the same place to make another picot, and taking up the top thread work 1 treble on each of the first and second treble stitches, make a picot, 5 consecutive treble, a picot, 2 treble, a picot, and fasten off evenly; this completes the four divisions. Now for the **Tufted Part**—This is worked in rows, and each row commences on the right-hand side and is fastened off at the end, the tags of cotton should be folded down and worked over in the next following row to ensure perfect neatness. **1st row**—Begin with 1 double crochet in the fifth picot (counting along the right-hand side from the centre of the semi-circle) 5 chain, 1 double crochet in the next picot, * 3 chain, 1 treble on the centre stitch of the five treble stitches between the picots, 3 chain, 1 double crochet in the next picot, 6 chain, miss a picot, and do 1 long treble in the next picot of the same division, 1 long treble in the corresponding picot of the next division, 6 chain, miss one picot, 1 double crochet in the next picot, and repeat from * twice, then 3 chain, 1 treble on the centre stitch of the five treble stitches between the picots, 3 chain, 1 double crochet in the next picot, 5 chain, 1 double crochet in the next picot, and fasten off. **2nd row**—Work 1 treble on the first double crochet stitch of preceding row, and proceed with 1 treble on each successive stitch till 45 treble are done, do 2 treble on the next stitch, then 44 successive treble to the end, and fasten off. **3rd row**—Work 15 consecutive double crochet, taking up the top thread of the stitches of previous row, cotton over the needle, insert the hook from right to left *under* the next treble stitch of last row and draw the cotton through, cotton over the needle and draw through 2 stitches on the needle, cotton over the needle and draw through the other 2 stitches on the needle; this is simply a treble stitch, and 4 more treble are to be worked in the same place in the same way, when the 5 treble are done take the hook out of the stitch and insert the hook in the first treble and draw the stitch through, so forming a "tuft." do 1 chain to tighten the tuft, miss one stitch behind the tuft, * do 11 double crochet, a

Raised Diamond Lattice Pattern.

tuft, and repeat from * till 6 tufts are done, then work 15 consecutive double crochet, and fasten off. **4th row**—Work 13 consecutive double crochet, * work a tuft into the lower part of the next double crochet stitch of last row, 1 double crochet, a tuft on the tuft of previous row, 1 double crochet, a tuft, 7 double crochet, and repeat from *, and end the row with 13 double crochet, and fasten off. **5th row**—Work 14 double crochet, * a tuft, 1 double crochet, a tuft, 9 double crochet, and repeat from *, and end with 14 double crochet, and fasten off. **6th row**—Work 15 double crochet, * a tuft, 11 double crochet, and repeat from *, and end with 15 double crochet, and fasten off. **7th row**—Treble, working 91 stitches in the row. When a sufficient number of scallops are worked in this manner join them by sewing together to the depth of seven stitches on each side. For the **Edge**—Begin crocheting on the eighth stitch of the first scallop, work 5 consecutive double crochet, * 5 chain, 1 single crochet in the fourth chain from the needle, miss three stitches of last row, 1 treble on the next (this should be the centre stitch over the group of tufts) § 5 chain, 1 single crochet in the fourth chain from the needle, another treble in the same place, repeat from § twice more, 5 chain, 1 single crochet in the fourth chain from the needle, miss three stitches of last row, 1 double crochet on the next, and work 4 more double crochet consecutively; repeat from * five times; and then proceed in the same way round the next scallop. For the **Heading—1st row**—Work single crochet along the thick part of the scallops, doing 2 chain or 3 chain as required across the space between the picots, and do 2 chain and 1 treble five times in the centre of each scallop where there are no picots; fasten off at the end of the row, and recommence on the right-hand side. **2nd row**—Plain double crochet. **3rd row**—Begin with a stitch secured on the needle, * pass the cotton twice round the needle, insert the hook in the first stitch of last row and draw the cotton through, cotton over the needle and draw through 2 stitches on the needle, cotton over the needle, miss two stitches of last row, insert the hook in the next stitch and draw the cotton through, then 4 times cotton over the needle and draw through 2 stitches on the needle, do 2 chain, cotton over the needle, insert the hook to take up the two centre threads of the twisted stitch just made, draw the cotton through, then twice cotton over the needle and draw through 2 stitches on the needle; the entire row is worked in the same manner, repeating from *, and presents the appearance of a number of small crosses. **4th row**—1 treble on the first stitch of preceding row, * 1 chain, miss one stitch, 1 treble on the next, and repeat from * to the end of the row.

BABY'S PILCH.

A WARM woollen pilch will prevent many a chill, and is almost a necessity in winter for a baby to wear in its perambulator. The pilch shown in our

the row, with of course 1 chain stitch between each double crochet stitch. **Next row**—Work as far as the twenty-first double crochet stitch; turn the work, miss the first double crochet stitch, and work back. **Next row**—Work as far as the nineteenth double crochet stitch; turn the work, miss the first double crochet stitch, and work back. **Next row**—Work as far as the seventeenth double crochet stitch; turn the work, miss the first double crochet stitch, and work back, and break off the wool. Recommence 21 stitches from the other side of the pilch, and work another side piece to correspond with the side piece you have just done. Now for the **Middle Piece** or **Flap**—Miss four double crochet stitches from the first side piece, and beginning with 1 double crochet upon the fifth stitch, work 1 chain and 1 double crochet alternately till 37 double crochet stitches are done, which will leave four double crochet stitches from the other side piece; turn the work, miss the first double crochet stitch, do 1 double crochet on the second double crochet stitch, and work 1 chain and 1 double crochet alternately till you come to the end, where leave 1 double crochet stitch unworked, and proceed in this manner, decreasing a stitch at the beginning and a stitch at the end of every row till you work 19 double crochet stitches in the row. Keep to 19 double crochet stitches for 20 rows. **Next row**—1 double crochet on the first double crochet stitch of preceding row, increase by doing 1 chain and 1 double crochet twice on the next double crochet stitch, then 1 chain and 1 double crochet alternately to the end. Repeat this row till you get 33 double crochets in the row. **Next row**—Work in the usual manner, no increase. For the **next 6 rows** decrease a stitch at the beginning of each row; and for the **next 15 rows** decrease a stitch at the beginning and at the end of each row, to form the point; and

D'Oyley with Fan Pattern Lace Border.

Little G

illustration is very simply made, the stitch being nothing more than chain and 1 double crochet worked alternately, always putting a double crochet stitch upon a double crochet stitch of the preceding row, yet though so easy, it is a pretty and tasteful little garment. Procure 3 ozs. of white Peacock fingering, a No. 10 bone crochet needle, 4 white linen buttons, and 1½ yards of inch-wide ribbon. Commence with 14 chain for the top of the pilch. **1st row**—Work 1 double crochet in the second chain from the needle, and continue plain double crochet to the end, doing in all 145 stitches. **2nd row**—Turn the work, do 1 double crochet on the first double crochet stitch of preceding row, * 1 chain, miss one stitch, 1 double crochet on the next, and repeat from * to the end, and there will be 73 double crochet in the row with a chain stitch between each double crochet stitch. **3rd row**—The same as the second row. **4th row**—Turn the work, do 1 double crochet on the first stitch of preceding row, 1 chain and 1 double crochet alternately 19 times, increase by doing 1 chain and 1 double crochet twice on the next double crochet stitch, which is the twenty-first double crochet stitch of the preceding row, then work 1 chain and 1 double crochet alternately till you come to the twenty-first double crochet stitch from the other end, increase again upon that stitch by doing 1 chain and 1 double crochet twice, then 1 chain and 1 double crochet alternately 20 times to the end of the row. **5th row**—Turn the work, do 1 double crochet on the first stitch of the preceding row, and 1 chain and 1 double crochet alternately to the end. Work 2 more rows the same as last row. Repeat from the fourth row until you work 87 double crochet stitches in

fasten off. For the **Edging round the Legs**—Work 1 row of plain double crochet along the opening for the leg, doing about 65 stitches; turn with 1 chain, * do 1 treble in the third stitch of double crochet of last row, § 3 chain, 1 single crochet in the third chain from the needle, another treble in the same stitch of double crochet, repeat from § twice, then miss two stitches, 1 double crochet on the next, miss two stitches, and repeat from * nine times, and fasten off. Work the same along the other leg. For the **Waistband**—**1st row**—Work double crochet into the commencing chain. **2nd row**—Long treble stitches, made by turning the wool twice round the needle, decrease twice on each side of the pilch by taking up two double crochet stitches together as one. **3rd row**—Double crochet. Run ribbon through the row of long treble stitches to tie in a bow in front. Make a buttonhole at each of the three points by sewing a chain stitch round with a needleful of wool, also make one buttonhole at the bottom of the front piece. Sew buttons on the corresponding part underneath.

RAISED DIAMOND LATTICE PATTERN.

FOR A SOFA BLANKET.

THIS handsome pattern looks well worked with four shades of Berlin, either crimson, art green, peacock blue, brown, or whatever colour will best harmonise or contrast with the furniture of the room. A blanket worked with double Berlin will be warm and useful, and the pattern looks just as nice in single

Berlin if a less weighty article is desired, work the former with a No. 8 bone crochet needle, the latter with a No. 12 needle. Commence with the darkest shade of wool with chain sufficient for the length of the sofa blanket, any number of stitches divisible by 6, and 4 stitches over. **1st row**—Work 1 double crochet in the second chain from the needle, and double crochet all along to the end. **2nd row**—Turn the work, and always inserting the hook to take up the two top threads of the stitches of preceding row, work 1 double crochet on the first stitch, and proceed in double crochet to the end, making any number of stitches divisible by 6, and 3 stitches over. **3rd row**—The same as the second row. **4th row**—Still with the darkest shade of wool, turn the work, do 4 consecutive double crochet, pass the wool thrice round the needle loosely, insert the hook from right to left to take up the chain stitch below the second double crochet on the first row and draw the wool through, wool over the needle and draw through two stitches on the needle, wool over the needle and draw through two more stitches on the needle, wool twice round the needle loosely, insert the hook from right to left to take up the chain stitch below the sixth double crochet from the previous lattice stitch and draw the wool through, wool over the needle and draw through two stitches on the needle, wool over the needle and draw through two more stitches on the needle, wool over the needle and draw through three stitches on the needle, miss one double crochet of last row, work 5 consecutive double crochet, * then wool twice round the needle loosely, insert the hook from right to left to take up the chain stitch next to the previous lattice stitch and draw the wool through, wool over the needle and draw through two stitches on the needle, wool over the needle and again draw through two stitches on the needle, wool twice round the needle

the row work the last lattice stitch off by drawing the wool through two stitches three times, miss one double crochet, and do 1 double crochet on the last stitch of previous row. Join on the next lightest shade of crimson, and work 3 rows the same as the second row; then work the lattice as directed in the fourth row, but looping the long lattice stitches into the lattices that are already made. Join the lightest shade of crimson and work 8 rows. Then do 4 rows with each shade back again to the darkest, with which work 8 rows, and continue shading in the same manner till the blanket is sufficiently wide, ending with 4 dark rows as it began. The blanket may be finished off with a knotted fringe, or with a border of tufted balls like those represented on the Cot Quilt, page 13 of this present issue.

D'OYLEY WITH FAN PATTERN LACE BORDER.

VERY pretty d'oyleys are made with a centre of diaper or fine damask linen, bordered with wide crochet lace. The diaper is cut to a convenient size, round or oval, as desired; the edge is then turned down and neatly hemmed, and ornamented with a feather stitching as shown in the engraving. For the feather stitching a reel of Evans' crochet cotton, No. 2, will be required; and for the border procure a ball of Finlayson's Scotch crochet thread, No. 40, or a reel of Evans' crochet cotton, No. 25, and a medium-sized steel crochet needle. When the centre is prepared take a crewel needle, and having threaded it with a rather long length of the same coarse cotton you have been using for the feather stitching, proceed to work the **1st round** by making a series of loops round the material as a foundation for crocheting into; thus—tie a knot at the

ock.

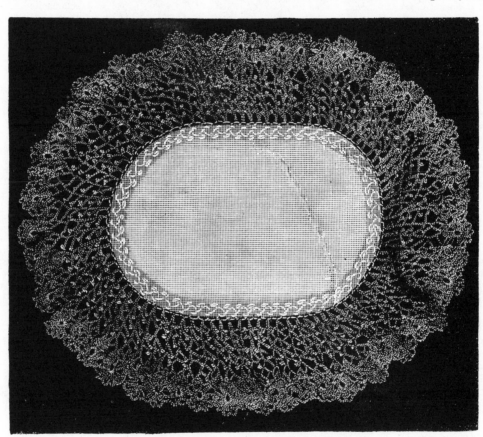

D'Oyley with Greek Lace Border.

loosely, insert the hook to take up the chain stitch below the sixth double crochet from the last lattice stitch and draw the wool through, wool over the needle and draw through two stitches on the needle, wool over the needle and draw through two more stitches on the needle, wool over the needle and draw through three stitches on the needle, repeat from * to the end, where work only 4 double crochet instead of five. Join on the next lightest shade of crimson, work 3 rows the same as the second row. **8th row**—Turn the work, and still with crimson the next shade to the darkest, do 1 double crochet on the first stitch, pass the wool twice round the needle loosely, insert the hook from right to left under the two lattice stitches of the fourth row and draw the wool through, wool over the needle and draw through two stitches on the needle, wool over the needle and draw through two more stitches on the needle, wool over the needle and again draw through two stitches on the needle, * miss one double crochet of last row, work 5 consecutive double crochet, wool twice round the needle loosely, insert the hook under the lattice stitch of the present row and under the same two lattice stitches that already have been worked under and draw the wool through, wool over the needle and draw through two stitches on the needle, wool over the needle and draw through two more stitches on the needle, wool twice round the needle loosely, insert the hook from right to left under the next two lattice stitches of the fourth row and draw the wool through, wool over the needle and draw through two stitches on the needle, wool over the needle and draw through two more stitches on the needle, wool over the needle and draw through three stitches on the needle; repeat from *; and at the end of

end of the needleful of cotton, bring the needle and cotton up from the wrong to the right side of the damask just on the margin of the hem, * let the cotton hang over the fingers of the left hand, insert the needle from the wrong side to the right side of the material about an eighth of an inch to the right of where it previously was brought up, and draw the cotton through in a rather loose loop; keep the cotton to the right, and insert the needle upwards through the loop and draw the cotton through; twist a similar stitch again in the loop, and then repeat from *, going all round the damask centre, and making the loops all the same size; join evenly at the end of the round, and fasten off. **2nd round**—With flax thread and crochet needle, work 3 treble stitches under the first loop, do 1 long treble under the next loop, then 1 chain and 1 long treble alternately four times in the same place, and continue the same all round, working loosely; and join evenly at the end of the round. **3rd round**—Still working loosely, do 1 double crochet on the centre stitch of the three treble of last round, 4 chain, 1 double crochet under the first loop of one chain, 2 chain, 1 double crochet under the next, 2 chain, 1 double crochet under the next, 2 chain, 1 double crochet under the next, 4 chain, 1 double crochet under the next, 2 chain; join at the end of the round, and fasten off. **4th round**—Begin with 1 treble under the first loop of four chain, 2 chain, 1 treble under the next loop of four chain, 2 chain, 1 treble under the centre loop of two chain, 2 chain, another treble in the same place, 2 chain, and repeat to the end of the round, and join evenly. **5th round**—Work 3 treble under the first loop of two chain of last round 1 chain, 1 long treble under the loop between the two treble stitches that are worked together, 1 chain and 1 long treble alternately four times in the same place. 1 chain, and repeat. **6th round**—Work just the same as the third round; you miss the one chain stitch on each side the three treble stitches, and fasten off at the end of the round. **7th round**—Same as the 4th round. **8th round**—Work 3 treble under the first loop of two chain of last round, 1 chain 1 long treble under the loop between the two treble stitches that are worked together, 1 chain and 1 long treble alternately six times in the same place, 1 chain, and repeat. **9th round**—Same as the sixth round, but do two more loops of 2 chain. 1 double crochet **10th round**—Begin with 1 treble under the first loop of four chain, 2 chain, 1 treble under the next loop of four chain. 3 chain 1 treble under the centre loop of two chain, 3 chain, another treble in the same place, 3 chain, and repeat to the end of the round, and join evenly **11th round**—Same as the eighth round. **12th round**—Same as the ninth round This completes the border, which is worked loosely throughout. It looks very light and lacy if crocheted with Coats No. 20 sewing cotton if the flax thread is not easily procurable.

LITTLE GIRL'S FROCK.

THIS pretty frock will fit a child of about three years of age; the body is worked in striped tricot and the skirt in crochet, and a handsome wide silk sash should be tied loosely round the waist, but is not represented in our engraving that the method of working the frock may be more clearly seen Procure 6 ozs. of Peacock Fingering wool, any colour that may be preferred, white always looks nice for a best frock, but of course a dark colour such as cardinal or peacock blue is more serviceable, use a No 9 bone tricot needle, and a No. 10 crochet needle Commence lengthways for the back of the body with 50 chain stitches. **1st row**—Pick up 1 tricot stitch in the second chain from the needle, and thence pick up 1 stitch in every chain to the end, making 49 tricot stitches on the needle, draw back in the ordinary manner. Work 2 more rows of plain tricot, 49 stitches in each row. **4th row**—

Full Size Working Design of Trimming for Chemise.

to shape the neck nicely. Next, **two Frills** are to be worked, the one to stand up round the neck, the other to fall over the body, the top frill is crocheted into the upper edge of the row of double crochet stitches, and the lower frill is fashioned by holding the body upside down and working into the lower edge of the same row of stitches; each row must be commenced on the right-hand side, holding the right side of the work towards you and fastened off at the end. **1st row**—Treble crochet, 1 treble in every stitch of the double crochet. **2nd row**—2 double crochet in the first stitch, * miss one stitch, 2 double crochet in the next, and repeat from * to the end. **3rd row**—1 double crochet on each of two double crochet stitches, 3 chain, 1 single crochet in the third chain from the needle, and repeat the same to the end. For the **Sleeves**—Work from where the armhole begins underneath to the same place again, forwards and backwards, in the same tricot stitch as used for the body, doing 3 plain rows and 3 fancy rows; next row, slip stitch; then 1 row of treble crochet; and then the last 2 rows of the frill. Sew up the under part of the sleeves. For the **Skirt**—Use the No. 10 crochet needle, and work a row of double crochet all along the bottom of the body getting 96 double crochet in the row, join the last stitch to the first, thereby uniting the two back pieces. Henceforth work in rounds, joining the work on the completion of every round. **1st round**—Work 1 double crochet on a double crochet stitch, miss one stitch, 4 treble on the next, miss one stitch, and repeat, and there will be 24 patterns in the round. **2nd round**—Work 1 double crochet, in the centre of the group of treble stitches in the last round, and 4 treble on the double crochet stitch. Work 2 more rounds the same. Then work 8 rounds with 5 treble in a group instead of four treble. Then 4 rounds with 6 treble stitches in a group. Then 3 rounds with 7 treble in a group. Now the skirt will probably be long enough, but if required longer more rounds can be done. Work a row of double crochet up each side the back of the body, and as you do this on the right-hand side work at intervals 2 chain stitches and miss two stitches of the body, so forming a little loop to use as a buttonhole. Sew on buttons to correspond. Run a length of narrow ribbon through the row of treble

Trimming for a Chemise.

You have 1 stitch already on the needle to begin with, wool over the needle and insert the hook to take up the second tricot stitch of the last row but one and draw the wool through, wool over the needle and draw through one stitch on the needle, wool over the needle and draw through two stitches on the needle, do 1 plain tricot stitch in the last row, do 1 raised tricot stitch in the last row but one, 1 plain tricot stitch in the last row, and so on, a raised stitch and a plain stitch alternately to the end. **5th row**—Pick up a plain tricot stitch in the second tricot stitch of last row, and work a raised stitch in the tricot stitch of the last row but one, in this way the raised stitches will come intermediately between the raised stitches of the last row. **6th row**—Work the same as the fourth row. There should be 24 raised stitches in the fourth row and in the sixth row and 23 raised stitches in the fifth row, and all the remaining stitches plain. Repeat these six rows till you have worked 18 rows in all from the commencement. You then begin to shape for the shoulder by making 10 chain at the end of the eighteenth fancy row and picking up these as additional tricot stitches at the beginning of the next plain tricot row, now doing 59 stitches in each row for 3 plain and 2 fancy rows, then slip stitch along 20 tricot stitches and work only 39 stitches of the next fancy row to allow of space for an armhole, and when drawing back do 20 chain at the end to restore the shoulder piece to its original height. Work 3 plain tricot rows and 2 fancy rows on 59 stitches; then at the beginning of the third fancy row slip stitch along 10 stitches and complete the row on 49 stitches as previously worked for the back of the body. Continue on 49 stitches for the front, doing altogether 6 stripes of plain and 5 stripes of fancy tricot, 33 rows in all. Next row do fancy tricot and work 10 chain at the end to shape for the other shoulder; do 2 rows of fancy tricot and 3 rows of plain tricot on 59 stitches, then slip stitch along 20 stitches and work only 39 stitches in the next fancy row and when drawing back do 20 chain at the end on which to complete the shoulder Work 2 fancy rows and 3 plain rows on 59 stitches; then at the beginning of the next fancy row slip stitch along 10 stitches and work along 49 stitches for the back of the body, continuing the striped pattern till 3 fancy stripes and 3 plain stripes are worked, slip stitch along the last row and fasten off. Sew the shoulder pieces together. Work a row of plain double crochet round the neck, using a No. 10 needle, and contracting a little

stitches at the bottom of the sleeves, and the same through the treble stitches in the upper frill.

D'OYLEY WITH GREEK LACE BORDER.

THIS useful d'oyley is composed of a centre of diaper or fine damask linen, bordered with a pretty crochet lace. Cut the damask the size the d'oyley is required to be, and after hemming it round, embroider the margin with feather stitching. The feather stitching should be done with coarse crochet cotton, the size of Evans' No. 2, while for the crochet border you will require a reel of No. 20 or No. 24, and a fine steel crochet needle. The **1st round** of the d'oyley consists of a series of buttonhole stitch loops, worked with a crewel needle and a rather long length of the same coarse cotton you have been using for the feather stitching, and is simply for the purpose of making a foundation for working the crochet into; proceed thus—tie a knot to secure the end of the needleful of cotton, bring the needle and cotton up from the wrong side to the right side of the damask, just on the margin of the hem, * let the cotton hang over the fingers of the left hand, insert the needle from the wrong side to the right side of the material, about an eighth of an inch to the right of where it previously was brought up, and draw the cotton through to form a rather loose loop, keep the cotton to the right while you insert the needle upwards through the loop and draw the cotton through twist another similar stitch in the loop, and then repeat from *, making the loops all of even size, and when you have gone entirely round the material, join neatly, and fasten off. **2nd round**—With No. 20 cotton and fine crochet needle—Work 1 double crochet under the first buttonhole stitch loop of last round, * 9 chain, 1 single crochet in the fifth chain from the needle, 5 chain, 1 double crochet under the next buttonhole loop, and repeat from *; fasten off at the end of this and every round, and recommence in a fresh place. **3rd round**—1 double crochet in the next chain stitch but one *after* the picot of last round, 9 chain, 1 single crochet in the fifth chain from the needle, 5 chain, and repeat to the end of the round. Work three more rounds the same as last round **7th round**—1 treble in the next chain stitch but one *after* the picot of last round, 8 chain, 1 single crochet in the fifth chain from the needle, 3 chain, another treble in the same place as last treble is worked into, 8 chain, 1 single crochet in the fifth chain from the neeedle, 5 chain, 1 single crochet in the same place, 5 chain, another single crochet in the same place (making three picots), 3 chain, and repeat. **8th round**—1 double crochet in the little picot of last round that stands by itself, 3 chain, 1 double crochet in the first picot of the group of three picots, 5 chain, 1 double crochet in the centre picot, 5 chain, 1 double crochet in the third picot, 3 chain, and continue the same to the end of the round. **9th round**—1 double crochet on the double crochet stitch that in last round is worked into the solitary picot, 5 chain, 1 double crochet in the fourth chain stitch of the first loop of five chain of last round, 5 chain, 1 double crochet in the second stitch of the next loop of five chain of last round, 5 chain, and repeat. **10th round**—1 double crochet on the double crochet stitch above the solitary picot, 5 chain, 1 double crochet in the centre loop of five chain of last round, 5 chain, another double crochet in the same place, 5 chain, another double crochet in the same place, 5 chain, another double crochet in the same place, 5 chain, 1 double crochet on the double crochet stitch above the next solitary picot, 5 chain, 1 double crochet in the centre loop of five chain of last round, * 3 chain, 2 treble in the same loop, 3 chain, 1 double crochet in the same loop, repeat from * twice, then do 5 chain, and repeat all. **11th round**—1 double crochet in the first of the chain picot loops of last round, 5 chain, 1 double crochet in the next loop, 5 chain, 1 double crochet in the next loop, 1 chain, * 1 double crochet in the loop of chain before the two treble stitches of last round, 5 chain, 1 double crochet in the loop of chain before the double crochet of last round, 5 chain, repeat from * twice, which makes five loops round the treble stitches of the scallop, 1 chain, and proceed in the same manner to the end of the round. This finishes the d'oyley.

of last row, 2 chain, 1 double crochet in the space to the left of the double crochet stitch of last row, 4 chain, and repeat from * to the end, where join neatly; this finishes the scalloped edge. For the **Heading**—Work along the opposite side of the insertion,—**1st round**—2 treble under the loop of chain at the top of a point, * 5 chain 2 treble under the loop of the next point, and repeat from * to the end of the round, and join neatly. **2nd round**—Slip stitch between the two treble stitches of last round, 5 chain, 1 treble in the centre stitch of the five chain of last round, 2 chain, 1 treble between the two next treble stitches, 2 chain, * 1 treble in the centre stitch of five chain of last round, 2 chain, 1 treble between the two next treble stitches, 2 chain, and repeat from *; and at the end of the round join to the third stitch of the chain with which the round commenced. Sew the trimming upon the chemise, and run the narrow blue ribbon in and out through the open part of the heading, finishing with a little bow in front and on the top of each shoulder, as represented in the engraving. This border is also very suitable as a trimming for drawers.

SET FOR CHEMISE TRIMMING.

THIS trimming is worked with Evans' crochet cotton, No. 24, of which two reels will be required, and a very fine steel crochet needle. Commence with 70 chain, and work closely and firmly. **1st row**—1 treble in the sixth chain from the needle, 2 chain, another treble in the same place, 1 chain, miss one, 1 double crochet in the next, 1 chain, miss one, 8 consecutive treble, 5 chain, miss one, 8 more consecutive treble, 1 chain, miss one, 1 double crochet in the next, 1 chain, miss one, 1 treble in the last, 2 chain, another treble in the same place. **2nd row**—5 chain to turn, 1 treble under the loop of two chain, 2 chain, another treble in the same place, 2 chain, 4 treble on the first four

Full Size Working Design for
Set for Chemise Trimming.

Set for Chemise Trimming.

TRIMMING FOR A CHEMISE.

PROCURE two reels of Evans' crochet cotton No. 18 or No. 20, a fine steel crochet needle, and 2 yards of blue ribbon measuring three-eighths of an inch in width. The trimming is first of all worked the short way, and when a sufficient length is thus executed the scallops and the heading are added on either side. Commence with 9 chain ; miss the eight chain stitches nearest the needle, and work 5 treble in the next stitch. **2nd row**—5 chain to turn, miss the first treble stitch, do 1 treble on the next, 2 chain, 1 treble on the next, 2 chain, miss one stitch, 1 treble on the next, 2 chain, 5 treble under the loop at the end **3rd row**—Do 5 chain to turn, miss the first treble stitch, and do 1 treble on the next, 2 chain, 1 treble on the next, 2 chain, miss one stitch, 1 treble on the next, 2 chain, 5 treble under the first loop of two chain of last row. Repeat the last row till you can count 102 points along each side of the insertion. Then work in the same manner 34 points for each sleeve. Join the pieces in three separate rounds. Now work for the **Scallop—1st round**—1 double crochet under a point of the insertion, 4 chain, 5 treble 2 chain and 5 treble all under the next point, * 1 double crochet, under the next point, 4 chain, 5 treble 2 chain and 5 treble all under the next point, and repeat from * to the end, where join neatly round. **2nd round**—Turn the work, recommence with 1 double crochet under the loop of four chain, * 2 chain, 1 treble on the second treble stitch, 2 chain, 1 treble on the third treble stitch, 2 chain, miss one, 1 treble on the fifth treble stitch, 2 chain, 1 treble under the loop of two chain at the point of the scallop, 3 chain, another treble in the same place, 2 chain, 1 treble on the first treble stitch, 2 chain, miss one, 1 treble on the third treble stitch, 2 chain, 1 treble on the next treble stitch, 2 chain, 1 double crochet under the loop of four chain, and repeat from * to the end of the round, and join neatly. **3rd round**—Turn the work, * do 1 double crochet under the space to the left of the first treble stitch, 4 chain, 1 double crochet under the next, 4 chain, 1 double crochet under the next, 4 chain, 1 double crochet under the loop at the point of the scallop, 4 chain, another double crochet in the same place, 4 chain, 1 double crochet under the next space, 4 chain, 1 double crochet under the next space, 4 chain, 1 double crochet under the next space, 4 chain, 1 double crochet in the space to the right of the double crochet stitch

treble of last row, 5 chain, 1 double crochet under the five chain of last row, 5 chain, 4 treble on the last four treble stitches, 2 chain, 1 treble under the loop of two chain, 2 chain, another treble in the same place. **3rd row**—5 chain to turn, 1 treble under the loop of two chain, 2 chain, another treble in the same place, 1 chain, 1 double crochet under two chain, 1 chain, 2 treble on the first two treble stitches, 4 chain, 1 double crochet under the first loop of five chain, 5 chain, 1 double crochet under the next loop of five chain, 4 chain, 2 treble on the last two treble stitches, 1 chain, 1 double crochet under two chain, 1 chain, 1 treble under the loop of two chain, 2 chain, another treble in the same place. **4th row**—5 chain to turn, 1 treble under the loop of two chain, 2 chain, another treble in the same place, 2 chain, 4 consecutive treble beginning over the two treble stitches of last row, 5 chain, 1 double crochet under the loop of five chain, 5 chain, 4 consecutive treble ending over the two treble stitches of last row, 2 chain, 1 treble under the loop of two chain, 2 chain, another treble in the same place. **5th row**—5 chain to turn, 1 treble under the loop of two chain, 2 chain, another treble in the same place, 1 chain, 1 double crochet under two chain, 1 chain, 8 consecutive treble beginning over the four treble stitches of last row, 5 chain, 8 more consecutive treble ending over the four treble stitches of last row, 1 chain, 1 double crochet under two chain, 1 chain, 1 treble under the loop of two chain, 2 chain, another treble in the same place. Repeat from the second row until 68 patterns are done, (or the length desired to go round the neck), then fasten off, and join the work in a round. Recommence with 30 stitches, and proceed with the same pattern for a sleeve ; when 12 patterns are done join the scalloped edge of the next 8 patterns to the edge of the 8 corresponding patterns of the neck piece ; work 12 more patterns, and fasten off Work for the other sleeve in the same manner, and join the 8 centre patterns to the opposite side of the neck piece. Join both the sleeve pieces in a round Now work for the **Scalloped Edge** on the top of the neck piece and on the outside of each sleeve piece —**1st round**—Do 2 long treble, 3 chain, and 2 long treble, all under every point of five chain stitches ; join evenly at the end of the round. **2nd round**—1 double crochet under a loop of three chain of last round, 1 chain, 1 treble under the next loop of three chain, 1 chain and 1 treble six times in the same place, 1 chain, and repeat to the end of the round. **3rd round**—1 double crochet under the chain stitch next after the double crochet stitch of last round, 5 chain, 1 double crochet under the next chain stitch, 5 chain and 1 double crochet six more times under successive chain stitches, and continue the same to the end of the round, where join neatly; this finishes the scalloped edge. For the **Heading**—Work along the under side of the neck piece and on the inside of the sleeves—3 treble under every point of five chain stitches, doing 2 chain between each group of treble stitches. This completes the trimming, which now is ready for sewing upon the chemise. The same border is also pretty as a trimming for drawers.

THE BURLINGTON CAPE.

THIS is one of the shoulder capes that are now so fashionably worn and gradually are usurping the place of shawls as they are warm and comfortable, and are not liable to fall off being secured round the neck with a ribbon. Our model is worked throughout in a pretty fancy stitch, with a soft shade of grey double Berlin wool, of which 10 ozs. are required, with 1¾ yards of two inch wide ribbon to match, and three bone crochet needles, No 9, No. 7, and No. 5. The pattern is worked in rows forwards and backwards. Wind two balls of

The Burlington Cape.

wool to begin with. Use No. 9 crochet needle, and commence with the first ball of wool with 63 chain stitches for the top of the cape. Leave this, and take the other ball, and leaving 17 chain unworked from the end where the first ball of wool is, begin with 1 double crochet in the eighteenth stitch of the chain, * miss one chain stitch, do 5 treble in the next, miss one, do 1 double crochet in the next, and repeat from * till 7 little patterns are worked, ending with a double crochet stitch as you began, and leaving 17 stitches unworked at the other end of the foundation chain. **2nd row**—1 chain to turn, and work back along the seven little patterns you have just done—thus—insert the hook from right to left behind the double crochet stitch and draw the wool through loosely, insert the hook from right to left behind the first treble stitch and draw the wool through loosely, insert the hook in the same manner behind the next treble stitch and draw the wool through loosely, now 4 loops are on the needle, wool over the needle and draw through all, do 1 chain to bind the cluster together, * insert the hook to take up the two top threads of the next treble stitch and draw the wool through, wool over the needle and draw through the two loops on the needle (this is practically a double crochet stitch and is always to be worked thus upon the centre treble stitch of a group), raise a loop upon the stem of each of the 2 next treble stitches (*always* inserting the hook from right to left at the back of the stitch), a loop upon the double crochet stitch, and a loop upon each of the 2 next treble stitches, all the loops to be as loose and as long as possible, now 6 loops are on the needle, wool over the needle and draw through all, do 1 chain to bind the loops together, and repeat from *, and when you come to the end of the seven patterns you will have only 3 stitches to raise loops upon for the last cluster, wool over the needle and draw through the loops, 1 chain, and break off the wool; tie the two ends of wool together **3rd row**—Resume the last stitch of the foundation chain, and proceed now with the first ball of wool; do 1 double crochet in the first chain stitch by the needle, * miss one, do 5 treble in the next, miss one, do 1 double crochet in the next, and repeat from * along the seventeen stitches of the foundation chain; when you get to the small portion that is already worked do a double crochet on the double crochet stitch of the first little row, and do 5 treble stitches in the loop of one chain that binds the little half pattern together, then * 1 double crochet on the double crochet of last row, and 5 treble in the one chain that binds the cluster of loops together, repeat from * five times, do 1 double crochet on the double crochet stitch, 5 treble in the loop of one chain that binds the half patterns together, 1 double crochet on the double crochet stitch at the end of the first little row, * miss one of the foundation chain, 5 treble in the next, miss one, 1 double crochet in the next, and repeat from * to the end of the row; there are 16 groups of five treble in this row, *i.e.*, 4 groups at each end of the foundation chain, and 8 groups on the little rows that are worked in the middle of the back; the object of working the little rows is to make the back of the cape longer than the front. **4th row**—1 chain to turn, and work as instructed for the second row, doing 15 clusters of five loops in a cluster, and half a cluster at the beginning and end of the row. **5th row**—1 chain to turn, work 6 treble in the chain stitch that binds the half cluster together, * 1 double crochet on the double crochet stitch of last row, 5 treble in the chain stitch that binds the entire cluster

together, repeat from *, and end the row with 6 treble stitches as it began; there are 17 groups in this row. **6th row**—1 chain to turn, and work as directed for the fourth row, but doing 16 clusters and two half clusters. **7th row**—The same as the fifth row, but doing 18 groups. **8th row**—Take the No 7 needle, and work as instructed for the sixth row, doing 17 clusters and two half clusters. **9th row**—Keep to No. 7 needle, and work in the same manner as the seventh row, but do 8 treble at the beginning of the row, 7 treble always in each pattern instead of five treble, and end with 8 treble; there will be 19 groups in the row. **10th row**—Work as the eighth row, but raise 7 loops in a cluster instead of five loops, and make 18 clusters and two half clusters. **11th row**—Work the same as the ninth row, but make 20 groups in the row. **12th row**—The same as the tenth row, but to consist of 19 clusters and two half clusters. **13th row**—The same as the eleventh row, but make 21 groups in the row. **14th row**—The same as the twelfth row, but to consist of 20 clusters and two half clusters. **15th row**—The same as the thirteenth row, but make 22 groups in the row. **16th row**—The same as the fourteenth row, but to consist of 21 clusters and two half clusters. **17th row**—The same as the fifteenth row, but make 23 groups in the row. **18th row**—Take the No 5 needle, and work the same as in the sixteenth row, but doing 22 clusters and two half clusters. **19th row**—Keep to No. 5 needle, and work in the same manner as the seventeenth row, but do 24 groups in the row. **20th row**—Work as the eighteenth row, but to consist of 23 clusters and two half clusters. **21st row**—2 chain to turn, 3 treble in the chain stitch that binds the half cluster together, 1 double crochet on double crochet stitch of last row, proceed as in the nineteenth row, and end with 4 treble stitches, this row therefore has no increase and will consist of 23 groups of treble stitches and two half groups. **22nd row**—Work a double crochet stitch on the first treble stitch of last row, then a cluster of 7 loops, a double crochet on double crochet, and continue to the end, where the double crochet must be worked upon the chain that turned, and there are 24 whole clusters in the row. **23rd row**—The same as the twenty-first row, and the same number of groups. **24th row**—The same as the twenty-second row. **25th row**—The same as the twenty-third row; leave the wool at the end of this row while you work a few rows for a neck-band. For the **Neck-band**—**1st row**—Use the second ball of the wool and No. 9 crochet needle, and holding the right side of the cape towards you, work along the commencing chain, 1 double crochet into about each alternate stitch of the chain, doing about 30 or 32 double crochet in the row. **2nd row**—Turn the work, and do another row of double crochet stitches. **3rd**

Gentleman's Mitten.

row—4 chain to turn, and work long treble stitches (the wool twice round the needle) through which to run the ribbon. **4th row**—Plain double crochet. Now continue the border from the bottom corner of the cape, rounding the corner nicely with additional treble stitches, do scallops up the front, along the neck, and down the other front, and join neatly at the corner. Run the ribbon at the neck through the row of long treble stitches, there will be long ends to tie in a nice bow in front.

GENTLEMAN'S MITTEN.

PROCURE 1½ ozs. of brown Berlin fingering, or a 2 oz. packet of Baldwin's Beehive yarn, and a No. 12 bone crochet needle. Commence with 61 chain for the length of the mitten from the wrist to the top of the hand. **1st row**—Miss the first chain stitch, and work 36 double crochet and 24 single crochet, that is, 60 stitches in the row. **2nd row**—1 chain to turn, and inserting the hook to take up the one thread at the back of the stitches of the preceding row, do 24 single crochet over the twenty-four single crochet and 36 double crochet over the thirty-six double crochet of last row. **3rd row**—1 chain to turn, work 36 double crochet and 24 single crochet in the row, always taking up the one back thread. **4th row**—Same as the second row. Repeat these two rows till 51 rows are done, or till the mitten is the right size to fit round the hand, the single crochet stitches form the wrist. **52nd row**—Beginning at the wrist end—Do 1 chain to turn, 24 single crochet, 26 double crochet and 6 chain, and leave the other ten double crochet unworked. **53rd row**—1 chain to turn, and work back 8 double crochet. **54th row**—Do 8 double crochet. **55th row**—1 chain to turn, and work 10 double crochet. **56th row**—Do 10 double crochet. **57th row**—1 chain to turn, and work twelve double crochet. Continue thus up and down, going 2 stitches further towards the wrist in every downward row till you work 16 stitches down and up again, and fasten off. Sew up the mitten, and work a row of double crochet along the top of the hand and thumb. Work a row of crazy stitch round the wrist, thus—1 double crochet on a rib of the mitten, 3 chain, 3 treble in the same place as the double crochet is worked into, and repeat the same, and join evenly at the end of the round. Crochet the other mitten in the same manner; and when sewing up be careful to fold this mitten to correspond with the mitten already made, one for the right hand and the other for the left, and the seam of each mitten must come inside the hand.

BABY'S PETTICOAT WITH BODICE.

WORKED IN RUSSIAN CROCHET.

THE petticoat from which our engraving is taken is very useful for summer wear, as it is worked with unbleached knitting cotton, Strutt's No. 10 being the size selected, and of which about 4 ozs. will be required, the work is done with a No. 14 steel crochet needle. A similar petticoat can of course be made

Baby's Petticoat with Bodice.

with Andalusian wool and a bone crochet needle if preferred. Begin for the bottom of the front of the petticoat with a chain of 170 stitches. **1st row**—Commence in the first chain stitch by the needle, and work 5 consecutive double crochet, 3 double crochet in the next chain stitch, 5 more consecutive double crochet, * miss two chain, work 5 consecutive double crochet, 3 double crochet in the next, 5 more consecutive double crochet, and repeat from * to the end of the row. **2nd row**—Turn the work, and now miss the first stitch, and inserting the needle to take up the back thread of the stitches of the previous row, do * 5 consecutive double crochet, 3 double crochet on the next stitch which is the centre stitch of the three double crochet of last row, 5 more consecutive double crochet, miss two stitches, and repeat from * to the end of the row, where you will leave the one last stitch unworked. Continue working every row the same as the second row till 40 rows are done. **41st row**—Turn the work, miss the first stitch, do 11 consecutive double crochet, * miss 2 stitches, 11 consecutive double crochet, and repeat from *; this forms the first decrease in the skirt. **42nd row**—Turn the work, miss the first stitch, * do 4 consecutive double crochet, 3 double crochet on the next stitch, which is the one stitch that in last row is worked upon the centre stitch of the three double crochet of previous rows, 4 more consecutive double crochet, miss two stitches, and repeat from * to the end, where as before, you will leave the one last stitch unworked. **43rd row**—Turn the work, miss the first stitch, do 9 consecutive double crochet, * miss two stitches, 9 consecutive double crochet, and repeat from *; this forms a second decrease in the skirt. **44th row**—Turn the work, miss the first stitch, * do 3 consecutive double crochet, 3 double crochet on the next stitch, which is the one stitch that in last row is worked upon the centre stitch of the three double crochet of previous rows, 3 more consecutive double crochet, miss two stitches, and repeat from * to the

end, where as usual you will leave the one last stitch unworked. **45th row**—Turn the work, miss the first stitch, do 7 consecutive double crochet, * miss two stitches, 7 consecutive double crochet, and repeat from *; this forms another decrease, and now the skirt is narrowed sufficiently for the waist. **46th row**—Turn the work, miss the first stitch, * do 2 consecutive double crochet, 3 double crochet on the next stitch, which is the one stitch that in last row is worked upon the centre stitch of the three double crochet of previous rows, 2 more consecutive double crochet, and repeat from * to the end, where as before you will leave the last stitch unworked. Work for the **Body** 20 more rows the same as the last row. Then for the shoulder pieces, work the first 12 stitches forwards and backwards in plain double crochet for 8 rows, and fasten off; work the last 12 stitches in the same manner for the other shoulder piece. The back of the petticoat commences with 170 chain, and is crocheted in the same manner as the front. Join the shoulder pieces together, and sew up the sides, leaving space at the top for armholes, round which is worked a little narrow edging, thus—* 1 double crochet, miss a little space, work 6 treble all in one loop of the foundation, miss a little space, and repeat from * and join evenly at the ending of the round. The petticoat has no opening at the back, but slips easily over the child's head.

COT QUILT.

THIS cot quilt is worked in squares of tricot, each square being surrounded with three rounds of crochet. It is easily and quickly made, and looks very bright and pretty. The same pattern will serve for a sofa blanket, for a cushion cover, and many other articles. Procure 10 ozs of pink and 10 ozs. of white double Berlin wool, a tricot needle No 6, a crochet needle No. 8, and odd lengths of filoselles of various colours. Commence with pink wool, with 15 chain, in which pick up 14 double crochet stitches, and draw back; continue in rows of plain tricot till you have made a perfect square. Then still with pink wool, and holding the tricot the wrong side towards you, take the crochet needle and work double crochet all round the square, doing three double crochet at the turning of the corners, join evenly at the end of the round, and fasten off. **2nd round**—With white wool, hold the tricot the right side towards you, and inserting the hook to take up the back thread of the stitches of last round, work round in treble, doing three or five treble to ease the corners, join at the end, and fasten off. **3rd round**—With pink wool, work a double crochet stitch on each of two successive stitches of last round, insert the hook into a double crochet stitch of the first round (the same stitch as the next treble stitch of last row is worked into) and draw the wool through, wool over the needle and draw through two stitches on the needle loosely, and repeat, and fasten off at the end of the round; this finishes one square. Work the tricot part of the next square with white wool, and border it with a round of pink, white, and pink again, like the square already done. On the white tricot square embroider a rose-bud spray, or other pretty device, with shaded filoselles. On the pink tricot square work five double perpendicular lines of coral stitch, all with pink filoselle. When a sufficient number of squares are worked join them together by a pink row of double crochet. For the **Border** round the **Quilt.** **1st round**—Hold the work the wrong side

Cot Quilt.

towards you, and taking up the one top thread, work with pink wool a round of double crochet. **2nd round**—With white wool, hold the work the right side towards you and insert the hook to take up the back thread of the stitches of last round, work 1 double crochet, 6 chain, miss two stitches, and repeat. **3rd round**—Still with white wool, do 1 double crochet under a loop of chain stitches, 6 chain and repeat. Make a number of daisy balls of pink and white wool mixed and sew one upon every alternate loop of chain stitches, as shown in the engraving, also place one daisy ball at every corner of the square sections.

ST. ANDREW'S CROSS.

SQUARE FOR A QUILT.

PROCURE sufficient quantity of Strutt's knitting cotton No. 6, and a medium sized steel crochet needle. Begin with 52 chain. **1st row**—Miss the two chain stitches nearest the needle and work 50 double crochet in the row, closely and firmly. **2nd row**—Turn the work, and proceed with double crochet, 51 stitches in the row, taking up the back thread of the stitches of the preceding row that the work may sit in ridges, the last double crochet stitch will come upon the chain that turned. Work 3 more rows of ridged crochet doing 51 stitches in each row. **6th row**—Turn, work 3 double crochet, 1 treble in the back thread of double crochet stitch of the second previous row, 3 double crochet, 1 treble in the lower rib, 3 double crochet, 1 treble in the lower rib, 9 double crochet, a tuft (4 treble stitches worked as a group in one stitch of the lower rib), 3 double crochet, a tuft, 3 double crochet, a tuft, 9 double crochet, 1 treble in the lower rib, 3 double crochet, 1 treble in the lower rib, 3 double crochet, 1 treble in the lower rib, 3 double crochet. The treble stitches which form the "cross" are always to be worked into the corresponding stitch of the second previous row, and so also are the groups of four treble stitches that form the "tufts." **7th row**—21 double crochet, 1 treble worked into the lower rib behind the tuft, 3 double crochet, 1 treble, 3 double crochet, 1 treble, 21 double crochet. **8th row**—5 double crochet, 1 treble, 3 double crochet, 1 treble, 3 double crochet, 1 treble, 9 double crochet, a tuft, 3 double crochet, a tuft, 9 double crochet, 1 treble, 3 double crochet, 1 treble, 3 double crochet, 1 treble, 5 double crochet. **9th row**—23 double crochet,

15 double crochet, 1 treble, 3 double crochet, 1 treble, 3 double crochet, 1 treble, 15 double crochet, a tuft, 5 double crochet. **25th row**—5 double crochet, 1 treble, 39 double crochet, 1 treble, 5 double crochet. **26th row**— 3 double crochet, a tuft, 3 double crochet, a tuft, 11 double crochet, 1 treble, 3 double crochet, 1 treble, 3 double crochet, 1 treble, 3 double crochet, 1 treble, 11 double crochet, a tuft, 3 double crochet, a tuft, 3 double crochet. **27th row**—3 double crochet, 1 treble, 3 double crochet, 1 treble, 35 double crochet, 1 treble, 3 double crochet, 1 treble, 3 double crochet. **28th row**—The same as the twenty-fourth row. **29th row**— Same as the twenty-third row. **30th row**—Same as the twenty-second row. And so on work backwards, each successive row, till you finish the square with 3 rows of plain double crochet. Do not break off the cotton but proceed for **the Edge**—After working the last double crochet stitch of last row, do 6 chain, 1 treble on that same double crochet stitch (which is a corner stitch), 2 chain, 1 treble on the tip of the second ridge along the side of the square, 2 chain, 1 treble in the depressed space midway between the third and fourth ridges, and continue 2 chain and 1 treble alternately, and get 18 treble stitches along the side of the square from corner to corner, do 3 chain to round the corner, another treble on the corner stitch, and work the same along each side of the square; and on completion of the round join with a single crochet to the third stitch of chain with which the round commenced. **2nd round**—Work 1 double crochet in every stitch of preceding round, and 3 double crochet in the corner stitch; join round neatly, and fasten off. A Border suitable for this quilt appears in No. 39 of "Weldon's Practical Needlework Series."

St. Andrew's Cross. Square for a Quilt.

1 treble, 3 double crochet, 1 treble, 23 double crochet. **10th row**—7 double crochet, 1 treble, 3 double crochet, 1 treble, 3 double crochet, 1 treble, 11 double crochet, a tuft, 11 double crochet, 1 treble, 3 double crochet, 1 treble, 3 double crochet, 1 treble, 7 double crochet. **11th row**—25 double crochet, 1 treble, 25 double crochet. **12th row**—9 double crochet, 1 treble, 3 double crochet, 1 treble, 3 double crochet, 1 treble, 15 double crochet, 1 treble, 3 double crochet, 1 treble, 3 double crochet, 1 treble, 9 double crochet. **13th row**—Plain double crochet, 51 stitches. **14th row**—11 double crochet, 1 treble, 3 double crochet, 1 treble, 3 double crochet, 1 treble, 11 double crochet, 1 treble, 3 double crochet, 1 treble, 3 double crochet, 1 treble, 11 double crochet. **15th row**—Plain double crochet. **16th row**—13 double crochet, 1 treble, 3 double crochet, 1 treble, 3 double crochet, 1 treble, 7 double crochet, 1 treble, 3 double crochet, 1 treble, 3 double crochet, 1 treble, 13 double crochet. **17th row**—Plain double crochet. **18th row**—15 double crochet, 1 treble, 3 double crochet, 1 treble, 3 double crochet, 1 treble, 3 double crochet, 1 treble, 3 double crochet, 1 treble, 3 double crochet, 1 treble, 15 double crochet. **19th row**—Plain double crochet. **20th row**—17 double crochet, 1 treble, 3 double crochet, 1 treble, 3 double crochet, 1 treble, 3 double crochet, 1 treble, 3 double crochet, 1 treble, 17 double crochet. **21st row**—Plain double crochet. **22nd row**—3 double crochet, a tuft, 15 double crochet, 1 treble, 3 double crochet, 1 treble, 3 double crochet, 1 treble, 3 double crochet, 1 treble, 15 double crochet, a tuft, 3 double crochet. **23rd row**— 3 double crochet, 1 treble behind the tuft, 43 double crochet, 1 treble behind the tuft, 3 double crochet. **24th row**—5 double crochet, a tuft,

WELDON'S
PRACTICAL CROCHET.

(ELEVENTH SERIES.)

HOW TO CROCHET HATS, PETTICOATS, QUILTS, BORDERS, PINCUSHIONS, HOODS, &c.

TWENTY-SIX ILLUSTRATIONS.

Telegraphic Address—
"Consuelo," London.

The Yearly Subscription to this Magazine, post free to any Part of the World, is 2s. 6d. Subscriptions are payable in advance, and may commence from any date and for any period.

[Telephone—
8745.

The Back Numbers are always in print. Nos. 1 to 90 now ready, Price 2d. each, or post free for 16s. Over 5,000 Engravings.

CHILD'S PETTICOAT.
SHELL PATTERN

THIS is a pretty and useful petticoat for a girl of about five years of age, and is worked with the best Peacock wool or Petticoat fingering, and a No. 8 or No. 9 bone crochet needle. Of Peacock wool 1 oz. of red and 3 ozs. of white will be sufficient, but of Petticoat fingering rather more will be required, as it is thicker and therefore weighs heavier, and will make a larger sized skirt. Commence with red wool for the 1st round, which forms a line of little scollops along the bottom of the skirt; * do 7 chain, pick up loosely 1 tricot stitch in each of 6 chain stitches, and there will be 7 stitches on the needle, wool over the needle and draw through all, do 1 chain to tighten the group of stitches; repeat from * till you have 37 of these shell-like scollops, (or more or less according as you desire for the width of the skirt); join round evenly, and fasten off the wool. 2nd round—With white—Join the white wool in the heading of the row of scollops, draw the wool through a round loop where the stitches of last row are gathered together, and do three chain, draw up a tricot stitch in each of the 2 chain stitches below the needle, a stitch in the round loop where the stitches of last row are gathered together, a stitch in the next thread of wool, and a stitch in the next thread of wool, now 6 stitches are on the needle, wool over the needle and draw through all, and do 1 chain to tighten the group; draw up a tricot stitch in the little round hole under the needle, a stitch in the lower back part of the shell just formed, a stitch in the thread of wool of last row where a stitch is already worked, a stitch in the next thread of wool, and a stitch in the next thread of wool, which is a little round loop where the stitches of last row are gathered together, now 6 stitches are on the needle, wool over the needle and draw through all, and do 1 chain to tighten the group; proceed in this shell pattern, working two shells above each scollop to the end of the round; which will make 74 shells in the round if you began with 37 scollops. 3rd round—Also with white wool—Work shell above shell; break off the wool at the end of this round. 4th round—Shell-stitch worked with red wool. 5th round—Shell stitch worked with white wool. Repeat the last two rounds twice more. Then continue entirely with white wool, retaining the same number of shells in every round, till 10 consecutive rounds are worked with white wool, when break off; and henceforth work in rows, doing 7 rows, and the beginning and at the end of the rows will form the opening of the placket hole at the back of the skirt. Decrease one shell in every six in the first row, and again one shell in every six in the fifth row. The waistband on our model is knitted with red wool

Child's Petticoat in Shell Pattern.

and a pair of No. 14 knitting needles, picking up a line of stitches along the top of the skirt and working in a rib of 1 stitch plain and 1 stitch purl for 10 rows, and cast off. Or you can make a calico waistband if you like, or work one in plain double crochet.

D'OYLEY WORKED IN MEDALLIONS.

A PRETTY dessert d'oyley can be worked according to the accompanying illustration by using Evans' crochet cotton, No. 18, of which two reels will be required, and a fine steel crochet needle, or for a toilet d'oyley employ red or blue crochet Maltese thread, No. 14. Commence with 8 chain, and join round. 1st round—Do 3 chain to stand for a treble, and work 23 treble stitches in the circle, and join evenly to the third chain with which the round began. 2nd round—3 chain, miss one treble stitch, 1 double crochet on the next, and repeat, doing 12 loops in the round, and join evenly. 3rd round—Slip-stitch to the middle of the loop of three chain, * 5 chain, 1 double crochet in the middle of the next loop, and repeat from * till 12 loops of five chain are done, and join round. 4th round—Slip-stitch to the middle of the loop of five chain, * 4 chain, 1 double crochet under the same loop, 3 chain, 1 double crochet under the next loop, and repeat from *, making 12 loops of four chain, and 12 loops of three chain, and join round. 5th round—Slip-stitch once into the four chain loop, do 3 chain to stand for a treble, 3 treble in the four chain loop, * 3 chain, 4 more treble in the same place, 3 chain, 4 treble in the next four chain loop, and repeat from *, making 12 groups of eight treble stitches, and join round. 6th round—Slip-stitch to the three chain loop in the centre of the group of treble stitches, * do 1 double crochet in the three chain loop, 5 chain, another double crochet in the same place, 5 chain, another double crochet, 5 chain, and another double crochet in the same place, 3 chain, miss one three-chain loop, and in the next loop repeat from *, and fasten off at the end of the round, which completes one medallion. Work 6 more medallions in the same manner, and unite them together in process of working the last round, as shown in the engraving. For the Border—1st round—1 double crochet in the centre loop of the first group of picots round the margin of a medallion, * 8 chain, 1 double crochet in the centre loop of the next group of picots, and repeat from *, doing 6 double crochet stitches into each medallion with 8 chain between; and join evenly at the end of the round. 2nd round—5 chain, miss one stitch of last round, 1 treble in the next, * 2 chain, miss one stitch, 1 treble in the next, and repeat from *; and join at the end of the round to the third chain with which the round commenced. **3rd round**—Slip-stitch under a space of last round, 6 chain, 1 treble in the same space, 2 chain, miss one space, * 1 treble in the next, 3 chain, 1 treble in the same space, 2 chain, miss one space, and repeat from *, and at the end join to the third chain with which the round commenced. **4th round**—Slip-stitch to the centre of a loop of three chain where do 1 double crochet, * 3 chain, 1 treble under the next loop of three chain, 2 chain, 1 treble in the same place, 2 chain, another treble, 2 chain, another treble in the same place, 3 chain, 1 double crochet under the next loop of three chain, and repeat from *; and join, and fasten off at the end of this round. **5th round**—1 double crochet under the centre loop of two chain of last round, 5 chain and 1 double crochet three times in the same place, 7 chain, and repeat; and join evenly at the end of the round, and fasten off.

TEA COSY.

REQUIRED, about 1 oz. of each of eight shades of crimson, and 1½ oz. of black single Berlin wool, and a No. 12 bone crochet needle. Begin for the fan-like semicircle with the fourth shade of crimson wool, counting from the lightest, make 37 chain stitches; and for the **1st row**—Work 8 double crochet in the second chain from the needle, 7 double crochet in the next, and continue the same number of double crochet alternately to the end of the foundation chain.

row—Sixth shade. **16th row**—Seventh shade. **17th row**—Darkest shade. **18th row**—Black. **19th row**—Lightest shade. **20th row**—Third shade, **21st row**—Fourth shade. **22nd row**—Sixth shade. **23rd row**—Black. This completes the fan. For the **Sunflower** in the Centre—Commence with the third shade of crimson wool, with 2 chain, and work 4 double crochet in the second chain from the needle, and join the last of the four stitches to the first, in a circle. **1st round**—With same shade of wool—Turn the work, and inserting the hook to take up the back thread of the previous stitches, work 8 double crochet in the round, that is, 2 double crochet on each stitch, and join round. **2nd round**—Still with the same wool—Turn the work, and again do 2 double crochet on each stitch of last round, making 16 double crochet, and join round. **3rd round**—Keep the work on the same side, do 3 chain to stand for a treble, insert the hook to take up both the front threads of last round and work 4 treble on the first stitch, withdraw the hook, insert it in the third stitch of chain and draw the wool through, which binds the treble stitches closely together in a knob, do 1 loose double crochet on the next stitch of last row, 5 treble on the same stitch, withdraw the hook and insert it in the first of the five treble stitches and draw the wool through, which produces another knob; make 7 of these knobs on seven stitches and 1 double crochet between each, then miss one stitch, and do 7 more knobs and 7 more double crochet stitches, making in all 14 knobs and 14 double crochet in the round. **4th round**—With the next darkest shade of crimson—Work 1 knob and 1

D'Oyley Worked in Medallions.

to the number of 269 stitches; fasten off at the end of this row and every row, and commence the following row on the right-hand side, always inserting the hook to take up the one top thread of the stitches of the previous row, and working closely and evenly. **2nd row**—With the third shade of crimson wool—Work 6 consecutive double crochet stitches (i.e., 1 stitch on each of 6 stitches), 3 double crochet on the next, * 6 consecutive double crochet, miss two stitches, 6 consecutive double crochet, 3 double crochet on the next, and repeat from *, making 18 points of three double crochet stitches, and end as you began with 6 consecutive double crochet. **3rd row**—With the lightest shade of crimson wool—Insert the hook to take up the first and second stitches of last row as one stitch in which to work 1 double crochet, do 5 consecutive double crochet, then 3 double crochet on the centre stitch of three double crochet of last row, * 6 consecutive double crochet, miss two stitches, 6 consecutive double crochet, 3 double crochet on the next, which again is on the centre stitch of three double crochet of last row, and repeat from *, and end the row as you began with 5 consecutive double crochet and the two last stitches taken together in 1 double crochet. Every succeeding row is worked in the same manner as this last row, the only difference being in the shade of the wool. For the **4th row**—Use black wool. **5th row**—The second shade of crimson. **6th row**—Darkest crimson. **7th row**—Sixth shade. **8th row**—Third shade. **9th row**—Black. **10th row**—Sixth shade. **11th row**—Fifth shade. **12th row**—Second shade. **13th row**—Black. **14th row**—Second shade. **15th**

double crochet on every stitch of the preceding round, making 28 knobs, and 28 double crochet in the round, join quite evenly, and fasten off. You now arrange the fan-like portion of the crochet upon the sunflower as shown in the engraving, it stretches over twenty-two of the knobs, and must be neatly joined thereto by stitching or by crocheting at the back; the remaining six knobs lie as they are to the bottom of the cosy. You now, with the darkest shade of crimson, work 2 rows of plain double crochet straight along the bottom of the cosy from end to end. Work the reverse side of the cosy in exactly the same manner. Join the two fan-like pieces together stitch by stitch along the scolloped edge, only when at the bottom of the hollows you take two stitches together twice, the better to preserve the shape of the scollops. The cosy is lined with nicely quilted satin, and finished off with a bow of ribbon on the top.

BULGARIAN HEAD-DRESS.
FOR EVENING WEAR.

THIS head-dress is a novel and exceedingly pretty style for the opera or theatre, and consists of a stiff coronet covered with satin on which a band of tricot is arranged, while the crochet falls like a veil down the back, and may be wrapped closely round the neck as a protection from draught, or be tastefully caught up on one side with a pretty pin or a small glistening brooch. Materials required—9 ozs. of white peacock fingering wool of A A quality, a No. 8 bone crochet needle and a No. 9 tricot needle, a piece of stiff buckram this shape, ⌒ measuring 14½ inches along the straight side and 4½ inches in width in the centre but rounded at the corners, ¼ yard of pale blue satin, and ⅓ yard of narrow white elastic. Commence for the top of the veil, with Peacock wool and No. 8 crochet needle, with 31 chain. **1st row**—Miss the three chain stitches nearest the needle, and work 5 long treble stitches (wool twice round the needle) in the fourth chain from the needle, miss two stitches, 1 double crochet in the next, * miss two, 5 long treble in the next, miss two, 1 double crochet in the next, and repeat from *, making five groups of long treble stitches in the row; always work loosely, and draw up the long treble stitches to stand as high as possible. **2nd row**—Make three chain to turn, work 5 long treble on the first long treble stitch of previous row, 1 double crochet on the third long treble which is the middle stitch of the group, * 5 long treble on the double crochet stitch of previous row, 1 double crochet on the middle stitch of the next group, and repeat from *, and at the end of the row work 5 long treble on the last long treble stitch of last row; this makes six groups of long treble stitches in the row. Every successive row is worked in the same way as the last row, and by the time you get 37 rows done for the length of the veil you will have 41 groups of long treble stitches in the row. Now work the **Border** which is crocheted all round the veil excepting along the foundation chain—**1st row**—Beginning on the side of the veil by the foundation chain, work 7 long treble stitches in a group, miss a row, work one double crochet, miss a row, and continue the same until the corner is reached; turn easily; then along the bottom of the veil you work the group of 7 long treble stitches on a double

stitch at the beginning and a stitch at the end of every row till 10 rows in all are worked for the width of the band. Stitch the tricoted band firmly and neatly upon the satin coronet, leaving a margin of satin showing in front, that is along the straight side of the coronet, place the commencing chain of the veil under the band on the opposite side, stitching both band and commencing chain of the veil neatly together : let the veil hang over the band while you stitch down on the slant about two scollops on each end of the coronet, then throw the veil back in its right position. Sew an elastic on each side of the coronet with a button to fasten.

PINCUSHION.

THIS pincushion is made in the shape of a brioche The cover is worked with red and pink D M C coton à tricoter, No. 20, a ball of each being required and a medium fine steel crochet needle. The cushion measures about 6 inches across, the top is covered with red satin on which the crochet is laid, and the bottom is of pink flannelette. Commence with pink cotton for the centre of the cover; work 8 chain, join round, do 14 double crochet in the circle, and again join evenly. **2nd round**—Do 3 chain to stand for 1 treble stitch, and work 5 treble on the first double crochet of last round, take the hook out and insert it in the top stitch of the three chain and draw the loop through, which binds the group of stitches in the form of a raised tuft, do 4 chain, * miss one double crochet, work 6 treble in the next, withdraw the hook and insert it in the top of the first treble stitch and draw the loop through, which again binds a group of stitches in the similitude of a raised

Tea Cosy.

crochet of last row, and a double crochet on the centre stitch of the previous group ; turn the other corner when you come to it, and then proceed up the other side to correspond with the side already done ; fasten off after doing the last group of 7 long treble stitches. **2nd row**—Recommencing on the right-hand side—Do 1 double crochet on the first long treble stitch, 1 double crochet on the second long treble stitch, 3 chain, 1 single crochet in the third chain from the needle, 1 double crochet on the third long treble stitch, 3 chain, 1 single crochet in the third chain from the needle, 1 double crochet on the fourth long treble stitch, 3 chain, 1 single crochet in the third chain from the needle, 1 double crochet on the fifth long treble stitch, 1 double crochet on the sixth long treble stitch, miss three stitches, and repeat the same upon every scollop round the veil; which now is completed. For the **Coronet**—Having the buckram cut to the required shape and size, cover it neatly on both sides with pale blue satin, and proceed to work a strip of tricot for the band. Take the tricot needle, and beginning with 62 chain, work a **1st row** of 60 stitches of plain tricot. **2nd row**—1 stitch remains on the needle, wool over the needle, insert the hook to take up the chain stitch below the second tricot stitch of last row, and draw the wool through very loosely, wool over the needle and draw through one loop, wool over the needle and draw through two loops, pick up a tricot loop in the next stitch of previous row, work another raised loop in the chain stitch below the next stitch of previous row, and continue the two stitches alternately to the end ; and draw back as in ordinary tricot. **3rd row**—Work alternately a plain tricot and a raised tricot, the raised tricot to be over the plain stitch of preceding row and the plain tricot over the raised stitch. Continue working in the same manner but decrease a

tuft, do 4 chain, and repeat from * five times, making in all 7 tufts in the round with 4 chain between each tuft ; join round **3rd round**—Slip stitch into a four chain loop, do 3 chain to stand for 1 treble stitch, and work 5 treble in the four chain loop, take out the hook and insert it in the top stitch of three chain and draw the loop through so as to bind the group of stitches into a tuft, then 4 chain, 6 treble stitches in the same loop and draw in a tuft, 4 chain, * 6 treble stitches in the next loop and make a tuft, 4 chain, 6 treble stitches in the same loop, and make a tuft, 4 chain, and repeat from * ; and make 14 tufts in the round with 4 chain between each tuft ; and join evenly. **4th round**—Work 1 tuft in each loop of last round, making again 14 tufts in the round with 4 chain between each tuft. **5th round**—Work the same as the third round, two tufts in each loop, making 28 tufts in the round with 4 chain between each tuft, and join round. **6th round**—Work 1 tuft in the first loop, 1 tuft in the next loop, and 1 tuft in the next loop, then 6 chain, 1 double crochet in the next loop, 6 chain, and repeat the same to the end of the round, and you will have 21 tufts in the round of seven groups of three tufts in a group. **7th round**—Do 1 tuft in the loop between the first and second tufts of preceding round, 4 chain, 1 tuft in the next loop between the second and third tufts of preceding round, 6 chain, 1 double crochet in the next loop, 6 chain, 1 double crochet in the next loop, 6 chain, * 1 tuft in the next loop, 4 chain, 1 tuft in the next, 6 chain, 1 double crochet in the next, 6 chain, 1 double crochet in the next, 6 chain, and repeat from * to the end of the round, and join evenly **8th round**—Do 1 tuft in the loop between the two tufts of last round, 6 chain and 1 double crochet in the next loop three times, 6 chain, and repeat the same to the end of the round, which brings each of the seven groups of tufts to a point of one tuft only. **9th round**—Slip-stitch to the centre of a loop of last round, do 1 double crochet in the loop, * 5 chain, 1 double crochet in the next loop, and repeat from *, and there will be 28 loops of chain in the round. **10th round**—The same. **11th round**—Slip-stitch to the centre of a loop of last round, do 1 double crochet in the loop, 7 chain, 1 double crochet in the fifth chain from the needle, 4 chain, 1 single crochet on the double crochet stitch, 4 chain, another single crochet in the same place where now there are three little pique loops of chain, 2 chain, and work the same to the completion of the round, where join evenly, and fasten off. **12th round**—With red

Bulgarian Head-Dress.

cotton—Work 1 double crochet in the centre pique loop of last round, * 6 chain, 1 double crochet in the next centre pique loop, and repeat from * to the end of the round. **13th round**—Also with red cotton—Plain double crochet. For the **Border**—With pink cotton, **1st round**—Work 1 double crochet on a double crochet stitch of last round, 5 chain, and repeat; you will generally miss two stitches, but occasionally miss three stitches of last round when doing the five chain, as there must be 68 loops of chain stitches in the round. **2nd round**—Work the same as the sixth round, and you will have 51 tufts in the round in seventeen groups of three tufts in a group. **3rd round**—Same as the seventh round. **4th round**—Same as the eighth round. **5th round**— With red cotton—Work 1 treble under a loop of last round, 3 chain, another treble in the same place, * 1 treble under the next loop, 3 chain, another treble in the same place, and repeat from * to the end of the round. **6th round**— Also with red cotton—Do 1 double crochet, 4 treble, 1 double crochet, all under each loop of three chain of last round, and join evenly, and fasten off. This finishes the crochet cover. The padded cushion should be just the size of the round of double crochet that is worked with red cotton; the first and second rounds of the cover are scarcely perceptible in the engraving as they sink into the hollow in the centre of the cushion. The cushion is very tightly stuffed with bran except in the exact centre where the red satin and the pink flannelette meet and are secured together by a few stitches.

BORDER FOR A QUILT.

THIS border is worked in rows lengthways, and though specially designed for trimming a quilt executed in the Raised Square Pattern, illustrated on page 13 of the present issue, it can be used with several patterns that have appeared in Nos. 6, 39, 42, and 51 of "Weldon's Practical Needlework Series," price 2d. each of all booksellers, or 2½d. each from this office. The first row may be commenced straight upon the margin or edge of the quilt itself, in

which case the additional fulness required for turning the corners can be ensured row by row, by working three or five extra stitches, in the same way as extra stitches are employed in turning the corners of the quilt squares; or it can be crocheted upon a foundation chain of the required length, with an ample allowance for fulling in round the corners. The same pattern is useful worked with macramé twine for a mantel-drape, or worked with coloured flax thread for furniture trimming. **1st row**—Plain double crochet. **2nd row**— Turn the work; do 1 treble in the back thread of a double crochet stitch of the preceding row, * 3 chain, another treble in the same place, miss two stitches, 1 treble in the back thread of the next double crochet, and repeat from * to the end of the row. **3rd row**—Keep the work on the same side, and do 1 double crochet in the centre stitch of three chain of last row, 2 chain, and continue the same. **4th row**—Plain double crochet. **5th row** —All treble, inserting the hook to take the one *top* thread of the stitches of the previous row, and increase one stitch in every ten. **6th row**—Work 1 double crochet in the *front* thread of a double crochet stitch of the fourth row, miss one stitch, 6 double crochet in the front thread of the next stitch, miss one, and repeat. **7th row**—Turn the work; and do plain double crochet, inserting the hook to take the back thread of the treble stitches of the fifth row. **8th row**—Turn the work; insert the hook into two top threads of the stitches of last row, and do 1 treble, 1 chain, miss one, and repeat. **9th row**—Turn the work; and do plain double crochet, inserting the hook to take the back thread of the stitches of last row. **10th row**—Same as the eighth row. **11th row**—Same as the ninth row. **12th row**—With the right side of the work to the front; work all treble, taking up the *back* thread of the stitches of last row, and increase one treble in every ten. **13th row**— Work 1 double crochet in the *top* thread of a double crochet stitch of the eleventh row, miss one stitch, 6 double crochet in the top thread of the next stitch, miss one, and repeat. **14th row**—With the right side of the work to the front, work double crochet on the treble stitches of the twelfth row. **15th row**—Same as the eighth row. **16th row**—Same as the ninth row. **17th row**—Turn the work; and again do plain double crochet, inserting the hook to take the back thread of the stitches of last row. **18th row**—The same. Now for the **Scollops**—Beginning with the wrong side of the work to the front—Do 1 double crochet on the first stitch, inserting the hook to take the top and back threads, * 5 chain, miss three, 1 double crochet on the next, and repeat from * three times, making four loops of chain stitches, and turn the work. **2nd row**—Do 6 double crochet under each of the three first loops, and 3 double crochet under the fourth loop. **3rd row**—Turn with 5 chain, 1 double crochet between the third and fourth double crochet stitches

Working Design of one Corner of the Bulgarian Head-Dress.

of the first loop, 5 chain, 1 double crochet between the third and fourth stitches of the next loop, 5 chain, 1 double crochet between the third and fourth stitches of the next loop, making three loops of chain stitches, and turn the work. **4th row**—Do 6 double crochet under each of the two first loops, and 3 double crochet under the third loop. **5th row**—Turn with 5 chain, 1 double crochet between the third and fourth double crochet stitches of the first loop, 5 chain, 1 double crochet between the third and fourth stitches of the next loop, making two loops of chain stitches, and turn the work. **6th row**—Do 6 double crochet under the first loop, and 3 double crochet under the second loop. **7th row**—Turn with 5 chain, 1 double crochet between the third and fourth double crochet stitches of the loop, forming one loop only for the top of the scollop, and turn the work. **8th row** —Do 2 double crochet under the loop, 4 chain, 2 more double crochet under the loop, 4 chain, again 2 double crochet, 4 chain, and again 2 double crochet under the loop, then 3 double crochet to fill in the vacant half space of the next loop to the left, 3 double crochet in the next loop, and 3 double crochet in the next loop, which finishes one scollop. The other scollops are formed in the same manner.

D'OYLEY, EDGED WITH VENETIAN LACE.

THE centre of this d'oyley is composed of an oval piece of fine linen damask measuring about six inches from end to end, which after being hemmed round, is bordered with a pretty crochet lace, worked shortways. For this lace procure a skein of Coats' crochet cotton, No. 20, and a fine steel crochet needle. Begin with 24 chain, do 1 treble in the eleventh chain from the needle, 5 chain, 1 treble in the next, 10 chain, miss ten stitches, 1 treble in the next, 5 chain, 1 treble in the next, which is the last of the foundation stitches : * 10 chain, turn the work, do 1 treble under the loop of five chain, 5 chain, another treble in the same place, 5 chain, 1 double crochet under the loop of ten chain, 5 chain, 1 treble under the loop of five chain, 5 chain, another treble in the same place ;

Pincushion.

10 chain, turn the work, do 1 treble under the loop of five chain, 5 chain, another treble in the same place, 10 chain, miss two loops of five chain, 1 treble under the next loop, 5 chain, another treble in the same place ; you are now on the side where the tag of cotton hangs, and must repeat from * twice more, when there will be three loops of ten chain protruding from the edge of the crochet on each side the work. Do 10 chain, turn the work, 1 treble under the loop of five chain, and now for a **Scollop**—1 chain, turn the work, do 11 treble under the last loop of ten chain, 10 chain, 1 treble in the second loop of ten chain (i.e., the second loop), that protrudes on that side the work, 5 chain, another treble in the same place ; 10 chain, turn, do 1 treble under the five chain just done, 5 chain, another treble in the same place, 10 chain, 1 double crochet between the first and second of the eleven treble stitches ; * 10 chain, turn, 1 treble under the last worked loop of five chain, 5 chain, another treble in the same place, 10 chain, turn, 1 treble under the five chain just done, 5 chain, another treble in the same place, 10 chain, 1 double crochet between the two next of the eleven treble stitches, and repeat from * till you have ten loops projecting in the form of a scollop, and ten double crochet stitches worked intermediately between the eleven treble stitches, work 1 single crochet on the one chain stitch with which the scollop began ; then, 5 chain, 1 treble in the same loop in which you see a treble is already worked, 5 chain, 1 double crochet under the loop of ten chain, 5 chain, 1 treble under the loop of five chain, 5 chain, another treble in the same place, and now you are at the top of the edging, and proceed with working the insertion or heading. Do 10 chain, turn the work, 1 treble under the loop of five chain, 5 chain, another treble in the same place, 10 chain, miss two loops of five chain, 1 treble under the next loop, 5 chain, another treble in the same place, 10 chain, turn the work, 1 treble under the loop of five chain, 5 chain, another treble in the same place, 5 chain, 1 double crochet under the loop of ten chain, 5 chain, 1 treble under the loop of five chain, 5 chain, another treble in the same place, which is the top of the edging ; 10 chain, turn the work, 1 treble under the loop of five chain, 5 chain, another treble in the same place, 10 chain, miss two loops of five chain, 1 treble under the next loop, 5 chain, another treble in the same place, then 5 chain, and do 1 double crochet in the five-chain loop in the last row of the scollop, 5 chain, turn the work, 1 treble under the ordinary five-chain loop, 5 chain, another treble in the same place, 5 chain, 1 double crochet under the loop of ten chain, 5 chain. 1 treble under the loop of five chain, 5 chain, another treble in the same place, and this brings you again to the top of the edging, and completes one scollop. Now proceed with working the insertion or heading forwards and backwards for 7 short rows in the manner already instructed, and when these are done crochet another scollop like the preceding,

only when you get to the first, also the second, projecting loops of ten chain, do 5 chain only, do 1 single crochet into the last projecting loop of last scollop, and another 5 chain, and this makes the ordinary projecting loops of the present scollop, and at the same time joins the present scollop to the preceding scollop. Continue the edging until twelve scollops are accomplished, which will be a sufficient length to go round a d'oyley of the size shown in our engraving, though a longer piece can be made if a larger d'oyley is required. Join the last row of the edging very neatly to the foundation row ; then sew the edging to the damask centre by two or three seam stitches set into the tip of each protruding loop. Work a row of coral stitching with coarse crochet cotton round the margin of the damask linen.

PRETTY DRESS FOR A CHILD.

THE dress shown in the accompanying illustration measures about 20 inches from the shoulder to the bottom of the skirt, and is intended for a child of about three years of age ; it is simply and easily made, and yet has a pretty and stylish appearance. The materials required are 5 ozs. of the best white Peacock fingering wool, a No. 10 bone crochet needle, five or six white pearl buttons, and a yard of ribbon to tie round the waist. A good warm petticoat for a poor child can be worked from the same instructions by using ordinary Scotch Yarn of strong quality. Begin with 80 chain for the length of the dress from the neck to the bottom of the skirt at the back. **1st row**—Do 1 treble in the fourth chain from the needle, 1 treble in the next chain, and so on, 1 treble in every stitch of chain, making 77 treble in all in the row. **2nd row**—3 chain to turn, 1 treble on the first treble stitch of preceding row, and 1 treble on each treble successively to the end, 77 treble in all, inserting the hook to take up the two top threads of the stitches. **3rd row**—3 chain to turn, 1 treble on the first treble stitch of last row, and 33 more treble worked consecutively ; then turn with 2 chain, miss the first treble stitch, and work again 33 consecutive treble ; and you are at the bottom edge of the skirt ; the short double row just worked, which is practically *two* rows, is repeated at regular intervals on purpose to increase the fulness of the skirt. **5th row**—3 chain to turn, 1 treble on the first treble stitch of last row, and continue in treble to the end, doing 1 treble on the chain where last row was turned, and making in all 77 treble in the row. **6th row**—3 chain to turn, and work 77 treble. Repeat from the third row twice. **15th row**—The same as the third row. **17th row**—Same as the fifth row, and do 14 chain at the end to heighten for the shoulder. **18th row**—Work 1 treble in the third chain from the needle, and treble all along 89 stitches to the bottom of the skirt. **19th row**—Same as the third row. **21st row**—3 chain to turn, and 89 treble in the row to the top of the shoulder. **22nd row**—3 chain to turn, and 89 treble to reach to the bottom of the skirt. **23rd row**—Same as the third row. **25th row**—3 chain to turn, and work 66

Tricot Design as used for the Coronet of Bulgarian Head-Dress.

treble, and leave the other stitches unworked to afford space for the armhole. **26th row**—3 chain to turn, and work 66 treble stitches. Repeat the last four rows. **31st row**—Same as the third row. **33rd row**—3 chain to turn, work 66 treble, and do 25 chain at the end to heighten for the shoulder. **34th row**—Work 1 treble in the third chain from the needle, and treble consecutively all along, 89 stitches to the bottom of the skirt. **35th row**—Same as the third row. **37th row**—3 chain to turn, and work 89 treble in the row to the top of the shoulder. **38th row**—3 chain to turn, and work 89 treble to reach to the bottom of the skirt. **39th row**—Here you begin the front of the dress by working a short double row the same as the third row. **41st row**—3 chain to turn, and work in all 77 treble in the row. **42nd row**—3 chain to turn, and work 77 treble to the bottom of the skirt. Repeat these four rows seven times, which will count 16 rows along the neck of the dress and 28 rows upon the skirt. **71st row**—Same as the third row. **73rd row**—Same as the seventeenth row. **74th row**—Same as the eighteenth row. And continue hence straight on, row by row, forming the other shoulder, till you come to a repetition of the forty-second row. Thence repeat the last four rows for the other half of the back of the dress till 10 rows are done along the neck, work the last row to the waist only, and fasten off. Sew up the back of the skirt, and sew the first two rows of the body to lap as it were over the last two rows. Join the shoulder pieces together. Work a **Crochet Edge** along the bottom of the skirt. **1st round**—1 double crochet under a loop of three chain, 4 chain, another double crochet in the same place, * 1 double crochet under the next loop of three chain, 4 chain, another double crochet in the same place, and repeat from * to the end of the round. **2nd round**—1 double crochet under a loop of four chain, 4 chain, another double crochet in the same place, and repeat. Work 2 more rounds the same. **5th round**—Work 6 double crochet under each loop of four chain of last round, and fasten off at the end of the round. Work the same crochet edge round the armholes, also round the neck, and down the right-hand side of the back as far as the waist, where put a stitch or two to cause the edge to fold over. Sew pearl buttons on the left-hand side of the back, and they will button into the first row of holes in the edging. Run a ribbon along the top of the skirt to tie round the waist. A broad handsome ribbon sash can be becomingly worn upon this little dress.

OPERA HOOD AND COLLARETTE.

WORKED WITH GIANT WOOL.

GIANT WOOL, or, as it is sometimes called, Leviathan Wool, is a soft wool of many plies, about the thickness of box-cord. Of course being so thick only a short length goes to an ounce, but it works up well in bulk, and the opera hood and collarette combined, as shown in our illustration, is a charming novelty, and is sure to be much liked by ladies who are partial to a pretty

Border for a Quilt.

treble, 3 treble on the centre stitch of three treble, 1 treble on treble, miss one stitch, 3 treble on the next, 1 treble on the next, 3 treble on the centre stitch of seven treble, 1 treble on the next, 3 treble on the next, miss one stitch, 1 treble on treble, 3 treble on the centre stitch of three treble, 1 treble on treble, 3 treble on the centre stitch of three treble, 1 treble on treble stitch at the end. **4th row**—2 chain to turn, 1 treble on the first treble stitch, * 3 treble on the centre stitch of three treble, 1 treble on treble stitch, and repeat from * six times. **5th row**—3 chain to turn, 3 treble on the centre stitch of three treble of last row, 1 treble on treble, 3 treble on the centre stitch of three treble, 1 treble on treble, 1 treble on the centre stitch of three treble, 1 treble on treble, 3 treble on centre stitch of three treble, 1 treble on treble, 1 treble on the centre stitch of three treble, 1 treble on treble, 3 treble on the centre stitch of three treble, 1 treble on treble, 3 treble on centre stitch of three treble, one treble on treble stitch at the end. **6th row**—3 chain to turn, 3 treble on the centre stitch of three treble of last row, 1 treble on treble, 3 treble on the centre stitch of three treble. 1 treble on treble, miss one stitch, 1 treble on the next, miss one stitch, 1 treble on the centre stitch of three treble, miss one stitch, 1 treble on t! e next, miss

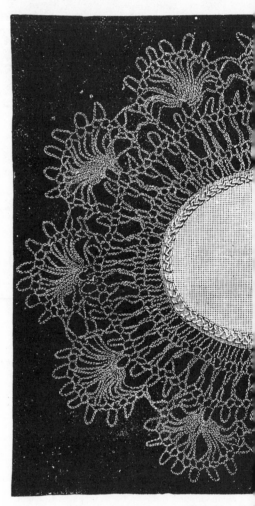

D'Oyley, Ed

head covering. Required, 6 ozs. of white and 2 ozs of a pale shade of greeny-blue giant wool, and a large wooden crochet needle of size to measure about 1½ inches round. Commence with white wool for the top of the head, make 2 chain, and work 6 double crochet stitches in the second chain from the needle. **2nd round**—Proceed in a circle, and do 2 double crochet on each of the six double crochet stitches taking up the one top thread. **3rd round**—Again do 2 double crochet on each stitch. **4th round**—Do 2 double crochet on the first stitch, 1 double crochet on the next, and repeat, and there will be 36 double crochet in this round. **5th round**—Do 2 double crochet on the first stitch, * 1 double crochet on each of the two next stitches, 2 double crochet on the next, repeat from * four times, and now turn, and work in rows. **1st row**—2 chain to turn, 1 treble on the first double crochet stitch taking up the two top threads, * miss one stitch, 3 treble on the next, miss one stitch, 1 treble on the next, and repeat from * four times ; the part now about to be done is for the back of the head. **2nd row**—2 chain to turn, 1 treble on the first treble stitch, 3 treble on the centre stitch of three treble of last row, 1 treble on one treble stitch, 3 treble on the centre stitch of three treble, 1 treble on one treble stitch, 7 treble on the centre stitch of three treble, 1 treble on one treble stitch, 3 treble on the centre stitch of three treble, 1 treble on one treble stitch, 3 treble on the centre stitch of three treble, 1 treble on treble stitch at the end. **3rd row**—2 chain to turn, 1 treble on the first treble stitch, 3 treble on the centre stitch of three treble, 1 treble on

one stitch, 1 treble on the next, 3 treble on the centre stitch of three treble, 1 treble on treble, 3 treble on the centre stitch of three treble, 1 treble on the chain that turned, and break off the wool. **7th row**—The beginning of the collarette,—Begin with 11 chain, do 1 treble on the treble stitch where you broke off, 3 treble on the centre stitch of three treble, 1 treble on treble, 3 treble on the centre stitch of three treble, 1 treble on treble, 3 treble on the next stitch, 1 treble on the next, 3 treble on the next, 1 treble on the next, 3 treble on the centre stitch of three treble, 1 treble on treble, 3 treble on the centre stitch of three treble, 1 treble on the chain at the end, 11 chain, and break off the wool. **8th row**—Begin with 16 chain, and turning the work so as to crochet in the chain where you broke off last row, do 1 single crochet in the first stitch of chain, 1 double crochet in each of the 2 next, 1 treble in the next, miss one, 3 treble in the next, miss one, 1 treble in the next, miss one, 3 treble in the next, miss one, then 1 treble on treble stitch of last row, 3 treble on the centre stitch of three treble, 1 treble on treble, 3 treble on the centre stitch of three treble, and now without missing any do 1 treble on the next stitch and 3 treble on the next stitch alternately six times, then miss one, 1 treble on treble, 3 treble on the centre stitch of three treble, 1 treble on the last treble stitch, miss one chain, 3 treble in the next. miss one, 1 treble in the next, miss one, 3 treble in the next miss one, 1 treble in the next, 1 double crochet in each of the 2 next, 1 single crochet in the last stitch of chain, do

16 chain, and break off. **9th row**—Recommencing now on the right-hand side, the same side where you began last row, work into the chain, 1 single crochet in the first stitch, 1 double crochet in each of the 2 next, 1 treble in the next, miss one, 3 treble in the next, miss one, 1 treble in the next, * miss one, 3 treble in the next, miss one, 1 treble in the next, and repeat from * till within 3 stitches of the end of the row, when do 1 double crochet in each of the 2 next, and 1 single crochet in the last stitch of chain, and break off; in the centre of this row the 3 treble stitches come always on the centre stitch of three treble of last row. **10th row**—Work into the stitches of last row in the manner there instructed. **11th row**—Work the same again. **12th row** —With blue wool. Holding the work the right side towards you, and working entirely round the hood and collarette, beginning at the corner of the sixth row to go first round the head, do 1 single crochet in a stitch of the hood, * 7 chain, 1 single crochet in the next stitch of the hood, and repeat from * to the opposite corner of the sixth row; then round the collarette do 7 chain, 1 single crochet in each of the two next stitches, till you meet the blue where you commenced, and join neatly. Then work with blue wool the trimming on the top of the head, holding the front of the hood with the blue edge

Venetian Lace.

towards you—Begin on the sixth round, and go just behind the first row of blue edging with 1 single crochet, 9 chain, alternately, always missing about half an inch of crochet between the single stitches, till you get to the fourth double crochet stitch from the middle of the top of the head, when break off, and work similar loops along the opposite side to correspond. The centre of the top of the head is worked with blue wool in the style of a rosette composed of loops of 4 chain, 1 single crochet in a double crochet of the top of the hood, till the front half of the circle of double crochet is covered with loops of blue. Make with blue wool a length of 25 chain, tie it in the back of the hood to embrace the five treble stitches in the middle of the sixth row; make a tassel at each end and tie the chain in a bow.

CHILD'S PELISSE.

THIS pelisse will fit a child of four or five years; it is Princesse shape, and measures 23 inches from the neck to the bottom of the flounce at the back. Materials required are, ¾ lb of pink Heather wool, a bone crochet needle No. 12, and 5 yards of ⅝ of an inch wide ribbon of colour to match the wool. The stitch used for the frock throughout is one row of plain double crochet, and turn, and work back the next row in point-neige or shell-stitch, this stitch is clearly described and illustrated on page 3 of this present issue. For the **Left Front**—Make 51 chain, along which work 50 stitches of double crochet, turn

with 3 chain, and work back 25 point-neige stitches. Begin each point-neige row with 3 chain, and the double crochet rows with 1 chain, to make a smooth edge. Decrease a point-neige stitch at the beginning of the sixth row, and at the beginning of every fourth row afterwards, till 30 rows are done, counting both double crochet and point-neige rows from the commencement; all these decreasings come at the same end (the right). In the 32nd row, and 2 following rows, decrease 3 stitches at the same end in each row, which shapes for the armhole. Do 6 rows without decreasing. Then for the shoulder, increase for 4 consecutive rows, and in the last of these leave 5 stitches unworked at the other end for the neck. Do 5 rows, decreasing 3 stitches at each end, and fasten off. **The Right Front** is to be worked in the same manner, but begin with 47 stitches, and make the decreasings come at the other end of the work. For the **Back** of the **Frock**—Make 63 chain, and work in the same stitch as the fronts. All decreasings and increasings are now to be done on *both* sides of the work, that is, at the end of the rows as well as at the beginning. Decrease every fourth row till the 16th row; then increase every fourth row till the 24th row; this brings you to the armhole, as the back of the frock is not required to be so long as the fronts in consequence of the flounce which is put on afterwards. Now decrease at the beginning and at the end of each row for 4 rows. Do 3 rows without decreasing. Decrease 2 stitches at each end for 7 rows, and fasten off. For the **Flounce**—Begin with 21 chain, and work forwards and backwards for 70 rows. This makes a long strip which is to be sewn in pleats to the foundation chain of the back piece, and then the whole back is to be joined to the two fronts as far as the armholes, and the shoulders also joined. For the **Sleeves**—Commence with 41 chain, and increase at the beginning and end of every fourth row till there are 56 double crochet worked in the 17th row of the sleeve; now slip along 4 stitches at the beginning, and leave 4 stitches unworked at the end of each row for 5 rows to make the slope for the shoulder, fasten off, and sew up as far as the 17th row. Make the other sleeve similarly. For the **Border** round the **Skirt**—Begin with a single

Pretty Dress for a Child.

crochet stitch into the commencing chain at the corner of the right front, do 10 chain, and now holding the *wrong* side of the frock towards you do 1 treble in the third chain from the needle, 1 chain, miss one stitch, 1 treble in the next, and continue the same all along the bottom of the frock till you get to the corner of the left front; this open row of treble and chain is to run a ribbon in, and the 10 chain with which you began makes a foundation to jut out to work the front trimming upon. You now do 6 rows of coiled crochet, thus—forwards and backwards, beginning with the right side of the frock towards you, and turning the work at the completion of every row—1 double crochet in the first stitch, insert the hook in the next stitch and draw the wool through and do 5 chain, at the last chain pulling the wool through both loops on the needle. repeat. In succeeding rows do double crochet on the double crochet and the 5 chain into the previous loops of five chain. When the 6 rows are worked round the bottom of the skirt do the same coiled crochet in little rows on the 10 extra chain added to the right front till sufficient length is worked to reach the neck, and sew it up the front. Work the same border, commencing with the 1 chain 1 treble row, round the neck and sleeves. Sew the sleeves in. Run ribbon in through the open treble row round the neck and sleeves, and round the bottom of the skirt, with ends sufficient to tie in bows. Place a ribbon over the pleating of the flounce at the back, with a bow in the centre. Add ribbon strings in front to tie in bows on the chest over the coiled trimming.

TAM O'SHANTER.

THE cap shown in our engraving is worked in a pretty combination of double crochet and point neige, or shell stitch, and can be suitably worn by a child of from five to ten years of age. Procure 2½ ozs. of pale blue single Berlin wool, and work with a No. 8 bone crochet needle. Commence for the centre of the cap with 3 chain stitches, and join round. **1st round**—2 chain to stand up to begin upon, and work 6 shell stitches in the round, and join evenly; shell stitch is fully explained in the instructions for working a Child's **Skirt**, see page 3 of the present issue. **2nd round**—Begin with 2 chain, and **work** 10 shell stitches over the six shell stitches of last round, and join evenly

Opera Hood and Collarette. Worked with Giant Wool.

to the commencement. **3rd round**—1 chain to begin, and work 27 double crochet stitches in the round, and again join evenly. **4th round**—1 chain to begin, turn the work, and do 30 double crochet stitches in the round, inserting the hook to take up the back thread of the stitches of the previous round. **5th round**—2 chain, turn the work, and do 25 shell stitches in the round. **6th round**—2 chain, and work 33 shell stitches in the round. **7th round**—1 chain to begin, and do 66 double crochet. **8th round**—1 chain, turn the work, and do plain double crochet, 66 stitches, into the back thread of the stitches of last round. **9th round**—2 chain, turn the work, and do 58 shell stitches in the round. **10th round**—2 chain, and work 64 shell stitches in the round. **11th round**—1 chain to begin, and do 128 double crochet. **12th round**—1 chain, turn the work, and do again 128 double crochet, working into the back thread of the stitches of last round. **13th round**—2 chain, turn the work, and do 80 shell stitches in the round. **14th round**—2 chain, and work 86 shell stitches in the round. **15th round**—1 chain, and do 145 double crochet. **16th round**—1 chain, turn the work, and do again 145 double crochet. **17th round**—Begin to draw in for the under part of the brim, and do 80 shell stitches in the round. **18th round**—74 shell stitches. **19th round**—110 double crochet. **20th round**—Turn, and decrease again, getting 94 double crochet into the back threads of the stitches of last round. **21st round**—Turn, and work 56 shell stitches. **22nd round**—50 shell stitches. **23rd round**—70 double crochet. **24th round**—70 double crochet. Work for the **Band** 6 or 8 rounds of single crochet, inserting the hook to take up the one top thread of the stitches of the preceding round. The tuft in the centre of the crown is made of a number of strands of wool

about 3 inches in length, tied tightly together in the centre; the thread of wool that ties them will do to secure the tuft to the cap, and the ends are then pulled into the shape of a pompon and cut smooth and even.

WIDE BORDER IN OPEN RAISED CROCHET.

THIS border is useful for a quilt or for any purpose for which a wide open raised border is desired. It is worked the short way. Begin with 43 chain. **1st row**—Work 1 treble in the third chain from the needle, 2 chain, miss two stitches, 1 treble in the next, 2 chain, miss two, 1 treble in the next, 2 chain, miss two, 1 treble in the next, 2 chain, miss two, 1 treble in the next, 2 chain, miss two, work 4 treble consecutive, 3 chain, miss three, 4 treble consecutive, 3 chain, miss three, 4 treble consecutive, 3 chain, miss three, 4 treble consecutive. **2nd row**—7 chain to turn, work 1 treble in the fourth chain from the needle and 8 more treble consecutive, on the next stitch which is the middle stitch of three chain of last row work a group of 5 treble stitches, withdraw the hook from the stitch on the needle, insert it in the top of the first of the five treble and draw the stitch through, do 1 chain to tighten the group, this is termed a "tuft," and is always to be worked thus, work 6 consecutive treble, then a tuft, 6 more treble, another tuft, 3 treble consecutive, 1 chain, 1 treble on last stitch of four of last row, 2 chain and 1 treble on treble five times, 1 treble on the chain that turned. **3rd row**—3 chain to turn, 1 treble on the treble stitch of last row, 2 chain and 1 treble on treble five times, 1 chain, 1 treble on first stitch of four of last row, 1 chain, miss one, 4 treble consecutive, 3 chain, miss three, 4 treble consecutive, 3 chain, miss three, 4 treble consecutive, 3 chain, miss three, 4 treble consecutive. **4th row**—7 chain to turn, work 1 treble in the fourth chain from the needle and 8 more treble consecutive, a tuft on the centre chain stitch, 6 consecutive treble, a tuft, 6 consecutive treble, a tuft, 3 consecutive treble, 1 chain, 1 treble on the last stitch of four of last row, 1 chain and 1 treble on treble three times, 2 chain and 1 treble on treble five times, 1 treble on the chain that turned. **5th row**—3 chain to turn, 1 treble on treble stitch of last row, 2 chain and 1 treble on treble five times, 1 chain and 1 treble on treble three times, 1 chain, miss one, 4 treble consecutive, 3 chain, miss three, 4 treble consecutive, 3 chain, miss three, 4 treble consecutive, 3 chain, miss three, 4 treble consecutive. **6th row**—7 chain to turn, work 1 treble in the fourth chain from the needle and 8 more consecutive treble, a tuft on the centre chain stitch, 6 consecutive treble, a tuft, 6 consecutive treble, a tuft, 3 consecutive treble, 1 chain, 1 treble on the last stitch of four of last row, 1 chain and 1 treble on treble four times, 2 chain and 1 treble on treble five times, 1 treble on the chain that turned. **7th row**—

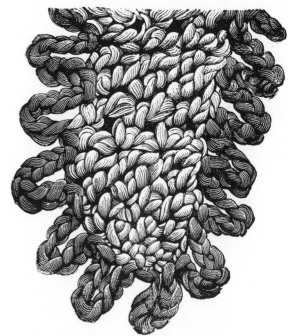

Working Design for Opera Hood and Collarette in Giant Wool.

3 chain to turn, 1 treble on treble stitch of last row, 2 chain and 1 treble on treble five times, 1 chain and 1 treble on treble five times, 1 chain, miss one, 4 treble consecutive, 3 chain, miss three, 4 treble consecutive, 3 chain, miss three, 4 treble consecutive, 3 chain, miss three, 4 treble consecutive. **8th row**—3 chain to turn, 1 treble on the first treble stitch of last row and 8 more treble consecutive, a tuft on the next treble stitch, 6 consecutive treble, a tuft on the next treble stitch, 3 consecutive treble, 1 chain and 1 treble on treble five times, 2 chain and 1 treble on treble five times, 1 treble on the chain that turned. **9th row**—3 chain to turn, 1 treble on treble stitch of last row, 2 chain and 1 treble on treble five times, 1 chain and 1 treble on treble three times, 1 chain, miss one, 4 treble consecutive, 3 chain, miss three, 4 treble consecutive, 3 chain,

miss three, 4 treble consecutive, 3 chain, miss three, 4 treble consecutive. **10th row**—3 chain to turn. 1 treble on the first treble stitch of last row and 8 more treble consecutive, a tuft on the next treble stitch, 6 consecutive treble, a tuft on the next treble-stitch, 6 consecutive treble, a tuft on the next treble stitch, 3 consecutive treble, 1 chain and 1 treble on treble 3 times, 2 chain and 1 treble on treble five times, 1 treble on the chain that turned. **11th row**—3 chain to turn, 1 treble on treble stitch of last row, 2 chain and 1 treble on treble five times, 1 chain, 1 treble on treble, 1 chain, miss one, 4 treble consecutive, 3 chain, miss three, 4 treble consecutive, 3 chain, miss three, 4 treble consecutive, 3 chain, miss three, 4 treble consecutive. **12th row**—3 chain to turn. 1 treble on the first treble stitch of last row and 8 more treble consecutive, a tuft on the next treble stitch, 6 consecutive treble, a tuft on the next treble stitch, 6 consecutive treble, a tuft on the next treble stitch, 3 consecutive treble, 1 chain, 1 treble on treble, 2 chain and 1 treble on treble five times,

Child's Pelisse.

1 treble on the chain that turned. Begin the next row with 3 chain to turn and work according to the first row of the pattern, and continue for the length required.

STRIPE FOR AN ANTIMACASSAR OR COUVRE-PIED PINE PATTERN.

THIS pattern may be worked in stripes with double Berlin wool of two good contrasting colours doing the whole of one stripe with one colour, or if preferred the colours may be arranged in rows, working three rows with each colour successively. Use a No. 6 tricot needle. Begin with a chain of 20 stitches. **1st row**—Wool over the needle and insert the hook in the third chain from the needle and draw the wool through, wool over the needle and draw through two threads on the needle, wool over the needle and insert the hook again in the same chain stitch and draw the wool through, wool over the needle and draw through two threads on the needle, wool over the needle and again insert the hook in the same chain stitch and draw the wool through, wool over the needle and draw through two threads on the needle, wool over the needle and draw through three threads on the needle, this group of stitches is termed "a pine," and every pine is worked in the same manner, raise a plain tricot stitch in the next stitch of the foundation, a pine in the next, a tricot stitch in the next, and so on to the end of the row, keeping all the stitches (19) on the needle; the plain tricot stitches should be raised very loosely; to work back, draw the wool through one stitch first, then wool over the needle and draw through two at a time till all the stitches are off. **2nd row**—Raise a plain tricot stitch over the pine of last row inserting the hook through the perpendicular thread only, * then a pine over the tricot stitch of last row taking up the stitch with a top thread of the chain that lies under it, and a tricot stitch over a pine, and repeat from *, and at the end there will be another plain tricot stitch to

pick up; work back as the first row. **3rd row**—Work a pine over the tricot stitch of last row, and a plain tricot stitch over a pine, and repeat, ending with a stitch of plain tricot. There will be 9 pines in the first row, 8 pines in the second, 9 pines again in the third, and so on alternately to keep the pattern straight. Repeat the second and third rows for the length required When a sufficient number of stripes are worked for the width of the article join them together with a row of plain double crochet, and finish off the top and the bottom with a fringe of four strands of wool knotted into each pine.

RAISED SQUARE PATTERN FOR A QUILT.

THIS very handsome square should be worked with Strutt's best knitting cotton, No. 6, and a steel crochet needle, No. 15. Begin in the centre by winding the cotton twice round the first finger of the left hand, work 8 double crochet in the loop, draw the loop in closely, then join the last stitch of the double crochet to the first stitch, and this forms the first round of the quilt square. Every successive round is to be joined in the same manner quite evenly to its own commencement, and unless otherways directed, always *turn* the work with 1 chain to re-commence a fresh round, and insert the hook to take up the one back thread of the stitches of the previous round, that the work may sit in ridges. **2nd round**—1 double crochet on the first stitch, 3 double crochet on the next stitch, and repeat the same three times, making 16 double crochet in the round. **3rd round**—1 double crochet on each of three double crochet along the side of the square, 3 double crochet on the centre stitch of three double crochet for the corner, making 24 double crochet in the round, and fasten off. **4th round**—Holding the wrong side of last round towards you, do 1 double crochet on the third stitch of the three double crochet at the corner, 1 double crochet on the next stitch, now a "tuft," that is 5 treble stitches worked into a thread of the second previous round, miss the next stitch of last round, 1 double crochet on the next stitch, 1 double crochet on the next, 3 double crochet on the centre stitch of three double crochet at the corner, and repeat the same three times. **5th round**—Plain double crochet, except behind the tufts, where a treble stitch is to be worked into the thread of the stitch that was missed in last round, and 3 double crochet are as usual to be worked on the centre stitch at each corner **6th round**—Work 1 double crochet on the third stitch of the three double crochet at the corner, 1 double crochet on the next, a tuft, miss one stitch of last round, 3 double crochet consecutive, a tuft, miss one stitch, 1 double crochet on the next, 3 double crochet on the centre stitch at the corner. **7th round**—Same as the fifth round. **8th round**—Work 1 double crochet on the third stitch of the three double crochet at the corner, 1 double crochet on the next, a tuft, miss one stitch of last round, 7 double crochet consecutive, a tuft, miss one stitch, 1 double crochet on the next, 1 double crochet on the next, 3 double crochet on the centre stitch at the corner. **9th round**—Same as the fifth. **10th round**—Work 1 double crochet on the third stitch of the three double crochet at the corner, 1 double crochet on the next, a tuft, miss one stitch of last round, 11 double crochet consecutive, a tuft, miss 1 stitch, 1 double crochet on

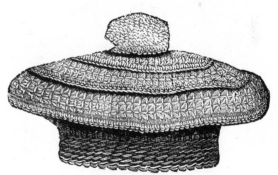

Tam O'Shanter.

the next, 1 double crochet on the next, 3 double crochet on the centre stitch at the corner. **11th round**—Same as the fifth. **12th round**—Work 1 double crochet on the third stitch of the three double crochet at the corner, 1 double crochet on the next, a tuft, miss one stitch of last round, 15 double crochet consecutive, a tuft, miss one stitch, 1 double crochet on the next, 1 double crochet on the next, 3 double crochet on the centre stitch at the corner. **13th round**—Same as the fifth. **14th round**—Work plain double crochet, with 3 double crochet on the centre stitch at each corner. **15th round**—The same; in this round there should be 27 double crochet along each side of the square and 3 double crochet at each corner; fasten off at the end of the round. **16th round**—Hold the right side of the work towards you, do 1 treble on the first of the three double crochet stitches at the corner, inserting the hook to take up the two front threads of the stitches of last round, 1 chain, 1 treble on the corner stitch, 1 chain, another treble on the corner stitch, 1 chain, another treble in the same place, 1 chain, 1 treble on the third of the three double crochet stitches; 1 chain, miss one, 1 treble on the next, and continue thus in 1 chain, miss one, 1 treble on the next, till you get in all, 5 treble worked at the corner, and 13 treble along the side of the square, with 1 chain between each; do 1 chain, and repeat the same to the end of the round, and join evenly. **17th round**—Turn, and work plain double crochet, with 3 double crochet on the centre stitch at each corner.

18th round—The same. **19th round**—Hold the right side of the work towards you, and insert the hook to take up the one *front* thread of the stitches of last round, 5 double crochet on one double crochet stitch of last round, miss one, 1 double crochet on the next, miss one, and repeat the same to the end of the round, and fasten off; this round sits in little scollops, and there must be a scollop at each corner and nine scollops along each side, making 40 scollops in the round. **20th round**—Hold the work the right side towards you and do a round of plain treble stitches, with 5 treble on the centre stitch at each corner, inserting the hook to take up the one *top* thread of the stitches of the eighteenth round, and keeping the little scollops down under the left-hand thumb. **21st round**—With the right side of the work still in front, do 1 double crochet into the top thread of a stitch of last row, do 1 double crochet into the

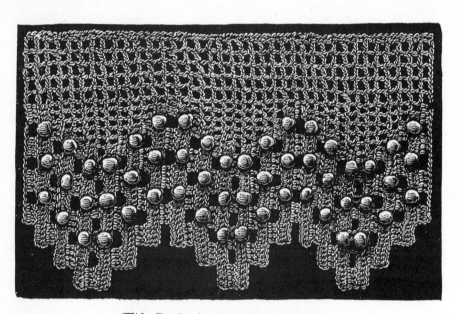

Wide Border in Open Raised Crochet.

front thread of a stitch of last row, and repeat this alternately all round, with 3 double crochet stitches at each corner. **22nd round**—Work in the same manner, taking the top thread now where in last round the front thread was taken. **23rd round**—Turn, and work plain double crochet into the back threads of the stitches of last round, and as before do 3 double crochet on the centre stitch at each corner. **24th round**—The same as last round. **25th round**—Work in little scollops, the same as the nineteenth round, a scollop at each corner and 12 scollops along each side, making 52 scollops in the round. **26th round**—The same as the twentieth round. **27th round**—Turn, and work plain double crochet into the back threads of the stitches of last round, and 3 double crochet on the centre stitch at each corner, and fasten off at the end of the round. **28th round**—Hold the right side of the work towards you and inserting the hook to take up the back thread of the stitches of last round, do 1 treble, 1 chain, miss one, and repeat the same all round, making a little increase to ease the corners. **29th round**—With the right side of the work still in front, do plain double crochet into the top thread of the stitches of last round, and 3 double crochet on the centre stitch at each corner. This finishes the square. When a number of squares are worked they may be joined together by a row of double crochet, or simply sewn together.

THE SYLVESTER CAPE.

For this very pretty and stylish cape procure 9 ozs of grey single Berlin wool, a No. 8 and No. 10 bone crochet needle, and 1½ yards of inch-wide grey ribbon for the neck. The cape is worked in four pieces, *i.e*, three frills as shown in the engraving, and an open-work foundation on which the frills are placed. Work first of all the foundation, using No 8 needle, and commencing for the neck with 71 chain. The **1st row** consists of double long treble stitches, worked thus—pass the wool three times round the needle, insert the hook in the sixth chain from the needle and draw the wool through, then four successive times pass the wool over the needle and draw through 2 stitches on the needle ; wool three times round the needle, insert the hook in the next stitch of the commencing chain and draw the wool through, and four successive times pass the wool over the needle and draw through 2 stitches on the needle ; every stitch is worked in the same manner, rather loosely, and there should be 66 stitches in the row, these form a wide insertion for the neckband in which afterwards to run a piece of ribbon. **2nd row**—3 chain to turn, 1 treble on the first stitch of previous row * 2 chain, miss one, 1 treble on the next, and repeat from * to the end, making in all 33 holes of two-chain stitches. **3rd row**—3 chain to turn, 1 treble on the first treble stitch of preceding row, 2 chain and 1 treble in the first space, * 2 chain and 1 treble in each of the four following spaces, 2 chain and 1 treble in the same place to increase, and

repeat from * to the end, making 42 holes of two-chain stitches. **4th row**—3 chain to turn, 1 treble on the first treble stitch of previous row, 2 chain and 1 treble in the first space, 2 chain and 1 treble in three successive spaces, 2 chain and 1 treble in the same place as last treble, * 2 chain and 1 treble in five successive spaces, 2 chain and 1 treble in the same space as the last treble, repeat from * six times, 2 chain and 1 double crochet in three successive spaces, 2 chain and 1 treble in the same space as the last treble, 2 chain and 1 treble on the chain that turned ; making 52 spaces in the row. **5th row**—3 chain to turn, 1 treble on the treble stitch, 2 chain and 1 treble in the first space, 2 chain and 1 treble in each successive space, and 1 treble on the chain that turned. **6th row**—3 chain to turn, * 2 chain and 1 treble in three successive holes, 2 chain and 1 treble in the same hole as the last treble, and repeat from *, and at the end do 2 chain and 1 treble twice, 2 chain and 1 treble in the chain that turned ; making 71 spaces in the row. **7th row**—3 chain to turn, 1 treble in the first space, 2 chain and 1 treble all along to the end of the row. **8th row**—3 chain to turn, 1 treble in the first space, do 2 chain and 1 treble sixteen times, 2 chain and 1 treble in the same space as the last treble, increase in the same way in the two next spaces, do 2 chain and 1 treble thirty-four times, 2 chain and 1 treble in the same space as the last treble, increase in each of the two next spaces, 2 chain and 1 treble sixteen times to the end. Work 11 more rows of open spaces without any increase, and fasten off, as now the foundation is long enough. For the **Frills**—Take the No. 10 crochet needle, and work firmer than you worked for the foundation. Begin for the **Top Frill** with 106 chain. **1st row**—1 treble in the third chain from the needle, * 1 chain, miss one stitch, 2 treble in the next, 2 chain, 2 treble in the next, 1 chain, miss one, 1 treble in the next, and repeat from * to the end, finish with 1 extra treble, and fasten off. **2nd row**—Commence this and every row on the right-hand side ; 2 treble stitches, 1 chain, 2 treble under the loop of two chain of last row, 2 chain, 2 more treble in the same place, 1 chain, 1 treble on the one treble stitch, and repeat from *, do 1 more treble at the end, and fasten off. Work 5 more rows the same as the last row. Also do 1 more row the same, but work also along the little side at the beginning of the rows and along the little side at the end. **9th row**—

Stripe for an Antimacassar or Couvrepied Pine Pattern.

Begin along the little side, * work 1 treble on the one treble stitch, 1 chain, 8 treble under the loop of two chain, 1 chain, and repeat from * to the end of the other little side. **10th row**—Single crochet along just below the chain edge of the stitches of last row. This finishes the first frill. For the second **Frill**—Begin with 172 chain—**1st row**—1 treble in the third chain from the needle, * 1 chain, miss two stitches, 2 treble in the next, 2 chain, 2 treble in the next, 1 chain, miss two, 1 treble in the next, and repeat from * to the end, finish with 1 extra treble, and fasten off. The remaining rows of the frill are worked in the same way as the corresponding rows in the first frill : there are 20 scollops along the first frill, 24 scollops along the second frill, and 28 scollops along the third frill. For the **Third Frill**—Commence with 256 chain. **1st row**—1 treble in the third chain from the needle, * 1 chain, miss three stitches, 2 treble in the next, 2 chain, 2 treble in the next, 1 chain, miss three, 1 treble in the next, and repeat from * to the end, finish with 1 extra treble, and fasten off. Work the remaining 9 rows in the same way as the corresponding rows of the first frill are worked, being careful to round the corners nicely in the 3 last rows. Sew the last frill upon the stitches of the fifteenth row of the foundation; sew the second frill upon the stitches of the eighth row; and sew the first frill just immediately below the neckband and above the first row of the open crochet; sew the front edge of the frills down in place as shown in the illustration. For the **Ruching** round the **Neck—1st row**—Work 4 treble stitches into every stitch of the foundation chain. **2nd row**—3 chain to turn, and work 1 treble on every stitch of last row. Fasten off all ends of wool securely. Run the ribbon through the open insertion of double long treble stitches weaving it over three and under three to the end.

MANTEL VALANCE, OR BRACKET DRAPE.

PROCURE a number of brass curtain rings about the size of a halfpenny, which can be procured at an ironmonger's for twopence the dozen, 1 oz. or 2 ozs. of shaded crimson Berlin wool, and a No. 10 bone crochet needle. Take the first ring, and to cover the brass outline, work one double crochet over the ring, * 3 chain, 2 double crochet, and repeat from * till you have 10 loops of three chain, when end with one double crochet as you began, join to the first stitch and fasten off; and draw in the ends of wool through two or three stitches on the wrong side of the work. Take the second ring, and work the same as

crochet just worked, 4 chain, 1 single crochet in the same place, 3 chain, another single crochet in the same place, 4 chain, 1 treble also on the double crochet stitch, 1 double crochet in the next loop of the same ring; 4 chain, 1 double crochet in the second loop of the ring at the point of the scollop, * 4 chain, 1 treble on the double crochet just done, 1 double crochet in the next loop of the same ring, repeat from * twice, then do 3 chain, 1 single crochet on the double crochet just worked, 4 chain, 1 single crochet in the same place, 3 chain, another single crochet in the same place, 4 chain, 1 treble on the same double crochet, 1 double crochet in the next loop of the ring, * 4 chain, 1 treble on the double crochet just done, 1 double crochet in the next loop of the same ring, repeat from * once; 4 chain, 1 double crochet in the first loop of the next ring, and proceed up this side of the scollop to correspond with the side already done; and edge along the remaining scollops in the same way. Cut a number of strands of wool in seven-inch lengths, and draw 18 or 20 strands through the centre loop at the bottom of each ring, fold the strands double, and bind the top in resemblance of a handsome tassel.

TOBOGGAN CAP.

PROCURE 3½ ozs. of brown Berlin fingering, and a No. 9 or No. 10 bone crochet needle. Commence with 80 chain for the bottom of the cap; join

Raised Square Pattern for a Quilt.

the first till you have done 8 loops and 2 double crochet stitches, then 1 chain join to a loop of the first ring, 1 chain, do 2 double crochet in the second ring, 1 chain, join to the next loop of the first ring, 1 chain, 1 double crochet in the second ring, and join and fasten off. Work in the same manner as many rings as you require for the length of the border, joining five rings in a straight line for one scollop, nine rings for two scollops, thirteen rings for three scollops, and so on. Then proceed with a second row of rings in the same manner, but joining them to the first row, as shown in the engraving, where also you will see how to place the additional seven rings to shape the scollops. For the **Edging** of the **Scollops**—Begin with a double crochet stitch in the fourth loop of the first ring of the second row, 4 chain, 1 treble in the double crochet just worked, 1 double crochet in the next loop, 3 chain, 1 single crochet on the double crochet just worked, 4 chain, 1 single crochet in the same place, 3 chain, another single crochet in the same place, 4 chain, 1 treble also on the double crochet stitch, 1 double crochet in the next loop of the same ring; 3 chain, 1 double crochet in the first loop of the next ring (the first ring on the first row of three), 4 chain, 1 treble on the double crochet just done, 1 double crochet in the next loop of the same ring, 4 chain, 1 treble on the double crochet just done, 1 double crochet in the next loop of the same ring, 4 chain, 1 treble on the double crochet last done, 1 double crochet in the next loop of the same ring; 3 chain, 1 double crochet in the first loop of the next ring (the first ring on the second row of three), * 4 chain, 1 treble on the double crochet just done, 1 double crochet in the next loop of the same ring, repeat from * three times, then do three chain, 1 single crochet on the double

round; and work in simple double crochet round and round continuously, inserting the hook to take up the one top thread of the stitches of the previous round, till 20 rounds are done. Continue working in the same manner, but now decrease 2 stitches in every round, at alternate intervals, till the cap is brought to a point at the top. For the **Brim**—Turn the cap upside down, and work a round of double crochet stitches into the commencing chain. **2nd round**—1 double crochet in the first stitch from the needle, insert the hook in the next stitch, draw the wool through and do 3 chain, wool over the needle and draw through the last stitch of the chain and through the stitch on the needle, and repeat the double crochet stitch and the raised chain stitch alternately to the end of the round; this fancy stitch must not take up any more room than the rounds of double crochet in which 80 stitches are worked, therefore if you find it becoming wider miss one stitch in every six or ten stitches to keep it to the required size. **3rd round**—Work a plain double crochet over a raised chain stitch of last round, and a raised chain stitch over a double crochet; and proceed working in the same manner till the turn-up brim is sufficiently deep, when join round evenly, work a round of single crochet stitches, and fasten off. Make a crochet chain with a wool pompon at each end, and loop the chain on the point of the cap as shown in the engraving. How to make a pompon or tuft is given at the end of description of Tam o'Shanter on page 10 of this issue.

LAMP MAT.

THIS lamp mat is crocheted with brown Macramé thread of a rather fine size, and a No. 10 bone crochet needle. Wind the thread once round the first finger of the left hand, and work 6 double crochet in the loop, draw in the loop closely to form a circle. Now proceed round and round in plain double crochet, inserting the hook to take up the top and back threads of the stitches. **1st round**—Work 2 double crochet on each stitch, 12 double crochet in all. **2nd round**—2 double crochet on the first stitch, 1 double crochet on the next, and repeat five times, making 18 stitches in the round. **3rd round**—2 double crochet on the first stitch, 1 double crochet on each of the two next stitches, and repeat five times, making 24 stitches in the round. **4th round**—2 double crochet on the first stitch, 1 double crochet in each of the three next stitches, * 3 double crochet on the next, 1 double crochet on each of the three next, and repeat from * four times. **5th round**—3 double crochet on the first stitch, 1 double crochet on each of the five next stitches, * 3 double crochet on the next, 1 double crochet on each of the five next, and repeat from * four times **6th round**—3 double crochet on the centre stitch of three double crochet of last round, 7 double crochet worked consecutively and repeat the same five times. **7th round**—3 double crochet on the centre stitch of three double crochet of last round, 9 double crochet worked consecutively, and repeat five times **8th round**—3 double crochet on the centre stitch of three

2 chain, and 1 treble, to be worked under every loop of chain of last round. **4th round**—1 treble in the small open space in the centre of 2 treble stitches at the point, 2 chain, another treble in the same place, 1 treble, 2 chain, 1 treble, as before, under every loop of chain along the sides of the mat. **5th round**—The same as the second round. **6th round**—Work 1 double crochet, 1 chain, 4 treble, 1 chain, 1 double crochet, *all* under a loop of 2 chain of last round, 1 double crochet in the small open space between 2 treble stitches, and repeat the same to the end of the round. This finishes the mat. A similar mat can be made by working the centre with single Berlin over a thin window blind cord, or picture cord, and doing the border with wool only.

SHORTWAY EDGING.

(Not illustrated.)

THIS simple edging, which is so useful for trimming underlinen, children's clothing, &c., may be worked with Coats' crochet cotton, No 25, and a fine steel crochet needle; or may be rendered still more lacy-looking by employing a finer cotton, thus rendering it suitable for infants tiny garments. Begin with 20 chain. **1st row**—1 double crochet in the eleventh chain from the

Sylvester Cape.

Mantel Valance,
or
Bracket Drape.

Toboggan Cap.

Section of Frill for Sylvester Cape.

Lamp Mat.

double crochet of last round, 11 double crochet worked consecutively, and repeat five times. **9th round**—3 double crochet on the centre stitch of three double crochet of last round, 13 double crochet worked consecutively, and repeat five times. Continue in this manner, always doing 3 double crochet on the centre stitch of the three double crochet of last round, and 1 double crochet on each of the intervening stitches, increasing 2 stitches on each of the six sides of the mat in every round, till in the 16th round you work 3 double crochet in every point, and 27 double crochet along each side of the mat; when join quite evenly, and fasten off. For the **Border—1st round**—Do 1 treble stitch on the centre stitch of three double crochet at the point, 2 chain, 1 more treble in the same place, miss two stitches, * 1 treble on the next, 2 chain, another treble in the same place, miss two stitches, and repeat from * till you get to the next point, which work the same as the first, and continue to the end of the round, where join to the first treble stitch with which the round began; and fasten off at the end of this and every following round, and commence the next round on one of the other points. **2nd round**—Do 1 treble under the loop of chain at the point, 2 chain, 1 more treble in the same place, 2 chain, another treble in the same place, * 1 treble under the next loop of chain of last round, 2 chain, another treble in the same place, and repeat from * till you get to the next point, which work the same as the first, and continue to the end of the round. **3rd round**—1 treble,

needle, miss two, 5 treble in the next, miss two, 1 double crochet in the next, 5 chain, miss two, 1 double crochet in the next. **2nd row**—3 chain to turn, 5 treble on the first double crochet stitch of last row, 1 double crochet in the centre stitch of five chain, 5 chain, 1 double crochet on the centre stitch of five treble, 5 chain, 1 double crochet in the third stitch of the chain that turned. **3rd row**—7 chain to turn, 1 double crochet on the centre stitch of next five chain, 5 chain, 1 double crochet in the centre stitch of next five chain, 5 treble on the double crochet stitch, 1 double crochet on the centre stitch of five treble of preceding row, 5 treble on the stitch at the corner. **4th row**—Slip-stitch over two first treble stitches of last row, 1 treble on the centre stitch of the five treble, 5 treble on the double crochet stitch, 1 double crochet on the centre stitch of the next five treble, 5 chain, 1 double crochet in the centre stitch of five chain, 5 chain, 1 double crochet in the third stitch of the chain that turned. **5th row**—7 chain to turn, 1 double crochet in the centre stitch of five chain, 5 treble on the double crochet stitch, 1 double crochet in the centre stitch of five chain, 5 chain, 1 double crochet on the centre stitch of five treble. Repeat from the second row for the length required. Now work the open edge round the bottom of the scollops: 1 treble on the end treble stitch of the fourth row, 3 chain, 1 treble at the point of the scollop, 5 chain, another treble in the same place, 3 chain, 1 treble on the end treble stitch of the second row; repeat the same on each scollop.

WELDON'S
PRACTICAL CROCHET.

(TWELFTH SERIES.)

How to Crochet Useful Garments for Ladies, Children, and the Home.

TWENTY-SEVEN ILLUSTRATIONS.

Telegraphic Address—]
"Consuelo," London.]

The Yearly Subscription to this Magazine, post free to any Part of the World, is 2s. 6d.
Subscriptions are payable in advance, and may commence from any date and for any period.

[Telephone—
8765.

The Back Numbers are always in print. Nos. 1 to 88 now ready, Price 2d. each, or post free for 15s. 8d. Over 5,000 Engravings.

LADY'S SHETLAND HOOD.

THIS hood is worked with pale blue Shetland wool in a very open lacy stitch ; a piece of thin silk of the same colour is required for lining, and four yards of inch-wide ribbon for trimming ; use a bone crochet needle, No. 7, as the work is done loosely ; the hood will take about 3 ozs. of wool.

Begin with 53 chain. **1st row**—1 double crochet in the first chain stitch by the needle, 3 chain, 1 double crochet in the third chain from the needle, 4 chain, 1 double crochet in the third chain from the needle, this makes two picots with one chain stitch between the picots, and is called a "bar," miss three of the foundation chain, 1 double crochet in the next, * work a "bar," miss three of the foundation chain, 1 double crochet in the next, and repeat from * to the end, when you will have thirteen picoteed bars in the row. **2nd row**—Make a bar, and turn the work, and do 1 double crochet under the one chain between two piques of last row, then a bar, and 1 double crochet under the chain stitch between the piques of the next bar, and so on, doing 13 bars in the row. Work 4 more rows like the second row ; then break off the wool. Gather up the foundation chain, and bring the crochet into a kind of semicircle or fan, this will be on the top of the head, and the gathering will be covered with a bow of ribbon ; the middle of row comes directly over the forehead, the opposite side, *i.e.*, the two *ends* of the rows (where turned) are now to be worked upon for the back of the hood. The two ends when brought together should measure about 14 inches across. Now work the pattern along the ends, proceeding forwards and backwards always in "bars": in the second row increase three bars in the middle of the row, increasing is done by working two bars where one bar should be. Increase one bar somewhere about the middle of every row till 12 or 14 rows are done, when the back of the neck will probably be reached. Continue now, increasing 2 bars in every row, for 6 or 8 rows. Then work a little row of 2 bars only, and turn back on the same. **Next row** —Work 3 bars, and then turn back thereon. **Next row**—Work 4 bars, and turn back on the same. And so on, increasing the number of bars in every forward row, till you get to the middle of the back of the hood, when fasten off. Recommence on the other side, and work it in the same manner. Then do 2 rows all along the bottom of the hood from end to end, and fasten off. For the **Border,** which is worked all round the hood—**1st round**—1 double crochet under the one chain stitch in the middle of a bar, * 6 chain, 1 double crochet under the stitch in the middle of the next bar, and repeat from * to the end of the round. **2nd round**—Work 1 double crochet on the double crochet of last round, and 10 treble under every loop of six chain ; and fasten off at the end of the round. Line the hood with silk throughout. Cut a fifteen-inch length of ribbon and

Lady's Shetland Hood.

run it through the fourteen loops of six chain at the top of the forehead securing it to the crochet at each end, this draws the frill prettily over the face. A thread of double wool is run a row or two behind the ribbon to still further confine the frill. A bow of ribbon is placed on the top of the head over the gathering of the foundation chain, and from this on each side two ribbons are run, as shown in the engraving. Tie a bow of ribbons in the crochet at the back of the neck. Make a bow to sew by the side of the chin, where also put strings to tie.

LADY'S PETTICOAT.
WORKED IN A VARIETY OF SHELL STITCH.

THE petticoat shown in our engraving can be made with petticoat fingering and a No. 8 crochet needle, or with fleecy wool and a No. 7 needle. Commence with sufficient chain for the length of the petticoat from the waist to the top of the border. **1st row** —Miss the chain stitch next to the needle, work 14 double crochet, then for shell stitch raise 1 stitch in the last double crochet, 1 stitch in the same chain the double crochet is worked into, 1 stitch in each of the next 2 chain, 5 now on the needle, wool over the needle and draw through all and do 1 chain to tighten the group, and now proceed in ordinary shell stitch to the end of the row. **2nd row**—Do 3 chain, and turn, raise 1 stitch in each of 2 chain stitches, 1 stitch in the chain that tightened the group of last row, and 1 stitch on the shell stitch taking up the one back thread, 5 now on the needle, wool over the needle and draw through all and do 1 chain to tighten the group, work ordinary shell stitch over the shell stitches of last row, always inserting the hook to take up the one back thread, work 14 double crochet on the double crochet of last row still taking the one back thread. **3rd row**—Do 1 chain, and turn, and always taking up the one back thread, work 14 double crochet, and then shell stitch as in the first row. Repeat the last two rows until the petticoat is the desired width. You will soon see how the work sits in small perpendicular stripes, and is alike on both sides, and how the double crochet contracts the top of the petticoat to the size of the waist. Sew up the petticoat from the bottom to within eight or nine inches of the top, which leave open for a placket ; strengthen the placket with a row of double crochet : work a row of 2 chain 1 treble along the top of the petticoat. For the **Border—1st round**—Work plain double crochet all round the bottom of the petticoat, and join evenly, and fasten off at the end of this and every succeeding round. **2nd round**—2 treble on a stitch of last round, 1 chain, 2 more treble in the same place, 1 chain, miss one stitch, insert the hook in the next stitch and draw the wool through, miss one stitch, insert the hook in the next stitch and draw the wool through, wool over the needle and draw through 3 stitches on the needle, 1 chain, miss one stitch, and repeat.

3rd round—2 treble under the chain stitch between the treble of last round, 1 chain, 2 more treble in the same place, 1 chain, insert the hook under the next chain stitch and draw the wool through, insert the hook under the next chain stitch and draw the wool through, wool over the needle and draw through 3 stitches on the needle, 1 chain, and repeat. **4th round**—Same as the third round. **5th round**—Double crochet in every stitch of last round. This completes the border. Run a ribbon through the open holes round the top of the petticoat to tie round the waist.

CHEMISE TRIMMING.

REQUIRED, Evan's crochet cotton No. 16 or No. 20, and a fine steel crochet needle. The buds are first to be worked. Begin with 20 chain; miss the first chain by the needle and work 18 double crochet stitches consecutively and 3 double crochet in the end stitch of the foundation chain, and work 16 double

Lady's Petticoat worked in a variety of Shell Stitch.

crochet along the other side of the foundation chain; * turn the work with 1 chain, do 17 consecutive double crochet, taking up always now the one back thread of the stitches of last row, do 3 double crochet on the centre stitch of the previous three double crochet, and 16 double crochet along the opposite side of the work, and repeat from * four times; then turn the work with 1 chain and do 17 double crochet stitches, which brings you to the bottom of the bud, and fasten off. This forms one bud. The other buds are all worked in the same manner, but each one is joined to the preceding with a single crochet worked (instead of the last chain stitch) into the corresponding point of the previous bud. Work sufficient buds to make a length to go round the neck, round the sleeves, and also for a **V**-shape in front, all in one piece, according to the shape shown in the engraving; and when this is arranged work a heading by which to sew the trimming on to the chemise, and finish off with a simple scolloped border. For the **Heading—1st round**—Do 1 long treble stitch in the fifth double crochet counting from the centre stitch at the bottom of one of the buds, * 4 chain (or 5 chain as may be necessary to make the buds lie flat and even), 1 single crochet in the point at the bottom of the bud, chain (or 5), cotton twice round the needle, insert the hook in the fifth double crochet stitch on the left side of the same bud and draw the cotton through cotton over the needle and draw through 2 loops on the needle, cotton over the needle and draw through 2 more loops on the needle, cotton twice round the needle, and proceed with a long treble stitch on the side of the next bud, finishing off the 2 long trebles as 1 stitch, and repeat from *. **2nd round**—1 treble, 1 chain, miss one, and repeat. For the **Scolloped Border**—Work the first two rounds the same as the two rounds of the heading. **3rd round**—2 treble stitches, 7 chain, miss six stitches, and repeat. **4th round**—3 treble in the second chain stitch, 3 chain, miss three stitches, 3 treble in the next, 3 chain, and repeat. **5th round**—1 double crochet under a loop of three chain, * 4 chain, 1 double crochet in the same loop, 4 chain, 1 double crochet under the next loop, and repeat from *. **6th round**—Work 1 double crochet in the upright loop of four chain of last round, * 3 chain, 1 long treble under the loop over the previous group of treble stitches, 4 chain, 1 single crochet on the long treble stitch, another long treble in the same loop, do another picot and another long treble till you have 3 picots and 4 long treble stitches, then 3 chain, 1 double crochet in the next loop, and repeat from * to the end of the round, which completes the trimming.

INFANT'S CAPE WITH WIDE COLLAR.

THE cape shown in our engraving is particularly handsome for an infant, and may easily be enlarged to suit a lady. Procure ¾ lb. of white double Berlin wool, Peacock quality, and a No. 4 bone crochet needle, 1½ yards of good sarcenet ribbon for strings, and about ½ yard of narrow ribbon to run through the crochet at the neck. Commence for the front of the cape, lengthways, with 36 chain. **1st row**—Miss the chain stitch nearest the needle, and work

35 double crochet along the foundation chain. **2nd row**—1 chain to turn, and work 35 double crochet upon the stitches of the preceding row, always throughout the cape inserting the needle to take up the one top thread of the stitches, that the work may appear as shown in the sectional illustration. **3rd row**—1 chain to turn, work 25 double crochet, and 5 single crochet, and leave 5 stitches at the end unworked, this end is the neck end, and the crochet is now to be shaped in a kind of gore. **4th row**—Do 5 single crochet on the single crochet, and 25 double crochet on the double crochet of the previous row. **5th row**—1 chain to turn, work 20 double crochet, and 5 single crochet, and leave 10 stitches unworked. **6th row**—Do 5 single crochet on the single crochet, and 20 double crochet on the double crochet of the previous row. **7th row**—1 chain to turn, work 15 double crochet, and 5 single crochet, and leave 15 end stitches unworked. **8th row**—Do 5 single crochet on the single crochet, and 15 double crochet on the double crochet of the previous row. **9th row**—1 chain to turn, and work all the way up to the neck end, doing 35 double crochet. **10th row**—1 chain to turn, and work 35 double crochet upon the stitches of the preceding row. Repeat from the third row twelve times, which will make 106 rows along the bottom of the cape but only 28 rows along the neck; thus, by means of the gores, the cape is brought to a nice circular shape. For the **Collar—1st row**—Work 42 double crochet along the edge of the stitches at the top of the neck; by doing 2 double crochet on one stitch, and 1 double crochet on the stitch following the required number is exactly managed. **2nd row**—Working as usual into the one top thread of the stitches, increase a stitch at the beginning and at the end, in the middle of the row, and on each shoulder, and so make 47 double crochet in the row. **3rd row**—Increase a stitch on each shoulder, but rather more to the back than the previous increase, and so make 49 double crochet in the row. **4th row**—Increase a stitch at the beginning, in the middle, and at the end, and so make 52 double crochet in the row. **5th row**—Increase twice upon each shoulder, and to make 56 double crochet in the row. **6th row**—Increase

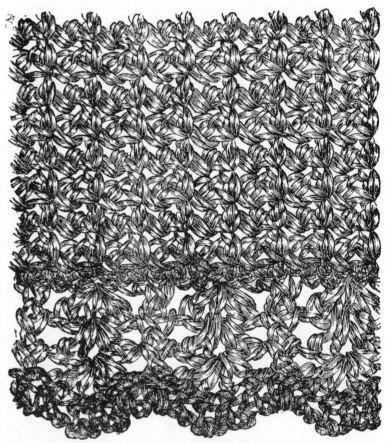

Details of a Lady's Petticoat.

four times at intervals in the row, and you will have 60 double crochet. **7th row**—Increase at the beginning, in the middle, and at the end, and so make 63 double crochet in the row. **8th row**—Increase six times at intervals in the row, and you will have 69 double crochet. **9th row**—Increase at the beginning and end and four times in the middle of the row, and so make 75 double crochet. **10th row**—Increase four times at intervals in the row, and there will be 79 double crochet. **11th row**—Plain double crochet without any increase. Fasten off. For the **Daisy Fringe**—Take about 14 long strands of wool and lay them all evenly together on the table before you, thread a rug needle or a tatting shuttle with another length of wool, and tie the end of this wool firmly round the strands of wool, beginning on the left-hand side about half an inch from the end; make another tie with the wool in the needle upon the stranded wool about an inch from the first tie, sewing it in a perfectly firm knot; and proceed in this manner till you have tied the stranded wool at regular intervals all along, when do more strands in the same way. When the needleful is used up thread another and tie it to the first with a knot. The strands of wool are then cut in the centre of every space between

...es; and a series of little tufts, or "daisies," is thus produced on the wool with which you have been sewing. This daisy fringe is now to be arranged in loops round the cape and round the collar; eight or nine daisies hang downwards in every loop, and two intermediate daisies are sewn straight upon the edge of the crochet, rather closely together, to simulate a kind of heading to the fringe. This daisy fringe uses up a quantity of wool but looks exceedingly stylish. Cut the narrow ribbon to the length required to go round the child's neck, and run it through the crochet, securing it at each end by a few stitches, thus the neck is drawn into shape and kept from stretching. Put on ribbon strings to tie in a bow in front of the neck.

A cape for a lady will take about 1 lb. of double Berlin wool, either grey, or ruby, or any colour that is desired. Begin with 44 chain, and work exactly as instructed above, only doing an additional 8 double crochet stitches always at the bottom of the cape to add to the length. The 106 rows along the bottom of the cape will probably make it quite sufficiently wide, but if for a stout figure another gore can be worked to increase the width. The collar forms a very pretty finish round the neck.

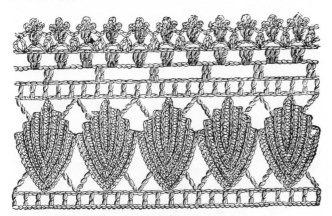

Section of Chemise Trimming.

ALBEMARLE PATTERN QUILT SQUARE.

WITH A PORTION OF BORDER.

THE handsome pattern represented in our engraving may be worked with either knitting cotton or crochet cotton, coarse or fine, according to taste. Strutt's No. 8 and No. 10 knitting cotton are nice sizes, or Coats' crochet cotton No. 12, and with either employ as fine a crochet-needle as you can conveniently use, that the work may be close and firm. Commence with 6 chain, and join round in a circle. **1st round**—Work 4 chain to stand for a long treble stitch, do 3 long treble (cotton twice round the needle) in the circle, * 5 chain, 4 long treble in the circle, repeat from * twice, and do 5 chain and join to the top stitch of the chain with which the round commenced. **2nd round**—Turn the work, and inserting the needle to take up the one back thread of the stitches of preceding round, do 1 double crochet on each stitch, and 3 double crochet on the centre stitch of chain at each corner. **3rd round**—Turn the work, slip invisibly to the centre chain stitch at the corner, do 4 chain to stand for a long treble stitch, * 2 long treble in the next chain stitch of the first round and 1 long treble in the next chain stitch, then inserting the needle to take always the one top thread of the stitches of the first round, work one long treble upon each long treble stitch, then 1 long treble on the first chain stitch, 2 long treble on the next chain stitch, 1 long treble on the centre stitch at the corner, 5 chain, 1 long treble again in the centre chain at the corner, and repeat from * three times; there should be 12 long treble stitches along each side of the square, and a loop of 5 chain at each corner; and finish by joining evenly to the top stitch of chain with which the round commenced: observe to work all the long treble stitches into the stitches of the first round and not into the double crochet stitches at all, these stand upwards in a kind of raised ridge upon the surface of the work as shown in the engraving. **4th round**—Work as instructed for the third round. **5th round**—Work as instructed for the third round, taking the long treble stitches into the one top thread of the stitches of the third round, and getting 20 long treble stitches along each side of the square, and a loop of 5 chain at each corner. It is a good plan to fasten off on the completion of some of the rounds and recommence in a fresh place, as thus any semblance of a seam on the surface of the work is avoided. Continue working a round of double crochet and a round of long treble stitches alternately, always *turning* the work on the completion of each round, and always working the double-crochet stitches in the one back thread of the stitches of last round, and the long treble stitches in the one top thread of the same round, and of course increasing the number of stitches in each round as the square gets larger, doing always eight more long treble stitches on each side of the square in each round, till you get to the **15th round**, where you will do 60 long treble stitches along each side of the square, and a loop of 5 chain at each corner; join evenly on completion, and fasten off. **16th round**—Beginning of the open crochet. Hold the right side of the work towards you, and now always inserting the needle to take up the tiny thread at the back of the stitches of last round, so as to leave the two front threads free, begin with 1 long treble in the centre stitch of chain at the corner, 5 chain, another long treble in the

same place, * cotton twice round the needle, insert the hook in the next chain stitch and draw the cotton through, cotton over the needle and draw through 2 loops on the needle, cotton over the needle, miss one chain stitch, insert the hook in the back thread of the treble stitch of last round and draw the cotton through, cotton over the needle, and draw through 2 loops on the needle four times in succession, 3 chain, cotton once over the needle, insert the hook to take up the two centre threads of the twisted stitch just done, and draw the cotton through, cotton over the needle and draw through 2 loops on the needle, cotton over the needle and draw through the last 2 loops on the needle, 1 long treble in the next stitch of last round, * 3 chain, miss three stitches, 1 long treble in the back thread of the next stitch and complete the "crossed stitch" as from * to * above, but miss two stitches where you before missed only one stitch; 3 chain, miss three stitches, 1 long treble, then a crossed stitch, and continue; and get 8 crossed stitches and 7 open spaces along the side of the square from corner to corner, missing two stitches instead of three under the last open space to get it in evenly, 5 chain at the corner, another long treble in the corner stitch, and repeat from * along the other three sides of the square; and join at the end of the round to the long treble stitch with which the round commenced. **17th round**—Keep the square the right side to the front, and now working always into the one top thread of the stitches of the preceding round, begin with 4-chain to stand for a long treble stitch, 2 long treble in the first chain stitch of the corner loop, 1 long treble in the next, 1 long treble in the next (which is the corner stitch), 7 chain, 1 long treble in the same place, 1 long treble in the next, 2 long treble in the next, 1 long treble on long treble stitch of last round, * 4 chain, miss the crossed stitch, 1 long treble on next long treble of last round, and 4 more long treble worked consecutively, and repeat from *; and get 9 groups of long treble stitches and 8 open spaces along each side of the square from corner to corner, with a loop of 7 chain at each corner; and join evenly at the end of the round. **18th round**—Work in cross stitches and spaces, getting 10 crossed stitches and 9 open spaces along each side of the square, with a loop of 7 chain at each corner. **19th round**—Work in long treble stitches and spaces, and get 11 groups of long treble and 10 open spaces along each side of the square and a loop of 7 chain at each corner. **20th round**—Same as the eighteenth round, but get 12 crossed stitches and 11 open spaces along each side, and a loop of 7 chain at each corner. **21st round**—Work long treble stitches consecutively along each side of the square, with 5 chain at each corner, and join evenly on completion, and fasten off. This completes one square. The number of squares to be worked will depend greatly upon the coarseness or fineness of the

Chemise Trimming.

cotton and the size the quilt is desired to be. When you have a sufficient number join them together with a row of double crochet, making the stitches stand up in a ridge, to correspond with the ridged rows in the centre of the square. For the **Border**—The border is, of course, worked round the outside of the quilt after all the squares are joined together. **1st round**—Double crochet, holding the wrong side of the quilt towards you, and inserting the hook to take up the back thread of the stitches. **2nd round**—Hold the right side of the quilt towards you, and work long treble into the top thread of the stitches the same as in the fifteenth round of the square, and do 3 chain at each corner. **3rd round**—1 double crochet on the centre stitch of three chain at the corner, 5 chain, 4 long treble on consecutive stitches taking up the one top thread, 5 chain, miss four stitches, 1 double crochet on the next, * 5 chain, miss four stitches, 4 long treble worked consecutively, 5 chain, miss four stitches, 1 double crochet on the next, and repeat from * till you get to the corner, where after working 4 long treble stitches close by the corner chain as shown in the engraving, do 5 chain, 1 double crochet on the centre stitch of three chain at the corner; and continue to the end of the round, and fasten off. **4th round**—1 double crochet between the second and third long treble stitches of last round, 12 chain, and repeat the same; do 13 chain on turning the corner. **5th round**—1 double crochet on double crochet of last round,

5 chain, miss four chain of last round, do 4 long treble worked consecutively, miss four stitches, 5 chain, and repeat; at the corner do two groups of 4 long treble stitches with the usual chain, and 1 double crochet on the centre stitch of chain, as shown in the engraving. **6th round**—Same as the fourth round. **7th round**—Same as the fifth round. **8th round**—Same as the fourth round, but 13 chain in each loop. **9th round**—1 double crochet on double crochet of last round, 6 chain, miss four stitches, do 5 long treble consecutively, 6 chain, miss four stitches, and repeat the same to the end of the round. **10th round**—Same as the eighth round. **11th round**—1 double crochet on double crochet of last round, 7 chain, 1 single crochet in the fifth chain from the needle, 2 chain, miss four stitches of last round, 1 long treble in the next, 4

Infant's Cape with Wide Collar.

chain, 1 single crochet in the top of the long treble stitch, 1 long treble on each of the three next stitches, 4 chain, 1 single crochet in the top of the last long treble stitch, 1 long treble on the next stitch, 7 chain, 1 single crochet in the fifth chain from the needle, 2 chain, and repeat the same to the end of the round; a double group of stitches is worked into each corner loop as will be seen by referring to the engraving. This finishes the border.

LADY'S WARM FLEECY PETTICOAT.

Procure 1¾ lbs. of grey four-thread superfine fleecy wool and a No. 8 bone crochet needle. The striped pattern, which constitutes the upper portion of the skirt, is first to be worked, and the skirt is afterwards brought to the length required by the addition of the insertion and the border. Commence therefore for the top of the skirt, lengthways, with 69 chain. **1st row**—Miss the first chain stitch by the needle, and work 7 single crochet, 7 double crochet, and then 1 treble and 1 double crochet alternately twenty-seven times. **2nd row**—3 chain to turn, 1 treble on double crochet stitch and 1 double crochet on treble stitch alternately twenty-seven times, always taking up the one back thread of the stitches of the preceding row that the work may sit in ridges, then 7 double crochet on double crochet, and 7 single crochet on single crochet, still working in the back thread of the stitches. **3rd row**—1 chain to turn, work 7 single crochet, 7 double crochet, and then 1 treble and 1 double crochet alternately twenty-seven times, always taking up the one back thread of the stitches of last row. Continue working up and down in a repetition of the last two rows, till 108 rows, or 120 rows, are worked for the width of the skirt. Do not make it too narrow, as the tendency of the skirt is to drop lengthways by reason of its own weight, and therefore in dropping it narrows itself slightly. You will see how the waist is shaped by the single crochet and double crochet stitches, which serve the purpose of a band; the single crochet should be worked rather tightly, so as to contract as nearly as possible to the size of the figure. In working the last row but one form a button-hole in the single crochet by doing 2 chain and missing two corresponding stitches of the preceding row when 3 stitches from the top, and in the following row work 2 single crochet on the two chain to restore the original number of single crochet stitches. Sew up the skirt from the bottom to within nine inches of the top, which space should be left open for a placket. Strengthen round the placket with a row of plain double crochet, and carry a line of open stitches—viz., 1 chain and 1 treble alternately—along the top edge of the single crochet, in which afterwards to run a tape or a ribbon to tie round the waist. For the **Insertion** round the **Bottom** of the **Skirt**—**1st round**—Work

in plain double crochet; notice how the pattern sits in ridges, each ridge comprising two rows of crochet; do 3 double crochet upon one ridge, and four double crochet upon the next following ridge, alternately, all round the bottom of the skirt; the number of double crochet in the whole round must be some number divisible by eight. **2nd round**—Work 7 double crochet consecutively on double crochet of last round, inserting the hook to take up the two front threads of the stitches, insert the hook to take up two threads of the next stitch, draw the wool through and do 3 chain, then draw the wool through the last stitch of chain and through the double crochet stitch on the needle, which makes a "knob" or "tuft;" repeat the same to the end of the round. **3rd round**—Work 1 knob to the left of the knob of last round, 5 double crochet, 1 knob to the right of a knob of last round, and 1 double crochet on the knob of last round. **4th round**—Extend the vandyke in the manner shown in the engraving, working 1 knob and 3 double crochet alternately to the end of the round. **5th round**—Still extending the vandyke, work 1 knob, 1 double crochet, 1 knob, 5 double crochet, and repeat the same to the end of the round. **6th round**—Close the vandyke by working 1 knob on the one double crochet stitch of last round, 7 double crochet consecutively, and repeat. **7th round**—Plain double crochet, taking up the two front threads of the stitches of previous round, and increase 1 double crochet on the centre stitch between each knob; this finishes the insertion. For the **Border**—Work now always into the one top thread of the stitches. **1st round**—Do 3 double crochet on one stitch, 1 double crochet on the next stitch, * miss one stitch, 1 double crochet on the next, 3 double crochet on the next, 1 double crochet on the next, and repeat from * to the end of the round. **2nd round**—Work 1 double crochet on the first of the 3 double crochet stitches of last round, 3 double crochet on the centre stitch, and 1 double crochet on the last stitch of the 3 double crochet stitches of

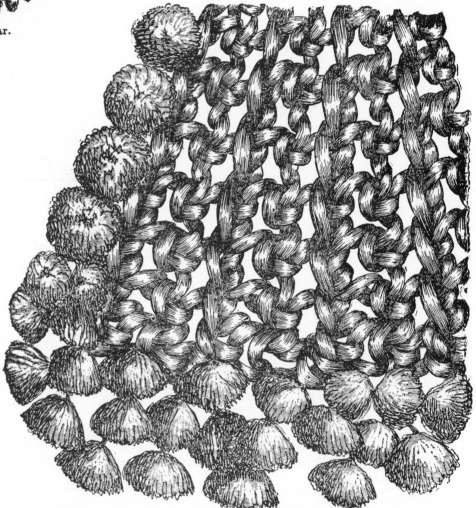

Section of Infant's Cape.

last round, miss two stitches, and repeat the same to the end. Repeat the 2nd round eight times, or till the border is as deep as is desired. **Last round**—To form **Scollops**—Work 3 treble on the centre stitch of the group of three double crochet, and do 1 double crochet on each of the other double crochet stitches, not missing any in the course of the round. Complete the skirt by sewing a button on the band to correspond with the button-hole; and run a tape or ribbon into the holes round the top of the skirt to tie round the waist.

D'OYLEY, EDGED WITH OLD ENGLISH LACE.

FOR the centre of this d'oyley procure a piece of fine diaper or damask linen measuring about six inches long by four inches and a half wide, or larger or smaller according to the size the d'oyley is required to be, cut this into a nice oval shape, and hem it neatly, either by machine or hand. The edging is crocheted upon this linen centre, working in rounds, with Ardern's crochet cotton, No. 24, and a fine steel crochet needle. **1st round**—Work 1 long treble, 1 chain, and repeat; the long treble stitches are formed by passing the cotton *twice* round the needle, and they are set rather closely together into the margin of the hem; join neatly on the completion of this and every round. **2nd round**—Work 1 double crochet under one chain space of last round, * 5 chain, miss three spaces, 1 long treble in the next, 1 chain, another long treble in the same place, do this twice more making in all 4 long treble divided by 1 chain under a one chain space of last round, 5 chain, miss three spaces, 1 double crochet in the next, and repeat from *. **3rd round**—Slip stitch to nearly the top of the five chain stitches of last round, do 6 chain to stand for a long treble stitch, * 1 long treble under the first one chain space of last round, loop, 2 chain, and repeat from *; and join at the end of the round to the fourth chain with which the round commenced. **8th round**—Slip stitch under the first two chain space of last round, * 2 chain and 1 treble under the next space four consecutive times, 6 chain, 1 treble under the first two chain space of the next group of stitches, and repeat from *. **9th round**—Slip stitch under the first two chain space of last round, * 2 chain and 1 treble under the next space three consecutive times, 7 chain, 1 treble under the first two chain space of the next group of stitches, and repeat from *; and fasten off at the end of the round. **10th round**—Begin with 1 double crochet under a loop of seven chain of last round, * 9 chain, 1 long treble under the centre space of two chain, 1 chain and 1 long treble three times in the same place, 9 chain, 1 double crochet under the loop of seven chain, and repeat from * **11th round**—Slip stitch along three chain stitches, 8 chain, 1 long treble under the first small space, * 2 chain, 1 long treble under the next which is the centre space, 2 chain, 1 long treble in the same place, 2 chain, 1 long treble in the same again, 2 chain, 1 long treble under the next space, 5 chain, 1 treble under the loop of nine chain, 1 treble under the next loop of 9 chain, 5 chain, 1 long treble under the first small space of the next group, and repeat from *; and join at the end of the round to the third chain stitch with

Albemarle Pattern Quilt Square, with a Portion of the Border.

2 chain, 1 long treble under the next space, 2 chain, 1 long treble under the next, 2 chain, 1 long treble under the next, 2 chain, 1 long treble under the five chain loop, 5 chain, 1 long treble under the next five chain loop, 2 chain, and repeat from *; and join at the end of the round to the fourth chain stitch with which the round commenced. **4th round**—Slip stitch under the first two chain space of last round, 5 chain to stand for a treble stitch, * 1 treble under the first space, 2 chain, 1 treble under the next space, 2 chain, 1 treble under the next space, 6 chain, and repeat from * to the end of the round, and join, and fasten off: the treble stitches in this round are ordinary treble worked with the cotton *once* round the needle. **5th round**—Begin with 1 double crochet under a loop of six chain of last round, * 5 chain, 1 long treble under the centre space of two chain, 1 chain and 1 long treble three times in the same place, 5 chain, 1 double crochet under the loop of six chain, and repeat from *; **6th round**—The same as the third round. **7th round**—Slip stitch under the five chain to the left, 6 chain to stand for a long treble stitch, * 1 long treble under the first two chain space, 2 chain, 1 long treble under the next two chain space three times, 2 chain, 1 long treble under the loop of five chain, 4 chain, 1 long treble under the same

which the round commenced. **12th round**—Work 5 double crochet under the loop of five chain, * 1 double crochet under the two chain space, 4 chain, 2 more double crochet under the same space, repeat the same under each of the next three spaces, 5 double crochet under the first loop of five chain, 5 double crochet under the next loop of five chain, and repeat from * to the end of the round, and fasten off. This finishes the d'oyley.

CROCHET SHAWL. HALF-CRAZY STITCH.

THIS shawl is extremely pretty worked with Shetland wool and a No. 10 bone crochet needle after the manner of the shawl from which our engraving is taken; or Pompadour wool can be employed if a handsome wrap is desired regardless of expense; while Andalusian wool is very suitable and will afford greater warmth. The shawl is worked lengthways, therefore commence with chain sufficient for the length required. **1st row**—1 double crochet in the second chain from the needle, 3 chain, 2 treble in the same stitch of the foundation as the double crochet is worked into, * miss three chain, 1 double crochet in the next, 3 chain, 2 treble in the same place, and repeat from * to the end of the row, where after missing three chain you do 1 double crochet on the last stitch of the foundation; it is wi e to make an *even* number of groups in the row. **2nd row**—1 chain to turn, 1 double crochet on the first double crochet stitch of previous row, inserting the needle to take up the two top threads, 3 chain, 2 treble in the same place, * 1 double crochet on the next double crochet of preceding row, 3 chain, 2 treble in the same place, and repeat from *; and end with 1 double crochet on the last double crochet stitch of last row. The remainder of the shawl is a repetition of the second row, working forwards and backwards till the required size is attained, when fasten off. For the **Border**—Beginning at the corner on the double crochet stitch with which you ended the last row of the shawl, and holding the wrong side of last row towards you in the usual way after having turned the work, do 2 treble on the corner stitch, 3 chain, 2 treble in the same place, 2 more treble in the same place, 2 chain, wool over the needle and insert the hook in the next stitch of double crochet of the last row of the shawl and draw the wool through in a loose long loop, * wool over the needle and insert the hook again in the same place and again draw the wool through in a loose long hoop, repeat from * twice more, and there will be 4 loose loops on the needle with the wool between each, pass the wool over the needle and draw through all the loops, wool over the needle and draw through 2 stitches on the

corner. **4th round**—Again beginning at the corner—Work 3 treble 3 chain and 3 treble under the loop of three chain between the treble stitches of last round, 2 chain, a tuft in the loop in front of the tuft of last round, 2 chain, a tuft in the next following loop, 2 chain, 3 treble 3 chain and 3 treble in the loop between the treble stitches of last round, * 2 chain, a tuft in the loop in front of the tuft of last round, 2 chain, a tuft in the next following loop, 2 chain, 3 treble 3 chain and 3 treble in the loop between the treble stitches of last round, and repeat from *; and work the other corners similarly to the first corner. **5th round**—Beginning with a double crochet in any loop between two tufts of last round, * do 3 treble under the three chain loop between the treble stitches of last round, 4 chain, 1 single crochet on the top of the treble stitch last done, 2 more treble in the same loop, 4 chain, 1 single crochet on the top of the treble stitch last done, 2 more treble in the same loop, 4 chain, 1 single crochet on the top of the treble stitch last done, 3 more treble in the same loop, this makes 10 treble in the loop of last round with three little piques jutting out, then do 1 double crochet in the loop between the two tufts of last round, and repeat from *; and work the other corners to corre pond; and join evenly at the end of the round, and fasten off securely. This a very handsome border and well worth the trouble of working.

Lady's Warm Fleecy Petticoat.

D'Oyley, Edged

needle, this forms a "tuft;" do 2 chain, then on the next double crochet stitch of last row work 2 treble 3 chain and 2 treble, do 2 chain, and on the next double crochet stitch make a tuft, and so on all along till you reach the corner, which work similarly to the first corner, and proceed along the other three sides of the shawl, and join evenly at the end of the round, and fasten off at the end of this and every round. **2nd round**—Work 2 treble under the first loop of three chain at the corner, 3 chain, 2 more treble in the same place; 2 chain, 2 treble 3 chain and 2 treble between the next two treble stitches of last round; 2 chain, 2 treble 3 chain and 2 treble under the other loop of three chain at the corner; * 2 chain, a tuft in the loop in front of the tuft of last round, 2 chain, a tuft in the loop following the tuft of last round, 2 chain, 2 treble 3 chain and 2 treble in the loop between the treble stitches of last round, and repeat from *; and work the other corners the same as the first corner. **3rd round**—Beginning by the corner in the same place as last round, do 3 treble 3 chain and 3 treble under the loop of three chain between the treble stitches of last round, 2 chain, a tuft under the next loop, 2 chain, 3 treble 3 chain and 3 treble in the corner loop, 2 chain, a tuft under the next loop, 2 chain, 3 treble 3 chain and 3 treble in the loop between the treble stitches of last round, * 2 chain, a tuft in the loop between the tufts of last round, 2 chain, 3 treble 3 chain and 3 treble in the loop between the treble stitches of last round, and repeat from *; and work the other corners the same as the first

COUVREPIED.

THIS couvrepied is composed of sectional squares worked in Russian crochet, each square being bordered with a round of open crossed stitches, through which a satin ribbon is run from side to side of the couvrepied. The process of working is clearly shown in the engraving. Select single Berlin wool of any colour that harmonises or contrasts well with the upholstery of the room. Crimson always looks bright and cheerful, and art green gives a pleasant, subdued colouring; a pretty way is to shade the wool from dark in the centre to light outside, doing four or six rounds with each shade. Use a No. 10 bone crochet needle, and work the Russian crochet closely and firmly. If you like to employ double Berlin wool use a No. 8 needle. Begin in the centre of the square with 2 chain; work 8 double crochet in the first stitch of chain, and join round quite evenly. **2nd round**—Turn the work, insert the hook always to take up the one *back* thread of the stitches of the previous round, do 1 double crochet on the first stitch of previous round, 3 double crochet on the next, repeat the same three times, and join evenly at the end of the round, this joining should be made quite invisibly, and that it may be so it is a good plan to break off the wool on the completion of every two or four rounds and recommence in a fresh place. **3rd round**—Turn the work, do 3 double crochet on the centre stitch at each corner, and 3 consecutive double crochet along each side of the square. **4th round**—Turn the work, do 3 double crochet on the centre stitch at each corner, and 5 consecutive double crochet along each side of the square. **5th round**—Turn the work, do 3 double crochet on the centre stitch at each corner, and 7 consecutive double crochet along each side of the square. Continue in this manner, always working 3 double crochet for corner stitches and consecutive double crochet along the sides of the square, till in the **18th round** you work 3 double crochet at the corner and 33 double crochet along each side, and join quite evenly, and fasten off. **19th round**—This round consists of open crossed stitches. Turn the work so as to have, as usual, the wrong side of last round uppermost, make a stitch on the needle, wool twice round the needle, insert the hook to take up the back thread of the centre stitch and draw the wool through, wool over the needle and draw through 2 loops on the needle, wool over the needle, miss one stitch of last round, insert the hook in the back thread of the next stitch and draw the wool through, wool over the needle and draw through 2 loops on the needle *four* times, 2 chain, wool over the needle, insert the hook to take up the two centre threads of the twisted stitch just made and draw the wool through, wool over the needle and draw through 2 loops on the needle, wool over the needle and again draw through 2 loops on the needle, this forms 1 crossed stitch, * 1 chain, wool twice round the needle, miss one

off. **2nd round**—Hold the right side of the work uppermost, and take up the one top thread of the stitches, * 3 double crochet in the centre stitch of the loop of eleven chain, 7 double crochet worked consecutively, miss two stitches, work 7 double crochet consecutively, and repeat from * to the end of the round. **3rd round**—Do 3 double crochet on the centre stitch of three double crochet of last round, 7 double crochet on the seven following stitches, miss two stitches, 7 double crochet on the following seven stitches, and repeat the same to the end of the round. Work 4 more rounds the same as last round. **8th round**—Work 1 double crochet on the second stitch of seven double crochet on the rising side of a scollop, then loops of 3 chain, miss one stitch, 1 double crochet on the next, seven times round the scollop, miss two stitches, and continue the same to the end of the round. The fringe is made by cutting strands of wool eight or nine inches in length and knotting 6 or 7 strands into each loop of chain. Procure good satin ribbon of a suitable width to run in through the open crossed stitches, as shown in the illustration : the ribbon is held in place by a few stitches at the beginning and at the end of each line.

CROCHET EDGING.
FOR A SHAWL, OR OTHER PURPOSE.

COMMENCE with a chain the length required, or otherwise work immediately

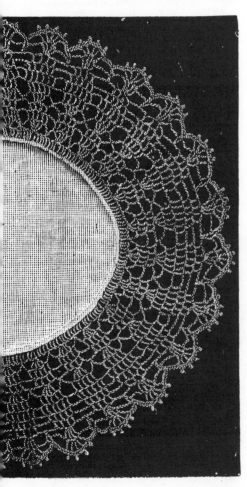

English Lace.

Crochet Shawl. Half-Crazy Stitch.

stitch of last round, insert the hook in the back thread of the next stitch and draw the wool through, wool over the needle and draw through 2 loops on the needle, wool over the needle, miss two stitches of last round, insert the hook in the back thread of the next stitch and draw the wool through, wool over the needle and draw through 2 loops on the needle *four* times, 2 chain, wool over the needle, insert the hook to take up the two centre threads of the twisted stitch just made and draw the wool through, wool over the needle and draw through 2 loops on the needle, wool over the needle and again draw through 2 loops on the needle, and repeat from * till you get to the centre stitch at the next corner, making 8 crossed stitches along the side of the square (one stitch only to be missed under the cross at the end the same as at the beginning), do 7 chain to turn round the corner, and continue the three other sides of the square in the same way, and join evenly at the end of the round, and fasten off. Work a sufficient number of squares for the size of the couvrepied and sew them together. When they are all joined, a row of crossed stitches is worked the whole way round the couvrepied, followed by six rounds of Russian crochet. For the **Border** and **Fringe—1st round**—Beginning on the double crochet stitch next after the three double crochet at the corner, * work 6 double crochet consecutively, 11 chain, miss seven stitches, and repeat from * ; make the stitches come in evenly at the corners where only three double crochet should be missed and join evenly at the end of the round, and fasten

upon the article for which the border is intended ; it is very pretty worked with Shetland wool and a fine crochet needle. **1st row**—1 double crochet in a stitch of the foundation, * 5 chain, a picot (that is 1 single crochet in the third chain from the needle), 6 chain, a picot, 2 chain, miss five stitches of the foundation, 1 double crochet in the next, and repeat from * to the end of the row ; break off the wool at the end of this and every row. The work may be turned or not, as preferred ; if it be turned, both sides of the edging will be alike, and if not turned, there will be a right side and a wrong side. **2nd row**—1 single crochet in the centre stitch of the three chain stitches between the picots of last row, * 5 chain, a picot, 6 chain, a picot, 2 chain, 1 single crochet in the centre stitch of the next loop of last row, and repeat from *. **3rd row**—Same as the second row. **4th row**—1 single crochet in the centre stitch of a loop of last row, 9 chain, 1 single crochet in the centre stitch of the next loop, 2 chain, turn the work, and do 7 treble and 1 double crochet under the loop of nine chain, 2 chain, turn the work and do 8 treble in the spaces of the little treble row just done, 6 chain, 1 single crochet in the centre stitch of the next loop of last row, * 2 chain, turn the work, and do 7 treble and 1 double crochet under the loop of six chain, 2 chain, turn the work, and do 8 treble in the spaces of the little treble row, 6 chain, 1 single crochet in the centre stitch of the next loop of last row, and repeat from *. **5th row**—1 single crochet in the two chain at the top of the little scollop of treb' stitches, * 5 chain, a picot, 6 chain, a picot, 2 chain, 1 single crochet in the two chain at the top of the next scollop of treble stitches, and repeat from *. **6th row**—Same as the second row. **7th row**—Also like the second row. **8th row**—Same as the fourth row. **9th row**—Same as the fifth row. **10th row**—Same as the second row. **11th row**—Also like the second row. This completes the edging.

INFANT'S BONNET IN TRICOT.

THIS warm comfortable bonnet for an infant is worked entirely in plain tricot, excepting the border which is done in looped knitting; it comes nicely upon the head, and protects the ears from cold winds. The materials required are 4 ozs. of white single Berlin wool, a No. 6 bone tricot needle, or a No. 7 if a loose worker, a pair of No. 14 steel knitting needles, 3 yards of ribbon for bows and strings, and 1 yard of narrow ribbon for drawing up the front, also a lace cap may be put in and is a decided improvement. Make 60 chain for the *front* of the *bonnet*, and work 14 rows of all plain tricot, 60 stitches in each

Section of Couvrepied.

row. **15th row**—Pick up 12 tricot stitches (1 stitch being already on the needle from last row makes 13 stitches on the needle), pick up 2 stitches together, 14 plain tricot, 2 stitches together, 14 plain tricot, 2 stitches together, 13 plain tricot, and draw back as usual. **16th row**—13 plain tricot, 2 together, 12 plain, 2 together, 13 plain, 2 together, 13 plain tricot. **17th row**—13 plain tricot, 2 together, 11 plain, 2 together, 11 plain, 2 together, 13 plain. **18th row**—13 plain tricot, 2 together, 9 plain, 2 together, 10 plain, 2 together, 13 plain. **19th row**—13 plain tricot, 2 together, 18 plain, 2 together, 13 plain. **20th row**—13 plain tricot, 2 together, 7 plain, 2 together, 7 plain, 2 together, 13 plain. **21st row**—12 plain tricot, 2 together, 6 plain, 2 together, 7 plain, 2 together, 12 plain. **22nd row**—11 plain tricot, 2 together, 6 plain, 2 together, 6 plain, 2 together, 11 plain. **23rd row**—10 plain tricot, 2 together, 5 plain, 2 together, 6 plain, 2 together, 10 plain. **24th row**—9 plain tricot, 2 together, 5 plain, 2 together, 5 plain, 2 together, 9 plain. **25th row**—8 plain tricot, 2 together, 4 plain, 2 together, 5 plain, 2 together, 8 plain. **26th row**—7 plain tricot, 2 together, 4 plain, 2 together, 4 plain, 2 together, 7 plain. **27th row**—11 plain tricot, 2 together, 12 plain tricot, which brings now only 24 stitches on the needle, draw back, and break off the wool with a long end; fold the 24 stitches to form the back of the crown, and sew up. Work a row of treble stitches along the bottom of the bonnet in which afterwards to run a ribbon to confine the bonnet in shape round the back of the neck, do 28 treble on each side and 1 treble on the join that runs up the back of the bonnet, 57 treble in all, and break off the wool. For the **Curtain**—**1st row**—Pick up 57 tricot stitches upon the edge of the treble, and draw back as usual. **2nd row**—Pick up 1 tricot stitch, increase 1, 22 plain, increase 1, 4 plain, increase 1, 5 plain, increase 1, 22 plain, increase 1, 2 plain. **3rd row**—Plain tricot, 62 stitches. **4th row**—Pick up 1 tricot stitch, increase 1, 20 plain, increase 1, 7 plain, increase 1, 4 plain, increase 1, 7 plain, increase 1, 20 plain, increase 1, 2 plain. **5th row**—Plain tricot, 68 stitches. **6th row**—Pick up 1 tricot stitch, increase 1, 24 plain, increase 1, 8 plain, increase 1, 8 plain, increase 1, 24 plain, increase 1, 2 plain. **7th row**—Plain tricot, 73 stitches. **8th row**—Pick up 20 tricot stitches, increase 1, 16 plain, increase 1, 16 plain, increase 1, 20 plain. **9th row**—Plain tricot, 76 stitches. Fasten off. For the **Looped Trimming**—Use the knitting needles and cast on 5 stitches. **1st row**—Plain knitting. **2nd row**—Insert the right-hand needle in the first stitch, pass the wool over the point of the needle and round the first and second fingers of the left hand twice, and then again over the point of the needle and knit the stitch

taking in all three threads of the wool, and knit the 4 other stitches in the same manner. **3rd row**—Plain, taking every group of threads as one stitch, so again you have 5 stitches on the needle. Repeat the last two rows till a sufficient length is knitted to go along the edge of the bottom of the curtain, when fasten off, and sew it on. Make another length of looped trimming to go along the edge of the front of the bonnet, from the bottom of the looped trimming on one side the curtain to the bottom of the looped trimming on the other side, and sew it on. Make a nice bow of ribbon to place on the top of the bonnet. Divide the remainder of the ribbon into four pieces; run two pieces through the row of treble stitches, securing an end firmly on each side under the looped trimming, and tying a bow at the back; use the other two pieces for strings. Run the narrow ribbon in the front of the bonnet along side the first row of the tricot, and draw it in slightly to suit the child's face, and the bonnet will appear as shown in the engraving. The bonnet may be lined with thin silk if desired, but it is not actually necessary.

SEXAGON FOR A QUILT.

OUR engraving shows a large handsome sexagon for a quilt, also a section of the same to more clearly illustrate the method of working. The model is executed with Coats' crochet cotton, No. 8, and a fine steel crochet needle; each sexagon measures nearly ten inches from side to side, therefore, though there is a great deal of work in the making of one sexagon, not a very great number will be required to complete a quilt, in fact eight or nine sexagons in width and the same number in length are sufficient for a good-sized quilt. Knitting cotton, No. 12, may be employed instead of crochet cotton, if preferred. The work is done closely and rather tightly. **Commence** in the centre of the sexagon, with 2 chain; work 4 double crochet in the second chain from the needle. **1st round**—Work 2 double crochet on each of the four double crochet stitches, inserting the needle to take up the one top thread. **2nd round**—Work again two double crochet on each stitch, making 16 double crochet, always inserting the hook in the one top thread of the stitches of previous round, and join evenly at the end of this and every following round. **3rd round**—In this round the raised tufts begin; if you look at the work you will see the front threads of the 4 first double crochet stitches visible in the middle of the circle, raise each a little so as to be more readily noticed, a "tuft" is to be worked into each of these four stitches; * cotton over the needle and insert the hook into the first of these stitches and draw the cotton through, cotton over the needle and draw through 2

Couvrepied.

stitches on the needle, § cotton over the needle and insert the hook again in the same place and draw the cotton through, cotton over the needle and draw through 2 stitches on the needle, repeat from § three times more, and there will be 6 stitches on the needle, cotton over the needle and draw through 5 of these stitches, cotton over the needle and draw through 2 stitches on the needle, miss the stitch of last round at the back of the tuft, do 1 double crochet on the next, 2 double crochet on the next, 1 double crochet on the next, and repeat from * three times, and there will be in all 20 stitches in the round. **4th round**—Double crochet all round, increasing eight times, and making 28 stitches in the round. **5th round**—Double crochet, increasing six times, and making 32 stitches in the round. **6th round**—You now should be in position for working directly beyond one of the tufts of the third round, work a tuft therefore into a stitch of the third round, miss one stitch of last round, 1 double crochet on the next, 2 double crochet on the next, 1 double crochet on the next, and repeat the same to the end of the round, making two tufts between each tuft of the third round, and there will be 8 tufts, and 40 stitches in all in the round. **7th round**—Plain double crochet, 40 stitches, and join *quite* evenly. **8th round**—This is an open round, do 5 chain to stand for a treble, 1 treble on the first stitch of the preceding round, 2 chain, 1 treble on the next, 2 chain, 1 treble on the next, 2 chain, miss 1 stitch, * 1 treble on the next, 2 chain, 1 treble on the next, 2 chain, miss one stitch, and repeat from *, and at the end of the round after doing 2 chain join to the third stitch of the chain with which the round began; the hook should be inserted into both the top and the back threads of the stitches of last round, and there will be 30 treble stitches and 30 open spaces in the round. **9th round**—The beginning of the raised pleated wheel—Do 3 double crochet on the treble stitch of last round, 1 double crochet on each of the two chain stitches, and repeat, working always now into the one top thread. **10th round**—3 double crochet on the centre stitch of the three double crochet of last round, 4 double crochet worked consecutively, and repeat; there should be 30 points of three double crochet stitches in each round. **11th round**—3 double crochet on the centre stitch of the three double crochet of last

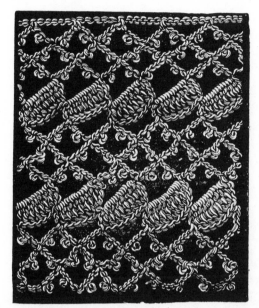

Crochet Edging for a Shawl or other purpose.

round, 6 double crochet worked consecutively, and repeat. **12th round**—3 double crochet on the centre stitch of the three double crochet of last round, 8 double crochet worked consecutively, and repeat. **13th round**—3 double crochet on the centre stitch of the three double crochet of last round, 10 double crochet worked consecutively, and repeat. **14th round**—3 double crochet on the centre stitch of the three double crochet of last round, 12 double crochet worked consecutively, and repeat. **15th round**—3 double crochet on the centre stitch of the three double crochet of last round, 14 double crochet worked consecutively, and repeat. Proceed working in the same manner as the last few rounds, always doing 3 double crochet on the centre stitch of the previous three double crochet, and always increasing two plain stitches in every round between the points, till in the **20th round** you do 3 double crochet on the centre stitch of the three double crochet of last round, and 24 double crochet worked consecutively, which completes the wheel, join round quite evenly, and fasten off. **21st round**—Beginning the plain double crochet behind the wheel—work 1 double crochet on the thirteenth stitch of the twenty-four consecutive stitches of the last round of the wheel, inserting the hook to take up the front and top threads of the stitch, * 4 chain, 1 double crochet on the thirteenth stitch of the next division of twenty-four stitches, 5 chain, 1 double crochet on the thirteenth stitch of the next division, 4 chain, 1 double crochet on the thirteenth stitch of the next division, 5 chain, 1 double crochet on the thirteenth stitch of the next division, 5 chain, 1 double crochet on the thirteenth stitch of the next division, and repeat from *, being very careful to make the right number of chain stitches; there should be 30 double crochet stitches and 30 loops of chain in the round, 168 stitches; keep the points of the wheel to the front of the loops of chain stitches, and join evenly on the completion of the round. **22nd round**—Plain double crochet, 168 stitches in the round. **23rd round**—Work 3 double crochet on the first stitch of last round (on the stitch above the double crochet of the preceding round), 27 consecutive double crochet, and repeat, working now into the one top thread of the stitches, and you will have 6 points of three double crochet to denote the six points of the sexagon. **24th round**—3 double crochet on the centre stitch of the three double crochet of last round, 29 double crochet worked consecutively, and repeat. **25th round.**—3 double crochet on the centre stitch of the three double crochet of last round, 31 double crochet worked consecutively, and repeat. **26th round**—3 double crochet on the centre stitch of the three double crochet of last round, 33 double crochet worked consecutively, and repeat. **27th round**—3 double crochet on the centre stitch of the three double crochet of last round, 35 double crochet worked consecutively, and repeat. **28th round**—3 double crochet on the centre stitch of the

three double crochet of last round, 37 double crochet worked consecutively, and repeat; and be careful to join quite evenly on the completion of the round, and fasten off. **29th round**—This is an open round; do 1 treble on the first of the three double crochet stitches on a point, 1 chain, 1 treble on the centre stitch of the point, 1 chain, 1 treble on the third of the three double crochet stitches, * 1 chain, miss one stitch, 1 treble on the next, and repeat from * till you get to the next point, which work like the first, and continue the same to the end of the round, when there should be 126 treble and 126 open spaces, that is 21 treble stitches and 21 open spaces on each of the six sides of the sexagon, and join round. **30th round**—Work 1 treble on the centre stitch of a point, 1 chain, 1 treble in the same place, 1 chain, another treble in the same place, * 1 chain, 1 treble on treble stitch of last round, and repeat from * till you get to the next point, which work like the first, and continue the same open stitch to the end of the round, when there should be 138 treble and 138 open spaces, that is 23 treble stitches, and 23 open spaces on each of the six sides of the sexagon, join round. **31st round**—Work 3 double crochet on the centre stitch of a point, 45 double crochet worked consecutively, and repeat. **32nd round**—Work 3 double crochet on the centre stitch of the three double crochet of last round, 47 double crochet worked consecutively, and repeat. **33rd round**—Beginning the triangles of tufts, * work 3 double crochet on the centre stitch of three double crochet at the point, 12 double crochet worked consecutively, a tuft into a stitch of the second previous round, 3 double crochet and a tuft alternately till 7 tufts are worked, 12 double crochet, and repeat from * to the end of the round. **34th round**—3 double crochet on the centre stitch of the point, 51 double crochet worked consecutively, and repeat. **35th round**—3 double crochet on the centre stitch at the point, 16 consecutive double crochet, a tuft into the middle double crochet between the tufts of the second previous round, 3 double crochet and a tuft alternately till 6 tufts are worked, 16 double crochet, and repeat the same. **36th round**—3 double crochet on the centre stitch at the point, 55 double crochet worked consecutively, and repeat. **37th round**—3 double crochet on the centre stitch at the point, 20 consecutive double crochet, a tuft into the middle stitch between the tufts of the second previous row, 3 double crochet and a tuft alternately till 5 tufts are worked, 20 double crochet, and repeat the same. **38th round**—3 double crochet on the centre stitch at the point, 59 double crochet worked consecutively, and repeat. **39th round**—3 double crochet on the centre stitch at

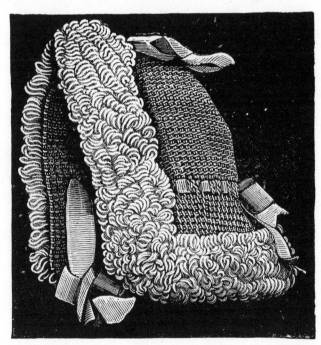

Infant's Bonnet in Tricot.

the point, 24 consecutive double crochet, a tuft into the middle stitch between the tufts of the second previous row, 3 double crochet and a tuft alternately till 4 tufts are worked, 24 double crochet, and repeat the same. **40th round**—3 double crochet on the centre stitch at the point, 63 double crochet worked consecutively, and repeat. **41st round**—3 double crochet on the centre stitch at the point, 28 consecutive double crochet, a tuft into the middle stitch between the tufts of the second previous row, 3 double crochet and a tuft alternately till 3 tufts are worked, 28 double crochet, and repeat the same. **42nd round**—3 double crochet on the centre stitch at the point, 67 double crochet worked consecutively, and repeat. **43rd round**—3 double crochet on the centre stitch at the point, 32 consecutive double crochet, a tuft into the middle stitch between the tufts of the second previous row, 3 double crochet, a tuft, 32 double crochet, and repeat the same. **44th round**—3 double crochet on the centre stitch at the point, 71 double crochet worked consecutively, and repeat. **45th round**—3 double crochet on the centre stitch at the point, 36 consecutive double crochet, a tuft, 36 double crochet, and repeat the same; this completes the triangles of tufts, join evenly, and fasten off. **46th round**—This is an open round, do 1 treble on the first of the three double crochet stitches on a point, 1 chain, 1 treble on the centre stitch of the point, 1 chain, 1 treble on the third of the three double crochet stitches, * 1 chain, miss one stitch, 1 treble on the next, and repeat from *, till you get to the next point, which work like the first, and continue the same to the end of the round. **47th round**—5 treble on the centre stitch at the point, and 77 treble worked consecutively, and repeat, and fasten off at the end of the round. This completes one sexagon. A number of sexagons are very easily joined together by sewing the straight side of one to the straight side of another. The spaces all round the edge of the quilt may be filled with *half* sexagons if the quilt is to be finished with a lace border; but if fringed a longer fringe can be put in the spaces than is put on the extreme outside margin.

INFANT'S BOOTS. TRICOT.

FOR an infant's first-size boots procure ¾ oz. of white and a little pale blue

tricot on the needle; and draw back. **3rd row**—Drop the tricot stitch off the needle, draw the wool through the twenty-second double crochet stitches, resume the dropped stitch, pick up 9 tricot on the tricot stitches, and 3 tricot on double crochet; 16 tricot on the needle; and draw back. **4th row**—Drop the tricot stitch off the needle, draw the wool through the seventeenth, eighteenth, and nineteenth double crochet stitche, resume the dropped stitch, pick up 15 tricot on the tricot stitches, and 3 tricot on double crochet; 22 tricot on the needle; and draw back. **5th row**—Drop the tricot stitch, pick up a tricot stitch in the fourteenth, fifteenth, and sixteenth double crochet stitches, resume the dropped stitch, pick up 5 tricot, pick up 2 stitches together, pick up 6 tricot, pick up 2 stitches together, pick up 6 tricot on tricot stitches, and 3 tricot on double crochet; 26 tricot on the needle; and draw back. **6th row**—Drop the tricot stitch, pick up a tricot stitch in the eleventh, twelfth, and thirteenth double crochet stitches, resume the dropped stitch, pick up 7 tricot, 2 together, 6 tricot for the instep, 2 together, pick up 8 tricot on tricot stitches, and 3 tricot on double crochet; 30 tricot on the needle; and draw back. **7th row**—Drop the tricot stitch, pick up a tricot stitch in the

Sexagon for a Quilt.

Andalusian wool and a No. 9 bone tricot needle; for larger boots 1 oz. of white and ¼ oz. of blue single Berlin and a No. 8 needle. The blue wool is only used as a trimming to edge the frill round the top of the boots. Commence for the bottom of the boot with white wool, with 55 chain, and work a row of 54 double crochet stitches, and break off the wool. Now proceed **in tricot**— Miss the first 24 double crochet stitches, draw the wool through the next double crochet and so form 1 tricot stitch, pick up 1 tricot stitch on each of the following 5 double crochet, making in all 6 tricot on the needle, and leave 24 double crochet at the end to correspond with the 24 left at the beginning, and draw back through the 6 tricot stitches in the ordinary manner. **2nd row**—Drop the tricot stitch off the needle for a moment, draw the wool through the twenty-third double crochet stitch, and the twenty-fourth double crochet stitch, resume the dropped stitch, pick up 5 tricot on 5 tricot stitches of last row, and 2 tricot on two double crochet stitches; making in all 10

eighth, ninth, and tenth double crochet stitches, resume the dropped stitch pick up 9 tricot, 2 together, 6 tricot for the instep, 2 together, pick up 10 tricot on tricot stitches, and 3 tricot on double crochet; 34 tricot on the needle; and draw back. **8th row**—Drop the tricot stitch, pick up a tricot stitch on the fifth, sixth, and seventh double crochet stitches, resume the dropped stitch, pick up 33 tricot on tricot stitches, and 3 tricot on double crochet; 40 tricot on the needle; and draw back. **9th row**—Drop the tricot stitch, pick up a tricot stitch in the first, second, third, and fourth double crochet stitches, resume the dropped stitch, pick up 14 tricot, 2 together, 6 tricot for the instep, 2 together, pick up 15 tricot on tricot stitches, and 4 tricot on double crochet; 46 tricot on the needle; and draw back. **10th row**— Keep the 1 tricot stitch on the needle, increase 1, pick up 17 tricot, 2 together, 6 tricot for the instep, 2 together, pick up 17 tricot, increase 1, pick up 1 tricot; 46 tricot on the needle; and draw back. **11th row**—Pick up 17 tricot,

2 together, 6 tricot for the instep, 2 together, 18 tricot; 44 tricot on the needle; and draw back. **12th row**—All plain tricot. **13th row**—Pick up 16 tricot, 2 together, 6 plain, 2 together, 17 plain; 42 tricot on the needle; and draw back. **14th row**—Pick up 15 tricot, 2 together, 6 plain, 2 together, 16 plain; and draw back. **15th row**—Pick up 14 tricot, 2 together, 6 plain, 2 together, 15 plain; and draw back. **16th row**—Pick up 2 together, 11 plain, 2 together, 6 plain, 2 together, 12 plain, 2 together; 34 tricot on the needle; and draw back. Work 5 rows of all plain tricot. **22nd row**—Pick up 2 tricot, increase 1, work plain tricot till within 3 stitches of the end, increase 1, pick up 3 tricot; and draw back. **23rd row**—Plain tricot. Work 4 rows with increase the same as the twenty-second row. **28th row**—Plain tricot, 44 stitches, and draw back. **29th row**—Plain tricot, and break off the wool. For the **Sole**—Pick up in tricot the 6 stitches of

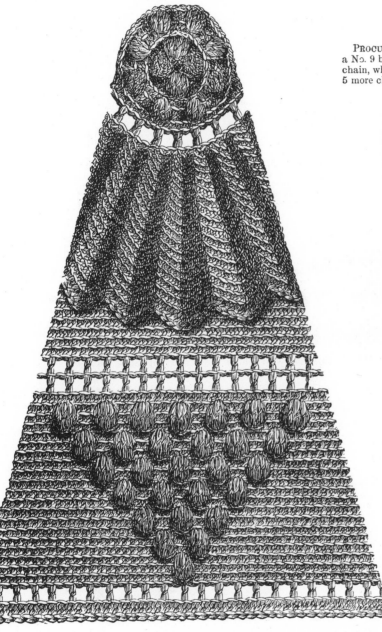

Section of Sexagon Quilt

the foundation chain that you used for the beginning of the toe, and work in plain tricot about 20 rows, or till the sole is about long enough to reach to the back of the boot, decrease one stitch on each side in course of doing the last row, and fasten off; sew up the back of the leg, then sew the sole neatly in its place, rounding the heel nicely. For the **Frill**—Begin by the seam, with white wool, and do a row of double crochet stitches along the top of the tricot, inserting the hook to take up the perpendicular threads, and join round. **2nd round**—Also with white wool,—Reverse the position of the boot, and hold the row you have just worked towards you, and insert the needle to take the threads that lie between those taken in the last row, that the scollops may turn downwards in the position shown in the engraving,—Do 1 single crochet in the stitch by the needle, miss one stitch, * do 5 treble in the next, miss one, do 1 single crochet in the next, miss one, and repeat from

* to the end of the round, and fasten off. Work three scollops on the front of the leg, beginning just underneath the scollops that run round the top of the boot and going only a little way down, as will be seen in the engraving. **3rd round**—With pale blue wool—Work a line of single crochet along the edge of the stitches of last round, inserting the hook to take the two front threads of the stitches; break off the wool on the completion of the round. **4th round**—With blue wool—Work upon the round of double crochet stitches, 1 double crochet on the first stitch by the seam, * 3 chain, miss one stitch, 1 double crochet on the next, and repeat from *; and fasten off at the end of the round. The other boot must be worked in the same manner, but the three scollops on the front of the leg should turn in the opposite direction; a small blue silk button is then placed on each of these scollops.

CUFF.

WORKED IN TRICOT WITH A CROCHET EDGE.

PROCURE 1 oz. of claret colour single Berlin wool, a No. 8 tricot needle, and a No. 9 bone crochet needle. Commence with the tricot needle by making 31 chain, which is a fair ordinary size to go round the arm, but, if required larger, 5 more chain must be added to allow for one more complete stripe of the tricot

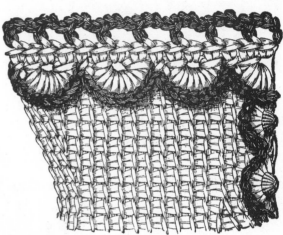

Section of Infant's Boot.

Infant's Boot in Tricot.

pattern. **1st row**—Pick up 1 tricot stitch in each stitch of chain, and you will have 31 stitches on the needle (or the same number with which you began), the tricot must be done moderately loosely, and work back in this manner,—draw through 1 stitch, * do 1 chain, draw through 3 stitches together, do 1 chain, draw through 2 stitches separately, and repeat from * till all the stitches are worked through. **2nd row**—Pick up 1 tricot stitch on the second stitch of previous row, * 1 tricot in the chain stitch, 1 tricot in the little thread at the back of the three stitches that are drawn together, 1 tricot in the next chain stitch, 1 tricot on each of the two plain tricot stitches, and repeat from * to the end, where will be only 1 plain tricot stitch to pick up, and there will be 31 stitches again on the needle, draw back through these as instructed in the first row. Continue working the same as the second row until 11 rows are done. **12th row**—With the crochet needle—work for the edge,—Insert the hook in the second stitch of previous row, draw the wool through and do 3 chain stitches, draw the wool through the last stitch of chain and through the other stitch on the needle, 1 double crochet on the chain stitch of last row, * insert the hook in the little thread at the back of the three stitches that are drawn together and draw the wool through, do 3 chain and draw the wool through the last stitch of chain and through the stitch on the needle, miss the chain stitch, do 1 double crochet on the first of the two plain tricot stitches, 1 picot (as above) on the second of the two plain tricot stitches, 1 double crochet on the chain stitch of last row, and repeat from * to the end of the row, and join *round* by making a single crochet to the beginning of the row. **13th row**—1 double crochet, 3 chain, 1 treble, 1 double crochet, all worked on each double crochet stitch of last row, taking up two front threads, and fasten off at the end of the round. Work a similar edge on the other side of the cuff. Join up the sides of the tricot work. Make the other cuff in the same manner.

'Cuff, worked in Tricot with a Crochet Edge.

SLIPPER FOR A CHILD OF EIGHT OR TEN YEARS.

THIS pretty slipper is worked in plain tricot, and is quickly and easily made. The same in a larger size is suitable for lady's wear. Required, single Berlin wool, scarlet, grey, and white, about 1 oz. of each colour, a No. 8 tricot needle, a No. 9 bone crochet needle, a pair of cork soles, a piece of scarlet flannel for lining, and 1½ yards of narrow scarlet ribbon. Begin with the tricot needle and scarlet wool and do 6 chain for the toe. **1st row**—Pick up 1 tricot stitch in the third chain from the needle, 3 in the next (1 in the front, 1 in the back, and 1 in the front again), and 1 in each of the two last, making in all 7 stitches on the needle; draw back in the usual manner, and when 2 stitches remain on the needle take the white wool and draw through the 2 stitches with white, which brings a white stitch on the needle for the beginning of the next row! **2nd row**—With white wool,—Pick up 1 tricot stitch in each of 2 stitches, 3 in the centre stitch (1 in the horizontal thread on each side it), and 1 in each of the 3 last, making 9 stitches on the needle; draw back, and when 2 stitches remain on the needle take the grey wool and draw through the 2 stitches with grey, and so you get a grey stitch on the needle for the beginning of the next row. **3rd row**—With grey wool,—Pick up 1 tricot stitch in each of 3 stitches, 3 in the centre stitch, and 1 in each of the 4 last, making 11 stitches on the needle; draw back, and when 2 stitches remain on the needle resume the scarlet wool and draw through the 2 stitches with scarlet. You will by this time see how the work is executed, one row with each colour, scarlet, white, and grey, in rotation, and the colour is always changed upon the two last stitches in drawing back. **4th row**—With scarlet,—Pick up 1 tricot stitch in each of 4 stitches, 3 in the centre stitch, 1 in each of 5 stitches, and draw back. **5th row**—With white,—Pick up 1 tricot stitch in each of 5 stitches, 3 in the centre stitch, 1 in each of 6 stitches, and draw back. **6th row**—With grey,—Pick up 1 tricot stitch in each of 6 stitches, 3 in the centre stitch, 1 in each of 7 stitches, and draw back. And continue in this manner, always changing the colour, and always increasing on the centre stitch of every row, till in the **15th row**, which is worked with grey wool, you get 35 stitches on the needle, and sufficient is done for the front of the slipper. **16th row**—Begin the side of the slipper by working with scarlet wool, 14 stitches only, and proceed on 14 stitches till about 20 little rows are done, or until enough is worked to reach to the back of the heel. Work the other 14 side stitches in the same way. Sew the two side pieces together at the back of the heel. A **Trimming** of **Looped Crochet** is worked round the ankle. **1st round**—With grey wool,—Do 1 double crochet stitch and 1 looped stitch alternately; a looped stitch is made by passing the wool three times round the first and second fingers of the left hand, then insert the hook in the tricot and also under the wool that lies over the first finger, draw the wool through and finish as a double crochet stitch. **2nd round**—With scarlet wool,—Work a looped stitch on the double crochet and a double crochet on a looped stitch of last round. **3rd round**—With white wool—Work the same as preceding round. Line the slipper with scarlet flannel, and sew on to the sole. Make the other slipper to correspond. Divide the ribbon, and run a piece through the stitches of double crochet, and tie in a bow in front. Strong useful slippers for a lady or gentleman can be made by working with 3-thread or 4-thread fleecy wool from the above instructions.

Slipper for a Child of Eight or Ten Years.

SHOOTING OR TRAVELLING CAP FOR A LADY.

THIS cap will be found very comfortable to wear in the country or when travelling. In the engraving the tabs are represented as being tied on the top of the cap, out of the way, but they can be let down at pleasure over the ears, and form a complete protection against wind and draughts. A peak in front of the cap rests upon the forehead, and a small plume of looped knitting ornaments the top. Procure a No. 8 bone crochet needle, and 1 oz. of each of two colours in Fleecy wool or double Berlin; grey and dark red are two useful colours and harmonise with almost any dress. Begin with red wool, with 6 chain, and in this pick up 5 stitches, wool over the needle and draw through all the stitches on the needle, do 1 chain to tighten the group, and thus one point neige stitch (or shell stitch) is formed for the centre of the crown of the cap. **1st round**—With red wool,—Do 8 point neige stitches round the centre stitch, and at the end of the round join quite evenly to the beginning, and fasten off. **2nd round**—With grey wool,—Work 16 point neige stitches in the round, and again and always join quite evenly to the beginning, and fasten off securely. **3rd round**—With red wool,—Work 22 point neige stitches in the round. **4th round**—With grey,—Work 28 point neige stitches. **5th round**—With red,—Work 30 point neige stitches. **6th round**—With grey,—Work 30 point neige stitches. **7th round**—With red,—Again work 30 point neige; and now the head of the cap will be sufficiently large. For the **Peak**—**1st row**—With grey wool,—Work 12 point neige stitches over ten point neige of the last round of the cap, and fasten off. **2nd row**—With red wool,—Work 8 point neige stitches on the centre eight of the stitches of last row, and fasten off. For the **Tabs**—Hold the cap the wrong side out, and beginning close by the peak, work with grey wool a row of 4 point neige stitches, and fasten off. **2nd row**—With red wool,—Work a row of 4 stitches over the last small row. **3rd row**—With grey wool,—Again do 4 stitches. **4th row**—With red wool,—Work 3 point neige stitches, which should come over the centre of the four stitches of last row, leaving a little space each side, as the tab is to slant off to a point in the centre. **5th row**—With grey wool,—Work 3 stitches over the three of last row. **6th row**—With red wool,—Work 2 stitches. **7th row**—With grey wool,—Work 1 stitch only. Work the other tab to correspond. Finish off all the margin of the cap, the peak, and the tabs, with a row of double crochet with red wool, on which afterwards a line of single crochet is to be worked with grey to simulate a chain stitch braid. Make a **Plume** of looped knitting with No. 11 knitting needles, casting on 4 stitches, and knitting about 12 rows with alternate colours; sew this on the front of the cap above the peak, as shown in the engraving. From each of the tabs make a short length of chain with parti-coloured wool, which finish off with a small tassel at the end. When the tabs are turned upwards, the right side of the crochet

Shooting or Travelling Cap for a Lady.

is folded on the right side of the cap, as is seen in the illustration, the chain and tassels being tied on the top; but when the tabs are brought over the ears, and tied under the chin, the wrong side of the work appears outside.

WELDON'S
PRACTICAL CROCHET.

(THIRTEENTH SERIES.)

How to Crochet Pretty Quilt Squares, Borders, and Edgings.

TWENTY-FIVE ILLUSTRATIONS.

Telegraphic Address—]
"Consuelo," London.]

The Yearly Subscription to this Magazine, post free to any Part of the World, is 2s. 3d. Subscriptions are payable in advance, and may commence from any date and for any period.

Telephone—
2745.

The Back Numbers are always in print. Nos. 1 to 86 now ready, Price 2d. each, or post free for 15s. 4d. Over 5,000 Engravings.

INSERTION AND EDGING FOR A QUILT.

THIS handsome pattern may be worked with coarse cotton such as No. 4 and hook No. 12, but it looks exceedingly pretty when executed in very fine lace cotton, such as No. 50 of the D.M.C. make and a hook No. 20, and it is then appropriate for trimming underlinen. It is worked shortways. Make a foundation of 20 chain. **1st row**—Miss 3 chain, 1 treble in the fourth, 3 chain, 2 treble in the same stitch, 3 chain, miss 2, 1 double crochet in the third, 6 chain, miss 5, 1 double crochet in the sixth, 3 chain, miss 2, 2 treble, 3 chain, 2 treble in the next, 3 chain, miss 3, 1 treble. **2nd row**—Turn, 6 chain, 2 treble, 3 chain, 2 treble in the hole made by the 3 chain of the first row, 3 chain, 11 treble in the large hole, 3 chain, 2 treble, 3 chain, 2 treble in the last hole, 5 chain. **3rd row**—Turn, 2 treble, 3 chain, 2 treble in the first hole, 3 chain, 7 double crochet over the seven middle treble, taking up the back thread of each stitch, 3 chain, 2 treble, 3 chain, 2 treble in the next hole, 3 chain, 1 treble in the third of the 6 chain at the end of the row, 6 chain. **4th row**—Turn, 2 treble, 3 chain, 2 treble in the first hole, 5 chain, 3 double crochet over the middle three of the seven double crochet of the third row, taking up the back threads as before, 5 chain, 2 treble, 3 chain, 2 treble, 5 chain. **5th row**—Turn, 2 treble, 3 chain, 2 treble, 3 chain, 1 double crochet in the middle of the large loop of 5 chain, 6 chain, 1 double crochet in the next large loop, 3 chain, 2 treble, 3 chain, 2 treble into the last hole, * 3 chain, 1 treble in the third of the six chain at the end of the row, 6 chain. **6th row**—Turn, 2 treble, 3 chain, 2 treble, 3 chain, 11 treble in the large loop, 3 chain, 2 treble, 3 chain, 2 treble in the last hole, 5 chain. **7th row**—Turn, 2 treble, 3 chain, 2 treble, 3 chain, 7 double crochet, 3 chain, 2 treble, 3 chain, 2 treble, 3 chain *, 1 treble in the third of the six chain at the end of the row, 8 chain, loop these back with a slip-stitch into the third treble along the edge of the insertion. **8th row**—Turn, 21 treble into the loop of 8 chain, 3 chain. Now work as in the 4th row. **9th row**—Work according to the 5th row as far as *, then 3 chain, 1 treble over the first of the 21 treble of the preceding row, 9 chain, 1 double crochet over the middle treble of the preceding row, 9 chain, 1 double crochet over the last treble, loop into the next treble but one of the insertion. **10th row**—Turn, 21 treble into each loop, 3 chain; continue as in the 6th row. **11th row**—Work as in the 7th row as far as *, then 1 treble in the first of the 21 treble, 2 chain, miss 3, 1 treble, 2 chain, 1 treble, 1 treble all in the same stitch, 2 chain, miss 3, 1 double crochet, 2 chain, miss 3, 1 treble, 2 chain, 1 treble, 2 chain, 1 treble all in the same stitch, 2 chain, miss 3, 1 double crochet, 8 chain, miss 10, 1 double crochet, turn, 21 treble in the 8 chain, loop the last treble into the last double crochet with a slip-stitch, turn, 2 chain, miss 3, 1 treble, 2 chain, 1 treble, 2 chain, 1 treble into the fourth stitch, 2 chain, miss 3, 1 double crochet, 2 chain, miss 3, 1 treble, 2 chain, 1 treble, 2 chain, 1 treble into the fourth stitch, 2 chain, miss 3, 1 double crochet, 2 chain, miss 3,

1 treble, 2 chain, 1 treble; repeat until there are seven groups of 3 treble and chain, miss two holes, 1 double crochet in the third. **12th row**—Turn, * 3 chain, 1 double crochet in the first hole of 2 chain, 5 chain, 1 double crochet in the second hole, 3 chain, 1 double crochet over the next double crochet; repeat from * round the three scollops, 3 chain, then work as in the 4th row. **13th row**—5 chain, 2 treble, 3 chain, 2 treble, 3 chain, 1 double crochet in the large loop, 6 chain, 1 double crochet in the next large loop, 3 chain, 2 treble, 3 chain, 2 treble in the last hole, 3 chain, 1 treble in the third of the six chain at the end of the row, 6 chain. Repeat from the 2nd row.

Insertion and Edging for a Quilt.

SQUARE FOR QUILT.

THIS square has the advantage of giving a good effect at the expense of very little time and trouble. It should be worked with Strutts' cotton, No. 6 and a steel hook, No. 15. The work is begun in the middle. Make a ring of 8 chain and into it put 12 double crochet. **2nd round**—1 double crochet over a double crochet of the first round, 24 chain, 1 double crochet in the next stitch, * 16 chain, 1 double crochet in the next stitch, 16 chain, 1 double crochet in the next stitch, 24 chain, 1 double crochet; repeat from * till there are twelve loops altogether, eight short and four long; loop the last set of chain into the top of the 1st double crochet with a slip-stitch. Fasten off and run in the end tidily. Join the thread to the top of one of the short loops of chain, work 1 double crochet into the top of the loop, * 6 chain, 1 double crochet into the next short loop, 8 chain, 1 double crochet into the next long loop, 8 chain, 1 double crochet into the next short loop; repeat from *, and finish by looping the last 16 chain into the first double crochet with a slip-stitch. Now work six rows of double crochet, putting one double into every stitch of the preceding row except at the corners, where three stitches are worked into one to make the necessary increase. There should be one hundred and forty-eight double crochet in the last row. Turn the work at the end of every row and take up the back loops of the stitches so as to give a ribbed effect. After the 6th row of double crochet, turn, so as to crochet on the right side as usual, and work all round the square, alternately 1 treble, 1 chain, missing one stitch between each treble. In the corners, work 1 treble, 3 chain, 1 treble into the same stitch. The last round is worked thus:—1 double crochet into a hole made by the 1 chain of the proceeding round, * 1 chain, 1 double crochet in the next hole, 5 chain, 1 treble in the next hole; repeat from *. In the corner hole work 1 double crochet, 5 chain, 1 double crochet into the same stitch, then continue as before. There should be nine loops of 5 chain along each side of the square exclusive of the corners, and in joining the squares these large loops are worked in together as the last row is made, thus saving the trouble of employing a needle and thread for this purpose.

HEXAGON FOR QUILT IN TREFOIL WREATH PATTERN.

Use Strutts' cotton No. 8 and a steel hook No. 17 for this very pretty pattern and work rather tightly. The effect is particularly good if coloured cotton be used for the raised leaves and ordinary white thread for the background. The hexagon is begun in the middle with a ring of 9 chain. **1st round**—2 chain (for the first double crochet), 17 double crochet. Loop the last stitch into the second of the first 2 chain to make the circle quite regular in shape. **2nd round**—3 chain (for one treble) * 1 chain, 1 treble in the next stitch; repeat from *, and at the end, loop the last stitch into the 1st. with a slip-stitch. **3rd round**—2 chain (for one double crochet), 4 double crochet, * 3 double crochet into the next stitch, 5 double crochet,

Square for Quilt.

repeat from * finishing off as usual with a slip-stitch at the end of the round. This row shapes the hexagon, so there should be six increasings with six sets of double crochet between them, making forty-eight stitches in all. **4th round**—Work 5 double crochet, 1 trefoil, 3 double crochet, increase in the corner, * 3 double crochet. A trefoil is worked thus :—After the third double crochet, work 1 single in the 4th, 5 chain, 1 double crochet, 3 treble into these chain, missing the one nearest the hook, then 1 single into the double crochet into which the previous single was worked, 7 chain, miss the one nearest the hook, and work into the others, 1 double crochet, 5 treble, 1 single into the double crochet, 5 chain, 1 double crochet, 3 treble, 1 single, then 3 double crochet, increase in the corner and repeat from *. **5th round**—Double crochet into every stitch. There should be nine stitches along each side. Increase as usual in the corners. **6th round**—Work 11 double crochet along each side and three in one at the corners. In making the first of the three corner stitches, put the hook through the tip of the side leaf of the trefoil that is nearest the corner, then work the second corner stitch, and in making the third, take in the next leaf of the next trefoil, work 11 double crochet and repeat, taking in each leaf in turn. **7th round**—Work 13 double crochet along each side; increase in the corners as usual. **8th round**—Increase as usual. At the sides, work 7 double crochet, with the 8th, take in the tip of the middle leaf of the trefoil, 7 double crochet. **9th round**—17 double crochet along each side. Increase as usual. **10th round**—5 double crochet, 1 trefoil, 7 double crochet, 1 trefoil, 5 double crochet along the sides. Work the corners in the usual way. **11th round**—Work 19 double crochet along each side, and increase at the corners. **12th round**—Work 1 double crochet only, in the corners, then one double crochet taking in a side leaf of a trefoil, 9 double crochet, take in the tips of the next trefoil with that of the first one, with the 10th double crochet, 9 double crochet, 1 double crochet taking in a leaf, 1 double crochet in the corner. Continue all round. **13th round**—Work 21 double crochet along each side and increase as usual in the corners. **14th round**—Double crochet into every stitch; work 23 along each side but do not increase in the corners. **15th round**—Along the side, work 7 double crochet, take in the extreme tip of the middle leaf of the trefoil in working the 8th, then work 7 double crochet, increase by working three stitches in one in each corner. **16th round**—Work one double crochet into every stitch of the preceding round. No increase will be needed in the corners, and there should be twenty-five stitches along each side. **17th round**—Increase by working three double crochet into the corner stitch, then make 1 double crochet, 1 leaf; (a leaf is made thus—5 chain, miss the stitch nearest the hook, and work 1 double crochet into the next, then 3 treble into the following

3 chain, miss 3 stitches of the preceding row, 1 double crochet into the 4th). After the last leaf of a side, work the double crochet which holds it in place, then the 3 double crochet into the corner stitch. There should be five leaves along each side. **18th round**—Behind each leaf work 3 chain, put 2 double crochet between each leaf and one into the corners. **19th round**—Work double crochet into every stitch not forgetting to put 1 into each of the three chain that were worked behind the leaves. Increase in the corners in the usual way. **20th round**—In this round must be taken in the tips of the leaves exactly as the tips of the trefoils were fastened in preceding rounds. The stitch which secures the leaves must be that which is worked exactly over the second chain of the three that were worked behind the leaves in the 18th round. This will leave 4 double crochet to be worked between each leaf. No increase will be needed in the corners. **21st round**—Work 1 double crochet into each stitch of the preceding row and increase in the corners in the usual way. These directions are according to the work as done by a very tight worker, but one who crochets loosely will perhaps find it necessary to make some alterations in the increasings in the corners, especially in the last few rounds; this will make no difference in the general appearance of the pattern provided that the stated number of stitches be left between each trefoil and each of the single leaves beyond them.

STRIPE FOR QUILT IN GREEK KEY PATTERN.

This favourite pattern looks well both in fine cotton, such as No. 10 (hook No. 18), and in coarse cotton, such as No. 6, (hook No. 15), but it is of course necessary that it shall be worked with two colours, scarlet and white having been used in the original. It is by no means difficult to execute, but care must be taken to get the position and number of the stitches correct or the pattern will not be perfect. Any geometric pattern can be worked in the way in which this is managed, and the quilts thus made have a remarkably bright and cheerful appearance. So great, too, is the variety to be had in coloured knitting cotton just now that the work can readily be made to match the predominating colour of any room. In working with two shades of cotton a little care is necessary in managing the two balls of thread that are required. The colour that is finished with for the moment must be kept on the wrong side of the work while the second colour is being used. When this is done with, it also is kept on the wrong side, the first thread being taken across the back of the work to the place where it is next required. Also, when working the last treble before beginning another colour, leave the two

Hexagon for Quilt in Trefoil Wreath Pattern.

last loops of the stitch on the hook and draw the second colour through them. The object of this is to prevent the second colour from straying into the first. The worker must not forget thus to take the second kind of cotton to complete the last worked stitch of the first colour. For the strip as illustrated, begin by making a foundation of chain the length required. **1st row**—3 chain (for one treble), 1 treble into every stitch. **2nd row**—Turn, 4 chain, miss 1 treble, 1 treble in the second stitch, * 1 chain, miss 1, 1 treble; repeat from *. **3rd row**—Turn, 3 chain (for one treble), 1 treble into every stitch. Fasten off at the end of the row. **4th row**—Join the cotton at the right-hand end of the strip, 3 chain (for one treble), 3 treble with white. Join on the colour and work 20 treble with it, 4 treble with white, * 20 coloured treble, 4 white treble; repeat from * all along. Fasten off and begin again at the other end. **5th row**—3 chain (for one treble), 3 white treble, * 4 red treble, 12 white treble, 4 red treble, 4 white treble; repeat from * all along. Fasten off and begin again as usual at the other end. **6th row**—3 chain (for one treble,

3 white treble, * 4 red treble, 4 white treble, 12 red treble, 4 white treble; repeat from *. **7th row**—3 chain (for one treble), 3 white treble, * 4 red treble, 4 white treble, 4 red treble, 12 white treble; repeat from * all along. **8th row**—3 red chain, and 7 red treble, 4 white treble, * 20 red treble, 4 white treble; repeat from * all along. **9th row**—Cut away the coloured cotton for the rest of the strip is worked with white only. 1 treble into every stitch. **10th row**—Like the 2nd. **11th row**—1 treble into every stitch. Run all the ends of cotton in neatly on the wrong side at the ends of the strip. Care must be taken that in passing the cotton across the back that it is not drawn too tightly, or it will be apt to pull the work out of shape.

EDGING FOR QUILT. TUFTED VANDYKE PATTERN.

THIS rich-looking lace is worked lengthwise, but it is not necessary to cut off th thread at the end of every row. The work should be turned, and the

Stripe for a Quilt in Greek Key Pattern.

stitches put into the back loops of those in the preceding row. It looks best in coarse cotton, such as No. 6, worked with a steel hook No. 15. Make a foundation chain the length required **1st row**—1 treble, * 1 chain, miss one, 1 treble: repeat from * all along. **2nd row**—Work this row all crossed trebles, thus * put the cotton twice round the hook, put it into the first chain of preceding row, cotton once round the hook, draw it through, cotton once round the hook, draw it through two loops, leave the three still there, put the cotton once round the hook, miss two stitches of the last row, put the hook into the third and draw the cotton through. There are now five loops on the hook, cotton round the hook, draw it through two loops, cotton round hook, draw it through two, cotton round hook, draw it through, 2 chain, 1 treble into the top of the two lower trebles. Repeat from * all along. **3rd row**—Like the 1st. **4th row**—18 double crochet, * 1 tuft made as in the centre of quilt, 3 double crochet; repeat from * six times more, making seven tufts, then repeat from the beginning of the row. **5th row**—5 double crochet, * 8 chain, miss 8 double crochet, 35 double crochet; repeat from *. **6th row**—3 double crochet, * 2 chain, miss 2 double crochet, 11 treble into the loop of 8 chain, 2 chain, miss 2 double crochet, 5 double crochet, work six tufts as above, 5 double crochet; repeat from *. **7th row**—Work double crochet behind the tufts as in the 5th row, 2 chain, miss the chain and the two last double crochet, 4 treble over the first 4 treble of the last row, 2 treble in the 5th stitch, 1 treble in the 6th, 2 treble in the 7th, 1 treble in each of the next four. **8th row**—There should be five tufts in this row, then after the 2 chain, work 5 treble, 2 treble into the sixth stitch, 1 treble in the 7th, 2 treble in the 8th, 1 treble into each of the next five. **9th row**—Work double crochet over and between the tufts. After the 2 chain, work 5 treble, 2 treble into the next stitch, 1 treble, 3 treble into the next stitch, 1 treble, 2 treble into the next stitch, 5 treble, 2 chain, miss 2 double crochet and repeat. **10th row**—Put 5 tufts into the vandykes in this row. After the first 2 chain, work 1 treble into the first of the 18 treble, * 1 chain, miss one, 1 treble on the second stitch; repeat from * eight times, then work the 2 chain, and the double crochet and tufts as usual. **11th row**—Work double crochet over and between the tufts. After the 2 chain, work the holes as in the preceding row, but put 2 chain instead of 1 between each treble. **12th row**—In this row do not miss the 2 double crochet before and after the tufts. Work 4 tufts and the holes as in the 11th row. **13th row**—Work double crochet as usual over and between the tufts and 3 chain instead of 2 for the holes. **14th row**—Miss 1 double crochet only, before and after the groups of tufts in future, 3 tufts and 3 chain for the holes. **15th row**—Double crochet over and between the tufts. Make the holes of 4 chain instead of three. **16th row**—Put two tufts only into the vandykes in this row and work 4 chain for the holes, as in the 15th row. **17th row**—Work double crochet above and between the tufts, then 2 chain, miss the first 2 chain of the

previous row, and work double crochet on the top of all the holes. **18th row**—After the first 2 chain of the 17th row, miss 2 and work 7 double crochet, * 1 tuft, 3 double crochet; repeat from * until there are nine tufts, 7 double crochet, 1 tuft; repeat from the beginning of the row. **19th row**—1 double crochet into every stitch. **20th row**—2 chain, 1 picot of 5 chain (5 chain, 1 double crochet into the first stitch), 2 chain, miss 2, 1 double crochet.

OCTAGON FOR QUILT. SCOLLOP PATTERN IN TWO COLOURS.

THIS pattern requires cotton No. 6, and a steel hook No. 15. The scollops should be worked with coloured cotton upon a white background, and in the original model the small squares which connect the octagons were worked with white cotton only. Commence the octagon by making the small cross in the middle—9 chain, 1 treble on the seventh chain from the hook, 3 chain, 1 single on the first of the nine chain, 5 chain, 1 treble at the bottom of the first-made treble, 4 chain, miss 2 chain, 1 single on the third. **1st round**—3 chain (for one treble), 2 treble, * 2 chain, 3 treble into one of the holes of the preceding round, 2 chain, 3 treble; repeat from * all round, and loop the last stitch to the third of the first three chain. Always remember thus to connect the first and last stitches of every round, so as to conceal as far as possible the place where each round is joined. **2nd round**—2 chain (for one double crochet), 1 double crochet into every stitch. **3rd round**—In the corner (the corners are made exactly over every hole made by the chain in the 1st round), work one double crochet, 2 chain, 1 double crochet in the next stitch. Then make 1 double crochet, take the coloured cotton, draw it through the loop on the hook and work with it 1 double crochet 5 treble, 1 double crochet in the next stitch, leave the coloured thread at the back of the work, draw the white cotton through the loop, and make one double crochet in the next stitch. Repeat from the beginning of the row. There should be eight coloured scollops altogether. **4th round**—In the corners work 1 double crochet, 2 chain, 1 double crochet; the rest of the round is done by working 1 double crochet into every stitch of the 3rd round and 1 chain behind each scollop. **5th round**—After working 1 double crochet, 2 chain, 1 double crochet in the corner, make 1 double crochet, 1 scollop, 3 double crochet (the second of which is put into the chain-stitch behind the scollops), 1 scollop, 1 double crochet; repeat from the beginning of the row. **6th round**—In the corner work * 1 treble, 2 chain, 1 treble, then 2 treble, 1 chain behind the scollop, 3 treble, 1 chain, 2 treble;

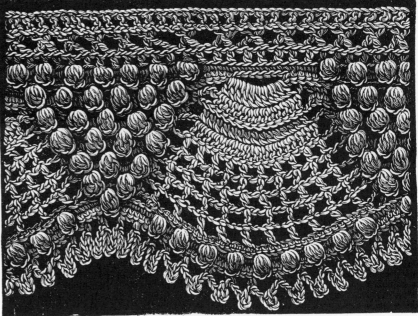

Edging for Quilt. Tufted Vandyke Pattern.

repeat from *. **7th round**—* 1 treble, 2 chain, 1 treble in the corner, 11 treble along the side; repeat from * all round. **8th round**—1 double crochet, 2 chain, 1 double crochet in the corner, * 1 double crochet, 1 scollop; repeat from * five times, 1 double crochet; then repeat from the beginning of the row. **9th round**—1 double crochet, 2 chain, 1 double crochet in the corner, 2 double crochet, * 1 chain behind the scollop, 1 double crochet over the double crochet of the 8th round; repeat from *, then work the corner. **10th round**—In the corner hole work 1 treble, 2 chain, 1 treble, 2 treble, * 1 chain, miss one, 3 treble; repeat from * till the corner is reached, then make 2 treble, 1 treble, 2 chain, 1 treble in the corner, 2 treble and repeat from * all round. **11th round**—Take the coloured cotton, which has until now been used for the scollops alone, and work with it a row of double crochet putting one into the back loop of every stitch of the preceding row. **12th round**—In the corner work 1 treble, 3 chain, 1 treble in the next stitch, then 3 treble, * 1 chain, miss 1, 3 treble; repeat from * till the corner is reached, then work again from the beginning of the round.

For the small square which connects the octagon, begin with 9 chain, 1 treble on the seventh chain from the hook, 3 chain, 1 single on the first of the 9 chain, 5 chain, 1 treble at the bottom of the first-made treble, 4 chain, miss 2 chain, 1 single on the third. **1st round**—3 chain (for one treble), 2 treble * 3 chain, 3 treble into one of the holes of the preceding round, 3 chain, 3 treble; repeat from * all round. **2nd round**—In the corner work 2 treble, 3 chain, 3 treble, then 6 treble on the top of the 6 treble of the preceding round, and taking up the back loops of the stitches; repeat from the beginning of the round. **3rd round**—Work 2 treble, 3 chain, 2 treble, in the corner, then 10 treble and repeat from the beginning of the round. **4th round**—* 2 treble, 3 chain, 2 treble in the hole in the corner, 14 treble; then repeat from *. If it is thought advisable to mix a little colour with the squares, it can best be done by beginning with it and working to the end of the 1st round; make the two following rounds white, and finish by taking

Octagon for Quilt. Scollop Pattern in Two Colours.

the colour again in the 4th round. The worker must be particularly careful to join the first and last stitches neatly in every round, as so simple and close a pattern as this would be greatly marred by any irregularity. It will be found far easier to manage if each round can be commenced in the corner, beginning with the first of the corner treble, which must of course be always represented by 3 chain. A practised worker will have no difficulty in thus managing to conceal any weak points there may chance to be in her pattern.

TASSEL FRINGE WITH OPEN-WORK HEADING FOR QUILT.

THIS fringe is worked shortways, the heading being made first and the strands looped in afterwards. Use a medium-sized cotton, such as No. 8 and a steel hook, No. 16. Begin with 16 chain, join them into a ring, 2 chain, 2 double crochet, 1 picot (5 chain with 1 double crochet in the first), * 2 double crochet, 1 picot, 3 double crochet, 1 picot, 2 double crochet, 12 chain, take the hook out of the last loop, put it into the second of the last 3 double crochet, draw the loop of chain through, work 1 chain and into the loop work 3 double crochet, 1 picot, 2 double crochet, 1 picot, 3 double crochet, 1 picot, 2 double crochet, 12 chain looped into the second stitch of the previous 3 double crochet; into this ring, work as before, 1 chain, 3 double crochet, 1 picot, 2 double crochet, 1 picot, 3 double crochet, 1 picot, 3 double crochet, 1 picot, 2 double crochet, 1 picot, 3 double crochet, 1 double crochet, in next ring of chain, 1 picot, 2 double crochet, 1 picot, 3 double crochet, 1 double crochet in last loop (that is, the second half of the ring of 16 chain with which the work was begun), 1 picot, 2 double crochet, 1 picot, 3 double crochet. This finishes the first row of three rings one above another. Begin with 20 chain, take out the hook, put it into the 5th chain and draw the last loop through. This makes a corresponding ring to the first one of 16 chain, work 1 chain, and put into the ring, 3 double crochet, 1 picot. In making this picot, take the hook out of the third chain, put it into the third stitch of the last picot on the first ring of the last row and draw it through. Remember always to loop the first picot of one ring to the last picot of the one next to it. Begin again from *. In this

second row, there should be five rings, and in the third row, three again like the first. Go on working in this way until a sufficient length has been made. The pattern of the heading is capable of infinite variations according to the number of rings worked in each row. By working three, six, ten, six, three rings, instead of three and five a pretty and deep vandyked border is made which needs a tassel only between each point. The straight edge of the heading is worked thus:—**1st row**—8 double into the rings, 6 double into the smaller spaces of 4 chain between the rings. **2nd row**—Turn and put * 1 treble, 3 chain, 1 treble into one of the double of the last row, 3 chain, miss 8 double; repeat from * all along. **3rd row**—Turn, * 3 chain, 1 double crochet, 3 chain, 1 double crochet, 2 chain, 1 double crochet into the first hole made by the 3 chain, 2 chain; repeat from *.

For each tassel, cut ninety-six strands of cotton about six inches long, draw them through the last ring of one of the rows, fold them in half and tie them round tightly just below the ring. Add one of these tassels to each of the edge rings, with care to tie them round very firmly. Finally, cut off the ends straight. In the original this fringe was worked with Strutts' cotton, No. 8 and a steel hook No. 18, but it must correspond with the size of those used for any quilt of which it is to form the finish. The fringe has a particularly handsome appearance if made in black silk and used as a dress or mantle trimming.

HEXAGON FOR QUILT IN FLUTED PATTERN.

THIS very handsome pattern looks well if worked either with Strutts' knitting cotton No. 6 and a steel hook No. 14, or with unbleached cotton. Indeed, a beautiful quilt may be made by working the centre in unbleached cotton, the openwork rows in white, and the border again in the unbleached thread. Begin with 6 chain and join them into a ring. **1st round**—3 chain, 17 treble into the ring, join the last treble to the last of the 3 chain with a slip-stitch. **2nd round**—2 chain, 1 double in the first stitch, * 2 double in the next stitch; repeat from * all round and fasten the last double to the second of the chain stitches with a slip-stitch. **3rd round**—7 chain, * miss 1, 1 double crochet in the second stitch, 5 chain; repeat from * all round. At the end of the round fasten the last of the 5 chain to the second of the

Tassel Fringe with Open-Work Heading for Quilt.

7 chain with which the row was begun. There should be eighteen holes. **4th round**—2 chain, 1 double crochet into the second stitch of last round, * 3 double crochet into next stitch (this gives an increase of two stitches and will in future be described by the word "increase" only), 2 double crochet, miss 1, 2 double crochet; repeat from * all round and at the end loop the last double crochet into the second of the 2 chain. These two chain represent a double crochet stitch, and it must be understood that every row of double crochet is thus begun. In future rounds, the number of the double crochet will be given without any special mention of the chain which are to represent the first stitch. **5th round**—* 3 double crochet, increase, 3 double crochet; repeat from *, and loop the last and first stitches together at the end of the round. **6th round**—* 4 double crochet, increase, 4 double crochet; repeat from * all round. **7th round**—* 5 double crochet, increase, 5 double crochet; repeat. **8th round**—* 6 double crochet, increase, 6 double crochet; repeat. **9th round**—* 7 double crochet, increase, 7 double crochet; repeat. **10th**

round—* 8 double crochet, increase, 8 double crochet; repeat. **11th round**—* 9 double crochet, increase, 9 double crochet; repeat. By this time the seven rows of double crochet have become very full, and, in order to make them set, they must be caught down into little pleats, thus—**12th round**—Fold two of the points made by increasing together and work 3 single stitches through both edges of the double crochet at the end of the pleat, that is, farthest away from the point, 3 chain, fold the next two points together, work 3 single, as before, through both edges, 3 chain, and repeat from the beginning of the round. The pleats should of course set quite evenly, and if the directions have been correctly followed, they should be eighteen in number. **13th round**—* 17 double crochet, increase; repeat from * five times. **14th round**—All double crochet, increasing at the corners in the usual way. **15th round**—All double crochet, increasing at the corners. **16th round**—1 double crochet, 6 treble in the next stitch, take out the hook, put it into the top of the first treble and draw the loop through, thus forming a tuft, * 2 double crochet, 1 tuft; repeat from * till within one of the corner, 1 double crochet, † increase in the corner, 1 double crochet, 1 tuft, 2 double crochet, 1 tuft; repeat from * five times, 1 double crochet, repeat from † four times, then 1 double crochet, 1 tuft, 1 double crochet. **17th round**—Work 1 double crochet over each tuft, and two between each tuft. Increase in each corner. **18th round**—All double crochet, increasing in the corners. **19th round**—All double crochet, increasing in the corners. There should be altogether 180 double crochet when this round is finished. **20th round**—4 chain, * miss 1, 1 treble in the second double crochet, 1 chain; repeat from * and in the corner stitch, work 1 treble, 1 chain, 1 long. Then 1 chain, † miss 1, 1 treble, 1 chain; repeat from † thirteen times, and increase in the corner by working two treble as before with 1 chain between them. Repeat, and after working the last corner, make 1 chain, 1 treble, 1 chain, 1 treble till the round is completed, making a slip-stitch to unite the first and last stitches. **21st round**—All double crochet, increasing at the corners by working three stitches in one as usual. **22nd round**—5 chain, * 1 double crochet into the third double crochet of last round, 3 chain; repeat from * and in the corner work 1 double crochet, 3 chain, 1 double crochet, † 3 chain, * miss 2, 1 double, 3 chain; repeat from * nine times, increase in the corner as above; repeat from † four times, and at the end work 3 chain, 1 double crochet, 1 slip-stitch into the first of the row. There should be eleven holes along each side, not including those in the corners. **23rd round**—* 1 double crochet, increase, 1 double crochet; repeat from * all round. **24th round**—* 2 double crochet, increase, 2 double crochet; repeat from *. **25th round**—3 double crochet, increase, 3 double crochet; repeat from *. In the **26th round** the three last rows of double crochet are pleated up as described in the 12th round, but, as the folds are smaller here, two single and two chain are worked instead of three. **27th round**—Work 1 double crochet between each pleat, and 2 double crochet over each pleat. Increase at the corners in the usual way. **28th round**—4 chain, * miss 1 stitch, 1 treble in the second, 1 chain; repeat from *. In the corner stitches work 1 treble, 1 chain, 1 treble into one stitch. There should be nineteen holes along each side, not counting those at the corners. At the end, loop the last chain into the third of the first 4 chain stitches with a slip-stitch, and fasten off the end of the thread neatly.

HEXAGON. STAR PATTERN.

FOR this very handsome and effective pattern it is well to use Strutts' cotton No. 6 and a steel hook No. 15. Begin in the middle by making a ring of 12 chain. **1st round**—3 chain (for one treble), 27 treble into the ring; loop the last treble to the third of the chain with a slip-stitch so as to hide the join in the circle. **2nd round**—4 chain (the first 3 serve as one treble), 5 treble into the first treble, take the hook out of the last loop, put it into the

top of the first of the 5 treble and draw the loop through, draw the cotton through the loop now on the hook to close the tuft at the top, * 1 chain, 1 treble in the next stitch, 1 chain, 1 tuft, as before, in the next stitch; repeat from *. There must be altogether fourteen tufts with 1 chain, 1 treble, 1 chain between each. Close the round by looping the last chain stitch to the third of the first 4 chain. **3rd round**—4 chain, 1 treble into the back of the first tuft, 1 chain * 1 tuft over the 1 treble of the preceding round, 1 chain, 2 treble over the next tuft; repeat from *. There should be fourteen tufts in this round also and they are arranged so as to alternate with these previously worked. **4th round**—3 chain (to serve as one treble stitch), 2 chain, 1 treble into the next stitch of the third round, * 2 chain, miss 2, 1 treble into the third stitch; repeat from * three times. There should be four holes; then work 2 chain, 1 treble into the same hole as the last; repeat from * all round, making thirty holes altogether. This round, it will be noticed, begins to shape the hexagon. **5th round**—2 chain (to serve as one double crochet stitch), then 1 double crochet into every stitch of the preceding round, taking up the back loop of the stitches. At the end, loop the last stitch into the top of the first 2 chain. **6th round**—In the corner holes work * 1 treble, 2 chain, 1 treble, then 1 treble into the next stitch (taking up the back loop), 1 tuft, 3 treble, 1 tuft, 3 treble, 1 tuft, 3 treble, 1 tuft, 1 treble; repeat from *. **7th round**—1 treble, 2 chain, 1 treble in the corner, then 4 treble, 1 tuft (this must come between two tufts of the preceding round), 3 treble, 1 tuft, 3 treble, 1 tuft, 4 treble; repeat from the beginning of the round. **8th round**—1 treble, 1 chain, 1 treble in the corner, then 6 treble, 1 tuft, 3 treble, 1 tuft, 6 treble; repeat from the beginning of the round. **9th round**—1 treble, 1 chain, 1 treble in the corner hole, 10 treble, 1 tuft, 10 treble; repeat all round. **10th round**—In the corner work 1 double crochet, 2 chain, 1 double crochet, and work 12 double crochet along each side. **11th round**—1 treble, 3 chain, 1 treble in the corner, then * 1 treble, 1 tuft; repeat from * until there are twelve tufts, and work from the corner in the same way. **12th round**—1 double crochet into every stitch along the sides, 5 double crochet into the hole in each corner made by the 3 chain of the preceding row. This row completes the hexagon.

OCTAGON FOR QUILT IN WATER-LILY PATTERN.

THIS pattern lends itself most satisfactorily to the use of rather coarse knitting cotton, such as Strutts' No. 6 and a steel crochet hook No. 15. Make a ring of 8 chain. **1st round**—2 chain (for 1 double crochet) 15 double crochet, join the last double crochet with a slip-stitch to the second chain. **2nd round**—2 chain (for 1 double crochet), 1 double crochet in the 2 chain with which the first round was begun, 2 double crochet in every stitch, making thirty-two double crochet in all. **3rd round**—5 chain (the first 3 answer to one treble), miss one, 1 treble in the second stitch, * 2 chain, miss 1, 1 treble; repeat from *. Loop the last two chain to the third stitch of the first five chain. There should be sixteen holes. **4th round**—1 double crochet into the first hole of the preceding row, * 17 chain, miss three, 14 treble on the remaining 14 chain, 1 double crochet in the same hole as that in which the first double crochet was worked, 2 chain, miss one hole, 1 double crochet in the next; repeat from * seven times. **5th round**—* 14 treble upon the bottom threads of the 14 treble of the last round, 1 double crochet in the top stitch, 14 single upon the top of the set of treble worked in the fourth round; repeat from * seven times. **6th round**—Work at the back of the first eight leaves, 1 double crochet into the hole that was missed between the first and second leaves of the fourth round, * 17 chain, miss 3, 14 treble on the remaining 14 chain, 1 double crochet in the hole in which the first double crochet was worked, 2 chain, miss 1 hole, 1 double crochet in the next; repeat from * seven times. **7th round**—* 14 treble, upon the bottom threads of the

Hexagon for Quilt in Fluted Pattern.

14 treble of the last round, 1 double crochet in the top stitch, 14 single upon the top of the set of treble worked in the 6th round; repeat from * seven times. At the end of the row work 14 single up the edge of the next leaf. **8th round—** * 1 double crochet in the double crochet that was worked at the tip of the leaf, 3 chain, 1 double crochet in the same stitch, 6 chain, 1 double crochet in the tip of the next leaf (this should be an underneath one), 6 chain; repeat from * seven times. **9th round—**1 single on the top of the first double crochet in the corner, 1 single in the hole, 3 chain (for a treble), 1 treble in the corner hole, 3 chain, 2 treble in the same hole, 6 chain, 1 double crochet over the double crochet in the tip of the leaf, 6 double crochet on the next 6 chain, * 2 treble in the corner hole, 3 chain, 2 treble in the same hole, 6 double crochet on the 6 chain, 1 double crochet in the tip of the leaf, 6 double crochet on the next 6 chain; repeat from * six times. Loop the last treble to the 3rd chain in the corner. **10th round—**1 single on the 2nd treble in the corner and 1 single in the hole, 3 chain (for 1 treble), 1 treble, 3 chain, 2 treble in the same hole, 2 chain, miss 2, 13 treble, * 2 chain, miss 2, 2 treble, 3 chain, 2 treble in the same hole, 2 chain, miss 2, 13 treble; repeat from * six times. Join the last treble to the 3rd of the first three chain in the corner. **11th round—**1 single on the second corner treble, 1 single in the hole, 3 chain (for 1 treble), 1 treble, 3 chain, 2 treble in the same hole, 2 chain, 2 treble in the next hole, 13 treble, 2 treble in the next hole, * 2 chain, 2 treble, 3 chain, 2 treble in the corner hole, 2 chain, 2 treble in the next hole, 13 treble, 2 treble in next hole; repeat from *. Loop the last chain to the top of the first treble in the corner. **12th round—**1 single on the second corner treble,

HANDSOME OPEN SQUARE.

THE sizes of the cotton and hook used for this square must depend upon the purpose for which it is wanted, and the pattern itself has the somewhat unusual merit of looking well, either in coarse cotton such as No. 6 (hook No 15) or fine cotton such as No. 12 (hook No. 18). The three large trefoils are made first. Begin with 12 chain joined in a ring. Into the ring work 40 treble (3 chain for the first one), join the last stitch to the 3rd chain stitch with a slip-stitch. **2nd round—**4 double crochet (2 chain for the first one), 1 single in the first, 10 chain, 1 single into the first, 8 chain, 1 single in the first, then 1 single again into the top of the first single that was worked after the first 8 chain. This forms three picots and full directions for making them will not be given again; 10 double crochet, 3 picots, 10 double crochet, 3 picots, 10 double crochet, 3 picots, 5 double crochet; loop the last stitch into the second of the first 2 chain with a slip-stitch. **3rd round—**10 chain, 1 double crochet into the middle of the second picot, 8 chain, 1 double crochet between the next two groups of picots, 6 chain, 1 double crochet into the next large picot, 6 chain, 1 double crochet between the next two groups of picots, 8 chain, 1 double crochet into the next large picot, 8 chain, 1 single into the second of the first ten chain. **4th round—**Turn, and work 3 chain, 19 treble into the space made by the 10 chain, 20 treble into the next space, 16 treble into

Octagon for a Qui

Hexagon. Star Pattern.

1 single in the hole, 3 chain (for one treble), 1 treble, 3 chain, 2 treble in the same hole, 2 chain, 2 treble in the next hole, * 2 chain, 2 treble, 3 chain, 2 treble in the corner hole, 2 chain, 2 treble in the next hole, 17 treble, 2 treble in the next hole; repeat from *. Loop the last chain to the top of the first treble in the corner. **13th round—**1 single on the 2nd corner treble, 2 chain (for one double crochet), 2 double crochet, 3 double crochet in the second of the corner 3 chain, 3 double crochet, miss 2, 21 double crochet, * miss 2, 3 double crochet in the corner stitch, 3 double crochet, miss 2, 21 double crochet; repeat from * and at the end catch the last loop to the first stitch and fasten off neatly.

To make the square for joining between the octagons—Work a length of 36 chain. **1st row—**Miss 4 chain and work 32 treble, putting one into each chain stitch. **2nd row—**Turn, 3 chain (for one treble), 2 treble, * 3 chain, miss 3 treble, 1 treble in the fourth; repeat from * 5 times, then 3 chain, 3 treble in the last three stitches. **3rd row—**Turn, 3 chain, 2 treble, 3 chain, miss 3, 21 treble, 3 chain, miss 3, 3 treble in the last three stitches. **4th row—**Turn, 3 chain, 2 treble, miss 3, 3 treble over the first three of the 21 treble, * 3 chain, miss 3, 1 treble; repeat twice from *, then 3 chain, miss 3, 3 treble, 3 chain, miss 3, 3 treble. **5th row—**Turn, 3 chain, 2 treble, 3 chain, miss 3, 3 treble, 3 chain, 9 treble, 3 chain, miss 3, 3 treble, 3 chain, miss 3, 3 treble. **6th row—**Like the 5th. **7th row—**Like the 4th. **8th row—**Like the 3rd. **9th row—**Like the 2nd. **10th row—**Like the 1st. Fasten off. Begin at a corner and work 2 treble, 3 chain, 2 treble into the same stitch *, 3 chain, miss 3, 1 treble in the 4th stitch; repeat from * all round.

the loop made by the 6 chain, 16 treble in the next, then 20 treble into each remaining space, loop the last stitch to the top of the 3 chain. **5th round—**Turn, and work 4 double crochet (2 chain for the first stitch), 1 picot of 5 chain with 1 single in the first, 4 double crochet, * 1 picot, 4 double crochet; repeat from * till within 2 stitches of the end of the scollop; miss these two and two of the next scollop, then 4 double crochet, 1 picot, repeat from * all round. In beginning and ending this round the two picots of eight chain made in the 2nd round must be looped in with the first and last stitches. In making the remaining three trefoils, the seventh and tenth and eleventh picots must be looped to those of the adjoining trefoil, as shown in the illustration.

The framework of the square is worked next. Begin by joining the thread to one of the picots of 10 chain at the base of one of the trefoils. **1st round—** 12 chain, miss 1 picot, 1 double crochet in the second, 4 chain, 1 treble in the next picot, * 39 chain, 1 treble in the third picot before the large picots of the next trefoil, 4 chain, 1 double crochet in the next picot, 9 chain, 1 treble in the large picot, 9 chain, miss 1 picot, 1 double crochet in the second picot, 4 chain, 1 double crochet in the next; repeat from *. After the last 9 chain, loop into the 3rd stitch of the first 9 chain, then work a row of double crochet, taking up the back threads of the chain stitches and putting 3 double crochet in the twentieth chain of the 39, to form the corners. **3rd round—**Turn and work double crochet as before, taking the back threads and putting three stitches into the corner stitch. **4th round**—Same as the 3rd round. **5th round**—There should be seventy-five double crochet along each side of the square; turn and work this round with the right side of the work towards you in the ordinary way. The round is begun in the middle of one of the sides. Work 1 tuft of 5 treble in one double of last round, take out the hook, put it into the top of the first treble and draw the last loop through. This tuft should come exactly in the middle of the side, * 5 double crochet, 1 tuft. Repeat from * five times; there should be seven tufts. Work 1 double crochet, † 1 tuft in the corner, 1 double crochet, 1 tuft * * 5 double crochet, 1 tuft; repeat from * * eleven times. This brings it to the corner again; repeat from †. After the last corner work six tufts with 5 double crochet between them, 5 double crochet and loop the last one into the first tuft. There should be thirteen tufts along each side, exclusive of the one in the corner, and fifty-six in all. **6th round**—All double crochet. Work 5 double crochet between each tuft, and one double crochet at the back of each. At the back of the corner tuft work 3 double crochet to make the necessary increase. There should be 312 double crochet in all. **7th round**—Turn. All double crochet with the usual increase in the corners. There should be 320 stitches. **8th round**—Turn, and work double crochet as before. **9th round**—Turn, and work alternately 1 long

SQUARE FOR QUILT IN RIB AND SHELL PATTERN.

THIS is a pattern which has a far better effect when worked in coarse cotton than when made with fine thread. Strutts' No. 4 and a bone hook No. 10 wi suit average workers, but those work very loosely may prefer a somewhat larger hook. Begin with a foundation of 12 chain for the small ribbed square in the middle, turn, miss 1, 10 double crochet, 2 chain, turn, 10 double crochet on the top of those first worked, taking up the back loops only, 2 chain, turn, 10 double crochet. Work thus till a square piece is done with four ribs on the right side, then begin at one of the corners of the square by working * 1 treble, 3 chain, 1 treble back into the same stitch, † 1 chain, miss one, 1 treble; repeat from † till the corner is reached, then work as from beginning of the row. There should be five holes along each side of the square. **2nd round**—Turn, and work double crochet into every stitch of the 1st round, taking the back loop of the stitches and putting three into one at the corners. **3rd round**—Turn, 1 double crochet into every stitch, and three in one at the corners as before. **4th round**—Turn, 1 treble, 3 chain, 1 treble in the corner stitch, * 1 chain, miss one, 1 treble; repeat from * till the corner is reached, then work as from the beginning of the row. There should be eight holes along each side and thirty-six in all. **5th round**—In the corner hole work 1 long treble (cotton twice round the hook),

Handsome Open Square.

ter Lily Pattern.

treble (cotton twice round the hook, 1 chain all round, missing 1 double crochet between each treble. In the corner stitch, work 1 long treble, 1 chain, 1 long treble. **10th round**—Turn and work 1 double crochet into every stitch and increase in the usual way at the corners. Fasten off the thread neatly; thus finishing the framework of the square.

Fill in the open corners by working four small wheels thus—Begin with 12 chain joined in a ring. **1st round**—Work 3 chain (for one treble), 39 treble into the ring, join the last stitch to the third of the 3 chain with a slip-stitch. **2nd round**—2 chain (for one double crochet), 4 double crochet, 5 chain, 1 single in the first, 5 chain, 1 single in the first, 5 chain, 1 single in the first and one single in the first made single. This makes 3 picots; the second of these picots must be looped into the fifth picot on the nearest trefoil, then work 10 double crochet, 3 picots, the second one being looped into the fifth picot of the next trefoil, 10 double crochet, loop the work into the ninth stitch (counting from the corner) of the 39 chain which formed the foundation of the framework. Make 10 double crochet, loop into the ninth stitch of the foundation, counting from the corner in the opposite direction. Work 5 double crochet, fastening off neatly to the first stitch of the row. Cut off the thread and run the ends in tidily.

1 chain, 1 shell in the next treble. A shell is made thus :—Wind the cotton twice round the hook, put the hook into the top of the treble stitch, draw the cotton through, cotton once round the hook, then through two loops, cotton once round the hook, through two loops again, leave two loops on the hook; wind cotton once round the hook, put it into the same treble into which the first long treble was worked, draw the cotton through, cotton once over the hook, draw it through two loops, cotton once round the hook, draw it through two loops. There are now three loops on the hook, make two more treble (four in all), when there will be five loops on the hook, draw the cotton through them all at once and make 1 chain to close the top of the shell. All the shells are made in this way. Continue the row by working * 1 chain, miss one, 1 long treble over the next long treble, 1 chain, miss one, 1 shell in the next treble; repeat from * till the corner is reached. Work a shell over the first treble in the corner, then 1 chain, 1 long treble into the hole, 1 chain, 1 shell in the second treble and repeat from *. There should be three shells along each, exclusive of the two in each corner, which make twenty in all. **6th round**—Like the 5th. Here each shell is worked over the single long treble between the shells of last round. In the corners, the first shell is placed in the hole made by the 1 chain, the long treble is worked into the corner long treble, and the second shell is placed in the second hole made by the 1 chain. There should be twenty-four shells altogether. **7th round**—Like the 6th. In the corner work one shell as in the 6th round, then 1 chain, 1 long treble in

into every stitch and increase in the usual way at the corners. Fasten off the thread neatly; thus finishing the framework of the square.

the corner long treble, 3 chain, 1 long treble in the same stitch, 1 long treble, 1 shell, as before, in the next hole. There must be altogether twenty-eight shells. **8th round**—Turn, and work 1 double crochet into every stitch of the preceding round, taking up the back loops. Put three stitches into one in the corners. **9th round**—Turn, and work double crochet as before, taking up the back loops of the stitches and increasing in the same way in the corners. This finishes the square.

SQUARE FOR SUMMER QUILT IN ROSE PATTERN.

THIS pattern can be effectively worked with Strutts' knitting cotton No. 8 and a steel hook No. 17. As it is rather an open design in some places the quilt made of it looks very pretty if it is mounted over Turkey twill or coloured sateen. Commence with the rose in the middle. Make a ring of

Square for Quilt in Rib and Shell Pattern.

6 chain **1st round**—4 chain, 1 double crochet in the first chain stitch, 4 chain, 1 double crochet in the next stitch. Repeat this, putting a double into each stitch so as to make six loops of chain. **2nd round**—* 1 double crochet, 4 treble, 1 double crochet into the first loop of 4 chain. Repeat from * five times putting a set of treble and double crochet into each loop. **3rd round** —3 chain, 1 double crochet into the back of the second double crochet of the 2nd round, 3 chain, 1 double crochet into the back of the next double crochet but one. Repeat four times more. **4th round**—1 double crochet, 6 treble, 1 double crochet into each loop of chain. **5th round**—4 chain, 1 double crochet into the back of the work as before; repeat until there are six loops as usual. **6th round**—1 double crochet, 7 treble, 1 double crochet into each loop. **7th round**—5 chain, 1 double crochet, six times. **8th round**— 1 double crochet, 8 treble, 1 double crochet into each loop. **9th round**— 5 chain worked very loosely, 1 double crochet, six times. **10th round**— 1 double crochet, 9 treble, 1 double crochet into each loop. **11th round**— 6 chain, 1 double crochet, six times. **12th round**—1 double crochet, 10 treble, 1 double crochet into each loop. This completes the rose. Make a foundation of loops of chain for the leaves as follows—5 chain, 1 double crochet into the back of the work eight times so as to make eight loops for the leaves. The positions of the double crochet stitches can best be marked by putting pins into those loops into which they are to be worked. For one leaf, * work 1 double crochet into one of the loops of 5 chain, 8 chain, 1 double crochet into the second stitch from the hook, 5 treble into the next 5 stitches, 1 double crochet in the last, 9 chain, 1 double crochet in the second stitch from the hook, 5 treble, 1 double crochet, 1 double crochet into the lower part of the first leaf. Then make the third leaf in the same way as the first, and 1 double crochet into the double crochet that was worked after the second leaf. Work 3 chain, 1 double crochet into the next loop of 5 chain, 3 chain, 1 double crochet into the next loop. Then repeat from *. There should be four sprays, each consisting of three leaves. When these are done, fasten off and run in the ends. Join the thread again at the tip of the middle leaf at one of the corners. **1st round**—Work 3 double crochet in this leaf, * then 8 chain, 1 double crochet in the next leaf, 8 chain, 1 double crochet in the next leaf, 8 chain, 3 double crochet into the next corner leaf; repeat from * and in the last corner loop the last chain to the top of the first

double crochet with a slip-stitch. **2nd round**—All double crochet, putting one into each chain and double crochet stitches of the 1st round and three into the middle of the three corner stitches. **3rd round**—3 double crochet in the corner stitch, 1 double crochet into the next stitch, then work 1 tuft (5 treble into one stitch, take the hook out of the last loop, put the hook into the first treble, and draw the last loop through. All the tufts are thus made), 3 double crochet, 1 tuft. Repeat till there are eight tufts with 3 double crochet between each, then work the double crochet as above in the corner, and continue all round. **4th round**—Like the 3rd, but with 7 tufts instead of 8. The tufts are worked into the second of the three double crochet stitches that were made between those of the preceding round, and three stitches are again worked between each. **5th round**—As before, but with 6 tufts along each side instead of 7. **6th round**—As before, but with 7 tufts. **7th round**— Like the third, but, of course, there will be a larger number of double crochet to be worked round the corners. **8th round**—1 double crochet into every stitch, and three in one at the corners. **9th round**—In the corner, work 1 treble into the middle stitch, 1 chain, 1 treble into the same stitch, * 1 chain, miss one, 1 treble, repeat from * till the second corner is reached, then repeat from the beginning of the round. There should be twenty-two holes along each side exclusive of the corners and ninety-two in all. **10th round**—1 double crochet over the first treble in the corner, 3 double crochet in the chain stitch, 1 double crochet in the second treble, * 5 chain, 1 double crochet into the stitch nearest the hook, 3 treble in the next three, miss 1 treble, 1 double crochet in the second. This completes one leaf; repeat from * till the next corner is reached, then repeat from beginning of the row. There should be eleven leaves along each edge of the square, forty-four in all. When several squares are finished, they may be joined by looping the last chain-stitch of each leaf to the tip of one of the leaves of another square. Thus the squares are joined as the work progresses instead of having to be patiently seamed together afterwards as is so often the case. This pattern lends itself specially well to the use of coloured cottons; thus, the rose may be pink, the leaves olive green, the rows of tufts may be worked with cotton of a fawn or brownish tint and the outer row of leaves with olive green to correspond with those in the middle.

COT COVER OR CENTRE FOR LARGE QUILT IN ROSETTE AND TUFT PATTERN.

THIS handsome centre is worked with Strutts' "bonnet" cotton and a large bone crochet hook, No. 6 or 7. This cotton it nearly as thick as double Berlin wool, is very soft, and can be had either bleached or unbleached. It has received the name of "bonnet" cotton because it is used as a sort of soft piping

Square for Summer Quilt in Rose Pattern.

cord in the gatherings of children's white cotton bonnets. It is not expensive in itself, except that it requires a very large quantity to work so elaborate a pattern as that given here. To make this square, begin with 3 chain and join them into a ring. **2nd round**—2 chain (for one double crochet), 7 double crochet into the ring, loop the last double crochet into the second chain with a slip-stitch. **3rd round**—2 chain (for one double crochet), 1 tuft (for each tuft, make 5 treble into one stitch, then take out the hook, put it into the top of the first treble, and draw the last loop through), * 1 double crochet in the next stitch, 1 tuft; repeat twice from *, loop the last double crochet into the first chain stitch. **4th round**—Work 3 double crochet behind each tuft, 1 double crochet between each tuft. **5th round**—Work one tuft in every alternate stitch and one double crochet as usual between each tuft. There should be eight tufts in all, one over each tuft of the 3rd round and one between each. **6th round**—Work 1 double crochet behind and between all the tufts, but over every alternate tuft put 3 double crochet into one stitch, thus beginning to shape the square. **7th round**—Alternately 1 chain, miss 1, 1 treble. In the corner stitches work 1 treble, 1 chain, 1 treble, 1 chain, 1 treble, 1 chain, 1 treble, thus making three holes. There should be twenty-four holes in all. **8th round**—All double crochet, putting three into the corner stitch. There should be fifty-six stitches altogether. **9th round**—Alternately 1 chain, miss 1, 1 treble. In the corner stitches work three holes as in the 7th round. There should be forty holes altogether. **10th round**—Work 1 treble into each hole and 1 chain between. At the corners put 1 treble into the centre hole, and 1 treble on the top of the treble stitch on each side of it. (Forty-eight holes in all.) **11th round**—Work 24 double crochet along each side of the square and three double crochet into each corner stitch. **12th round**—5 chain, miss 4, 1 double crochet; repeat this all round making five holes along each side. In the corner stitches work 1 double crochet in the first stitch, 3 chain, 1 double crochet, 5 chain, 1 double crochet in the second stitch, 3 chain 1 double

crochet in the third stitch, thus making three loops. **13th round**—Into each loop of 5 chain, * work 2 treble in the first two stitches, 1 treble, 1 chain, 1 treble in the third stitch, 1 treble in each of the next two stitches, work 1 double crochet over the double crochet between each loop of chain; at the corners, after the double crochet stitch, work 3 chain, 1 double crochet, 3 chain, 1 double crochet into the centre loop, then 3 chain, 1 double crochet on the top of the next double crochet; repeat from * along the next side. **14th round**—* 3 treble over the 3 treble of 12th round, 1 treble, 1 chain, 1 treble into the centre chain stitch, 3 treble, 1 double crochet; repeat from *. The corners are worked as in the 12th round. **15th round**— * 4 treble, 1 treble, 1 chain, 1 treble in the centre stitch, 4 treble, 1 double crochet; repeat from *. Work the corners as before. **16th round**—* 5 treble, 1 treble, 1 chain, 1 treble in the centre stitch, 5 treble, 1 double crochet; repeat from *. Work the corners in the usual way. **17th round**—* 6 treble, 1 treble, 1 chain, 1 treble in the centre stitch, 6 treble, 1 double crochet; repeat

Cot Cover or Centre for Large Quilt in Rosette and Tuft Pattern.

from *. Work in the corners as usual. **18th round**—7 treble, 1 treble, 2 chain, 1 treble, 4 chain, 1 treble, 2 chain, 1 treble in the centre loop, 7 treble, 1 double crochet; repeat from *. Work the corners as before. **19th round**—* 7 treble, 1 treble, 1 chain, 1 treble, 3 chain, 1 treble, 1 chain, 1 treble into the centre hole, 7 treble, 1 double crochet; repeat from *. Work the corners as usual. There should be five pleats along each side. **20th round**—* 7 chain, 1 double crochet on the double crochet of 18th round; repeat from *. Work the corner as usual. **21st round**—All double crochet. Work 3 double crochet into the middle stitch at each corner. There should be two-hundred and eight double crochet in all. **22nd round**—Treble all round, 3 stitches into each corner stitch. **23rd round**—1 chain, miss one, 1 treble all round. In the corner work 1 treble, 1 chain, 1 treble. There should be twenty-seven holes along each side, and one at each corner, making one-hundred and twelve in all. **24th round**—1 chain, 1 treble into each hole. At the corners work 1 treble into the centre stitch and one on each of the two treble on each side of it with one chain between them. There should be thirty holes along each side. **25th round**—* 7 treble, 1 tuft; repeat from * along each side. Before the corner (after a tuft) work 1 treble, 3 treble in the centre stitch, 1 treble, then make a tuft, and work along the side as before. There should be eight

Stripe for Counterpane in Shell Pattern.

tufts along each side. **26th round**—Work seven tufts along each side putting one between each tuft of the preceding round. In each corner (after the seventh tuft) work 6 treble, 3 treble in the next stitch, 6 treble, and then the tufts as before. **27th round**—Work 6 tufts, putting one between each tuft of preceding row as before, and 7 treble between each. In each corner (after the sixth tuft) work 11 treble, 3 treble into the next stitch, 11 treble. **28th round**—Make 5 tufts along each side, 16 treble, 3 treble in one, 16 treble in the corners. **29th round**—Work 4 tufts, 21 treble, 3 treble in one, 21 treble. **30th round**—Work 3 tufts, 26 treble, 3 treble in one, 26 treble. **31st round**—Work 2 tufts, 31 treble, 3 treble, 31 treble. **32nd round**—Make 1 tuft in the middle of each side, 36 treble, 3 treble in one, 36 treble. **33rd round**—Work 1 treble into every stitch, increase in the corners. There should be seventy-five treble altogether. **34th round**—1 chain, miss 1, 1 treble all round. In the middle stitch of the corner work 1 treble, 2 chain, 1 treble. Finish off neatly and fasten in any joins and loose threads there may be. This square is an extremely rich one if worked with fine cotton such as No. 10 or 12. The pieces are then only about a foot or so across. Should the pattern as given here be used as the centre to a large quilt the remainder should be made up of the centre part of this square, working as far as the end of the 11th round. If it is proposed to use it as a quilt for a child's cot, all that will be required is an edging, and an appropriate one is shown on page 13. This should, of course, be worked with the same cotton as that used for the square.

STRIPE FOR COUNTERPANE IN SHELL PATTERN.

WHAT would be generally considered as the wrong side of the crochet is really the right side of this pattern, owing to the more raised appearance of the shells upon the reverse side. The design is one which looks better in coarse cotton than in fine, and a suitable size is No. 6 used with a bone hook, No. 10. Make a length of chain the proper size, work a row of double crochet, putting one into every stitch, turn and work a second row of double crochet, taking up the back loop of each stitch. At the end of the row, break off and begin again at the opposite end. Do this with every row until further notice. **3rd row**—3 chain (for 1 treble), 1 chain, miss 1,

1 treble in the second, 1 chain, miss 1, 1 treble in the second, 1 chain, miss 1, 1 treble in next. Continue thus all along. **4th row**—5 chain (the first 4 are for the first long treble), * 1 shell over the next treble. A shell is made of four long treble all worked into the same stitch, leave the last loops unworked and draw the cotton through them all at once, close the tip of the shell by working 1 chain, then 1 long treble on the top of the next treble; repeat from * until there are five shells, then 1 long treble on the next treble, 1 long treble over the chain, 1 long treble on the next treble, 1 chain, 5 shells as before; repeat from * all along. **5th row**—4 chain (for 1 long treble), 2 long treble, * 4 shells, 7 long treble; repeat from * all along. **6th row**—4 chain (for 1 long treble), 4 long treble, * 3 shells, 11 long treble; repeat from *. **7th row**—4 chain (for one long treble), 6 long treble, * 2 shells, 15 long treble; repeat from *. **8th row**—4 chain (for 1 long treble), 8 long treble, * 1 shell, 19 long treble; repeat from *. **9th row**—Like the 7th. **10th row**—Like the 6th. **11th row**—Like the 5th. **12th row**—Like the 4th. **13th row**—Like the 3rd. **14th row**—Like the 2nd. **15th row**—Like the 1st. Fasten off and run in all the ends with a needle and thread. The cotton is not broken off at the end of a row after working the 13th, 14th, or 15th rows.

SIMPLE QUILT PATTERN.

THIS square is worked with Strutts' white knitting cotton, No. 6 and a stout steel crochet hook, such as No. 14 or 15. For the foundation make a chain of 53 stitches. **1st row**—1 treble in the fourth chain stitch and one treble in every following stitch. **2nd row**—Turn, 3 chain, 1 treble over the last treble but one of the 1st row, and 1 treble in the next stitch, * 2 chain, miss 2, 1 treble in the third; repeat from * fourteen times, then 2 chain, miss 2, 3 treble in the three last stitches. **3rd row**—Turn, 3 chain, 2 treble, * 2 chain, miss 2 chain, 1 treble over the next treble; repeat from * six times, 6 treble in the six following stitches, * 2 chain, miss 2, 1 treble; repeat six times from *, 3 treble at the end. **4th row**—Like the 3rd. **5th row**—Turn, 3 chain, 2 treble, * 2 chain, miss 2, 1 treble; repeat four times from *, 18 treble, * 2 chain, miss 2, 1 treble; repeat four times from *, 3 treble at the end. **6th row**—Like the 5th. **7th row**—Turn, 3 chain, 2 treble, 2 chain, miss 2, 1 treble, 2 chain, miss 2, 1 treble, 2 chain, miss 2, 7 treble, 2 chain, miss 2 treble, 1 treble in the 3rd, 2 chain, miss 2, 1 treble in the 3rd, 6 treble, 2 chain, miss 2, 1 treble, 2 chain, miss 2, 7 treble, 2 chain, miss 2, 1 treble, 2 chain, miss 2, 1 treble, 2 chain, miss 2, 3 treble. **8th row**—Like the 7th. **9th row**—Turn, 3 chain, 2 treble, 2 chain, 43 treble, 2 chain, 3 treble at the end. **10th row**—Like the 9th. **11th and 12th rows**—Like the 7th and 8th. **12th and 13th**

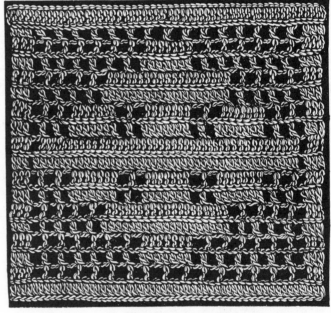

Simple Quilt Pattern.

rows—Like the 5th and 6th. **14th and 15th rows**—Like the 3rd and 4th. **16th row**—Like the 2nd. **17th row**—Turn, 3 chain, one treble into every stitch.

This pattern is one which lends itself well to being worked in a stripe instead of a square. At the beginning, instead of one row of open holes such as the 2nd, work three such rows, and at the end again work three open rows instead of one, and omit the row of treble until the end of the stripe is reached. Begin to work the cross again in the 21st row. Every alternate stripe should be worked in this way, the remaining ones should commence with the three open-work rows and then with the 9th row. This will cause the crosses to set less formally when a number of the stripes are joined than were they all to be begun in exactly the same place in each one. The work should be executed rather tightly in order to set well and closely. The pattern also has a pretty effect if the cross be worked with coloured cotton. Care must then be taken to leave the thread very loose when it is passed from place to place across the back. It can then be caught down with a needle and thread here and there at the back to prevent it from showing through the open-work part of the pattern.

LACE EDGING.

THIS lace matches the square for Quilt on page 4, and is worked with Strutts' cotton No. 6 and a steel hook No 15. Begin by working a chain the length required. Into this put 1 treble, * 1 chain, miss 1, 1 treble in the 2nd; repeat from *. **2nd row**—2 treble, * 5 chain, miss 3, 2 treble in the 4th and 5th; repeat from *. **3rd row**—Like the 1st. **4th row**—1 double crochet in a hole made by 1 chain of preceding row, * 1 chain, 1 double crochet in the next hole, 5 chain, 1 double crochet in the next hole; repeat from *. Fasten off at the end of this row. Make the half stars next. 8 chain joined in a ring 12 double crochet. **2nd row**—4 single, loop each one of these single into a stitch of the foundation chain, then work 1 double crochet, 24 chain, 1 double crochet in the next stitch, 16 chain, 1 double crochet, 16 chain, 1 double crochet, 24 chain, 1 double crochet, 16 chain, 1 double crochet, 16 chain, 1 double crochet, 24 chain, 1 double crochet; fasten off neatly. Forty-seven stitches of the foundation must be left between each star. When a sufficient number is finished, join the thread to the 23rd stitch between two stars, work 5 double crochet, * then 3 chain, 1 double crochet into the first loop

Lace Edging.

of 24 chain, 6 chain, 1 double crochet into the first loop of 16 chain, 6 chain, 1 double crochet into the second loop of 16 chain, 8 chain, 1 double crochet into the second loop of 24 chain, 8 chain, 1 double crochet into the next short loop, 6 chain, 1 double crochet into the next short loop, 6 chain, 1 double crochet into the last loop of the star, 3 chain, 5 double crochet as before into the foundation between two stars, and repeat from *. **2nd row**—Turn the work and make * 27 double crochet (2 chain for the first double) over the chain, and double crochet of preceding row. At the top of the long loop in the middle of the star, work 3 double crochet in the same stitch, then 27 double crochet again, 2 chain, 1 double crochet in the middle stitch of the 5 double crochet that were worked between the stars, 2 chain; repeat from *. **3rd row**—Turn, make 2 chain, miss 1 double crochet, 26 double crochet, 3 double crochet into the top stitch, then 27 double crochet, * 2 chain, miss the two holes in the preceding row, also the first double crochet of next vandyke, 27 double crochet, 3 double crochet in the tip, then 27 double crochet again and repeat from *. Repeat the 2nd and 3rd rows, until there are six rows of double crochet or three ribs on the right side, remembering always to pick up the back loop of the stitches in working the double crochet. **8th row**—1 double crochet in the 1st double crochet of a vandyke, * 5 chain, miss 3, 1 double crochet in the 4th; repeat from * and at the tip put 1 double crochet, 5 chain, 1 double crochet into the same stitch; repeat again till the end of the vandyke is reached, work 2 chain, 1 double crochet into the loop of chain between the points, 2 chain; repeat from the beginning of the row. There should be seven loops down each side of the vandykes, not including that at the tip of the point. **9th row**—Like the 8th, putting 1 double crochet into every hole made by the 5 chain of the 8th row. When the end of the vandyke is reached, make 5 chain, miss the two small holes of the preceding row and work 1 double crochet in next loop of 5 chain of the 8th row. **10th row**—1 double crochet in a loop of 5 chain, * 1 chain, picot of 5 chain, 1 double crochet into the next loop. A picot is here made by working 5 chain, 1 single in the first. Repeat from *. At the tip of the vandyke, work 1 double crochet in the top loop, 1 chain, picot. 1 chain, 1 double crochet back into same loop, then continue as before. This looks still more handsome with tassels at the tip and between each vandyke. It is also a very suitable design for the introduction of colour—the ribbed rows, for instance, may be of a totally different tint from the loops and the half stars.

EDGING FOR QUILT IN CROCHET APPLIQUÉ.

THIS edging must be worked with some of the same cotton as that used for the quilt it is intended to trim. It is most effective if the background is worked with No. 10 cotton and a hook No. 18, No. 8 cotton and a hook No. 16 being used for the flowers. The pattern loses all its effect unless made in two colours or in two shades of the same. The name "appliqué" is given because the flowers are made quite separately and are sewn to the background afterwards; the edging, comprising as it does, so many different kinds of work, will be found a particularly interesting one to execute. When the worker is tired of making the flowers, she can get on with the background, or can sew the sprays into place. In attaching the sprays, care must be taken to get them exactly the same distance apart. This can only be done accurately by counting the holes between them in the background. It is easier (and the stitches are less likely to show if this is done) to sew the sprays on from the wrong side. The worker then runs little risk of spoiling the effect by stitches on the right side, for it must be a very clumsy stitch indeed that is long enough to go completely through the two thicknesses of the crochet. When it is necessary to pass the thread from one leaf to another, care too must be taken to slip it across those portions in which the work is double, for, if the cotton were laid across the background, it would be very likely to show on the right side between the holes. These are small details in themselves, but attention or inattention paid to them marks the difference between a piece of work worthy of all admiration and one which shows the careless disposition of the maker.

It is well to begin by making the background. Work a chain the length required. This must be about an eighth as long again as the sides of the quilt, for, as will be shown hereafter, the edging is not sewn on as flatly as it is worked. **1st row**—1 treble into the 5th chain from the hook, * miss 1 stitch, 1 treble, 1 chain, 1 treble into the next; repeat from * all along. **2nd row**—Turn, 4 chain, 1 treble into the last hole between two treble of the first row, * miss 2 treble, 1 treble, 1 chain, 1 treble over the next hole made by the 1 chain of last row; repeat from * all along. Repeat this row till fifteen rows are done, then fasten off. This part of the work should be executed with one colour only, and that the darker of the two chosen for it.

It is advisable to attach the flowers to this foundation before adding the scollops or the gathering at the top. To make a flower :—* work 6 chain, join

Edging for Quilt in Crochet Appliqué.

them into a ring, then 2 chain (for one double crochet), 17 double crochet into the ring. Loop the last stitch with a slip-stitch to the first of the 2 chain, 1 double crochet on the second chain stitch, 6 chain, miss 1 chain, 1 double crochet in the second, 1 long double crochet, 3 treble, miss 2 double crochet of the ring and work 1 double crochet in the third; repeat five times from *, then fasten off. In working the second flower, join two of its points to the first one. In working the third flower, join one of the points to a point of the second next to one of the points that are joined to the first flower. This will be better understood by reference to the illustration. For the stem of the spray, join the cotton to the tips that are joined of the first and second flowers, work 5 chain, loop the last into the free point of the third flower that is next to the one that joins the second flower, 15 chain, miss 3 chain, 1 treble in the fourth from the hook, 2 treble in the next two stitches, 3 treble in the next stitch, 3 long double crochet, double crochet into the rest of the chain, 1 single into the point from which the stem was begun. Fasten off. These sprays are of course made of a different coloured cotton to that used for the foundation and it should be of a lighter shade. A pretty effect is given on a white background if the middle ring of the flowers is worked with yellow, the petals being crimson and the stem dull green; in short, the pattern is open to endless variation as far as colour is concerned.

Now continue the foundation of the edging and work a row in the lighter shade of cotton, exactly as the other fifteen rows were done. Fasten off and join the dark cotton at the commencement of this row, 8 chain, 1 triple long treble (cotton three times round the hook), into the 1st hole made by the 1 chain of the preceding row, * 1 chain, 1 triple long treble into the same hole; repeat from * five times more, when counting the first 7 chain as a long treble, there should be eight in the hole altogether. Miss one pair of treble of the preceding row and work one double crochet into the next, then miss another pair of treble and make a set of eight triple long treble with 1 chain between each into the next hole. Continue thus all along and at the end fasten off. Join the lighter shade of cotton at the right-hand end of the first scollop and work one double crochet between the first and second trebles, then 3 chain, 1 double crochet between the second and third trebles, 3 chain, 1 double crochet between the next two trebles. * Work thus till there are six loops of three chain. After the seventh double crochet, miss the last treble of this scollop and the first treble of the next and work 1 double crochet into the hole between the first and second trebles, 3 chain, 1 double crochet into the next hole; repeat from * all along, thus finishing the work on this side of the background. Take the paler cotton and begin at the right-hand corner of the other edge of the foundation. Work one treble into every edge loop of the chain with which the background was begun. When the end is reached fasten off and begin again at the right-hand end. Work, still with the paler colour, 2 double crochet, putting one into each of the preceding treble, * miss one, 2 double crochet into the two next stitches; repeat from * all along. The object of missing every fourth stitch is to gather the trimming slightly, as the pattern is one which looks far better if used full than quite plain, but at the same time must not be so full as to spoil the effect of the design.

STRIPE IN PICOT PATTERN.

THIS stripe is most effective when executed with Strutts' No. 4 cotton and a small bone hook No. 11 or No. 12. The small picots which form one of the main features of the pattern then stand out in bolder relief than when a finer cotton is used for them. The design is one which makes a far handsomer quilt if alternated with strips of a close pattern than if used alone. If, however, it is not convenient to vary the design, the quilt should be lined with a coloured material. Few fabrics are more satisfactory for this purpose than fine cashmere, this being preferable to sateen owing to the greater durability of the colour. A very pretty coverlet can be made by using a thick cretonne for the alternate stripes. A cretonne should be chosen that is rather firm in quality and of a good bold design; very rich patterns may often be had woven in stripes which only require cutting up, and hemming down the sides. An ingenious worker by giving the matter a little thought will soon find many other materials that can effectively be mixed with open stripes of this kind. To work the stripe as illustrated make a length of 35 chain. Use the last three as a treble stitch and work thirty-two treble along the remaining thirty-two stitches. **2nd row**—Turn, 3 chain (for one treble), 2 treble, * 1 chain, picot, 1 chain, miss 3, 3 treble over the next three; repeat from * all along, finishing the row with three treble. A picot is made here of 3 chain with one double crochet in the first chain. **3rd row**—Turn, 4 chain (for one long treble), 2 long treble (cotton twice round the hook), * 3 chain, miss the chain stitches and the picot, 3 long treble over the three treble of the preceding row; repeat from *, finishing the row with three long treble. **4th row**—Turn, 2 chain (for one double crochet), 1 double crochet into every stitch of the preceding row, taking up the back loop of the stitches. There should be thirty-two double crochet without counting the two chain which serve as a double crochet at the beginning of the row. **5th row**—Turn, 2 chain, double crochet into the back loop of every stitch of the 4th row. After this repeat from the 2nd row and continue to work thus until the stripe is long enough. Finish it after a row of long treble by working a row of ordinary treble to correspond with that with which the stripe was begun and fasten off. The stripe may be made wider than this by beginning with more chain, but the number must be always divisible by three and there must be an odd number of sets of three. A variety may easily be made by working three or five ribs of double crochet between the open rows, instead of two rows only. A pretty effect, too, may be gained by working the ribs with a different colour to the rest of the stripe. It must be noted, too, that if the pattern has been correctly worked, the wrong side of the picots forms the right side of the design, which in this way becomes rather more raised than it would otherwise be.

Stripe in Picot Pattern.

VANDYKE BORDER FOR QUILT.

THIS border is far more effective with coarse than with fine cotton, but this must correspond in size with that used for the rest of the quilt that is to be trimmed with the edging. It looks best with cotton No. 6 and a steel hook No. 14. Begin by working a foundation of chain stitches, the number of which must be divisible by eleven, the entire length of the chain being about double that required altogether. **1st row**—Miss 2 chain, 3 double crochet, * 3 double crochet in the next stitch, 4 double crochet, miss 2, 4 double crochet; repeat from * all along. **2nd row**—Turn, miss one stitch, * 4 double crochet, 3 double crochet in the middle of the vandyke, 4 double crochet, miss 2; repeat from *. Work the double crochet stitches in each row into the back loops of those in the preceding row to form the ribs. Repeat the 2nd row till eight rows are finished, which form four ribs on the right side of the work. **9th row**—Turn, miss one, * 1 double crochet on the second stitch, 4 chain, miss 2, 1 double crochet on the third stitch which should be the first of the three double crochet in the tip of the vandyke, 4 chain, miss 1, 1 double crochet into the third of the three double crochet in the tip of the vandyke, 4 chain, miss 2, 1 double crochet into the third stitch, miss the last stitch of one vandyke and the first stitch of the next and repeat from * all along. **10th row**—Turn, 3 double crochet into the first loop of 4 chain, * 2 chain, 1 treble into the loop at the top of the vandyke, 1 chain, picot, 1 chain, 1 treble into the same loop. (A picot is made by working 4 chain, 1 double crochet into the first stitch.) Continue by working 2 chain, 3 double crochet into the next loop, 3 double crochet into the first loop of 4 chain on the next vandyke. Repeat from * all along. At the other edge of the lace work * 1 double crochet into the tip of the point, 4 chain, 1 double long treble between the vandykes, 4 chain; repeat from * all along. **2nd row** — Alternately 1 treble, 1 chain, miss 1, 1 treble all along, taking up the back loops of the stitches in the preceding row.

EDGING FOR WATER-LILY PATTERN.

(Not Illustrated.)

THIS edging must be worked with the same size of cotton and hook as was used for the Octagon for a Quilt in Water-lily Pattern on centre page. In the original, this was Strutts' cotton No. 6 and a steel hook No. 15. It is made in sections which are joined as each one is completed. Begin with 1? chain, miss 5, work 1 treble, 1 chain, miss 1, 1 treble in the next, 1 chain, miss 1, 1 treble in the next, 1 chain, miss 1, 1 treble, 20 chain, turn, 1 double crochet into the last made hole of 1 chain, turn, and put 14 treble into the loop of 20 chain, 10 chain, turn, and work 1 double crochet into the second hole, turn, 14 treble into the loop, 10 chain, turn, 1 double crochet into the third hole, turn, 14 treble, * 10 chain, turn, 1 double crochet into the top hole, turn, 14 treble; repeat from * four times, then make 10 chain, turn, 1 double crochet into the next hole, turn, 14 treble. Work two more leaves into the next two holes, making eleven in all, 10 chain, turn, 1 double crochet into the first chain of the foundation, turn, work 15 double crochet into the loop of 10 chain, * 6 chain, 1 double crochet into the next loop of chain between two leaves; repeat from * till there are eleven of these sets of chain, work the last one into the loop of 10 chain, and put 14 double crochet into the loop, 2 double

Vandyke Border for Quilt.

crochet into the hole in the middle of the scollop, 15 single on the top of the next 15 double crochet, * * 3 double crochet into the next loop of 6 chain, 1 picot of 5 chain (5 chain, 1 single in the first stitch), 3 double crochet into the same loop; repeat from * * all round. Loop the last double crochet into the first of the fifteen double crochet, and fasten off. The scollops are joined by looping the last picot into the corresponding picot on the next scollop. When a sufficient length is done, fasten the thread to one of the double crochet along the upper edge and work 3 treble, * 2 chain, miss 2, 3 treble; repeat from *. **2nd row**—1 double crochet into every stitch to make a firm edge. This border would also prove effective used as a finish to the Hexagon for Quilt in Fluted Pattern, as illustrated on page 7; or worked with same size cotton as that employed for the Cot Cover on page 11, it could be used as a bordering. It would also work up well in Macramé twine, forming a handsome bracket valance, &c., or it would be very suitable for an edging to a gipsy table, and from each loop could be suspended a tassel, if a still more elaborate design be needed.

WELDON'S
PRACTICAL CROCHET.

(FOURTEENTH SERIES.)

How to Crochet Useful Articles for Home and Personal Adornment.

TWENTY-EIGHT ILLUSTRATIONS.

Telegraphic Address—]
"Consuelo," London.]

The Yearly Subscription to this Magazine, post free to any Part of the World, is 2s. 6d.
Subscriptions are payable in advance, and may commence from any date and for any period.

[Telephone—
2745.

The Back Numbers are always in print. Nos. 1 to 86 now ready, Price 2d. each, or post free for 15s. 4d. Over 5,000 Engravings.

GENTLEMAN'S COTTON NIGHTCAP.

A COMFORTABLE nightcap for a gentleman can be crocheted as shown in our engraving, by using Strutt's knitting cotton, No. 8, and a No. 12 bone crochet needle, that is the smallest size that is made in bone, or a good-sized steel needle will do equally well. Commence with 75 chain for the length from the tassel to the bottom of the cap. **1st row**—Miss the first chain stitch by the needle, work 12 single crochet stitches, 12 double crochet, then 1 treble and 1 double crochet alternately twenty-five times. **2nd row**—2 chain to turn, 1 treble on a double crochet stitch and 1 double crochet on a treble stitch alternately twenty-five times, always taking up the one back thread of the stitches of previous row that the work may sit in ridges, then 12 double crochet on double crochet, and 12 single crochet on single crochet, still in the back thread of the stitches. **3rd row**—1 chain to turn, work 12 single crochet, 12 double crochet, and then 1 treble and 1 double crochet alternately twenty-five times, always taking up the back thread of the stitches of last row. Continue working forwards and backwards in repetition of the two last rows, till from 56 rows to 60 rows are worked, according to the size needed to fit nicely round the head. Sew the last row neatly to the commencing chain. Make a nice full tassel; draw up the top of the cap, and put the tassel on. Turn up about two inches of the crochet round the bottom of the cap, which now will be finished.

Gentleman's Cotton Nightcap.

between the fourth and fifth long treble stitches, 2 chain, 8 long treble under the loop of chain at the end of the row, 2 chain, another long treble in the same place. **4th row**—5 chain to turn, 8 long treble under the loop of two chain, 1 double crochet between the fourth and fifth long treble stitches, * 2 chain, 9 long treble under the loop of two chain of last row, 1 double crochet between the fourth and fifth long treble stitches, repeat from *, then 2 chain, 8 long treble under the loop of chain at the end of the row, 2 chain, another long treble in the same place. You now continue working as the last row, doing always one more repeat between * and *, till 52 rows are done, when you get 52 groups of long treble stitches in the row, and the row from end to end will be about one and a half yards long. Then for the **Border**—Take the pink wool, and beginning on the right-hand side of the last row of the shawl, do * 1 treble under a loop of two chain, 1 chain and 1 treble alternately eight times in the same place, 1 chain, 1 double crochet between the fourth and fifth long treble stitches of last row, 1 chain, and repeat from * to the end of the row, and then go along the other two sides of the shawl in the same manner working the groups of treble and chain stitches in one loop, and 1 double crochet in the next successive loop, and so on. **2nd round**—Also with pink wool, work loosely, 1 double crochet under a chain stitch of last round, * 30 chain, 1 double crochet under the next chain stitch, and repeat from *; so making a full fringy edge, which finishes off the shawl in a very attractive manner.

SHOULDER SHAWL OR FASCINATOR.

WORKED IN TORONTO STITCH.

THIS is an elegant and comfortable thing to wear as a shoulder-wrap to the theatre, or when any light wrap is needed in the house, or it can be thrown over the head as a fascinator, in the manner shown in the engraving. The shape may be described as three-sided, and a sectional example of the stitch will be found on page 4. Procure 3 ozs. of white and 2 ozs. of pink Shetland wool, and a No. 15 steel crochet needle. The entire centre of the shawl or fascinator is worked with white wool and the border with pink. Commence with white wool, with 9 chain; join round in a circle; do 5 chain, 8 long treble in the circle, 2 chain, 1 more long treble in the circle. **2nd row**—5 chain, turn the work, do 8 long treble under the loop of two chain, 1 double crochet between the fourth and fifth long treble stitches of the first row, 2 chain, 8 long treble under the loop of two chain at the end of the row, 2 chain, another long treble in the same place. **3rd row**—5 chain to turn, 8 long treble under the loop of two chain, 1 double crochet between the fourth and fifth long treble stitches, 2 chain, 9 long treble under the loop of two chain of last row, 1 double crochet

TORONTO STITCH.

FOR A SQUARE SHAWL OR SCARF.

OUR engraving shows a pretty new stitch for a shawl or scarf; the same stitch is employed for the shoulder shawl, or fascinator, illustrated on page 4 of the present issue, but that is shaped, and of course requires definite instructions for the shaping, while we here describe the working of the pattern as it would be used for making a square shawl or scarf. The finer the material the better the work will look, therefore procure Shetland wool, or the new fine Fife Lace yarn, and a No. 15 steel crochet needle. Commence with chain for the length required. **1st row**—Work 1 long treble (wool twice round the needle) in the sixth chain from the needle, 2 more long treble in the same place, miss three chain stitches, 1 double crochet in the next, * 2 chain, miss three foundation stitches, 5 long treble in the next and 4 long treble in the next, making 9 long treble in all in a group, miss three foundation stitches,

1 double crochet in the next, and repeat from * to the end of the row. **2nd row**—5 chain to turn, work 3 long treble on the double crochet stitch with which you ended the preceding row, * 1 double crochet between the fourth and fifth long treble stitches of preceding row, 2 chain, 9 long treble under the loop of two chain of last row, and repeat from * ; and at the end of the row work 1 double crochet on the top stitch of the chain with which the row turned. Every succeeding row is worked the same as the second row. When the shawl is finished, it may be bordered with the same fringy edge as seen upon the shoulder shawl, or fascinator, as below, or with a deep lace border.

THE ADELAIDE MUFF AND BOA COMBINED.

THIS comfortable article is intended to be worn by children of from three to seven years of age. It is worked in fancy tricot and looped crochet. Required, 6 ozs. of white double Berlin wool, a No. 5 bone tricot needle, and a No. 7 crochet needle, ½ yard of pale blue pongée silk for lining, 1 yard of silk cord

Shoulder Shawl or Fascinator. Worked in Toronto Stitch.

to match, and a piece of wool wadding. For the centre portion of the muff, take the tricot needle and begin with 16 chain. **1st row**—Pick up 15 tricot stitches, which with one on the needle makes 16 stitches, and draw back in the usual manner. **2nd row**—Increase one stitch at each end, now there will be 18 stitches on the needle picked up as in plain tricot, and draw back one by one to the end. **3rd row**—Pick up the perpendicular threads at the back of the stitches of last row, by which means an ornamental ridge is thrown on the front of the work, get 18 stitches in the row, and draw back as usual. **4th row**—Pick up the front loops as in plain tricot, and increase again 1 stitch at each end. **5th row**—Pick up the back threads, 20 stitches in the row. **6th row**—Plain tricot, increasing at each end. **7th row**—Pick up the back threads, 22 stitches in the row. **8th row**—Plain tricot, increasing at each end. **9th row**—Pick up the back threads, 24 stitches. **10th row**—Plain tricot, increasing at each end. **11th row**—Pick up the back threads, 26 stitches. Repeat a plain row and a ridged row on 26 stitches, till you can count 12 ridged rows across the work. **26th row**—Pick up in plain tricot, 26 stitches, and decrease in drawing back by taking the 2 first stitches and the 2 last stitches together. **27th row**—Pick up the back threads, 24 stitches. Continue now a plain tricot row with decreasings and a ridged row, alternately, till the work is reduced to 16 stitches, when fasten off, and sew the end to the commencement. Use the crochet needle for working the boa, do 12 chain, and join round: now work n looped crochet round and round, making one loop to each stitch of double crochet, thus pass the wool once round the first finger of the left hand (going first over and then under), insert the hook in the work and also through the loop on the finger, and draw the wool and the loop through, and then finish the stitch as a double crochet stitch, every stitch is worked in the same manner, until a length of about 24 inches or 26 inches is crocheted to go from the top of the muff and round the child's neck: then work on 6 stitches only in rows forwards and backwards, always making the loops come on the right side of the work, till a sufficient length is done to go round one end of the muff, when fasten off, and sew on beyond the tricot.

Work a similar piece from the other end of the boa to go round the opposite end of the muff. Quilt the lining upon the wadding, and line the muff. The boa is confined at the throat by a bow of silk cord, and a fancy knot of cord is arranged on the front of the muff.

BEEHIVE PATTERN JACKET.

THIS is a warm and useful jacket for a child about three years of age. Procure 5 ozs. of Andalusian wool, or a good soft make of fingering wool, and a No. 9 bone crochet needle. The work is done in rows, breaking off the wool at the end of every row. Commence with 78 chain for the neck. **1st row**—Do 1 double crochet in the second chain from the needle, * miss one chain, 5 treble in the next, miss one chain, 1 double crochet in the next, and repeat from * to the end of the row and there will be 19 groups of treble stitches and 20 double crochet stitches in the row. **2nd row**—Beginning again on the right-hand side—Do 1 treble on the first double crochet stitch of last row, wool over the needle, insert the hook from back to front between the double crochet stitch and the first treble stitch and pass it from front to back between the first and second treble stitches and draw the wool through in a long loose loop, wool over the needle and draw through two stitches on the needle, wool over the needle, insert the hook from back to front between the first and second treble stitches and pass it from front to back between the second and third treble stitches and draw the wool through in a long loose loop, wool over the needle and draw through two stitches on the needle, there now are 3 stitches on the needle, 2 looped stitches and the treble stitch with which you began, wool over the needle and draw through the 3 stitches on the needle and do 1 chain to confine the group, remember all *looped stitches* are to be drawn up in

Toronto Stitch.

this manner leaving the top of the treble stitches free to stand in raised honeycomb as shown in the engraving, * now do 1 double crochet inserting the hook to take the two top front threads of the centre stitch of the group of treble stitches, then raise a looped stitch in each of the 5 following stitches of the previous row, wool over the needle and draw through all the stitches (6) on the needle, 1 chain to confine the group, and repeat from * to the end of the row, where you will make half a group of stitches to correspond with the beginning. **3rd row**—Commence on the right-hand side,—4 treble on the first stitch of the preceding row, * 1 double crochet on the double crochet of preceding row, but inserting the hook in the lower part of the stitch instead of on the top as usual, 7 treble in the stitch that draws together the beehive of last row, and repeat from * to the end, finishing with 4 treble upon the last stitch. **4th row**—1 double crochet on the first stitch of the preceding row, * raise a looped stitch in each of the 7 following stitches, wool over the needle and draw through all the stitches (8) on the needle, 1 chain to confine the group, 1 double crochet on the centre stitch of the group of trebles of preceding row, and repeat from * to the end of the row where the double crochet will come upon the very last stitch ; be sure and draw the looped stitches well up, particularly those in the hollow of the beehive, for upon this the beauty of the pattern greatly depends. **5th row**—1 double crochet on the first stitch of previous row, * 7 treble in the stitch that draws together the beehive of last row, 1 double crochet in the lower part of the double crochet stitch of last row, and repeat from * to the end ; there are 19 groups of treble stitches in this row. **6th row**—1 treble on the first stitch, raise 3 loops and draw in to form a beehive, 1 double crochet on the centre stitch of trebles, raise 3 loops and form a

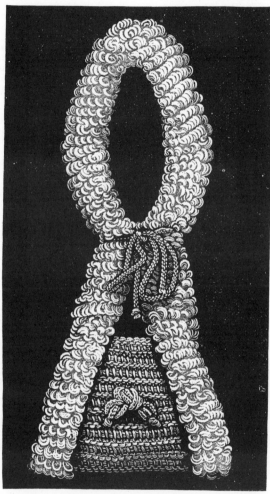

The Adelaide Muff and Boa Combined.

beehive, raise 4 loops and form a beehive, so making two small hives instead of one, do 16 beehives, then another increase, and finish the row with half a beehive as it began. **7th row**—This row will consist of 20 groups of treble stitches, and half a group at the beginning and end. **8th row**—1 double crochet on the first stitch, raise 3 beehives, increase, 1 beehive, increase, 4 beehives, increase, 4 beehives, increase, 1 beehive, increase, 3 beehives, 1 double crochet on the last stitch. **9th row**—Same as the fifth row, but 26 groups in the row. **10th row**—Same as the sixth row, but instead of increasing in the front increase twice on each shoulder. **11th row**—As seventh row, with 29 groups of treble stitches, and half a group at the beginning and end. **12th row**—This row will consist of 30 beehives. **13th row**—Work as the fifth row. **14th row**—Work as the sixth row. **15th row**—Work as third row. **16th row**—Work as fourth row, when 6 beehives are done make 21 chain for an armhole, miss five patterns, do 1 double crochet on double crochet, 8 beehives, 1 double crochet on double crochet, miss five patterns doing 21 chain for an armhole, do 6 beehives to the end. **17th row**—Work as the fifth row, proceeding over the beehives of last row and also along the chain stitches, and get, according to the size of the child's waist, either 26 or 28 groups of treble stitches in the row. Proceed now in pattern till the jacket is long enough,— about 16 more rows,—ending with the row of treble stitch groups corresponding to the fifth row of the above instructions. The same treble stitch groups are to be worked as an edge up each side the front of the jacket, and two rows of the same round the neck for frills, as represented in the engraving. For the **Sleeves**—Begin upon the armhole, and get 9 patterns in the round ; work now in rounds, in the beehive pattern ; do 4 rounds. Next round decrease one pattern under

the arm. Do 6 rounds with 8 patterns in the round. Decrease again under the arm. Do 11 rounds with 7 patterns in the round, and fasten off. Work the other sleeve in the same manner. Make a crochet chain to run in round the neck of the jacket, and put tassels on the ends to tie and hang down in front.

CHEMISE TRIMMING.

PROCURE two or three reels of Evans' crochet cotton No. 18, and a fine steel crochet needle. Begin in the centre of one of the medallions, 6 chain, join round in a circle ; work 12 double crochet in a circle, and join the last double crochet to the first ; then 12 chain to start the first wing, do 1 single crochet in the first stitch of the chain, turn the work, do 20 double crochet in the loop of chain, then join with 1 single crochet to the next double crochet stitch of the central round ; turn the work, and proceed again round the wing, with 1 double crochet on each of the 4 double crochet stitches nearest the needle, * 4 chain for a picot, 3 double crochet, and repeat from * four times, then 1 more double crochet on the last stitch of the wing, and 1 single crochet on each of the 3 next stitches of the central round ; for the second wing, 12 chain, 1 single crochet in the first stitch of the chain, turn the work, do 20 double crochet in the loop of chain, then join with 1 single crochet to a stitch of the central round ; turn the work, and proceed again round the wing, do 1 double crochet on each of the 2 double crochet stitches nearest the needle, join with a single crochet to the corresponding stitch of the previous wing, 2 more double crochet worked consecutive, * 4 chain for a picot, 3 double crochet, and repeat from * four times, then 1 double crochet upon the last remaining stitch of the wing, and 1 single crochet on each of the 3 next stitches of the central round : work two more wings like the foregoing ; the only difference will be to join the last wing to the first wing in the same manner as the previous wings have been joined. Work a sufficient number of medallions for the length to go round the neck, and round the armholes, and also for a V-shape in front, all in one piece, according to the shape of the entire trimming as shown in the engraving, connecting them together in process of working, by a single crochet from a picot of a wing to the corresponding picot of the previous wing. For the **Heading**—Work 1 double crochet in the second picot to the right upon the top edge of the medallions, * 2 chain, 1 single crochet in the centre picot, 2 chain, 1 double crochet in the next picot, then either 6 or 8 chain according as you find reach nicely along the edge, cotton three times round the needle

Beehive Pattern Jacket.

and work off in a double long treble in the second picot in the side wing of the medallion, 2 more double long treble in the same place, keeping the top stitch of all three on the needle, 3 double long treble in the corresponding picot of the next medallion, cotton over the needle and draw through all six double long treble together, cotton over the needle and draw through the two stitches remaining on the needle, do 6 chain or 8 chain as before, 1 double crochet in the second picot of the top wing of the next medallion, and repeat from *, and fasten off at the end of the round. **2nd round**—1 treble on the double long treble stitch of last round, * 1 chain, miss one stitch, 1 treble on the next, and repeat from * to the end of the round. **3rd round**—1 treble on the treble over the double long treble stitch, 1 treble in the next stitch which is a chain stitch, * 4 chain, miss four stitches, do 2 treble, and repeat from * to the end of the round. **4th round**—Same as the second round. **5th round**—1 single crochet on a chain stitch of last round, * 7 chain, miss two spaces, 1 single crochet on the chain stitch of the next space, and repeat from * to the end of the round·

6th round—3 double crochet along the first part of the loop of seven chain, 3 double crochet in the centre stitch of the loop, 3 double crochet along the other part of the loop, miss the single crochet stitch and repeat. **7th round**—Miss the first stitch of the group of last round, * work three consecutive double crochet, 4 chain, 1 double crochet on the centre double crochet of the group, 4 chain, another double crochet in the same place, 4 chain, another double crochet in the same place, 3 double crochet worked consecutive, miss the last stitch of the group and also miss the first stitch of the next group, and repeat from * to the end: this finishes the scolloped edge on the top of the trimming. Repeat the first and second rounds along the bottom of the trimming to give a level edge whereby to sew the trimming on the chemise. When the trimming is finished and sewn on, run a ribbon through the row of open treble stitches, to tie in a bow in front.

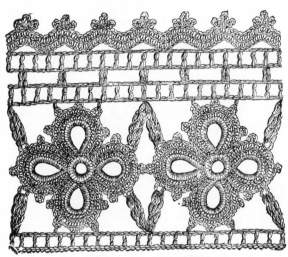

Details of Chemise Trimming.

NIGHTDRESS SACHET.

THIS pretty sachet is crocheted with single Berlin wool, either white or coloured as preferred, about 4 ozs. of wool will be required, also a No. 10 bone crochet needle, a piece of sateen for lining, 1 yard of silk ribbon for bows, and three small fancy buttons. The sachet is worked all in one piece, in Russian crochet, in rows forwards and backwards. Begin with 96 chain. **1st row**—Do 14 consecutive double crochet, 3 double crochet in the next stitch of chain, 14 consecutive double crochet, miss four stitches, and repeat the same twice, which will bring you to the end of the row. **2nd row**—Turn the work, miss the first double crochet stitch, * work 14 consecutive double crochet taking up the one back thread of the stitches of the previous row, 3 double crochet on the next which is the centre stitch of three double crochet of last row, 14 consecutive double crochet, miss two stitches, and repeat from * twice; and there will be one stitch to leave unworked at the end of the row. Continue working the same as the second row till about 68 rows or 70 rows are done. **Last row**—Turn the work, miss the first double crochet stitch, 1 double crochet on the next, * miss one stitch, 4 treble, 2 chain, and 4 more treble on the next, miss one, 1 double crochet on the next, and repeat from * six times, which brings you round the first scollop or point, and work the other two scollops in the same way, with a group of treble stitches always to come on the centre double crochet stitch at the tip of each scollop; fasten off at the end of this row. The commencing chain is the top of the pocket of the sachet, the last row of crochet is the ending of the flap. Fold the crochet in the shape of an envelope, and sew up the sides of the pocket. All round the outside edge of the sachet work a row of crochet,—thus—1 double crochet in a stitch of the sachet, * miss a stitch or two, 4 treble in the next, miss a stitch or two, 1 double crochet in the next, and repeat from *, and join evenly at the end of the round. Line the sachet throughout, cutting the points to the shape of the crochet. Make two pretty bows of ribbon, and put one by the right-hand top corner and the other by the left-hand bottom corner, as in the engraving. Put buttons on the pocket to button the points into.

COSY ANTIMACASSAR.

WORKED WITH MACRAMÉ TWINE.

THE engraving shows a serviceable antimacassar to draw over the back of a chair that is in constant use, it will not slip out of place and therefore always looks tidy; the two sides vary in pattern but are equally pretty and may be reversed to front and back at pleasure. Required, six balls of salmon pink rather coarse macramé twine, and six balls of chestnut brown of a finer size, a bone crochet

needle, No. 8, and 1½ yards of pink ribbon. Commence for the first side with brown thread, with 49 chain for the length of the antimacassar. Work 4 rows of Russian double crochet, doing 48 stitches in each row, this is the same thing as ordinary double crochet but you take up always the one back thread of the stitches that the work may sit in ridges. Do 1 row of Point-neige or shell stitch, 24 stitches in the row. Next 1 row of double crochet. Then another row of Point-neige. And then 3 rows of Russian crochet with 48 stitches in each row. Now cut off the brown thread and join on pink, and change the pattern to crazy stitch, still inserting the needle always to take up the back thread of the stitches of the previous row, do 1 double crochet and 3 treble stitches in every fourth stitch of last row, making 12 groups of stitches in the row; next row work 1 double crochet and 3 treble on each double crochet stitch, again 12 groups of stitches in the row; repeat this row until 6 rows are worked with pink. Then repeat the brown stripe and the pink stripe alternately till you have four pink stripes and five brown stripes, which are sufficient for one side of the antimacassar. The other side is worked in a variety of crazy crochet. Continue using the brown thread, and for the **1st row** on this side do 1 double crochet, 3 chain, and 3 treble a'l on the fourth stitch of double crochet of last row, and the same on every fourth stitch, making 12 groups of stitches in the row. **2nd row**—Turn, and work 1 double crochet, 3 chain, and 3 treble under each loop of chain of last row. Work 2 more rows in the same manner. Then do 4 rows in the same way with pink thread, then 4 rows with brown, and continue till four pink and five brown stripes are worked in this crazy stitch. Sew the last row to the commencing chain; and join the top of the antimacassar, making the stripes meet evenly together. The **Edging** round the bottom of the antimacassar is worked entirely with brown thread. **1st round**—1 treble, 1 chain, and repeat; do the treble just close enough together to lie flat and even, and join the last chain stitch at the end of the round to the first treble stitch with which the round commenced; this round is to be threaded with ribbon. **2nd round**—Scollops—Do 1 double crochet under a loop of chain of last round, * 6 chain, 1 single crochet in the sixth chain from the needle, and in the little circle thus made work 19 treble stitches, thus, 3 ordinary treble, 3 treble with the thread passed twice round the needle, 3 treble with the thread three times round the needle, 1 treble with the thread four times round the needle, 3 treble with the thread three times round the needle, 3 treble with the thread twice round the needle, 3 ordinary treble, then 1 double crochet in each of the four next spaces, and repeat from *; in working the successive scollops attach at the fourth treble stitch to the corresponding stitch of the previous scollop; and at the end of the round join the last scollop to the first, and fasten off. Run the piece of pink ribbon through the row of holes, and tie a bow on each side the antimacassar.

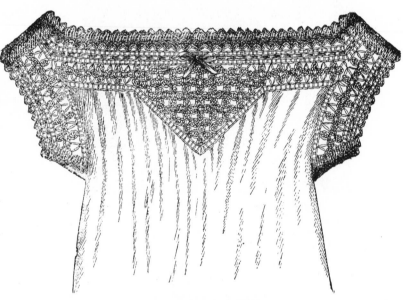

Chemise Trimming.

DOLL, DRESSED IN CROCHET.

THE dolly represented in our engraving has blue eyes and golden hair, and stands between 12 inches and 13 inches high, her body is made of composition, her arms, legs, and head are jointed, and will move in any position. She wears a combination garment and a petticoat, a pretty frock and a hat, all worked in crochet; her socks are woven, and her kid shoes have tiny buckles in front. Procure 1 oz. of white and ½ oz. of pale blue Andalusian wool, 1 oz. of white Shetland, and a No. 14 and No. 9 crochet needle. The white Andalusian is used for the underclothing, the pale blue for the frock and hat, and the white Shetland for the looped trimming on the frock and hat; the Shetland must be wound in two balls to be worked together. For the **Combination of Drawers** and **Body**—Begin the body at the waist, with 50 chain, employing white Andalusian wool and No. 14 crochet needle. Work closely and firmly. **1st row**—Do 1 double crochet in the second chain from the needle, and proceed in double crochet to the end, 48 stitches. **2nd row**—Turn the work, do 1 double crochet on the first stitch by the needle, and work in double crochet to the end, inserting the hook to take up the front and top threads of the stitches of the previous row. Continue as the second row till 20 rows are done. **21st row**—Turn the work, do 1 double crochet on the first stitch by the needle and work 12 double crochet; and turn, and work in little rows on the 12 stitches till 6 rows are done, and fasten off; this is the first side of the back; work the other side to correspond: miss one stitch against those for the armholes, and work double crochet on 22 stitches for 6 rows for the front. **27th row**—Recommence on the right-hand side, do 10 double crochet over the 12 on the first back, 4 chain for a shoulder strap, 20 double crochet along the front, 4 chain for the other shoulder strap, and 10 double crochet on the other back. **28th row**—Turn, and work 48 double crochet tightly to the end of the row, and fasten off. Now resume on the foundation chain and work for the drawers, do 12 double crochet, 3 double crochet in the next stitch, 24 double crochet, 3 double crochet in the next, 12 double crochet; fold the work in a round, and now do 3 or 4 rounds of 54 stitches in a round taking up the front and top threads. **Next round**—Do 27 double crochet, fold the work for shaping a leg, and work on the 27 stitches round and round for 20 rounds, but decrease one stitch on the inner side of the leg in the 16th, 17th, and 18th rounds. For an **Edge**—Work 1 double crochet on one stitch, 3 chain, another double crochet on the same stitch as last double crochet, miss two stitches, and repeat. Work the other leg in the same manner. The **Sleeves** are made by working double crochet round the armhole, about 20 stitches in a round for 4 rounds, and then a round of edging the same as at the bottom of the drawers. Begin by the waist and work a row of double crochet up one side of the back of the body, work a row of edging along the neck, and a row of double crochet down the other side of the back, and finish by the waist with a few buttonhole stitches to strengthen the opening; four or five very tiny pearl buttons must be sewn on the left-hand side of the back and will secure into the crochet on the opposite side.

For the **Petticoat.** With white Andalusian wool commence at the waist with 52 chain, and join round. Do 3 or 4 rounds of 52 double crochet; then increase 1 stitch in every round, not always in the same place, till 60 double crochet are in the round; do 3 rounds on 60 double crochet, always in this petticoat taking up the front and top threads; do 3 rounds of treble stitches; then three more rounds of double crochet; and then for the flounce. **1st round**—1 double crochet on double crochet, * 3 chain, 1 double crochet on the next double crochet, and repeat from *.

Nightdress Sachet.

2nd round—1 double crochet under a loop of chain of last round, * 3 chain, 1 double crochet under the next loop, and repeat from *. **3rd round**—The same as last round but do only 2 chain. **4th round**—1 double crochet under each loop and 1 chain between; and fasten off at the end of the round. Work a row of treble along the top of the petticoat, and make a chain to run through the stitches and tie round the waist.

For the **Frock.**—Use blue Andalusian wool and a No. 10 bone crochet needle, and work moderately loosely. Begin the skirt at the waist with 72 chain. **1st row**—Do 1 double crochet in the second chain from the needle, 2 chain, another double crochet in the same place, * miss one stitch, 1 double crochet in the next, 2 chain, another double crochet in the same place, and repeat from * to the end. **2nd row**—2 chain to turn, * do 1 double crochet in the first of the two chain stitches of last row, 2 chain, another double crochet in the same place, and repeat from * to the end, there will be 36 patterns in the row, and the work should appear rather open. Work as the second row till 10 or 12 rows are done for the length of the skirt: finish off evenly, and sew up the back. Now to work the **Body**, begin by the seam, and first work a row of 36 long treble stitches, that is, putting 1 long treble stitch to each striped pattern of the skirt, work high and rather loosely to afford space for a ribbon to run through. **2nd row**—Work in pattern as on the skirt, get 22 patterns along the row. Do 3 more rows the same. **6th row**—Work five patterns for one side of the back, turn, and again do 5 patterns: work 4 patterns, and turn, and work 4 patterns again; fasten off. Work the other side of the back to correspond. Along the front, missing one pattern on each side for armholes, work a row of 10 patterns, and turn and work 10 patterns back; omit one pattern on each side and work 2 rows with 8 patterns in each row, and fasten off. Join the shoulders across with from 4 to 6 chain. Begin a sleeve by the arm-pit, work about 11 patterns round the armhole, and

turn, and work the same number of patterns again: in the 2 next rows omit one pattern at the end of each row: do 2 or 3 rows without decrease; then 2 rows omitting the last stitch again, now 7 patterns; and work on till sleeve is sufficiently long. Work the other sleeve in the same manner, and sew the sleeves up. For the **Looped Trimming.**—Use the Shetland wool double, *i.e.*, taking a thread from each of two balls: begin round the bottom of the skirt,—**1st row**—Work 1 double crochet stitch and 1 looped stitch alternately,—The looped stitch is made thus—pass the double wool three times round the first and second fingers of the left hand, then insert the hook in the previous row of the crochet and also under the wool that lies over the first finger, draw the wool through and finish as a double crochet stitch. **2nd row**—Work a double crochet over a double crochet and a looped stitch over a looped stitch of preceding row, and repeat. Continue till 4 rows are worked round the bottom of the skirt. Work 3 rows of the same looped trimming round the wrists, and 2 rows along the neck. Then run in a piece of inch-wide ribbon through the long treble stitches at the waist, and a narrower ribbon to tie round the neck, and place a little bow in front at the neck and waist, and also on the wrists.

For the **Hat.**—This is a toque shape. Commence with blue wool with 3 chain: do 3 double crochet in the first stitch of chain, and continue in double crochet round and round, increasing a stitch here and there as necessary to keep the work nearly flat till you have a circle measuring about 2 inches across or a little more. Round this work with white wool 4 rounds of looped trimming the same as on the bottom of the skirt. Run a double thread of wool through the last round of crochet to keep the hat to the size of the doll's head. Trim the hat with a little bow of ribbon as represented in the engraving.

COSY CHAIR-BACK.

WORKED WITH MACRAMÉ TWINE.

THE front of this chair-back is worked in stripes with macramé twine of two good contrasting colours, forming a series of checks or squares; the back is simple open crochet; the two parts are joined together somewhat in the shape of a cosy, and when drawn over the back of a chair the antimacassar will remain in position without fear of falling off. Procure six balls of salmon-pink, and seven balls of chocolate-brown macramé thread of medium thickness, and a No. 8 bone crochet needle. For the **First Stripe of Squares** for the *Front* of the chair-back, — Begin with brown twine, with 18 chain. **1st row**—Do 1 treble in the third chain from the needle, 1 chain, miss one, 6 treble in the next, withdraw the needle from the last treble stitch and insert it in the top of the first stitch of the group of six stitches, and draw the dropped stitch through to confine the group of six stitches in a close tuft, *. 1 chain, miss one, 1 treble in the next, 1 chain, miss one, a tuft in the next, and repeat from * twice, making a series of four tufts in the row. **2nd row**—3 chain to turn, * work 1 treble on the back of the tuft of last row, 1 chain, 1 tuft on the treble stitch of last row, 1 chain, and repeat from * to the end; the tufts should stand raised on the same side as the tufts of the first row. Work the same till 5 rows of tufts are completed, when one square will be finished. Join on the pink twine, and do plain double crochet forwards and backwards for 13 rows, having 15 double crochet stitches in each row, and inserting the needle to take up both top threads; this is the second square. Then do another square of 5 tufted rows with brown twine, and another square of 13 plain double crochet rows with pink twine; and fasten off. For the **Second Stripe of Squares,**—Commence with 16 chain with pink twine and work 13 rows of plain double crochet, 15 stitches in each row, for the first square; then 5 tufted rows with brown twine for the second square; and repeat the same, and fasten off. Do two more stripes like each of the above, making six stripes in all, and sew them together, pink against brown, and brown against pink, in an arrangement of "checks," as shown in the engraving. The **Back** of the antimacassar is crocheted entirely with brown twine.—Commence upon the piece of work that is already done, and work along the top edge of the six stripes—which will be the top of the chair-back,—2 long treble stitches in one stitch of the striped work, * miss two stitches, 2 long treble in the next, and repeat from * to the end: turn with 4 chain, and do 2 long treble in each space between the long treble stitches of last row. Continue thus till a sufficient length of open long treble is worked to correspond with the length of the striped crochet. Join up the sides of the antimacassar. For the **Border**—This is worked all round the bottom of the antimacassar with pink twine. **1st round**—1 double crochet in a stitch of the antimacassar, * 2 chain, miss three stitches, 3 treble in the next, 2 chain, 3 more treble in the same place, 2 chain, miss three stitches, 1 double crochet in the next, and repeat from * ; and join evenly at the end of the round. **2nd round**—1 double crochet on a double crochet stitch of last round, * 3 chain, 3 treble, 2 chain, and 3 treble all under the two chain in the centre of the previous group of treble stitches, 3 chain, 1 double crochet on double crochet, and repeat from * ; and fasten off at the end of the round. The chair-back is now finished, and may be ornamented with one or two bows of ribbon if desired.

PASSEMENTERIE DRESS TRIMMING.

As braiding will this season be a most fashionable trimming for dresses and mantles, our subscribers will be pleased to learn a clever way of reproducing in crochet a pattern of antique wheels in exact imitation of braiding, and particularly handsome for using upon silk or woollen dresses; and our engravings show two styles of this trimming, one being wider and more elaborate than the other, but both crocheted in the same manner. The trimming may be made with tolerably coarse purse silk, or with a medium size crochet flax thread, or Maltese crochet thread, and a rather fine crochet needle. For the **First Wheel**—Commence with 10 chain, and join round in a circle. **1st round**—Do 18 double crochet in the circle, and join evenly at

HARLEQUIN BALL.

THIS attractive ball is made with odds and ends of wool of various colours, and is very bright and pretty. Single Berlin wool, or Andalusian wool, either may be employed, with a fine crochet needle to work closely and firmly. In the model ball cardinal is used for the groundwork and the tufted rows are crocheted in a different colour in every successive row, in this rotation,—amber, brown, amber, violet, amber, orange, amber, pink, amber, blue, amber, rose,—making 12 lines of raised tufts running perpendicularly from the top to the bottom round the ball, as shown in the engraving : three plain rows of cardinal are worked between each line of colour. Begin with cardinal wool for the flat circle at the bottom of the ball ; do 2 chain, 3 double crochet in the first stitch of chain, and proceed round and round in double crochet, taking up top and back threads, working tightly, and increasing as necessary to keep the circle flat till there are 24 stitches in the round ; break off. Make another similar circle for the top of the ball, and when this is complete with 24 stitches in the round, instead of breaking off make 29 chain, and join to a stitch of the bottom circle, now turn the work and on the chain, for the **1st row** of the pattern—work 6 single crochet, 17 double crochet, 6 single crochet, and join to the same stitch of the circle from which the chain started. **2nd row**—Turn, and go back on the stitches of last row, doing again 6 single crochet, 17 double crochet, 6 single crochet, and join to the same stitch as you previously joined on the circle. **3rd row**—Do 6 single crochet, 17 double crochet, and 6 single crochet, and join to the next stitch of the top circle, fasten off cardinal wool, and run the end in neatly. **4th row**—Take amber

Cosy Antimacassar worked with Macramé Twine.

Doll Dres

the end of the round. **2nd round**—Do 14 chain, turn, and work 22 double crochet firmly *over* the line of chain stitches just done (by managing carefully the stitches will not fall off the end of the chain) and do 1 double crochet on the first double crochet stitch of the circle inserting the hook into the two front threads ; turn the work, and along the little bar or strip do 22 double crochet over the last twenty-two double crochet working into the one back thread of the stitches ; turn with 1 chain, * do 1 double crochet on each of 4 double crochet of last row, inserting the hook to take up the one back thread of the stitches, 4 chain, 1 double crochet in the fourth chain from the needle, and repeat from * till four of the chain picots are done, then 1 double crochet on each of the 5 remaining stitches of the bar, and 1 double crochet on a double crochet stitch of the first round where miss one from the stitch last worked upon and take up the two front threads instead of working upon the one back thread as on the bar ; next do 14 chain for another bar, and to connect this with the preceding work a single crochet in the third picot from the end of the last bar, turn, and work 22 double crochet under the loop of fourteen chain, and continue this bar similarly to the last bar. Six of these bars constitute a wheel, and when working the last of the bars make the circle complete by joining in the proper place to the first bar. When working successive wheels connect them together by the picots in the manner shown in our engraving, either to make a narrow passementerie trimming as the top engraving, or a wider and more important trimming as the lower engraving shows.

---

wool, and bringing it up in the next stitch of the bottom circle, work 6 single crochet on the single crochet of last row, then for tufts, do 4 treble stitches in a stitch of the second previous row, take the hook from the last treble stitch, insert it in the top of the first treble stitch, pick up the wool of the fourth stitch again on the needle and draw it through the first treble stitch closely for a tuft, miss one stitch of last row, do 1 double crochet on the next, then another tuft on the next stitch of the second previous row, and repeat a double crochet and a tuft till you have 8 tufts worked, then 6 single crochet on the single crochet of last row, and join to the same stitch of the top circle as last row is joined, and fasten off. Join cardinal wool to the bottom circle, and repeat the first, second, and third rows of the pattern. The next row will be worked with brown wool in tufts as the fourth row. And now continue in plain crochet, and every fourth row a line of tufts, through the gradations of colour stated above, when the circle will be completed ; and the ball may be stuffed with wool or horse-hair, and sewn up.

LADY'S MANTELETTE.

THIS handsome mantelette is intended for out-of-door wear, to go to the theatre or opera, or to drive to a dinner party. It is thick and warm, and the pattern, as shown in the sectional engraving, is alike on both sides. Procure 1½ lbs. of white, or if preferred pale blue or pink, double Berlin wool, and a No. 5 bone crochet needle. Commence for the front of the mantelette, working lengthways, and making 86 chain from the top to the bottom. **1st row**—Insert the hook in the second chain from the needle and draw the wool through, wool over the needle and insert the hook again in the same place and draw the wool through, now there are 4 loops on the needle, wool over the needle and draw through the 4 loops ; * insert the hook in the next stitch of the commencing chain and draw the wool through, wool over the needle and insert the hook again in the same place and draw the wool through, wool over the needle and draw through the four loops on the needle, and proceed from * to the end of the row, making 84 of these compound stitches in the row. 2nd row—Do 2 chain and turn the work, insert the hook to take up the one back thread of the first stitch of previous row and draw the wool through, wool over the needle and insert the hook again in the same place and draw the wool through, wool over the needle and draw through 4 loops on the needle, and continue the same stitch, always working into the one back thread of the stitches of last row, and doing again 84 stitches in the row. 3rd row—Do 2 chain to turn, work 84 compound stitches, and increase by working an extra stitch in the last stitch of previous row. 4th row—Work 85 compound stitches ; always in this and every row turn with 2 chain. 5th row—Work 85 stitches and an extra stitch at the end ; this end of the row where the increasing is made is the neck end where shaping is required, the other end is the bottom of the mantelette and is kept straight for the present. 6th row—Work 86 stitches. 7th row—86 stitches and increase at the end. 8th row—87 stitches. 9th row —87 stitches and increase at the end. 10th row—88 stitches. 11th row—88 stitches and increase at the end. 12th row—2 chain to turn, increase by working 1 compound stitch into the second chain from the needle, then do 89 stitches consecutively to the end of the row. 13th row—Work 90

and increase at the end. Do 3 rows upon 44 stitches. 59th row—43 stitches, omit the last stitch. 60th row—Turn with 1 chain, miss this and miss one stitch, and do 42 stitches. 61st row—41 stitches, omit the last stitch. 62nd row—Turn with 1 chain, miss this and miss one stitch, and do 40 stitches. 63rd row—39 stitches, omit the last stitch. 64th row—Turn with 1 chain, miss this and miss one stitch, and do 38 stitches. 65th row—38 stitches. 66th row—Increase at the beginning of the row, and work thence 38 consecutive stitches. 67th row— 39 stitches. 68th row—Increase, work 39 stitches. 69th row—40 stitches. 70th row—Increase, and work 40 stitches. 71st row—41 stitches, and increase at the end. 72nd row—Increase, and work 42 stitches, and at the end make 52 chain for the other side of the front. 73rd row—Work 50 stitches along the chain, work 43 stitches over stitches of last row, and increase at the end. 74th row—Turn with 1 chain, miss this and miss one stitch, and do 93 stitches. 75th row—92 stitches, omit one stitch at the neck. 76th row—Decrease at neck and work 91 stitches. 77th row—90 stitches, omit the last stitch. 78th row—Decrease at neck, and work 89 stitches. 79th row—88 stitches, omit the last stitch. 80th row—88 stitches. 81st row— 87 stitches, omit the last stitch. 82nd row—87 stitches. 83rd row—86 stitches, omit the last stitch. 84th row—86 stitches. 85th row—85 stitches, omit the last stitch. 86th row—85 stitches. 87th row—84 stitches, omit the last stitch. 88th row—84 stitches. Fasten off. Sew up the shoulders. Work a row of plain double crochet along the neck, rather tightly, to draw the work in to the size required. The mantelette is trimmed with pompons which are made after the manner of a child's soft wool ball :—

Cosy Chair-Back worked with Macramé Twine.

stitches and increase at the neck end. 14th row—Increase at the beginning of the row and work 91 stitches to the end. 15th row—Work 92 stitches and increase at the neck. 16th row—Increase at the beginning of the row and work thence 43 consecutive stitches, and leave 50 stitches unworked for the lower end of the front of the mantelette. 17th row—Work 43 stitches, omit one stitch at the end. 18th row—Turn with 1 chain, miss this and miss one stitch, and do 42 stitches. 19th row—2 chain to turn as usual, work 41 stitches, omit one stitch at the neck. 20th row—Turn with 1 chain, miss this and miss one stitch, and do 40 stitches. 21st row—40 stitches. 22nd row—Turn with 1 chain, miss this and miss one stitch, and do 39 stitches. 23rd row—39 stitches. 24th row—Turn with 1 chain, miss this and miss the first stitch, and do 38 stitches. 25th row—38 stitches. 26th row—Increase 1 stitch at the beginning, and work to the end. 27th row—39 stitches, increase by doing another stitch at the end. 28th row— Increase 1 stitch at the beginning, and work to the end. 29th row—41 stitches, increase by doing another stitch at the end. 30th row—Increase 1 stitch at the beginning, and work to the end. 31st row—43 stitches, increase by doing another stitch at the end. Do 3 rows upon 44 stitches. 35th row—43 stitches, omit one stitch at the end. 36th row—43 stitches. 37th row—42 stitches, omit the last stitch at the end. 38th row—42 stitches. 39th row—41 stitches, omit the last stitch at the end. 40th row—41 stitches. Now work for the middle of the back, and do from 10 rows to 20 rows, as required for the width of the back, whether for a slim or a stout figure. 51st row—Work 41 stitches, and increase by doing another stitch at the end. 52nd row—42 stitches. 53rd row—42 stitches, and increase at the end. 54th row—43 stitches. 55th row—43 stitches,

Cut a skein of wool in half and take about 20 of the long strands and lay them all evenly together on the table before you, thread a rug needle or a tatting shuttle with another length of wool, and tie the end of this wool firmly round the strands of wool beginning on the left-hand side about half an inch from the end : make another tie with the wool in the needle upon the stranded wool about an inch or a little further from the first tie, sewing it in a perfectly firm knot ; and proceed in this manner until you have tied the stranded wool at regular intervals all along, when do more strands in the same manner ; and continue till a sufficient length is made to go twice the whole way round the mantelette. The strands of wool are then cut in the centre of every space between the ties, of course not cutting the wool with which you have been sewing, as the pompons hang on this, pull the pompons into shape clipping them if needful : now arrange the trimming in two rows round the mantelette, as shown in the engraving. The mantelette should fasten from the throat to the waist with buttons and loops. If a high collar is liked, several rows of plain double crochet, worked tightly, may be put round the neck, and be covered with pompon trimming.

FASCINATOR.

THIS fascinator is worked in a simple open stitch of treble and chain. Either Shetland wool or Andalusian wool can be employed, and the fascinator will take about 2 ozs. of the former, or about 3 ozs. of the latter, using a No. 10 bone crochet needle. Begin in the centre of the square, with 4 chain, which join in a circle, and proceed to work in rounds. 1st round—Do 4 chain to stand for a treble stitch, 1 treble in the circle, * 2 chain, 2 treble in the circle, repeat from * twice, then 2 chain, and join to the top stitch of the chain with which the round began. **2nd round**—Turn the hook, and put it in the hole to the right of the join, and draw the wool through the stitch on the needle, do 4 chain to stand for a treble stitch, 1 treble in the same hole, * 2 chain, 2 treble in the next hole or space, 2 chain, and 2 more treble in the same place, repeat from * twice; 2 chain, 2 treble in the next space, 2 chain, and join to the top stitch of chain with which the round commenced. **3rd round**—Turn the hook and put it in the space to the right of the join, and draw the wool through the stitch on the needle, do 4 chain to stand for a treble stitch, 1 treble in the same space (which is a corner space), * 2 chain, 2 treble in the next space, 2 chain, 2 treble in the next space, 2 chain, and 2 more treble in the same place (which is another corner), repeat from * twice; 2 chain, 2 treble in the next space, 2 chain, 2 treble in the next space, 2 chain, and join to the top stitch of chain with which the round began. The remainder of the square is worked similarly to the third round, the only difference being that as the square gets larger you work one additional group of 2 chain 2 treble along each side of the square in each successive round; the corners are always turned by working two groups of 2 treble with 2 chain between the same as in the third round. When 15 rounds are done the square will be sufficiently large. From the corner where you are finishing off, work a 16-inch length of chain, and break off. Work a similar length of chain from the opposite corner; these are for the ends of the fascinator. Hold the work the right side towards you, and begin on the twenty-first stitch of chain from the corner of the square, do 2 single crochet, 6 double crochet, then treble to the end of the chain and round the point and along the opposite side, and end with 6 double crochet opposite the six double crochet stitches, and 2 single crochet opposite the two single crochet stitches, and fasten off. Recommence upon the fifth double crochet stitch, and work another row of single, double, and treble stitches round the end of the fascinator. Work the other end in the same manner. For the **Border**—**1st round**—Tuft stitch—Begin with a stitch tied on the needle and the wool over the needle, * insert the hook under one of the spaces on the square and draw the wool through, wool over the needle, insert the hook in the same place and draw the wool through, do this four more times, drawing all the loops up as long and loosely as possible, wool over the needle and draw through the bunch of loops, wool over the needle and draw through two stitches on the needle, 3 chain, and repeat from *; the tuft stitch is similarly worked round the ends of the fascinator as well as along the intervening twenty chain stitches that connect the ends to the square. **2nd round**—Scollops—Work 1 double crochet on the tuft stitch of last round, 2 chain, 2 treble, 3 long treble, and 2 treble, *all* under the loop of three chain of last round, 2 chain, and repeat the same to the end of the round. The square, as described above, if worked with thicker wool, and continued to a larger size, is a useful pattern for a shoulder shawl for charity purposes.

SLUMBER ROLL.

WORKED IN MUSCOVITE TRICOT.

THIS pretty head-rest or slumber roll is intended to hang on the back of an easy chair to support the head when sleeping. It is worked in Muscovite tricot, with double Berlin wool of two good contrasting colours, such as pale blue and dove grey, of which half a pound of each colour will be required, and

a No. 4 or No. 5 bone tricot needle, also **2 yards of pale blue silk cord**, and 4 silk pompons, and half a yard of pale blue sateen to make the bolster case. Make the bolster case the size you desire the roll to be, and draw the ends up with a gathering thread, having previously stuffed the bolster with feathers, wool-wadding, or scraps of rags cut very small and fine. For the tricot, commence with 60 chain stitches with blue wool. **1st row**—With blue wool,—pick up every stitch as in tricot; and work back in this manner, wool over the needle and draw through 1 tricot stitch, wool over the needle and draw through the stitch just made and through the next tricot stitch, * do 3 chain, wool over the needle and draw through the last stitch of chain and through 1 tricot stitch, wool over the needle and draw through the stitch just made and through the next tricot stitch, and repeat from * to the end of the row, and you will have 29 picot loops of three chain in the row with 2 picot stitches between each. **2nd row**—Take grey wool,—pick up every tricot stitch of last row, taking the front threads and keeping the loops of chain on the front of the work, you should have 60 stitches on the needle in this and every row; to draw back, wool over the needle and draw through 3 tricot stitches in succession, * do 3 chain, wool over the needle and draw through the last stitch of chain and through 1 tricot stitch, wool over the needle and draw through the stitch just made and through the next tricot stitch, and repeat from *, and when you have 28 picot loops of chain, you will end the row with 3 plain tricot stitches as it began. Repeat these two rows till you have 40 rows worked, then join the first row to the last, and put the tricot over the bolster, gathering up the ends neatly; and finish off with double loops of cord to throw over the back of the chair to hold the slumber roll in position convenient to rest the head: two pompons are placed on each end where the work is gathered up, if not easy to get silk ones, these may be made of wool over two circles of cord in the same manner as children's soft wool balls are made.

TEA COSY IN TRICOT.

LIMPET SHELL PATTERN.

FOR this pretty tea cosy procure 3 ozs. of shrimp pink single Berlin wool, 1 yard of figured pongée silk and two yards of silk cord to match, a good supply of wadding, and a No. 6 bone tricot needle. Commence for the bottom of one side of the cosy, with 39 chain. **1st row**—Pick up all the stitches in tricot, 39 on the needle, and draw back in the usual manner, that is, the wool over the needle and draw through 1 tricot stitch, * wool over the needle and draw through the stitch just made and through the next tricot stitch, and repeat from * till all the stitches are worked through and 1 stitch only remains upon the needle. **2nd row**—Pick up 3 tricot stitches, making with the 1 stitch already, 4 stitches on the needle, * put the wool in a kind of loop over the first finger of the left hand, the thread of wool that comes from the needle being below and behind the finger and the end of wool from the ball over the finger and in front, put the hook over the front wool and into the loop and slip the loop off the finger on to the needle, make in all 8 of these loops loosely upon the needle, then wool over the needle (as see the position in the sectional engraving) and draw through the 8 loops, wool over the needle and draw through the 1 stitch to hold the limpet shell in its place, miss one tricot stitch of last row, pick up the next 5 tricot stitches, and repeat from * to the end of the row, where there will be 4 tricot stitches to correspond with the four at the beginning, and draw back as usual. **3rd row**—Plain tricot. 39 stitches in the row. **4th row**—Pick up 6 tricot stitches, * make a limpet shell over the centre stitch between the shells of the previous row, 5 tricot stitches, and repeat from *, and the row will end with 7 tricot stitches as it

Narrow Passementerie Dress Trimming.

Wide Passementerie Dress Trimming.

began, draw back as usual. **5th row**—Plain tricot. Thus the pattern consists of four rows, as the work is continued by repeating from the second row. **6th row**—Tricot the same as the second row, but when drawing back draw through the 2 first stitches together and the 2 last stitches together, so decreasing a stitch on each side to shape the cosy. Similar decreases are made henceforward in each pattern row, and of course in working, as there are fewer stitches, you must make allowance for those that are decreased, and remember to keep the shells in perpendicular line over the shells of the second row and fourth row. By the time you have done the twenty-fourth row you will have reduced to 23 stitches, 3 shells, in the row. Then work 1 row of plain tricot, and slip-stitch along the top, and fasten off. The other side of the cosy is worked to correspond. When both sides of the tricot are accomplished the tea cosy must be made up. Cut two pieces of pongée silk the required size, quilt them thickly with wadding, and put a full fluting of double silk all round the top to keep the two sides of the cosy together; edge all round the tricot with silk cord. Make four wool pompons, and place two on each side the top of the cosy mixed with ornamental loops of cord; and cord for handles in the manner shown in the engraving.

—With amber, or lemon colour. Do 3 treble under a loop of three chain of last round, 3 chain, 3 more treble in the same place, * 3 treble under the next loop, 3 chain, 3 more treble in the same place, and repeat from * twice, and join to the treble stitch with which the round commenced, and fasten off. **3rd round**—With ruby, green, blue, or any colour—Do 3 treble, 3 chain, 3 treble, *all* under a loop of three chain of last round, which is a corner loop, 3 treble in the little space between the groups of treble stitches on the side of the square, repeat this three times; join to the treble stitch at the beginning of the round, and fasten off. **4th round**—With black—Do 3 treble, 3 chain, 3 treble, all under the loop of three chain of last round, which is a corner of the square, 3 treble in the first space along the side of the square, 3 treble in the next space, and repeat three times, and join to the treble stitch with which the round began, and fasten off. Work a number of these squares, and sew them together. All ends of wool should be crocheted over as the work proceeds, or may be drawn in neatly afterwards, if preferred. For the **Border—1st round**—With black wool—Work 3 treble, 3 chain, 3 treble, *all* under the loop of three chain at the corner of the piece of work, and 3 treble in every space along the side, and repeat, and fasten off at

Details of Stitch used for Lady's Mantelette.

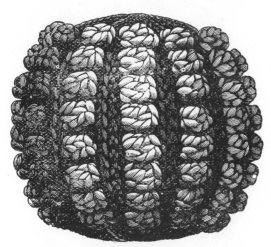

Harlequin Ball.

PATCHWORK CROCHET.

FOR USING ODD LENGTHS OF WOOL TO MAKE QUILTS, BASSINETTE COVERS, &C.

THE pattern consists of a number of small square sections, in the making of which any odd lengths of wool of various colours may be employed with a due proportion of white and black. Very pretty sofa antimacassars, couvrepieds, &c., may be fashioned in this manner. Use a rather fine bone crochet needle and work firmly. Commence with white wool, with 5 chain, and join round in a circle. **1st round**—With white—Do 3 chain to stand for a treble. 2 treble in the circle, * 3 chain, 3 treble in the circle, repeat from * twice, 3 chain, and join to the top stitch of chain with which the round began, and fasten off. **2nd round**

Lady's Mantelette.

the end of the round. **2nd round**—With white—1 double crochet in the space between the groups of treble stitches, 4 chain, 1 double crochet in the next space, and repeat; make an extra loop on turning the corners. **3rd round**—With pink—Do 1 double crochet, 1 chain, 2 treble, then a picot of 4 chain, 1 single crochet on the last treble stitch, then 2 more treble, 1 chain, and 1 double crochet, *all* under each loop of four chain of last round, taking care to draw the treble stitches to stand up high. **4th round**—With white—Do 1 treble (well drawn up) between the two double crochet stitches of last round, 2 chain, 1 double crochet in the round picot, 2 chain, and repeat; and make two loops of 2 chain and 1 double crochet at the corners. **5th round**—With white—* 1 double crochet in the space next after a treble stitch of last round, 5 chain, 1 double crochet in the fifth chain from the needle, 5 chain, 1 double crochet in the fifth chain from the needle, 1 double crochet in the space next after a double crochet stitch of last round, and repeat from *; make increase at the corners sufficient to turn round them nicely, in the manner shown in the engraving.

BABY'S LONG BOOTS.

WORKED IN POINT NEIGE OR SHELL STITCH.

PROCURE 2 ozs. of white Peacock fingering and a No. 9 bone crochet needle. Commence with 36 chain for the top of the leg, and join in a round. Work 1 round of double crochet. The next and all the following rounds are worked in point neige, or shell stitch, which has many times been described in these columns (See page 3, No. 56 of "Weldon's Practical Needlework Series "). Work 18 shell stitches in a round for 3 rounds. Put in a coloured thread to denote the back of the leg, or an imaginary seam, and there decrease 1 stitch in each successive round till reduced to 14 stitches in the round. Work then without further decreasing till there are 15 rounds in all for the length of the leg. For the heel, work 8 stitches across the back of the leg, that is, 4 stitches on each side the imaginary seam, turn, and work back over the 8 heel stitches in double crochet, 16 double crochet in a row for 4 rows, and 2 more rows decreasing twice in the centre of each row, when the heel will be long enough. Fold the last row of the heel and join it at the bottom. Now work all round the foot, doing 18 point neige stitches in the round: then two rounds decreasing a stitch at the gusset on each side the 6 instep stitches and so bringing the foot to 14 stitches in the round, on which to do 4 rounds, when the foot will be nearly long enough. Do 2 rounds or three rounds decreasing two or three stitches in each round for the toe, and fasten off, and sew up. A row of crazy stitch is worked to form an edge round the top of the leg, 1 single crochet in a stitch of the foundation chain, 3 chain, 2 treble in the same stitch with the single crochet, miss two stitches and repeat; and join evenly at the end of the round.

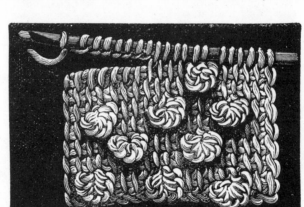

Details of Tricot Stitch for Tea Cosy.

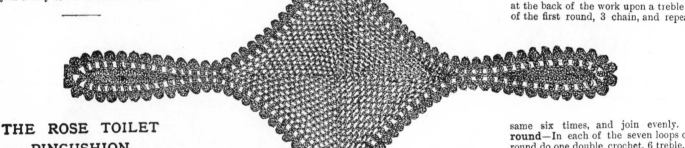

Fascinator.

THE ROSE TOILET PINCUSHION.

THE pincushion, of which we here give an illustration, stands about 2½ inches high, and measures rather more than 6 inches in diameter, it is made in the shape of a brioche cushion, and has a hole in the centre of a size to hold a small tumbler to contain flowers. Procure six skeins of Ardern's crochet cotton No. 18, and a fine steel crochet needle. For the **Large Roses,** — of which there are six round the top of the pincushion,—begin with 12 chain, and join round ; then do 7 chain, 1 treble in the circle, * 4 chain, 1 treble in the circle, repeat from * twice, then 4 chain, and join to the third stitch of chain with which the round commenced. **2nd round** —In each of the five loops of last round work

Slumber Roll worked in Muscovite Tricot.

double crochet in each of the five loops of last round. **9th round**—Do 1 double crochet at the back of the work above a double crochet stitch of the seventh round, 11 chain, and repeat the same four times, and join evenly. **10th round**—Work 1 double crochet, 2 treble, 11 long treble, 2 treble, and 1 double crochet in each of the five loops of last round. **11th round**—Do 1 double crochet at the back of the work above a double crochet stitch of the ninth round, 12 chain, and repeat the same four times, and join evenly. **12th round**—Work 1 double crochet, 2 treble, 2 long treble, 9 double long treble, 2 long treble, 2 treble, and 1 double crochet, *all* in each of the five loops of last round, and join evenly, and fasten off ; this completes the first rose. Work five more roses in the same manner, and as you work join one of the petals in the course of the last round to a corresponding petal of the previous rose, that is, miss one petal on the inside and miss two petals on the outside between the joinings, and so make the six roses assume the form of a wreath, as represented in the engraving. This wreath is to be laid on the top of the pincushion, the foundation of which should be made up firmly and covered with pale blue sateen. And now a network of chain and double crochet is carried on from the wreath of roses to cover the intermediate spaces that occur between the roses, and also to cover and closely envelop round the side of the pincushion ; while a similar network is arranged to the shape of the hole in the centre of the pincushion. For the **Outside Border of Small Roses.** Make 8 chain, and join round in a circle ; do 5 chain, 1 treble in the circle, * 2 chain, 1 treble in the circle, and repeat from * four times, then two chain, and join to the third stitch of chain with which the round commenced. **2nd round** —In each of the seven loops of last round do 1 double crochet, 4 treble, and 1 double crochet, and join evenly at the end of the round. **3rd round**—Do 1 double crochet at the back of the work upon a treble stitch of the first round, 3 chain, and repeat the same six times, and join evenly. **4th round**—In each of the seven loops of last round do one double crochet, 6 treble, and 1 double crochet, and join evenly. **5th round** —Do 1 double crochet at the back of the work above a double crochet stitch of the third round, 5 chain, and repeat the same six times, and join evenly. **6th round**—In each of the seven loops of last round do 1 double crochet, 8 treble, and 1 double crochet, and join evenly. **7th round** — Do 1 double crochet at the back of the work above a double crochet stitch of the fifth round, 7 chain, and repeat the same six times, and join evenly. **8th round**—In each of the seven loops of last round do 1 double crochet, 11 treble, and 1 double crochet, and join evenly, and fasten off. Work nine more roses, joining each to the one previous, in the form of a circular wreath, as see engraving. A network

1 double crochet, 5 treble, and 1 double crochet, and join evenly at the end of the round. **3rd round**—Do 1 double crochet at the back of the work upon a treble stitch of the first round, 5 chain, and repeat the same four times, and join evenly. **4th round**—In each of the five loops of last round work 1 double crochet, 7 treble, 1 double crochet, and join evenly. **5th round**—Do 1 double crochet at the back of the work above a double crochet stitch of the third round, 7 chain, and repeat the same four times, and join evenly. **6th round**—Work 1 double crochet, 2 treble, 6 long treble, 2 treble, and 1 double crochet in each of the five loops of last round. **7th round** —Do 1 double crochet at the back of the work above the double crochet stitch of the fifth round, 9 chain, and repeat the same four times, and join evenly. **8th round**—Work 1 double crochet, 2 treble, 8 long treble, 2 treble, and 1

of chain and double crochet, or chain and treble stitches, will connect the inner side of this wreath to the chain network that has been carried from the top to the bottom of the pincushion. For the **Scollop** round the **Border of Roses. 1st round**—Begin with 1 double crochet on a petal, where two of the roses are joined together, 8 chain, 1 double crochet on the third treble stitch of the next petal, 8 chain, miss six stitches, 1 double crochet on the next stitch, 11 chain, 1 double crochet on the centre stitch of the next petal (which is the centre petal of three that were missed upon the outside when joining), 6 chain, another double crochet in the same place, 11 chain, 1 double crochet on the third treble stitch of the next petal, 8 chain, miss six stitches, 1 double crochet on the next stitch, 8 chain, 1 double crochet on the next petal ; and continue the same on each rose all round the wreath. **2nd round**—Work 2 treble, 3 chain, and 2 more treble in each loop of chain of last round. **3rd round**—Work 2 treble, 3 chain, and 2 treble under each three chain loop of previous round, and 2 chain between the groups of stitches : this finishes the scollop. Cut a circular piece of cardboard for the bottom of the pincushion, letting it be large enough to extend below the border of small roses, and scolloping it in vandykes to correspond with the crocheted scollops : this cardboard is covered on both sides with sateen, and makes a stiff foundation for both cushion and border, the crochet scollops being tacked thereupon to spread out as shown in the engraving. The top of the pincushion is decorated with three or four pretty bows of narrow blue ribbon.

Tea Cosy in Tricot. Limpet Shell Pattern.

LADY'S BOA.

A HANDSOME boa for the neck can be made in loops of crochet chain in imitation of an ostrich feather boa. Required, 10 ozs. of double Berlin wool, or best superfine peacock quality 3-thread fleecy, either white, grey, or black, as preferred, and a No. 6 bone crochet needle. Commence by making a length of from 1¾ yards to 2 yards of crochet chain as a foundation for working the boa. **1st row**—Do 1 double crochet in the nineteenth stitch from the needle ; 18 chain, 1 double crochet in the next stitch of the foundation ; 18 chain, 1 double crochet in the next stitch ; and so on in loops to the end of the foundation. **2nd row**—Turn, and work into the opposite side of the stitches of the foundation chain ; 18 chain, 1 double crochet in the first stitch of the foundation ; 18 chain, 1 double crochet in the next ; and continue to the end, and fasten off. **3rd row**—Hold the work with the loops hanging downwards double, and now work inserting the hook below the foundation chain *between* the double crochet stitches already worked ; miss the first two spaces, 1 double crochet in the third space ; 18 chain, 1 double crochet in the next space, and repeat till within two spaces of the end of the row, which must be missed to correspond with the beginning. **4th row**—Turn, and work in the same way in loops along the opposite side, inserting the needle to take up the two lower threads of the double crochet stitches of last row. If these four rows are not considered enough to make the boa sufficiently thick and "feathery," work two more rows in the same way. The boa may be fastened with a hook and eye, and a bow of ribbon, as shown in the engraving.

CROCHET BUTTERFLY.

(Not Illustrated.)

CROCHET butterflies are used to appliqué to the corners of teacloths, sideboard cloths, and pocket-handkerchiefs, either by themselves or accompanied with embroidery ; they also are very suitable for decorating photograph frames, fancy boxes, work-baskets, pen-wipers, and other articles, for which latter purposes a wire is run behind the crochet to raise and support the wings. Procure a fine size of brown, gold, or cardinal crochet thread, or flax thread, and a fine steel crochet needle, and work tightly and firmly. Begin for the lower part of a wing, make 13 chain, do 1 long treble in the fourth chain from the needle and 1 long treble in each of the 3 following chain stitches, 1 treble in each of the 4 next stitches, 1 double crochet in the next, and 1 single crochet in the next ; * 2 chain, turn the work, miss the single and double crochet and do 1 double crochet on the first treble stitch of previous row, 1 chain, miss one, 1 treble on the next, 1 chain, miss one, 1 treble on the next, 2

chain, miss two, 1 treble on the next ; for another wing, 7 chain, turn the work do 1 treble in the fourth chain from the needle, 1 long treble on each of the next 5 **stitches**, 1 treble on each of the next 4 stitches, 1 double crochet on the next, 1 single crochet on the **next** which is the double crochet stitch of last row ; repeat from *, do 1 single crochet under the loop of chain ; and one wing will be crocheted ; fasten off. Make another wing in the same manner. Do not fasten the last wing off but connect it to the first wing by a single crochet worked into the last stitch of the first wing ; the right side of the crochet will be uppermost on one wing and the reverse side uppermost on the other wing ; and then for the open crochet all round the wings, do 4 chain, 1 double crochet on the first of the treble stitches of the first wing, 2 chain, miss two, 1 treble in the next, 2 chain, miss one, 1 treble in the next, 2 chain, miss one, 1 treble in the next, then 2 chain and 1 treble in the next till 8 treble stitches in all are done round the first section of the wing, there should be one stitch left between your last treble stitch and the open treble stitch to the left of the section ; then do 1 treble on the next section of the wing in the next stitch to that occupied by the open treble stitch, 2 chain and 1 treble four times on this centre section ; then 1 treble on the next section in the stitch following that occupied by the open treble stitch, 2 chain and 1 treble in the next four times, 2 chain, miss one, 1 treble in the next, 2 chain, miss one, 1 treble in the next, 2 chain, connect this wing to the other wing by a single crochet, and openwork round the other wing to correspond with the wing already worked ; and join evenly at the end of the round, and fasten off ; sew up the gap between the two wings. For the **Body**—Begin with a stitch on the needle, hold the tail part of the butterfly upwards, take up a thread of the crochet in the centre of the join between the wings and draw the cotton through, do 9 chain, 1 treble in the fourth chain from the needle, 4 more consecutive treble, 1 double crochet in the last stitch, and fasten off ; take the ends of cotton to the back of the work and secure them neatly in ; pull the piece of crochet in position to simulate the body of the butterfly. For the **Head**—Do 5 chain to project for the *antennæ* of the butterfly, hold the tail part of the butterfly downwards, cotton twice round the needle and work 4 double long treble by the join between the wings, all in one thread of the crochet and just above the body, withdraw the hook from the last stitch, insert it in the first stitch, then take up the stitch again and draw it through to confine the group of stitches, then 5 chain for the other *antennæ*, and fasten off. The ends of the cotton must be threaded in a needle and drawn invisibly through the back of the chain stitches. Stretch the wings, and the butterfly is finished.

ELYSEE ANTIMACASSAR.

(Not Illustrated.)

THIS is a pretty, light antimacassar formed of cotton crochet combined with cross-stitch embroidery on canvas ; it is oval in shape, and measures about 21 inches in length and 16 inches in width across the widest part. The crochet

Patchwork Crochet.

may be executed with white or with coloured crochet cotton according to taste ; if the former is preferred procure five skeins of Coats No. 12 or No. 14, if the latter use the D M C Coton à tricoter No. 20, this is made in all shades and will wash nicely ; a small steel crochet needle is employed, and you will require about a quarter of a yard of single thread flax canvas, and filoselles of four or five shades of olive greens, pinks shading to crimson, three shades of blue, and a little gold and orange colour

For the **Stripe of Crochet up the Centre of the Antimacassar:** Commence with 6 chain, and join round in a circle. **1st round**—Work 3 chain to stand for a treble, and do 19 treble stitches in the circle, working closely and firmly, and join round. **2nd round**—7 chain to stand for a long treble stitch, 1 long treble (cotton twice round the needle) on the first treble stitch of previous round taking up both front threads, * 2 chain, 1 long treble on the next treble, and repeat from * till 19 long treble are done, then 2 chain, and join to the fifth stitch of the chain with which the round commenced. **3rd round**—4 chain, * cotton twice round the needle and insert the hook under the loop of two chain of last round and draw the cotton through, cotton over the needle and draw through 2 stitches on the needle, cotton over the needle and again draw through 2 stitches on the needle, repeat from * twice, and there will be 4 stitches on the needle, cotton over the needle and draw through all, do 3 chain, repeat from * to the end of the round, and join evenly. **4th round**

—1 double crochet under the loop of three chain of last round, 7 chain, and repeat; join at the end of the round, and fasten off; this forms one medallion. In working the next successive medallions join three of the loops of the last round of the medallion to the three corresponding loops of the previous medallion by a single crochet after doing the third of the seven chain stitches. Continue till you have eleven medallions joined together in a stripe. Next, work a crochet border along each side and round the ends of the stripe: Begin on the right-hand side of the end medallion, which hold in position for working into each of the seventeen loops, and under the next loop to where it is joined to the preceding medallion do 1 double crochet, 12 chain, 1 long treble under the next loop, 5 chain, 1 treble under the next, 4 chain, 1 double crochet under the next, 4 chain, 1 treble under the next, 5 chain, 1 long treble under the next, 5 chain, 1 double long treble under the next, 7 chain, 1 long treble in the same place, 5 chain, 1 treble under the next, 4 chain, 1 double crochet under the next, 4 chain, 1 treble under the next, 5 chain, 1 long treble under the next, 7 chain, 1 double long treble in the same place, 5 chain, 1 long treble under the next, * 5 chain, 1 treble under the next, 4 chain, 1 double crochet under the next, 4 chain, 1 treble under the next, 5 chain, 1 long treble under the next, 12 chain, 1 double crochet under the next which is the last loop of the end medallion, 4 chain, 1 double crochet under the first loop of the next medallion, 6 chain, 1 single crochet in the sixth stitch of the loop of twelve chain just done, 5 chain, 1 long treble under the next, and repeat from * to the end of the stripe, where work round the last medallion, and proceed in the same manner along the opposite side, join evenly to the commencement of the round, and fasten off. Now, holding the right side of the work towards you, begin with 1 double crochet in the fifth stitch of the seven chain at the right-hand corner of the straight side of the stripe, * 2 chain, miss two stitches of previous row, 1 treble in the next, and repeat from * till you get to the loop of seven chain at the left-hand corner, when fasten off; and work the same row along the other side of the stripe. Next, you will work two triangular pieces of crochet to go one on each side of the centre stripe. Begin by working three medallions in a straight line, then do another medallion to join outside the centre medallion of these three. Next, work a portion of a medallion to be joined from the top medallion of the three to the medallion at the side—4 chain, join in a circle, do 3 chain to stand for a treble, 9 treble in the circle, turn the work, do * 6 chain, 1 double crochet on the second treble stitch, repeat from * four times, which will bring you to the last stitch, turn, do 1 chain, 1 double crochet under the first loop of six chain, 3 chain, 1 single crochet to catch into the medallion, 3 chain, 1 double crochet in the same loop last double crochet is worked into, 3 chain, 1 single crochet to catch into the next loop of the medallion, 3 chain, 1 double crochet under the next loop of the section; 7 chain, 1 double crochet under the next loop twice, 3 chain, 1 single crochet in a side loop of the top medallion, 3 chain, 1 double crochet into the next loop of the section, 3 chain, 1 single

crochet into the next loop of the medallion, 3 chain, 1 double crochet under the same loop of the section, and work 5 chain and 1 double crochet alternately five times along the side of the little section to get to the double crochet stitch with which this round began, and fasten off. Work another similar section to fill in the space between the bottom medallion of the three and the medallion at the side. Then in the intervening spaces between the sections and the medallions do a star of 8 groups of long treble stitches as worked in the third round of the medallions, but make no chain between the stitches, and join in such a way that the tops of the eight groups are drawn closely together. Now work above the top medallion of the three, doing loops of 7 chain and 1 double crochet, in little rows to produce an angular corner. Make a similar angular corner on the lower of the three medallions. The piece of crochet should now be three-cornered. Work now the same border round this three-cornered piece that you before worked round the long stripe. Cut four pieces of canvas into triangular shape, each a trifle larger than the three-cornered piece of crochet, to allow for a hem all round, and after embroidering a pretty pattern in cross-stitch, do an edge of feather-stitch with the darkest green filoselle over the hem. Arrange the pieces of canvas thus : two pieces of canvas on each side the central stripe with the three-cornered piece of crochet in the middle ; sew the two corners of the canvas together with a stitch or two, and unite the central stripe to the sides of the canvas, thus, work 1 double crochet in the canvas, 3 chain, 1 double crochet under the loop of two chain of the crochet stripe, * 3 chain, 1 double crochet in the canvas, 3 chain, 1 double crochet under the next loop of the crochet stripe, and repeat from *.

Join the three-cornered pieces of crochet to the canvases in the same way. When all this is in place work the **Border** in medallions as directed for the central stripe, and edge one side of the medallions with the first row of edging as already described, but doing one chain or two chain less in each loop to contract it to the oval shape of the antimacassar; sew the border on, making it lie flat and even.

The Rose Toilet Pincushion.

A HANDSOME SHAWL KNITTED WITH ASTRA-CHAN WOOL.

(Not Illustrated.)

THE variety of wool known as "Astra-chan" is spun in a series of little loops or rings, after the manner of Ice wool, to which it is immeasurably superior, while it is to be had in many beautiful colours. There are two qualities of Astrachan wool, the most silky should be procured. This wool does not lend itself favourably to fancy patterns, and is nearly always used for quite plain knitting, and the effect when worked up bears a great resemblance to Astrachan fur. A handsome shawl can be knitted in the following manner: Procure several balls of Astrachan wool, either white or coloured, according to taste, and a pair of No. 7 or No. 8 bone knitting needles. Cast on 126 stitches, or any number divisible by 8, and 6 stitches over. Work all in plain knitting to the size required, either for a square shawl or a long scarf shape. Then for the last row—Cast off 6 stitches, * drop 2 stitches, cast off 6 stitches, and repeat from * to the end of the row ; a long loose stitch must be drawn over the gap where the two stitches are dropped ; it will be advisable to do all the casting off rather loosely. Now, run down the dropped stitches right to the very first row of the knitting, and the work will be transformed into a pattern of plain knit stripes with a ladder-like open work running between. For the Border—Use a good sized bone crochet needle,—Do 1 double crochet in a stitch of the knitting, * 25 chain worked loosely, 1 double crochet in the second stitch of the knitting, and repeat from *, working the whole way round the shawl : this makes an elegant fringy border, and of course adds greatly to the beauty of the shawl.

Baby's Long Boot.

Lady's Boa.

WELDON'S
PRACTICAL CROCHET.

(FIFTEENTH SERIES.)

How to Crochet Useful Articles for Home and Personal Adornment.

TWENTY-EIGHT ILLUSTRATIONS.

Telegraphic Address—]
"Consuelo," London.]

The Yearly Subscription to this Magazine, post free for United Kingdom and all Parts of the World, is 2s. 6d. Subscriptions are payable in advance, and may commence from any date and for any period.

Telephone—
2745.

The Back Numbers are always in print. Nos. 1 to 77 now ready, Price 2d. each, or post free for 13s. 10d. Over 4,000 Engravings.

BABY'S BOOTS.
WORKED IN PLAIN AND FANCY TRICOT.

REQUIRED, 1 oz. of white and ½ oz. of red single Berlin wool, and a No. 7 bone tricot needle. Commence for top of leg with red wool and make 30 chain stitches. **1st row**—Using red wool,—Pick up a stitch in each stitch of chain, and when 30 stitches are on the needle draw back as follows, put the wool over the needle and draw through 1 stitch, wool over the needle and draw through another stitch, * do 3 chain, wool over the needle and draw through the last stitch of chain and through 1 stitch of tricot, wool over the needle and draw through another stitch of tricot, and repeat from * to the end of the row; there will be 14 tufts of chain in the row. **2nd row**—With white wool—Pick up a stitch in each perpendicular thread of the tricot stitches of last row, raising 30 stitches on the needle, and to draw back, put the wool over the needle and draw through 1 stitch, * do 3 chain, wool over the needle and draw through the last stitch of chain and through 1 stitch of tricot, wool over the needle and draw through another stitch of tricot, and repeat from *; and at the end of the row there will be only 1 tricot stitch after the chain, and there will be 15 tufts of chain in the row. **3rd row**—With red wool—Pick up 30 stitches, and draw back as in the first row. **4th row**—With white wool—Work alternately 1 treble stitch and 1 rice stitch all along; a rice stitch is made by winding the wool 6 times round the needle, then insert the hook in the tricot and draw the wool through and also through the roll of stitches on the needle, as see example on page 13, No. 6, of "Weldon's Practical Needlework Series;" break off the wool at the end of the row. **5th row**—With red wool—Work the same as the third row. **6th row**—Same as the second row. **7th row**—Same as the third, and break off the red wool; this finishes the fancy tricot. The remainder of the boot is worked entirely with white wool in plain tricot, of which do 4 rows, decreasing a stitch at the beginning and at the end of the second row and the fourth row. Then do 3 rows with 26 stitches in each row. Now for the **Instep**—Work upon the 6 centre stitches for 6 rows, and break off. Work a row of single crochet with red wool all along the bottom of the foot, and then do 5 rows of tricot in each of which increase a stitch at each corner of the instep, do 1 row without increase, and 2 rows gathering in 4 or 5 stitches at the toe to round it in nicely into shape. Sew up the foot and leg. For the **Edging** round the top of the leg—Use red wool,—do 1 double crochet in a stitch of the commencing chain, * 3 chain, 1 double crochet in the third chain from the needle, miss one stitch, 1 double crochet in the next, and repeat from *; and fasten off evenly at the end of the round. Make a crochet chain to run in the first row of the tricot to tie round the leg, placing a tassel at each end of the chain.

Baby's Boot.
WORKED IN PLAIN AND FANCY TRICOT.

ANTIMACASSAR.

THE Antimacassar shown in the engraving is a combination of crochet and canvas embroidery; the crochet is worked in small round medallions either in Arkwright's white, cream, écru, coral pink, or red crochet cotton, nine medallions being united together in the form of a square, and when nine squares are accomplished they are arranged in diamond fashion in conjunction with four similar sized squares made of canvas and previously embroidered in cross-stitch with Maygrove's Improved Filoselles, in a design consisting of a narrow insertion round the margin of the canvas and an effective-looking star in the centre. No. 65 of "Weldon's Practical Needlework Series" is devoted to canvas work and here many designs are shown for all purposes. Procure ½ yard of flat canvas, 4 skeins of Arkwright's crochet cotton, No. 12, and a medium-sized steel crochet needle. Commence a **Medallion** by winding the cotton about 20 times round a black-lead pencil, and in the circle work 16 double crochet, and join evenly round; the circle will by this means be solid and raised. **2nd round**—Do 4 chain, 1 treble inserting the hook to take up both front threads of the first stitch of last round, * 1 chain, 1 treble on the next, and repeat from * till 16 treble are worked, counting the commencing chain as one, then 1 chain, and join to the third stitch of the commencing chain. **3rd round**—Work 1 double crochet under the chain stitch of last round, 5 chain, and repeat; there should be 16 loops of chain. **4th round**—Slip-stitch to the centre stitch of the first loop of chain and there work 1 double crochet, * 7 chain, 1 double crochet in the next loop, and repeat; join evenly at the end of the round, and fasten off. Work 8 more medallions for the first square. To **Join** the medallions together and at the same time to fill in the spaces between, do 2 treble under each of two loops of each of four medallions, unite the last treble stitch to the first, and fasten off; this small circle of treble is illustrated in detail in connection with one of the medallions in full working size. When all the diamonds are completed and properly joined together the antimacassar is finished off with large tassels made by grouping about 40 strands of crochet cotton in a bunch and tying them together with a thread that has been passed into the medallion where the tassel is to hang.

HEAD-REST FOR THE BACK OF A CHAIR.
HONEYCOMB LATTICE PATTERN.

EVERYONE has seen the brocaded cushions that have lately been so fashionably used in pairs, thrown over the backs of chairs in the place of antimacassars, and which, hanging one at the back and the other at the front of the chair, form such a comfortable rest for the head when reading or dozing. The cushions are padded with wadding, horse-hair, or feathers, and therefore are very soft; they are made in every size, from 10 inches to 12 inches square for a small drawing-room chair, to from 12 inches to 18 inches for an easy chair. Our engraving represents one of these cushions worked in crochet in a very pretty stitch known as Honeycomb Lattice; it is for a small chair, and it measures about 10 inches across from side to side; another cushion is joined to this by the loops of cord at the top. Procure two shades of peacock-blue double Berlin wool, one shade considerably lighter than the other, 4 ozs. of the darkest shade and 1½ oz. of the lightest, a No. 8 bone crochet needle, two pieces of gold coloured sateen 12 inches or so square for the backs of the cushions, some sheets of wool wadding, and 3 yards of gold silk cord for trimming. The crochet is executed in rows forwards and backwards, turning the work at the end of every row, and always taking up two threads of the stitches. Begin with the darkest shade of wool with 34 chain. **1st row**—Plain double crochet, miss the first stitch of chain, and do 33 double crochet in the row. **2nd row**—Turn the work, insert the hook in the same stitch of the commencing chain that the third double crochet of last row is worked into, draw the wool up from the back in a long loop loosely, wool over the needle and draw through the long loop, wool over the needle and draw through the two stitches on the needle, this stands for the first stitch, * work 1 double crochet on each of 3 consecutive stitches of last row, insert the hook in the same chain stitch the last long loop is worked into and draw up a long loop loosely, insert the hook in the fourth chain stitch from the last long loop and draw up another long loop, wool over the needle and draw through the two long loops, wool over the needle and draw through the two stitches on the needle; repeat from *; and the row must end with the first long loop that is worked after the 3 double crochet stitches. **3rd row**—Turn, and work 33 stitches of plain double crochet. **4th row**—Turn, work 2 double crochet, * insert the hook in the top part of the long loop to the right of the needle (that is, in the centre of the little stitch that looks like a ring) and draw up a long loop, insert the hook in the top part of the long loop to the left of the needle and draw up another long loop, wool over the needle and draw through the two long loops, wool over the needle and draw through the two stitches on the needle, 1 double crochet on each of 3 consecutive double crochet of last row, and repeat from *; and the row must end with 2 double crochet stitches as it began. Repeat these 4 rows with the same shade of wool. Then work 4 rows with the lightest shade. Work 8 rows with the dark shade. Work 4 rows with the light shade. Work 8 rows with the dark shade, and fasten off. Take the light shade, and holding the right side of the work towards you, do a row of double crochet along the commencing chain, along the end of the work, and up the last row, that is, round three sides of the lattice pattern; the fourth side is the top of the cushion and is not margined; the stripes run perpendicularly from the top to the bottom of the cushion. Do another similar piece of crochet. Now to make up the cushion, place each piece of crochet on the table the right side downwards, arrange two layers of wool wadding on each piece of crochet, and cover that with sateen of which the edge has previously been turned in to the required size; sew the edge of the sateen to the edge of the crochet with neat stitches. Then having made both cushions in this way, trim them round with cord, and make loops of cord at the top to connect the cushions one to the other and at the same time to hang them in position over the back of a chair.

The honeycomb lattice stitch is very effective for sofa rugs, cot-covers, and other purposes, and may be executed in many varieties of colours.

Full Size Working Design for Antimacassar.

Antimacassar.

on the last stitch. Proceed thus in rows, in double crochet, always increasing a stitch at the end of every row, till in the **13th row** you work 1 double crochet on each of 12 stitches, and 2 double crochet on the last stitch. **14th row**—Work 1 double crochet on each of 5 stitches, then to begin the honeycomb trellis, turn the cotton twice round the needle, insert the hook from right to left to take up the centre stitch at the base of the third preceding row and draw the cotton through, then draw off the 4 threads on the needle as a long treble stitch, miss one stitch of preceding row, do 1 double crochet on each of the three next stitches, then 1 long treble in the same place as the last long treble (making the two long treble stitches incline right and left in the form of a $\vee$), miss one stitch of preceding row, then 1 double crochet on each of the 3 next stitches, and two double crochet on the last stitch. **15th row**—Plain double crochet, 16 stitches. **16th row**—Double crochet, 17 stitches. **17th row**—Double crochet, 18 stitches. **18th row**—Work 1 double crochet on each of 5 stitches, cotton twice round the needle, insert the hook from right to left under the first long treble stitch of the fourteenth row and draw the cotton through and complete the long treble stitch in the usual way, miss one stitch of last row, do 1 double crochet on each of the 3 next stitches, cotton twice round the needle and insert the hook in the same place as before (*behind* the long treble just done) and draw the cotton through, cotton over the needle and draw through 2 threads on the needle, cotton over the needle and again draw through 2 threads on the needle, cotton twice round the needle and insert the hook from right to left under the second long treble stitch of the fourteenth row and draw the cotton through, and complete this long treble by working off 2 threads at a time till the stitch is finished; miss one stitch of last row, do 1 double crochet on each of the 3 next stitches, cotton twice round the needle and insert the hook in the same place but *in front* of the long treble just done, and draw the cotton through, and complete the long treble stitch as usual, miss one stitch of last row, do 1 double crochet on each of the 3 next stitches, and 2 double crochet on the last stitch. **19th row**—Plain double crochet, 20 stitches. **20th row**—Double crochet, 21 stitches. **21st row**—Double crochet, 22 stitches. **22nd row**—Work 1 double crochet on each of 5 stitches, 1 long treble under the first long treble stitch of the eighteenth row, miss one stitch of preceding row, 1 double crochet on each of the 3 next stitches, 1 long treble in the same place as the last long treble is worked (but *behind* that), and 1 long treble under the combined long treble of the eighteenth row, miss one stitch of preceding row, 1 double crochet on each of the 3 next stitches, 1 long treble in the same place as the last long treble is worked (but *behind* that), and 1 long treble under the next long treble of the eighteenth row, miss one stitch of preceding row, 1 double crochet on each of the 3 next stitches, 1 long treble in the same place as the last long treble is worked (but this time *in front* of that), miss one stitch of preceding row, 1 double crochet on each of the 3 next stitches, and 2 double crochet on the last stitch. Continue in this manner, always increasing at the end of every row, and doing 3 rows of double crochet between every row of trellis honeycomb, till in the forty-second row the diamond reaches its widest point with 16 long treble stitches from side to side of the trellis honeycomb, and of course the usual double crochet stitches intervening. Henceforward decrease in every row, by taking up together the two last stitches in the row and working them as one stitch, and diminish the long treble stitches of the trellis honeycomb in regular symmetry, as represented in the engraving, till the trellis is brought to a point of two long treble stitches slanting thus $\wedge$; after which proceed entirely in double crochet and bring the diamond to a point of one stitch only. Now work, all round this diamond, a row of open crochet—beginning with 7 chain, do 1 treble on the point where the cotton is, * 2 chain, 1 treble on the next ridge of the foundation, and repeat from * to the next point, where do 4 chain and 1 treble twice to ease round the point; when repeat again from *; and when you get to the commencing point, finish with 4 chain, and join into the third chain stitch with which the round commenced, and fasten off. For the **Floral Sprays**—Make 12 chain, and join in a circle. **1st round**—Do 24 double crochet in the circle, and join evenly. **2nd round**—Do 1 chain, miss two stitches, 1 double crochet on the next, * 6 chain, miss three stitches, 1 double crochet on the next, and repeat from *, and end with 8 chain, and join evenly. **3rd round**—Work 7 double crochet under a loop of chain of last round, 9 chain, 1 single crochet in the sixth chain from the needle, 11 chain, 1 single crochet in the sixth chain from the needle, 11 chain, 1 single crochet in the sixth chain from the needle, 5 chain, join to the third space along the side of the diamond (as shown in the engraving), do three single crochet along the chain, leaving the chain stitch next by the picot unworked, 7 chain, 1 single crochet in the sixth chain from

CROCHET SQUARE FOR ANTIMACASSAR OR COUNTERPANE.

THIS square may be utilised for an antimacassar by working it with fine crochet cotton, such as Ardern's, No. 14, or it will serve for a summer quilt if No. 8 cotton be employed, using in either case as fine a steel crochet needle as convenient. In coloured crochet cotton it is very effective too. The centre of the square is composed of a diamond of solid crochet, on which a pattern of trellis honey-combing stands in prominent relief; the corners are occupied by ornamental floral sprays; and the whole is surrounded by a border, or insertion, of open trebles and close crochet to match the centre. Commence with 2 chain; and work 2 double crochet in the second chain-stitch from the needle. **2nd row**—Turn the work, and inserting the hook to take up the two top threads of the stitches of the previous row, do 1 double crochet on the first stitch, and 2 double crochet on the other stitch. **3rd row**—Turn the work, do 1 double crochet on each of the 2 first stitches, and 2 double crochet on the last stitch, always now taking up the two top threads. **4th row**—Turn the work, do 1 double crochet on each of the 3 first stitches, and 2 double crochet the needle, 1 chain, 1 single crochet on each of the 3 centre stitches of the chain bar between the picots, 7 chain, 1 single crochet in the sixth chain from the needle, 1 chain, 1 single crochet on each of the 3 centre stitches of the next chain bar between the picots, 7 chain, 1 single crochet in the sixth chain from the needle, 1 chain, 1 single crochet on each of the two chain by the double crochet stitches, 7 double crochet in the loop where seven double crochet are already done; 7 double crochet in the next loop of eight chain, 9 chain, 1 single crochet in the sixth chain from the needle, 4 chain, join to the fourth open space further along the side of the diamond, do 2 single crochet along the chain, leaving the chain stitch next by the picot unworked, 7 chain, 1 single crochet in the sixth chain from the needle, 1 chain, 1 single crochet on each of the 2 chain by the double crochet stitches, 7 double crochet to fill up the loop where seven double crochet are already done; and proceed, doing a small spray from the next loop of the flower, and join to the diamond; then a long spray from the next loop of the flower, and join to the diamond at a corresponding distance from the corner to the first long spray; then a small spray from each of the two next loops to correspond with the foregoing small sprays, but simply standing out from the flower without at present being joined to any other portion of the crochet; fasten off at the completion of the flower. Work similar sprays on the three other corners. For the **Border** or **Outside Insertion—1st round**—Work 1 long treble on the treble stitch that stands at the point of the diamond, 5 chain, another long treble in the same place, then work as many chain (joining at intervals to the sprays as shown in the engraving) as will form a "corner" and extend to the next point of the diamond, where work 1 long treble, 5 chain, and another long treble, and repeat the same, and at the end of the round join evenly, and fasten off. **2nd round**—Begin with 1 treble on a corner stitch of the chain of last round, 2 chain, another treble in the same place, * 2 chain, miss two stitches, 1 treble in the next, and repeat from * to next corner, where work 2 chain, 1 treble on the same stitch as last treble which is a corner stitch, 2 chain, another treble in the same place, and continue from * to the end of the round, and join evenly. **3rd round** —Turn the work, and go round in plain double crochet the same as the double crochet worked in the diamond, putting, however, 3 double crochet on the centre stitch at each corner. Work 2 more rounds the same as last round. **6th round** — Turn the work, and proceed in trellis honeycomb as worked in the diamond, but doing still an increase on the centre stitch at each corner. **7th round** —The same as the third round. Work 2 more rounds the same. **10th round**—Turn the work, and continue the formation of the trellis honeycomb. **11th round** — The same as the third round. **12th round** — Open crochet like the second round. **13th round**—Plain double crochet. This finishes the square. When a number of squares are worked, they are sewn together with a needle and cotton, or may be crocheted together if preferred.

Head-Rest for Back of a Chair.
HONEYCOMB LATTICE PATTERN.

BABY'S WARM OVER-BOOTS.
POINT MUSCOVITE AND LOOPED CROCHET.

BABIES in perambulators should be provided in severe weather with a pair of warm woollen over-boots as an additional covering on their feet and legs to guard against chills and keep the blood in healthy circulation. This result will be attained by the use of crocheted boots similar to the one represented in our engraving, which is worked throughout in Point Muscovite stitch and headed with looped crochet. Procure 1 oz. of white and 1½ ozs. of red single Berlin wool, and a No. 9 bone crochet needle. Commence with white wool, with 35 chain. **1st row**—Work 1 single crochet in the first stitch from the needle,* insert the hook in the next stitch and draw the wool through and do 3 chain, draw the wool through the last chain and also through the stitch on the needle, 1 single crochet in the next stitch of the foundation, and repeat from * to the end of the row, making in all 17 stitches of Point Muscovite; the single crochet must be done rather loosely; turn the work, and slip-stitch (that is, single crochet) back. **2nd row**—Proceed in the same manner, but alternate the tufts by working a point stitch over the single crochet of the previous row and a single crochet over a point stitch. Continue till nine rows are worked. Then for the **Instep**—Leave 4 tufts each side, and work a row of 9 tufts, followed by a row of 8 tufts; then a row of 7 tufts, and a row of 6 tufts; next a row of 5 tufts, and a row of 4 tufts; and then a row of 3 tufts, and a row of 2 tufts, and fasten off; all this is to be done with white wool. Sew up the leg. Then still with white wool work in the same stitch for the **Foot**, but now in **rounds**; do one round on all the stitches, then 2 rounds or

3 rounds decreasing at the toe and heel, but chiefly at the toe for the purpose of bringing it to a nicely rounded shape; seam up the middle of the sole. Proceed now to the **Top** of the **Leg** and work in looped crochet with red wool. Tie a stitch on the needle, * insert the hook in a stitch of the foundation chain, pass the wool over the the hook and round the first finger of the left hand, pass it round in the same manner twice more, then pass it only over the hook and draw the loops (4 threads of wool) through, wool over the needle and draw through the loops and also through the stitch on the needle, 1 chain, miss one stitch of the foundation, and repeat from * to the end of the round; there will be 15 bunches of loops in the round. Work 4 more rounds in the same manner, but now inserting the hook under the chain stitches. In the **next round** the top of the boot is finished with a little scollop,—thus,—do 1 double crochet under a stitch of chain, do 3 treble under the next stitch of chain, 1 chain, and 3 more treble in the same place, and repeat the same to the end of the round, and fasten off. A bow of narrow red ribbon may be placed upon the instep if liked, or a ribbon may be run in to tie round the leg below the looped crochet.

BABY'S HIGH BOOTIKINS.
WORKED IN FANCY TRICOT AND CROCHET.

THESE pretty bootikins may be worked throughout with white Berlin fingering, of which 1½ ozs. will be required; or if preferred the foot may be tricoted with colour and the upper part of the leg crocheted with white wool, taking about ¾ oz. of each. Employ a No. 8 bone tricot needle and a No. 10 bone crochet needle, and have at hand eight fancy silk buttons. Begin for the tricot with 34 chain. **1st row**— Pick up 1 stitch in each stitch of chain, and when 34 stitches are on the needle draw back in the usual manner. **2nd row**—In this row, and in every successive row, the hook is to be inserted into the small horizontal thread at the back of the stitches of the previous row, instead of as in ordinary tricot into the front perpendicular loop; 34 stitches should be on the needle, and draw back in the usual manner. **3rd row**—Decrease at the beginning and at the end of this row by drawing back through the first 2 and the last 2 stitches together. **4th row**—Work the fancy tricot stitch without decrease. Repeat the last two rows twice. **9th row**— Increase a stitch when 2 stitches from the beginning, also each side the 6 centre stitches, and again when 2 stitches from the end, and draw back as usual. Work two more rows the same. **12th row**—Slip over the first 3 stitches, pick up till 14 stitches are on the needle, increase 1, pick up 6 centre stitches, increase 1, pick up 14, omit the 3 last stitches, and draw back as usual. **13th row**—Slip over the first 3 stitches, pick up 12, increase 1, pick up 6 centre stitches, increase 1, pick up 12, and omitting the last 3 stitches, draw back as usual. **14th row**—Slip over the first 3 stitches, pick up 10, increase 1, pick up 6 centre stitches, increase 1, pick up 10, omit the last 3 stitches, and draw back. **15th row**—Slip over the first 3 stitches, pick up 22 stitches, omit the last 3 stitches, and draw back. **16th row**—Slip over the first 3 stitches, pick up 16 stitches, omit the last 3 stitches, and draw back; break off the wool. **17th row**—Work the same fancy tricot stitch the whole way along the bottom of the foot, 46 stitches in the row. **18th row**—Pick up about 38 stitches, missing 6 or 8 alternate stitches round the toe to draw the toe in to shape, and draw back through 2 together at the beginning and 2 together at the end of the row. Break off the wool, and sew up the foot and the back of the leg. The **crochet** round the top of the bootikin is worked in Point Muscovite. Hold the boot the right side out, and beginning by the seam, work 1 double crochet in the first stitch of the commencing chain, insert the hook in the next stitch and draw the wool through and do 3 chain stitches, draw the wool through the last stitch of chain and through the stitch on the needle, and continue the double crochet stitch and the point stitch alternately to the end of the round, getting 16 double crochet and 16 points in the round. The following rounds are worked in the same manner, doing always a double crochet stitch upon a point, and a point stitch upon a double crochet, for 10 rounds. Then for the **Edge**—Work 1 double crochet on a point stitch, 1 chain, miss two stitches, 1 treble on the next, * 4 chain, 1 double crochet on the treble to form a picot, 1 treble in the same place as last treble, repeat from * twice more and there will be 3 picots and 4 treble stitches, 1 chain, miss two, 1 double crochet on the next, 1 chain, miss two, 1 treble on the next, and repeat the same to the end of the round, and join evenly, and fasten off. Sew four buttons down the centre of the instep, as shown in the engraving; and on each side, by the increasings, work a line of fancy chain stitch with a rug needle.

SQUARE FOR ANTIMACASSAR OR BASSINETTE COVER, WITH BORDER.

TWISTED RINGS PATTERN.

THIS is a particularly pretty pattern for a drawing-room antimacassar, and may also be used for a bassinette cover or for a cot quilt. Procure three or four balls of white or cream and the same quantity of Arkwright's coral pink, red or blue crochet cotton, No. 18, and a medium-sized steel crochet needle; this make of cotton is perfectly fast coloured and will stand any amount of washing. Begin for the twisted rings, using blue cotton, with which work 17 chain, join round, and work 40 double crochet in the ring, join neatly, and break off the cotton, and draw the end through a few stitches at the back of the work. Again do 17 chain, pass the chain through the first ring, join it round, and work 40 double crochet in this ring the same as in the first. Continue until you come to the eighth ring, when pass the chain through the seventh and also through the first, and you will

which the round commenced. **2nd round**—Work 2 double crochet on the first chain stitch at the corner, 3 double crochet on the centre chain stitch, 1 double crochet on the third chain stitch, and 29 consecutive double crochet along the side of the square, and repeat, making in all 140 double crochet in the round; join quite evenly, and fasten off. **3rd round**—Still with white cotton,—Begin at a corner, work 2 treble on the centre stitch of three double crochet of preceding round, 3 chain, 2 more treble in the same place, and along the side do * 2 chain, miss two, 2 treble, and repeat from * seven times, then 2 chain, miss two, which brings you to the next corner, where work the same as the first, and continue to the end of the round. **4th round**—A double crochet on each stitch of last round, excepting at the corners, where do 3 double crochet on the centre stitch of chain and 2 double crochet on the next chain stitch to the left, 44 double crochet on each side, 176 double crochet in all in the round, and fasten off. **5th round**—With blue cotton,—Do 2 treble, 3 chain, and 2 treble in the centre stitch at the corner, * 1 chain, miss one, 1 treble in the next, 1 chain, miss one, 6 treble in the next, withdraw the needle and insert the hook in the first of the six treble

Crochet Square for Antimacassar or Counterpane.

have a square of rings. Do 17 chain for the ring that is to fill up the centre of the square, pass the chain under the second and fourth rings, over the fourth and sixth, and under the sixth and eighth, these being the four rings at the centre of each side of the square, join the chain, and work 40 double crochet in this ring as in the previous rings, and fasten off. Proceed now to work round the outside of the square of twisted rings. **1st round**—With white cotton,—Begin on the first ring, which is a corner ring, work 1 treble on one of the double crochet stitches,* 1 chain, miss one, 1 treble in the next, repeat from * until 5 treble stitches are done (the double crochet upon which the last stitch is worked is to be considered a "corner" stitch), do 3 chain, 2 more treble in the corner stitch, and then 1 chain, miss one, 1 treble in the next four times, making in all 10 treble on the corner ring, work 1 chain, 1 treble on the next ring, and 1 chain, miss one, 1 treble in the next, till here 5 treble stitches are worked; and continue as above, doing 10 treble upon each corner ring, and 5 treble upon each of the other rings, with always 1 chain between each treble, then 1 chain, and join to the first treble stitch with

stitches, take up the dropped stitch and draw it through to make a tuft, and repeat from * till 10 tufts are worked, then 1 chain, miss one, 1 treble in the next, 1 chain, miss one, and you are by the centre stitch of the next corner, proceed as before to the end of the round. **6th round**—With white cotton,—Work 2 treble, 3 chain, and 2 treble in the centre stitch at the corner, 1 chain, miss one, 1 treble on the next, 1 chain, a tuft on the treble stitch of last row, 1 chain, a treble on a tuft, and continue this till 11 tufts are worked, then 1 chain, miss two, 1 treble on the next, 1 chain, turn the corner, and work on to the end of the round. **7th round**—With blue cotton,—Work as last round, but there will be 12 tufts on each side of the square. **8th round**—At the corner work 1 treble in the centre stitch, 6 chain, 1 single crochet in the sixth chain from the needle, 5 chain, 1 single crochet in the same place, 5 chain, another single crochet in the same place, 1 treble in the centre stitch where a treble is already worked, 4 chain, 1 double crochet on the first single treble stitch of last round, * 3 chain, 1 treble on the next treble stitch between the tufts, 6 chain, 1 single crochet in the sixth chain from the needle, 5 chain,

1 single crochet in the same place, 5 chain, another single crochet in the same place, 1 treble on the same treble stitch, 3 chain, 1 double crochet on the next treble stitch between the tufts, and repeat from * five times, then 4 chain, and turn the corner, and continue to the end of the round, and fasten off. This completes one square. Make as many squares as are required, 20 will be sufficient for a good-sized antimacassar, and join them together picot to picot in the course of working the last round. For the **Border—1st round—** With blue cotton,—1 double crochet in the centre loop of a picot on the side of the antimacassar, * 8 chain, 1 double crochet in the centre loop of the next picot, and repeat from *, and at the corner do 12 double crochet on each side the corner picot. **2nd round**—1 treble in every successive stitch of last round, and three treble at the corners, and fasten off. **3rd round**—Still with blue cotton,—Work in tufts as described in the fifth round of the square, but at the corners work 7 tufts and treble stitches with a chain between each and without missing one stitch, to round the corner as shown in the engraving.

Baby's Warm Overboots.

4th round—With white cotton,—Work a treble over a tuft, and a tuft over a treble, with 1 chain between each. **5th round**—With blue cotton.—Work similarly to last round. **6th round**—With white cotton,—Double crochet on every stitch, and 2 double crochet on each tuft in rounding the corner. **7th round**—2 treble, 2 chain, miss two, and repeat. **8th round**—Double crochet in every stitch. **9th round**—1 double crochet on a stitch of last round, 6 chain, 1 single crochet in the fifth chain from the needle, 6 chain, 1 single crochet in the fifth chain from the needle, 6 chain, 1 single crochet in the fifth chain from the needle, 1 chain, miss five stitches of last row, 1 double crochet in the next, 9 chain, 1 single crochet in sixth chain from needle, 3 chain, miss three stitches of last row, 1 double crochet in the next, and repeat these two patterns the whole way round. **10th round**—Work 1 double crochet in the first top loop of preceding round, * 6 chain, 1 single crochet in the fifth chain from the needle, repeat from * till you have 7 loops of chain, then 1 chain, 1 double crochet in the same loop with the last double crochet, 3 chain, 1 double crochet into another loop of preceding round, and repeat from *, working the same to the completion of the round.

CHILD'S OVERALLS.

THIS useful garment, which is suitable for a child from one to two years of age, is worked nearly entirely in close ridged crochet, and will be found very warm and comfortable. Required, 8 oz. of white Peacock wool, a No. 9 or No. 10 bone crochet needle, and 1 yard of white ribbon. Commence with 138 chain to go round the waist. Work in rows forwards and backwards, turning the work at the end of every row. **1st row**—1 treble in the fourth chain from the needle, and 1 treble in every stitch thence to the end of the row. **2nd row**—Plain double crochet, 136 stitches in the row. **3rd row**—4 chain to turn, miss one stitch, 1 treble in the next, * 1 chain, miss one, 1 treble in the next, and repeat from * to the end. **4th row**—4 chain to turn, and work 2 treble in every space of chain of last row. **5th row**—4 chain to turn, and 2 treble intermediate between the groups of treble of last row. Work 2 more rows the same. **8th row**—Plain double crochet, there should still be 136 stitches in the row. **9th row**—Plain double crochet, but now taking up the one back thread of the stitches of last row that the work may sit in ridges. Proceed till in all 32 rows are done of the ridged crochet, that is, making 16 raised ridges on each side the work. **Next row**—Divide for the legs—Work still in ridged crochet along half the stitches (68 stitches); turn, and work back in the same way. Now do 30 rows of ridged crochet, decreasing a stitch at the end of every row, which will reduce to 38 stitches for the ankle. Work 10 rows on the 38 stitches for the ankle; break off the wool. Work in ridged crochet upon the 16 centre stitches for 12 rows for the instep; break off the

wool. For the **Shoe**—Work 12 rows of ridged crochet all along the foot increasing 1 stitch at each corner of the instep for 10 rows, and 2 rows without increase, and fasten off. Sew up the foot and leg. Work the other leg and foot in the same manner. Join up the back of the garment, and run ribbon through the holes made in the third row, which ribbon will serve to secure the garment round the child's waist.

RED AND WHITE SQUARE FOR COVERLET.

THIS square is worked with Strutt's red and white knitting cottons, No. 8, and a steel hook, No. 17, but any other two colours may be substituted, to suit one's taste. Begin with a foundation of 55 chain worked with the white cotton. **1st row**—1 long treble (cotton twice round the hook) in the fifth chain from the hook, 23 long treble. Leave the last two loops of the twenty-third long treble unworked off, take the red cotton and finish these loops with it. Remember always to do this when about to change cotton. Leave the white cotton at the back of the work and make 4 long treble with red, then put the red cotton at the back and bring forward the white, with care not to draw it so tightly across as to pull the work out of shape, work 24 long treble with the white. **2nd row**—Turn, 4 chain (these serve as one long treble), 3 long treble, taking the stitches through both the top loops of the trebles of the preceding row, leave the white cotton in the front as the work is now held, and make 4 long treble with red, 12 white long treble, 12 red, 12 white, 4 red, 4 white long treble. **3rd row**—Turn, 4 chain, 7 white long treble, 8 red, leaving the white cotton at the back of the work, 4 white, 12 red, 4 white, 8 red, 8 white long treble. **4th row**—Turn, 4 chain, 7 white, 12 red, 4 white, 4 red, 4 white, 12 red, 8 white long treble. **5th row**—Turn, 4 chain, 11 white long treble, 28 red, 12 white long treble. **6th row**—Turn, 4 chain, 3 white, 8 red, 4 white, 8 red, 4 white, 8 red, 4 white, 8 red, 4 white long treble. **7th row**—Turn, take the red, 4 chain, 19 red, 4 white, 4 red, 4 white, 20 red. **8th row**—Turn, take the white, 4 chain, 3 white long treble, 8 red, 4 white, 8 red, 4 white, 8 red, 4 white, 8 red, 4 white long treble. **9th row**—Turn, 4 white, 11 white, 28 red, 12 white long treble. **10th row**—Turn, 4 chain, 7 white, 12 red, 4 white, 4 red, 4 white, 12 red, 8 white. **11th row**—Turn, 4 chain, 7 white, 8 red, 4 white, 12 red, 4 white, 8 red, 8 white long treble. **12th row**—Turn, 4 chain, 3 white, 4 red, 12 white, 12 red, 12 white, 4 red, 4 white long treble. **13th row**—Turn, 4 chain, 23 long treble, 4 red, 24 long treble. Fasten off, thus completing the middle

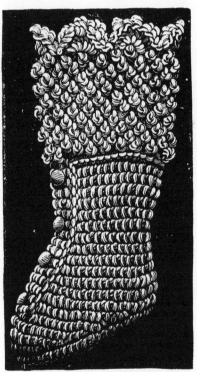

Baby's High Bootikins.

part of the square. For the **1st round** of the border, join the white cotton at one of the corners, work 3 double crochet in one stitch, 1 double crochet into every stitch all along the side, making 50 double crochet in all; put 3 double crochet into the next corner and continue all round. It will be found rather a troublesome matter to pick up the stitches along the edges of the treble rows and the worker must be particular in counting them or the sides will be irregular. **2nd round**—Take the red and work a round of long treble, taking up the back loops and putting 7 into the corner stitches. **3rd round**—All ordinary treble with white cotton, taking up the back loops as before, but putting 5 instead of 7 into the corners. **4th round**—All treble with red cotton and 5 into each corner. **5th round**—All treble with white cotton, again putting 5 into each corner. **6th round**—Double crochet with red cotton into every stitch as usual, 3 in the corners. **7th round**—All treble with white cotton and 5 in the corners. **8th round**—All single with red cotton and 3 in the corners. **9th and last round**—All treble with white and 5 in the corner stitches. This square, with the exception of the 8th round, requires to be worked very tightly, or it will not have a sufficiently close, firm appearance. The single stitches have to be worked rather loosely as the tendency of this stitch is to draw the work, and if this is done, the square will not set flat.

TOY LAMB.

A TOY LAMB is a very pretty plaything, and will give great delight to its small owners. Procure ¾ oz. of white Scotch fingering and ½ oz. of creamy white single Berlin wool; the former is for the legs, face, and lower part of the body, the latter is to represent the fleece of the lamb. First, mould the body of the lamb with stout paper and white wadding; the legs of our model are 3 inches long, the total height is 7 inches, and the length from the head to the root of the tail is 10 inches. With fingering wool and a rather small bone crochet needle commence for the sole of the foot with 4 chain, join round, and in the circle work 10 double crochet; do another round, taking up the one top thread and increasing in every alternate stitch, this is sufficiently large for the pad; next round decrease by taking up 2 stitches together alternately, and so get 11 stitches in the round, on which continue to work double crochet round

is already done; join round; do 3 chain to stand for a treble stitch, and do 2 treble in every stitch all round, loosely; next, do 2 rounds of treble loosely without increase; and then 6 rounds of double crochet, which probably will be sufficient to go down the neck and reach to the fore legs: from this the work is done in treble stitch in rows of 22 stitches in the row, loosely, till sufficient is done to extend to the tail, when the row is folded together and sewn to shape. For the **Tail**, use Berlin wool, work 14 chain, and do 4 rows of treble stitches, fold the last row to the commencing chain, and join up, taking the stitches through the crochet to keep the work flat; sew it on. Pull the loose crochet well over the head to produce a high forehead. Sew on the ears, and sew on two black beads for eyes. Tie a narrow ribbon round the lamb's neck; also a bell if liked.

TOY ELEPHANT.

A TOY ELEPHANT is an attractive novelty that will sell well at bazaars and also will afford great pleasure in a nursery, as children can play many merry games with it. The body of the elephant can be manufactured at home by cutting out the shape of the limbs in brown paper, stuffing each with wool wadding, sewing into shape, and covering the whole with coarse grey serge, preparatory to putting on the outer covering, or hide, which is worked in crochet.

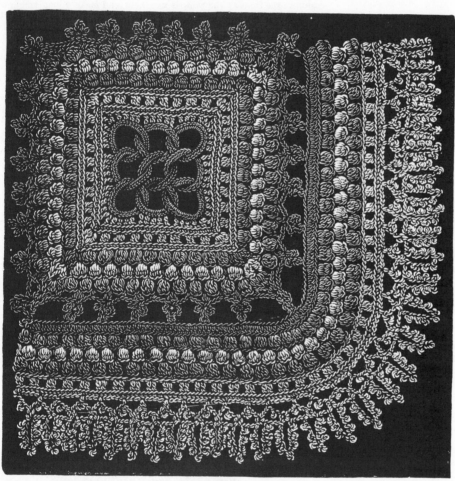

Square for Antimacassar or Bassinette Cover with Border. TWISTED RINGS PATTERN.

and round, but increase 3 or 4 stitches as you get towards the top of the leg and fasten off when sufficiently long; this is for one of the fore-legs; make the other to correspond. The hinder legs are similar, but they get a little thicker as they approach the top. The under part of the body consists of a piece of plain crochet commenced on 20 stitches, on which double crochet forwards and backwards until a piece is done long enough to reach from the hinder to the fore legs, and wide enough to extend a little way up each side of the body, at each end of this work a few rows on the centre 8 or 9 stitches only; draw the crochet legs upon the model, and sew the crochet in position attaching the legs to it as neatly as possible. The **Head** is partly worked with yarn, and is begun at the nose with two chain, do tightly 4 double crochet in the first stitch of chain; work round 8 double crochet; again work round 10 double crochet; then gradually increase in each successive round to the shape of the model till about 8 rounds are done; this is drawn on with the rough side of the crochet outside, and a stitch of red wool is sewn through to simulate the mouth, and another stitch for the nostrils. For the **Ears**, with fingering do 9 chain, 1 treble in the fourth chain from the needle, and 5 more treble along the other chain stitches; turn, and work 2 rounds of double crochet outside the treble stitches, increasing at the ends to preserve the oval shape; the ears are folded lengthways and sewn in position when the woolly part of the fleece is completed. Take Berlin wool and a larger crochet needle, and make 15 chain, or as many as are needed to go round the head on the margin of the crochet that

Our engraving shows a model elephant, standing 11 inches high, whose whole length from head to tail measures 12½ inches; the legs are 5½ inches high by 6 inches in circumference, the trunk extends 5 inches from the head, and the tail is 4 inches long; he wears a saddle made of black and blue serge, both pinked round the edges, and decorated with all manner of fancy stitches embroidered with filoselles and wool in immense variety of colours, and ornamented with spangles; the valance on each side the saddle is formed of red and white striped material embroidered with yellow wool, the stitches are taken through, and thereby the saddle is secured in position on the elephant. If a few beads are put in a small box, and the box placed inside the body, the elephant will rattle.

The crochet with which the elephant is covered is worked with coarse grey fingering, an iron grey is most suitable, in quantity about 3 ozs., and a No. 9 bone crochet needle. Begin with 4 chain, join round, and work 8 or 9 double crochet in the circle, and proceed round and round, working into the one top thread, and increasing in the second round in every stitch, in the third round in each alternate stitch, and subsequently in every third or fourth stitch, keeping the work perfectly flat till the circle measures 3¼ inches in diameter; this forms the pad of the foot, it sets flat on the ground, and bulges out in a kind of rim beyond the circumference of the leg; the next round must contract the crochet to the size of the leg by taking up 2 stitches together and getting about 20 double crochet in the round; from this continue round and round in double crochet till 22 rounds are done for the length of the leg, which as it nears the top should be widened by increasing a stitch or two as required: this is a fore leg, and another must be worked to correspond. The two hinder legs are worked in the same manner but are shorter, being only 18 rounds in length. The head is commenced at the mouth and worked upwards to the top of the forehead—do 15 chain, and work double crochet backwards and forwards, increasing a stitch at the end of each row till 27 stitches are attained, work 6 or 8 rows on 27 stitches, and then to shape the forehead decrease a stitch at the end of each row for 4 rows, do the same and also decrease in the centre by taking up the 3 centre stitches as 1 stitch till only 5 stitches are worked, and fasten off. Resume on the commencing chain, 15 double crochet, 4 chain, and join round, and now crochet round and round, decreasing a stitch in about every alternate round as required to fit the trunk, till the work is brought to 4 or 5 stitches in the round and the trunk is covered, then 9 chain, 1 single crochet in the chain stitch nearest the needle, 2 double crochet, 6 treble, and fasten off, and sew the end of wool to the end of the trunk. Draw the trunk and head upon the model, also the legs. Now crochet for the neck, beginning round the head-piece, and working in double crochet in rounds over the model and fitting the work to the model till the crochet reaches the fore-legs, here divide and crochet for the back and for the under part separately, joining the work to the legs at the end of every row; stop when you get to the middle of

last increase in every third stitch that the flap may fall full and frilly. Make the other flap to correspond. Sew the two flaps on in correct position, the widest part on the top of the head. Sew on two black boot buttons to simulate eyes. Then when you have arranged the saddle the elephant is completed.

BABY'S RATTLE.

THIS novel rattle bears a great resemblance to a dressed doll. To make it, procure a skeleton rattle, consisting of a rag doll's face on the end of a stick. Or get a stick about as thick as a black-lead pencil and a little longer, and contrive a rag ball on the top of it, and cover the front of the ball with a piece of fine muslin that previously has been painted to represent a doll's face, and glue a fringe of hair on the top of the head to fall over the forehead, as shown in the engraving. A small pill-box containing three or four dry peas should have been placed in the middle of the ball (or head) to rattle. Surround the face with a bit of muslin frilling to simulate a cap. You will require ½ oz. of white and ½ oz. of pale blue single Berlin wool and a medium-sized bone crochet needle. Begin the **Hood** with white wool, which wind five or six times round a penholder, and work 30 long treble stitches very loosely in the circle, join evenly round, and fasten off. On this piece of crochet work 26 long treble

ralls.

Red and White Square for Coverlet.

the top of the back, and thence work the under part only to reach to the extent of the hinder legs. The remaining portion of the top of the back is commenced by the tail, work 10 chain, do 1 double crochet in each stitch of chain (8 double crochet), 3 double crochet in the top stitch, and 8 double crochet along the other side of the chain; turn, do 1 double crochet in each of 8 stitches, 2 in the next, 3 in the next, 2 in the next, and 1 in each of the remaining 8 stitches; turn, 1 double crochet in each of 9 stitches, 2 in the next, 3 in the next, 2 in the next, and 1 in each of 9 stitches; and so on, in a horse-shoe shape, till the crochet is the right size to fit nicely on the hind quarters of the elephant, when work without further increase, and join at the end of the rows to the hinder legs, till sufficient is done to finish the covering of the back, when join the last row of this to the last row of the piece you previously worked. For the tail, make 24 chain, and work 3 rows of double crochet, make half-a-dozen loops of wool at the end that is to be the tip of the tail, and sew up the tail lengthways, and attach it to its place on the body of the animal. For the two flaps on the neck, work chain sufficient to reach from the top of the head to behind the ear, work double crochet forwards and backwards; **1st row**—Double crochet to within 6 stitches of the end. **2nd row**—Work to the end. **3rd row**—Work to within 8 stitches of the end of the first row. **4th row**—Work to the end. **5th row**—Work to the end of the commencing chain. **6th row**—Work to end, and break off. **7th row**—Work again on the same side as last row, and break off. In *all* these rows excepting the two

stitches consecutively, and join the last stitch to the first, and fasten off, so forming the front of the hood; the four stitches that are omitted working come at the back of the neck. Take the blue wool, and round the front of the hood, inserting the needle in the one top thread of the stitches, work 1 double crochet on a long treble stitch, 1 chain, which pull out to about half an inch long, 1 double crochet on the next long treble stitch, and repeat from *. Work another round with blue wool in the same manner, but now taking up the one front thread of the stitches; the two rows form a pretty double ruche round the face. Run a gathering thread through the margin of the last row of long treble stitches and draw the hood to fit closely on the head. The stick, or handle, is bound round with blue wool. Now cut all the remaining white wool in strands of 6 inches long, lay it evenly all round the stick in such a manner that about 1½ inch stands above the neck and the remainder below, and tie it securely in this position round the stick. Cut the remaining blue wool in strands the same length, lay this evenly all round the white wool and tie it firmly in the same position. Then fold the short ends down to simulate a boa or muffler, and the long ends will fall round the stick, the white wool appearing like a petticoat, and the blue wool in resemblance of a dress skirt. Three little brass bells are tied on in front, and a tiny bow of white satin ribbon is sewn under the chin, as shown in the engraving. Bore a hole through the base of the stick in which to run a ring of wire, and crochet over this ring with double crochet with blue wool.

BABY'S MUFF.

WORKED IN MUSCOVITE TRICOT.

THE muff shown in the engraving is a convenient size for a baby or very young child. Procure 2 oz. of white single Berlin wool, a skein of white knitting silk, a ¼ yard of sateen, and a sheet of wool wadding for lining, and a No. 6 bone tricot needle. Commence with wool by making 46 chain. **1st row**—Plain tricot. **2nd row**—Pick up each tricot loop in the usual way, making 46 stitches on the needle, and to draw back, draw through 2 stitches, * take the silk with the wool and do 3 chain, with wool alone draw through 2 stitches, and repeat from * to the end of the row; break off the silk. **3rd row**—Plain tricot, keeping all the raised tufts in front of the work. **4th row**—Pick up each tricot loop and to draw back, draw through one stitch, * with silk and wool together do 3 chain, with wool alone draw through 2 stitches, and repeat from *, and there will be only 1 stitch to draw through at the end of the row as at the beginning; break off the silk; all the tufts in this row come intermediately between the tufts made in the second row. Repeat these four rows till 24 rows are done; then join the last row to the first row. Line

Toy Lamb.

the muff with sateen and wadding. Crochet a length of chain by which to suspend the muff round the neck, using wool and silk together; this chain is brought over the seam and tied in a bow on the front of the muff, and the ends are nicely finished off with tassels.

CHILD'S DRESS IN TRICOT AND CROCHET.

OUR engraving represents a very pretty dress worked partly in tricot and partly in crochet; the body and garniture are tricot, the flounce is crochet. The dress is suitable for a girl about four years of age. Procure 13 ozs. of ruby-coloured single Berlin wool, a No. 7 long bone tricot needle, a No. 8 bone crochet needle, and 2 dozen ruby silk buttons. Commence with the tricot needle for the back of the body with 68 chain. Work 16 rows of plain tricot. **17th row**—Begin a gore—Take up 48 stitches only, and draw back. **18th row**—Take up 44 stitches, and draw back. **19th row**—Take up 40 stitches, and draw back. **20th row**—Take up 36 stitches, and draw back. And proceed thus, picking up 4 stitches less in each successive row till in the 28th row you pick up only 4 stitches, and draw back, and the gore is finished. **29th row**—Take up the whole row of 68 stitches, and draw back. Work 6 more rows of plain tricot. **36th row**—For under the arm—Take up 49 stitches only, and draw back. **37th row**—The same. **38th row**—Take up 49 stitches, then do 35 chain for the front and the shoulder, and break off the wool; resume by drawing the wool through the top stitch of tricot where the chain commenced, and draw back the tricot stitches as usual. **39th row**—Pick up 49 tricot stitches also 35 stitches on the chain, 84 stitches in all, and draw back. Work 6 more rows with 84 stitches in each row. **46th row**—Begin another gore—Take up 4 stitches only, and draw back. **47th row**—Take up 8 stitches, and draw back. **48th row**—Take up 12 stitches, and draw back. Proceed thus, picking up 4 additional stitches in every successive row till when doing the 57th row you pick up 48 stitches, and draw back, which finishes the gore. **58th row**—Take up the whole length of 84 stitches and draw back. **59th row**—This row is to resemble a raised seam, to effect which you pick up the perpendicular loops at the *back* instead of at the front of the stitches of last row, do 84 stitches in the row, and draw back as usual, this row finishes the shoulder. **60th row**—Begins the **Front** of the dress—Take up 68 stitches in the ordinary manner, and draw back. Do 5 more rows the same. **66th row**—A raised seam row—Pick up 68 stitches, taking the *back* perpendicular loops of last row, and draw back thus for the beginning of the fancy pattern on the front of the dress—draw through 6 stitches, * do 4 chain, draw through 2 stitches, do 4 chain, draw through 2 stitches, do 4 chain, draw through 6 stitches, repeat from * four times, and then draw through the remaining 2 stitches. **67th row**—Pick up 68 tricot stitches in the usual way, and as you pick up keep all the little knobs of chain on the front of the work, and coming back draw through 7 stitches, * do 4 chain, draw through 2 stitches, do 4 chain, draw through 2 stitches, do 4 chain, draw through 8 stitches, repeat from * four times, and then draw through the 1 last stitch. **68th row**—Pick up 68 tricot stitches in the usual way, keeping the little knobs of chain to the front, and coming back draw through 6 stitches, * do 4 chain, draw through 2 stitches, do 4 chain, draw

through 2 stitches, do 4 chain, draw through 2 stitches, do 4 chain, draw through 6 stitches, repeat from * four times, and then draw through the remaining 2 stitches. Repeat the last two rows five times, and you will have done 13 rows in all of raised knobs. **79th row**—Take up 68 stitches in the ordinary manner, and draw back. **80th row**—A raised seam row—Pick up 68 stitches, taking the *back* perpendicular loop of last row, and draw back. Work 4 rows of plain tricot. **85th row**—Take up 68 stitches, then do 16 chain for the shoulder, and break off the wool; resume by drawing the wool through the top stitch of tricot where the chain commenced, and draw back the tricot stitches as usual. **86th row**—Take up 68 stitches on the tricot and 16 stitches on the chain, 84 stitches in all, and draw back. **87th row**—A raised seam row, and also the commencement of a gore—Pick up 48 stitches taking the *back* perpendicular loops of last row, and draw back in the usual manner. **88th row**—Take up 44 stitches in plain tricot, and draw back. **89th row**—Take up 40 stitches, and draw back. And proceed thus picking up 4 stitches less in each successive row till in the 98th row you pick up only 4 stitches, and draw back, which finishes the gore. **99th row**—Take up 48 stitches in plain tricot and take up 36 stitches at the *back* in continuation of the raised row which was interrupted on account of fashioning the gore, 84 stitches in all, and draw back. Work 6 rows of plain tricot with 84 stitches in each row. **106th row**—For under the arm—Take up 49 stitches only, and draw back. **107th row**—The same. **108th row**—Take up 49 stitches, then do 19 chain for the back of the dress, and break off the wool; resume by drawing the wool through the top stitch of tricot where the chain commenced, and draw back the tricot stitches as usual. **109th row**—Take up 49 tricot stitches, also 19 stitches on the chain, 68 stitches in all, and draw back. Work 6 rows of plain tricot. **116th row**—Begin another gore—Take up 4 stitches only, and draw back. **117th row**—Take up 8 stitches, and draw back. **118th row**—Take up 12 stitches and draw back. Proceed thus, picking up 4 additional stitches in every successive row till when doing the 127th row you pick up 48 stitches, and draw back, which finishes the gore. **128th row**—Take up 68 stitches, and draw back. Work 20 rows of plain tricot on 68 stitches. This completes the body; the five plain rows that are worked over and above the number of plain tricot rows at the commencement of the body are to form an under wrap to stitch the buttons on. For the **Flounce**—This is worked in ridged Russian crochet—Use the No. 8 crochet needle and make a length of 37 chain. Work 36 double crochet in a row, with always 1 chain to turn the rows, and always inserting the hook in the back thread of the stitches of the preceding row to form ridges. A sufficient length must be crocheted for the flounce to hang nice and full, probably about 220 rows; when enough is done, sew the last row to the commencing chain, and sew one edge of the flounce to the bottom of the dress body. Work a row of scollop along the bottom of the

Toy Elephant.

flounce—thus—2 double crochet on one of the depressed ridges, * 4 chain, 1 double crochet on the fourth chain from the needle, 2 double crochet on the next depressed ridge, and repeat from * to the end of the round. For the **Trimming** on the **Skirt**—The skirt trimming is composed of two pieces of tricot, both alike, and worked in a raised pattern to correspond with the front of the body. Begin with 78 chain, and do 2 rows of plain tricot. **3rd row**—A raised row—Decrease a stitch at the beginning and also at the end of the row—take up the perpendicular loops from the *back* of the preceding row, and draw back as usual. **4th row**—Plain tricot, but decrease a stitch at the beginning and at the end, and also at the beginning and end of *every* following row. **5th row**—The same. **6th row**—A raised row—Take up the *back* perpendicular loops, and draw back for the beginning of the knobbed pattern, thus, draw through 4 stitches, * do 4 chain, draw through 2 stitches, repeat from * to the end. **7th row**—Pick up in the usual way, and in drawing back let the raised knobs come intermediate between the knobs of the preceding row. Work 2 more rows the same, slanting the knobs at the beginning and end of the rows as the stitches are there decreased. **10th row**—Plain tricot. **11th row**—A raised row. Work two plain rows. **14th row**—Single crochet or slip stitch, inserting the hook into the *back* perpendicular loop of the stitches of last row. **15th row** —Scollop—1 double crochet on a slip-stitch of last row,* 5 chain, 1 double crochet in the fourth chain from the needle, 1 chain, miss one single stitch, 1 double crochet on the next, and repeat from *; this row and the preceding row are worked along each slope of the decreased ends as well as along the bottom of the trimming. Make another similar piece of trimming. Sew the trimming on the lower part of the body, at the back and front ; it is just above the flounce and secured with a button, as shown in the engraving; it is raised nearly two inches above the flounce on the hips. For the **Sleeves**—These are worked in tricot—Begin at the wrist with 34 chain. Work 2 rows of plain tricot. **3rd row**—A raised row. **4th row**—Plain. **5th row**—A raised row. **6th row**—Plain, increase a stitch at the beginning and at the end of the row. **7th row**—Knobs—Take up the stitches in the usual manner, and coming back draw through 2 stitches, * do 4 chain, draw through 2 stitches, and repeat from * to the end. **8th row**—The same, but in drawing back work 3 plain stitches at each end, that the knobs may come intermediate between the knobs of last row. **9th row**—Same as the seventh row. **10th row**—Plain, increase at each end. **11th row**—A raised row. **12th row**—

Baby's Rattle.

Plain, increase at each end. **13th row**—Plain, without increase. Repeat the last two rows twice, and there will be 44 stitches in the row. Do 8 rows of all plain tricot. Next row increase at each end. Do 6 rows of plain tricot. To shape the top of the Sleeve: Leave 10 stitches at each end, and work 1 row on the centre 26 stitches. Next row work the centre 24 stitches. And so on decrease a stitch at each end till reduced to 10 stitches for the highest part of the sleeve; work a row of slip-stitch along the top of the sleeve, and fasten off. Sew up the sleeve. Make the other sleeve in the same manner. Sew up the shoulder seams on the body, and set the sleeves in the armholes. For the **Neck Band**—**1st row**—Plain tricot along the top of the body. **2nd row**—Pick up the *back* perpendicular loops of the preceding row, and when drawing back make a series of knobs as instructed for the seventh row of the sleeves. Work 2 more rows of knobs as the eighth and ninth rows of the sleeves. **5th row**—Plain tricot, decreasing a stitch here and there to draw in the neck. **6th row**—A raised row. **7th row**—Slip stitch. **8th row**—Scollop, the same as round the bottom of the trimming. A row of the same scollop is required to edge the wrists; and also a row is worked down the commencement of the body where it forms a convenient fastening for the row of buttons which are to be sewn on the opposite side. Thirteen buttons are arranged down the front of the dress, as shown in the engraving.

INFANT'S SHAWL AND HOOD.

WORKED IN FAN STITCH.

THIS useful head-wrap may be worked with Shetland wool or andalusian wool as preferred, and may be either white or coloured. It consists of a square piece of crochet worked in Fan stitch, and one corner of the square is afterwards gathered up with ribbon to form a hood. From 2½ ozs. to 3½ ozs. of wool will be required, a No. 10 bone crochet needle, and 2 yards of inch wide ribbon. Begin by making a chain about a yard in length; the pattern is done in rows forwards and backwards. **1st row**—Work 3 long treble stitches (wool twice round the needle) in the fourth chain from the needle, * miss three of the foundation chain, 1 double crochet in the next, miss three, 7 long treble in the next, and repeat from * to the end of the row, where however finish by doing only 4 long treble instead of seven. **2nd row**—Turn the work, and do 1 double crochet on the first long treble stitch by the needle, *

7 long treble on the double crochet stitch, 1 double crochet on the centre stitch of the group of seven long treble of last row, and repeat from * to the end of the row, where the double crochet stitch should come on the very last stitch of last row. **3rd row**—Do 3 chain to turn, 3 long treble on the double crochet stitch by the needle, * 1 double crochet on the centre stitch of the group of long treble of preceding row, 7 long treble on the double crochet stitch, and repeat from * to the end, where finish with 4 long treble stitches instead of seven. Repeat the two last rows till the shawl is a perfect square. The last row must be taken round the other three sides of the shawl as well as straight along the top. Then for the **Border**—Work all round the shawl—1 double crochet on double crochet of the last round of the shawl, 3 chain, 9 long treble on the centre stitch of the group of long treble stitches, 3 chain, and repeat the same ; and fasten off at the end of the round. **To Make up the Hood**—Cut the ribbon in two equal lengths, and divide one piece in half again. The longest piece is to be run in a semicircular direction to define the shape of the hood from one corner of the shawl, in the manner so clearly shown in the engraving, and when the hood is worn this ribbon will pass round the infant's neck and will tie in a bow under the chin. The other two pieces of ribbon are to be run along the front of the hood, beginning close to the ribbon that is already put in for the neck, and being sewn thereto, will pass to the top of the head, and finish off in a good sized bow.

CHEMISE TRIMMED WITH CROCHET.

THIS trimming is a combination of crochet and fancy woven braid, the braid is a little more than a ¼ inch but not quite ⅜ inch in width, and quite plain except for the little pin-hole edge on each side ; it is obtainable at most wool repositories, procure also two reels of Evans' No. 16 crochet cotton, and a fine steel crochet needle. Commence by planning, upon a piece of stout paper, the shape you desire your chemise top to be, marking out the space the braid is to occupy, and tracing the outline of the "zigzag" as shown in the illustration ; fold the braid in accordance with the tracing and tack it lightly down to retain it in position ; each little square space will measure about ½ inch from side to side. When the braid is fully arranged, begin crocheting along the top edge, and working into the pin-holes along the side of the braid, do 1 double crochet on the right-hand corner of a level fold, 1 chain and 1 double

Baby's Muff.

crochet three times to reach the left-hand corner of the same fold, 1 chain and 1 double crochet three times to reach the entrance to a little square, 1 chain and 1 double crochet three times to the inner corner of the entrance, 2 chain, * cotton over the needle and insert the hook in a pin-hole of the braid along the side of the square and draw the cotton well through, cotton over the needle and draw through two loops on the needle, work as from * twice on each side and once at each corner of the square, when in all there will be 12 stitches on the needle, cotton over the needle and draw through all, 2 chain, 1 double crochet at the inner corner of the entrance (you are now of course on the opposite side of the entrance), 1 single crochet in a chain stitch on the first side, 1 double crochet in the folded braid ; do this twice more to reach the outer corner of the entrance ; then 1 chain and 1 double crochet three times to reach the next corner of the braid, which is by the outside fold, and repeat as above, zigzagging in and out the whole way round the top of the braid trimming ; and then work in the same manner round the bottom. Next do the **Heading** along the bottom of the trimming by which the work is to be sewn to the chemise. **1st row**—1 double crochet in the space of chain before the first double crochet stitch on the level fold of the braid, 2 chain and 1 double crochet four times in succession, 2 chain, cotton twice round the needle, insert the hook in the second loop down the hollow and draw the cotton through, cotton over the needle and draw through two loops on the needle, cotton over the needle and draw through 2 loops, make another similar long stitch in the same place and 2 corresponding long stitches on the opposite side of the hollow, cotton over the needle and draw through 5 stitches on the needle, 2 chain, and repeat the same: when at the corner by the sleeve go round with 3 chain, 1 treble, 3 chain, as shown in the engraving. **2nd row**—1 chain and 1 treble all round. For the **Edging** —Work the first 2 rows as described for the heading, with a difference only at the corners which now are rounded by working a set of three double-long-stitches on each of the three sides of the corner and drawing them closely together. **3rd row**—Crossed trebles; —1 chain, cotton twice round the needle, insert the hook in a stitch of last row and draw the cotton through, cotton over the needle and draw through 2 loops on the needle, cotton over the needle, insert the hook in the same stitch and draw the cotton through, cotton over the needle and draw through 2 loops on the needle; again cotton over the needle, miss three stitches, insert the hook in the next stitch and draw the cotton through, cotton over the needle and draw through two loops on the needle, cotton over the needle, insert the hook in the same place and draw the cotton through, cotton over the needle and draw through 2 loops on the needle, cotton over the needle and draw through 5 loops, cotton over the needle and draw through the re-maining 2 loops; cotton over the needle, insert the hook to take up the two centre threads of the twisted stitch just done and draw the cotton through, cotton over the needle and draw through 2 loops on the needle, cotton over the needle and draw through the

Child's Dress in Tricot and Crochet

treble and a long treble stitch to the end. **4th row**—1 chain and 1 treble the same as the second row. **5th row**—1 double crochet on a treble stitch of last row, * 2 chain, miss one space; 1 treble in the next space, 3 chain, another treble in the same space, 2 chain, miss one space, 1 double crochet on a treble stitch, and repeat from *: this finishes the trimming. A narrow ribbon is to be run under the crossed-treble stitches of the neck and sleeves.

INFANT'S HOOD AND SHAWL COMBINED.

A DAINTY hood and shawl for an infant is shown in our engraving, and being a new adaptation of an old stitch presents no difficulty in working, but will form a most acceptable and useful gift for a young child. Or a shawl can be crocheted without the hood if a combined garment is not desired. Procure 2½ ozs. of white and ½ oz. of pale blue Shetland wool, a No. 10 bone crochet needle, and 2 yards of pale blue satin ribbon. The white wool is employed for the shawl and the hood, the blue is only used for the border; the work is executed in rows forwards and backwards, and the peculiarity of the pattern lies in the height to which the treble stitches are drawn up, giving a very pretty effect. Begin—For the **Shawl**—With white wool, with 8 chain, which join round in a circle. **1st row**—Do 4 chain to stand for a treble, and work 11 treble stitches in the circle, and now and always be careful to draw up the first part of the treble stitches to stand about half an inch high. **2nd row**—Do 4 chain, and turn the work, do 8 treble between the second and third treble stitches from end of last row, do 4 treble between fourth and

Infant's Shawl and Hood, Worked in Fan Stitch.

other 2 loops, 3 chain, cotton over the needle, insert the hook again to take up the two centre threads of the twisted stitch and draw the cotton through, cotton over the needle and draw through 2 loops on the needle, cotton over the needle, insert the hook in the same place and draw the cotton through, cotton over the needle and draw through 2 loops on the needle, cotton over the needle and draw through 3 loops on the needle; do 1 long treble on the next stitch of last row, and proceed working a "crossed"

fifth treble stitches, 8 treble between the six and seventh treble stitches, 4 treble between the eighth and ninth treble stitches, 8 treble between the tenth and eleventh treble stitches, and 1 treble under the space of chain at the end. **3rd row**—Do 4 chain, and turn the work, do 4 treble between the second and third treble stitches of the first group of last row, 4 treble between the fourth and fifth, and 4 treble between the sixth and seventh treble stitches of the first group; 4 treble in the centre of the four treble stitches of the next group;

4 treble between the second and third, also between the fourth and fifth, and also between the sixth and seventh treble stitches of the middle group; 4 treble in the centre of the four treble stitches of the next group; 4 treble between the second and third, also between the fourth and fifth, and also between the sixth and seventh treble stitches of the last group, and 1 treble under the space of chain at the end of the row; there should be 11 groups of four treble stitches in the row. **4th row**—Do 4 chain, and turn the work, do 8 treble between the second and third treble stitches of the first group, do 4 treble in the centre of the four treble stitches of the next group, 4 treble in the centre of each of the next three groups, 8 treble in the centre of the next group of four treble which is the middle of the row, 4 treble in the centre of each of the next four groups, 8 treble in the centre of the last group, and 1 treble under the space of chain at the end. **5th row**—Do 4 chain to turn, and work in groups of 4 treble as directed in the third row, but now there will be 17 groups in the row, and conclude with 1 treble under the space of chain at the end. **6th row**—

Chemise Trimmed with Crochet.

Do 4 chain, and turn the work, do 8 treble between the second and third treble stitches of the first group, 4 treble in the centre of each of the next seven groups, 8 treble in the centre of the next group which is the middle of the row, 4 treble in the centre of each of the next seven groups, 8 treble in the centre of the last group, and 1 treble under the space of chain at the end. **7th row**—Work as instructed in the fifth row, but now there will be 23 groups in the row. Proceed after the manner of the two last rows, always increasing, so you get six additional groups in every repetition of the seventh row; and when 29 rows are worked the shawl will be large enough, and may be fastened off. For the **Hood**—Hold the top of the shawl towards you, and with white wool begin on the seventh row to the right of the ring of chain with which the shawl was commenced, do 1 treble on the edge of the seventh row (taking two treble stitches on the needle to work under), do 4 treble under the edge of each of the next six rows, 4 treble in the circle of chain, 4 treble under the edge of each of the next six rows, and 1 treble under the edge of the next (the seventh) row. **2nd row**—Do 4 chain, and turn the work, and do 4 treble in the centre of every group of four treble of last row, making 13 groups, and 1 treble on the treble stitch at the end. **3rd row**—Do 4 chain, and turn the work, and do 4 treble again in the centre of every group, making 13 groups, and 1 treble under the space of chain at the end. Work 6 more rows the same as last row. Then the hood is to be shaped and rounded as follows. **10th row**—Do 4 chain, and turn the work, do 2 treble in the centre of the first group of treble stitches, do 4 treble in the centre of each of the following 11 groups, do 2 treble in the centre of the last group, and 1 treble under the space of chain at the end. **11th row**—Do 4 chain, and turn the work, do 4 treble in the centre of each of the 11 groups of treble stitches of last row, and 1 treble under the space of chain at the end. **12th row**—Do 4 chain, and turn the work, do 2 treble in the centre of the first group, do 4 treble in the centre of each of the following 9 groups, do 2 treble in the centre of the last group, and 1 treble under the space of chain at the end. **13th row**—Do 4 chain, and turn the work, do 4 treble in the centre of each of the 9 groups of last row, and 1 treble under the space of chain at the end. **14th row**—Do 4 chain, and turn the work, do 2 treble in the centre of the first group, do 4 treble in the centre of each of the following 7 groups, do 2 treble in the centre of the last group, and 1 treble under the space of chain at the end, and fasten off. **Work a row** with white wool round the hood (not round the shawl),—Begin in the place where the hood began, and do 3 treble under each loop of chain up the side of the hood; then 3 treble in the centre of groups and also 3 treble in the spaces between the groups of the last row at top of the hood; then 3 treble under each loop of chain down the opposite side of the hood, and 1 treble into the seventh row of the shawl where 1 treble stitch is already worked, and fasten off. For the **Border**—The border is crocheted entirely with blue wool. The wide border as shown in the sectional engraving is worked only along the bottom of the shawl, and a simple edge constitutes the trimming up the fronts of the shawl and round the hood. Begin for the wide border by first doing 6 treble in the centre of the sixth group of four treble stitches counting from the front left-hand corner; thence go perpendicularly *up* the five bottom rows of the shawl, do 1 chain, 1 double crochet inserting the hook under the last treble of the group of treble stitches of the bottom row of the shawl (near by the group of the six treble just worked), * 3 chain, 1 double crochet inserting the hook under the last treble stitch of the group in the next row above, and repeat from * three times, the last double crochet being on a treble stitch of the fifth row from the bottom, then 3 chain, reverse the position of the work in the hands so as now to proceed downwards towards the edge, 1 double crochet inserting the hook under the first treble stitch of the next group in the fifth row, * 3 chain, 1 double crochet inserting the hook under the first treble stitch of the group in the next row below, and repeat from * three times; then 1 chain, 6 treble in the centre of the next group of stitches on the edge of the shawl, and repeat from * till you get to the point in the middle of the shawl where graduate the height of the border to fit nicely on the angle; from this work on to the next corner and there also fit the border to shape on the angle. Up the front of the shawl you do a simple row of scollops, 2 treble 2 chain and 2 treble in the edge of every row; the same in every space between the groups of treble stitches round the hood; and the same down the other front of the shawl; and finish the corner (which will be the corner where the border began) to correspond with the corner that is already worked.

Run one yard of ribbon through the stitches of the first row of the hood, this will be to tie round the infant's neck; cut the other yard of ribbon in two pieces, and run each of these half-way round the front of the hood within the two edge rows; attach one end of each ribbon to the neck ribbon, and tie the other ends in a bow on the top of the hood drawing the hood in to the size of the child's head.

GIMP TRIMMING.

A USEFUL trimming in imitation of gimp, for the adornment of mats, fancy tablecloths, and other miscellaneous purposes, or for braiding a dress, can be

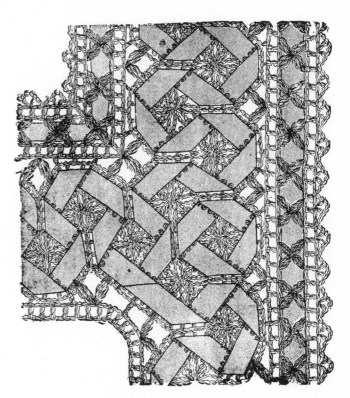

Details of Chemise Trimming.

made by working double crochet over a foundation cord and twisting the same in a series of looped rings as shown in the engraving. A piece of macramé twine will answer for the foundation, or several strands of the wool or thread of which the trimming is to be composed may be laid together and crocheted over. Begin by doing 24 double crochet upon the foundation, then, having the crochet the right side up, bend the work in the direction indicated in the illustration till the last stitch with the strand of foundation cord is brought to lie above the beginning of the double crochet, with the wool to the left, and while holding the ring in this position do a single crochet in the fifth double crochet stitch from the beginning, this will hold the ring in place; * you then work 18 double crochet along the foundation bend the work as shown in the engraving, and with the wool and foundation held towards the left, make a single crochet to connect the present loop to the side of the previous ring, do 6 more double crochet on the foundation, then 1 single crochet on the top edge of the trimming, missing 4 double crochet from the double crochet you before made on the top edge of the trimming, and repeat from * till a sufficient length of the trimming is worked. The top edge of the

centre stitches of the next group; turn the work, and under the first loop of chain do 5 double crochet, 4 chain, 4 double crochet, 4 chain, 5 double crochet, and under the second loop of chain do 5 double crochet, 4 chain, 2 double crochet; then turn the work, do 7 chain, 1 single crochet on the first of the 2 centre stitches of the group; turn the work, and under the loop of chain just done, work 5 double crochet, 4 chain, 2 double crochet, 4 chain, 2 double crochet, 4 chain, 5 double crochet; in the unfinished portion of the next loop do 2 double crochet, 4 chain, 5 double crochet; and in the unfinished portion of the next loop do 2 double crochet, 4 chain, 5 double crochet, which completes the point of the first scollop, and the needle and cotton are in proper position for the working of another scollop, for which repeat the instruction as detailed above.

Infant's Hood and Shawl Combined.

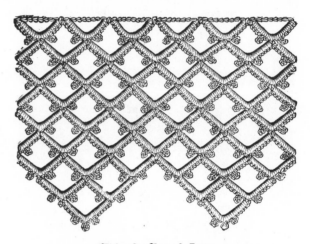

Wide Scolloped Lace.

Gimp Trimming.

trimming is strengthened by working a row of plain double crochet all along it. The trimming can be made wider or narrower by working a greater or less number of double crochet stitches in each ring, and it can be worked in coloured crochet cotton or silk, according to the purpose for which it is required.

WIDE SCOLLOPED LACE.

SELECT cotton and a steel crochet needle of suitable size for the purpose for which the lace is required, and work closely and firmly in rows from right to left. In Arkwright's coloured crochet cotton it is pretty, or done in coloured or black twist it would serve for trimming dresses. Commence with a length of chain. **1st row**—Work a single crochet in each of the 2 stitches nearest the needle, * 7 chain, miss three stitches, 1 single crochet in each of the 2 next stitches, and repeat from * to the end of the row, and break off the cotton. **2nd row**—Recommence on the right-hand side. Do 5 double crochet under the first loop of chain of last row, 4 chain for a picot, 4 double crochet, 4 chain for another picot, 5 double crochet, *all* under the same loop of chain of last row, and the same under every loop of chain to the end of the row, and fasten off. **3rd row**—Begin on the right-hand side—Work a single crochet on each of the 2 centre double crochet stitches between the picots of last row, * 7 chain, 1 single crochet on each of the 2 next centre stitches between the picots, and repeat from *, and fasten off. **14th row**—To point off the scollops. Recommence as usual on the right-hand side. Under the first loop of chain do 5 double crochet, 4 chain, 4 double crochet, 4 chain, 5 double crochet; do the same under the second loop of chain, and under the third loop of chain do 5 double crochet, 4 chain, 2 double crochet; then turn the work, do 7 chain, 1 single crochet on each of the 2 centre stitches between the picots of the first group of stitches of last row, 7 chain, 1 single crochet on the first of the

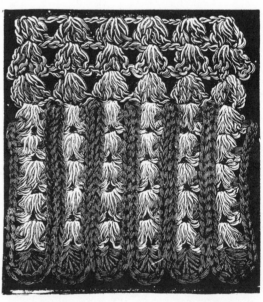

Details of Stitch and Border for Shawl.

WELDON'S
PRACTICAL CROCHET,

WITH COLOURED THREADS AND MOULDS.

(SIXTEENTH SERIES.)

New and Original Designs for Brackets, Cosies, Sideboard Cloths, Piano Covers, &c.

NINETEEN DESIGNS.

Telegraphic Address—]
"Consuelo," London.]

The Yearly Subscription to this Magazine, post free to any Part of the World, is 2s. 6d.
Subscriptions are payable in advance, and may commence from any date and for any period.

[Telephone—
2745.

The Back Numbers are always in print. Nos. 1 to 84 now ready, Price 2d. each, or post free for 15s. Over 5,000 Engravings.

CROCHET WITH COLOURED THREADS AND MOULDS.

A WONDERFUL advance in the ART OF CROCHET has lately been induced by the introduction of a new manufacture of coloured crochet twist and stiff moulds, by means of which, together with a special make of untarnishable gold thread, the most handsome and effective trimmings can be made, as well as many articles both for personal wear and for household adornment, that have never hitherto been considered within the possibilities of even the best crochet workers to accomplish. The old-fashioned white cotton crochet, though often very elaborate in detail, and very useful in its limited capacity for edging under-linen and making strong and serviceable antimacassars and cover-alls, could never, even by the highest stretch of the imagination, be considered artistic, and is now seldom seen in the best houses, having been almost totally eclipsed by the numerous art embroideries that have been in vogue of late years. Hence the revival of crochet, always a favourite work, is to be welcomed.

The new COLOURED CROCHET can be utilised for almost any and every purpose, and certainly supplies a long unsatisfied craving for a work that is durable as well as handsome, and at the same time has the desirable qualification of being tolerably easy of execution; it makes charming trimming for dresses and jackets, borders for window-blinds, mantel-valances, bracket-drapes, and other furniture trimmings, besides sofa-backs, chair-backs, cushions, cosies, wall-pockets, work-bags, &c.

The moulds impart a solidity to the crochet that is unattainable by any other means; they are not visible, being entirely covered with stitches, and they do not add to the weight of the work, but by their use a decided and raised appearance is given to all the prominent parts of the pattern, which thus stand in relief above the light and open stitches of the crochet. The "brilliant" colours of the new crochet twist shine almost like silk, indeed the work at first sight would undoubtedly be taken for silk crochet; and the gold thread, which is employed to make lace wheels, spiders, and trellis to fill open spaces, and for an ornamental edging, together combine to render this new work especially attractive.

The designs contained in the following pages and the subject matter explaining the same, are the copyright of Messrs. Weldon and Co., while the materials and moulds are manufactured solely by Messrs. Carl Mez and Söhne, whose goods are stocked by every fancy depôt and art needlework establishment.

Ring Pattern Border.

REQUISITES—CROCHET WORK WITH COLOURED THREADS AND MOULDS.

Two kinds of crochet twist are employed in working the patterns illustrated in this issue of our "Practical Needlework Series;" both are conveniently done up in ready-wound balls, but they are perfectly distinct one from the other, and are never, or very rarely, used together in the same piece of work. The finest of the two, called "Brilliant Crochet Twist," partakes of the nature of flax thread, and really is flax, spun very smoothly, with a glossy surface that shines like silk; it is made in every colour, and in almost all shades of colour—white, cream, dark and light blue, pink, red, cardinal, salmon, flesh, olive green, olive brown, tabac, terra-cotta, sea green, sage, fawn, crushed strawberry, old gold, and others too numerous to mention; this is the kind most generally used for dress trimming. It is strong and will wear well, and is warranted to wash. A variety of the same "Brilliant" crochet twist goes by the name of "Glanz Häkelgarn," and is shaded throughout the ball in the sweetest imaginable tints of art shades, running from pink through salmon to sap green, from gold through tabac to rich dark brown, from salmon through pale greeny-blue to apple green, from white through pale yellow to guinea gold, and other mixtures and shades of self-colour. The other kind of crochet twist is termed "Original Glanzgarn." It also is made of flax and has a glossy surface, but it is considerably thicker than "Brilliant" crochet twist; in fact, is almost as thick as whipcord, or a medium size of macramé twine, to which it bears a great resemblance. It is in all shades of colour, and is thoroughly suitable for decorative purposes. Every ball of twist is labelled with the manufacturers' names, Messrs. Carl Mez and Söhne, of Aldermanbury, London, E.C. All the different colours and shades are denoted by numbers, so that when ordering, through your nearest fancy repository, it is only necessary to state the number, and you are sure of obtaining exactly what is required. The patterns in this issue are described in their actual colours and the numbers are given accordingly, that anyone desiring to work an exact copy can do so. At the same time it is possible to arrange many equally pleasing combinations by carefully consulting the shade pattern books of the above-named firm.

On page 4 will be seen an engraving of some of the stiff moulds as they appear before being covered with crochet, and other shapes will be noticed in the worked examples. They are all denoted by numbers, and, though stiff, are not at all heavy nor cumbrous.

A few steel crochet needles must be procured of various sizes, a rather fine steel needle for working the Brilliant crochet twist, and one a trifle larger for using with the Original Glanzgarn. Penelope needles are the best, as their stem is the same consistency all the way up, which conduces a great deal to the evenness of the work. You also should have one or two crochet needles with stems larger round the top than by the hook, and keep these specially for doing "rice stitches," because the size at the top of the stem makes a larger roll of stitches for the hook to draw through and saves a great deal of unnecessary pulling.

A good make of Japanese gold thread is required, avoiding the cheap sorts which always tarnish and make the work look shabby before it is half worn out. Gold braid is employed in some of the patterns to run through the open crochet stitches of the heading, thereby adding to the handsome appearance of the work. And last, but not least, be sure and have a sharp pair of scissors handy to cut the twist.

STITCHES USED IN COLOURED CROCHET WORK.

ANYONE who can crochet at all may enter upon this work without the slightest hesitation. The very simplest stitches are used—single crochet, double crochet, chain, treble, and rice stitch. Rice stitches make a very effective edging round the outside of the moulds, and are besides employed for tufts

crochet on double crochet, taking up always the one top thread of the work, and join at the end of the round, and break off. **3rd round**—With lightest shade of twist, and holding the wrong side of the last round towards you, work 3 double-crochet stitches, and a picot of 3 chain, and repeat the same to the end of the round, and break. All the large moulds are crocheted thus, and they are joined one to the other in a straight line by 3 connecting picots. The small moulds are covered first with a round of double crochet worked with the lightest shade of twist, and this is edged with picots like the third round of the large moulds, but worked with the medium shade of twist; a pendant is sewn over and over with overcast stitches of the lighter shade of twist, and here and there a gold stitch, and is joined to the small mould, which after having its centre embellished with a lace spider executed with gold thread, is sewn on inside the large crocheted mould, as shown in the engraving.

For the **Heading—1st row**—With darkest crochet twist—Work 2 double long treble in one of the picots of the first large ring, 2 long treble in the next picot, 2 chain, 2 treble in the next picot, then 3 chain, 1 double in the next picot, and 2 chain and 1 double in the next picot three times, when reverse the stitches and complete the heading of the first ring as it began, and continue similarly to the end of the row. **2nd row**—With medium shade of twist, and holding the wrong side of last row towards you, work along in plain double crochet. **3rd row**—Work a picot edge with the lightest shade of twist, to correspond with the outside round of the large rings. This finishes the border.

Some of the Moulds used in the New Coloured Crochet Work.

and tassels. When you once get into the method of working them they are as easy as any other stitch. There must be a stitch on the needle to begin with; you then wind about ten turns of the thread round the needle, insert the hook in a stitch of the foundation and draw the thread through, thread over the needle and draw through *all* the lot of coiled stitches on the needle without in the least disarranging the position of the coil, and when all are drawn through, you do 1 chain or 1 treble, as the case may be. If a treble, the rice stitch will stand upright to the same height as the treble stitch; it is seen thus in the headings of many borders; while if a chain, it will curl gracefully under to the wrong side of the work, making a pretty crinkly edge, as see round the Fleur de Lis design in this issue.

RING PATTERN BORDER.

AN effective border, worked with Brilliant crochet twist in three shades of crushed strawberry over ring-like moulds. The twist bears the numbers 247, 251, and 241. The moulds are 121 and 101. Commence with the darkest shade of twist and one of the largest moulds, and using a fine steel crochet needle, fill the mould quite closely with double-crochet stitches, and when it is quite full, join evenly, and break off. **2nd round**—With medium shade of twist, and holding the wrong side of the crochet towards you, work double-

CROCHET BORDER FOR TRIMMING DRESSES.

OUR engraving shows a border eminently suitable for dress trimmings, worked in crochet in passementerie style, with Messrs. Carl Mez and Söhne's Brilliant Crochet Twist over moulds. The twist is highly glazed and will wash perfectly, and may be had in every variety of colour, each shade bearing its own respective number by which it can always be identified; our example is executed with art green No. 78, and pale salmon No. 247; and the moulds are numbered 103 and 114. A fine steel crochet needle is required, and a skein of Japanese gold thread must also be procured.

Take the smaller of the two moulds, and work it over in double crochet with green twist, doing 39 double crochet stitches, or as many as will cover the mould closely and evenly; break off, and join as neatly as possible: cover all the small moulds in the same manner; and complete them by threading a needleful of gold twist with which to fabricate a few long stitches across and across the centre of the mould as "wheels" and "spiders" are formed in lace work. Proceed to the large moulds, and work one of these likewise with green twist, getting 70 double crochet stitches round the mould, and join, and break off. Do a 2nd round with salmon colour, beginning at the top of the mould to work down the left-hand side, the right side of the green crochet being towards you—work 2 double crochet on stitches of last round, taking up the one top thread, do 1 chain and join with a single crochet to the side of the small mould as represented in the engraving, 1 chain, 3 double crochet or consecutive stitches of the large mould, 3 chain, 3 double crochet, 3 chain, 3 more double crochet, then 1 chain and join with a single crochet to the same small mould, missing eight stitches from the last join, 1 chain, 3 double crochet upon the large mould, and continue 3 chain and 3 double crochet till you have done 8 picots and 8 lots of 3 double crochet, then 3 chain, 6 double crochet, which 6 double crochet are to stretch over the indented bend at the bottom of the mould, then 3 chain, 3 double crochet, 3 chain, and this, the eleventh picot, should come exactly in the centre of the bottom of the mould, do 3 double crochet, and work up the other side to correspond with the side already done, annexing another small mould level with the first, and ending with a picot of 3 chain at the top point of the mould, and join to the first double crochet, and break off. More large moulds are crocheted similarly, and these are joined each to the preceding by the sixth and seventh picots: they all are filled in with a lace stitch "spider" of gold thread.

Crochet Border for Trimming Dresses.

For the **Heading—1st row**—With gold tinsel thread. Do 1 double crochet on a double crochet at the right-hand top corner of a small mould, 3 chain, 1 double crochet on the centre stitch of the same mould, 1 double crochet at the left-hand top corner, 3 chain, miss two stitches of the same mould and do 1 treble in the next, 1 long treble in the picot at the point of the large mould, 1 treble in the side of the next small mould, 3 chain, and repeat the same for the length of the border. **2nd row**—With green crochet twist. Work 1 treble on the first stitch of the previous row, * 4 chain, 1 single crochet in the top of the treble stitch just done (this forms a picot), 1 chain, miss one stitch of previous row, 1 treble on the next, and repeat from *. The pendants or tassels are covered with double crochet worked with green twist, and completed by a short length of chain to connect the pendant to the border as represented in the engraving.

TRIPLE WHEEL BORDER.

This border is composed simply of small wheels, three of which are joined together to form a scollop. It is quite easy to work, and makes a neat and pretty trimming. Our example is crocheted in shaded Brilliant Crochet Twist, No. 613, in tints of light art green, flesh colour and fawn. Shades of crushed strawberry as No. 609, and shades of brown and gold, as No. 600, are also very tasteful. The moulds are No. 101. A skein of Japanese gold thread is required for filling the centres of the wheels. Use a rather fine steel crochet needle. Take the **First Mould** and work with the shaded twist 44 double crochet round it. This should completely cover the surface of the mould. Join the last stitch to the first stitch evenly, then do 1 double crochet on each of 2 stitches of last round with the work the right side towards you, and inserting the hook to take up the one top thread, * 5 chain, 1 double crochet on each of the 2 next stitches, and repeat from *, and end with 5 chain, and join to the beginning of the round. There will be 22 picots of chain in the round, and fasten off. The **Second Mould** is worked in the same way till you have made 18 picots of chain, then 2 double crochet, and do 2 chain, join with a single crochet stitch to a picot of the previous wheel, 2 more chain, and 2 double crochet as usual, join the next two picots to picots of the previous wheel in the same way, and when you have completed the twenty-second picot, join round and fasten off. The **Third Mould**, or wheel, comes intermediately under the two first wheels, and is connected to each by 3 picots, with 2 picots standing between, consequently there are 14 picots extending round the lower portion of this wheel. Thread a crewel needle with gold thread and take long stitches across and across the centres of the wheels on the wrong or under-side of the crochet, and darn a spot in the middle where the stitches cross each other. The manner of doing this is clearly shown in the engraving, and the effect in the actual work is very good. The pendants are made by com-

mencing with 2 or 3 chain, which join round, and work in double crochet round and round, the wrong side of the stitches outside, increasing to about 6 double crochet in the round, more or less, according to the size of the pad that is to be put in the crochet, and reducing to the top, and ending with a loop of chain stitches by which to attach the pendant to the wheel, as in the engraving. For the **Heading—1st row**—1 treble in the seventh picot to the right of the first joining, 4 chain, miss one picot, 1 double crochet in the next, 1 chain, 1 double crochet in the next picot, * 4 chain, thread over the needle, and missing one picot insert the hook in the next and draw the thread through, thread over the needle and draw through 2 stitches on the needle, thread over the needle, miss one picot of this wheel and one picot of the next wheel, insert the hook in the next and draw the thread through, thread over the needle and draw through 2 stitches, thread over the needle and draw through 2 stitches, and again thread over the needle and draw through 2 stitches, 4 chain, miss 1 picot, 1 double crochet in the next, 1 chain, 1 double crochet in the next, and repeat from * to the end of the row, finishing with 4 chain and 1 treble as you began. **2nd row**—Work 1 treble on the first stitch of previous row, * 6 chain, 1 treble in the sixth chain from the needle, miss three or four stitches of last row, 1 treble on the next, and repeat from * to the end of the row. This finishes the border.

FLEUR DE LIS DESIGN.

A Fleur de Lis is a crocheted ornament that will be found useful for many purposes. Our model is worked with shaded brilliant crochet twist called Häkelgarn in tints of greeny blue, pale strawberry, and flesh colour, as numbered 619 in the sample books of Messrs. Carl Mez and Söhne. The Fleur de Lis moulds are 117. You also will require a skein or two of Japanese gold thread. Commence by winding the Brilliant Crochet Twist firmly round and round the two branching points of the mould and wind also a little way beyond where the points meet, as will be seen by referring to the engraving, then change to double crochet over the mould until the neck of the mould is attained, about 24 double crochet stitches, when resume the twining till you get to the situation where, as represented in the engraving, the double crochet is again taken up and continued round the three divisions of the fleur de lis to the opposite side, about 30 double crochet each side and 34 in the middle division; then stop, turn the mould the wrong side uppermost, and go back round the scollops in double crochet, working in the one back thread of the previous row of stitches; turn again with 3 chain, and now always taking up the one back thread, proceed in rice stitch, doing one rice stitch on each double crochet round the scollops, but missing one or two stitches in the

Triple Wheel Border.

indents to ensure a nice shape; break off the Häkelgarn when this part of the work is complete. Finish the mould to correspond with its commencement, and also wind Häkelgarn on the inside points of the scollops. Work along the top of the fleur de lis in double crochet and in rice stitch as on the scollops. Take the gold thread, and with the right side of the mould towards you work this edge as a margin to the rice stitches—single crochet round the corner of the first rice stitch, then 1 double crochet between the first and second rice stitches, * 5 chain, 1 double crochet in the fifth chain from the needle, miss one space, 1 double crochet in the next space, and repeat from * The three pendants are tiny solid moulds, or peas, covered with rice stitches. Commence with 3 chain, and join round; do 4 chain, and work 3 rice stitches in each stitch of the commencing chain, put in the mould, and draw the top in closely, and fasten off with an end an inch or two in length; the three ends are knotted together a little way up, and a bunch of stitches is worked with gold thread over the knot, from thence one only of the first threads is carried on to secure the bunch to the lowest point of the fleur de lis. With a needleful of gold thread embroider a fancy network of herring-bone stitch up the centre of each scollop, and make a spider in each circle at the top of the fleur de lis.

BORDER OF FLEUR DE LIS AND TREFOILS.

THIS handsome border, which measures 6½ inches in depth, inclusive of tassels, is worked over moulds, 117 fleur de lis, and 119 trefoil, with the shaded brilliant crochet twist known as 607 Häkelgarn in lovely tints of pink. Commence by winding the crochet twist firmly and smoothly round and round the double upper points of the **Fleur de Lis Mould**, winding also a little way

Fleur de Lis Design.

beyond the meeting of the points, as will be seen by referring to the engraving; along the top of the mould work 30 double crochet on one side the neck and 30 double crochet on the other side; turn the work, do 4 chain, miss the double crochet by the needle, and work 1 rice stitch of 6 coils in the back thread of the next, and then proceed; 1 chain, miss one, 1 rice stitch, till 27 rice stitches are worked along the top of the fleur de lis (the middle stitch will come in the centre of the neck and there will be 3 double crochet missed each side it), end with 3 chain and 1 single crochet on the last double crochet stitch, and break off; join the twist on the right-hand side the row of rice stitches, do 3 double crochet in the little loop of chain, 5 chain, 1 double crochet in the fifth chain from the needle to form a picot, 1 double crochet in the space made by the one chain stitch of last row, and continue in picots and double crochet, ending with 3 double crochet in the little loop of chain at the end, and fasten off. Begin the crochet round the lower scollops of the fleur de lis, 25 double crochet on the first scollop, 35 on the centre, and 25 on the last; turn, and proceed in rice stitch as already instructed; two double crochet stitches are missed on each side the indentation and 3 rice stitches are worked on one double crochet at each tip, so you get 13 rice stitches upon the side scollops and 17 rice stitches on the centre scollop; then follows a row of picots in which to make the work sit flat you will have to miss two chain stitches by the indentations. Finish the fleur de lis by winding twist round the neck from one part of the crochet to the other part of the crochet, also on the inside points of the scollops, and embroider the inside of the scollops with herringbone stitch and the curves with spiders of gold thread. Work the **trefoil** to correspond with the fleur de lis; on this there should be 34 double crochet and 15 rice stitches and 13 picots round each top leaf, and 30 double crochet and 13 rice stitches, and 11 picots round the bottom leaf, with 1 rice stitch on each indentation with three double crochet missed on each side of it; the trefoil is filled with spiders embroidered with gold thread. For the **Heading**—Make 32 chain, 1 double crochet in the centre of the top of a fleur de lis, * 16 chain, 1 double crochet in the fourth picot of the leaf to the right of a trefoil, 1 chain, 1 double in the next picot, 1 chain, 1 double crochet in the next picot, 14 chain, miss two picots, 1 double crochet in the next, 1 chain, 1 double crochet in the

next, 1 chain, 1 double crochet in the next, 7 chain, 1 double crochet in the third picot of the next leaf, 1 chain, 1 double crochet in the next, 1 chain, 1 double crochet in the next, 14 chain, miss two picots, 1 double crochet in the next, 1 chain, 1 double crochet in the next, 1 chain, 1 double crochet in the next, 16 chain, 1 double crochet in the centre of the top of the next fleur de lis, and repeat from *. **2nd row of Heading**—Beginning on the right-hand side, do 4 double crochet in consecutive stitches of the chain, 3 double crochet in the next, * 26 double crochet will bring you to the fleur de lis, where miss one double-crochet stitch and one chain stitch on each side thereof, 26 double crochet, 3 double crochet in the next, 31 double crochet in a straight line over the trefoil, 3 double crochet in the next, and repeat from *. **3rd row**—Work 1 chain and 1 rice stitch alternately, and in general miss one double crochet between the rice stitches, but over the fleur de lis six double crochet must be missed to form a good angle, and where you worked 3 double crochet together in the last row, you are now to work 3 rice stitches on the centre stitch, which is a corner stitch. **4th row**—Do 1 double crochet in the space of one chain of last row, and 1 chain between the double crochet stitches. **5th row**—Work 1 double crochet on the corner stitch at the right-hand side of the first V, 15 chain, 1 double crochet over the fourth rice stitch from the corner, 9 chain, 1 double crochet over the third rice stitch, 5 chain, 1 double crochet over the third rice stitch from the last double crochet, then 1 double crochet on the opposite side of the V, 1 chain, 3 single crochet up three of the five chain stitches, 1 chain, 1 double crochet opposite the corresponding double crochet on the first side of the V, 3 chain, 1 single crochet in the centre stitch of the loop of nine chain, 5 chain, 1 double crochet on the side of the V, 5 chain, 1 single crochet in the sixth stitch of the first loop of chain, 8 chain, 1 double crochet on the left-hand corner of the V, then 16 chain to reach along the top of the V opening, and join to the corner where you just now commenced; then for the picot edge work straight along the top of the border, * 2 double crochet, 5 chain, 1 double crochet in the fifth chain from the needle, miss one stitch of the previous row, and repeat from *. For the **Tassels**—Make 4 chain and unite in a circle; do 5 chain, then work 12 rice stitches of 14 coils in the circle, insert the tassel mould, and draw the stitches up closely, fastening off with a length of thread; make two more similar tassels; knot the three threads together with a thread of gold twist about ⅓ inch above the tassels, make a little ball of gold tinsel to stand over the knot, carry on the three coloured threads to the place where the tassel is to hang and secure it there.

Border of Fleur de Lis and Trefoils.

CHEVASSE PATTERN.

THE scollop from which our engraving is taken measures nine inches in depth, inclusive of tassels, and is particularly handsome for a mantel border or bracket drape. It is worked with Original Glanzgarn, as numbered, 736 tabac, 739 eau de nil, and 726 dark art green; over moulds No. 110 pear shape and No. 240 medium-sized rings; eight of the former and five of the latter in each scollop; and you also will require a skein of gold thread and a yard or more of half-inch wide gold braid. Commence with the **Pear-shaped Moulds**, and using tabac Glanzgarn work forty double crochet on each mould, beginning and ending at the point, and join, and fasten off neatly. Three of the moulds are hereby completed, and to finish the other five you will take the dark green Glanzgarn and do a rice stitch in every alternate stitch of double crochet, holding the work the right side towards you and inserting the hook to take up the two front threads of the tabac stitches; the thread is passed ten times round the needle for these rice stitches, and is drawn rather tightly through, that the stitches may "curl" under, and 1 chain is made between each rice stitch to compensate for the stitch that is missed. Work each of the **Ring-shaped Moulds**, in double crochet with eau-de-nil Glanzgarn, doing twenty-six stitches in the circle, and join evenly round; then with gold thread, keeping the ring the right side towards you and inserting the hook to take up the one top thread of the stitches, margin the edge with a line of single crochet. For the **Heading.**—Use tabac Glanzgarn, and make a chain the length the border is required to be; and for the **1st row**—Work 1 treble in the seventh chain from the needle, * 1 chain, miss one stitch of the foundation, 1 rice stitch (11 turns of the thread) in the next, 1 chain, miss one stitch, 1 treble in the next, and repeat from * to the end of the foundation. **2nd row**—Turn the work, and do double crochet the whole way round the heading, that is to say on both sides of the strip of crochet and round the ends.

The different parts of the pattern are arranged together as shown in the engraving, and are to be sewn one to the other and to the heading with a few stitches of black sewing cotton. A rosette of six rice stitches worked with tabac Glanzgarn is placed on the join where the points of the three pear-shaped moulds meet. Two little tabac tassels, also worked in rice stitch, are sewn below the heading at a little distance from the scollop, so as to hang *between* the scollops when a whole length of border is completed; other tassels worked with green Glanzgarn hang round the bottom of the scollop, three

follows, ten discs measuring 2 inches in diameter, six thick rings 400, four double-heart moulds 209, four curved hearts 204, two pear-shaped 20, two indented triangles 242, four lobes 109, and eight V-shaped moulds.

Cover the moulds with original Glanzgarn, passing it over and over as smoothly and as evenly as you would work overcast stitches in embroidery; cover four discs with the lightest shade of electric blue, four with ivory, and two with the lightest shade of terra-cotta; these are placed, the blue at the lower corners of the cosy, the ivory on each side, reaching from 4 inches to 6 inches from the bottom, and the light terra in the middle of the cosy; an indented triangle covered with the lightest shade of electric blue occupies a space below the terra-cotta disc; and has curved hearts in the darkest terra-cotta on each side of it; a thick ring covered with the lightest shade of art green is dotted close to each of the three points of the triangle; then to the right and left of the cosy above the ivory discs there are other V-shaped moulds in dark terra-cotta; and again above these, and inclining more towards the top of the cosy, are the double-heart moulds in the darkest shade of electric-blue; between which, and immediately over the terra-cotta disc, we find room for a pear-shaped mould covered with the darkest shade of art green, and a lobe of ivory colour in the intermediate space to the right and left at quite the top of the cosy. Before the moulds are attached to the felt their centres are filled with gold thread in wheels, spiders, network, and trellis, more or less

Chevasse Pattern.

being dependent from the centre mould and one from each of the other pear-shaped moulds. The gold braid is threaded through the rice stitches and treble stitches of the heading, bringing the rice stitches to the front and the treble stitches to the back of the braid.

TEA COSY.

OUR illustration shows an example of the New Rococo Work, the size of the original tea cosy being 15½ inches wide by 11½ inches high. This work is not crochet, but the moulds are simply covered, or overcast, with original Glanzgarn twist; they then are laid upon an olive-brown felt foundation as shown in the illustration—in point of fact the felt may be bought with the design ready printed for working. The reverse side of the cosy is the same as the front, and it is a really beautiful piece of work. The requirements are original Glanzgarn shades 704 and 705 terra-cotta, 710 ivory, 724 and 726 art green, and 732 and 734 electric blue; shades 242 and 247 terra-cotta Brilliant Crochet Twist for embroidering fancy stitches; a skein each of gold thread and gold cord, the former for filling in the centres of the moulds and the latter for couching round the outlines; and various moulds as

elaborately, according to taste; the stitches are plainly depicted in the engraving, and may readily be copied therefrom. When all this is accomplished, the moulds are placed one by one upon the felt, each in its own respective place as detailed above, and they are retained in position by sewing the felt to that part of the Glanzgarn that passes under the moulds, the sewing of course being performed on the inner or wrong side of the work; the felt is cut clear away from the open part of the moulds, and this can be done before the sewing on, or afterwards, whichever the worker considers most convenient to herself. Turning again to the engraving, it will be observed that five of the moulds are surrounded by a little pointed border or edging—to work this you will take a crewel needle threaded with Brilliant crochet twist (the lightest shade of terra-cotta goes round four of the moulds and the darkest terra-cotta round the centre disc only), and embroider smooth satin stitches close beside the mould, making the stitches of graduated length; a couching of fine gold cord is then laid round the outline of these moulds, and also round the outline of all the other moulds on the cosy; and streaks of satin stitch are worked on the felt in the places where represented in the engraving.

When both halves of the cosy are complete, a piece of satin must be pasted all over their wrong sides, behind the work, and which will show the threads of the fancy network. It is wadded and lined, then made up, and a dark terra-cotta silk cord is put round the edge and made into a loop at the top.

CREAM CANVAS SLIP FOR PIANO TOP.

EMBROIDERED WITH GLANZGARN AND SILK, WITH ENDS AND TASSELS OF CROCHET.

OUR engraving represents a new and charming method of employing the Original Glanzgarn twist for decorative purposes, other than crochet, and the manner pursued in finishing off the ends of a fabric material with crochet trimming and tassels. The canvas used in the example is manufactured to the width of 13 inches, and is sold by the yard, so that any length may be procured. It has a woven insertion of gold threads running up each side, about 1½ inches within the selvedge. The space between the gold thread insertion and the selvedge is occupied with a running zigzag border that goes the entire length of the slip, and is worked with No. 732 electric blue Original Glanzgarn. This zigzag gives the clue to the more elaborate design that engages the centre of the slip (but extends only 18 inches up, where it is worked off to a point), as the stitches follow the same rule of placing, lying always in a straight direction on the canvas, either perpendicularly upright, or horizontally from right to left, always for the most part taking 5 threads of the canvas upon the needle. In the narrow border all the Glanzgarn stitches are taken over 5 threads from right to left, slanting one thread in each of 11 stitches, and then reversing the slant till in 10 stitches more the

are russet brown, cerise, guinea gold, and light olive green. The basket stitch in the lowest device is worked in the two latter colours, the gold in the *upper* half of the band and the green in the other half. The smallest diamonds and the uppermost and the lowest of the block of four diamonds are russet brown. The latter have gold spots in the centre, while the other two diamonds are cerise with green spots. The central diamond in the ornament above and also the triangles in the wings are worked with green silk. The large diamond in outline is russet brown, and the mitred angles are cerise. Tiny gold spots appear in the interstices of some of the Glanzgarn stitches. The four corner points of the large cross are filled with green and gold, each occupying one-half of the space, and the four interior diamonds correspond with the diamonds in the first device, but are minus the spots, and instead are decorated with a little tuft of self-coloured stitches. The lozenge with which the device is brought to a close is worked up with russet brown and cerise, the former as a section of a diamond, the latter as a filling. All the tiny diamonds, of which

Tea Cosy.

THE NEW ROCOCO WORK.

Cream Canvas

5 threads parallel to the first stitch are worked again. Little stars embroidered with russet brown silk in cross stitch and plume stitch are ranged in the interstices of the zigzag. Within the insertion of gold threads there is a narrow line of drawn thread embroidery. You leave 3 canvas threads (it is a double-thread canvas and the two threads count as one), draw out 1 thread, leave 5, draw out 1 thread, and then over the 5 threads that are left you embroider in herringbone stitch with guinea gold silk.

The central design is commenced above the hem at the bottom of the slip by working with Glanzgarn a horizontal stitch over the 1 centre thread, a stitch above this over 3 threads, and so on, extending the size of the stitch by one thread on each side till the sixth stitch occupies a width of 9 threads; over this divide to the right and to the left, 5 threads on each side, till five more stitches are done, when narrow gradually on the right-hand side to 4 threads and 2 threads, but keeping the left-hand side in a slant always 5 threads in width, till, as you see in the engraving, you get to another cross-bar with stitches 5 threads in width, for which you have to make way, but resume the original slant on the other side of the cross bar, and proceed in pattern, always consulting the engraving with regard to the position of the stitches. Be careful in mitring the corners when changing from the horizontal to the perpendicular stitches, and keep the wrong side of the work neat. The outline of the Glanzgarn upon the canvas is accentuated by a series of back stitches worked with silk in a shade to match. The shades of silk used for the filling

no special mention has been made, consist of green stitches, excepting those on each side the lozenge, which are gold.

For the **Crochet End and Tassels**— Use No. 761 Original Glanzgarn, which is most exquisitely shaded through salmon pinks and greeny blues. Make a chain the width of the canvas, allowing a few stitches for turning over the side. **1st row**—Work 1 treble in the sixth chain from the needle, * 1 chain, miss one stitch of the foundation, 1 rice stitch of 6 coils in the next, 1 chain, miss one stitch, 1 treble in the next, and repeat from * to the end of the commencing chain. **2nd row**—Turn the work, and do a row of double crochet stitches above the rice stitches, and also along the foundation chain. **3rd row**—With gold thread and the wrong side of the double-crochet stitches uppermost, work single crochet along each side of the heading. The little tassels are formed of 5 loosely made long rice stitches (20 coils or so), clustered together in a bunch and secured at intervals in the gold stitches of the heading by loops of twist. Run a piece of gold braid through the rice-stitch row of the heading, bringing the rice stitches to the front and the treble stitches to the back of the braid. Sew the heading of the crochet neatly over the hem of the canvas, and the slip is ready for use when the other side is finished to correspond.

FELT DESIGN FOR THE END OF A SIDEBOARD SLIP OR PIANO COVER.

THE example from which our engraving is taken is another specimen of the New Rococo Work, attained by the use of the new crochet twist called "Original Glanzgarn," combined with stiff-shaped moulds. In this

Piano Top.

wrong side or under side of the material, behind the work, becomes visible through the threads of the ornamental network.

To make a sideboard slip or piano cover after the style of the sectional piece shown in our engraving, the requirements are as follows: A piece of olive brown felt, measuring 16 inches in width and about 2 yards in length. The ends of the felt are scolloped, and the margin is "pinked" all the way round; the embroidery is executed at both the ends of this piece of felt, which can, if required, be purchased with the design printed thereon. Original Glanzgarn in shades as numbered, 731 and 732 electric blue, 716 art green, 710 ivory, 721 apricot, 722 crushed strawberry, and 706 chocolate; to use over moulds, six 112 discs, two 207 large hearts, four 231 small hearts, six 20 pear shape, six V-shaped, and four pines: also copper-coloured iridescent metallic thread for embroidering the centres of the moulds, gold cord and green and strawberry-coloured iridescent metallic cord for couching round the outsides of the moulds, and pale electric blue and pale crushed strawberry embroidery silk for working fancy stitches on the felt. Cover the largest hearts with chocolate Glanzgarn, the smaller hearts with ivory, the pines with pale electric blue, the discs with green, four of the pear-shaped moulds with crushed strawberry and two with apricot, four V-shaped moulds with dark

Felt Design for the End of a Sideboard Slip or Piano Cover.

THE NEW ROCOCO WORK.

electric blue, and two with ivory. Fill the centres of the moulds with net work as represented in the engraving, using the copper-coloured metallic thread. When this is accomplished the moulds are grouped together in the manner seen in the illustration, and they are attached to the felt by sewing through the felt to the under threads of the Glanzgarn; the sewing is not at all visible on the surface of the work. The felt may be cut to the inner shape of the mould either before or after the mould is affixed, whichever appears most convenient to the worker. The embroidery stitches round the large heart and the three pines are executed with pale electric blue silk, and consist of small points or vandykes made of one strand of silk, with a small French knot in the centre of each point; the same is applied to the small hearts and to two of the discs, but using strawberry-coloured silk.

A clever worker will discover very many uses to which this class of work can be devoted. It looks well for the borders of table-cloths, for mantel-drapes, and other hangings; and may even be introduced to a certain extent into church needlework.

instance, as likewise in the tea cosy, the Glanzgarn instead of being crocheted, is simply wound very smoothly and evenly round and round the contour of the mould, of course securing the ends firmly and evenly by underlaying them or darning them in at the commencing and ending of the winding, and paying special attention to the shaping of the angles and corners to preserve the exact shape of the mould. When the moulds are thus covered with the Glanzgarn, the open spaces in the centres thereof are embroidered in ornamental network with gold thread or the new iridescent metallic thread, and the moulds are mounted upon a foundation of felt or other material by means of sewn stitches on the reverse side. A few simple stitches of silk embroidery may be worked at pleasure upon the surface of the felt round the margin of the moulds, or round some of the moulds, but whether this is done or not, the moulds are each separately outlined with a couching of gold thread or metallic lustre thread; then the felt is cut away (within the radius of the sewn stitches) from under the open spaces of the moulds, and a piece of satin that is pasted all over the

FOUR-RINGS PATTERN BORDER.

THE engraving shows a most effective little pattern, about 5 inches in depth, worked with original Glanzgarn thread in crushed strawberry No. 723, and green No. 715, and suitable for bracket drapes, for trimming baskets, and other purposes. A skein or two of Japanese gold thread is required for embellishment, and a length of ¼-inch wide gold braid is run through the stitches of the heading. Use a medium sized steel crochet needle, and work as firmly and evenly as possible. Commence the **first ring** with crushed strawberry Glanzgarn with 34 chain, join round in a circle, work 48 double crochet in the circle, and join the last stitch evenly to the first; turn the work, and, taking up the one back thread as in Russian crochet, do again a round of 48 double-crochet stitches, and unite evenly at the end of the round; then, turning the crochet to bring the right side of the work uppermost, proceed in single crochet in each back thread of the previous round, and join, and fasten off. Keep the right side of the ring towards you, and take the gold thread, and work with it an edge of single-crochet stitches round the ring, and fasten off. Make 2 more terra-cotta rings in the same manner. For the **fourth ring**, take green Glanzgarn and make 34 chain, place the three crushed strawberry rings in the position of the three outside rings of the scollop illustrated in the engraving, with of course the right side of the crochet uppermost, pass the end of the green chain through and under the ring on the right hand side, then over and through and under the lowest ring, and also under and through the ring on the left-hand side, and join round in a circle, crochet this ring similarly to the other rings, and when finished take a needle and sewing cotton and sew the four rings one to the other in places where they cross each other, thus retaining them all firmly together. For the **Heading** —Work with green Glanzgarn a chain the length required; when sufficiently long, do 1 treble in the sixth chain from the needle, * 1 chain, miss one stitch, 1 rice stitch (with 7 twists of the thread round the needle) in the next, 1 chain, miss one stitch, 1 treble in the next, and repeat from *, and break off at the end of the row. Then work double crochet with crushed strawberry Glanzgarn the whole way round the green crochet. And finally, take the gold thread, and proceed along the top of the heading in single crochet, going a few stitches round the corner at either ends. Sew the rings tastefully to the heading in such a way that the green ring just touches the bottom row of crushed strawberry crochet, and the two crushed strawberry rings rest upon the row of foundation chain. The little tassels with which the border is ornamented are commenced with 3 chain joined in a circle, 5 long rice stitches (10 twists in each) are single crocheted round the circle, which then is suspended in its place by a loop of the Glanzgarn thread; a crushed strawberry tassel hangs from each of the two upper crushed strawberry rings, and green tassels are placed at the bottom of the scollop and on the heading between the scollops. A piece of gold tinsel braid is run through the treble stitches and rice stitches in the heading; and the border is ready for use.

BELBROUGHTON BORDER.

A HANDSOME border for draping furniture, trimming fancy articles, and other purposes. Procure a supply of moulds, No. 400 circular, and Nos. 134 and 124 elongated lozenge shape, in the proportion of two of the latter to one

Four Rings Pattern Border.

The Belbroughton Border.

of the former; a ball each of 721 apricot coloured, and 724 and 726 art green original Glanzgarn; and also a skein of gold thread. Use a medium-sized crochet needle. On a **Circular Mould**, with the darkest shade of green Glanzgarn, work 33 double crochet stitches, and join evenly and fasten off; turn the wrong side of the work towards you and go round the margin with apricot colour in single crochet, taking up the one back thread of the stitches of the previous round, fasten off on completion of this round; turn the work again, and edge the ring with gold tinsel, doing 3 single crochet on three consecutive stitches of last round (taking up the one back thread), 4 chain, 1 double crochet by the last single crochet, and 3 single crochet on three consecutive stitches of last round, and repeat the picot and the 3 single crochet till 11 picots in all are made, and join neatly round, and fasten off; the picot that is intended for the bottom of the ring must have 2 additional loops of 4 chain, making in reality 3 picots instead of 1 picot, and an apricot-coloured pendant is afterwards to be suspended from the middle picot of the three. Take three of the **Lozenge-shaped Moulds**, two small ones and one large one, and first of all secure them by binding them together, with a little apricot-coloured Glanzgarn, the largest lozenge in the centre, in the position shown in the engraving; proceed to cover each in its turn with apricot double crochet, doing 30 double crochet on the largest mould and 24 double crochet on each of the two top moulds, and bind the last stitch firmly over the junction of the two top moulds; turn the work, and go round the leaf with the lightest shade of green in single crochet taking up the one back thread of the apricot stitches; turn the work again, and with gold thread make a picot edge similar to that already worked round the ring, but do the first 6 and last 6 stitches on the large lozenge without a picot, so that you get 7 picots on each lozenge; the fifth picot from the junction of the two small lozenges is used to connect the leaves to the rings, and it is quite easy to do this as you work, though they may be sewn together afterwards if preferred. A dark green pendant is attached to the middle picot at the bottom of the leaf. For the **Heading—1st row** —With the lightest shade of green Glanzgarn, and holding the right side of the border towards you, work 1 double crochet in the thread of apricot behind the fourth picot (counting from the middle of the leaf) on the first lozenge, 11 chain, 1 single crochet in the fifth chain from the needle, * 6 chain, 1 double crochet in the thread of apricot behind the third picot, 3 chain, 1 single crochet in the third chain stitch from the Glanzgarn picot, 6 chain, 1 double crochet in the thread of apricot behind the first picot, 2 chain, 1 double crochet in the thread of apricot behind the first picot of the next lozenge,

3 chain, 1 single crochet in the third chain from the last single crochet, 6 chain, 1 double crochet in the thread of apricot behind the third picot, 3 chain, 1 single crochet in the third chain from the last single crochet, 7 chain, 1 single crochet in the fifth chain from the needle, 6 chain, 1 double crochet in the thread of apricot behind the fourth picot, 2 chain, 1 double crochet in the thread of apricot behind the first picot on the ring, 3 chain, 1 single crochet in the third chain stitch from the Glanzgarn picot, 7 chain, 1 single crochet in the fifth chain from the needle, 5 chain, 1 double crochet in the thread of apricot behind the second picot on the ring, 3 chain, 1 single crochet in the second stitch from the last Glanzgarn picot, 3 chain, 1 double crochet in the thread of apricot behind the third picot, 3 chain, 1 single crochet in the same place as last single crochet, 7 chain, 1 single crochet in the fifth chain from the needle, 6 chain, 1 double crochet in the thread of apricot behind the fourth picot on the ring, 2 chain,

1 double crochet in the thread of apricot behind the fourth picot of the next lozenge, 3 chain, 1 single crochet in the third chain stitch from the last Glanzgarn picot, 7 chain, 1 single crochet in the fifth chain from the needle, and repeat from * for the whole length of the border, and fasten off. **2nd row**—With dark shade of green, and holding the wrong side of the work towards you, do 1 single crochet in each uppermost stitch of last row, and keep all the little picots turned downwards. **3rd row**—With gold thread, and the right side of the work towards you, work a line of open crochet, 1 treble, 1 chain, miss one. **4th row**—With dark shade of green, and the right side of the work towards you, do 2 double crochet in each space of chain of last row ; but if the work seems any too full you may occasionally do only 1 double crochet in the spaces. **5th row**—With light green, and holding the wrong side of the work towards you, proceed in single crochet in the one back

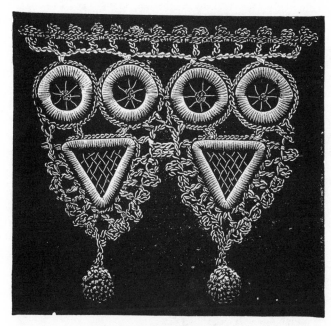

Wheel and Triangle Design.

thread of the stitches of last row. **6th row**—With apricot colour, and the right side of the work towards you, begin with a stitch on the needle, insert the hook to take up the one back thread of a stitch of last row and draw the Glanzgarn through, insert the hook in the next stitch and draw the Glanzgarn through, glanzgarn over the needle and draw through 3 stitches on the needle, * 5 chain, miss three stitches, insert the hook in the next stitch and draw the Glanzgarn through, insert the hook in the next stitch and draw the Glanzgarn through, glanzgarn over the needle and draw through 3 stitches on the needle, this makes a kind of compound double crochet stitch ; repeat from * to the end of the row. **7th row**—With gold thread, and the right side of the work towards you, do a compound double crochet stitch from loop to loop over the compound double crochet of last row, 2 chain, 1 double crochet in the centre stitch of the loop of five chain, 3 chain, another double crochet in the same place, 3 chain, and again another double crochet in the same place, 2 chain, and repeat the same to the end ; which completes the heading. The **Pendants** are made over small solid moulds—You begin with 3 chain and join round, do 2 double crochet in each stitch of chain, increase a stitch or two in the next round, put the mould in the crochet, the wrong side of the work outside, continue it to fit the mould contracting the top as needful, and when closed up make a loop of chain to attach the pendant in its position on the border.

WHEEL AND TRIANGLE DESIGN.

A NEAT and effective border for dress and mantle trimming, measuring 3½ inches in width and is executed with No. 78 dark green brilliant crochet twist, and Japanese gold thread, using moulds No. 101 small rings and 102 small triangles. Cover each **ring** with green twist, doing about 44 double crochet stitches, join the last stitch to the first, and fasten off neatly ; unite each successive ring to its predecessor in a straight level row by catching with a single crochet from one to the other ; there must be an even number of rings in the row. Work the **Triangular Moulds** in a similar manner, getting 18 double crochet on each side of the triangle, and as you proceed along the top and complete the third stitch from the right-hand corner, do 2 chain, and join with a single crochet to a stitch of the ring, 2 chain, 12 double crochet on the triangle, 2 chain, join with a single crochet to a stitch of the next ring, 2 chain, and continue on the triangle till the mould is full. For the **Scolloped Edge**—Hold the right side of the crochet towards you, and keeping for the present to the dark green crochet twist, work 1 treble in the corner stitch of the first triangle, * 5 chain for a picot, 1 treble on the treble stitch just worked, miss two double crochet, 1 treble on the next, and

repeat from * till 7 picots are done, and you find yourself at the bottom corner of the triangle ready to make 2 additional picots, 5 chain, 1 single crochet on the last treble stitch, 5 chain, 1 treble on the single crochet, and 1 treble in the same stitch of double crochet at the bottom of the triangle, continue thence as from * to * till 7 treble are worked up the opposite side, then 1 chain, 1 treble on the ring, 1 chain, miss two stitches of the ring, 1 treble on the next stitch of the same ring, 1 treble on the next ring, 1 chain, miss two stitches of the ring, 1 treble on the next, 1 chain, 1 treble on the corner stitch of the next triangle, 2 chain, join by a single crochet to the top picot of the first triangle, 2 chain, 1 treble on the treble stitch last worked, and continue hence as on the first triangle, and go on in scollops all along the border. For the **Heading—1st row**—With gold thread, make 5 chain, 1 double crochet on the centre stitch at the top of a ring, * 9 chain, 1 double crochet on the next ring, and proceed from * to the end of the row. **2nd row**—With brilliant green twist—Work open crochet of 1 treble, 2 chain, miss two stitches. **3rd row**—Do 2 double crochet in the space of two chain of last row, 7 chain, 1 single crochet in the fifth chain from the needle, and repeat the same ; this finishes the heading. The interior of the triangles is filled with open diamond darning, and the rings with spider stitches, worked after the fashion of drawn thread embroidery. The pendants consist of small solid moulds closely covered with double crochet, and secured to the border by a little loop of chain, as represented in the engraving.

HEART DESIGN BORDER.

THIS is a most exquisite little border worked in the original with No. 247 apricot and No. 301 eau de nil Brilliant Crochet Twist, which is a particularly pleasing combination of colour, though of course other colours may be substituted if these are not appropriate to the purpose for which the border is required. As a dress trimming it is eminently suitable. The moulds are small hearts numbered 103, and small beads are used to give substance to the tassels. Upon one of the **Small Hearts**, with eau de nil, work 33 double crochet smoothly and evenly, and join and fasten off. Take apricot, and beginning in the depression at the top of the heart, do 2 double crochet, now inserting the hook to take up the front and top threads of the eau de nil stitches, 5 chain, 1 double crochet on the double crochet last done, 3 double crochet on three consecutive stitches, * 5 chain, 1 double crochet on the double crochet last done, 2 double crochet on the following consecutive stitches, and repeat from * till you have made 14 picots round the heart (the eighth picot should come just on the point of the heart), then add 1 more double crochet to the 2 already worked, 5 chain, 1 double crochet on the double crochet last done, and 1 double crochet on the next following stitch will complete the circumference of the

Heart Design Border.

heart, join evenly and fasten off. The next heart is worked in precisely the same manner, but you will unite the first picot and the last picot to the first and last picots of the preceding heart. The third heart, which forms the point of the scollop, is also similarly worked, and is united to each of the above hearts by picots as shown in the engraving. With the fourth heart you commence another scollop, therefore unite the eighth picot, that is the "point" picot, to the picot at the "point" of the first heart, and proceed with this scollop in the same manner as you have already worked the first scollop ; and continue for the entire length of the border. For the **Heading**—Commence on the right-hand side of the line of hearts, and with eau de nil, work 1 double long treble in the picot next above the point, 2 chain, 1 long treble in the next picot, 2 chain, 1 treble in the next picot, 2 chain, 1 double crochet in the next, 2 chain, 1 double crochet in the next,

2 chain, 1 treble in the next, all these 6 stitches being on one heart, then 2 chain, 1 treble in the corresponding picot of the next heart, 2 chain, 1 double crochet in the next picot, 2 chain, 1 double crochet in the next, 2 chain, 1 treble in the next, 2 chain, 1 long treble in the next, 2 chain, 1 double long treble in the next, this same double long treble extends to the first picot of the next heart and they both are drawn together at the top, as see engraving ; continue this heading along the length of the row. **2nd row of Heading**—Work upon the stitches of the previous row, still using eau de nil twist—1 treble on the first stitch, * 4 chain, 1 double crochet on the treble stitch just done, miss two stitches of last row, 1 treble on the next and repeat from * to the end. For the **Tassels**—Use eau de nil, and commencing with 3 chain, join round, do 6 double crochet in the circle, and proceed round and round in double crochet, increasing as necessary to the size of your bead, put the bead inside, with the crochet the *wrong* side out, decrease the number of stitches, and draw the remaining ones up closely over the bead, and make a few chain stitches by which to attach the tassel to the border in the position occupied in the engraving.

a marginal edge of single crochet into the one back thread of the stitches of the second round, and fasten off. Commence the **second ring** with brown Glanzgarn, with 34 chain, pass the end of the chain *upwards* through the first ring, unite in a circle, and proceed in exactly the same manner as the first ring. You have to make this ring pass *above* the join of the first ring, and subsequently the third ring will pass *above* the join of this ring ; a clever worker can manage to connect the rings together by taking a stitch *through* when passing, but if this is difficult, they may be sewn in position after they all are worked. The next three rings are crocheted with salmon colour, and they each are linked to the preceding in the same way that the second ring is linked to the first. The sixth ring reverts to brown. After this recommence with a first ring for the opposite side of the scollop, and do six more rings exactly as the first six rings are done. For the **thirteenth ring,** which forms the point at the bottom of the scollop and is rather larger than the other rings, make 40 chain with brown Glanzgarn, pass the end of the chain upwards through the last brown ring on the right-hand side of the scollop and downwards through the last brown ring on the left-hand

Linked Rings Pattern

LINKED RINGS PATTERN.

OUR engraving represents a scollop crocheted with original Glanzgarn in a bold and handsome pattern of linked rings and roses. The rings run down the sides of the scollop and meet in a point, and the roses, three in number, occupy the centre, and are surmounted with a kind of spreading plume; the actual depth of the pattern is 11½ inches ; it is eminently suitable for a mantel drape. Procure several balls of Glanzgarn in shades numbered 717 salmon, and 745 russet brown—these are for the rings ; 701 cream for the roses ; and 739 eau de nil for the plume ; also some skeins of Japanese gold thread for margining, and a length of ½ inch wide gold braid to pass through the open stitches in the heading. No moulds are required. For the **first ring**—Make a chain of 34 stitches with the russet brown Glanzgarn, and join round in a circle ; work 48 double crochet in the circle, and join quite evenly the last of these stitches to the first. Turn the work, and inserting the hook always to take up the one back thread of the stitches of the previous row, work double crochet round again, stitch over stitch, and join on the completion of the round, and fasten off. Take the gold thread, and holding the ring as you had it to work the first round (which is the right side of the crochet), do

side, and unite in a circle, in which work 54 double crochet, and complete the ring in the usual manner. For the **First Rose**—Use cream Glanzgarn, make 6 chain, and join round ; * do 1 double crochet in the circle, then 2 treble, 2 long treble, and 2 more treble all in the top thread of one stitch of chain, 1 double crochet in the circle, 2 treble, 2 long treble, and 2 more treble all in another stitch of chain, and repeat from *, and join round ; there will be four petals in the round. **2nd round**—Keep the petals to the front, and do 1 single crochet at the back of the double crochet of last round, 4 chain, and repeat, making four loops of chain, and join round. **3rd round**—Work 2 treble, 5 long treble, and 2 more treble all in the chain loop of last round, and 1 double crochet on the single crochet stitch, and repeat the same, making another four petals, and join evenly, and fasten off. **4th round**—With gold thread—Do 1 double crochet in the front thread of the single crochet stitch, then 1 double crochet between each stitch of last round, and repeat ; join evenly at the end of the round, and fasten off. Make two more roses in the same manner. For the **Plume**—With eau de nil Glanzgarn work 37 chain, do 1 double crochet in the third chain from the needle, and 1 double crochet in each of 7 consecutive stitches, 1 rice stitch of 8 coils in the next stitch, 1 chain, miss one stitch of the foundation, and continue 1 rice stitch and

1 chain alternately, always missing a stitch of the foundation under the chain stitch, and increasing the height of the rice stitch by an additional coil or two in every stitch till you come to the tenth rice stitch, which should consist of 20 coils; after this go on with the high rice stitches to 22 and 24 coils, still with chain between, but do not miss any stitch of the foundation; work 3 stitches of 24 coils, and in the next 4 stitches diminish by 2 coils in each stitch, and fasten off. The opposite side of the plume is worked reversely, consequently you do the high rice stitches first, and end with the short rice stitches, which are extended to within the last 3 chain stitches of the foundation, those being for 3 double crochet, and fasten off. This end of the plume is to be sewn over the first 3 or 4 double crochet stitches of the other side of the plume. Take gold thread and margin along the foundation chain with double crochet. Bend the 4 top stitches on either side against the 4 next stitches, and sew them in this position, to form the "curl" at the top of the plume. For the **Heading**—Begin with a chain the length the drape is required to be. For this use salmon-coloured Glanzgarn; work 1 treble in the sixth chain from the needle, * 1 chain, miss one stitch of the foundation, 1 rice stitch of 10 coils in the next, 1 chain, miss one stitch, 1 treble in the next, repeat from * till you reach the end of the foundation chain; then turn the work, and proceed the whole way round the heading in double crochet, and fasten off. Take russet-brown Glanzgarn, and holding the work with the right side of the rice stitches towards you, margin the heading with single crochet worked into the one back thread of the stitches of last round; this finishes the heading.

brown Glanzgarn and work 56 double crochet over a mould, and unite the last stitch evenly to the first; turn the work, and do another round of 56 double crochet, always inserting the hook in the one top front thread of the stitches of the previous round, and join at the end of the round, and fasten off; the double-crochet stitches of this last round will curl slightly over the front of the stitches of the first round. Now to **edge** the circular mould and to **attach** the heart within it,—Use gold twist from two balls together, hold the circular mould in the same position as you had it when doing the first round of double crochet, and so working with a double thread of gold twist, do a round of double-crochet stitches with the hook at the back of the work to take up the one back thread of the stitches of the first round, and at the completion of every fourth stitch of double crochet insert the hook from the back to the front through the crochet, bringing it out above the little thread on the front of the stitches of the first round, place the heart in position in the centre of the ring and insert the hook in the top thread of one of the stitches of the heart, draw the gold twist right through in a long loop stitch that will hold the two pieces of work together in the manner shown in the engraving. There will be 14 of these long loop stitches extending from the ring to the heart, i.e., one in the centre of the top of the heart, one in the point at the bottom, and six on each side; the gold thread does not show very conspicuously round the edge of the ring, as it lies for the most part *behind* the second round of olive-brown double crochet, but still you can see that it is there; thread a needleful of black sewing cotton,

Viola Pattern Border.

Arrange the several parts of the pattern and sew them one to the other with a few stitches of cotton on the wrong side of the work, making the design appear as shown in the engraving. The tassels are formed by bunching up a circle of six long loose rice stitches, tying the same firmly together, and then placing them on the scollop as you see them in the engraving.

VIOLA PATTERN BORDER.

THIS is a bold and striking pattern, very easy of execution, and very suitable for any purpose for which a deep border is required, as it measures almost 9 inches. The example is crocheted with original Glanzgarn No. 741, a new olive brown, 701 cream, 704 light terra-cotta, and 739 eau de nil; and the moulds are of two forms, No. 233 large circular, and 231 heart shaped; three moulds of each form are employed in each scollop of the border, and, as represented in the engraving, the heart-shaped mould is always fitted in the middle of the circular mould. The **Heart-shaped Moulds** are each worked in a different colour; thus in the same scollop one heart is eau de nil, another is cream colour, and another is light terra-cotta; the method of working is similar for each, i.e., to cover the mould with double crochet, about 48 stitches, and finish off with a tuft of 3 loose rice stitches to hang pendulous from the top of the heart. For the **Large Circular Moulds**—Take the olive-

and sew the rings in position one to the other. For the **Heading**—Commence with a length of crochet chain worked with olive-brown Glanzgarn; do 1 treble in the seventh chain from the needle, * 1 chain, miss one stitch of the foundation, 1 rice stitch (Glanzgarn 11 times round the needle) in the next, 1 chain, miss 1 stitch, 1 treble in the next, and repeat from * to the end, and fasten off. Turn the row of rice stitches the wrong side towards you, and complete the heading by working double crochet along both sides of the same, going also round the ends. The heading is joined to the rings by a few stitches sewn with a needle and cotton; also two short lengths of chain are made and sewn from the heading to the rings, as see engraving; a piece of ½-inch wide gold braid is run in the open row of the heading; the rice stitches come on the front of the braid and the treble stitches lie at the back. For the **Tassels**—Make a tuft of 5 loose rice stitches with Glanzgarn of colour to correspond with the Glanzgarn near which the tassel is to be placed, thus for a tassel to be sewn on a ring where the heart is worked with cream, use cream for the tufts, and where the heart is terra-cotta let the tufts be terra-cotta, and so on; draw the tufts compactly together, and break off with an end, and there should have been an end left likewise at the beginning of the tuft: the balls upon every tassel are worked with olive brown. Begin with 4 chain, and join round; do 4 chain, and then work 10 or 11 treble in the circle of commencing chain, join; pick up the top threads of the stitches as if about to work double crochet, keep all the stitches on the needle, pass the Glanzgarn over the needle and draw through all, and break off: pass the two ends from the tuft up through the centre of the ball, tie all the ends in a knot together as near the ball as possible, and cutting off the olive-green end, carry the other ends on, and after passing them through a crocheted stitch in the place where the tassel is to hang, sew them neatly and securely at the back of the work. The position of the tassels is clearly shown in the engraving. The tassels that depend from the heading have each a double tuft of rice stitches.

BRIGADIER BORDER.

THE handsome border represented in our engraving is worked with Original Glanzgarn twist in two shades of brown combined with cream colour and a little gold thread. It measures 8 inches in depth. The shades are known by their respective numbers in Carl Mez and Söhne's shade pattern book, 701 cream, 702 light art brown, 703 snuff brown; procure also a good supply of moulds, 105 small rings, 131 very tiny rings, 127 tiny drops, 134 oval shaped, and 103 small heart shaped; together with a skein or two of gold thread. Work a small ring with light brown, doing 32 double crochet on the ring, and join evenly, and fasten off: work a tiny ring with snuff brown, with 14 double crochet stitches, join, and fasten off; take a needleful of gold thread and embroider a star on the surface of the tiny ring, and carry a few stitches at

rings; embroider a trellis of herringbone stitch with light brown Glanzgarn up the open space in the centre of the mould. A similar mould is employed on the opposite side of the design. Also two more ovals are placed lower down on each side of the design reaching from the compound mould at the bottom of the heart-shaped medallion to the compound moulds on each side thereof. Hold the work in such a position as to proceed along the lower edge of the bottom compound ring, begin close to the place where this is joined to an oval, and work double crochet with cream colour along to the join on the opposite side; there should be 22 cream-coloured stitches, and fasten off. Take gold thread, which join to the gold margin of the oval, do 1 treble in the top thread of the first cream-coloured double crochet, 2 chain, 1 treble on the next double crochet, and continue till 22 treble are worked, join to the gold margin of the other oval, and fasten off, and over the open row work 2 double crochet (with here and there 3 double crochet) in each space. Now work four tiny drops with snuff colour, doing about 13 double-crochet stitches, and three tiny drops with light brown in the same manner, beginning at the top of each and working round, and as you join round, join also to the semicircle of gold at the bottom of the scollop, and get the seven drops, in alternate colours, nicely arranged round the semicircle in the manner you see in the engraving. Edge the tiny drops with a gold margin, thus—join the gold thread to the gold margin of the oval, do 1 double crochet in third double crochet of the first drop, join to the oval, * 1 double crochet in each of

Brigadier Border.

the back of the work to attach this ring within the diameter of the larger ring; then leave this for the present; and work similarly two more compound rings. Next, take another of the tiny rings and cover it with 24 double crochet worked with gold thread, which join round, and fasten off; this is the tiny ring you will observe in the centre of the pattern; another tiny gold ring is wanted to place above under the heading. Now upon a heart-shaped mould work 26 double crochet with cream Glanzgarn, going from the point of the heart round to the point again, join, at the same time joining also to one of the tiny gold rings, and fasten off; keep the heart-shaped mould the right side up and work round the margin with snuff colour in single crochet, and fasten off. Three more similar hearts are required to complete the medallion in the centre of the scollop: each of these is to be joined to the preceding after working the ninth cream double crochet, and after the twenty-sixth double crochet you will join to one of the compound rings, and fasten off: place the tiny gold ring in the centre of the four hearts and keep it in position by long snuff-coloured stitches wound over the top of the heart and reaching thence to a thread of the gold stitches, as shown in the engraving. Take an oval-shaped mould, and snuff-coloured Glanzgarn, and work 34 double crochet and fasten off; use gold thread to edge the margin, which consists of single crochet in the one top thread of each of the snuff-coloured stitches; in this margin you join on one side to the tiny gold ring under the heading and also join at the point to one of the compound

the 3 next stitches of the drop, 4 chain, 1 double crochet in the centre stitch of the drop, 5 chain, another double crochet in the same place, 4 chain, 1 double crochet in each of the 3 next stitches, thence repeat from * round the half of each little drop, and end as you began with joining to the gold margin of the oval. This completes the first scollop; add as many more scollops as you require for the length of the border. Then you must make rings to occupy the several spaces at the top of the border between the scollops, proceeding similarly to the tiny embroidered rings you have already worked, but do the double crochet with light brown instead of snuff colour, and finish with an edge of single crochet worked with snuff colour, in the course of which you will join to the oval moulds on either side For the **Heading—1st row**—With light brown Glanzgarn, and the right side of the border towards you—Make 7 chain, 1 double crochet in the third gold stitch to the right of the first oval, 7 chain, 1 double crochet on the tiny gold ring, 7 chain, 1 double crochet in the third gold stitch to the left of the second oval, 7 chain, 1 double crochet on the embroidered ring, and repeat the same, and at the end do 7 chain as at the beginning, and fasten off. **2nd row**—Recommence on the right side, and work plain double crochet all along the row. **3rd row**—With snuff colour—1 treble on the first stitch of the preceding row, * 1 chain, miss one stitch, 1 treble on the next, and repeat from * to the end. **4th row**—With light brown—Work plain double crochet all along.

WELDON'S
PRACTICAL CROCHET.

(SEVENTEENTH SERIES.)

Showing Borders and Articles Trimmed with the New Ivory Crochet.

TWENTY-SIX ILLUSTRATIONS.

Telegraphic Address—
"Consuelo," London.]

The Yearly Subscription to this Magazine, post free to any Part of the World, is 2s. 6d.
Subscriptions are payable in advance, and may commence from any date and for any period.

[Telephone 2745.

The Back Numbers are always in print. Nos. 1 to 83 now ready, Price 2d. each, or post free for 14s. 10d. Over 5,000 Engravings.

IVORY CROCHET BORDERS.

THE introduction of IVORY CROCHET COTTON for the purpose of crocheting BORDERS for small fancy table-cloths, toilet covers, side-board slips, berceaunette quilts, nightdress sachets, and the many useful articles that now are made with ivory congress canvas, marks a new departure in the always favourite work of crochet, and has led to the invention of a number of handsome patterns for borders and laces, mostly quite novel in style, and calculated to rouse the enthusiasm of all lovers of crochet work. The ivory tint on both cotton and canvas is something that must be seen to be realised, it is so delicate and charming; the cream colour that once was so much admired is nothing to it. This ivory cotton is done up in balls, Ardern is the chief maker, and No. 16 to No. 20 are the most useful sizes. A moderately fine steel crochet needle should be used that the work may be tolerably firm; very few patterns are at all loosely executed, as if the work is too loose it looks slovenly. The new "Brilliant" crochet twist, manufactured by Carl Mez and Söhne, and sold at all fancy repositories, in white shades, is splendid for borders to trim things made with white linen material; it is very strong, and shines with the brilliancy of the linen itself. And for flax thread in écru and brown we have Finlayson's make of Scotch linen thread in balls, of which No. 35 is a useful size; Harris's; and Kerr's egg-shaped balls; affording ample variety, together with Strutts' well-known cottons, and Evans' Maltese thread, to gratify the most fastidious taste.

The following pages contain a selection of original designs for borders and laces, clearly engraved, and accompanied by fully detailed instructions for working.

IMITATION TORCHON LACE.

FOR TRIMMING HOUSEHOLD LINEN, ANTIMACASSARS, &c.

THIS charming border is a perfect imitation of the Torchon lace that is so fashionably used at the present time for trimming every variety of household linen and fancy linen antimacassars, and even window blinds. It is crocheted

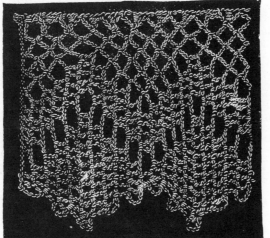

Imitation Torchon Lace for Trimming Purposes.

shortways. Worked with Finlayson's écru Scotch linen crochet thread No. 35 and a fine steel crochet needle it will measure 2 inches wide; but any other make, say Carl Mez and Söhne's No. 20 white brilliant crochet twist, or Evans' coloured Maltese thread, or Ardern's cream crochet cotton, may be employed at pleasure according to the purpose for which the lace is required. Begin with 33 chain and work firmly. **1st row**—Do 1 treble in the fifth chain from the needle, 3 chain, miss three stitches, 1 treble in the next, 1 chain, miss one, 1 treble in the next, 1 chain, miss one, 1 treble in the next, 3 chain, miss three, do 4 consecutive treble, 3 chain, miss three, 1 treble in the next, 1 chain, miss one, 1 treble in the next, 1 chain, miss one, 1 treble in the next, 3 chain, miss three, 2 consecutive treble. **2nd row**—Turn with 4 chain, 1 double crochet under the first loop, 4 chain, 1 treble in the second one chain space, 1 chain, 1 treble in the loop of three chain, 1 chain, another treble in the same place, 3 chain, 1 treble between the first and second treble stitches of last row, 1 chain, 1 treble between the second and third, 1 chain, 1 treble between the

third and fourth treble stitches, 3 chain, 1 treble in the loop of three chain, 1 chain, another treble in the same place, 1 chain, 1 treble in the first one chain space, 3 chain, 1 treble in the loop of three chain, 1 chain, another treble in the same place, 1 chain, 1 treble in the end loop, 1 chain, another treble in the same place. **3rd row**—Turn with 4 chain, 1 treble in the first space of previous row, 1 chain, another treble in the same place, 1 chain and 1 treble alternately in the 3 following spaces, 1 chain, another treble in the three chain space, 3 chain, 1 treble in the second one chain space, 1 chain, 1 treble in the loop of three chain, 1 chain, another treble in the same place, 3 chain, 1 treble between the first and second treble stitches, 1 chain, 1 treble between the second and third treble stitches, 3 chain, 1 treble in the loop of three chain, 1 chain, another treble in the same place, 1 chain, 1 treble in the first one chain space, 4 chain, 1 double crochet in the loop of four chain, 4 chain, 2 treble in the small loop at the top. **4th row**—Turn with 4 chain, 1 double crochet in the first loop of four chain of last row, 3 chain, 1 double crochet in the next loop of four chain, 4 chain, 1 treble in the second one chain space, 1 chain, 1 treble in the loop of three chain, 1 chain, another treble in the same place, 3 chain, 1 treble in the next loop of three chain, 1 chain, another treble in the same place, 1 chain, 1 treble in the first one chain space, 3 chain, 1 treble in the loop of three chain, 1 chain, another treble in the same place, 1 chain and 1 treble alternately in the 5 following spaces, and 1 chain and 1 treble again in the same place as the last treble; and leave the end space unworked to shape the scollop. **5th row**—Turn with 4 chain, 1 treble in the first space of preceding row, 1 chain, another treble in the same place, 1 chain and 1 treble alternately in the following 7 spaces, 1 chain, another treble in the three chain space, 3 chain, 1 treble in the second one chain space, 1 chain, 1 treble in the central loop of three chain, 1 chain, another treble in the same place, 1 chain, 1 treble in the first one chain space, 4 chain, 1 double crochet in the loop of four chain, 3 chain, 1 double crochet in the next loop, 4 chain, 2 treble in the small loop at the top. **6th row**—Turn with 4 chain, 1 double crochet in the first loop of four chain of last row, 3 chain, 1 double crochet in the next loop, 4 chain, 1 treble in the loop of three chain, 1 chain, another treble in the same place, 1 chain, 1 treble in the first one chain space, 3 chain, 1 treble in the third one chain space, 1 chain, 1 treble in the loop of three chain, 1 chain, another treble in the same place, 3 chain, miss one little space, 1 treble in the next, and 1 chain and 1 treble alternately in the 7 following spaces. **7th row**—Turn with 4 chain, 1 treble in the first space of previous row, 1 chain and 1 treble alternately in the five following spaces, 3 chain, 1 treble in the loop of three chain, 1 chain, another treble in the same place, 1 chain, 1 treble in the first one chain space, 3 chain, 1 treble in the central loop of three chain, 1 chain, another treble in the same place, 3 chain, 1 treble in the second one chain, 1 chain, 1 treble in the loop of three chain, 1 chain, another treble in the same place, 4 chain, 1 double crochet in the loop of three chain, 4 chain, 2 treble in the small loop at the top. **8th row**—Turn with 4 chain, 1 double crochet in the first loop, 4 chain, 1 treble in the second loop, 1 chain, another treble in the same place, 1 chain, 1 treble in the first one chain space, 3 chain, 1 treble in the loop of three chain, 1 chain, 1 treble in the one chain space,

1 chain in the loop of 3 chain, 3 chain, 1 treble in the second one chain space, 1 chain, 1 treble in the next loop, 1 chain, another treble in the same place, 3 chain, 1 treble in the second one chain space, 1 chain and 1 treble alternately in the 3 following spaces. **9th row**—Turn with 4 chain, 1 treble in the first space by the needle, 3 chain, 1 treble in the loop of three chain, 1 chain, another treble in the same place, 1 chain, 1 treble in the first one chain loop, 3 chain, 1 treble in the loop of three chain, 1 chain, 1 treble in the first one chain loop, 1 chain, 1 treble in the next one chain loop, 1 chain, 1 treble in the loop of three chain, 3 chain, 1 treble in the second one chain space, 1 chain, 1 treble in the space of three chain, one chain, 1 treble in the same place, 3 chain, 2 treble in the small loop at the top. Repeat from the second row for the length required.

UNION PATTERN BORDER.

THIS border is composed of medallions and a heading. Procure a steel crochet needle and suitable cotton, and commence a **Medallion** with 10

Union Pattern Border.

chain, and join in a circle. **1st round**—Do 4 chain to stand for a long treble stitch, work 2 long treble (cotton twice round the needle) in the circle, * 3 chain, 3 long treble in the circle, repeat from * till 8 groups of long treble are done, then 3 chain, and join to the top stitch of the four chain that stand for a treble stitch. **2nd round**—1 double crochet on the centre stitch of the group of three long treble stitches of the preceding round, 4 chain, 1 treble in the loop of three chain, 3 chain, another treble in the same place, 4 chain, and repeat the same to the end of the round, and join evenly, and fasten off. Work successive medallions in the same manner, and join each to the foregoing by a single crochet at one of the little points. For the **Heading**—Make a stitch on the needle, cotton twice round the needle, insert the hook in the centre stitch of one of the points (that to the right of the centre point at the top of the medallion), and draw the cotton through, cotton over the needle and draw through 2 stitches on the needle, cotton over the needle and draw through 2 more stitches on the needle, cotton twice round the needle and repeat the process, again cotton twice round the needle and again repeat the process, now 4 stitches are on the needle, cotton over the needle and draw through all, * 8 chain, 1 double crochet in the centre chain stitch of the centre point of the medallion, 8 chain, a compound stitch (as before) in the next point of the medallion, and another compound stitch in the corresponding point of the next medallion, and repeat from * to the end of the row, and fasten off. **2nd row**—Open crochet, 1 treble, 1 chain, miss one, and repeat. **3rd row**—Do 1 long treble on the second treble stitch of last row, 4 chain, 1 double crochet in the same place, * 9 chain, miss four stitches, 1 double crochet on the next, 4 chain, 1 long treble in the same place, miss four stitches, 1 long treble on the next, 4 chain, 1 double crochet in the same place, and repeat from *. **4th row**—Work a compound long treble stitch on the first long treble stitch of the row, * 1 long treble in the centre stitch of the loop of nine chain, 3 chain, another long treble in the same place, a compound stitch on the next long treble stitch of last row, 3 chain, another compound stitch on the adjoining long treble stitch of last row, and repeat from * to the end. **5th row**—Same as the second row. Work a **Scolloped Edge** along the bottom of the border —thus,—1 double crochet on a double crochet of the medallion, 1 chain, 7 treble in a point of the medallion (this point is the one to the right of the centre point at the bottom of the medallion), 1 chain, 1 double crochet on double crochet, 1 chain, 7 treble in the centre point of the medallion, 1 chain, 1 double crochet on double crochet, 1 chain, 7 treble in the next point of the medallion, 1 chain, 1 double crochet on double crochet, 3 chain, and proceed on the successive medallions in the same way.

SIDEBOARD CLOTH,

WITH HANDSOME CROCHET BORDER.

A SIDEBOARD cloth may be of canvas, linen, or damask material, and the cloth represented in our engraving is made of plain ivory congress canvas, which can be bought by the yard in all widths, or may be purchased ready hemmed for bordering; it is not customary, however, to use the canvas in this simple condition, and more often than not it is elaborately embroidered, either in the new work known as "Ivory work," for instructions and designs of which see No. 63 and No. 75 of "Weldon's Practical Needlework Series," or in "Drawn Thread Embroidery," as treated in No. 52 and No. 53 of the same series, or it may be worked in cross-stitch with coloured cotton. Many of the best needlework depôts keep sideboard cloths of all descriptions with a design ready traced and commenced for working. For the **Crochet Border** as shown in the engraving procure several balls of Ardern's No. 18 ivory crochet cotton and a rather fine steel crochet needle. Work the **1st round** immediately upon the edge of the cloth—1 treble, 1 chain, and repeat; leave just as much space below the chain stitch as will keep the work flat, ease the corners with a loop of 3 chain instead of only one chain, and join evenly the first stitch to the last on the completion of the round, and fasten off. **2nd round**—Do 1 treble on a stitch of previous round, taking up one top thread, miss three stitches, 1 treble on the next, 2 chain, work 3 treble under the treble stitch last worked (these will fall slantways as in crazy crochet), * miss three stitches, 1 treble in the next, 2 chain, 3 treble under the last treble stitch, and repeat from *; work an extra block of stitches at each corner, and join and fasten off at the end of the round. **3rd round**—1 treble at the top of the point under the loop of two chain of last round, 2 chain, 3 treble under the treble last worked, and repeat the same: here again do an extra block at each corner, and join and fasten off at the end of the round. **4th round**—1 double crochet at the top of a point under the loop of two chain of preceding round, 3 chain, and repeat the same; at the corner do 4 chain, 1 treble in the corner stitch, 5 chain, another treble in the corner stitch, 4 chain; and continue as before. **5th round**—Plain double crochet, and 3 double crochet on the corner stitch. **6th round**—Turn, and work with the wrong side of the crochet towards you, 1 double crochet on every stitch, taking up the one back thread of the stitches of last round, and 3 double crochet on the centre stitch at the corner. **7th round**—Turn, and with the right side of the work towards you proceed as last round. **8th round**—Turn the wrong side of the crochet towards you, work 6 double crochet as in the sixth round, then a tuft of 3 treble in the ridged thread of the second previous round, remove the needle from the third treble stitch, insert it in the top of the first treble stitch, pick up the dropped stitch, and draw it through to close the tuft, miss one

Sideboard Cloth, with Handsome Crochet Border.

double crochet of last round, and repeat, so you get a tuft at intervals of every six double crochet; turn the corner with 3 double crochet together on the corner stitch. **9th round**—With the work the right side towards you, proceed as the seventh round. **10th round**—The Scollop—Hold the right side of the crochet towards you and take up the front and top threads of the stitches; 1 treble on the seventh stitch from the corner stitch, 2 chain, miss two stitches, 1 treble on the next, and repeat the same till 4 treble stitches are done, making 3 spaces, * then 7 chain, miss two, 1 treble on the next, 2 chain, miss two, 1 treble on the next, turn the work and do 7 treble under the loop of seven chain, 2 chain, 7 more treble under the loop, 1 double crochet on the treble stitch to the left, 2 double crochet under the space of two chain, and 1 double crochet on the next treble stitch to the left; 2 chain, turn the work, miss one treble stitch of the scollop, 1 treble on the next, 2 chain, miss one, 1 treble on the next, 2 chain, miss one, 1 treble on the next, 2 chain, miss one, 1 treble in the loop of two chain at the point, 3 chain, another treble in the same place, then 2 chain, miss one, 1 treble, and do this four times, which brings you on the last stitch of the scollop, miss two stitches of the preceding row and do 1 treble on the next, 2 chain, miss two, 1 treble on the next, 2 chain, miss two, 1 treble on the next, and again 2 chain, miss two, 1 treble on the next, when 6 treble stitches (5 spaces) will be done from the middle of the last scollop, and you do 7 chain to begin another scollop, as from preceding *, and finish the round of cloth. **11th round**—For **Edge**—Hold the right side of the work towards you, do 1 double crochet in the space of two chain between the scollops of last round, and loops of 3 chain and 1 double crochet in every space round the scollop, with an additional loop in the point at the top of the scollop.

LITTLE ROSE BORDER.

AN extremely pretty border, consisting of roses and sprays of leaves, may be worked with Evans' maltese thread, using pink or red for the roses and green for the leaves; or with Brilliant crochet twist No. 4 pink and No. 77 green; and a fine steel crochet needle. For a **Rose**—With pink—Begin in the centre of a flower with 6 chain, and join in a circle. **1st round**—Do 5 chain, 1 treble in the first stitch of the foundation chain, * 2 chain, 1 treble

Little Rose Border.

in the next, repeat from * three times more, 2 chain, and unite to the centre stitch of the five chain with which the round commenced. **2nd round**—Work 1 double crochet, 1 treble, 3 long treble, 1 treble, 1 double crochet, *all* under each of the six spaces of two chain, and join evenly at end of this and every round. **3rd round**—Do 1 double crochet on a treble stitch of the first round, 5 chain, and repeat, making 6 loops of five chain behind the petals of the second round. **4th round**—Work 1 double crochet, 2 treble, 4 long treble, 2 treble, 1 double crochet, under each of the loops of five chain. **5th round**—Do 1 double crochet on a double crochet of the third round, 6 chain, and repeat. **6th round** —Work 1 double crochet, 2 treble, 6 long treble, 2 treble, 1 double crochet, under each of the loops of six chain. **7th round**—Do 1 double crochet on a double crochet of the fifth round, 8 chain, and repeat. **8th round**—Work 1 double crochet, 2 treble, 7 long treble, 2 treble, 1 double crochet, under each of the loops of eight chain, and fasten off; this finishes the rose. Work more roses in the same manner, joining each to the preceding by a single crochet from the centre long treble stitch of an outside petal to the corresponding stitch of a petal on the preceding rose, till the row is the length the border is required to be. Next, work the **Heading** of the border: **1st row**—With green thread—Do 5 chain, * 1 treble on the third long treble stitch of one top petal of a rose, 1 chain, 1 treble on the fifth long treble stitch of the same petal, 5 chain, 1 treble on the third long treble stitch of the next petal, 1 chain, 1 treble on the fifth long treble stitch of the same petal, 11 chain, and repeat from * to the end of the row. **2nd row**—Also with green, and recommencing on the right-hand side—Work in open crochet, 1 treble, 1 chain, miss one. For the **Leaves**— With green—Work 9 chain; 1 double crochet in the second chain from the needle, 6 consecutive double crochet, 3 double crochet in the top chain stitch, 7 double crochet down the other side of the chain; * turn the work, 2 chain, miss one double crochet, work 7 consecutive double crochet, 3 double crochet in the centre stitch of three double crochet at the top, 7 more consecutive double crochet, all this taking up the one back thread of the stitches that the work may sit in ridges, and working firmly, miss the end stitch; repeat from * six times; and one leaf will be fashioned; fasten off. Make two more similar leaves, and sew the three in a group, placing the sides of two leaves together, and the third leaf below between the two top leaves. Then for the mid-rib, bring the cotton to the front by the tip of the leaf at the bottom of the spray, do 12 chain, 1 single crochet in the top of the same leaf, 8 or 10 chain, and 1 single crochet at the top of the two upper leaves, where they are sewn together, 12 chain, 1 single crochet where two roses are joined together, 10 chain, and 1 single crochet in the foundation chain of the heading above, and fasten off, securing the end neatly. Rib the other leaves similarly, bring up the cotton by the tip of the leaf to the right of the spray, 12 chain, 1 single crochet in the place where the two leaves are joined and where the central mid-rib is already affixed, 12 chain, 1 single crochet by

the tip of the leaf to the left of the spray, and fasten off, and secure the ends. The other sprays of leaves are worked in the same way; the position of both roses and leaves is clearly shown in the engraving.

BORDER FOR A TRAY SLIP.

THIS border is useful for a tray slip, an afternoon tea-cloth, a toilet cloth or other purpose; it is particularly pretty, and at the same time is not at all difficult to work, the heading is crocheted upon the edge of the material, the scollops are worked "short way," and the two parts are then joined together with single crochet. Our model slip is of ivory congress canvas, and the crochet border is executed with Ardern's Ivory crochet cotton, No. 16, of which four or more balls will be required, as some will be needed to work an insertion either of drawn threads or of ivory work round the inside margin of the material, which in our illustration is shown as simply hemmed, but of course the slip is so much more handsome if it be embroidered in some way or other. Work the **1st round** of the **Border** immediately upon the hem of the material, using a fine steel crochet needle—1 treble in the material, 1 chain, and repeat; and leave just as much space below the chain stitch as will serve to keep the work flat, and ease the corners with a loop of 3 chain instead of one chain only. **2nd round**—Crossed trebles—Carry on 3 chain from the join of last round and it will stand for a treble stitch, miss the two first stitches of last round, do 1 treble on the next, 5 chain, 1 treble on the top of the treble stitch last done, * 2 chain, cotton twice round the needle, miss two stitches of last round, insert the needle in the third stitch and draw the cotton through, cotton over the needle and draw through 2 stitches on the needle, cotton over the needle and insert the hook in the third stitch of last round from that last worked into and draw the cotton through, now cotton over the needle and draw through 2 stitches till all the stitches are drawn off the needle, then, do 2 chain, 1 treble in the centre threads of the long stitch just worked, and repeat from *; the corner is turned by doing 7 chain between two crossed treble stitches: join evenly on the completion of the round, and break off the cotton; the heading is thus finished. Now for the **Scollops**, which are worked the short way in rows forwards and backwards. Make 5 chain, do 3 treble in the fourth chain from the needle, 3 chain, 3 treble in the next chain stitch. **2nd row**—Turn with 3 chain, do 3 treble in the loop

Border for a Tray Slip.

of three chain of preceding row, 3 chain, 3 more treble in the same place, 2 chain, 1 treble at the end upon the last treble stitch. **3rd row**—Turn with 5 chain, 1 treble on the first of the three treble stitches of last row, 2 chain, 3 treble in the loop of three chain, 3 chain, 3 more treble in the same place. **4th row**—Turn with 3 chain, do 3 treble in the loop of three chain of previous row, 3 chain, 3 more treble in the same place, 2 chain, 1 treble on the last of the three treble stitches of last row, 2 chain, 1 treble on one treble stitch, 2 chain, 1 treble in the centre stitch of the chain that turned. **5th row**—Turn with 5 chain, 1 treble on treble stitch of last row, 2 chain, 1 treble on the next treble stitch, 2 chain, 1 treble on the first of the three treble stitches, 2 chain, 3 treble in the loop of three chain, 3 chain, 3 more treble in the same place: this completes the first scollop. **6th row**—Which is practically the first row of the second scollop—Turn with 3 chain, do 3 treble in the loop of three chain of preceding row, 3 chain, 3 more treble in the same place, 2 chain, 1 treble on the last of the three treble stitches of preceding row. Work on now from the third row till you have made as many scollops as are required, allowing for fulness to be gathered in round the corners of the slip. Head the border with a row, thus—3 treble in every loop of three chain that turned the rows of the border, 3 chain between the groups of treble stitches. With single slip-stitch crochet join together the heading of the scollops to the crochet that is worked on the cloth, inserting the hook to take one thread of each and draw through. A **Picot Edge** is crocheted round the scollops, and may be done either before the above-mentioned joining takes place, or afterwards, as seems most convenient; the last scollop is, of course, to be sewn to the commencing chain of the first scollop to make the round of scollops complete. Begin the edge with 1 double crochet on the last of the three treble stitches at the foot of a scollop where one treble is already worked, * 4 chain, 1 double crochet in the fourth chain from the needle, 1 double crochet at the foot of the next treble stitch, and repeat from * twice more, which gives three picots along the side of the scollop, then a picot and 1 double crochet in the centre stitch of chain at the point of the scollop, another picot, and one more double crochet at the point of the scollop, and work in the same manner picots and double crochet four times, which will bring you to the foot of the next scollop; and proceed in the same manner to the end.

PRIMROSE BORDER.

THE engraving represents a useful border that may be worked with any variety of cotton to suit the purpose for which it is required. The lower

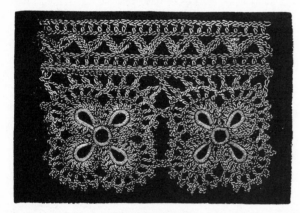

Primrose Border.

part of the border consists of medallions, or "primroses," and a heading is added on the top when a sufficient number of these are crocheted and joined together in a row. Begin a **Medallion** with 12 chain, and join round. **1st round**—Work 3 double crochet in the circle, * make 12 chain, 1 single crochet in the twelfth chain from the needle, and then keeping the work the same side uppermost, do 15 double crochet in the chain loop and close with a single crochet, do 5 double crochet in the circle, repeat from * three times, but the last time do only 2 double crochet as 3 are already worked at the beginning of the round, join neatly. **2nd round**—Now taking up the front and top threads of the stitches, work 1 double crochet on the centre stitch of five double crochet of last round, 1 treble on the first double crochet of the petal, * 1 chain, 1 treble on the next double crochet, and repeat from * till 15 treble are worked round the petal, then 1 double crochet on the centre stitch of five double crochet, and the same round each of the other petals, and join at the end of the round. **3rd round**—Slip along to the fourth treble stitch up the side of the petal, and from that do 8 chain, 1 double crochet in the fifth chain from the needle to make a picot, 1 treble on the next treble stitch (now taking the top and back threads), * 5 chain, 1 double crochet in the fifth chain from the needle (a picot again), 1 treble on the next treble stitch, repeat from * till 8 picots and 9 treble stitches are done (counting the commencing chain as 1 treble stitch), then 1 treble on the fourth treble stitch of the next petal, and work the same picots and treble stitches, and repeat to the end of the round, and join, and fasten off. Work more primrose medallions, and join each to the one previous in the course of the picots, as shown in the engraving. For the **Heading**—Do 1 long treble in the fifth and 1 long treble in the fourth picot to the right of the primrose, these long treble being drawn together in one at the top, 3 chain, 1 double crochet in the next picot, * 2 chain, 1 double crochet in the next picot, and repeat from * till in all 6 double crochet are done, then 3 chain, and compound long treble in the next two picots, and go on to the next primrose in the same way. **2nd row**—Turn, and work along in double crochet. **3rd row**—Turn with 4 chain, and proceed in open stitch, 1 treble, 1 chain, miss one, and repeat; break off at the end of the row. **4th row**—Recommence on the right-hand side—1 double crochet on the first treble stitch of the previous row, 4 chain, 1 long treble in the same place, * miss five stitches, 1 long treble on the next, 4 chain, 1 double crochet in the same place, 4 chain, 1 long treble in the same place, and repeat from * to the end, and fasten off. **5th row**—Do 2 double crochet on the point of the stitches of last row, 5 chain, and repeat. **6th row**—Open stitch of 1 treble, 1 chain, miss one.

WHEEL BORDER.

AN effective border can be worked with small crochet wheels arranged in groups of threes in triangular fashion, forming scollops, surmounted with a crochet heading. The engraving shows a corner of an afternoon tea-cloth edged with a wheel border worked with Ardern's Ivory crochet cotton No. 16, and a fine steel crochet needle. Commence a **Wheel** by winding the cotton nine times round the forefinger of the left hand. **1st round**—Work 40 double crochet in the circle, and join evenly the last stitch to the first at the end of the round. **2nd round**—Work 1 double crochet on each of 2 double crochet stitches, taking up the front and top threads, 5 chain, miss three stitches, 1 double crochet on each of the two next, 5 chain, miss three stitches, and repeat the same, and join evenly at the end of the round. **3rd round**—Work 7 double crochet under each loop of five chain of last round, and join, and fasten off; this forms one wheel. Continue crocheting in wheels, and join each to the preceding by a single crochet as you work, till you have done a sufficient length of scollops for the purpose required. For the **Heading**—**1st row**—Do 1 treble on the centre double crochet stitch of the first of the three groups of seven double crochet along the top edge of the wheels, 5 chain, 1 double crochet on the centre stitch of the centre group, 5 chain, 1 treble on the centre stitch of the third group, 5 chain, and repeat the same; and at the corner instead of 5 chain do 2 chain, 1 long treble in the centre stitch of the corner wheel, 2 chain, and continue thence as before. **2nd row**—Open crochet of 1 chain and 1 treble alternately, and miss one stitch between the trebles; a treble should in every case come over a stitch of the previous row, and three trebles are drawn together to shape at the corner. **3rd row**—Do 1 treble on a treble stitch that stands over one of the stitches worked in the first row, * cotton twice round the needle, insert the needle in the third treble stitch of last row and draw the cotton through, cotton over the needle and draw through 2 stitches on the needle, cotton over the needle and again draw through two stitches on the needle, cotton over the needle and once more draw through 2 stitches on the needle, then 3 chain, and 5 treble stitches under the long treble stitch just worked, and repeat from *. **4th row**—Work 1 double crochet in the chain stitch at the top of the little point of last row, * 5 chain, 1 double crochet in the chain stitch at the top of the next point, and repeat from *. **5th row**—Open crochet as the second row; and this finishes the border.

WINDOW BLINDS EDGED WITH CROCHET LACE.

BLINDS of both plain and coloured linen or holland edged with lace are very fashionable, and to make them still more elaborate, an insertion is often used. Crochet lace is extremely pretty, and suitable for decorating blinds,

Wheel Border.

and our left-hand sketch shows a bordering after the style of the Union Pattern Border, while the right-hand sketch shows the Wheel Border, both of which would be worked with coarse cream or white cotton. The Union Pattern Border could well be converted into an insertion by repeating the border on the other side of the wheels, and the Wheel Border could have two straight rows of wheels and the heading crocheted on either side for an insertion.

HONITON LACE BORDER.
FOR THE ENDS OF A SIDEBOARD CLOTH.

THE border shown in our engraving is used to ornament the ends of a fine white linen sideboard cloth, and is crocheted finely with Coats' No. 16 white crochet cotton and a fine steel crochet needle. The ends of the linen cloth above the border are embroidered with a design in drawn threads, which also is represented in the engraving, and may easily be copied therefrom; should, however, any difficulty appear it may be explained by turning to No. 52 and No. 53 of "Weldon's Practical Needlework Series," where full instructions are given for working these stitches, and where also many other lovely designs are illustrated and explained. The **Border** consists of sprays of leaves and roses in scollops. Commence with a **rose**. Do 5 chain, unite in a ring. **1st round**—Do 6 chain, 1 treble in the ring, * 3 chain, 1 treble in the ring, and repeat from * three times, then 3 chain, and join to the third stitch of chain with which the round commenced; there should be six loops of three chain stitches. **2nd round**—Work 1 double crochet, 1 treble, 3 long treble, 1 treble, and 1 double crochet, *all* in each loop of three chain, and join evenly at the end of this and every round. **3rd round**—Work behind the little petals of last round, 1 double crochet on a treble stitch of the first round, 4 chain, and repeat, making as before six loops of chain. **4th round**—Do 1 double crochet, 2 treble, 5 long treble, 2 treble, 1 double crochet, under each loop of four chain of last round. **5th round**—1 double crochet on double crochet of the third round, 5 chain, and repeat, again making six loops of chain. **6th round**—Work 1 double crochet, 2 treble, 7 long treble, 2 treble, 1 double crochet, under each loop of five chain of the preceding round; join quite evenly: this rose stands to the right of the spray: do 24 chain for part of the stem and the foundation of the leaf to the left. For the **Leaf**—Work 1 double crochet in the third chain from the needle, 1 treble in the next, 5 long treble consecutively, 1 treble in the next, 1 double crochet in the next: then 3 chain, and turn and go round the leaf, 1 treble on the double crochet stitch, 3 chain, 1 treble on the

stitch of the third scollop of the first leaf; on the completion of the rose do only 6 chain for a stem, unite to the seventh chain stitch of the long stem, unite also to the chain stitch above, then do 6 double crochet back to the rose, and fasten off: this forms one spray. Work as many sprays as you will require scollops for the length of the border. To **connect** the **sprays** together —Do 1 double crochet on the middle treble of the seventh little scollop of the third leaf, 8 chain, 1 double crochet in the fifth chain from the needle, 10 chain, 1 double crochet in the fifth chain from the needle, 10 chain, 1 double crochet in the fifth chain from the needle, 3 chain, 1 double crochet in the middle treble stitch of the sixth little scollop of the first leaf of the spray to the right, and you have a bar of three picots in five loops of chain reaching from one spray to the other, do 4 chain, 1 double crochet on the centre stitch of the nearest petal of the rose above; turn the work so that all future picots may point upwards, and work thus along the bar you have just made, 1 chain, 1 picot (a picot is always 5 chain and 1 double crochet stitch in the first of these chain stitches), 1 chain, 1 treble in the loop of chain to the left of the first picot of the bar, 1 chain, 1 picot, 1 chain, 1 treble in the same loop, 3 chain, 1 treble in the loop to the left of the next picot of the bar, 1 chain, 1 picot, 1 chain, 1 treble in the same loop, 1 chain, 1 picot, 1 chain, 1 treble on the seventh little scollop of the third leaf where the first double crochet stitch is worked, 3 chain, 1 double crochet on the centre stitch of the petal of the rose above; turn for another short row, 1 chain, 1 picot, 1 chain, 1 treble on the first treble stitch of the previous short row, 1 chain, 1 picot, 1 chain, 1 treble in the loop of three chain, 1 chain, 1 picot, 1 chain, 1 treble on the fourth

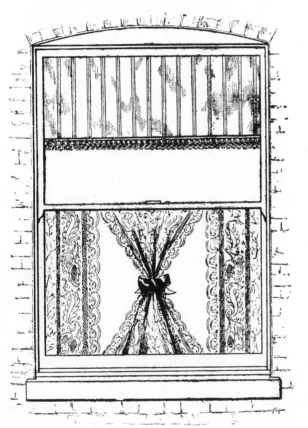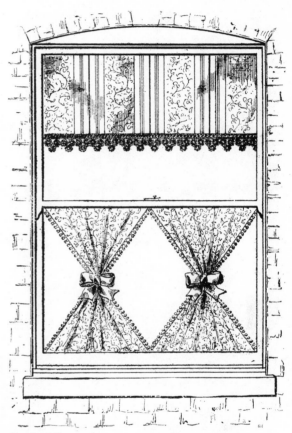

Window Blinds edged with Crochet Lace.

first long treble stitch, 3 chain, 1 treble on the third long treble stitch, 3 chain, 1 treble on the fifth long treble stitch, 3 chain, 1 treble on the double crochet stitch, 3 chain, 1 treble at the tip of the leaf, work 6 spaces in the same way along the opposite side of the leaf, and 1 single crochet in the nearest stitch of the stem chain: turn, do 1 double crochet on a treble stitch, and 3 treble on the three following chain stitches, and repeat the same to form as it were 12 little scollops round the leaf, and end with 1 double crochet on the last treble stitch, and finish the leaf neatly with 1 double crochet in the nearest stitch of the stem chain (the twelfth stitch of chain from the rose) and take also the first of the double crochet stitches on the outside margin of the leaf. For the remainder of the stem and the **Bottom Leaf** work 16 chain, fashion the leaf as instructed above, only join the middle treble stitch of the second scollop in the outside round to the middle treble stitch of the corresponding scollop of the first leaf, as see engraving; after the completion of the leaf do 3 double crochet stitches along the 3 chain stem stitches that intervene between this leaf and the first leaf. For the **Third Leaf** work 13 chain, and proceed like the other leaves till you get to the outside round, and there join the middle treble stitch of the second scollop to the middle treble stitch of the corresponding scollop of the bottom leaf, and join the middle treble stitch of the tenth scollop to a long treble stitch on the first outside petal of the rose, finish the leaf neatly, and work 11 double crochet along the 11 chain stem stitches up to the rose, and fasten off. Crochet another **rose** by the instructions given for the first; join the centre stitch of the first outside petal to the corresponding petal of the first rose, and join a stitch of the last petal to the centre

treble stitch of previous row, 1 chain, 1 picot, 1 chain, 1 double crochet on the petal of the rose close by the preceding join, 3 chain, 1 double crochet on the centre stitch of the next petal above; turn for another short row, 1 chain, 1 picot, 1 chain, 1 treble on the treble after the picot of the preceding row, do this twice more, then 1 chain, 1 picot, 1 chain, 1 treble on the petal where a double crochet is already worked, 3 chain, 1 double crochet on the next petal above; turn for another short row which work as the last row; then 3 chain, 1 double crochet on the petal above; turn, 3 chain, 1 picot, 1 chain, 1 treble under the one chain before the picot of last short row, * 1 chain, 1 picot, 1 chain, 1 treble under the one chain before the next picot of last row, repeat from * till 4 treble stitches are done, then 1 chain, 1 picot, 3 chain, unite to the first treble stitch of the next petal of the rose, and fasten off. Join the other sprays in the same manner. Then work for the **Heading**—Do 1 double crochet in the centre stitch of the centre petal at the top of the rose, 2 chain, 1 picot, 1 chain, 1 treble in the second long treble stitch of the next petal, 2 chain, 1 picot, 1 chain, cotton three times round the needle, insert the hook in the sixth long treble stitch of the same petal and work off two threads of cotton, cotton twice round the needle, insert the hook in the second long treble stitch of a petal of the next rose, and now work off all the threads one by one till all are worked off, 2 chain, 1 picot, 1 chain, 1 treble on the sixth long treble stitch of the same petal, 2 chain, 1 picot, 1 chain, 1 double crochet on the centre stitch of the next petal, * 2 chain, 1 picot, 1 chain, 1 treble in the chain before the next picot of the short row, and repeat from * five times, then 2 chain, 1 picot, 1 chain, 1 double crochet on the centre stitch of the centre petal at the top of the rose, and continue hence to the end of the row. **2nd row**—Do 1 treble under the chain before a picot, * 2 chain, 1 picot, 1 chain, 1 treble under the chain before the next picot, and repeat from *. **3rd row**—The same. **4th row**—Do 1 treble under the chain before a picot, * 4 chain, 1 treble under the chain before the next picot, and repeat from *. **5th row**—Work 4 double crochet under every loop of four chain, or 5 double crochet if required to keep the border flat; this finishes the heading. For the **Edge** round the **Scollops** —Do 1 long treble on the centre stitch of the seventh little scollop of the leaf to the right of the spray, 3 chain, 1 long treble on the next little scollop, 3 chain, 1 long treble on the next, 3 chain, cotton three times round the needle, insert the hook in the centre stitch of the next little scollop, and work off 2 threads of cotton, cotton twice round the needle, insert the hook in the centre stitch of the third little scollop of the middle leaf, and now work off all the threads one by one, 3 chain, 1 long treble on the next little scollop, 3 chain, 1 long treble on the next, 3 chain, 1 long treble on the next, 5 chain, 1 long treble on the double crochet stitch at the point of the leaf, 5 chain, 1 long treble on the next little scollop, and proceed in the open work of 3 chain, 1 long treble to correspond with the half of the scollop that is already worked, there should be 14 loops of chain and 15 long treble stitches; then 1 long treble stitch in the open work to the right of the picot, 3 chain, 1 long treble stitch between the picots, 3 chain, 1 long treble stitch between the two next picots, 3 chain, 1 long treble stitch to the left of the

NIGHTDRESS CASE,
BORDERED WITH CROCHET.

THIS nightdress case is made of ivory congress canvas in the usual oblong bag shape, about 13 inches long by 11 inches deep; the front of the bag under the flap reaches very nearly to the same height as the back; the flap is 10 inches long and 4½ inches deep. The canvas should be embroidered with a pretty design of drawn threads, or ivory work, executed with the same ivory crochet cotton, Ardern's No. 16, that is used for the border. Commence the **Border** upon a foundation chain the length required, allowing sufficient to mitre over at the corners, and employing as fine a crochet needle as convenient. **1st row**—Open crochet, 1 treble, 1 chain, miss one, and repeat. **2nd row**—Crossed trebles—Make a stitch on the needle, cotton twice round the needle, insert the hook in the first stitch of previous row and draw the cotton through, cotton over the needle and draw through 2 stitches on the needle, cotton over the needle, miss two stitches of the previous row and insert the hook in the next and draw the cotton through, and now cotton over the needle and draw through 2 stitches at a time till all the stitches are worked off, do 2

Honiton Lace Border.

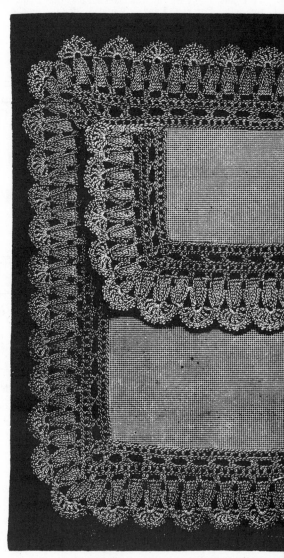

Nightdress Ca

last picot, and 1 long treble on the centre treble stitch of the seventh little scollop of the leaf of the next spray; and continue. **2nd row**—Under every loop of three chain of last row do 3 double crochet, 5 chain, and 3 more double crochet, and in those two loops of five chain at the point of the scollop do 4 double crochet, 5 chain, and 4 more double crochet. **3rd row**—1 treble on the first double crochet stitch, * 4 chain, 1 treble between the double crochet stitches of last row and directly over the long treble stitch of the first row, repeat from * till 6 loops are worked, then 4 chain, 1 treble between the first and second double crochet stitches, and 4 chain, 1 treble between the fifth and sixth double crochet of the same group, 4 chain, 1 treble over the long treble stitch in the exact middle of the point of the scollop; 4 chain, 1 treble between the first and second double crochet stitches, and 4 chain, 1 treble between the fifth and sixth double crochet of the same group, then work as from * to * down the opposite side of the scollop, and also along the open work. **4th row**—1 treble under the loop of four chain of last row, * 2 chain, 1 picot, 1 chain, 1 treble under the next loop, and repeat from * all round the scollop; contract in the centre of the open work between the scollops by doing 2 treble stitches without any chain or picot between; and continue to the end of the row.

chain, 1 treble in the centre threads of the long treble just worked, then 2 chain, cotton twice round the needle and work another crossed treble stitch, missing two stitches of the previous row from the stitch you have just made. **3rd row**—Open crochet like the first row. **4th row**—Spear-points—Work 2 treble in the first space of one chain of last row, * 10 chain, 1 double crochet in the third chain from the needle, 1 double crochet in the next, 3 consecutive treble (making each treble stitch a little taller than the foregoing), and 3 consecutive long treble, miss two spaces of last row, 2 treble in the next space, and repeat from *. **5th row**—Work 1 double crochet in the fourth chain stitch up the side of the first spear point (counting from the two treble stitches of the preceding row), 4 chain, 1 double crochet in the little loop of chain at the top of the spear point, 4 chain, another double crochet in the little loop, 4 chain, 1 double crochet on the third treble stitch down the side of the spear point, 1 chain, go to the next spear point and work similarly, and so on, to the end of the row. **6th row**—Work 2 double crochet in the loop of four chain at the top of the first spear point, 1 long treble in the loop of four chain at the top of the next spear point, 4 chain, 1 double crochet on the top of the long treble stitch just done (making a picot), and repeat the long treble and the picot till you have 8 long treble stitches and 7 picots spreading out in the shape of a fan from the loop of four chain at the top of this spear point; then 2 double crochet in the loop of the next spear point, a fan on the next, and continue to the end of the row. This finishes the border. A shorter length is worked in the same way to trim the flap. Sew the border neatly on the nightdress case.

CRESCENT BORDER.

FOR this pretty border select crochet cotton suitable for the material on which the border is to be placed, and use a steel crochet needle. Begin with 7 chain; do 1 treble in the seventh chain from the needle: this makes a circle. **1st row**—Turn with 1 chain, and work 31 treble in the circle. **2nd row**—Turn with 3 chain, miss two treble stitches, 1 treble on the next, * 1 chain, miss one, 1 treble on the next, and repeat from * till 14 treble stitches are worked. **3rd row**—Turn with 6 chain, 1 double crochet in the space of one

lered with Crochet.

chain of last row, * 6 chain, 1 double crochet in the next space, and repeat from * till you have 11 loops of chain, then do 7 chain, and 1 double crochet at the end of the row. **4th row**—Turn with 1 chain, and work 31 treble under the loop of seven chain of previous row, 2 chain, miss one of the loops of six chain, 1 double crochet in the next. **5th row**—Turn with 1 chain, miss two treble stitches, 1 treble on the next, * 1 chain, miss one, 1 treble on the next, and repeat from * till 14 treble stitches are worked, then do 1 double crochet in the nearest loop of six chain of the previous scollop. **6th row**—Turn with 6 chain, 1 double crochet in the first space of preceding row, * 6 chain, 1 double crochet in the next space, and repeat from * till there are 11 loops of chain, then do 7 chain, and 1 double crochet at the end of the row. Repeat from the fourth row. For the **Heading**—Work along one side of the line of crescents. **1st row**—Do 1 long treble in the first loop of six chain, * 2 chain, 1 treble in the next loop, and repeat from * four times, then 2 chain, 1 long treble in the next loop; all this goes upon one crescent; continue the same to the end of the row. **2nd row**—Work 2 treble under every space of two chain of last row. Sew the border to the margin of the cloth, which should previously have been hemstitched round.

GRECIAN BORDER.

THIS border is worked lengthways. Procure Ardern's crochet cotton, No. 20, and a steel crochet needle. Make a foundation chain the length required. **1st row**—Double crochet in every stitch of the foundation chain, and break off at the end of the row. **2nd row**—Recommence on the right-hand side, 1 treble on the first stitch, * 1 chain, miss one, 1 treble on the next, and repeat from * to the end, and fasten off. **3rd row**—Double crochet. **4th row**—Same as the second row. These four rows form the heading. **5th row**—Begins the scollops,—Do 12 double crochet ; * 12 chain, 1 double crochet in the seventh chain from the needle and 3 more double crochet worked consecutively, and leave the last 2 chain stitches void, repeat from * four more times ; then 10 chain, 1 double crochet in the sixth chain from the needle and 2 more double crochet worked consecutively, and leave the last 2 chain stitches void; 8 chain, 1 double crochet in the fifth chain from the needle and 1 double crochet in the next, 2 more double crochet, and leave 2 stitches void; 6 chain, 1 double crochet in the fifth chain from the needle, and 1 double crochet in the next; 6 chain again, 1 double crochet in the fifth chain from the needle, and 1 double crochet in the next, this is the top of the scollop; now do 2 double crochet in two chain stitches that were left void, 8 chain, 1 double crochet in the sixth chain from the needle and 2 more double crochet worked consecutively, and two double crochet in two

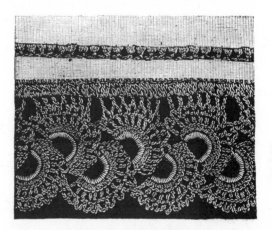

Crescent Border.

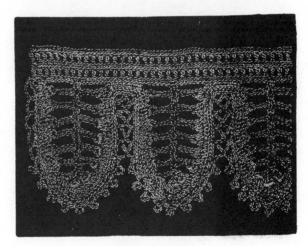

Grecian Border.

chain stitches that were left void, * 10 chain, 1 double crochet in the seventh chain from the needle and 3 more double crochet worked consecutively, and two double crochet in the two void chain stitches ; repeat from * four times and you have shaped the scollop ; miss three stitches of the fourth row, do 23 double crochet consecutively ; then begin another scollop, and continue to the end of the row, where should be 12 double crochet stitches to match the beginning. **6th row**—Do 1 double crochet on each of the 5 first double crochet stitches of the preceding row, miss the other 7 double crochet, do 4 treble in each of the five first spikes of the scollop, 5 treble in the next spike, 6 treble in the next, 7 treble in the next (which is the top spike), 6 treble in the next, 5 treble in the next, and 4 treble in each of the five last spikes, then miss 7 of the 23 double crochet stitches, work 9 double crochet on the nine middle stitches, miss the other 7 double crochet ; and continue the same upon each scollop to the end of the row ; and do not break off here, but **turn** the work. **7th row**—Plain double crochet, taking up the one back thread of the stitches of last row to make a ridge, the first stitch and the last stitch of the nine double crochet of last row are to be missed ; turn again at the end of this row. **8th row**—Double crochet, again taking up the back threads of the stitches of last row, and likewise missing the first and last stitches of the seven double crochet ; break off at the end. **9th row**—With the right side of the work next you, do 1 double crochet on the first double crochet of the previous row, * 5 chain, miss three stitches, 1 double crochet on the next, repeat from * till 5 loops of chain are done, then * 6 chain, 1 double crochet in the fifth chain from the needle to make a picot, 1 chain, miss two, 1 double crochet in the next, repeat from * twice ; then 7 times do the same picot loop and miss only one stitch ; again do 3 picot loops missing two stitches ; and then 5 loops of 5 chain missing three stitches, which completes one scollop ; connect four of the plain loops of the second scollop to the corresponding four loops of the first scollop as shown in the engraving, then work picoted loops as before, and again do five plain loops ; and continue the same the whole length of the border.

CROCHET BORDER FOR AN AFTERNOON TEA-CLOTH.

AN afternoon tea-cloth is one of the most useful and necessary requirements of the present day, and consequently is a favourite subject on which clever workers can display their taste and skill ; it is a thing too that always fetches a fair price at a bazaar or fancy sale. Of course an essential qualification of a tea-cloth is that it be made of a washable material, as it will be likely

WIDE SCOLLOPED BORDER.

THIS border is worked shortways, and the example is crocheted with Finlayson's Scotch flax linen thread, No. 35 brown, and a No. 3 Penelope steel crochet needle. Commence with 23 chain. **1st row**—Work 1 treble in the sixth chain from the needle, 1 chain, miss one stitch, 1 treble in the next, 1 chain, miss one, 1 treble in the next, 1 chain, miss one, 1 treble in the next, 1 chain, miss one, do 8 consecutive treble, 1 chain, miss one, 1 treble in the next which is the end of the commencing chain. **2nd row**—Turn with 5 chain, 6 treble on the six centre stitches of the eight treble of last row, 2 chain, 1 treble on treble, 1 chain, 1 treble on treble, 1 chain, 1 treble on treble, 1 chain, 1 treble on treble, 1 chain, miss one chain stitch of last row, and do 1 treble in the next chain stitch. **3rd row**—Turn with 4 chain, 1 treble on treble, do 1 chain and 1 treble on treble three times, 4 chain, 2 treble on the two centre stitches of the six treble of last row, 4 chain, 1 treble in the third stitch (the corner stitch) of the chain that turned. **4th row**—Turn with 5 chain, miss two chain stitches of last row, do 6 consecutive treble (the two centre of these will come over the two treble stitches of last row), 2 chain, 1 treble on treble, do 1 chain and 1 treble on treble three times, 1 chain, miss one chain stitch of last row and do 1 treble in the next chain stitch. **5th row**—Turn with 4 chain, 1 treble on treble, do 1 chain and 1 treble on treble three times, 1 chain, miss one

Crochet Border for an Afternoon Tea-Cloth.

to be often in the laundry, therefore the new ivory congress canvas with its appropriate trimming of ivory cotton crochet would seem to be exactly suitable for the purpose, being both light and pretty and withal strong. Our engraving represents this description of cloth ; the canvas can be bought by the yard, any width. It should be hemstitched round, and decorated with an insertion of ivory work (see No. 75 of " Weldon's Practical Needlework Series") or drawn thread embroidery (see Nos. 52, 53, and 58 of " Weldon's Practical Needlework Series," price 2d. each, post free 2½d. each). Cross-stitch work in red or blue cotton also affords a change. The **Border** shown on the corner of the tea-cloth is worked with Ardern's Ivory crochet cotton No. 16, and six or more balls will be required, according to the size of the cloth, our example measuring from 1 yard to 1½ yards square. Use a rather fine steel crochet needle. The pattern is almost identical with the border used upon the nightdress case in present issue, and the instruction need not be repeated. The only difference is that the border now under consideration is commenced by working the first row of open crochet into the edge of the material, so dispensing with a commencing chain ; the corners are eased round by increasing a few stitches in the pattern as you work ; and in the fourth round 2 double crochet stitches are here substituted in the place of 2 treble stitches, and you join evenly at the end of every round.

chain of last row, do 8 consecutive treble (the six centre of these will come over the six treble stitches of last row), 1 chain, 1 treble in the corner stitch at the end. **6th row**—Same as the second row. **7th row**—As third. **8th row**—As fourth. **9th row**—As fifth row, and then for the scollop do 8 chain and 1 single crochet to join to the end of the eighth row, and 2 chain and 1 single crochet to join to the end of the seventh row. **10th row**—Turn, and work 15 treble in the hole of eight chain, 1 treble on treble stitch of last row, 2 chain, 6 treble on the six centre stitches of the eight treble of last row, 2 chain, 1 treble on treble, do 1 chain and 1 treble on treble three times, 1 chain, miss one chain stitch of last row and do 1 treble in the next chain stitch. **11th row**—As third row, only that the last treble stitch will come on a treble instead of coming in a chain, and then for the scollop do 2 chain, miss two treble stitches, do 2 treble on the next, 2 chain, miss two stitches, 2 treble on the next, 2 chain, miss one stitch, 2 treble on the next, 2 chain, miss one, 2 treble on the next, 2 chain, miss two, 2 treble on the next, 2 chain, and join by 1 single crochet to the end of the fifth row, and single crochet along two chain stitches to get to the end of the fifth row. **12th row**—Turn with 3 chain, and work 3 treble over the first group of two treble of last row, * 3 chain, 3 treble over two treble, repeat from * three times more, then 3 chain, 1 treble on one treble, 2 chain, 6 treble (the two centre of these will come over the two treble stitches of last row), 2 chain, 1 treble on treble, do 1 chain and 1 treble on treble three times, 1 chain, miss one chain stitch of last row and do 1 treble in the next chain stitch. **13th row**—As fifth row, only the last treble stitch will stand on a treble instead of coming in a chain, and then for the scollop, * 4 chain, 4 treble over three treble stitches, and repeat from * four times more, then 4 chain, 1 single crochet in the end of the fourth row, and single crochet along two chain stitches to get to the end of the third row. **14th row**—Turn with 4 chain, and work 6 treble over the first group of four treble of last row (that is, 1 in the first, 2 in the second, 2 in the third, and 1 on the fourth stitch), * 4 chain, 6 treble over four treble, repeat from * three times more, then 4 chain, 1 treble on one treble, 2 chain, 6 treble on the six centre stitches of the eight treble of last row, 2 chain, 1 treble on treble, do 1 chain and 1 treble on treble three times, 1 chain, miss one chain stitch of last row and do 1 treble in the next chain stitch. **15th row**—As third row, only the last treble stitch will come on a treble instead of coming in a chain, and then for the scollop,* 4 chain, 1 treble on each of 3 treble stitches of the group of last row, 3 chain,

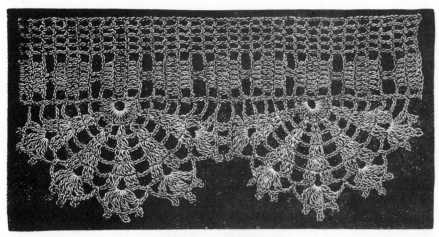

Wide Scolloped Border.

1 treble on each of the other 3 stitches of the same group, and repeat from * four times more, then 4 chain, 1 single crochet in the end of the second row, and single crochet along two chain stitches to get to the end of the first row. **16th row**—Turn with 3 chain, do 2 long treble stitches (cotton twice round the needle) in the loop of three chain of last row, * 5 chain, 1 double crochet in the fifth chain from the needle (to form a picot), 2 more long treble stitches in the same loop of three chain, repeat from * twice more, making in all four groups of long treble stitches and three picots; then 3 chain, 1 double crochet under the loop of four chain; 3 chain, and repeat the groups, with the chain and the double crochet between the groups, until you have five groups done; then 3 chain, 1 treble on one treble, 2 chain, 6 treble (the two centre of these will be on the two treble stitches of last row), 2 chain, 1 treble on treble, do 1 chain and 1 treble on treble three times, 1 chain, miss one chain stitch of last row and do 1 treble in the next chain stitch. This practically finishes one scollop. The **1st row** of the second scollop is worked thus,—Turn with 4 chain, 1 treble on treble, do 1 chain and 1 treble on treble three times, 1 chain, miss one chain of last row, and do 8 consecutive treble, 1 chain, miss one chain of last row, and do 1 treble on one treble stitch; now go to the second row; and work onwards for the length required. The scollops are joined one to the other by uniting the two first picots to the two corresponding picots of the preceding scollop.

TORCHON BORDER IN A DIAMOND PATTERN.

THIS elegant border may be worked immediately upon the edge of a square of canvas or linen material, or in the usual manner upon a length of chain crocheted for the purpose of a foundation. We will suppose you have procured suitable cotton and a crochet needle, and that you are going to work on a chain, commencing at a corner. **1st row**—Do 1 treble in the first stitch of chain, 1 chain, miss one, 1 treble in the next, 3 chain, miss two, 1 treble in the next, 1 chain, miss one, 1 treble in the next; 3 chain, miss two, 1 treble in the next, 1 chain, miss one, 1 treble in the next, * 3 chain, miss two, 1 treble in each of 3 consecutive stitches; 3 chain, miss two, 1 treble in the next, 1 chain, miss one, 1 treble in the next; 3 chain, miss two, 1 treble in the next, 1 chain, miss one, 1 treble in the next; 3 chain, miss two, 1 treble in the next, 1 chain, miss one, 1 treble in the next, and repeat from *; the repetition should come in exactly to the opposite corner; all the corners are alike with 3 chain, as the one shown in the engraving; the other sides are worked in the same manner; you had better join and break off the thread at the completion of every round, and recommence the next round at one of the other corners, and so avoid an unsightly seam anywhere in the border. **2nd row**—3 treble in the loop of three chain at the corner, 5 chain, 3 more treble in the same place; * 3 chain, miss three stitches, 1 treble in the first stitch of three chain of last row, 1 chain, 1 treble in the third chain stitch, 3 chain, 1 treble

in the first stitch of the next three chain of last row, 1 chain, 1 treble in the third chain stitch, 3 chain, 3 treble in the space to the right of the three treble of last row, 3 chain, 3 treble in the space to the left of the three treble, and repeat from *; do 3 chain in front of the next corner; and at the end 3 chain, and join. **3rd row**—1 treble in the first of the five chain stitches at the corner, 1 chain, miss one, 1 treble in the next, 5 chain, 1 treble in the same stitch as last treble, 1 chain, miss one, 1 treble in the fifth chain stitch; * 3 chain, 3 treble in the space to the left of the three treble of the previous row, 3 chain, 1 treble in the first stitch of three chain of previous row, 1 chain, 1 treble in the third chain stitch, 3 chain, 3 treble in the space to the right of the three treble of the previous row, 3 chain, 1 treble in the first stitch of three chain, 1 chain, 1 treble in the third chain stitch, and repeat from *; and do 3 chain in front of the corner. **4th row**—Work the corner by the instruction in the third row; then * 3 chain, 1 treble in the first stitch of three chain of preceding row, 1 chain, 1 treble in the third chain stitch, 3 chain, 3 treble in the space to the left of the group of preceding row, 3 chain, 3 treble in the space to the right of the next group of preceding row, 3 chain, 1 treble on the first of three chain stitches, 1 chain, 1 treble in the third chain stitch, and repeat from *; do 3 chain in front of the next corner. **5th row**—Work the corner as before; * 3 chain, 3 treble in the space of three chain of last row, 3 chain, 1 treble in the first of three chain stitches, 1 chain, 1 treble in the third chain stitch, 3 chain, 3 treble in the space between the groups of last row, 3 chain, 1 treble in the first of three chain stitches, 1 chain, 1 treble in the third chain stitch, and repeat from *, 3 chain to corner. **6th row**—Work the corner as before; * 3 chain, 3 treble in the space of three chain of previous row, 2 treble on the three treble of previous row, taking up the front and top threads, 3 treble in the next space (making 8 treble), 3 chain, 1 treble in the first of three chain stitches, 1 chain, 1 treble in the third chain stitch, 3 chain, 1 treble in the first of three chain stitches, 1 chain, 1 treble in the third chain stitch, and repeat from *; 3 chain to corner. **7th row**—Work the corner as before; * 3 chain, 3 treble in the space, 7 treble on the eight treble of last row, 3 treble in the next space (making 13 treble), 3 chain, 1 treble in the first stitch of three chain of last row, 1 chain, 1 treble in the third chain stitch, and repeat from *; 3 chain to corner. **8th row**—Work 7 treble in the loop of five chain at the corner, * 3 chain, 3 treble in the space, miss one treble stitch and work 4 treble consecutively, 3 chain, miss

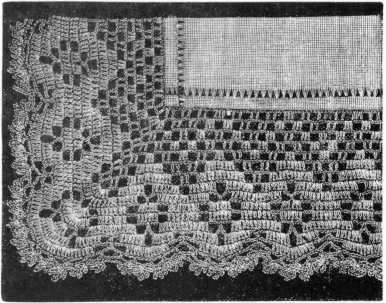

Torchon Border in a Diamond Pattern.

three treble stitches, work 3 treble consecutively, miss a stitch, do 1 treble on the last stitch of the group of last row and 3 treble in the next space. and repeat from *; 3 chain in front of the 7 treble at the corner. **9th row**—Work 1 treble on each of the 4 first of the seven treble at the corner, 5 chain, 1 treble in the same stitch as the last treble and 1 treble on each of the remaining 3 treble stitches, 3 treble in the space, and 5 consecutive treble on treble stitches of last row (making 12 treble); * 3 chain, 1 double crochet in the space of three chain of last row, 3 chain, miss two treble stitches, do 5 consecutive treble, 3 treble in the space, and 5 more consecutive treble (making 13 treble), repeat from *; and fashion the other corner to correspond with the part of the corner that is already done. **10th row**—Work 7 treble in the loop of five chain at the corner, 3 chain, miss two treble, work 7 treble consecutive; * 3 chain, 3 treble in the first loop of chain of last row, and 3 treble in the second loop, 3 chain, miss three treble stitches, and repeat from *; always now fashion the corner to correspond with the part of the corner with which you began. **11th row**—Work 13 treble over the seven treble stitches at the corner (making the increase by doing 3 treble on the third, fourth, and fifth stitches); * 3 chain, 7 treble, 3 chain, 6 treble, and repeat from *, the treble in every case being over the treble stitches of the previous row. **12th row**—Do 1 double crochet between the third and fourth treble stitches at the corner, 4 chain, 5 treble on the centre stitch at the corner, 4 chain, 1 double crochet between the tenth and eleventh treble stitches; 4 chain; * 3 treble in the space, 7 treble over seven treble of last row, 3 treble in the next space, 4 chain, 1 double crochet between the third and fourth stitches of the group of six treble of last row, 4 chain, and repeat from *. **13th row**—Begin in the loop to the right of the five corner trebles of last row and do 3 treble, do 7 treble over the five treble (making the increase on the centre stitch), and do 3 treble in the first loop to the left ; * 3 chain, 3 treble in the next loop and 1 treble on each of 4 treble stitches, 3 chain, miss two treble, 3 treble, 1 double crochet on the next, 3 chain, miss two treble, work 4 treble consecutive and 3 treble in the first loop, and repeat from *. **14th row**—Begin with a double crochet on the double crochet stitch to the right of a corner, 4 chain, and now

Imitation Limouges Lace for Cuffs and Dress Trimming.

follows a considerable number (33) of treble stitches round the corner, thus, miss the two first trebles of last row, do 5 treble consecutive, 3 treble in the loop of chain, 5 treble consecutive, 2 treble on the next, 3 treble on the centre stitch, 2 treble on the next, 5 treble consecutive, 3 treble in the loop of chain, and 5 treble consecutive, 4 chain, 1 double crochet on double crochet of last row ; * 4 chain, miss the chain loop and miss two treble stitches of last row, do 5 consecutive treble, 3 treble in the space, and 5 more consecutive treble, 4 chain, 1 double crochet on double crochet of last row, and repeat from * **15th row**—Do 1 double crochet on the third of the thirty-three treble at the corner, 5 chain, miss three stitches, 1 double crochet on the next, and continue this till you have seven loops of chain round the corner, then * 5 chain, 1 double crochet in the second stitch of the first loop of chain, 5 chain, 1 double crochet in the fourth stitch of the next loop of chain, 5 chain, 1 double crochet on the third treble stitch, 5 chain, 1 double crochet on the seventh (the centre) treble stitch, 5 chain, 1 double crochet on the eleventh treble stitch, and repeat from *. **16th row**—Edging of picots—Do 1 double crochet in the centre stitch of the loop of chain between the scollops, 4 chain, 1 double crochet in the centre stitch of the next loop of chain, * 5 chain, 1 double crochet in the same place, 6 chain, 1 double crochet in the same place, 5 chain, again 1 double crochet in the same place, 4 chain, 1 double crochet in the centre stitch of the next loop of chain, and repeat from * ; there must be four groups of picots above each scollop, and nine groups of picots round the corners.

IMITATION LIMOUGES LACE FOR CUFFS AND DRESS TRIMMING.

PROCURE écru or brown flax thread rather fine in size and a fine steel crochet needle. The lace is crocheted the short way. Commence with 56 chain. **1st row**—Work 1 double crochet in the sixth chain from the needle. * 7 chain, 1 double crochet in the fifth chain from the needle (to make a picot). 4 chain, miss five stitches of the foundation, 1 double crochet in the next, and repeat from * to the end of the row. **2nd row**—Turn with 8 chain, 1 double crochet in the chain stitch before the picot, 7 chain, picot, 4 chain, 1 double crochet in the stitch before the next picot, 7 chain, picot, 4 chain, 1 double crochet in the stitch before the next picot, 6 chain, withdraw the hook from the last stitch of chain, insert it in the double crochet stitch to the right, take up the chain stitch and draw it through, work 1 double crochet, 7 treble, and 1 double crochet in the loop of six chain, then * 7 chain, picot, 4 chain, 1 double crochet in the stitch before the next picot, repeat from * twice more, then 6 chain, withdraw the hook from the chain stitch on the needle, insert it in the double crochet stitch to the right, take up the chain stitch and draw it through, and in the loop of six chain do 1 double crochet, 7 treble, and 1 double crochet ; and repeat from * which will bring you to the end of the row, the double crochet previous to the six chain being worked in the third stitch of the chain that turned. **3rd row**—Turn with 4 chain, * do 1 treble on the

first treble stitch of the group, 1 chain and 1 treble on a treble stitch alternately six times, 3 chain, 1 double crochet in the stitch before the picot, 7 chain, picot, 4 chain, 1 double crochet in the stitch before the next picot, 7 chain, picot, 1 chain, repeat from * till the third group of crested treble are worked, then 3 chain, 1 double crochet in the stitch before the picot, 7 chain, picot, 4 chain, 12 treble in the loop of eight chain at the end. **4th row**—Turn with 4 chain, do 1 treble on the second treble stitch from the needle, and 1 chain and 1 treble on treble alternately ten times, 3 chain, 1 double crochet in the stitch before the picot, * 7 chain, picot, 4 chain, 1 double crochet in the first space of one chain of the group, 7 chain, picot, 4 chain, 1 double crochet in the sixth space of one chain of the group, 7 chain, picot, 4 chain, 1 double crochet in the stitch before the picot, and repeat from * till you end the row with 1 double crochet in the sixth space of one chain of the top group. **5th row**—Turn with 7 chain, picot, 4 chain, 1 double crochet in the stitch before the picot, 7 chain, picot, 4 chain, 1 double crochet in the stitch before the next picot, 7 chain, picot, 4 chain, 1 double crochet in the stitch before the next picot, then 6 chain, withdraw the hook from the last stitch of chain, insert it in the double crochet to the right, take up the chain stitch, and draw it through, and work 1 double crochet, 7 treble, and 1 double crochet in the loop of six chain, repeat the same twice more, and after the third group of stitches in the six chain loop, do 3 chain, 1 treble in the first one chain space of the scollop, and 2 chain and 1 treble alternately ten times round the scollop ; in future workings of this pattern you will join here with a single crochet to a point of the preceding scollop. **6th row**—Turn with 3 chain, work 1 double crochet in the first one chain space of the scollop, 2 chain, 1 treble in the second space, and *on this treble* do a point of 4 chain, 1 double crochet, 5 chain, 1 double crochet, 4 chain, 1 double crochet, then 2 chain, 1 double crochet in the next space, 2 chain, 1 treble in the next space, do a point on this treble, and repeat the same till you have worked 5 points on five treble stitches round the scollop ; then 3 chain, 1 double crochet in the loop of three chain of last row, 3 chain, 1 treble on the first treble stitch of the group, 1 chain and 1 treble on a treble stitch alternately six times, 3 chain, 1 double crochet in the stitch before the picot, 7 chain, picot, 4 chain, 1 double crochet in the stitch before the picot, * 7 chain picot, 1 chain, 1 treble on the first treble stitch of the group, 1 chain and 1 treble on a treble stitch alternately six times, 3 chain, 1 double crochet in the stitch before the picot, 7 chain, picot, 4 chain, 1 double crochet in the stitch before the picot, and repeat from *, which will bring you to the end of the row ; this row completes the first scollop. **7th row**—or the first row of the next scollop,—turn with 7 chain, picot, 4 chain, 1 double crochet in the stitch before the picot, 7

Argyle Scollop, showing a Corner.

chain, picot, 4 chain, 1 double crochet in the first space of one chain of the group, 7 chain, picot, 4 chain, 1 double crochet in the sixth space of the group, and repeat the same to the end of the row, that is till you come to the double crochet stitch in the sixth space of the last group. Repeat from the second row for the length required. For the row of **Heading** along the top of the lace—Work open crochet of 1 treble and 2 chain alternately into the chain loops or on the double crochet stitches at the top edge of the lace.

ARGYLE SCOLLOP, SHOWING A CORNER.

THIS handsome lace can be employed for many purposes, according to the material with which it is worked, thus, supposing it to be executed with écru or white flax thread, it is useful for trimming window blinds and household linen ; borders for fancy table covers, sideboard slips, bags, &c., can be made with ivory or coloured cotton ; with knitting cotton it makes a good quilt border ; and if brilliant crochet twist be employed it results in a charming trimming for dresses. The scollops are worked separately and joined together: a corner scollop can be fitted or not as required. Use a fine steel crochet needle and work closely. A scollop is commenced with 12 chain, which unite in a circle; then work 32 double crochet in the circle, and join round. Henceforward work in rows backwards and forwards. **2nd row**—Do 5 chain, miss one double crochet stitch of the circle and work 1 treble in the next, * 2 chain, miss one stitch, 1 treble in the next, and repeat from * till you have done 5 treble stitches, taking up the front and top threads of the double crochet of preceding row, then 3 chain, another treble in the same place as last treble; this is the beginning of the point at the bottom of the scollop, then repeat from * to * five times; leave 11 double crochet stitches unworked at the top of the ring, and turn the work. **3rd row**—Do 1 double crochet on each consecutive stitch to the point, 3 double crochet in the centre stitch of three chain at the point, and 1 double crochet on each consecutive stitch up the opposite side of the scollop; in this row there are 17 double crochet stitches up each side and 3 double crochet at the point of the scollop. **4th row**—Turn the work, and now insert the needle always to take up the one back thread of the stitches of last row, do 1 double crochet on each consecutive stitch, 3 double crochet on the centre stitch at the point, and 1 double crochet on each consecutive stitch up the opposite side. Work 3 more rows the same as the last row: in the last of these there will be 45 double crochet stitches. **8th row**—Turn with 6 chain, work 2 long treble on the fourth stitch of double crochet, * 3 chain, miss two stitches, 2 long treble on the next, taking up now the two top threads of the stitches, and drawing the two long treble into one stitch at the top, repeat from * five times, then 3 chain, 2 long treble on the next stitch which is the centre stitch of the three double crochet at the point, 3 chain, 2 long treble on the next stitch, and then proceed up the opposite side to correspond with the first, and end with 3 chain, 1 long treble in the top corner stitch, and fasten off. **9th row**—With the right side of the preceding row towards you work 1 double crochet, 3 treble, 1 double crochet, *all* under each loop of three chain of preceding row, and fasten off; this finishes the scollop. More scollops are crocheted in the same way, and joined each to the foregoing by a single crochet from the middle treble stitch at the end of the ninth row to the corresponding treble stitch of the previous scollop. The **Corner Scollop** is not quite so large as the others; it begins with a circle of 8 chain, in which work 24 double crochet; the next

end of the row. **2nd row**—Turn with 6 chain, 1 treble under the loop of three chain, 3 chain, another treble in the same place, 9 chain, miss the long loop of last row, 2 treble under the loop of three chain, 3 chain, 2 more treble in the same place, 2 chain, 1 treble on one treble stitch, 2 chain, miss two stitches, 1 treble on the next which is the corner stitch of the chain that turned. **3rd row** —Turn with 5 chain, 1 treble on one treble stitch of last row, 2 chain, 2 treble under the loop of three chain, 3 chain, 2 more treble in the same place, 9 chain, 2 treble in the next loop of three chain, 3 chain, 2 more treble in the same place, 1 chain, 1 treble in the loop of six chain, and 1 treble alternately till in all 7 treble are worked in the loop of six chain, then do 1 chain and 1 double crochet in the end stitch of the foundation chain. **4th row**—Turn with 3 chain, do 1 double crochet in the first space of one chain, 3 chain and 1 double crochet in the next space, and repeat from * till 7 double crochet stitches are worked, then 3 chain, 1 treble in the loop of three chain of last row, 3 chain, another treble in the same place, 4 chain, 1 double crochet under the loop of nine chain in the first row (embracing also both the other bars of nine chain), 4 chain, 2 treble in the loop of three chain, 3 chain, 2 more treble in the same place, 2 chain, 1 treble on one treble, 2 chain, 1 treble in the corner stitch. **5th row**—Turn the work with 5 chain, 1 treble on one treble stitch of last row, 2 chain, 2 treble under the loop of three chain, 3 chain, 2 more treble in the same place, 4 chain, 1 long treble in the top thread of the treble stitch last done, 2 long treble in the second of the two treble stitches of last row, 2 long treble on the next one treble stitch of last row, 4 chain, 1 long treble in the top thread of the long treble last worked, 2 treble in the loop of three chain of last row, 3 chain, 2 more treble in the same place. **6th row**— Turn with 6 chain, 1 treble under the loop of three chain, 3 chain, another treble in the same place, 2 long treble in the centre of the star of long treble stitches, 9 chain, 2 more long treble in the centre of the star, 2 treble under the loop of three chain, 3 chain, 2 more treble in the same place, 2 chain, 1 treble on one treble, 2 chain, 1 treble in the corner stitch. **7th row**—Turn with 5 chain, 1 treble on one treble stitch of last row, 2 chain, 2 treble under the loop of three chain, 3 chain, 2 more treble in the same place, 9 chain, 2 treble under the next loop of three chain, 3 chain, 2 more treble in the same place, 1 chain, 1 treble in the loop of six chain, and 1 chain and 1 treble alternately till in all 7 treble are worked in the loop of six chain, then do 1 chain and 1 double crochet in the first loop of three chain belonging to the

Border worked Short-way.

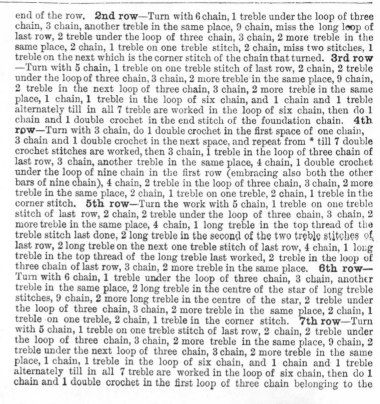

Border for Sideboard Cloth.

following 6 rows are worked as above, the only difference being that there are fewer stitches: the 8th and 9th rows are worked the whole way *round* the scollop, as will be understood by consulting the engraving, which also shows how the scollop is joined in its place. For the **Heading—1st row**—Beginning on the right-hand side of the top of a scollop—Do 1 treble at the corner, * 1 chain, miss a little space, do 1 treble, and repeat from * till in all 9 treble stitches are worked, and the last should come on the second double crochet stitch of the centre circle, 1 chain, miss one, 1 double crochet on the next, 1 chain, miss one, 1 double crochet on the next, 1 chain, miss one, 1 treble on the next, then 1 chain and 1 treble alternately eight times, and the last of these treble stitches will come at the left-hand corner of the scollop; repeat the same on every scollop; and at the corner work just 1 treble in the centre of the corner piece. **2nd row**—Treble stitches. **3rd row**—Work 1 treble on a stitch of treble of last row, 5 chain, another treble in the same place, miss three stitches, and repeat the same. **4th row**—Do 1 double crochet in the centre stitch of the loop of five chain, 3 chain, and repeat. **5th row**— Open crochet of 1 treble and 1 chain alternately, miss one stitch. This completes the border.

BORDER WORKED SHORT-WAY.

A PRETTY border is worked with old gold, shade 16, brilliant crochet twist, or it may otherwise be crocheted with white or with écru flax thread, or with Ardern's ivory cotton, and a fine steel crochet needle. Begin with 26 chain. **1st row**—Work 1 treble in the eighth chain from the needle, 2 chain, miss two stitches, 2 treble in the next, 3 chain, 2 treble in the next, miss four stitches, cotton twice round the needle, insert the hook in the next stitch of chain and draw the cotton through, cotton over the needle and draw through 2 stitches on the needle, cotton over the needle, insert the hook again in the same place and draw the cotton through, cotton over the needle and draw through 2 stitches on the needle, cotton over the needle and again draw through 2 stitches on the needle, cotton over the needle and draw through 2 more stitches on the needle (this proceeding is henceforth termed 2 long treble stitches), 9 chain, 2 long treble in the next, miss four stitches, 2 treble in the next, 3 chain, 2 treble in the next, and leave two of the foundation chain at the

preceding scollop. **8th row**—Turn with 3 chain, do 1 double crochet in the first space of one chain, * 3 chain and 1 double crochet in the next space, and repeat from * till 7 double crochet stitches are worked, then 3 chain, 1 treble in the loop of three chain of last row, 3 chain, another treble in the same place, 9 chain, 2 treble under the next loop of three chain, 3 chain, 2 more treble in the same place, 2 chain, 1 treble on one treble stitch, 2 chain, 1 treble in the corner stitch. **9th row**—Turn with 5 chain, 1 treble on one treble stitch of last row, 2 chain, 2 treble under the loop of three chain, 3 chain, 2 more treble in the same place, 4 chain, 1 double crochet under the lowest of the three loops of nine chain (which will of course embrace all *three* loops), 4 chain, 2 treble in the loop of three chain, 3 chain, 2 more treble in the same place. **10th row** —Turn with 6 chain, 1 treble under the loop of three chain, 3 chain, another treble in the same place, 4 chain, 1 long treble in the top thread of the treble stitch last done, 2 long treble on the second of the two treble stitches of last row, 2 long treble on the next treble stitch of last row, 4 chain, 1 long treble in the top thread of the long treble stitch last done, 2 treble in the loop of three chain of last row, 3 chain, 2 more treble in the same place, 2 chain, 1 treble on one treble stitch, 2 chain, 1 treble in the corner stitch. **11th row**—Turn with 5 chain, 1 treble on one treble stitch of last row, 2 chain, 2 treble under the loop of three chain, 3 chain, 2 more treble in the same place, 2 long treble in the centre of the star of long treble stitches, 9 chain, 2 more long treble in the centre of the star, 2 treble under the loop of three chain, 3 chain, 2 more treble in the same place, 1 chain, 1 treble in the loop of six chain, and 1 chain and 1 treble alternately till in all 7 treble are worked in the loop of six chain, then do 1 chain and 1 double crochet in the first loop of three chain on the previous scollop. **12th row**—Turn with 3 chain, do 1 double crochet in the first space of one chain, * 3 chain and 1 double crochet in the next space, and repeat from * till 7 double crochet stitches are worked, then 3 chain, 1 treble in the loop of three chain of last row, 3 chain, another treble in the same place, 9 chain, 2 treble in the next loop of three chain, 3 chain, 2 more treble in the same place, 2 chain, 1 treble on one treble stitch, 2 chain, 1 treble in the corner stitch. This completes three scollops of the pattern, there being four rows in each scollop; but the stars and open bars in the centre of the pattern occupy seven rows; and you therefore must adapt the one to the other as you proceed, and as you will understand by consulting the piece already done.

BORDER FOR A SIDEBOARD CLOTH.

HERE is a particularly attractive border that will please many workers as it can be quickly and readily accomplished and though simple is effective. The sideboard cloth is composed of ivory congress canvas embroidered with an "all round" margin of fancy stitches or drawn threads according to taste. The border is crocheted short-way, and sewn on the hem of the canvas. Procure two or three balls of Ardern's ivory crochet cotton, No. 16, and a rather fine steel crochet needle. Begin with 8 chain; work 1 treble in the first of these chain stitches (that is, in the eighth chain from the needle); * 5 chain, turn the work, miss the treble stitch and two of the chain stitches and do 1 treble in the next chain stitch, repeat from * three times, and you will find a straight line of five square holes—this is a portion of the "heading;" now do 4 chain, turn the work, and having the wrong side of these last chain towards you, miss the chain stitch nearest the needle and do 1 single crochet in each of 3 chain stitches to form a spike, then 1 double crochet on the treble stitch of the heading, 2 double crochet down the chain side of the last square hole and 1 double crochet at the far corner of the hole (in the corner stitch of chain); 5 chain, turn, 1 treble on the fourth double crochet from the needle to form another square hole in the heading; 6 chain, 1 single crochet in the top of the spike, 6 chain, 1 single crochet in the chain stitch in which a treble is worked at a distance of one square on the left-hand side of the spike (this begins a scollop); turn with 1 chain, do 8 double crochet under each loop of six chain of the scollop, 1 chain, 2 double crochet under the two chain down the side of the last square hole, 1 double crochet in the chain stitch at the far corner of the hole; 5 chain, turn, 1 treble on the treble stitch of the last square (working *over* the one chain stitch), 8 chain, 1 double crochet on the fourth double crochet from the end of the first group of double crochet stitches, 9 chain, 1 double crochet on the fourth double crochet from the beginning of the second group, 8 chain, 1 single crochet in the treble stitch at the distance of one square to the left of the heading; 1 chain, turn the work, 3 double crochet under the loop of eight chain, * 6 chain, 1 double crochet in the sixth chain from the needle to make a picot, 3 double crochet under the same loop of

chain, repeat from * once; then in the loop of nine chain do 3 double crochet, and work from * to * four times, and in the next loop of eight chain work the same as in the first loop, then do 1 single crochet on the treble stitch of the heading to retain the scollop securely; 5 chain, 1 treble in the centre stitch of five chain at the top corner of the heading; * 5 chain, turn, 1 treble in the centre stitch of last five chain, and repeat from * till you have six square holes worked beyond the scollop to produce a further extent of "heading," then do 4 chain, turn the work, miss the stitch by the needle and do 1 single crochet in each of 3 chain stitches to form a spike; and continue the pattern from the last spike as instructed above. When required to turn a corner, work three square holes beyond a scollop, do a fourth hole angle-ways above the last, and another hole above this, then make a spike, and proceed in pattern as before.

CREMORNE LACE.

OUR model is worked with pink or any coloured silk twist or with cream cotton over ring and pear-shaped moulds, employing a fine steel crochet needle. Cover all the rings with 3 double crochet and all the pear-shaped moulds with 60 double crochet. Then proceed to work the **1st row** of the **Scollops**—Do 1 double crochet on the fourteenth stitch from the top of a pear-shaped mould, 3 chain, miss three, 1 double crochet on the next, * 3 chain, miss two, 1 double crochet on the next, repeat from * till nine loops of chain are made, then 3 chain, miss three, 1 double crochet on the next; 2 chain, take a ring mould, 1 double crochet on a stitch of it, ‖ 3 chain, miss two, 1 double crochet on the next, and repeat from ‖ five more times; then two chain, take another pear-shaped mould and work it as the first, and then a ring mould, and continue for the length the border is required to be. **2nd row**—Omit the first loop of three chain upon a pear-shaped mould, work 1 double crochet, 5 treble, and 1 double crochet all in the next loop, and the same in eight loops altogether round the pear, miss the last loop; do 1 double crochet in the second loop of the ring, 3 chain, 1 double crochet in the next loop, 7 treble on the double crochet stitch, 1 double crochet in the next

loop, 3 chain, 1 double crochet in the next loop; and repeat the same. Now for the **Heading : 1st row**—Work 1 long treble in the side of a pear-shaped mould, 5 chain, 1 double crochet on the point, 5 chain, 1 long treble on the opposite side of the mould, 1 long treble at the side of the ring mould, 5 chain, 1 double crochet in the centre stitch of the ring, 5 chain, 1 long treble on the other side of the ring, and repeat the same to the end of the row. **2nd row**—Plain double crochet. **3rd row**— 1 double crochet on the first stitch of preceding row, 5 chain, 2 long treble in the same stitch as the double crochet, miss five stitches, * 2 long treble on the next, 5 chain, 1 double crochet in the same place, 5 chain, 2 long treble in the same place, miss five stitches, and repeat from * to the end. **4th row**— Work the same as the last row, and put the groups of stitches on the groups of last row. **5th row**—Do 1 double crochet in the loop of four chain, 2 long treble stitches, 5 chain, and repeat the same. **6th row**—Work double crochet in every stitch along the top of the heading. Now complete the lace by covering little pea-shaped moulds with double crochet, close the top and fasten the pendant with 5 chain to the point at the top of the pear-shaped mould, as represented in the engraving, and secure it firmly.

PINE-APPLE BORDER.

THE border shown in the engraving is crocheted short-ways; and may be worked with ivory crochet cotton or flax thread for trimming household linen, with coloured brilliant crochet twist for decorative purposes and dress trimmings, or with silk as preferred; using in each case as fine a crochet needle as may be convenient. Make a foundation of 35 chain. **1st row**—Work 1 treble in the thirteenth chain from the needle, 3 chain, 1 treble in the next, 2 chain, miss four stitches of the foundation, 1 treble in the next, 1 chain, 1 treble in the next, 1 chain, 1 treble in the same place, 1 chain, 1 treble in the next, 1 chain, 1 treble in the next, 1 chain, 1 treble in the same place, 1 chain, 1 treble in the next; this makes a group of 7 treble stitches with 1 chain between each ; 2 chain, miss four stitches, 1 treble in the next, 3 chain, 1 treble in the next,

Cremorne Lace.

Pine-Apple Border.

2 chain, miss four stitches, 1 treble in the next, and 1 treble in the last stitch of the foundation. **2nd row**—Turn with 3 chain, do 1 treble on the treble stitch next by the needle, 2 chain, 7 treble in the loop of three chain of last row, 2 chain, 1 double crochet in the second space of one chain, 4 chain, 1 double crochet in the next space, 4 chain, 1 double crochet in the next space, 2 chain, 7 treble in the loop of three chain, 2 chain, 12 treble in the loop at the end. **3rd row**—Turn with 6 chain, do 1 double crochet in the fourth chain from the needle, 1 treble on the second stitch of the twelve treble of last row, * 4 chain, 1 double crochet in the fourth chain from the needle, miss one treble stitch, 1 treble on the next, repeat from * four times, and you will have 6 picots and 6 treble stitches ; then 2 chain, 1 treble on the first of the seven treble stitches of last row, and 1 chain and 1 treble alternately six times, that is, until 7 treble with 1 chain between each are worked over the seven treble of last row, then 2 chain, 1 treble in the centre loop of four chain, 3 chain, another treble in the same place, 2 chain, 1 treble on the first stitch of the next group of seven trebles and do 1 chain and 1 treble alternately six times, then 2 chain, 1 treble on one treble stitch, and 1 treble on the top stitch of the chain that turned. **4th row**—Turn with 3 chain, 1 treble on the treble stitch next by the needle, 2 chain, 1 double crochet in the second space of one chain, 4 chain, 1 double crochet in the next, 4 chain, 1 double crochet in the next, 2 chain, **7 treble** in the loop of three chain, 2 chain, 1 double crochet in the second of the two chain spaces, 4 chain, 1 double crochet in the next, 4 chain, 1 double crochet in the next, 4 chain, 1 double crochet in the next. **5th row**—Turn with 9 chain, do 1 treble in the centre loop of four chain of last row, 3 chain, another treble in the same place, 2 chain, 1 treble on the first of the seven treble stitches, and 1 chain and 1 treble alternately six times, then 2 chain, 1 treble in the centre loop of four chain, 3 chain, another treble in the same place, 2 chain, 1 treble on one treble stitch, and 1 treble on the top stitch of the chain that turned. Repeat from the second row for the length required. In every repetition of the second row you must, after working the 12 treble stitches, do 1 single crochet in the first picot of the preceding scollop, which will connect the scollops neatly together.

WELDON'S
PRACTICAL CROCHET,
WITH COLOURED THREADS AND MOULDS.

(EIGHTEENTH SERIES.)

New and Original Designs for Mantel Valances, Brackets, Borders for Sideboard Cloths, Piano Covers, &c.

EIGHTEEN DESIGNS.

Telegraphic Address—] "Consuelo," London.]   The Yearly Subscription to this Magazine, post free to any Part of the World, is 2s. 6d. Subscriptions are payable in advance, and may commence from any date and for any period.   [Telephone— 2745.

The Back Numbers are always in print. Nos. 1 to 85 now ready, Price 2d. each, or post free for 15s. 2d. Over 5,000 Engravings.

CROCHET WITH COLOURED THREADS AND MOULDS.
(SECOND SERIES.)

THE preliminary instructions for working this novel style of Crochet, now so fashionable for brackets, mantel valances, gipsy tables, &c., together with the fullest information regarding coloured threads, moulds, crochet needles, and other details, will be found in No. 81 of "Weldon's Practical Needlework Series," to which we beg to refer our readers, not only for the sake of these preliminary instructions, however valuable they may be to beginners, but also for the many elegant and effective original designs contained in its pages. These designs are now supplemented with a further collection of beautiful and original patterns all fully explained and illustrated; while they are worked with Messrs. Carl Mez and Söhne's Glanzgarn and Brilliant Crochet Twist, using moulds of various shapes as our illustrations clearly define. Designs worked with Brilliant Crochet Twist have all the effect of passementerie, and there is no reason why this crochet worked over moulds should not be used for dress and mantle trimmings, for it is effective and very quickly executed.

Trinity Border.

moulds, 101 small rings and 102 small triangles, in quantity of two of the latter to three of the former; a skein or two of the best gold thread, and a fine steel crochet needle. Work very closely. Take one of the **Small Ring Moulds**, and with the medium shade of blue twist work 42 double crochet round the mould, join the last stitch evenly to the first; then, holding the ring in the same position, go round again, inserting the hook to take up the one top thread of the stitches, and now work in picots, * 1 double crochet on each of 3 consecutive stitches, 5 chain, 1 single crochet on the last double crochet stitch, and repeat from * till 14 picots are done, when join round as invisibly as possible, and fasten off; which finishes the first ring. The **Second Ring** is worked in the same way till you come to the thirteenth picot, where instead of working 5 chain all at once, work 2 chain, join with a single crochet to a picot of the preceding ring, 2 chain, 1 single crochet on the last double-crochet stitch, 3 double crochet on three consecutive stitches, 2 chain, join with a single crochet to the next picot of the preceding ring, 2 chain, 1 single crochet on the last double-crochet stitch, and join and fasten off. A straight line of rings worked in this manner with the medium shade of blue is arranged to run the whole length of the border. The **Third Ring**, which forms the point of the scollop and comes intermediately under two of the upper rings, is crocheted with the lightest shade of blue, working as directed above until you come to the tenth picot, where, as well as at the eleventh picot, you will join to two picots in the ring on the right-hand side above, work the twelfth picot

TRINITY BORDER

THE engraving shows a border prettily worked in a design of rings and triangles, with Brilliant crochet twist in three shades of blue; it is not at all difficult of execution, and is well suited for dress and mantle trimmings. If any other colour is preferred to blue it can of course be substituted, as this Brilliant crochet twist is made in many shades of every colour. Or a stylish trimming can be made by using black silk. To work according to model procure Brilliant crochet twist Nos. 52 light blue, 56 medium, and 57 dark blue;

with 5 chain as usual, and join the thirteenth and fourteenth picots to two picots in the ring on the left-hand side above; the position of the rings and the joining of the same are plainly set forth in the engraving. For the **Triangles** use the darkest shade of twist, and work 70 double crochet closely over the mould, and join evenly; a second round is worked in picots, inserting the hook to take up the front and top threads of the stitches of the first round, begin at the top right-hand corner of the triangle with 5 double crochet *exactly* at the corner, then a picot (of 5 chain) and 3 double crochet alternately till 7 picots are made along the top of the triangle, do 5 double crochet at the corner to match the first corner, and continue with a picot and a double crochet till 15 picots are formulated to reach round the triangle to the corner where you commenced, and where you are now to fasten off; with the sixth and seventh of these picots you must join to picots of the ring to the left, the eighth picot stands free at the lowest point of the triangle, and the ninth and tenth picots must join to picots of the ring to the right. Succeeding triangles are all worked in the same manner, but are joined by the fourteenth and fifteenth picots to corresponding picots of the previous triangles. For the **Heading**— **1st row**—With gold thread. Work 1 chain and 1 treble alternately the whole way along the top of the border; you will thus get a treble stitch in each of the seven picots on the upper side of the triangles. **2nd row**—With medium blue twist—Work 1 treble in the space of one chain of previous row, 2 chain, and repeat. **3rd row**—With lightest shade of blue twist, 2 double crochet under the chain of preceding row, 4 chain, 1 single crochet in the last

Pendulum Border.

double-crochet stitch (to form a picot), and repeat the same to the end. You now will finish off the border by embellishing the interior of the triangles with open diamond darning, and the rings with spiders, worked with gold thread in embroidery stitches. The **Pendants** consist of double crochet worked over small pea-shaped moulds; you begin with 3 chain and join round, and proceed in double crochet, increasing in each round to the size of the mould, put the mould in the crochet, the wrong side of the work outside, continue it to fit the mould, contracting the top as needful, and close up with a loop of chain to attach the pendant in position. The pendants that hang from the point of each scollop are worked with medium shade of blue, and those between the scollops with the lightest shade of blue twist.

PENDULUM BORDER.

THIS border may be employed for dress trimming, made in whatever shade of Brilliant Crochet Twist best harmonises with the material on which the trimming is to be placed; No. 78, a pretty olive-green, is used for our example, and the moulds are No. 110 pear shaped, a little gold thread is required, and a fine steel crochet needle. The moulds are covered with double crochet, doing 68 stitches, and join and fasten off. The two "ears" at the top of the mould are now to be added,—join by a single crochet to the ninth stitch to the left from the top of the mould, do 9 chain, 1 single crochet to the right in the seventh stitch above the first single crochet, then 1 double crochet, 20 treble, 1 double crochet, all in the loop of nine chain, and join neatly and fasten off. Join by a single crochet to the second stitch to the right from the top of the mould, do 9 chain, 1 single crochet in the seventh stitch further to the right, then 1 double crochet, 17 treble in the loop of chain, join to a treble stitch of the first "ear" (above the point of the mould) 3 more treble, 1 double crochet, and fasten off. Work another mould in the same manner. A small ring is required to fill the space between the "ears" of the two moulds; this is begun with 6 chain, unite in a circle, do 3 chain to stand for a treble, and work 11 treble in the circle, join to a treble stitch of one of the ears, 11 more treble in the circle, join to a treble stitch of the opposite ear, unite the ring, and fasten off. Continue thus for the length the border is desired to be. For the **Edge**—Work 1 double crochet on a treble stitch of the ear, 5 chain, 1 double crochet on the double crochet just worked (forming a picot), 1 treble on the second double crochet stitch of the mould, * 5 chain, 1 double crochet on the treble stitch last worked, miss one stitch of the mould, 1 treble on the next, repeat from * till 7 treble are worked on the mould, then do a treble instead of a double crochet, and miss two stitches of the mould till 7 more

treble are worked on the mould, then again as at first for 7 treble more, when make a picot as usual and do 1 treble on the ear, 1 chain, 1 treble on the centre stitch of the little ring, 1 chain, 1 treble on the next ear, a picot, and 1 treble on the second stitch of the next mould, and proceed in the same manner for the length of the border. Thread a needle with gold twist and embroider "a spider" in the centre of every mould; this is done on the wrong side of the work by taking long stitches from side to side across the open space. When doing the last stitch sew it once or twice over the other stitches in the centre of the mould to confine the stitches together as will be understood by consulting the engraving. For the **Heading**—1st row—With gold thread—Work 4 chain, 1 treble on the first ear on the right-hand side of the border, 4 chain, thread over the needle, insert the hook in the third treble to the right of the joining of the ears and draw the thread through, thread over the needle and draw through 2 stitches on the needle, thread over the needle, insert the hook in the third treble of the next ear and draw the thread through, thread over the needle and draw through 2 stitches on the needle, thread over the needle and draw through 3 stitches on the needle, 4 chain, 1 treble on the ear, 4 chain, 1 double crochet on the centre stitch of the little circle, and repeat the same. **2nd row**—With Brilliant Crochet Twist—Work 1 treble in the first chain stitch on the right-hand side, * 2 chain, miss two, 1 treble in the next, and repeat from * to the end of the row. **3rd row**— Resume on the right-hand side—Do 2 double crochet below the two chain of last row, 4 chain, 1 double crochet on the double crochet last worked, and repeat thus in double crochet and picots of chain to the end of the row. For the **Drops**—Procure small pea moulds to solidify the drops; work 4 chain, join round, proceed in double crochet round and round to the shape of the pea that is to be enclosed within the crochet, draw the last round of double crochet closely over the pea, make 3 chain, join to the centre picot on a pear-shaped mould, 3 chain, and break off, and sew the end of the crochet twist firmly on the drop.

PINE-CRESTED BORDER.

THIS charming little border is worked in the original with Nos. 240 and 247 shades of crushed strawberry, and No. 21 art green Brilliant crochet twist combined with gold thread and copper-coloured iridescent metallic thread over moulds 128 tiny rings, 127 small pear shapes, 129 small fan shapes, and 132 pines. Begin with the **Three Tiny Rings** at the top of the border; these are worked with the lightest shade of crushed strawberry, doing 24 double crochet, and join and fasten off; reverse the position of the moulds, and margin the

Pine-Crested Border.

edge of each with copper-coloured thread, taking up the two top threads of the stitches of the preceding round with single crochet stitches; sew the three rings together with the ends of the metallic thread, and pass it also two or three times over the surface of the crochet from ring to ring. Next make two small pear-shaped moulds to place below the rings, work with the darkest shade of strawberry and edge with copper thread; place the points of the moulds together, and sew them to each other and to the lowest of the three tiny rings. The **Fan** is crocheted with green twist, working as many double crochet stitches as the mould will conveniently hold; it then is edged with gold thread in single crochet, and the centre is embroidered with perpendicular stitches reaching from the top to the bottom of the fan, with a little crossway darning, as you will best understand by a study of the engraving, where the stitches are all very clearly visible. Now fashion the **Scollop** by working five small pear-shaped moulds with a covering of dark strawberry double-crochet stitches, and as you join each and fasten off sew it in its position to the back of the fan in a kind of semi-circle; edge the scollop with copper-coloured iridescent thread, thus—Begin on the first small mould close by the fan, and do single crochet stitches in the usual manner till you reach the centre of the bottom of mould and make a picot, 6 chain, 1 single crochet in next stitch, 6 chain, 1 single crochet in the next, 6 chain, and single crochet half way down the side of the mould, then stop and go hence to edge half a side of the next mould, here also do a picot at the top, and go half way down the side, and proceed till you finish the last small pear shape to correspond with the first, and fasten off. A **Pine-shaped Mould** is placed within every scollop; it is worked with green double crochet till quite covered with stitches, taking care to round the head nicely, then reverse the work and margin the edge with gold thread, fill the centre with a series of herringbone stitches worked from side to side, and attach it neatly to the one small ring on the right-hand side of the top of the border and to the four nearest adjoining pear-shaped moulds next adjacent. For the **Heading—1st row**—With green crochet twist—Do 4 chain, 3 long treble near the top of a pine, 10 chain, 1 single crochet at the

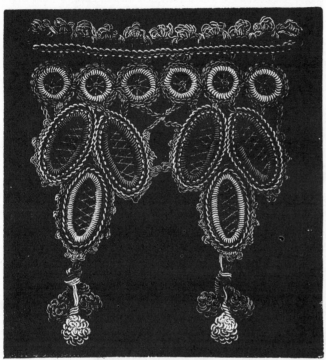

Montpellier Border.

back of a ring, 6 chain, 1 single crochet at the back of the next ring, 16 chain to reach the top of the next pine, where work 3 long treble as before, and continue to the end of the row. **2nd row**—Still with green, and the work the right side towards you—Do double crochet in every stitch of the preceding row. **3rd row**—Work with the lightest shade of crushed strawberry,—4 double crochet, * 5 chain, 1 single crochet on the last double crochet stitch, 5 double crochet on consecutive stitches, and repeat from *, a picot and 5 double crochet alternately to the end.

MONTPELLIER BORDER.

HERE is a particularly elegant design for a border worked with art green and terra-cotta Original Glanzgarn, numbered 716 and 704 respectively, and the combination of colour is very pleasing to look upon. Procure with the Glanzgarn an assortment of moulds, 101 small rings, and 134 oval, in equal numbers of each, and a skein or two of gold thread. Take first the **Oval Moulds.** Work two of these with a covering of green double crochet, about 40 stitches on the mould, and then, reversing the position, go round the margin with terra cotton in single crochet, working into the one back thread of the green stitches; fasten both colours off neatly. For the third oval use terra cotton for covering and green for margining. Sew the three ovals in the position shown in the engraving by a stitch or two on the wrong side of the work; these form one scollop. Upon the **Ring-shaped Moulds** work with terra-cotta Glanzgarn about 24 or more double crochet stitches, join each ring to its predecessor in the process of working this double crochet, and so get them all in a straight line one with the other for the entire length to which you make your scollops. Go round every ring with a margin of gold thread, taking the hook right through the work below the front thread of the stitches; as you go thus round the rings catch by a chain stitch and a double crochet into the ovals in two places on each oval as is shown in the engraving. Thread a crewel needle with gold thread and embroider a spider in the centre of each ring. For the **Heading—1st row**—With green Glanzgarn, and holding the right side of the border towards you,—Do 5 chain, 2 double crochet in the centre stitch at the top of the ring, and repeat the same all along, ending with 5 chain and break off. **2nd row**—With terra cotton,—on the reverse side of last row, do single crochet into the back threads of the stitches. **3rd row**—With green—and the border the wrong side towards you,—2 double crochet in one stitch of the preceding row, 2 chain, miss two, and repeat the

same to the end. **4th row**—With gold thread, and the border the right side towards you—1 double crochet in a stitch of last row, * 4 chain, another double crochet in the same place, repeat from * till three loops of chain and 4 double-crochet stitches are worked, then 2 chain, miss two stitches, and repeat the picot, and continue in the same manner to the end of the row. For the **Scollops** to be margined with picots in gold—Work 1 double crochet in the lower part of a ring, 4 chain, 1 double crochet on the edge of an oval, 3 chain, 2 single crochet in consecutive stitches of the oval, and continue all round the three ovals in these little picots of chain and single crochet, till you get close to rings on opposite side of the scollop, then 4 chain, 1 treble on the ring, and also 1 treble on the next ring, whence do 4 chain as at the beginning of the first scollop, and proceed in just the same manner, only joining the picot at the bottom of the top oval to its predecessor. For the **Tassels**—These are made over beads, working a little case of double crochet in which the bead can be inserted, two beads are covered with green and one with terra-cotta Glanzgarn; the ends of the threads (6 ends) are sewn at the back of the work, as seen in the engraving, after tying a knot to keep all the threads closely together.

UTRECHT MEDALLION.

AN eight-sided medallion or star can be turned to account for an endless variety of purposes, and affords considerable scope for ingenuity in producing the most charming result with a moderate amount of labour. The example which forms the subject of the present description is a particularly tasteful and at the same time simple medallion crocheted with Glanzgarn, 701 cream, 704 terra cotta, and 742 sage green, and requiring four 124 oval moulds and eight 106 heart-shaped moulds, also a skein of gold thread. Or, 702 light fawn, 725 art green, and 712 cherry, are a pretty combination. Begin working upon one of the four **Oval Moulds** that compose the centre of the medallion, and with terra-cotta Glanzgarn do 5 double crochet, 4 chain, 1 single crochet on the last double crochet (this makes a picot), 3 double crochet, a picot, 3 double crochet, a picot, 5 double crochet, *all* along one side of the mould; a picot at the tip; 5 double crochet, a picot, 3 double crochet, a picot, 3 double crochet, a picot, 5 double crochet along the opposite side; then a picot at the opposite tip, and fasten off. Work another oval in a similar manner till you get to the place where the last picot should be formed, and there instead of working a picot in the regular way do 2 chain, join with a single crochet to the first

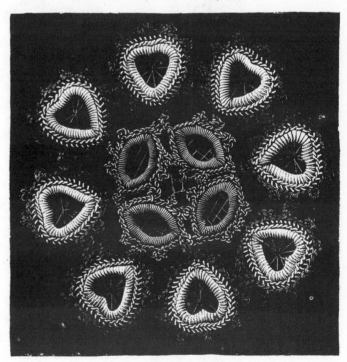

Utrecht Medallion.

picot of the first oval, 2 chain, 1 single crochet on the last double-crochet stitch, 5 double crochet, a picot, and fasten off. The third oval is joined in like manner to the second oval. And the fourth oval is joined by the fifth picot to the first oval as well as by the seventh picot to the third oval; and thus the centre of the medallion will appear as represented in the engraving. Now for the **Heart-shaped Moulds**—Use cream Glanzgarn to work 34 double crochet upon a mould, beginning and ending at the point, and fasten off; work round the same mould again with green Glanzgarn, keeping the right side of the crochet towards you and taking up the one top thread of the stitches, 4 double crochet, 4 chain, 1 single crochet on the last double crochet stitch (for a picot), 3 double crochet, a picot, 3 double crochet, a picot, 3 double crochet, a picot, 4 double crochet, a picot (this last picot should come exactly over the centre of the top of the heart), 4 double crochet, a picot, 3 double crochet, a picot, 3 double crochet, a picot, 3 double crochet, a picot, 4 double crochet, 2 chain, 1 single crochet in the centre picot along the side of one of the ovals, 2 chain, 1 single crochet in the last double crochet, and join evenly to the first double crochet stitch, and fasten off. Proceed with another heart similar to the one just worked, but join the second picot to the eighth picot (the next picot but one to the point) of the first heart, and join the last picot to the *two* picots that lie close together from the tips of two adjacent ovals. Continue working hearts, joining each successive heart to the preceding and also to the ovals, till the medallion is complete, as will clearly be seen by consulting the engraving. Then for the gold thread embellishment, do first of all a little square of gold stitches in the very centre of the medallion, and afterwards fill the ovals with open diamond net-work, and embroider the hearts with "spiders."

HANDSOME BORDER FOR BRACKET OR MANTEL VALANCE.

THIS is a bold and important-looking design for a border measuring 10

join, make 1 chain to carry the Glanzgarn to the outer margin, and turn the work, and do double crochet in the one back thread of each cream-coloured stitch; join firmly at the top of the heart, turn the work to the right side, work a single crochet or two to get back upon the inner rim, pass the Glanzgarn 18 times round the needle to make a long loose rice stitch, glanzgarn over the needle and draw through the coil, which coil is to hang like a loop dependent from the top of the heart, as see engraving; break off, and sew the end securely at the back of the work. Now with gold thread double, that is, using from two balls at the same time, and having the right side of the heart towards you, begin at the top, and work single crochet in the back thread of the row of cream-coloured stitches, and at intervals of generally three but sometimes four stitches insert the hook through the work from the back to the front between the two double-crochet rounds, catch it in a top thread of the eau de nil round, and draw the gold thread right through. You will find this procedure will make a loop stretching across the vacant space between the moulds and will apparently hold the two hearts together; make five loops on each side and one at the point of the hearts, as see in the

Handsome Border for Bracket or Mantel Valance.

inches in depth. Our model is executed with Glanzgarn in four colours, 701 cream, 701 terra cotta, 739 eau de nil, and 742 sage green; the moulds are 209 double hearts, of which six are employed to make a scollop, and 240 rings which are utilised merely for the heading; a few skeins of gold thread must be procured, and also a piece of gold braid. Commence with the **Centre Heart** of the three at the top of the scollop; this is crocheted with cream and eau de nil. With the cream Glanzgarn work 46 compound double crochet stitches, beginning and ending at the top of the mould,—you have a stitch on the needle, insert the hook below the rim of the mould and draw the Glanzgarn through, glanzgarn over the needle and draw through one stitch on the needle, insert the hook again in the mould and draw the Glanzgarn through, glanzgarn over the needle and draw through three stitches on the needle—this is one compound stitch; they all are made in the same way, and produce a thicker and slightly taller stitch than simple double crochet; join evenly on the completion of the round, and fasten off. Take eau de nil, and, beginning at the top, work 31 plain double-crochet stitches upon the inner rim of the heart,

engraving. On each side of this central heart is a heart worked with cream and sage green. Immediately below these you will see two hearts which are both crocheted with cream and terra-cotta. And the scollop is brought to a point by one heart worked like the first with cream and eau de nil. They all are sewn in position with a needle and cotton, and the heading when finished is sewn along the top. For the **Heading**—Use the ring moulds and sage-green Glanzgarn, and work 28 double-crochet stitches round the ring, and join evenly; upon these stitches do an edging of rice-stitches, 14 coils in each stitch, and missing one double crochet as you work 1 chain between each rice stitch, there will be 14 rice stitches in the round; join evenly on its completion. These rings are sewn together in a straight line, and so form the heading; gold braid is passed along the back, and drawn to the front through the centre of each ring in similitude of a fan; it is held in place by a stitch passing through the crochet to the top and bottom of the braid. Tassels made of clusters of rice stitches surround the scollop in the manner shown in the engraving.

ROSETTE BORDER FOR VALANCES AND FURNITURE TRIMMING.

A VERY pretty border is crocheted in rosettes of rice stitch, using Original Glanzgarn of two nicely contrasting colours; dark art green, No. 726, and light terra-cotta, No. 704, is an excellent combination, as also is green, No. 726, and tabac, No. 736, or olive-brown, No. 741, and shrimp-pink, No. 744. The rosettes are arranged three in a group, triangular fashion, to form a scollop, and they will keep in shape without the assistance of stiff moulds. Besides the Glanzgarn you will require one or two skeins of gold thread, and a piece of ½-inch wide gold braid, a medium-sized steel crochet needle, with the stem of equal thickness all the way up, and another steel crochet needle with similar hook, but the stem increasing in thickness from the hook upwards; this latter is conveniently employed for working the rice stitches. Commence a **Rosette** with terra-cotta Glanzgarn with 26 chain, and join round; the circle should measure 1½ inches in diameter; work 52 double crochet round the circle, and join evenly. **2nd round**—Still with terra-cotta,—Do 3 chain, 1 rice stitch of 18 coils on the first double-crochet stitch of last round, taking up the front and top threads, * 1 chain, miss one stitch, 1 rice stitch of 18 coils on the next,

of 10 coils in the next, 1 chain, miss one, 1 treble in the next, and repeat from *. **2nd row**—Turn the work, and do double crochet in the back thread of every stitch all round the heading. Now the rosettes have to be joined with a needle and cotton in the position shown in the engraving; the two top rosettes of a scollop are sewn to the heading, allowing for about half an inch of space to be left between these rosettes, and the third rosette is sewn intermediately below to form a point to the scollop. About two inches or rather more of space is left between the scollops. The space in the centre of the scollop is filled with a crochet chain worked with gold thread double,—Begin with a single crochet at the back of the heading over the rosette to the left, do 9 chain, 1 double crochet in the side of the rosette to the right, 7 chain, 1 double crochet in the side of the rosette to the left, 7 chain, 1 double crochet lower down the rosette to the right, 7 chain, 1 double crochet lower down the rosette to the left, 10 chain, 1 double crochet in the rosette to the right just over the place where this rosette is sewn to the third rosette, 7 or 8 double crochet along the top of the rice stitches of the third rosette, 1 double crochet in the rosette to the left just over the place where this rosette is sewn to the third rosette, 10 chain, cross the previous ten chain and work 1 double crochet in the rosette to the right, 7 chain, cross the previous seven chain, and work a

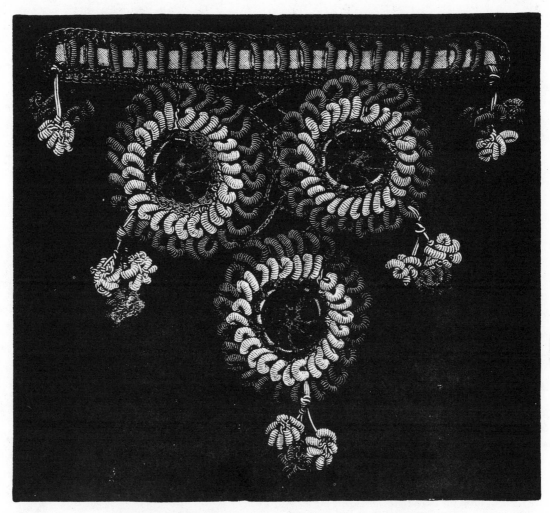

Rosette Border for Valances and Furniture Trimming.

repeat from *, and at the end of the round join to the top stitch of chain with which the round began, and fasten off. **3rd round**—With green Glanzgarn,—Work 1 rice stitch of 20 coils in the one loose thread between the rice stitches of the preceding round, 1 chain, and continue the same; and join at the end of the round, and fasten off. Now take the gold thread, which previously should have been wound in two balls, and crocheting from both balls together make an open-work circle to go in the centre of the rosette,—do 8 chain, join in a circle; do 9 chain, 1 treble in the fifth chain from the needle, 1 long treble (thread twice round the needle) in the circle, * 4 chain, 1 treble on the long treble stitch to make a picot, 1 long treble in the circle, and repeat from * till you have made 10 picots, and join to the fifth stitch of the chain by the first picot, and fasten off; thread a needleful of gold thread, and tack the open-work circle within the rosette by laying the treble stitches and picots upon the round of double-crochet stitches; this completes one rosette. Make as many rosettes as you consider necessary for the length of your border, calculating three for each scollop. Then proceed to the **Heading**, for which use green Glanzgarn, making a chain the length required. **1st row**—Work 1 treble in the sixth chain from the needle, * 1 chain, miss 1 stitch, 1 rice stitch

double crochet in the rosette to the left, 7 chain, again cross and do a double crochet in the rosette to the right, 7 chain, once again cross and work a double crochet near the top of the rosette to the left, then 9 chain, and crossing the first nine chain join with a single crochet in the back of the heading about an inch to the right of the place where the chain commenced, and fasten off; the double-crochet stitches, five on each rosette, should be exactly opposite each other, and the chain will form a kind of diamond trellis between the rosettes. The **Tassels** consist of three bunches of 6 long loose rice stitches; begin and finish each bunch with a short length of Glanzgarn and tie these ends together in a knot over the bunch, then knot all the six threads together a little distance above, and carry them on from the front to the back through the crochet where the tassel is to hang, and sew securely. Those tassels that depend from the rosettes comprise two bunches of terra-cotta and one bunch of green rice stitches, while the tassels on the heading between the scollops are of reverse colouring. The gold braid is run in the open row of the heading, the rice stitches come on the front of the braid, and the treble stitches lie at the back.

SAXON MEDALLION.

A SIMPLE eight-sided medallion is crocheted with Glanzgarn over stiff moulds; and pretty chair-backs, cushion centres, and other useful things may be quickly and easily made by joining several of these together and laying them on a background of cloth or satin. Procure shades 701 cream, 721 apricot, and 752 electric blue, original Glanzgarn; four 124 oval moulds, four 240 rings, and four 119 trefoil moulds; and a skein of gold thread. Commence with cream Glanzgarn on one of **Oval Moulds**, work 3 double crochet, 3 chain, 1 single crochet in the last double-crochet stitch to make a picot, and repeat the same till you have made 12 groups of double crochet and 12 picots, when join evenly to the first stitch, and fasten off. Work 3 more ovals in the same way, but stop when you get to the twelfth picot of the fourth oval, and instead work 3 chain, * 1 single crochet in the top picot of one of the other moulds, 1 chain, 1 single crochet in the second stitch of the chain you have just done, 1 chain, repeat from * twice, when you will find all four of the ovals nicely joined together, do 1 chain, unite by a single crochet to the last double-crochet on the fourth mould, and join evenly, and fasten off. For the **Trefoils** use apricot Glanzgarn, and work in double crochet and picots in the same manner as you worked the ovals, get if possible 6 picots on each section of the trefoil, with the second picot join to the second picot from the top of the oval to the right, and with the last picot but one (i.e., the seventeenth picot presumably) join to the second picot from the top of the oval to the left; join the last double-crochet stitch to the first, then for the stem (which may be cut off the mould as crochet stitches are sufficient) do 7 chain, join with a single crochet to the second picot of the oval (counting from the connec-

Saxon Medallion.

tion in the centre of the medallion), do 1 chain, 1 double crochet in the fifth stitch of the seven chain, 1 chain, join to the second picot of the next adjoining oval, 1 chain, 1 single crochet on each of four chain stitches up the stem, and join firmly to the trefoil. The other three trefoils are worked to correspond, each occupying their allotted position as will be understood by consulting the engraving. The **Four Rings** are covered with electric blue, doing 11 groups of 3 double crochet and 11 picots in the round; with the seventh picot join to a picot of the trefoil to the left, with the ninth picot join to the picot at the top of an oval, and with the eleventh picot join to a picot of the trefoil to the right, then unite the ring and fasten off. Now complete the medallion by embroidering the centres of the ovals and trefoils with a neat close net-work darning of gold thread, and fill the centres of the rings with gold spiders.

ANTIMACASSAR IN VIENNESE EMBROIDERY.

THIS illustration shows a new and most charming embroidery upon net, worked with Carl Mez and Söhne's Brilliant Embroidery Thread, in delicate shades of pink, pale blue, maize, and brown. The design is woven in a fine solid ground upon net, and entirely outlined with a fine gold cord, which, being woven in the actual material, is wonderfully durable, and is of the best gold, warranted to clean or even wash perfectly, and always retain its rich colour. The work is supplied ready commenced and with materials to finish, while the stitches are most simple, being nothing more nor less than satin and

stem stitches, varied with feather and herringbone stitches. This effective work has all the delicacy and delightful colouring of Eastern embroidery, and is admirably suited to antimacassars, small table covers, piano tops, drawing-room mats, duchesse table-cloths, mats, &c. We are sure our readers will be charmed with this latest novelty in fancy work, for it is so quickly done, and so effective and lasting. For embroidery purposes our readers will find Carl Mez and Söhne's Brilliant Embroidery Thread equal, we may say, to silk in

Antimacassar

effect, for it has a beautiful lustre and silky finish, and can be had in about 300 shades, each one of which is numbered, so that on requiring any more of one colour, the number only has to be quoted, and the exact tint is always in stock. Brilliant Embroidery Thread also crochets nicely into mats, sponge bags, dress trimmings, &c., and, as before said, it is admirably suited to every kind of embroidery on flannel, silk, material, velvet, or velveteen. All colours are guaranteed fast and warranted to wash perfectly.

FIVE-POINTED STAR.

THE engraving shows a pretty five-pointed star crocheted with Original Glanzgarn in two nicely contrasting artistic colours, 710 ivory and 722 crushed strawberry, and the moulds required are one 101 small ring, five 124 ovals, and five 119 trefoils. Procure also a skein of gold twist. Use a medium-sized steel crochet needle. Commence with the **Small Ring** which forms

crochet on the last double-crochet stitch, and join by a single crochet to the beginning of the mould, and fasten off. Work the other four ovals in exactly the same manner, joining each to the small ring at intervals of four stitches; but these ovals are *not* joined one to the other. Now upon a **Trefoil Mould** with terra-cotta Glanzgarn, beginning in the centre of the top of the mould, work 7 double crochet, 1 chain, join by a single crochet to the fourth double crochet from the top of an oval, 1 chain, 3 double crochet, 4 chain, 1 single crochet on the last double crochet (this makes a picot), 3 double crochet, a picot, 3 double crochet, a picot, 3 double crochet, all this on the first section of the trefoil; then on the second or middle section of the trefoil do 5 groups of 3 double crochet with 4 picots intermediate; and on the last section work 3 double crochet and a picot alternately three times, 3 double crochet, 1 chain, join with a single crochet to the fourth stitch from the top of the adjacent oval, 1 chain, 7 double crochet, join to the first double crochet of the trefoil, do 7 chain, join with a single crochet to the sixth stitch further down the same oval, do single crochet in 2 of the chain stitches, 1 chain, join with a single crochet to the fifth stitch lower on the oval to the right (the one on which the first join was made), 1 single crochet on each chain stitch up to the trefoil, and there join and fasten off. Work four more trefoils in the same manner. The little stiff stem which is attached to the trefoil moulds is to be cut off before commencing the work, as its place is taken by the single crochet stitches that are described above. The star is thus complete with only the exception of the lace stitches, which you now proceed to work with gold thread and a crewel needle, taking long stitches from side to side across the open centres of the several moulds, and with the last stitch darn a spot in the middle where the gold threads cross each other.

nnese Embroidery.

Five-Pointed Star.

SQUARE IN ARABESQUE STYLE.

HERE is a light and elegant square to use as a centre for a cushion, or for any purpose for which a square may be desired. It measures about nine inches across from side to side. The various sections are all worked separately and sewn together with a needle and thread. Procure Brilliant crochet twist Nos. 240 and 247, two shades of crushed strawberry, and 234, a pretty bright ash green; moulds fifty-six 128 tiny rings, eight 131 slightly larger rings, sixty-eight 127 tiny pear-shaped, and sixteen 125 larger pear-shaped; also a skein of copper-coloured iridescent metallic thread, and a fine steel crochet needle. The whole of the fifty-six **Tiny Rings** are to be covered with double crochet worked with green twist, getting about 24 stitches, more or less, in the circle, join the last stitch to the first when the circle is full, and fasten off neatly; turn the mould the reverse side up, and with metallic thread, and always inserting the hook to take the two top threads of the green stitches, margin the edge with single crochet, and join this evenly and fasten off; the side on which the margin is crocheted is the right side of the work. These tiny rings are the only moulds that are elaborated with a margin of metallic thread; all the other moulds are simply worked with double crochet and then are finished, and remember the reverse side of the double crochet is in this pattern considered to be the right side of the work. Now take four 127 moulds, work two with light and two with dark strawberry twist, arrange them **like a star,** two dark ones opposite each other and two light ones opposite each other, stitch the points slightly together, and ornament the centre by winding iridescent thread from mould to mould and across and across; this star is practically the **Centre of the Square.** Round it you may now sew eight of the tiny rings, i.e., two on the top of each pear-shaped section, almost close

the centre of the star, and on it with terra-cotta Glanzgarn work 20 double crochet stitches, join quite evenly the last stitch to the first, and fasten off invisibly. Take ivory Glanzgarn, and along one side of an **Oval Mould** work 15 double crochet, at the tip do 1 chain, unite by a single crochet to a stitch of the small ring, taking up the front and top threads, 1 chain, 1 single crochet on the last ivory double-crochet stitch, 15 double crochet along the other side of the mould, and at the top do 3 chain, 1 single together and yet not quite touching each other; next cover four 127 moulds with the lightest shade of strawberry, and sew these by their widest end between the pairs of tiny rings; their points will be turned towards the outside of the square, and on these points may be sewn, endways, a block of four tiny rings that have previously been joined closely one to the other in a kind of lozenge-shaped medallion; the progress of the work can be clearly seen by studying the engraving. Now make **Four Rosettes**, consisting each of eight small pear-shaped moulds worked in alternate shades of crushed strawberry, round a 131 green mould; the points of the pear-shaped moulds are stitched to the green ring by their own working threads, then the iridescent thread is wound from the centre of the ring through the open spaces of the moulds, and being caught together by lace stitches in the ring, a pretty and uncommon effect is attained. Attach the rosettes to each pair of tiny rings in the position they hold in the engraving, and also let them be connected to the green medallions on either side by one or two loose stitches made with iridescent thread. For the **Corners**—Make four square medallions, consisting each of a 131 ring mould covered with green twist, round which four large pear-shaped moulds worked with dark strawberry and four small pear-shaped moulds worked with light strawberry are alternately grouped; the centre of this medallion is decorated to correspond with the centre of the rosettes, and the large pear-shaped moulds have their centres filled with open diamond net-work; sew a

forty 125 larger pear-shaped, four 109 still larger pear-shaped, four 110 largest pear-shaped, and four 106 hearts; also one or two skeins of gold thread, and a fine steel crochet needle. Commence for the centre of the square with the four 109 **Pear-shaped Moulds**, and, using green crochet twist, work closely and evenly over each of these moulds, doing as many double-crochet stitches as will sit together and completely cover the rim; it probably may take 60 stitches or thereabouts; the exact number will necessarily vary by the skill of the worker, and is not particular if only the mould be properly covered. Unite the last stitch carefully to the first, and fasten off green; turn the work the reverse side up, and with gold thread, and always inserting the hook to pick up the two top threads of the previous stitches, margin the edge with a line of gold single crochet, and join this evenly and fasten off; the side on which the gold margin is crocheted is the right side of the work. Take four 127 tiny pear-shaped moulds and cover them with double crochet with gold thread, break off with a long end after joining round, thread the end through a crewel needle, and placing a tiny gold mould (with the reverse side of its crochet to the front) in the centre of a larger green mould, sew herringbone stitches across from one to the other, on the wrong side of the work, to retain the two in relative position one to the other; and when this is accomplished arrange the four green moulds as you see them in the engraving and join them neatly by a few stitches at the back of the work. Next do a **Corner**—cover

Square in Arabesque Style.

corner of a medallion to a rosette and arrange blocks of four tiny rings on each side, and when you have done four groups of three small pear-shaped moulds with shades of crushed strawberry, and affixed them between the blocks of tiny rings as shown in the engraving, the square will be finished.

HANDSOME SQUARE OR SMALL MAT WORKED IN TWO COLOURS.

OUR engraving represents a specially handsome square for the centre of a small fancy table cover, or for the centre of a cushion; it is worked in only two colours of Brilliant crochet twist, but these are so harmonious and glossy-looking and blend together so charmingly with a plentiful use of gold Japanese thread, that nothing more effective can be imagined. The various sections composing the square are for the most part sewn together with a needle and cotton after the actual crocheting is accomplished, though in some places they are united in the course of the work, as will be explained below. The requirements are Brilliant crochet twist, No. 77 art green, and No. 141 golden brown; a supply of moulds, twelve 128 tiny rings, forty-four 127 tiny pear-shaped,

two 125 moulds with brown and two with green, also one 110 mould with green, working as described above, and of course edging each with gold thread; break off the gold thread with an end, with which work herringbone stitches from side to side of the moulds to fill the open spaces in the centres; group these five sections together something in the form of a pansy, the largest mould in the centre at the top, a green one on each side below, and a brown one on each side below these, with all their points nearly meeting, and sew each to the other by a stitch or two a little above the points, then sew the two brown sections over the point of one of the central green sections, and carry a few long gold threads in a decorative way from join to join and over the points of the two brown sections, making all the long threads meet at the junction of the five sections. Work three 125 moulds with golden brown, and in edging these stop when you get a little further than half way down the second side of the first mould, go hence and edge the upper half (in point of fact rather *more* than the actual half) of the second mould, then go to the corresponding side of the third mould and finish to the point of that, join slightly to the point of the first mould, and break off with an end to embroider herringbone stitch inside each mould, also to carry ornamental threads from the points upwards over the stitch that retains the moulds together; work three more 125 moulds to correspond; sew these on each side the large green mould and likewise to the smaller green moulds as represented in the engraving. Take five 127 moulds and with brown twist work about 30 double crochet upon each; begin the gold margin in the usual manner and when you get to the top of the first mould do a picot, thus, 5 chain, 1 single crochet on the last single crochet stitch, 3 chain, join to a gold stitch of the first brown mould to the right of corner, 3 chain, 1 single crochet again where last single crochet is worked, 5 chain, another single crochet in the same place; carry the margining half way down the side of the mould, then stop and go hence to edge half a side of the next mould, at the top do 3 chain, join to a gold stitch of the third brown mould to the right, 2 chain, 1 single crochet on the last single crochet stitch, 5 chain, another single crochet in the same place, 5 chain, one more single crochet in the same place, resume the margining till you get half way down the side of the mould; go thence upon the third mould, work a picot of three loops on the top of this, and margin half way up the fifth mould; margin half way up the fourth mould, work a picot at the top and in the third loop, join to a gold stitch of the uppermost brown mould to the left, continue half way down the side; thence go half way up the fifth mould, and in the centre loop at the top of this join to the lower of the brown moulds to the left, then margin onwards to the point, and break off with a long end of gold thread; sew the first and last moulds of the group to the top of the large green mould by a slight stitch or two, and use the end of gold thread to ornament the junction of the five brown points: this completes one corner; and the other

SQUARE BLOCK BORDER.

THIS pretty border is worked with the new shaded Glanzgarn, No. 760, in exquisite tints ranging through pale art greens and light strawberry pinks, and as the required moulds are all the same square shape, No. 236, and are simply sewn together after the crochet is accomplished, there is no difficulty whatever in the execution of the pattern. The squares are margined, and also filled in with sparkling gold thread, and a gold braid is run through the open stitches in the heading. Take the **first Square Mould,** and with Glanzgarn cover the surface full of double-crochet stitches; the exact number is immaterial so long as the mould is well covered, probably there will be 58 or 60 double crochet, then join evenly the last stitch to the first, and fasten off. Work with gold thread a line of single crochet, inserting the hook to take up the one top thread of the double-crochet stitches, join evenly, and break off with an end of 7 or 8 inches, which thread into a crewel needle, slip under the Glanzgarn to the centre of the mould, whence darn from side to side of the centre, letting all the long stitches cross one another in the centre of the space, like a spider in drawn thread embroidery, darn once or twice in the centre of the threads, and fasten off neatly. Work two more squares in the same manner. Sew the third square angle-ways against the other two squares as you see the representation in the engraving. This forms one point or scollop. The

Handsome Square or Small Mat Worked in Two Colours.

three corners must be fashioned to correspond. Next work the twelve **tiny Rings** with brown double crochet, and edge them gold, and work a gold spider in the centre of each; these go in groups of threes. You may unite the second to the first and the third to the second in triangular form in process of working the gold edge, or you may sew them together when you sew each group in its place round the centre of the star, as you will observe in the engraving. Now take the four **Heart-shaped Moulds,** cover them with green double crochet, margin them with gold, embroider a series of perpendicular gold stitches from the bottom to the top of the heart, and make a little darning in and out of these threads in a fan shape at the bottom of the heart, and when finished join each heart to one of the tiny ring moulds on each side of the square. Work five 127 moulds with brown double crochet, doing about 30 double-crochet stitches upon each, and sew these five moulds (by the ends of the thread) round the top of a heart in a kind of semi-circle as represented in the engraving; margin them with gold in the same manner as you have already margined similar small moulds at the corners of the square, uniting the first and the last moulds by their picots to the nearest brown mould of the adjacent corner, and with a stitch or two attaching the sides of these to the top of the green mould immediately below; the centres of all the 127 moulds are left open. When you have finished the four sides as thus instructed, the square will be complete. It measures about ten inches across.

Heading is worked separately, and sewn on. Commence with chain the length required; do 1 treble in the sixth chain from the needle, * 1 chain, miss one stitch of the foundation, 1 rice stitch of 10 coils in the next, 1 chain, miss one, 1 treble in the next, and repeat from * to the end of the length. Turn the reverse side of the heading towards you, and work double crochet into every stitch round the heading. Use the right side of the heading against the right side of the moulds, and simply sew them together by an invisible stitch or two at the back of the work; the two top moulds of the scollop do not require to be united together, as the joining upon the heading retains them in place. The **Tassels** are made by working 5 long loose rice stitches into 1 stitch of chain; draw the rice stitches together at the top, confine both ends of your Glanzgarn together by a knot, and draw through a stitch of the crochet where the tassel is to hang, return them through the threads of the tassel, and secure by a knot.

WELLESLEY BORDER.

THIS is a most elegant border for gipsy tables, brackets, mantel valances, and drapes of all descriptions; it measures 6¼ inches in depth, and no more pleasing combination of colours can be imagined than those selected for the example, while the stitches employed are of the simplest. To work it procure

Glanzgarn numbered 739 eau de nil and 733 electric blue ; moulds 101 small ring, and 228 pear-shaped; a scollop will take five of the latter to one of the former and 2 or 3 skeins of gold thread, with a rather fine steel crochet needle. Work upon the **Small Ring** with eau de nil Glanzgarn, doing 24 double-crochet stitches, and join, and fasten off; employ gold thread, and keeping the right side of the crochet towards you and working into the one front thread thereof, do 3 consecutive single crochet, * 4 chain, 1 single crochet in the same place the last single crochet is worked and 2 more single crochet on consecutive stitches, and repeat from * till you have made 8 picots or loops of chain, when join to the first stitch with which the round commenced. For the **first Pear-shaped Mould** at the top left-hand side of the scollop, do 36 double crochet with eau de nil Glanzgarn, and join evenly, and fasten off. This should begin and end at the point of the mould; turn the work, and go round the mould with electric blue, working a single crochet into the one back thread of the eau de nil stitches, join this quite neatly, and

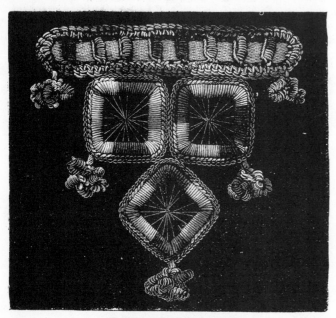

Square Block Border.

fasten off; then with the work the right side front margin a gold edge, beginning at the point and taking up the one back thread of the electric blue stitches, 3 consecutive double crochet, * 4 chain, 1 single crochet in the same place the last single crochet is worked, and 2 more single crochet on consecutive stitches, repeat from * till 11 picots and 12 groups of single crochet are worked, then 2 chain, join with a single crochet to a picot of the small ring, 2 chain, join to the first gold single crochet stitch, and fasten off. Work a corresponding pear-shape mould for the top right-hand side of the scollop, and join this to the opposite side of the small ring, leaving on this latter two void picots at the bottom for other pear-shaped moulds to be united, and four void picots at the top next against the heading. For the **third Pear-shaped Mould**, work the first round with electric blue and the second round with eau de nil, the stitches being precisely the same as the former moulds, but the colours reversed ; then, when proceeding with the gold edge, join the first and second picots to the eleventh and tenth picots respectively of the first pear-shape, and join the twelfth picot to the nearest picot of the small ring. Do another pear-shaped mould to stand level with this, with the same arrangement of colours, and join the first and second picots to the eleventh and tenth picots respectively of this mould, the tenth and eleventh picots to the second and first picots of the mould on the top right-hand side, and the twelfth picot to the picot of the small ring. Work the **fifth Pear-shaped Mould** the same as the first, and when you get to the edge join the first picot to the eighth picot of the mould on the left-hand side of the scollop, the eleventh picot to the fourth picot of the mould on the right-hand side of the scollop, and the twelfth picot to *both* the intervening picots of these two moulds by 1 chain and a join, 2 chain and a join, 1 chain and unite and fasten off. This completes the working of the scollop ; the interior of every mould is to be embroidered with a spider in gold thread, which may be taken in hand now or after the border is crocheted, whichever seems most convenient to the worker. For the **Heading—1st row**—With electric blue, do 12 chain, 1 single crochet in the seventh chain from the needle, 9 chain, 1 single crochet in the same place, 6 chain, 1 single crochet again in the same place (making three loops to hang downwards from the heading), 3 chain, 1 compound double crochet in the fourth picot to the right of the pear-shaped mould, 2 chain and 1 treble twice in the eau de nil threads at the back of the mould, 7 chain, 1 single crochet in the sixth chain from the needle, 2 chain, glanzgarn twice round the needle, insert the hook again in an eau de nil thread of the same mould and draw the Glanzgarn through, glanzgarn over the needle and draw through one stitch on the needle, glanzgarn over the needle, insert the hook in a back thread on the side of the small ring and draw the Glanzgarn through, and now glanzgarn over the needle to draw through 2 stitches at a time till all are drawn off, 3 chain, 1 treble on the centre stitch at the back of the small ring, 3 chain, a double long treble as before, 7 chain, 1 single crochet in the sixth chain from

the needle, 2 chain and 1 treble twice in the eau de nil threads at the back of this mould, 2 chain, 1 compound double crochet in the fourth gold picot, 9 chain, 1 single crochet in the seventh chain from the needle, 9 chain, 1 single crochet in the same place, 6 chain, again 1 single crochet in the same place, and continue in the same manner along the other scollops to the length the border is required. **2nd row**—With eau de nil—Turn the work, and go in single crochet along the back threads of the stitches of the previous row. **3rd row**—With gold thread and the work the right side towards you, proceed in open crochet of 1 treble, 1 chain, miss one, and repeat. **4th row**—With eau de nil and the right side of the work in front, do 2 double crochet in every loop of two chain. **5th row**—With electric blue—Turn the work, and go in single crochet in the back threads of the stitches. **6th row**—With eau de nil and the right side of the crochet towards you, begin with a stitch on the needle, insert the hook to take up the one back thread of a stitch of last row, and draw the Glanzgarn through, insert the hook in the next stitch and draw the Glanzgarn through, glanzgarn over the needle and draw through 3 stitches on the needle, * 5 chain, miss three stitches, work another compound stitch in like manner, and repeat from * to the end of the row. **7th row**—With gold thread and still the right side of the crochet towards you, 1 double crochet under the first loop of five chain, * 2 chain, 1 double crochet in the centre stitch of the loop of five chain, 3 chain, another double-crochet in the same place, 3 chain, and again another double crochet in the same place, 2 chain, insert the hook under the same loop of chain and draw the thread through, insert the hook in the next loop of chain and draw the thread through, thread over the needle and draw through 3 stitches on the needle, and repeat from * to the end of the row. The **Pendants** are made over small solid moulds,—you begin with 3 chain, and join round, do 6 double-crochet in the circle, increase again in the next round, put the mould in the crochet, and gradually narrow to the shape of the mould, draw in the top, and tie a knot with the two ends of the Glanzgarn over the pendant. A pendant of each colour is knotted together and suspended from the two centre pear-shaped moulds of the scollop, and a bunch of three pendants hangs from the point of the scollop.

Wellesley Border.

FRENCH LACE.

THIS lace is worked with ordinary white or ivory crochet cotton over moulds. Procure two or three balls of Ardern's Ivory Crochet Cotton, No. 16, together with a supply of moulds, No. 110 pear shaped, 101 small ring, and 129 shield shaped, and a rather fine steel crochet needle. Cover the **Pear-shaped Moulds** by working 55 double crochet, or as many as each will take, join the last stitch to the first, and fasten off. In the same way cover the **Shields** with 35 double crochet. Then take the **Ring Moulds** and on each work 5 double crochet and a picot of 4 chain alternately till you get 30 double crochet and 6 picots, when join evenly, and fasten off. When you think you have a sufficient number of moulds prepared to make the required length of lace you may begin the process of joining. Commence with the

Scolloped Edge, which consists of rings and shields. Take a shield and work 1 double crochet in the sixth stitch from the top of the mould (counting from the point downwards), 2 chain, miss two stitches, 1 treble in the next, 3 chain, another treble in the same place, 2 chain, miss two, 1 double crochet in the next, * 2 chain, miss one, 1 treble in the next, 3 chain, another treble in the same place, 2 chain, miss one, 1 double crochet in the next, repeat from * twice, 2 chain, miss two, 1 treble in the next, 1 chain, 1 single crochet in a picot of a ring, 1 chain, another treble in the same place as last treble, 2 chain, miss two, 1 double crochet in the next. You now should be exactly opposite the spot on which you began, and there will be ten stitches unworked between; 9 chain, 1 single crochet in the next picot of the ring, 9 chain, take another shield and work 1 double crochet in the sixth stitch from the top, 2 chain, miss two stitches, 1 treble in the next, 3 chain, another treble in the next picot of the ring, 1 chain, another treble in the same place as last treble, 2 chain, miss two, 1 double crochet in the next, and repeat as before, and join

French Lace.

on successive moulds as you see them in the engraving. This finishes the edge and you now go on with the middle portion of the lace. **1st row**—With the right side of the small crocheted moulds towards you,—1 double crochet at the point of the shield, 5 chain, 1 treble on the first of the nine chain stitches, 2 chain, miss two, 1 treble on the next, do this till you have **7** treble stitches and 6 spaces, then 5 chain, 1 double crochet at the point of the next shield, and continue. **2nd row**—Turn, work double crochet in the back thread of the stitches of last row. **3rd row**—Turn, work 3 consecutive treble on stitches of the preceding row, * 6 treble on the next stitch, withdraw the hook from the last stitch, insert it in the first treble of the group, retake the dropped stitch and draw it through, so making a "tuft;" do 3 consecutive treble, and repeat from *. **4th row**—Turn, do 1 double crochet on the first stitch of the previous row, * take a pear-shaped mould and do 1 double crochet on the point of it, work 6 consecutive double crochet on stitches of last row and 1 treble in the sixth stitch up the side of the mould, 6 more consecutive double crochet on stitches of last row and 1 long treble in the seventh stitch of the mould beyond the treble stitch, 3 more consecutive double crochet on stitches of last row, and repeat from * to the end. For **1st row** of **Heading** over the pear-shaped moulds—Hold the right side of the work towards you,—Do 1 long treble in the eighth stitch of the mould above the long treble already worked, * 4 chain, miss four stitches of the mould, 1 double crochet on the next, 4 chain, miss five stitches, 1 double crochet on the next, 4 chain, miss four stitches, 1 long treble on the next, 1 long treble on the eighth stitch of the next mould, and repeat from * ; the moulds all lie on the slant, as you will observe in the engraving. **2nd row**—Turn, and work double crochet along the row. **3rd row**—Open crochet, 1 treble, 1 chain, miss one, and repeat. **4th row**—Plain double crochet.

ANTIQUE STAR.

THIS charming star is finely worked with Brilliant crochet thread, and shines with silken lustre. It is useful for any purpose to which a star can be applied, and may be crocheted in any two nicely harmonising colours. We have selected No. 122 olive green and No. 240 crushed strawberry Brilliant crochet thread for our model, employing stiff moulds, one 101 small ring, five 102 triangles, and five 120 fleurette-shaped moulds, to afford substance to the star. The embroidery in the centre of the moulds is executed with gold thread. Commence with the one **Small Ring** in the centre of the star, and with green crochet twist work 40 double crochet smoothly and evenly over the mould, join the last stitch to the first, and fasten off invisibly; take gold twist and edge the ring, do 4 double crochet, inserting the hook to take up the one top thread of the green stitches, 5 chain, 1 single crochet on the last double crochet stitch to form a picot, and repeat 4 double crochet and a picot until you have 10 of each round the circumference of the ring, join the last gold stitch to the first, and fasten off. Next use a **Fleurette-shaped Mould** and

work with crushed strawberry twist, begin crocheting at the narrow point of the mould, and on the first section work 4 double crochet, a picot, 5 double crochet, a picot, 5 double crochet, a picot, 3 double crochet; on the second section work the same; and at the top, on the two upper sections, work 4 double crochet, a picot, * 6 double crochet and a picot, and repeat from * till 11 picots are worked (the centre one of these eleven picots should come on the depression at the top of the mould), then 3 double crochet; and do the two last sections to correspond with the two first; and after the 4 double crochet at the point, work 2 chain, join with a single crochet to one of the picots of the small ring, 2 chain, join evenly round the mould, and fasten off. The remaining four fleurette moulds are crocheted in like manner, and each are joined to a picot of the small ring, leaving one picot of the ring free between each joining. For the **Triangular Moulds** take green twist, and beginning at a corner, work 5 double crochet and a picot four times along the side of the triangle; the fourth picot should come exactly on the opposite corner (you may do more than five double crochet between the picots if required, as the number of stitches is not absolute, but the mould must be well covered); proceed in the same manner along the next side of the triangle, and join the corner picot to the middle picot on the second section of the fleurette to the left, continue along the third (or lower) side of the triangle and join the last picot to the middle picot on the second section of the fleurette to the right. Work the other four triangles, and join them likewise in position between the fleurettes as you see them in the engraving. With gold thread passed through the eye of a needle, pick up every alternate picot between a triangle and the ring in the centre of a star, seven in all, darn round the top of the stitches to form a lace-work wheel, and fasten off; and do a similar lace-work wheel in every corresponding space. Embroider a spider-like network of gold threads in the small ring, in the fleurettes, and in the triangles, following as nearly as possible the direction of the stitches as they are represented in the engraving.

HANDSOME BORDER FOR TRIMMING FURNITURE.

THIS effective border measures 10 inches in depth. It is executed with Original Glanzgarn in colours, 701 cream, 739 eau de nil, 740 pale sea-green, and 704 terra cotta; also there will be required a few skeins of gold thread,

Antique Star.

and a piece of ¾-inch wide gold braid; besides the following moulds to work over, 240 and 400 small rings, 209 double hearts, and 228 pear-shaped moulds. There are three double hearts, seven pear shapes, and two larger and five smaller rings used in every scollop, the latter being employed exclusively for the heading, while the former are grouped together in the centre of the scollop. Commence with a **Heart-shaped Mould,** take cream Glanzgarn, and round the outside rim work 46 compound double-crochet stitches, and join evenly, and fasten off; these make a thicker stitch than the ordinary double crochet, and are worked thus:—have a stitch on the needle, insert the hook under the rim of the mould and draw the Glanzgarn through, glanzgarn over the needle and draw through one stitch on the needle, insert the hook again in the mould and draw the Glanzgarn through, glanzgarn over the needle and draw through three stitches on the needle. Then round the inner rim, with eau de nil, and beginning at the top, work 31 plain double-crochet stitches; make 1 chain to carry the Glanzgarn to the outer margin, and turn the work, and do double crochet in the one back thread of each cream-coloured stitch; join evenly at the top of the heart, turn the work to the right side, do a single crochet or two to get back upon the inner rim; in fact, do any little cluster of stitches that will serve to cover whatever bit of mould may be visible, put the Glanzgarn 18 times round the needle, insert the hook in a thread of a double-crochet stitch, glanzgarn over the needle, and draw through the coil, which will result in a rice stitch in the form of a loop, as see engraving; break off with an end, which thread in a wool needle, and sew securely at the back of the crochet. Now with gold thread double, *i.e.*, from two balls together, and the crochet the right side towards you, begin at the top of the heart and do single crochet in the one back thread of the row of cream stitches, and at intervals of nine times in the course of going round insert the hook through the work from the back to the front between the two double-crochet rounds, catch it into a top thread of the eau de nil round, and draw the gold thread right through; the loop will stretch across the vacant space between the hearts and will apparently hold the two together; there is one loop at the tip of the heart and four on each side, as in the engraving; join neatly when the round is complete. Make

double-crochet stitches worked with eau de nil, and the same colour is employed for the surrounding edging of rice stitches, which have 14 coils of Glanzgarn in each stitch, and correspond in appearance with the green rice stitches that surround the pear-shaped moulds; these rings form the **Heading,** and they are sewn together in a straight line by two connecting rice stitches, and also are sewn in position above the scollop as represented in the engraving. Now there only remains the **Tassels,** which consist of bunches of five long rice stitches looped upon the scollop by the two ends of the Glanzgarn; begin with green Glanzgarn with 2 loose chain, work 5 rice stitches of 14 coils in the first chain stitch, and fasten off; tie the two ends together just above the bunch, loop them through a rice stitch at the bottom of one of the pear-shaped moulds on the side of the scollop, carry them back to the tassel, and sew or knot them securely. A similar tassel is placed on each of three other pear-shaped moulds; two green, and one cream tassel are knotted in a bunch at the point of the scollop; and two eau de nil tassels depend from the heading between the scollops. Pass the gold braid along the back of the heading, drawing it through the centre of each ring in similitude of a fan, and retain

Handsome Border for Trimming Furniture.

another heart similar to this, and sew the points together with a needle and cotton. In the third heart use terra cotton where you before used eau de nil; sew this intermediately between the other two hearts. Take two of the **Pear-shaped Moulds,** and round each do 40 double crochet with terra-cotta Glanzgarn; then margin the edge with gold thread, doing single crochet in the one top thread of the double-crochet stitches; sew these to each other, and sew each over an eau de nil heart, in the position represented in the engraving. Work the other 5 pear-shaped moulds with 40 double crochet with cream-colour; take green Glanzgarn, do 1 double crochet in the top thread of the stitch at the point of the mould, * 1 chain, miss one stitch, 1 rice stitch of 6 coils in the next, and repeat from *, but in each rice stitch increase the number of coils, so you get longer stitches round the bottom of the mould than at the top, and they all curl prettily round, and as you go on you will diminish the size of the stitches, making both sides of the mould to correspond. Work the two larger rings with terra-cotta Glanzgarn in 20 compound double-crochet stitches, and join, and fasten off. Sew these and the five pear-shaped moulds in position on the scollop. The smaller rings are covered with 28

it in place by a stitch passing through the crochet at the top and bottom of the braid.

WELDON'S
PRACTICAL CROCHET.

(NINETEENTH SERIES.)

How to Crochet Shawls, Petticoats, Capes, Hats, and Fancy Articles.

TWENTY-TWO DESIGNS.

Telegraphic Address—]
" Consuelo," London.]

The Yearly Subscription to this Magazine, post free to any Part of the World, is 2s. 6d. Subscriptions are payable in advance, and may commence from any date and for any period.

[Telephone— 2754.

The Back Numbers are always in print. Nos. 1 to 87 now ready, Price 2d. each, or post free for 15s. 6d. Over 5,000 Engravings.

LOTUS PATTERN.

FOR A SHAWL OR SCARF.

THE pretty lacy pattern shown in the engraving is crocheted in a very similar manner to the well-known " crazy " stitch, but the effect is altogether different, for here the stitches fall into narrow perpendicular stripes. Procure 4 ozs. of Shetland wool, white, or any colour you prefer, and a No. 10 bone crochet needle. Commence with chain the length required for the width of the scarf or shawl. Work in rows, beginning on the right-hand side of every row and fastening off at the end. **1st row**—Do 1 treble in the seventh chain from the needle, and 3 more treble in the same place, * miss three stitches of the foundation, 1 double crochet in the next, 5 chain, 4 treble in the same stitch as the double crochet is worked into, and repeat from * ; and at the end, after doing 4 treble, miss three stitches of the foundation, do 1 double crochet in the next, and fasten off: the treble stitches should all be drawn up to a fair height. **2nd row**—Resuming on the right-hand side—Do 1 double crochet in the loop of chain at the beginning of the previous row, 5 chain, 4 treble in the same loop of chain, * 1 double crochet in the next loop of chain of previous row, 5 chain, 4 treble in the same place, and repeat from * ; and at the end, after doing 4 treble, do 1 treble on the stitch at the end of the row, and fasten off. Every following row is worked the same as the second row. The right side of the shawl is the side that is away from you in working. For the **Border**—Recommence as before on the right-hand side—Do 1 double crochet in the loop of chain at the beginning of last row, * 7 chain, 1 single crochet in the sixth chain from the needle, 4 chain, and crossing as it were over the little round circle work 12 treble in the circle, fold the treble stitches over each other in the shape of a " tab " (or section of an orange), do 1 single crochet in the top stitch of the four chain stitches, and make 1 chain to tighten the tab, then 1 double crochet in the next loop of chain of last row, and repeat from * to the end of the row : there, after the last tab, do 1 treble on the treble stitch at the end of the row, make a tab on this treble to turn round the corner, and continue the same tabs along the side of the shawl, doing one tab to each row of the crochet. Work likewise round the other two sides of the shawl or scarf, which then will be finished.

CHEMISE TRIMMING.

PROCURE 4 skeins of Ardern's or Coats' crochet cotton, No. 16, and a fine steel crochet needle. The straight piece of crochet that goes across the **Front** of the chemise from arm to arm is worked in the style of an insertion. Begin with 40 chain. **1st row**—Miss the four chain next the needle, and work 36 treble along the row. **2nd row**—Do 3 chain to turn (these stand up like a treble stitch), miss the first treble stitch of the previous row, work 3 treble consecutively, * 2 chain, miss two stitches, 1 treble on the next, 2 chain, miss two, 1 treble on the next, 2 chain, miss one, 1 treble on the next, 2 chain, miss two, 1 treble on the next, 2 chain, miss two, 3 treble consecutively, repeat from *, and then do 1 more treble, which will complete the row. **3rd row**—3 chain to turn, miss the first treble stitch, 3 treble consecutively on treble of last row, * 2 chain, 1 treble on treble, 2 chain, 3 treble in the central open space of last row, 2 chain, 1 treble on treble, 2 chain, 3 treble on three treble of last row, repeat from *, and then do 1 more treble, which will complete the row. **4th row**—3 chain to turn, miss the first treble stitch, 3 treble

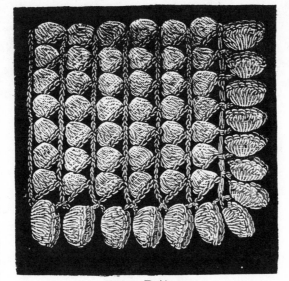

Lotus Pattern.

consecutively on treble of last row, * 3 chain, 3 treble in the space to the right of the three treble of last row, 2 chain, 3 treble in the space to the left of the three treble of last row, 3 chain, 3 treble on three treble, repeat from *, and end the row with 1 more treble stitch. **5th row**—3 chain to turn, miss the first stitch, 3 treble consecutively on treble of last row, * 2 chain, 1 treble on the first of the three treble stitches, 2 chain, 3 treble in the open space, 2 chain, 1 treble on the last stitch of the next group of trebles, 2 chain, 3 treble on three treble, repeat from *, and end the row with 1 more treble stitch. **6th row**—3 chain to turn, and work 36 treble along the row. Repeat from the second row. Thus you will do 5 rows in each square check of the pattern till 17 patterns are done in the breadth across the chemise ; or the breadth may be extended to 19 or 21 patterns if needful. Work a similar piece of insertion for the back of the chemise. For the **Shoulders**—Take the front piece of insertion, and beginning at the right-hand corner, work along the **side** of the insertion—Do 4 treble on the edge of the treble row, * 2 chain and 1 treble alternately 4 times along the four next rows, 2 chain, 3 treble on the edge of the next line of treble stitches, repeat from * twice, and then do 1 more treble close by the last treble stitch to complete the row ; you will see this corresponds in pattern to the second row of the insertion, but now there are three squares of check in the row, and as you proceed you will find you now have 52 treble in the 6th row of the pattern. Work until 7 patterns are done (35 rows) ; then break off the cotton. Work a similar shoulder at the other end of the front piece of insertion. Then reverse the position of the insertion, and to make **Gussets**, crochet as instructed above, till, at each end of the insertion, you have worked a perfect square of 3 checks wide and 3 checks (15 rows) long. Sew the shoulder pieces to the insertion that is to form the back of the chemise trimming, also join the gussets thereto. For the **Lace Edging** round the **Neck**—This is worked in rounds, joining evenly, and breaking off on the completion of every round. **1st round**—Open crochet, 1 treble, 2 chain ; and repeat the same ; get 1 treble stitch on every row of the check pattern crochet. **2nd round**—Treble ; contract at each of the four corners by drawing 4 or 5 treble stitches together in 1. **3rd round**—1 treble, 2 chain, miss two, and repeat the same ; the open spaces in this round must be counted, and arranged in such a number as to be divisible by seven. **4th round**—Do 3 treble in one space, 3 treble in the next space, 2 chain, 3 treble in· the next space, and 3 treble again in the next space, 3 chain, miss one space, 1 treble in the next space, 3 chain, miss one space, and repeat the same to the end of the round. **5th round**—Miss the two first treble stitches, work 4 treble consecutively, 3 ·chain over the 2 chain of previous round, 4 consecutive treble, here again two treble stitches must be missed, 3 chain, 1 treble on the 1 treble of previous round, 3 chain, and repeat the same. **6th round**—Miss the first of the four treble stitches of last round, work 3 treble consecutively, 4 chain over the 3 ·chain of last round, 3 treble on treble stitches, missing the last one of the group of four, 3 chain, 1 treble on the 1 treble of last round, 3 chain, another treble in the same place, 3 chain, and repeat. **7th round**—Do 6 treble over the four chain of previous round, that is, do 1 treble in each chain and 1 treble on the treble stitch on each side, 3 chain, 1 treble in the loop of chain between two treble stitches of previous round, 3 chain, 1 treble in the same place, 3 chain, again 1 treble in the same place, 3 chain, and repeat. **8th round**— Work 4 treble on the 4 middle stitches of the six treble of last round, 3 chain, 1 treble in the first loop of chain between two treble stitches of last round, 2 chain, 1 treble in the same place, 2 chain, again 1 treble in the same place, 1 treble in the next loop, 2 chain, 1 treble in the same place, 2 chain, again 1 treble in the same place, 3 chain, and repeat. **9th round**—Work 2 treble on the 2 middle stitches of the four treble of previous round, 3 chain, 1 double crochet in the loop of 3 chain, 3 chain, 1 double crochet in the first of the two ·chain loops, 9 chain, 1 double crochet in the last of the two chain loops, 3 ·chain, 1 double crochet in the loop of three chain, 3 chain, and repeat. **10th**

round. **1st round** of **Shell Stitch** for the **Boot**—Beginning at the back of the leg—Do 3 chain, wool over the needle, insert the hook in the chain stitch by the needle and draw the wool through, wool over the needle, insert the hook in the next chain stitch and draw the wool through, wool over the needle, insert the hook in the stitch of last round where the chain springs from and draw the wool through, wool over the needle, insert the hook in the next stitch of the previous row and draw the wool through, then wool over the needle and draw through all the 9 stitches on the needle, and do 1 chain to tighten the group ; * wool over the needle, insert the hook in the little hole formed by the one chain stitch and draw the wool through, wool over the needle, insert the hook in a back thread of the lower part of the stitch just made and draw the wool through, wool over the needle, insert the hook in the next stitch of the previous row and draw the wool through, wool over the needle, insert the hook in the next following stitch of the previous row and draw the wool through, then wool over the needle and draw through all the 9 stitches on the needle, and do 1 chain to tighten the group ; work 4 more shell stitches as from * ; then increase by getting 2 shell stitches over the next two stitches of last row ; then 3 shell stitches to come over the six middle stitches of last row ; another increase of 2 shell stitches over two double crochet stitches ; and 6 more shell stitches to complete the round, and join evenly to the first stitch of the round, and break off the wool. For the **Instep**—Draw the wool through the little hole to the left of the seventh shell stitch, do 3 chain, and work 5 shell stitches over the centre five stitches of last row, and break off wool. **2nd row** of the Instep—Draw the wool through the uppermost of the three chain stitches with which the last row began, and work in the same manner 5 shell stitches over five shell stitches. Work 2 more instep rows of 5 stitches in each row ; and work another row of 3 shell stitches

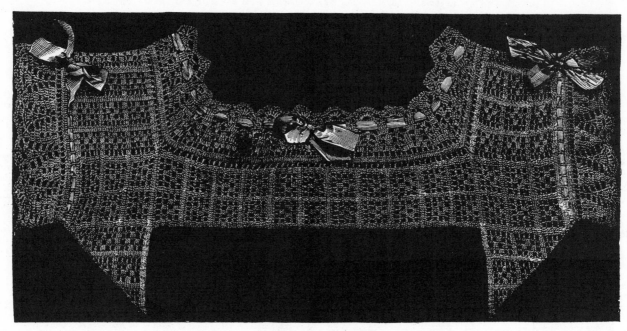

Chemise Trimming.

round—1 double crochet between the two treble stitches at the top of the pyramid, 5 chain, 1 treble in the loop of nine chain, 2 chain and 1 treble alternately five times in the same place, 5 chain, and repeat. **11th round**— 1 double crochet in a loop of chain of the previous round, 3 chain, 1 double crochet in the next loop, 3 chain, and repeat. This finishes the lace. The same lace is worked round the armholes, and then the chemise top is ready for use. A ribbon is run through the first round of lace trimming of the armholes, and through the holes of the ninth round of the neck.

LITTLE HAROLD BOOT.

POINT MUSCOVITE AND SHELL STITCH.

REQUIRED, 1 oz. of white Andalusian wool and a No. 13 bone crochet needle. Commence with 34 chain for the top of the leg, and join round. **1st round**—Do 1 double crochet in the first chain stitch, insert the hook in the next stitch and draw the wool through, work 3 chain, wool over the needle and draw through 2 stitches on the needle, and continue thus, doing 1 double crochet and 1 point alternately ; and proceed round and round for 12 rounds, always working 1 double crochet stitch over a point stitch and a point stitch over a double crochet stitch. **13th round**—This is an "open" round in which to run a tie round the ankle ; it should begin under the tag end of wool at the back of the leg ; make 3 chain to stand for a treble, 1 treble on the next stitch, * 1 chain, miss one, 1 treble on the next and again 1 treble on the next, and repeat from * ; and end 1 chain, miss one, 1 treble close to the chain with which the round commenced, and join evenly ; there should be 11 groups of 2 treble stitches. Work 2 rounds of double crochet with 34 stitches in each

over the three centre stitches, which completes the instep. For the **Boot**— **2nd round**—Begin at the back of the leg on the first round of the shell stitches—Work 6 shell stitches over six stitches, 7 more shell stitches to come up to the corner of the instep, 1 shell stitch at the corner, 3 at the toe, 1 at the other corner, and 13 along the opposite side to correspond with the first side of the boot ; join at the end of the round : in this round there are 31 shell stitches. **3rd round**—Do 6 shell stitches over six, then 1 over the two next, 1 over each of the fifteen next, 1 over the two next, and 1 over each of six, making 29 shell stitches, and join round. **4th round**—Do 1 shell stitch over each of twelve stitches, 1 over the two next, 1 over the next stitch which is the centre stitch of the toe, 1 over the two next, and 1 over each of twelve stitches, 27 shell stitches in the round, and join evenly. **5th round**—Do 1 shell stitch over two stitches of last round, 1 over each of nine, 1 over two, 1 over the next stitch which is the centre stitch of the toe, 1 over two, 1 over each of nine, and 1 over the two last stitches, making in all 23 stitches, and join evenly. Break off with a long end of wool, and sew along the sole of the boot : and in case any holes appear down the back of the heel where the rounds are joined, darn such neatly up. A double chain is worked to run round the ankle, thus—Work 2 chain stitches as usual, then insert the hook in the first chain stitch and draw the wool through, wool over the needle and draw through 2 stitches on the needle, * insert the hook in the stitch to the left and draw the wool through, wool over the needle and draw through 2 stitches on the needle, repeat from * for the length required : then run the chain through the holes that already have been prepared to receive it, join it in front, and make a small rosette of double crochet stitches as shown in the engraving.

CHILD'S PELISSE.

THE model is suitable for a child from 2 to 3 years old, and would require 1 lb. of eider or Andalusian wool, 2 bone crochet needles, Nos. 7 and 10, and 9 pearl buttons. Make a chain of 247 for the bottom of pelisse, and 1 more to turn. **1st row**—Loop crochet, which is worked thus: insert the needle in 2nd chain, and * put the wool over the needle and your 2 first fingers, then once over needle only and draw them through the chain stitch, wool over the needle and draw it through the 2 loops on needle, insert the needle in next stitch and repeat from * to end of row. **2nd row**—Double crochet, taking up both threads of stitches in previous row. Repeat these 2 rows 4 times. **11th row**—240 stitches in double crochet, the last 7 stitches in loop crochet. **12th**

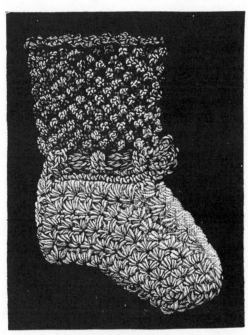

Little Harold Boot.

row—Double crochet all along. Repeat these two rows 28 times. **69th row** —Like the 11th row. **70th row**—Stick pins in the 64th, 84th, 104th, 124th, 144th, 164th, and 184th stitches. Now pleat up the back so that the 1st pin comes over the 3rd, the 2nd over the 4th, the 6th over the 4th, and the 7th over the 5th, and you will have 2 pleats meeting in the centre. Now work all along in double crochet; where it is pleated you will have to take up 6 threads instead of 2, as you have 3 thicknesses instead of 1, and you will have 167 stitches in the row. Now to reduce the size for the **Body** use the smaller needle. **1st row**—160 stitches in double crochet and the last 7 in loop crochet. **2nd row**—Double crochet all along. Repeat these 2 rows 17 times, when you must divide for the armholes. **37th row**—Like the 1st. **38th row**—54 stitches in double crochet and turn. **39th row**—Miss 1 instead of making 1 chain to turn, 46 stitches in double crochet, and 7 in loop crochet. **40th row**—47 stitches in double crochet (leave the last 6 stitches to shape the armhole), turn. **41st row**—Miss 1, double crochet to within 7 stitches of the end, which are worked in loop crochet. **42nd row**—Double crochet all along. **43rd row**—Like the 41st row, only you miss 2 stitches instead of 1 at beginning of row. **44th row**—Double crochet all along. Repeat the last 2 rows till you have only 35 stitches, then work 10 rows without decreasing. You must now decrease at the neck. **64th row**—Miss 2, 33 double crochet. **65th row**—28 double crochet and 5 loop crochet. **66th row**—Miss 2, double crochet all along. **67th row**—28 double crochet and 3 loop crochet. **68th row**—Like the 66th. **69th row**—28 double crochet and 1 loop crochet. **70th row**—Like the 66th. **71st row**—Double crochet. Repeat the last two rows till you have only 15 stitches, then work 3 rows without decreasing, then decrease 3 stitches at the end of every other row on the armhole side till you have only 3 stitches left. Break off. Make the other front to correspond with this one. For the **Back**—Work the remaining 60 stitches in double crochet, then miss 1 at the beginning of each row till you have only 54 stitches. Work 16 rows without decreasing, then miss 3 at the beginning of each row till you have only 32 stitches, break off and sew up the shoulders. For the **Sleeves**—Make a chain of 47, 1 row of loop crochet, and 1 row of double crochet for 4 times. This forms the cuff. Then 32 rows of double crochet. Increase a stitch at the beginning of each of the next 6 rows. Two rows without increasing. Then decrease at the beginning of every row till you have 47 stitches again. Break off, sew up the sleeves, and stitch them in. For the **Cape**—Make a chain of 172, 1 row of loop crochet, and 1 row of double crochet for 4 times. **9th row**—Double crochet except the first and last 7 stitches, which are worked in loop crochet. **10th row**—Double crochet. Repeat the last two rows 16 times. **43rd row**—Miss every other stitch. **44th row**—Double crochet. Place the cape on the pelisse and crochet them together. For the **Neck**—Work back in loop crochet, 1 row of double crochet and 1 row of loop crochet. Break off. For the **Collar**—Make a chain of 7 and work backwards

and forwards in alternate rows of double crochet and loop crochet, till you have done a piece long enough to go round the neck. Break off and sew it on. For the **Buttonhole Strip**—Make a chain of 9. Work 1 row in double crochet. **2nd row**—3 stitches in double crochet, 3 chain, miss 3, 2 double crochet, * 17 rows of double crochet, then make another buttonhole. Repeat from * till 9 buttonholes are worked. A few more rows of double crochet to make it the same length as the pelisse. Hem it on to the inside of pelisse under the loop crochet, so that the first buttonhole comes at the neck. Catch it at the edge half way between each buttonhole, and sew on the buttons. The total length of pelisse is about 21 inches. The centre of the back just at the waist is finished off with a chain prettily looped with wool pompons added to either end of chain.

LADY'S EVENING MANTLE.

PROCURE 1 lb. of thick astrachan wool, a bone crochet needle No. 4, and 1½ yards of ribbon. Commence with 5 chain. **1st row**—Double crochet in every stitch taking up both threads of stitches in previous row. **2nd row**—Increase 2 stitches at the beginning of the row by making 3 chain instead of 1 to turn. Repeat this 2nd row till you have 77 stitches, then make 2 chain, and work * 1 double crochet stitch in every row till you come to the point and work 3 double crochet in the centre stitch. Work up the other side and make 2 chain to turn. Repeat from * 7 times. For the **Front**—**1st row**—Make 1 chain and work 36 double crochet stitches across the top and turn with 1 chain. **2nd row**—Double crochet, and at the end of the row make 24 chain and 2 more to turn. * **3rd row**—Double crochet and 1 chain to turn. **4th row**—Double crochet and 2 chain to turn. Repeat from * 7 times, and break off. Work the other front the same way, and for the **Neck** work rather tightly 1 double crochet in every other row to draw up the neck to the required size. For the **Fringe**—Make 14 chain and 1 double crochet into every stitch round the neck, and 14 chain and 1 double crochet into every other stitch down the fronts, and 20 chain and 1 double crochet into every other stitch all round the mantle. Put on ribbon strings to tie at the neck.

Child's Pelisse.

TEA-COSY WORKED IN POINT MUSCOVITE.

THE model tea-cosy is prettily worked with single Berlin wool in four shades of art blue, in the stitch known as Point Muscovite. The front, back, and two side pieces are made separately, and sewn together; the join is concealed with silk cord trimming. It requires 1 oz. of the lightest shade and 1½ ozs. of each of three graduated darker shades of wool, a No. 7 bone crochet needle, 2 yards of silk cord, and a piece of silk and wadding for the lining. Commence with the lightest shade of wool, and make 27 chain moderately loosely for the height of the middle of the cosy. **1st row**—Miss the first chain stitch by the needle; * work 1 double crochet in the next, insert the hook in the next stitch of the foundation chain and draw the wool through, do 4 chain.

wool over the needle and draw through the last chain stitch and through the stitch on the needle: repeat from *, and you will get 13 double crochet and 13 Muscovite stitches or "picots" in the row; do a single crochet to secure the last picot in its place, and break off the wool. **2nd row**—Recommence with 1 single crochet on the first double crochet stitch at the bottom of the cosy, and work into the two front threads of the stitches of the previous row; * insert the needle to take up the two front threads of the double crochet stitch, do 4 chain, wool over the needle and draw through the last stitch of chain and through the stitch on the needle, 1 double crochet on the picot stitch of the previous row, repeat from * to the end of the row, and break off the wool. Reverse the position of the foundation chain, which is the exact centre of the cosy, and down the opposite side thereof repeat the 1st row and 2nd row as

Lady's Evening Mantle.

above, remembering always to work a double crochet stitch on a picot, and a picot on a double crochet stitch: this makes four rows done. **5th row**—Use the second shade of wool and revert to the right-hand side of the cosy, beginning at the bottom (that is, beginning where the 1st row and 2nd row began); work 1 double crochet on the picot stitch and a picot on a double-crochet stitch, this is practically the same as the first row, and there will be 13 double crochet and 13 picots in the row; finish with a single crochet to hold the last picot in place, and fasten off. **6th row**—With the second shade of wool, work as directed in the second row. Repeat these two rows. Go to the left-hand side of the cosy and work the same four rows, which will make 12 rows done. **13th row**—Use the third shade of wool and return to right-hand side, beginning at the bottom of the cosy,—Work as the fifth row, a double crochet and a picot alternately to the end of the row. **14th row**—Do a picot and a double crochet alternately till 11 of each are done, and fasten off, omitting 4 stitches at the top for the shaping of the cosy. **15th row**—Work a double crochet and a picot alternately till 8 of each are done, and fasten off, omitting 10 stitches at the top of the cosy. **16th row**—Do a picot and a double crochet alternately the entire length of the row. Go to the left-hand side of the cosy and work to correspond, that is to say, the 17th row begins at the top of the cosy, and is continued the whole way down; the 18th row begins on the fifth stitch from the top; the 19th row begins on the eleventh stitch from the top; and the 20th row begins at the top and is continued, of course, to the bottom of the cosy. **21st row**—Use the darkest shade of wool and revert again to the right-hand side, beginning at the bottom of the cosy—Work as the fifth row, a double crochet and a picot alternately to the end of the row. **22nd row**—Work a picot and a double crochet alternately till 10 of each are done, and fasten off, omitting 6 stitches at the top of the cosy. **23rd row**—Work a double crochet and a picot alternately till 7 of each are done, and fasten off, omitting 12 stitches at the top of the cosy. **24th row**—Work

a picot and a double crochet alternately the entire length of the row, doing 13 of each. Go to the left-hand side of the cosy and work to correspond, to effect which you will begin the 25th row at the top of the cosy, and continue it all the way down; begin the 26th row from the seventh stitch from the top; the 27th row on the thirteenth stitch from the top, and the 28th row begins at the top and is continued to the bottom, and comprises 13 double crochet and 13 picots. This finishes the front. Work another similar piece for the back. For the **Sides** or **Gussets**—Take the lightest shade of wool, and make as for the front, 27 chain, moderately loosely, and work 4 rows as directed for the front. **5th row**—Take the second shade of wool, and beginning at the bottom of the right-hand side of the gusset, work a double crochet and a picot alternately all along the row, 13 of each. **6th row**—On the same side, work a picot and a double crochet alternately till 11 of each are done, and fasten off, omitting four stitches at the top. Work on the left side to correspond, doing 1 row from the top to the bottom, and 1 row beginning on the fifth stitch from the top, and going thence to the bottom. **9th row**—Use the third shade of wool, and beginning at the bottom of the right-hand side of the gusset work a double crochet and a picot alternately till 9 of each are done, and fasten off, omitting 8 stitches at the top. The row corresponding to this is worked on the left-hand side of the gusset, beginning on the ninth stitch from the top, and going thence to the bottom. **11th row**—Use the darkest shade of wool, and work as the second row from the bottom to the top of the gusset. **12th row**—The same, working on the left-hand side from the top to the bottom of the gusset. Make another gusset in the same way. Wad the front and back of the cosy with cotton wool, and line them with silk. The gussets are lined with silk, but are not wadded. Sew the pieces together, and trim the cosy with silk cord over all the seams, and put silk cord across the top for handles, with bows of cord on each side; make wool pompons to be placed two on each side above the bows, as shown in the engraving, and the cosy will be ready for use.

TOBOGGAN CAP.

REQUIRED, nearly 4 ozs. of electric blue fingering, such as Paton's 4-ply, and a No. 9 bone crochet needle. Commence with 80 chain, or a sufficient length to go round the head of the child for whom the cap is intended; join in a round. Proceed in double crochet, working round and round continuously, inserting the hook to take up the top and back threads of the stitches of the previous round, until a depth of about 4 inches is done. After that the rounds must be gradually decreased; 2 stitches in every round (at alternate intervals) for 4 rounds, and then 1 round without decrease, and so you will bring the cap to a point at the top, and fasten off. The **Trimming** round the head is worked in Looped Knitting and sewn over the first few rounds of the crochet.

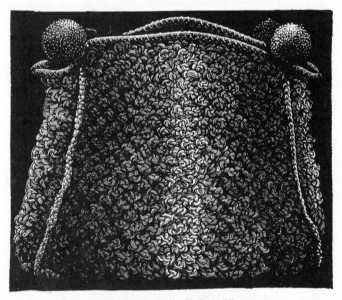

Tea Cosy Worked in Point Muscovite.

Use No. 10 bone needles, and cast on 12 stitches. Knit 1 plain row. **2nd row**—Slip the first stitch, * insert the needle in the next stitch, pass the wool over the point of the needle and round the first and second fingers of the left hand three times, then again over the point of the needle, and knit the stitch drawing all four threads of wool through, repeat from * to the end of the row. Repeat these two rows alternately until a sufficient length is knitted to go round the cap; finish with a plain row, and cast off. Join the trimming, the cast-off stitches to the cast on; and sew it on the crochet as it appears in the engraving. Work a length of chain with double wool, make two wool pompons upon the ends of the chain, and arrange the latter in loops on the point of the cap. Fold the point on one side and retain it in place by a few sewn stitches.

LADY'S SHOULDER CAPE.

AN elegant and nicely-shaped shoulder cape for a lady is made by a simple arrangement of single crochet, double crochet, and treble stitches, as represented in the accompanying engraving. Procure about 8 ozs. of coral pink single Berlin wool, a No. 9 or No. 10 bone crochet needle, and 2 yards of inch wide ribbon of colour to match the wool. Commence with a chain of 78 stitches for the length of the front of the cape. **1st row**—Work 8 single crochet, 18 double crochet, and 52 treble stitches in the row. **2nd row**—Do 52 treble stitches on the treble of last row (the first of these must be executed by 3 chain which will turn the row and stand for a treble), 18 double crochet on the double crochet, and 8 single crochet on the single crochet of last row. Repeat these two rows till you have done 21 rows from the commencement; the single crochet forms the neck band, the treble is the lower portion of the cape. **22nd row**—Beginning of a gore to shape the shoulder—52 treble, 5 double crochet, and turn the work. **23rd row**—5 double

Toboggan Cap.

crochet, 52 treble. **24th row**—52 treble, 18 double crochet, 8 single crochet; in this row, and in successive rows when working over "a turn," be careful to take up an extra thread of wool to avoid making a hole in the crochet. **25th row**—8 single crochet, 18 double crochet, and 52 treble. **26th row**—52 treble, 11 double crochet, and turn the work. **27th row**—11 double crochet, 52 treble. **28th row**—52 treble, 18 double crochet, 8 single crochet. **29th row**—8 single crochet, 18 double crochet, 52 treble. **30th row**—52 treble, 17 double crochet, and turn the work. **31st row**—17 double crochet, 52 treble. **32nd row**—52 treble, 18 double crochet, 8 single crochet. **33rd row**—8 single crochet, 18 double crochet, 52 treble. **34th row**—52 treble, 11 double crochet, and turn the work. **35th row**—11 double crochet, 52 treble. **36th row**—52 treble, 18 double crochet, 8 single crochet. **37th row**—8 single crochet, 18 double crochet, 52 treble. **38th row**—52 treble, 5 double crochet, and turn the work. **39th row**—5 double crochet, 52 treble. **40th row**—52 treble, 18 double crochet, 8 single crochet. **41st row**—8 single crochet, 18 double crochet, 52 treble. Repeat the last two rows 14 times, when there should be 69 rows done, counting the outside edge of treble stitches. **70th row**—Work the same as the twenty-second row, and continue thence as far as the thirty-ninth row inclusive. Then crochet 21 rows the whole length, the same as at the commencement of the cape, and fasten off. For the **Border**—The border is worked all round the cape, and upon the neck band; it does not add at all to the length of the cape, as it is crocheted upon the surface thereof, after the manner of a flat trimming. Begin at one end of the neck, and do 1 double crochet on the top stitch of the band, 5 chain, 1 double crochet on the third single crochet in the same row lower down on the band, 5 chain, 1 double crochet on the third single crochet in the same row still lower down the band, 5 chain, 1 double crochet on the double crochet stitch next by the neck band; now turn upwards, 5 chain, 1 double crochet on stitch of the next row but one of single crochet, 5 chain, 1 double crochet on the third single crochet in the same row higher up on the band, 5 chain, 1 double crochet on the third single crochet still higher up the band, 5 chain, 1 double crochet on a single crochet at the top of the band, and proceed zigzagging up and down the surface of the band till the end is reached, and you fasten off. Recommence on the front edge of the cape, close to the neck, and work a similar trimming, but now only miss one stitch under the five chain as the stitches are farther apart; the trimming down the fronts is about the same width as that on the neck band, or it may be a little wider; it is widest of all (about three inches deep) along the bottom of the cape. Cut the ribbon in half, and sew a piece upon each end of the neck band to tie in front of the neck; put one or two hooks and eyes to keep the cape closed upon the chest.

BABY'S SHETLAND PETTICOAT WITH BODICE.

WORKED IN DOUBLE CROCHET.

THIS dainty petticoat is intended for a baby of from nine to twelve months old; the skirt is worked in "waived" double crochet, and as the stitches slant some to the right and some to the left in regular alternation, a very pretty reflection of light and shadow is imparted to the work, giving it almost

the appearance of stripes; the body is in plain double crochet. Required, 4½ oz. of white Shetland wool, a ball of white knitting silk, 2½ yards of narrow white ribbon, and a fine bone crochet needle. Begin for the **Bottom** of the **Petticoat** with 374 chain, and join round. **1st round**—Work 7 consecutive double crochet, 3 double crochet in the next, 7 more consecutive double crochet, miss two stitches of the chain, and repeat the same to the end of the round; there will be 22 scollops of 17 stitches in each scollop. **2nd round**—The needle is to be inserted to take up the one top thread of the previous stitches, miss the first double crochet of last round, * work 7 consecutive double crochet, 3 double crochet on the centre stitch of three double crochet of last round, 7 more consecutive double crochet, miss two stitches of last round, and repeat from *. Proceed according to the second round, crocheting round and round continuously and always taking up the one top thread of the stitches, till 44 rounds are done, which brings you to the opening of the placket: break off the wool. Continue in the same manner but working now *in rows*, breaking off at the end of every row, for 14 rows, for the opening of the placket: 58 rows in all from the commencement, and 374 double crochet in every row. **59th row**—The waved crochet of the skirt is completed, and you now work in plain double crochet for the purpose of decreasing the width of the skirt and bringing the work in a straight line for the waist; miss the first double crochet of the last row, * do 1 double crochet on each of 7 stitches, 1 double crochet on the centre stitch, one double crochet on each of 7 stitches, miss two stitches, and repeat from * to the end of the row; there will be 330 double crochet in this row. **60th row**—Miss the first stitch, * do 13 consecutive double crochet, miss two stitches, and repeat from *; there will be 286 double crochet in this row. **61st row**—Commence on the first stitch, work 12 double crochet, * take up the next two stitches together in 1 double crochet, work 11 double crochet, and repeat from * to the end, where there will be 12 double crochet as at the beginning; 265 double crochet in all in the row. **62nd row**—Plain double crochet, 265 stitches. **63rd row**—This is the waist, and you work treble stitches to run ribbon in, take up two double crochet stitches together in 1 treble until 57 treble are done, then 1 treble on one double crochet, * 1 treble on two double crochet taken together, and 1 treble on one double crochet, repeat from * eleven times, then 1 treble on two double crochet together till 57 treble are done, making in all 139 treble in the row, and break off the wool at the end. For the **Body**—Work forwards and backwards in plain double crochet, taking up the one top thread, and doing 139 double crochet in the row for 24 rows. **25th row**—Work 33 double crochet, and turn the work. **26th row**—Again 33 double crochet. **27th row**—Do 32 double crochet,

Lady's Shoulder Cape.

omit one stitch at the armhole end, turn. **28th row**—Again 32 double crochet. **29th row**—Do 33 double crochet, the increase of one is to come in the last stitch by the armhole. **30th row**—Again 33 double crochet. **31st row**—Do 34 double crochet, the increase to be in the last stitch by the armhole. **32nd row**—Again 34 double crochet. **33rd row**—Do 35 double crochet, the increase to be in the last stitch. **34th row**—35 double crochet, and break off; this forms one side of the back. Recommence upon the stitches of the twenty-fourth row, miss six stitches for the armhole, work 61 double crochet for the front of the body; turn, and crochet back omitting 1 stitch at the end of every row for four rows; then do 2 rows of 57 double crochet in each row; and then increase 1 stitch at the end of every row for four rows; after which crochet the first 12 stitches forwards and backwards for 12 rows for a shoulder strap, and fasten off; and crochet the 12 stitches on the opposite side in the same way for the other shoulder, and fasten off. Recommence again upon the stitches of the twenty-fourth row, miss six stitches for the other armhole, work 33 double crochet to the end, and do this half of the back to correspond with the first half. Sew the shoulder-straps upon the back pieces. For the **Edging** round the **Neck: 1st row**—Work treble along the top of the neck, and go down the backs and round the placket opening in double crochet. **2nd row**—Along the neck only—Do 1 double crochet on a treble stitch of previous row, * miss one treble stitch, 6 treble between that and next treble stitch of last row, miss one, 1 double crochet on the next treble stitch and repeat from *. **3rd row**—With white silk—Work a line of single crochet as an edge along the front of the top of the stitches of last row. Work the same three rows of crochet edging round the armholes. For the **Edging** round the **Bottom of the Skirt: 1st round**—Do 4 treble in the space where three double crochet are worked into one stitch of the commencing chain, miss three chain stitches, 4 treble in the next, miss three stitches, 4 treble in the space where two chain stitches were missed, miss three stitches, 4 treble in the next, miss three stitches, and repeat the same; you will get 3 groups of treble stitches upon each scollop and 1 group in each hollow between the scollops. **2nd round**—1 double crochet in the space between the groups of treble stitches, and 5 treble between the second and third treble stitches of the group; and repeat the same. **3rd round**—With silk—Work a margin of single crochet along the front of the top of the stitches of last round: this finishes the edging. Run a length of ribbon through the treble stitches of the waist, neck, and round the armholes; tie the ends of the latter in bows on the shoulders as shown in the engraving. Additional ribbon strings may be placed to tie at the back of the body if required.

back. **3rd row**—Pick up 6 stitches, 2 together, 22 stitches, 2 together, 28 stitches, 2 together, 8 stitches, 2 together, 28 stitches, 2 together, 22 stitches, 2 together, 6 stitches, and draw back. **4th row**—Pick up 6 stitches, 2 together, 21 stitches, 2 together, 26 stitches, 2 together, 8 stitches, 2 together, 26 stitches, 2 together, 51 stitches, 2 together, 6 stitches, and draw back. **5th row**—Pick up 6 stitches, 2 together, 20 stitches, 2 together, 24 stitches, 2 together, 8 stitches, 2 together, 24 stitches, 2 together, 20 stitches, 2 together, 6 stitches, and draw back. **6th row**—Pick up 6 stitches, 2 together, 19 stitches, 2 together, 22 stitches, 2 together, 8 stitches, 2 together, 22 stitches, 2 together, 19 stitches, 2 together, 6 stitches, and draw back. **7th row**—Pick up 6 stitches, 2 together, 18 stitches, 2 together, 20 stitches, 2 together, 8 stitches, 2 together, 20 stitches, 2 together, 18 stitches, 2 together, 6 stitches, and draw back. **8th row**—Pick up 6 stitches, 2 together, 17 stitches, 2 together, 18 stitches, 2 together, 8 stitches, 2 together, 18 stitches, 2 together, 17 stitches, 2 together, 6 stitches, and draw back. **9th row**—Pick up 6 stitches, 2 together, 16 stitches, 2 together, 16 stitches, 2 together, 8 stitches, 2 together, 16 stitches, 2 together, 16 stitches, 2 together, 6 stitches, and draw back. **10th row**—Long treble stitches, in which a ribbon is to threaded. **11th row**—Double crochet on the long treble stitches, and also double crochet round the placket; this finishes the band. For the **Border** round the bottom of the petticoat. Use a No. 7 crochet needle. **1st round** —Work 2 treble in a stitch of the tricot, 2 treble in the next stitch of the tricot, miss one, 1 treble in the next, miss one, and repeat the same, and join evenly on the completion of the round. **2nd round**— With ruby—Work 5 treble on the one treble stitch of last round, and 1 treble

Baby's Shetland Petticoat with Bodice.

Lady's Petti

LADY'S PETTICOAT IN KILTED TRICOT.

REQUIRED, 16 ozs. of grey and 3 ozs. of ruby petticoat wool, 5-ply fingering, or Alloa, whichever is preferred, a long bone No. 5 tricot needle, and 1½ yards of grey ribbon. The petticoat hangs in graceful kilts from a shaped waistband; the kilts are formed by doing a few rows of tricot with the right side of the work to the front and then a few rows with the wrong side to the front, alternately, and the effect is excellent: the bottom of the petticoat is finished with a crochet border in which the second colour is introduced. Commence with grey wool, with 90 chain, for the **length** of the **kilted** portion of the petticoat. Work 4 rows of tricot in the usual manner, having 90 stitches in each row. Then work along the row in slip-stitch or single crochet. * Turn the work, pick up in tricot the one back thread of the slip stitches, and do 4 rows of plain tricot of 90 stitches in each row; and then work along in slip-stitch. Repeat from * till you find you have accomplished 40 kilts for the width of the petticoat. Both sides of the work are alike; you will find 20 raised and 20 depressed kilts on each side. Sew the last row to the commencing chain, leaving space at the top for a placket opening. For the **Waistband**—With grey wool. **1st row**—Pick up tricot stitches along the top edge of the skirt, 3 tricot stitches on each of the first 12 kilts, 4 tricot stitches on each of the 16 kilts forming the front of the skirt, and 3 tricot stitches on each of the last 12 kilts—136 stitches in all, and draw back. **2nd row**—Pick up 6 stitches, pick up 2 stitches together, pick up 54 stitches, 2 together, 8 stitches, 2 together, 54 stitches, 2 together, 6 stitches, and draw

in the centre of the four treble stitches, and repeat the same, and join at the end of the round. **3rd round**—With grey—5 treble on the one treble stitch, 1 treble on the centre stitch of the group of five treble, and repeat. **4th round**—With ruby—Work 6 treble on the centre stitch of the group of five treble of last round, and 1 double crochet on the one treble stitch, and repeat. **5th round**—With grey—Work single crochet on the margin of the stitches of the preceding round. This finishes the border. Darn in all the ends of wool. Run ribbon through the long treble stitches of the waistband. Put a button and a loop at the bottom of the waistband.

LITTLE PETTICOAT WITH BODICE.

A PRETTY petticoat for a child from one to two years of age, measuring 17 inches from the shoulder to the bottom of the petticoat; the body is worked in single crochet, the skirt is in double crochet, certain rounds of which are the ordinary plain stitch and other rounds are the Russian stitch, and the dark shaded lines that appear in the engraving are due to the introduction of the Russian stitch and the ridges that thereby are made, and not as you would imagine to the employment of a second and darker shade of wool. The petticoat does not open at the back, it slips over the child's head. Procure 5 ozs. of Paton's best quality electric blue 4-ply fingering, a No. 5 bone crochet needle, and 3 yards of narrow ribbon to match the wool. Begin with the **Bodice**, and for the part under the arm do 21 chain rather loosely. **1st row**—Miss the first stitch by the needle, and do 20 single crochet. **2nd row**—Turn with 1 chain, and taking up the one back thread of the stitches of previous row and drawing the wool up easily on the needle, again work 20 single crochet, and at the end of the row do 35 chain to reach over the shoulder. **3rd row**—Miss the first chain by the needle, work 34 single crochet along the 34 chain and 20 single crochet on the single crochet of the preceding row, 54 stitches in all. **4th row**—Beginning on the side by the waist,—Turn with 1 chain, do 4 single crochet, 2 chain, miss two stitches (this makes a hole through which the waist ribbon is to be run), and thence work in single crochet to the end; a similar hole is to be made in every fourth row that begins at the waist. **5th row**—Turn with 1 chain, do 54 single crochet. Continue this long row till 4 ribs (8 rows) are worked the whole length of the 54 stitches. **10th row**—Turn with 1 chain, work 34 single crochet; turn here with 1 chain as usual, and repeat this row till 22 ribs (44 rows) are done for the front of the body, remembering always in every fourth row to make the hole for the ribbon to pass through. At the end of the last front row add 20 chain for the other shoulder, and work 4 ribs on 54 stitches. Then do 2 ribs on 20 stitches for under the arm. After this add 14 chain, and work in rows of 34 stitches for the back of the body till 30 ribs are accomplished. Let the next row consist of 20 stitches for under the arm, do a return row to the waist, and up again; then break off the wool, and sew the last row to the commencing chain. Join the shoulder straps to the corresponding ribs on the back of the body.

FROCK FOR CHILD OF TWO YEARS.

This pretty little frock measures 19 inches from the neck to the bottom of the skirt and is worked in ridged crochet with fancy border. Required, 9 ozs. of the best Andalusian wool, any colour preferred, a No. 9 bone crochet needle, 1½ yards of narrow ribbon, and three buttons.

For **Border** at the **Bottom of Skirt**—The border is joined at the end of every row by drawing the first stitch through the last. Commence with 380 chain. **1st and 2nd rows**—Double crochet. Turn. **3rd row**—Make a chain of 3 and work * 5 treble in the first stitch, take out the hook and insert it in the first treble stitch, and draw the fifth treble stitch through it, 1 chain, miss 1, and repeat from * to the end of the row. **4th row**—Same as third. Turn. **5th and 6th rows**—Double crochet. **7th row**—3 chain, insert the hook in second chain from needle, and draw wool through so as to form a loop, take up the first chain and 2 first stitches in the same way, and you will have 5 loops on the needle; draw the wool through all five loops at once, and make 1 chain. This completes the first shell, * insert the needle in hole made by 1 chain, and draw the wool through, put the needle in the stitch which holds the last loop of the previous shell, and draw the wool through, take up the next two stitches in the same way, and draw the wool through all 5 loops at once as before, 1 chain, and repeat from * to the end of the row. **8th and 9th rows**—Double crochet. Turn. **10th and 11th rows**—Like 3rd. Turn. **12th and 13th rows**—Double crochet, and at the end of the 13th row make a chain of 50 and 1 more to turn. Now you begin the ridged crochet for **Top of Skirt**, which is worked backwards and forwards, but taking up back thread only of stitches in pre-

Quilted Tricot.

Little Petticoat with Bodice.

For the **Skirt—1st round**—Hold the body conveniently and begin at the centre of the back; work 1 double crochet on each rib of the single crochet and 1 double crochet between the ribs, and get 128, or more, double crochet stitches in the round; join evenly at the end of this and every round, and be careful to keep the seam *straight* down the back of the skirt. Work 8 more rounds of plain double crochet inserting the hook to take up the two front threads of the stitches of the preceding round; you may increase a few stitches, or not, in these rounds, according if you wish the skirt to hang full or otherwise. **10th round**—Turn the work, and proceed in double crochet, but now take up the one *back* thread of the stitches of last round. Do 2 more rounds the same. **13th round**—Turn the work to get that side uppermost on which you before did the plain double crochet, and work this round and the 2 next rounds as at first, taking up the two front threads of the stitches. Repeat the 3 ridged rounds and the three plain rounds alternately five times. The reverse or rough side of the plain rounds is to be considered the right side of the work. Work 2 additional plain rounds and also a scolloped round to complete the skirt. The scollops are formed thus—1 double crochet on a stitch of the petticoat, miss one stitch, 7 treble on the next, miss one, and repeat. Similar scollops, but consisting of 5 treble instead of seven, are to be crocheted round the neck and armholes; and ribbon is run round these, and round the waist, as shown in the engraving.

vious row. **1st row**—Double crochet in each of 50 chain, insert the needle in third stitch of last row in border, and draw it through the stitch already on the needle. **2nd row**—Ridged crochet, 1 chain to turn. **3rd row**—Ridged crochet, and take up the fifth stitch of 13th row, like you did the third, and turn. Repeat the 2nd and 3rd rows until you have worked right round the skirt. Break off the wool and sew up to within 20 stitches from top of skirt to form a placket hole. Work 6 rows of ridged crochet on the 20 stitches on the button side of skirt for a wrap, and stitch it carefully across the bottom on the wrong side. For the **Waistband**—With the right side of the work towards you work 1 double crochet in every ridge at top of skirt and you will have 190 stitches, 1 chain to turn. **2nd row**—Double crochet, taking up both threads of stitches in last row, 1 chain to turn. **3rd row**—1 double crochet, miss 1 for 15 times, then 1 double crochet in each of the next 130 stitches, then 1 double crochet, miss 1 for 15 times, and you will have 160 stitches. **4th row** —Same as 3rd row in band. **5th row**—Double crochet. Repeat the 4th and 5th rows twice more. **10th row**—Double crochet and make a chain of 40 and 1 more to turn for the **Bodice—1st row**—Double crochet in each of the 40 chain, insert the needle in the 3rd stitch of 10th row in band, and draw it through the stitch already on the needle. **2nd row**—Ridged crochet, 1 chain to turn. **3rd row**—Ridged crochet, and at the end of row take up the 5th stitch of 10th row in band, like you did the third, and turn. Repeat the 2nd and 3rd rows 19 times and you will have done 20 ridges, and have picked up 20 stitches. **41st row**—Ridged crochet in each of next 16 stitches, 1 chain to turn. **42nd row**—Ridged crochet, and take up a stitch and draw it through as usual. Repeat the 41st and 42nd rows once more. **45th row**—Ridged crochet and make a chain of 24, and 1 more to turn. Now work backwards and forwards on these 40 stitches as before for 72 rows. Repeat from 41st to 45th rows inclusive, then work backwards and forwards on these 40 stitches for 38 rows, and you will have worked 158 rows altogether on the bodice. **159th row**—7 ridged crochet, 3 chain, miss 3, 9 ridged crochet, 3 chain, miss 3, 9 ridged crochet, 3 chain, miss 3, 6 ridged crochet. **160th row**—Ridged crochet in each stitch of last row. Break off and fasten the end in securely. For shoulder sew up 6 ridges from either side of armholes. For the **Neck—1st row**—2 double crochet in each ridge right across. **2nd row**—3 chain to turn, 1 treble in the second stitch, * 2 chain, miss 2, 2 treble, and repeat from * to end of row. **3rd row**—1 chain to turn, * 1 double crochet, 2 treble, 1 chain, 2 treble, 1 double crochet in the same stitch, miss 3, and repeat from * to end of row. Break off. Work the last row round bottom of skirt. **Sleeves**—Make a chain of 24 and work backwards and forwards in ridged crochet for 80 rows. 3 chain to turn. 1 double crochet in each of the 40 ridges. Make holes and edge same as in 2nd and 3rd rows of neck. Sew up the sleeves and stitch them in. Thread the ribbon in the holes in sleeves and the remainder in the neck, leaving ends to tie. Sew the buttons on and the frock is finished.

BOLSOVER PATTERN FOR A SHAWL.

THE Bolsover pattern is equally suitable for shawls, scarfs, and fascinators, is crocheted in rows forwards and backwards, and the work is alike on both

the needle and draw through 2 stitches on the needle, wool over the needle and draw through 3 stitches on the needle, and repeat from * to the end of the round : the corners are eased by 5 times missing only one stitch instead of missing two stitches, and by 5 times doing 3 chain instead of two chain ; join evenly when the round is completed. **3rd round**—Work 3 treble under a loop of two chain of preceding round, 1 chain, 3 treble in the next loop, and repeat : and at the corners work double groups of 3 treble stitches in the three corner loops : join at the end of the round and break off the wool. **4th round**—Begin with 3 chain, * wool over the needle and insert the hook in the space of one chain of last round and draw the wool through loosely, wool over the needle and draw through 2 stitches on the needle, wool over the needle and insert the hook in the next space of last round and draw the wool through loosely, wool over the needle and draw through 2 stitches on the needle, wool over the needle and draw through 3 stitches on the needle, then 3 chain, and repeat from * : in this round there is no increase at the corners. **5th round**—Do 1 double crochet under a loop of three chain of previous round, * 1 chain, 1 treble under the next loop of three chain, and 1 chain and 1 treble alternately 4 times in the same place (that is 5 treble stitches with 1 chain between each), 1 chain, 1 double crochet under the next loop, and repeat from * all round ; but at the corner make a pattern with 7 treble stitches in a loop, as seen in the engraving. **6th round**—Work 1 double crochet on the first treble stitch of a group of stitches of last round, 2 chain, 1 treble on the next treble stitch, 4 chain, 1 double crochet on the treble stitch last worked (which forms a picot), 1 treble on the centre stitch of the 5 treble of last round, 4 chain, 1 double crochet on the treble stitch last worked (forms another picot),

Frock for a Child of Two Years.

sides. Procure 8 ozs. of Andalusian wool, or more, according to the size the shawl is required to be, and a No. 8 bone crochet needle. Make a chain the necessary length. **1st row**—Work 1 double crochet in the second chain from the needle, and 1 double crochet in the next stitch of chain, * wool over the needle, insert the hook in the next stitch of chain and draw the wool through loosely, wool over the needle, insert the hook again in the same place and draw the wool through loosely, again wool over the needle, insert the hook in the same place and draw the wool through loosely, wool over the needle and draw through all the 7 stitches on the needle, work 1 double crochet in each of 2 consecutive stitches of the foundation, and repeat from * to the end of the row, which must finish with only 1 double crochet after the raised tuft. **2nd row**—Do 1 chain and turn the work, now take up the one back thread of the stitches of the previous row, 1 double crochet on the double crochet stitch, and 1 double crochet on the tuft stitch, * a tuft (worked as instructed above) on the next stitch, then 1 double crochet on each of 2 consecutive stitches, and repeat from * ; and this row will end as the preceding with 1 double crochet after the last raised tuft, the number of tufts being the same as were worked in the first row. Every succeeding row is worked the same as the second row, until the shawl is brought to the dimension required.

For the **Border : 1st round**—Do double crochet all round the shawl. **2nd round**—Work 1 treble in a stitch of double crochet, * 2 chain, wool over the needle, insert the hook in the same double crochet as the treble is worked into, and draw the wool through loosely, wool over the needle and draw through 2 stitches on the needle, wool over the needle, miss two double crochet, insert the hook in the next double crochet and draw the wool through loosely, wool over

1 treble again on the centre stitch of the 5 treble, 4 chain, 1 double crochet on the treble stitch last worked (a third picot), 1 treble on the fourth of the 5 treble stitches, 2 chain, 1 double crochet on the last treble of the group ; repeat the same scollop upon every group of 5 treble stitches, and at the corners, where there are 7 stitches in a group, work 2 extra treble stitches and 2 extra picots : join round evenly, and fasten off.

WORK BOX.

REQUIRED, ½ yard each of crimson satin and sateen, 2 yards of crimson cord, 1 yard of crimson satin ribbon ½ inch wide, some stout cardboard, a little wadding, 1 ball of fine crochet macramé twine (tan colour), and a fine steel crochet needle. Make a box with the cardboard 9 inches square and 2½ inches deep, line it with satin, and cover the outside with sateen. The bottom of the inside of the box and the outside of cover are to be padded. For the **Cover**—Make a chain of 4 and join. You must join at the end of every row when working the cover. **1st row**—Work 3 double crochet in each of the 4 chain to form the corners. Work 5 more rows of double crochet, increasing 3 stitches at each corner so as to keep the work square throughout. **7th row**—In point neige or shell stitch, which is worked as follows,—Insert the needle in the first stitch and draw the thread through so as to form a loop, raise 3 more loops in the same way in the 3 next stitches, and draw the thread through all 5 loops at once and make 1 chain ; this completes the first shell, * raise a loop in hole formed by 1 chain, another in the stitch which holds the last loop of first shell, and 2 more in the 2 next stitches, and draw the thread through all 5 loops at once, make 1 chain and repeat from * to the end of row. **8th row**—Double crochet. **9th row**—Like the 7th. **10th row**—Double crochet. **11th row**—Turn, work 5 treble in the first stitch, take out the needle and insert it in the first treble stitch and draw the fifth treble stitch through it, 1 chain, miss 1, and repeat. **12th row**—Turn, double crochet. **13th row**—Like the 7th. **14th row**—Double crochet. **15th row**—Like the 11th. **16th row**—Like the 12th. **17th row**—1 treble in each of the first two stitches, 2 chain, miss 2, and repeat. **18th row**—Double crochet. **19th row**—Like the 11th. **20th row**—Like the 12th. **21st row**—Like the 7th. **22nd and 23rd rows**—Double crochet. **24th row**—Like the 7th. Work 7 more rows in double crochet and fasten off. Cover a piece of cardboard 1¾ inches square first with wadding, and then with the satin, and stitch it in the centre so as just to cover the first six rows. Thread the ribbon through the holes, stitch the crochet on the cover, and sew on the cord, making a loop with the cord at each corner as shown in the illustration. For the **Sides** of **Box**—Make a chain of 24 and work backwards and forwards in double crochet, taking up the back thread only of stitches in previous row till you have done a piece long enough to go round the box, then join up the sides and work 1 row of double crochet and 1 row like the 11th round the top and bottom; fasten off and sew it on to the box, then stitch on the cover.

row—Work 2 treble, 2 long treble, and 2 more treble stitches in the first hole of 3 chain, take out the hook and insert it in the first treble stitch, and draw the last treble stitch through it, make 4 chain and repeat in every hole and join round. Thread the cord through the holes and sew it round the top of the box. For the lid work three triangular pieces as follows: Make a chain of 29 and turn and work backwards and forwards in double crochet, always missing the first stitch in every row and taking up the back thread only of stitches in previous row till you have only 1 stitch; then break off and draw the end through and work a row of 1 treble. 3 chain, miss 2, all round each, then sew them on to the lid as shown in the illustration, after stitching the little piece of plush in the centre. Thread the ribbon through the holes that border the plush and tie in a bow at each corner, then thread remainder of cord through the holes round the outside. Tie the two pieces of cord in a knot and fray out the ends, then stitch the lid on to the box at the two corners.

BLOTTER.

PROCURE the same materials as for the work box, with the addition of a few sheets of blotting paper, as this blotter is made to exactly match the work box. Make the cover as described for the work box cover, and on the

Bolsover Pattern for a Shawl.

TRINKET BOX.

A BOX to hold trinkets or odds and ends is a very useful article on a toilet table and may be quite an ornament as well. Our model is triangular in shape and is made on a foundation of stout cardboard measuring 5¾ inches each way, and 2½ inches deep; thus, you require three pieces of cardboard these dimensions and two triangular pieces measuring 5¾ inches each way, one for the lid and the other for the bottom of box. The box being made is then covered inside and out with pale blue silk or sateen, the lining round the sides being put on rather full, while the *bottom* of the box and the *outside* of lid should have been previously padded. About ⅛ a ball of old gold crochet macramé thread will be required with a tiny three-cornered piece of olive green plush, 1 yard of bébé ribbon to match, a yard of pale blue silk cord and a fine steel crochet hook. Commence with a chain of 29 for the **Sides** of **Box** and turn with 1 chain. **1st row**—Work 14 double crochet in the first 14 chain, 2 double crochet in the fifteenth chain, and 1 double crochet in each of the remaining 14 chain. Turn without making a chain. **2nd row**—Miss the first stitch and work 14 double crochet, 2 double crochet in next stitch, then 14 double crochet, taking up back thread only of stitches in previous row and turn. Repeat the second row until you have done a piece long enough to go round the box, then join and sew it on the box. For the knobby pattern round the **Top**, make a chain the same length as the crochet strip and turn. **1st row**—2 double crochet, 3 chain, miss 2, and repeat. **2nd**

inside there would be a pocket (made of thin cardboard and covered with satin) to hold note paper and envelope. For the **Pad**—Cover a piece of cardboard first with wadding, and then with the satin, and paste a piece of white paper on the inside. Sew on a little three-cornered piece of satin across each corner and slip in the blotting paper, which must be cut the same size as the cardboard. Bind the cover and the pad with a piece of satin (doubled) about 1¼ inches wide, and the opening of pocket should be inside and parallel with the binding.

ACORN PINCUSHION.

REQUIRED, a little green plush or velvet, some fine brown crochet macramé twine, a steel crochet needle, a little fine wire, and some wadding for stuffing the acorn, which, when completed, should measure 5 inches long and 7 inches round. Fill a linen case with wadding, the bottom half of which is to be covered with plush, the top half being covered with the crochet cup. For the stalk—Work a piece of wire 1½ inches long closely over in double crochet and twist the work round so as to give the stalk a natural bend. For the **Cup**—Raise 3 stitches and work 2 double crochet in each stitch for two rounds. **3rd round**—Work 5 treble in 1 stitch, take out the hook and insert it in the first treble stitch and draw the fifth treble stitch through it, 1 chain and repeat. **4th round**—Like the third, only you miss a stitch after making the 1 chain. **5th round**—Like the fourth, but increasing occasionally by making 2 chain instead of 1. **6th round**—Like the fifth. Work 4 more rounds without increasing, and fasten off. Slip the acorn into the cup, run a thread through the top of the cup, draw it up tightly so as to keep the acorn from slipping out, and fasten the end off securely. It is as well also to slip-stitch the edge of the crochet down to the plush.

DOLL DRESSED IN CROCHET SAILOR COSTUME.

REQUIRED, a doll with movable joints, 2 ozs. of pale blue Andalusian wool, and a small quantity of white Andalusian for the vest, 1 oz. of white Shetland, half a yard of narrow ribbon, a little white crochet cotton for the lanyard and

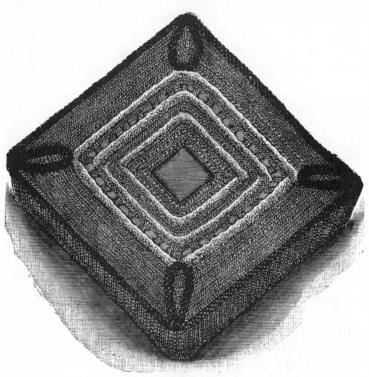

Work Box.

socks, some very tiny wire and elastic for the hat, and buckles for the slippers, if you can get them (if not, you could make little rosettes with the ribbon), and a very small quantity of cream twine for soles of slippers, a pair of bone knitting needles No. 9, a pair of steel needles No. 14, a bone crochet needle No. 10, and a fine steel crochet needle. For the **Vest**—White Andalusian and bone knitting needle. Cast on 68 stitches and knit 1 row plain, and 1 row purl for 28 rows, then divide for the armholes, 34 stitches for the front and 17 for each of the backs. Work backwards and forwards on each of these pieces for 24 rows, then cast off and sew up 8 stitches on either side of the armholes for the shoulders. Work 1 row of double crochet down the button side of back, across the bottom and up the buttonhole side of back, making 4 buttonholes at regular distances, and sew on the buttons. For the **Drawers**—Use the Shetland wool and bone crochet needle No. 10. Make a chain of 64, and work 1 row of double crochet. **2nd row**—2 treble, 2 chain, miss 2, and repeat. **3rd row**—Double crochet. **4th row** and 7 succeeding rows—Treble. **12th row**—32 treble and turn. Work backwards and forwards on these 32 stitches as before for 8 rows, then 1 row of double crochet, 3 treble, 1 double crochet in one stitch, miss three, and repeat to the end of row. Break off and work the other leg in the same way, and sew up the legs. Make a chain and thread it through the holes at waist. **Petticoat**—Same wool and needle as for drawers. Make a chain of 120 and join, then work one round of double crochet, one round of holes and one more round of double crochet, 1 round of treble, 2 rounds of double crochet, 1 round of point neige, 1 round of treble, another round of point neige, then 7 rounds of treble. For the **Border—1st round**—5 treble in one stitch, miss 2, and repeat. **2nd round** and two succeeding rounds—5 treble in the centre stitch of the 5 treble in previous round, and 1 double crochet between every set of 5 treble. Make a chain and thread it through the holes at waist. For the **Dress**—Use the pale-blue Andalusian wool and bone crochet and knitting needles. Cast on 142 stitches and knit 1 row plain, 1 row of holes, 2 rows plain. **5th row**—Knit 1, purl 1, and repeat. **6th row**—Purl 1, knit 1, and repeat. Repeat the last two rows 14 times and cast off. The remainder of the **Skirt** is crocheted. **1st row**—2 double crochet, then 3 in the same stitch, 2 double crochet, and repeat. **2nd row**—* Miss 1, 2 double crochet, 3 double crochet in the next stitch, 2 double crochet, miss 1, and repeat from * to end of row. In the border you only take up the back thread of stitches in previous row so as to form little ridges. Work 10 more rows like the 2nd. Break off and sew up the skirt. Make a chain and thread it through the holes at waist. **Blouse**—Use the Andalusian wool and knitting needles No. 9. Cast on 60 stitches and knit 1 row plain, 1 row of holes, 2 rows plain. **5th row**—Knit 1, purl 1, and repeat. **6th row**

—Purl 1, knit 1, and repeat. Repeat these two rows 7 times, then decrease a stitch at the beginning and end of every row for 8 rows. Then divide for the armholes—30 stitches for the back and 15 for each front. Work 16 more rows on each of these three pieces, decreasing in the fronts as before for the vest. Cast off and sew up 6 stitches on either side of armholes for the shoulders. Cut out a collar in blue sateen, and stitch it round twice with a chain-stitch machine so that the chain comes on the outside, or else make a chain with white crochet cotton and sew it on. Stitch the collar on the blouse and add ribbon strings to either end. For the **Sleeves**—Cast on 20 stitches with No. 14 steel needles. **1st row**—Knit 1, purl 1, and repeat. **2nd row**—Purl 1, knit 1, and repeat. Repeat these two rows three times and work 4 more rows with the bone needles, then increase a stitch at the beginning of every row for 10 rows and work 8 more rows without increasing, and cast off. Sew up the sleeves, stitch them in, and turn up the cuffs. Make a chain to thread through holes at waist. **Lanyard**—Use crochet cotton and steel hook. Make a chain and join just large enough to slip over the doll's head, then make a chain about 3 inches long and work back in double crochet. **Hat**—Andalusian wool and bone crochet needle No. 9. Make a loop and work 9 double crochet into it and draw the end of wool tight so as to close up the hole. Work round and round in double crochet, increasing occasionally so as to keep the work perfectly flat till it measures about 2 inches across. Then work 8 rounds without increasing. Next round, increase in every other stitch for the brim, then work three rounds, increasing occasionally so as to keep the work flat. In the next round you must crochet in the wire and when that is done break off. Turn up the brim at the back and crinkle it. For the feather, make a chain of 7 with the white Shetland and work backwards and forwards in loop crochet for about 5 inches and fasten off. Fasten it on the hat and make three little pompons with the Shetland and one each with the white and blue Andalusian; stitch them on the crown at back and sew on the elastic. **Socks**—Use the crochet cotton and steel crochet hook. Make a chain of 30. Join and work round and round in double crochet for 18 rounds, then decrease 2 stitches at the back (where the seam stitch would come) in every alternate round till you have only 6 stitches. Break off and sew up the toe. Work a little edging round the top of sock of 1 double crochet, 3 treble, 1 double crochet in 1 stitch, miss 3, and repeat. Make the other sock in the same way. **Slippers**—Use the Andalusian wool and steel crochet hook. Make a chain of 7 and 1 more to turn. Work backwards and forwards in ridged crochet, increasing 2 stitches in the centre stitch of each row till you have 21 stitches in the row. Now work backwards and forwards on 7 stitches only for 20 rows. Break off and sew up the end of this strip to the toe part. For the **Sole**—Use the cream twine and steel needle. Make a chain of 16, turn and work round and round in double crochet, increasing at both ends so as to keep it flat for 3 rounds. Fasten off. Work the other slipper in the same way and the sole, and sew on the soles. Put on the buckles with a little ribbon bow, or ribbon rosettes only.

Trinket Box.

BASKET PINCUSHION.

REQUIRED, a small quantity of fine brown crochet macramé twine, a steel crochet hook, a small piece each of green plush and salmon-pink silk, a yard each of green and pink bébé ribbon to match, some wire or a brass ring for the handle, and wadding to stuff the cushions. For the **Basket**—Make a chain of 12, and 1 more to turn, and work round and round in double crochet, increasing occasionally at each end, so as to keep it perfectly flat for 6 rounds. **7th round**—1 treble, 1 chain, miss 1, and repeat. **8th round** —* Thread forward, and insert the needle in the first hole, and draw through so as to form a loop, and repeat from * 3 times, and you will have 9 loops on the needle, thread forward, and draw through all together, 1 chain, and repeat from † to the end of the round. **9th round**—Double crochet, increasing every 7th stitch. **10th round**—Like the 7th. **11th round**—

Like the 8th. **12th round**—Like the 9th. **13th round**—Like the 7th. **14th round**—Like the 8th. **15th round**—1 double crochet, 2 chain, miss 1, and repeat all round. Cover an oval piece of cardboard 3 inches by 1¾ inches with pink sateen, and stitch it on to the bottom of the basket. Thread the pink ribbon through the holes in 10th row, leaving ends to tie on both sides, and thread the green ribbon through the holes in the 13th row, leaving ends to tie on both sides, then tie all the ends together in a bow. Line the basket with pink silk, gathering it neatly so as to form a frill round the edge. Make two little cushions, one of plush and the other of silk, and fix in the basket. For the handle make a ring of wire 1½ inches in diameter, and cover same by working a row of double crochet over it, which you must wind round the wire to give it a twisted appearance. Catch both sides of the basket together as shown in the illustration, and fasten on the handle.

Blotter.

CHILD'S CROCHET PELISSE.

(Not Illustrated.)

A PRETTY little outdoor garment arranged to button down the front, with fancy trimming on either side, also round skirt part. Required, 1 lb. of single Berlin wool, a long bone No. 6 tricot needle, also a bone crochet needle No. 7 for the bordering, 3 yards of 1½-inch wide satin ribbon to match the wool, and a dozen pearl buttons. The length of the model pelisse from the collar to the bottom of the skirt is 25 inches, and the size round the waist about 23 inches. A smaller pelisse can be made by working the tricot with a No. 7 needle. And if petticoat fingering be used with a No. 6 or No. 5 tricot needle it will result in a larger and stronger garment. Commence for the **Bottom** of the **Skirt** with 213 chain, and work 4 rows of plain tricot. **5th row**—Pick up 54 tricot stitches, pick up 2 stitches together, 22 stitches, 2 stitches together, 53 stitches, 2 stitches together, 22 stitches, 2 stitches together, and thence 54 stitches to the end, and draw back as usual. Do 3 plain rows. **9th row**—Pick up 3 stitches, pick up 2 together, pick up 48, pick up 2 together, 22 stitches, 2 together, 51 stitches, 2 together, 22 stitches, 2 together, 53 stitches; and draw back, and when 4 stitches from the right-hand edge of the tricot do 1 chain to replace the stitch lost by picking up 2 stitches together, and draw back to the end; thus a buttonhole will be made, and similar buttonholes must be formed at intervals of every eighth row up the right-hand side of the front. Do 3 plain rows. **13th row**—Pick up 52 stitches, 2 stitches together, 22 stitches, 2 together, 49 stitches, 2 together, 22 stitches, 2 together, 52 stitches. Do 2 plain rows. **16th row**—Pick up 51 stitches, 2 together, 22 stitches, 2 together, 47 stitches, 2 together, 22 stitches, 2 together, 51 stitches. Do 2 plain rows. **19th row**—Pick up 50 stitches, 2 together, 22 stitches, 2 together, 45 stitches, 2 together, 22 stitches, 2 together, 50 stitches. Do 2 plain rows. **22nd row**—Pick up 49 stitches, 2 together, 22 stitches, 2 together, 43 stitches, 2 together, 22 stitches, 2 together, 49 stitches. Do 2 plain rows. **25th row**—Pick up 48 stitches, 2 together, 22 stitches, 2 together, 41 stitches, 2 together, 22 stitches, 2 together, 48 stitches. Do 2 plain rows. **28th row**—Pick up 47 stitches, 2 together, 22 stitches, 2 together, 39 stitches, 2 together, 22 stitches, 2 together, 47 stitches. Do 1 plain row. **30th row**—Pick up 46 stitches, 2 together, 22 stitches, 2 together, 37 stitches, 2 together, 22 stitches, 2 together, 46 stitches. Do 1 plain row. **32nd row**—Pick up 45 stitches, 2 together, 22 stitches, 2 together, 35 stitches, 2 together, 22 stitches, 2 together, 45 stitches. Do 1 plain row. **34th row**—Pick up 68 stitches, miss 37 stitches to form a box pleat at the back of the skirt, pick up 68 stitches; now there are 136 stitches on the needle, and draw back as usual. Do 2 plain rows. **37th row**—Pick up 44 stitches, 2 together, 44 stitches, 2 together, 44 stitches. Do 4 plain rows. **42nd row**—Pick up 43 stitches, 2 together, 44 stitches, 2 together, 43 stitches. Do 4 plain rows. **47th row**—Pick up 42 stitches, 2 together, 44 stitches, 2 together, 42 stitches. Do 4 plain rows. **52nd row**—Pick up 41 stitches, 2 together, 44 stitches, 2 together, 41 stitches. Do 4 plain rows. **57th row**—Pick up 40 stitches, 2 together, 44 stitches, 2 together, 40 stitches. Do 2 plain rows on 126 stitches. **60th row**—Begins the **First Front**—Pick up 42 stitches, and draw the same back. **61st row**—Pick up 36 stitches, pick up 6 stitches together, making 37 on the needle, and draw back. **62nd row**—Pick up 31 stitches, pick up 6 stitches together, making 32 on the needle, and draw back. **63rd row**—Pick up 28 stitches, pick up 4 stitches together, making 29 on the needle, and draw back. **64th row**—Pick up 26 stitches, pick up 3 stitches together, making 27 on the needle, and draw back. **65th row**—Pick up 25 stitches, pick up 2 stitches together, making 26 on the needle, and draw back. Do 6 plain rows on the 26 stitches. **72nd row**—Pick up 25 stitches, increase 1 stitch by picking up a stitch in the horizontal thread before the tricot stitch at the end of last row, pick up the last tricot stitch. **73rd row**—Plain, 27 stitches. **74th row**—Increase 1 stitch as before at the shoulder. **75th row**—In picking up increase 1 stitch at the shoulder, and in drawing back draw through 4 stitches together at the neck. **76th row**—Plain, 26 stitches, and in drawing back draw through 4 together at the neck. **77th row**—Increase 1 stitch at the shoulder, and draw through 4 together at the neck. **78th row**—Increase 1 stitch at the shoulder, and draw through 3 together at the neck. Do 3 more rows the same as last row. **82nd row**—Begin to slant the shoulder—Pick up 15 stitches, pick up 2 stitches together, making 16 on the needle; and in drawing back draw through 3 together at the neck. **83rd row**—Pick up 12 stitches, pick up 2 together, making 13 on the needle; and in drawing back draw through 2 together at the neck. **84th row**—Pick up 9 stitches, pick up 3 together, making 10 on the needle; and draw through 2 together at the neck. **85th row**—Pick up 7 stitches, pick up 2 together, making 8 on the needle; and draw through 2 together at the neck. **86th row**—Pick up 4 stitches, pick up 3 together, making 5 on the needle; and draw through 2 together at the neck. **87th row**—Pick up 2 stitches, pick up 2 together, making 3 on the needle; draw through the 3 stitches together, and break off the wool. For the **Other Side** of the **Front**—Pick up the 42 stitches at the end of the fifty-ninth row, and work to correspond with the front already done. For the **Back**—**1st row**—Pick up 42 tricot stitches, and decrease by drawing through 2 stitches together at the beginning and at the

Acorn Pincushion.

end of the row. **2nd row**—Pick up 40 stitches, and decrease in the same way. **3rd row**—Pick up 38 stitches, and again decrease. Work 10 rows on 36 tricot stitches. **14th row**—Increase 1 stitch at each end, and so get 38 stitches on the needle, and draw back. **15th row**—Increase 1 stitch at each end, and there will be 40 on the needle, and draw back. **16th row**—Again increase 1 stitch at each end, and get 42 on the needle, and draw back. **17th row**—Begin to slant the shoulders—Pick up 42 stitches, and decrease by drawing through 3 together at each end. **18th row**—Pick up 38 stitches, and again draw through 3 together at each end. **19th row**—Pick up 34 stitches, and decrease by drawing through 2 together at each end. **20th row**—Pick up 32 stitches, and draw through 3 together at each end. **21st row**—Pick up

23 stitches, and draw through 2 together at each end. Now slip along the 26 stitches, and break off the wool, the back is finished. Sew the shoulder pieces neatly together. For the **Sleeves**—Begin at the top of the sleeve with 54 chain, and break off. **1st row**—Miss the first 22 stitches of the chain, commence on the twenty-third, and pick up 10 tricot stitches, and draw back, this is the centre or highest part of the sleeve, then slip the wool stitch by stitch along 3 stitches of the foundation chain. **2nd row**—Pick up 3 tricot stitches on those you have just slipped, 10 stitches on the ten of the previous row, and 3 stitches in the chain to the left, and draw back, and slip the wool along 3 more of the foundation chain. **3rd row**—Pick up 3 tricot stitches on those you have just slipped, 16 stitches on the sixteen of previous row, and 3 stitches in the chain to the left, and draw back, and slip the wool along 3 more of the foundation chain. **4th row**—Pick up 3 tricot stitches on those just slipped,

Doll Dressed in Crochet Sailor Costume.

22 stitches on the twenty-two of previous row, and 3 stitches in the chain to the left, and draw back, and slip the wool along 3 more of the foundation chain. **5th row**—Pick up 3 tricot stitches on those just slipped, 28 stitches on the twenty-eight of previous row, and 3 stitches in the chain to the left, and draw back, and slip the wool along 3 more of the foundation chain. **6th row**—Pick up 3 tricot stitches on those just slipped, 34 stitches on the thirty-four of previous row, and 3 stitches in the chain to the left, and draw back, and slip the wool along 3 more of the foundation chain. **7th row**—Pick up 3 tricot stitches on those just slipped, 40 stitches on the forty of previous row, and 3 stitches in the chain to the left, and draw back, and slip the wool along the 4 remaining stitches of the foundation chain. **8th row**—Pick up 4 tricot stitches on those just slipped, 46 stitches on the forty-six of previous row, and 4 stitches in the chain to the left, making 54 stitches in all on the needle, and draw back. * Work 4 rows of plain tricot on the 54 stitches; but in drawing back the fourth of these rows, stop at 6 stitches from the end, pick up again to within 6 stitches of other end, and then draw back through all; this makes a *short* and *additional row* to ease the back of the sleeve. Repeat from * three times more. Then work 1 plain row on 54 stitches. **26th row**—Pick up 24 stitches, pick up 2 stitches together, pick up 2 stitches separately, then 2 stitches together, pick up 24 stitches to the end of the row, and draw back. **27th row**—Plain, 52 stitches, and in drawing back stop at 6 stitches from the end, pick up again to within 6 stitches of the other end, and draw back through all. **28th row**—Pick up 23 stitches, and then 2 together, 2 stitches, and then 2 together, 23 stitches, and draw back. **29th row**—Plain. **30th row**—Pick up 22 stitches, and then 2 together, 2 stitches, and then 2 together, 22 stitches, and in drawing back stop 6 stitches from the end, pick up again to within 6 stitches of the other end, and draw back through all. **31st row**—Plain. **32nd row**—Pick up 21 stitches, and then 2 together, 2 stitches, and then 2 together, 21 stitches, and draw back. **33rd row**—Plain, 46 stitches, and in drawing back stop 6 stitches from the end, pick up again to within 6 stitches of the other end, and draw back through all. **34th row**—Pick up 20 stitches, and then 2 together, 2 stitches, and then 2 together, 20 stitches, and draw back. **35th row**—Plain. **36th row**—Pick up 19 stitches, and then 2 together, 2 stitches, and then 2 together, 19 stitches, and in drawing back stop 6 stitches from the end, pick up again to within 6 stitches of the other end, and draw back through all. **37th row**—Plain. **38th row**—Pick up 18 stitches, and then 2 together, 2 stitches, and then 2 together, 18 stitches, and draw back. **39th row**—Plain.

40 stitches, and in drawing back stop 6 stitches from the end, pick up again to within 6 stitches of the other end, and draw back through all. **40th row**—Pick up 17 stitches, and then 2 together, 2 stitches, and then 2 together, 17 stitches, and draw back. **41st row**—Plain, 38 stitches: slip stitch along, and break off the wool with a long end. Make the other sleeve like this one; and sew the sleeves up, and put them in the armholes. Work a row of slip stitch on the 37 stitches missed at the back of the skirt, and sew them to form a box pleat. Up the front edge on the buttonhole side work this scollop,—1 single crochet at the lowest corner of the tricot,* miss two loops of the tricot, 6 treble in the next, miss two loops, 1 single crochet in the next, and repeat from *: do double crochet round the neck, also down the edge of the left hand front, and the whole way round the bottom of the skirt.

The **Crochet Trimming** may be made upon lengths of foundation chain and afterwards sewn down either front and along lower edge, or it may be crocheted directly upon the tricot, as seems most convenient; if on the tricot you work upon the eleventh line of stitches from the front edges, on the ninth row of tricot from the bottom of the skirt, and on the eleventh row from the bottom of the sleeves. For the **Trimming** up the **Front**—**1st row**—Work *loosely*, 4 treble on the first stitch, * miss two stitches, 6 treble on the next, miss two stitches, 1 single crochet on the next, and repeat from *, and turn at the end of the row, and go down the opposite side of the foundation in the same way, single crochet opposite to the single crochet that is already worked and 6 treble opposite to the previous 6 treble. **2nd row**—1 single crochet on the first treble stitch of the foregoing row, * 3 chain, insert the hook to take up the two back threads of the stitches, and pick up (like tricot but much more loosely) 1 stitch on each of the following 7 stitches of previous row, then wool over the needle and draw through the 8 stitches on the needle, 3 chain, 1 single crochet on the third of the six treble stitches of previous row, and repeat from *, and go round the top of the strip and down the other side in the same way. **3rd row**—1 single crochet in the same treble stitch as the single crochet of last row is worked into, 7 treble in a group under the stitch that draws together the cluster of stitches of last row, and repeat the same; the treble is to be drawn up as high as possible; you will go round the top of the strip, and down the other side in the same way. **4th row**—Work single crochet along the margin of the stitches of last row. This finishes the trimming up one of the fronts: do another piece of trimming in the same manner for the other front, and if these have not been worked upon the tricot, sew them thereto; they need not come any lower down the skirt than the ninth row from the bottom. For the **Trimming** round the **Skirt**—The first row consists of double long treble stitches, the wool passed three times round the needle; the stitches must stand at least 1½ inches in height to admit of ribbon of that width being afterwards run through them; break off the wool at the end of the row. The next three rows are identical with the first three rows of the front trimming, excepting that the first row is crocheted upon the double long treble stitches, and you break off when you get to the end of the row. The following row is a repetition of the second row, which has the effect of widening the trimming. The next row is like the third row, but it begins upon the first of the double long treble stitches and margins the *side* of the four previous rows, then the corner is rounded, and you proceed along the stitches of the last row and round the opposite corner to correspond. The border is to be completed with a line of single crochet to margin the scollops. The last three rows of

Basket Pincushion.

the border hang below the tricot work of the skirt. Border the **Sleeves** in the same manner, but after the double long treble row is done work a little more tightly. For the **Neck Trimming**—Work a row of double long treble stitches to stand up round the neck, and break off the wool; a ribbon is afterwards passed through these long treble stitches (3 stitches to show in front of the ribbon and 3 stitches at the back) and is tied in a bow under the chin. The collar turns downwards, and to produce this effect you must hold the garment conveniently for crocheting into the double crochet at the base of the double long treble stitches: do 4 rows as instructed for trimming on the bottom of the skirt; then carry the last row of scollops the whole way round the collar and also along the top of the double long treble stitches; and margin it with single crochet. Put white pearl buttons down the front to fasten into the buttonholes.